THE COURSE OF IRISH HISTORY

THE COURSE

OF

IRISH HISTORY

EDITED BY

T. W. MOODY AND F. X. MARTIN

Published in association with
Radio Telefís Éireann
by

MERCIER PRESS

Mercier Press

Trade enquiries to Columba Mercier Distribution
55A Spruce Avenue
Stillorgan Industrial Park
Blackrock County Dublin
Tel: (01) 294 2556; Fax: (01) 294 2564
E-mail: cmd@columba.ie

First published 1967
Fifteenth impression 1980

Revised and enlarged edition 1984
Seventeenth impression 1993

Revised and enlarged edition 1994
Tenth impression 2000

Revised and enlarged edition 2001

10 9 8 7 6 5 4 3 2

ISBN 1 85635 370 2

A CIP record for this title is available from the
British Library

Cover design by SPACE
Typeset by *Deirdre's Desktop*
Printed in Ireland by ColourBooks

To the memory of Theo Moody (1907–1984) and Frank X. Martin (1922–2000) in appreciation of their lifetime of work as historians and their pioneering contribution to the academic broadcasting of their subject on television.

Contents

The death occurred of Professor Frank X. Martin between the publication of the revised edition of *The Course of Irish History* in 1994 and the appearance of this 2001 edition. Theo Moody, his co-editor, died in 1984. As the conceivers of a major television history series, they were successful pioneers in the art of adapting an academic subject like history and helping to shape it into the original twenty-one-part *Course of Irish History*. Many historians – some of a younger generation than the authors – were slower to grasp the mass appeal and power of the new medium of television, which was very much there to stay. In the Ireland of the 1960s, television contributed to a revolution in popular culture.

It is difficult to convey the impact that the original series – on which this book was subsequently based – had on an Irish audience in 1966. Radio Telefís Éireann, the national television station, had only been set up in 1961. Up to that point, television-owners in the border counties and those along the eastern seaboard were able to receive BBC and ITV, but the reception was generally poor in quality. By the middle of the 1960s, many Irish homes had their own television sets and RTÉ reception was usually strong and clear. The medium was a departure for Irish broadcasting; the genre of the history documentary was also a novelty for a young station careful to husband its scarce resources. The decision to commission a twenty-one-part series and to broadcast it from 24 January to 13 June 1966 – the year of the fiftieth anniversary of the 1916 Rising – was as imaginative as it was daring. In the modern world, which has grown accustomed to the History Channel, five months seems a long time to attempt to hold a loyal audience.

The series proved to be both a critical and a popular success, as did the companion volume, *The Course of Irish History*. The decision to publish a book to accompany the programmes might appear to have been an obvious undertaking in a pre-video era. But that, too, was an innovation, not least because of the exacting task the two editors set their twenty-one contributors. As Moody and Martin wrote in the preface to the first edition:

> The aim of the series was to present a survey of Irish history that would be both popular and authoritative, concise but comprehensive, highly selective while at the same time balanced and fair-minded, critical but constructive and sympathetic.

The many tens of thousands of readers who purchased this volume may have had divided opinions on its content. But the unceasing demand for the book nearly forty years after it first appeared attests to its enduring quality and, in the words of its editors in the preface to the 1984 edition, 'This book, we are persuaded, continues to serve a useful purpose.' Many households in Ireland still have copies of the 1966 edition, the blue cover now separated or still precariously clinging to the body of the volume, as the glue binding was fragile.

The Course of Irish History is a point of departure and of reference for the lifelong student of Irish history. It is a tribute to the two editors and their original team of contributors that the content has stood the test of time. It must, however, be stressed that the volume is of major historiographical significance. It presents a unique view of Irish history, written, broadcast and published in the year of the fiftieth anniversary of the 1916 Rising. It is a snapshot of the work of the Irish historical profession, as selected by Moody and Martin in that context. The series and book differed from later generations of historical documentaries in their format, and that also has major historiographic significance. A single historian, for the most part, scripted each programme and wrote each chapter. That gave the individual historian the opportunity to develop a personal thesis and retain control over his or her script. In later generations of history programme-making, the historian is at the mercy of the editor, who takes a pre-recorded interview and cuts sections of it into a text scripted by someone else and usually read by somebody else again.

There are ways in which this book shows its age. The number of women contributors was and remains very small. There is no entry in the index under 'women'. There is a reference to *cumal*, meaning a female slave, and there are two entries under 'Cathleen Ní Houlihan'. The volume was of its time.

In 1984, both editors recorded sadly that five of the original twenty-one contributors had died. Alas, by 2001, several other members of the original team had also died. Professor John H. Whyte, having written one of the chapters in the original volume, was commissioned to add a chapter entitled 'Ireland: 1966–82'. He died in 1990. A new and revised edition was published in 1994, when Dr Richard English contributed the chapter entitled 'Ireland: 1982–94'. He became the twenty-second contributor. In the 2001 edition, it has fallen to me to write a chapter on 'Ireland at the Turn of the Century: 1994–2001'. New illustrations have been included. The chronology has been brought up to date and the index revised.

I was also asked to commission the compilation of bibliographies to supplement the reference material in the existing volume. I would like to thank the following colleagues in the History Department, University College Cork: Drs Damien Bracken, David Edwards, Larry Geary and Dónal Ó Drisceoil. I am also grateful to Dr Daire Keogh, St Patrick's College, Drumcondra, for compiling the bibliography on the eighteenth century.

Nothing has been done to disturb the original contributors' pristine prose or to update the contents of their essays. The chapters remain as left by Martin and Moody after they undertook to revise the edition in 1984.

I vividly recall watching the original series in 1966 and being aware of the significant impact that it was having on myself and on the wider public. Every programme in the series was the subject of topical conversation and public comment.

At a critical juncture for the country in the turbulent 1960s, the series and the book helped develop the critical faculties of Irish citizens. The series reinforced among its viewers the desire to acquire a good knowledge of the nation's past. It also encouraged an independence of judgement and warned against a partisanship about the past that reduces 'history' to a tool of propaganda. The growing crisis in Northern Ireland in the late 1960s fuelled emotions and strengthened the temptation to plunder the past to serve the politics of the present. *The Course of Irish History* helped warn against over-simplification and cultivated a more critical public understanding of the island's past. It was a timely contribution to Irish popular education.

The Course of Irish History remains, nearly forty years later, a book I would strongly recommend to anyone wishing to gain a professional overview of Irish history.

DERMOT KEOGH
DEPARTMENT OF HISTORY
UNIVERSITY COLLEGE CORK

A Geographer's View of Irish History
J. H. Andrews

Throughout the twentieth century Ireland has been among the weaker countries of the western world. It is small in area and population and has been slow in achieving success as a producer of non-agricultural wealth. Geographically it stands on the edge of things, a wallflower at the gathering of west-European nations, and despite its popularity with the tourist it has failed to attract any large body of permanent immigrants. Not all these characteristics are deeply rooted in the past. Ireland has been a small and sea-bound country, admittedly, for at least 8,000 years, ever since the upward movement of sea level that finally separated it from the Continent, and it has never been a great military power. Nevertheless, there have been times when its fertile soils, its copper and its gold have attracted some of Europe's most vigorous colonising peoples and, later, when its scholars and missionaries have moulded the intellectual life of other lands. Before trying to understand these changes of fortune, we must look at the different regions of our country and study their relations both with each other and with the world outside.

In many parts of Ireland, nature has remained inhospitable for long periods, in some cases down to the present day. Around the edges, especially, much of its surface is raised or crumpled into highland masses and steep-sided glens, their upper slopes seared by winter gales, the goodness washed from their soils by drenching rain, their coarse grass and heather of little value except as rough grazing. In these areas the stony roots of the Irish landscape reach the surface – in the basalt cliffs of Antrim, for example; the spiky quartzite mountains of Donegal, Mayo and Galway; the bare and fissured limestone pavements of north Clare; the sandstone masses of Kerry; and the schist and granite of the Wicklow glens. These hills, though they are seldom out of sight, make up only one eighth of Ireland's total area; but this is not to say that all the rest is fertile lowland. In much of the north, particularly, the lowland shown on the ordinary school-atlas map is really a maze of tightly packed small hills known as drumlins, low but quite steep, and patched together with fragments of bog or lake. For much of their history the drumlin belts have made a surprisingly effective obstacle to movement. Southwards they give way to smoother country, but this in turn is interrupted by thousands of acres of bare and lonely peat bog, some of it in the very centre of the island – another difficult kind of country in both the military and the agricultural sense.

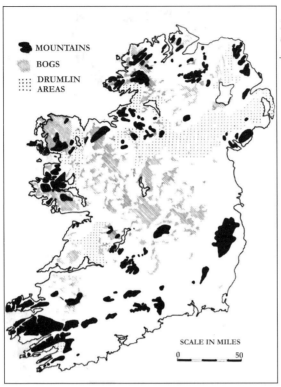

1
Mountains, bogs and
drumlins
J.H. Andrews

This still leaves a large part of Ireland – half, at least – as fully productive, but much of the good land is inextricably mixed with the bad, and until a few centuries ago the pattern was further complicated by the numerous patches of forest that fringed the bogs and clothed the lower slopes of many of the hills. Bog, mountain and forest, though unfitted for tillage, provided useful summer grazing land for nearby farmers and a refuge where life could be sustained even when invading armies had burned the corn from the lowland fields. These strips of relatively unattractive country have many times helped to channel the course of Irish history, but their influence has never been quite decisive. Ideas and attitudes have flown freely around and between them. One such attitude, perhaps the oldest Irish national characteristic, is our love of celebrating death, which was implanted as long ago as 3000 BC by the builders of the megalithic tombs. These imposing stone structures are found in every corner of the island and the same is true of many of our other pre-Christian and early Christian antiquities, several of which are distinctively Irish and found in hardly any other country. This cultural identity has prompted Irishmen to seek political union and political independence as well, but here they have been less successful in overcoming geographical difficulties. The traditional centre of the island, the hill of Uisneach, was not, as might have been expected, a national capital, but part of a political frontier zone, the meeting place of independent kingdoms. And although these kingdoms have long since passed into history or legend, there is nothing legendary about the international boundary that still divides the country fifty miles further north. Nobody would claim that such political divisions, old and new, have been 'caused' by geography in any simple sense. Nothing about Irish geography is simple. But emerging from this intricate pattern we can distinguish at least two broad regional themes that no historian can ignore. One of them is the tendency for the north to stand aloof from the rest of the country; the other, which we shall look at first, is the gap between the east of Ireland and the west.

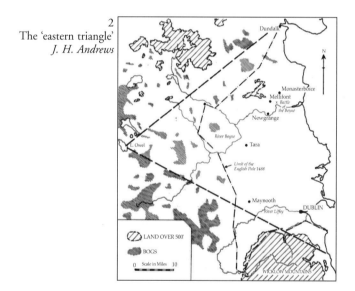

2
The 'eastern triangle'
J. H. Andrews

As one travels westwards from the Shannon, unfriendly and inaccessible regions crowd more closely together. In the east, the land is generally kinder, and if we draw one line from Lough Owel to Dundalk and another to meet the coast just south of Dublin (Fig. 2) we have marked off the heart of this eastern zone, a part of Ireland which receives less rain and contains less bog and mountain than any other compact area of similar size, and which forms a junction for routes that thread their way between the bogs and mountains to give access to smaller but equally fertile districts like the lowlands of the Suir, Nore and Barrow. Almost every period of our history has left conspicuous traces in this eastern triangle. Here is Newgrange, the most impressive of our prehistoric monuments, and Tara, the focus of an ancient road system and the most famous of the early centres from which Irishmen have sought political unification. Here was found the richest of our illuminated manuscripts, the *Book of Kells*, while the highest of our high crosses stands at Monasterboice and the earliest of our great Cistercian monasteries at Mellifont. In this triangle, at Dublin, the Norsemen placed the largest and most powerful of their Irish city states, so vital a centre that Strongbow the Norman hurried north to possess it within a month of his first landing at Waterford harbour. At Dublin, too, the English kings established their deputies, and at the other end of the triangle, at Dundalk, the Scottish invader Edward Bruce challenged them by having himself crowned king of Ireland. Here, in the pale, the fifteenth-century English government resolved to keep one last precarious foothold; and here, at Maynooth, stood the fortress of their strongest and most ungovernable vassal, the great earl of Kildare. Here the primate of the Irish church placed his residence, at Termonfeckin, at a time when the archiepiscopal seat of Armagh was too much threatened by war and disorder to be considered safe. Here, finally, beside the Boyne, was fought the last great battle of Irish history. The eastern triangle is the geographical nucleus from which men have seen their best chance of commanding the whole country. And yet the same district is also one of the most vulnerable parts of Ireland, the longest break in its defensive mountain ring, with the estuaries of the Liffey and the Boyne to beckon the invader onwards. The sea that washes its shore is too narrow to make an effective geographical barrier, and there have been many times when a united Irish Sea must have seemed as likely a prospect, politically, as a united Ireland. From this triangle, then, we are inevitable drawn eastwards to consider Ireland's relations with the outside world.

Our most distinguished geographer, Professor Estyn Evans, has placed the coastlands of the Irish Sea among what he calls the 'Atlantic ends of Europe', a geographical province that stretches all the way from Norway to Brittany and Spain but which excludes eastern and central England. He has pointed out, for instance, that Ireland's first taste of civilisation and its first knowledge of metals came from prehistoric seafarers making their way from island to island and peninsula to peninsula across these western seas. Historians tell of many other important journeys among the Atlantic ends of Europe. But as they take the story forward, one trend is inescapable: when we compare our modern emigrants with the saints and scholars of the past, Ireland's role in western Europe appears increasingly passive, involuntary and dominated by England. Consider a few examples. The Romans brought their armies no further west than Pembrokeshire. Ireland viewed their empire with detachment, appropriated some of their best ideas, and then drew on this

Roman legacy to maintain its own spiritual ascendancy of the Irish Sea long after the last of the legions had been disbanded. The Norsemen were more aggressive, and although their territorial conquests were confined to small areas near the coast, they struck two blows at the native civilisation of the interior, firstly by attacking the monasteries which were the custodians of this civilisation and secondly by securing each of the chief harbours with a fortified town. Towns were a new and alien settlement form, and one that Gaelic Ireland has never succeeded in fully assimilating. But the next invaders, the Normans, appreciated their value at once, and by stringing others along the well-articulated river systems of the south and east they drew this part of Ireland into feudal dependence on the English kings. Their Tudor successors completed the sequence by going one stage further: starting from a narrow foothold in the Pale, they reconquered the area of Norman influence and went on to conquer the north and west as well.

3   The mountains of Connemara

Bord Fáilte Éireann

Behind this sequence we can see a general European trend. Under the Tudors, England had emerged as one of a number of large, compact, land-based nation states, each well integrated within itself, but each in conflict with one or more of the others. Several of them owed much of their power to the quickening economic life of Europe's northern lowlands, and central England was one of the lowland areas most affected by this trend: from being a prehistoric barrier region, it had become the obvious link between London and the Irish Sea – a shorter route, of course, and now an easier one, than any of the sea routes from Ireland to the Continent. Even if Ireland had been united, England would still have been larger, richer and more in touch with

Continental technology and military science. But Ireland was not united. It had remained an exception to the west-European rule. No Irish leader had recaptured the nucleus of the eastern triangle, or even sought to dominate any of the inland towns – such as Athlone, Kilkenny or Athy – which have from time to time been suggested as alternative capitals of a united Ireland. By the standards of the middle sixteenth century, almost the whole island was a political vacuum, like the newly discovered countries of America. The conflict between the English and other European powers made it necessary to fill this vacuum, and it eventually became clear to the statesmen and strategists of Spain and France that the idea of the Atlantic ends of Europe could not be translated into political terms. While English troops poured into Dublin from Chester and Liverpool, Continental forces had to seek a timid foothold on the extremities of Munster, and after they had been defeated, Ireland's southern traffic dwindled down to a trickle of spies, smugglers and fishermen.

4   Drumlins in south Donegal

J.C. Brindley, UCD

Today it is in the older details of our countryside and its folklore that the idea of Atlantic Europe must be sought: in the design of the Irish peasant house and much of its furniture, and in the stories, songs, attitudes, and some of the farming practices of its inhabitants. The student who seeks to understand the history of more recent times will find an interesting contrast to Professor Evans's view in the ideas of the English geographer Halford Mackinder. In a map published in 1902 in his book *Britain and the British Seas*, Mackinder described the Irish Sea as 'the inland sea of Britain' – not very tactfully put, perhaps, but we must admit that what has mattered most in the last few centuries of our history is the easy passage from Britain to Ireland's eastern coastlands. Because of it, our present-day laws and institutions have their origins in England.

5   Bogland in County Offaly

Bord na Móna

There were limits to the process of Anglicisation, however, and insofar as Ireland today enjoys political independence, the English conquest may be regarded as a failure. It certainly did not fail for want of thought or planning. The Elizabethans, for example, made a great effort to master the geography of the country, as we can see by studying the maps collected by their capable chief minister, Lord Burghley. His earliest specimens were crude and distorted, with little but artist's licence in the west and north-west. But he was constantly seeking out better ones, correcting and augmenting them with his own hand, and finding expert surveyors to supply new detail. As the map of Ireland was painfully filled in, key river-crossings and mountain passes were fully appreciated by English strategists for the first time. But in many areas – the far west for instance – there was little of importance apart from physical geography for the mapmakers to add, and indeed the blankness of much of the Irish landscape was one of the most difficult problems facing the conquerors. They soon discovered that military victories were not enough: Ireland could not be secured without being brought to what the Elizabethans called 'civility', and to an Englishman civility meant towns, villages and enclosed fields – the sort of orderly landscape that was still missing from Tudor Ireland except for a few favoured districts in the east. It was easy enough to plan such improvements on paper – not so easy to establish them on the ground. One method was by parcelling out tracts of land to English proprietors with English tenants, in the somewhat naive hope that Irishmen would be so impressed by these newcomers that they would hasten to imitate their way of life. Deciding where to put these colonies was an interesting geographical exercise. But it remained, for the most part, no more than an exercise. The new ruling class could carve out estates, build forts and barracks, cut down woods, and drive new roads across the bogs; and in the seventeenth and eighteenth centuries they were doing all these things. But what they could not do, except in some parts of Ulster, was to persuade any large number of their countrymen to come and till the soil of Ireland.

It was a familiar problem in colonial territories. Where immigrant meets native in a landed society, economic war may go on smouldering long after the military conquest is over. The native is content with a lower standard of living than the settler. So unless the settler can earn more, acre for acre, from his farm, the native can outbid him by offering the landlord a higher rent. This is one reason why so many of the British immigrants stayed in the towns. It also explains why Scotsmen made better colonists than Englishmen: their expectations were more modest. The outcome of this economic competition depends to some extent on local geography, for it is on the better land that the progressive newcomer is likely to have an advantage over his less efficient native rival. Outside Ulster, the planters of the seventeenth century were nowhere numerous enough to displace the previous inhabitants completely, and their biggest successes, such as they were, occurred in areas of fertile land and good communications. In the rural areas of the west they made hardly any impression. Yet the west was the very part of Ireland that had been most in need of civility when the Tudor conquest had begun.

So for all their efforts the English had not managed to wipe out the distinction between the richer east and the poorer west. This distinction appeared again with harsh clarity in a great series of official maps, memoirs and statistical reports compiled in the decades that followed the union, and especially in the early years of Queen Victoria, many of them prepared under the direction or influence of Captain Thomas Larcom of the Ordnance Survey, whom we may perhaps regard as the ablest practical geographer ever to have worked in Ireland. The landscape revealed by the ordnance surveyors was much better furnished and more closely occupied than the one depicted on Lord Burghley's maps. Nevertheless, Ireland could still be divided into two broad regions, and with the important exception of Ulster these were pretty much the same two regions that could have been distinguished 300 years earlier. In the east and south, the resident gentry were more numerous and more progressive; society was more diversified, both economically and in religious terms; farms were larger and farming more commercialised; towns were larger and more closely spaced; people were better housed and better educated. In all these matters the west lagged behind and in general the further west one travelled the poorer were the land and the people, until one reached the westernmost peninsulas of Europe, the 'parishes next to America'. The remarkable thing, though, was how little difference America had made to Ireland. In other west European countries, economic geography had been revolutionised by the discovery and development of the new world. But these changed space-relationships brought no great benefits to Ireland under British rule, certainly not to western Ireland. America had provided the potato in the sixteenth century; and now, in the nineteenth, it provided somewhere to emigrate to after the ruinous upsurge of population that the potato had helped to bring about. Through these changes, the west remained the most secluded and in some ways the most Irish part of Ireland.

6   Hill and lowland in County Tipperary

Bord Fáilte Éireann

East and west were not clearly distinct. Among most of their boundary they either overlapped, interpenetrated or merged into one another. But in parts of Munster at least, where fertile bog-free lowland laps against the upland blocks of the south, the contrast between English and Gaelic influences was more abrupt and historically more consequential. One of our leading geographers, Professor T. Jones Hughes, has pointed out that it was not in the east or west but in this critical frontier region that modern Irish nationalism found some of its earliest expressions, ranging for example from a high incidence of agrarian unrest to the beginnings of the cooperative movement. Here then is a possible view of Ireland in the decades before the treaty of 1921: the west, and especially the far west, remote on every side and for the most part crushingly poor; the east, and especially the old English Pale, attractive and accessible by land and sea; with the two finally integrated, one hopes, in the Ireland of today and tomorrow. It is an interesting view; but like many pictures drawn in Dublin, it leaves out the north. Ulster has always had its own geographical personality, formed, as we might imagine, by taking qualities from each of the other regions, accentuating them and combining them into something dramatic and highly coloured. Like the west – only more so – Ulster for long remained somewhat inaccessible by land, kept apart from the south by mountains, drumlins, forests and water, which together formed the nearest Irish equivalent to the uplands that divided England from Scotland, just as the prehistoric earthworks known as the Black Pig's Dyke are the nearest Irish equivalent of Hadrian's Wall. What lay beyond this barrier, however, was not a handful of impoverished peninsulas, but something more like a whole Ireland in miniature, with its own version of the eastern triangle in the valleys of the Lagan and the Bann. For the English government, Ulster was the most intractable part of Ireland, and in trying to breach its frontiers they suffered several particularly humiliating defeats, defeats which stung them, when the wars were over, to devise the most thoroughgoing of all their plantation schemes.

7   The Glen of Aherlow, County Tipperary: sixteenth–century forest, twentieth-century farmland

Bord Fáilte Éireann

Remoteness from Dublin was what gave Ulster a certain resemblance to the west. But like Dublin – only, again, more so – Ulster lay open to outside influence. A narrow gap, at its narrowest a mere thirteen miles, separated it from Scotland and along the shores of this gap English, Irish and Scots had for many centuries confronted each other in a confused and shifting pattern of wars and alliances. A new era was inaugurated, however, when England and Scotland were united under James I in 1603. As king of Ireland, James had two advantages denied to his predecessor Elizabeth: his kingdom of Scotland gave him command of the narrow North Channel, and from the manpower of that kingdom he could stiffen his Ulster colony with energetic lowlanders who were reinforced by a new wave of immigration in the last decades of the seventeenth century. By combining agriculture with their national industry of linen-making, these Scottish immigrants became almost the only people in modern Ireland to combine a high rural population density with a relatively high level of prosperity. Irishmen, who have a habit of confusing Britain with England, often forget that James I's two British crowns played an important part in the division of their own country.

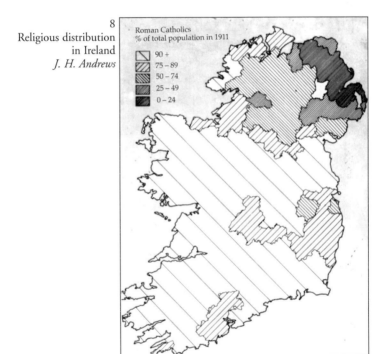

8
Religious distribution
in Ireland
J. H. Andrews

Roman Catholics
% of total population in 1911

90 +
75 – 89
50 – 74
25 – 49
0 – 24

Ever since the Tudor conquest, most of our new settlers have been Protestants, and as religious conversion is a rare experience in Ireland, a twentieth-century denominational map (Fig. 8) is the best way of measuring the overall effect of the plantation policy. Outside the north, this policy was clearly a failure. In the north it enjoyed considerable success. But the north, in common with the rest of Ireland, had its upland refuges, like the Sperrin Mountains and the northern glens of Antrim, where the older communities survived almost intact. This mixture of Catholic districts and Protestant districts was to be further complicated when Ulster, more than any of the other provinces of Ireland, experienced the Industrial Revolution of the nineteenth century, and when new factories attracted the descendants of pre-plantation Ulstermen to help to populate its growing towns. Some urban Catholic majorities now appeared in certain rural hinterlands that remained predominantly Protestant; and within the typical northern town each religious denomination kept to its own streets. Like Ireland as a whole, Ulster has remained divided within itself.

The geographical factors in Irish history cannot be adequately summarised in a short survey. They have helped to unite Ireland and to divide it, just as they have helped both to divide and to unite the British Isles. Their significance has changed and is still changing, generally for the better. Rivers have been harnessed; hillsides have been afforested with productive timber; bogs have been exploited for fuel and electric power, and will in future give way to cultivated land; and new industries are at last beginning to exploit the advantages of Ireland's central position among the land masses of the world. Geographical barriers are disappearing, and in time the consequences of these barriers will themselves begin to fade away – not only within Ireland but between Ireland and other countries.

Prehistoric Ireland
G. F. Mitchell

Everybody has some interest in the past: not only their own past, but also that of the society to which they belong. The past has made us what we are, and we must all at some time have asked: where and what do I come from? What does it mean to be Irish? Historians can tell us a good deal of Ireland's and our forefathers' past. They work by studying what man wrote years or centuries ago, and from these documents they try to reconstruct the story of a society. But men did not always write. In Ireland, writing began about 1,500 years ago. What happened before then, before history, we call prehistory, and for many people there is a fascination in the mute testimony of the peoples who lived thousands of years ago: a massive stone fort on the Atlantic cliffs, a great earthen mound on a hilltop, a circle of standing stones in some farmer's field.

The archaeologist investigates the forts and other monuments: he asks questions about them; he searches for smaller and less obvious works of early man. He goes to work like a detective piecing together clues to reconstruct a story: he removes from the earth scraps of pottery, implements of bone or flint or a polished axe-head. He is not primarily interested in the objects – often dull enough – which he finds, and he is not seeking for treasure in his excavations. He is trying to find out in the only way possible what people were like in prehistoric times.

The story the prehistorian has to tell must be related to its geographical setting. When we look at a map (Fig. 9) of western Europe at the end of the ice age we see that Spain and Portugal, and England and Ireland, stick out from the west of Europe into the Atlantic. While England and Ireland are now detached from the mainland, they nonetheless remain part of Europe. These areas which jut out from Europe, together with Scandinavia, are highland areas. Lowlands extend from western France along both sides of the English Channel, and stretch far to the east through the Low Countries and northern Germany.

In the last ice age, which lasted from over 100,000 until about 15,000 years ago, conditions were too cold over much of Europe for trees to grow. Ice covered the highlands of the north and the mountains of central Europe. On the lowlands we had rich and fertile grassy plains, with great herds of deer and horses in western France, but farther north the grass was sparser and poorer, and the big game were fewer. At this time there must have been, in western

France and parts of Spain, a large population who lived by hunting this big game. They lived in caves, and at Lascaux and other places they painted wonderful pictures of the animals they hunted on cave walls. This palaeolithic (or old Stone Age) art was the earliest art in the world. From it and from the tools of stone and bone we get a vivid picture of the way of life of these early men. These hunters moved on following the game into England, for the English Channel did not then exist. In England they have not left any pictures, but their flint implements have been found, and their living conditions must have been much the same as in France. They do not seem to have reached Ireland, because for a hundred years archaeologists have searched in vain for this type of tool. I do not believe they will ever be found here, because there were not enough animals in Ireland then to provide food for these hunting people.

9
Western Europe at the end of the Ice Age, c. 15,000 BC
G. F. Mitchell

Here in Ireland at the end of the ice age it must have been much as Lapland is today, with boggy grassland on flat ground and little vegetation on the hill slopes. As the climate got warmer, bushes began to grow again, just as in warmer parts of Lapland. It was at this time, about 10,000 BC, that the giant deer became common in Ireland. These animals would have provided food for the hunters, but although there were hunting peoples in Holland and Denmark at the time, we have found no traces of them in Ireland. The country seems to have been still unpopulated, and the giant deer were more common here than elsewhere – probably because there were no men to hunt them.

Before we come to the first inhabitants of Ireland, we must look at the way Europe was changing. During the ice age a great deal of the world's water was frozen solid on higher ground; there was much less water in the sea, and the sea level was low. As a result, land connected Ireland with England and England with the Continent. When the ice melted, sea levels rose again, and by 6000 BC Ireland had been cut off from Britain, but the floor of the future North Sea still stood above sea level; forests and swamps stretched from Yorkshire to Denmark (Fig. 9). As the ice sheets retreated northwards, the warmer climate allowed trees to grow again, and Europe, except for its lakes and rivers, became entirely covered by dense woodland. The deer and the horses that had roamed the grassy plains were driven out by the expanding forests: the hunters now had no big game, and had to live on birds and fish. Their movements too were restricted because of the growth of forests, and the people migrated along the rivers and by sea and lake shores, to wherever they could find food.

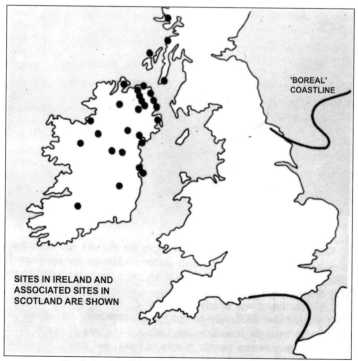

'BOREAL' COASTLINE

SITES IN IRELAND AND ASSOCIATED SITES IN SCOTLAND ARE SHOWN

10 Ireland and Western Britain in mesolithic times

G. F. Mitchell

These were the first people to come to Ireland. They had crossed from Scandinavia to Britain, and at about 6000 BC, or perhaps a little earlier, they moved still farther west, probably across narrow straits of water towards the highlands of Antrim and Wicklow, as these could be clearly seen from the British shore. We find them first near Coleraine in Derry and Tullamore in Offaly. As time went on, they seem to have preferred the north-eastern half of the country to the south-western. Lakes are more common in the north-east, and food would have been more abundant there.

We can tell little about our first ancestors – these middle Stone Age or mesolithic people. We know that at the Coleraine site they lived in round huts with a central hearth, but we do not know how they disposed of their dead. All we have are the rubbish-dumps or kitchen middens they left behind them near the swamps and waters where their food supplies were stored. The first arrivals used microliths, tiny blades of flint which were probably set as barbs in a wooden shaft. But these implements, very handy in arrows for shooting birds, do not seem to have been used by the later mesolithic people. Their tools are less exciting – a limited range of flint implements, used for skinning and cleaning birds and fish; hardly any bone; and a few stones for rubbing and hammering.

Barbed harpoons of bone are known outside Ireland, and were almost certainly used here also, not only for chasing seals and porpoises in the sea, but also for hunting deer, which could be ambushed when crossing rivers or venturing into woodland clearings. Deer like young shoots, and there is now evidence that mesolithic man made deliberate clearings, where the deer could be easily killed when they came to graze.

Man the hunter was utterly dependent on the bounty of nature. To feed himself and his family he had to hunt incessantly throughout the year, often by night as well as day. Only a tiny group of people could win sustenance from a very large area of forest and marsh, where they were in competition with other beasts of prey. But even before the first aborigines entered Ireland to try to scrape a living by hunting along the banks of its rivers and lakes, elsewhere in the world the great revolution was taking place, which was to win for mankind the empire of the earth – the first farmers were at work in the Middle East.

This neolithic or new Stone Age revolution was perhaps the most significant step forward in the history of man. From now on, instead of being at the mercy of nature, man could control his environment. He learned from observing wild plants and grasses that by scattering the seeds he could cultivate grain. Wild beasts who came to graze in the special clearings were gradually tamed, perhaps by capturing a young animal, a calf or a kid, and rearing it to maturity. These domestic herds provided not only meat and hides, but also milk and hair. Food was stored in baskets and leather bags, and this led eventually to the discovery of pottery. Someone probably had the idea of daubing a basket with clay to make it waterproof. When it was baked by the sun it became hard and firm, and then it was found possible to make containers wholly of clay. This was the first manufacture, and the earliest pots are round-bottomed and bag-shaped, resembling the baskets and bags from which they derive. At the same time, people learned to polish their rough stone tools and to make a more effective hoe or axe. As land was cultivated and exhausted, more land was needed, and the clearing of forests began. The felling axe was invented (Fig. 11). Later Egyptian paintings show us the whole process – the trees being cut down with stone axes, the ground broken with stone hoes, and the crop being raised and harvested.

11
Polished stone axe with wooden handle
c. 3000 BC
National Museum of Ireland

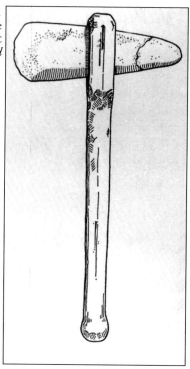

Expanding population in the Middle East forced these farming people to spread out in the never-ending search for new land. They pushed west along the Mediterranean to Spain and France, moved up through France to the Channel coast and on into Ireland, Great Britain and the Low Countries (Fig. 12). This expansion took quite a long time, but by various dating methods we can say that the neolithic colonisers reached north-west Europe by about 3000 BC.

At Lough Gur in County Limerick we can observe the way of life of the first people to till the soil of Ireland. They were practical and observant, and knew that the soil would be richest where elm trees grew most freely, and so they settled on light limestone soils such as we have in south Limerick – an area that is still fertile and suitable for cattle-raising. At Lough Gur the late Professor Seán Ó Ríordáin excavated many of their houses. What the archaeologist finds are stains in the soil where wooden posts have rotted away, or remains of stone foundations. The houses must have had walls of turves on a wooden frame, and were thatched with rushes from the lake shore. Some of the houses were round – others were rectangular. By piecing together some of the many pottery fragments found, Ó Ríordáin showed that these people made round-bottomed pots with decorated rims for storing their food, and heavier flat-bottomed cooking pots. They used stone axes of various sizes for cutting trees and hoeing the ground, and antler picks were also used in agriculture. Many small bone implements – borers, needles, awls – had domestic uses, and whorls of bone and stone were used in spinning wool for clothing. The women ground the grain by pushing a heavy rubbing implement across a block of stone.

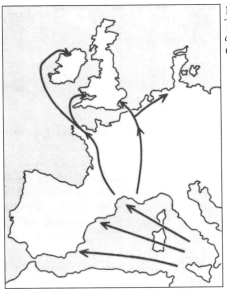

12
The expansion of neolithic farming
c. 3000 BC
G.F. Mitchell

As well as the crops they grew, these people ate great quantities of meat – from the refuse bones, we know that they kept cows and also pigs and sheep. Arrows or spears with flint tips were probably used for hunting small game birds, and flint blades and scrapers took the place of our modern knives. Not all the objects left behind by these early farmers are utilitarian, for many beads of bone and stone and bracelets of lignite show they adorned themselves and were interested in their appearance, just as we are today.

We can still read the record of this first farming in the muds on the bottom of the lake. The plants which grew by its shores scattered their pollen in the air and much of this fell in the lake. If we take samples of the lake mud and count the pollen grains in it, in the lower levels we see much elm pollen coming from the virgin woodlands before the colonisers arrived. The farmers killed off the trees and the amount of elm pollen fell. In its place we find at a higher level in the mud the pollen of the cultivated fields – grasses, cereals and weeds. These first farmers had no idea of using manure, and after a time the productivity of the fields was drastically reduced. The farmers moved on to new lands, and then the tree pollen reaching the mud increased again as the trees invaded the abandoned fields.

The people who lived at Lough Gur were self-sufficient in most things, but a certain amount of trading went on. Some of the axes found were of local stone, but others were imported from further afield, where particularly suitable rocks were available. Tievebulliagh in County Antrim and Rathlin Island were two such places, and here stone axes were mass-produced in the first Irish factories. From the factories, axes of a characteristic speckled stone were traded, not only to the surrounding counties, but also to Dublin, to Lough Gur, and to the south of England, in what was Ireland's first export-drive, 5,000 years ago.

Lough Gur was naturally not the only settlement of neolithic people, but it is the only place where many dwellings have so far been found. Others lived and worked at the axe factories, and there must have been a considerable settlement at Lyle's Hill, County Antrim. Here hundreds of fragments of neolithic pottery have been found, and no doubt many other sites still await discovery.

Not only do we know how these early farmers lived, we can tell something of their religious beliefs from the massive monuments they raised for their dead. Some of these are in the form of long galleries of huge stones in which the burials were placed, with a forecourt or central open court where ceremonies could be held. These court cairns, as they are called, are found mainly in the northern half of the country. At Ballyglass, in Mayo, the cairn had been built on top of the ruins of a wooden house.

The general term for such burial places is megalithic tombs (from the Greek megos, 'large', and lithos, 'stone'), and it is easy to see why they are so called, even when we look at the simplest tombs which survive. Dolmens – stone tripods with a capstone – are common throughout the country. All that now remains are the huge stones which formed the burial chamber, but originally they may have been covered by a cairn of stones or mound of earth. The most spectacular of the neolithic graves are the great megalithic cairns which we find in groups on the hills to the west of Lough Arrow, County Sligo; on the Lough Crew Hills in County Meath, in the valley of the Boyne; and on the Dublin–Wicklow Mountains. Inside the cairns are elaborate burial chambers approached by a passage, and the type is known as a passage grave.

Such great cairns were constructed by a tribal group, and an immense amount of social organisation was required in their building. Many people were buried in the one passage grave – their bodies were burnt, and then the cremated bones were placed in the burial chambers, sometimes with pottery, beads of stone and bone, and tools for use in the next life. Great quantities of burnt bone have been found in some excavated tombs, showing that they were used over quite a long period of time. We do not know exactly what beliefs the builders held, but some of them may have worshipped the sun, since some tombs are placed with their entrances towards the rising sun. But their religion was a compelling one, and similar types of burial structures are known over large areas of Europe.

Another clue to their religious belief is the elaborate decoration of the stones in some of these tombs, such as Newgrange, County Meath, where the finest passage grave in the country is to be seen. The spirals, lozenges and zigzag patterns which ornament the stones must have had a religious significance, and some are thought to be highly stylised versions of the human face and figure. These may represent the death-goddess worshipped for so long in the Mediterranean world.

While some of these tombs were still in use, other groups of people had reached Ireland's shores. A further great technological advance had taken place in the Middle East, where men had learnt to recognise ores and make metal objects. Early prospectors were probably first attracted by the bright colour of gold, but then they became aware of other metals such as copper. By fairly complicated processes, they had learnt to reduce the ores to molten metal and then cast objects in moulds. Metal objects could be made in any size, and another advantage was that broken or unfashionable articles could be melted down and remade.

Prospectors and metalworkers reached Ireland around 2000 BC and began their search for metallic ores – a search that continues to the present day. In nearly every case where a copper deposit has been worked in more recent times, the miners have come across evidence of prehistoric mining. In any case there can be no doubt that these new colonisers were successful in their search, for many objects of bronze were soon being made: first of all simple flat axes, and then others decorated with zigzag or spiral ornamentation. These are found in great quantity here, but were also exported to Britain and as far afield as Scandinavia. There is gold in the gravels of the Wicklow rivers, and distinctive gold ornaments were made in Ireland in this period, which we call the early Bronze Age. One type of necklet was named a lunula (Fig. 13) because its outline resembled the crescent moon, and the lunulae were also exported to Britain and the Continent.

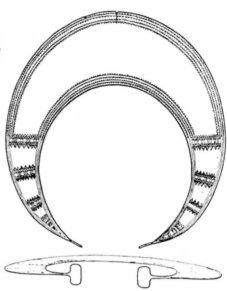

13
Gold lunula from Trillick, County Tyrone, *c.* 1800 BC
National Museum of Ireland

The early metalworkers introduced a new type of pottery vessel into Ireland – very well made and beautifully decorated. The vessels probably were drinking cups, and are known by the term 'beaker'. Pottery of this type has been found in Ireland in megalithic tombs. But in this early part of the Bronze Age (from about 2000 to 1200 BC), a new style of burial was coming into fashion. Some groups were burying their dead, no longer cremated but each in a single grave, with a new style of decorated pot placed beside the body. Archaeologists assume that food for the dead man was placed in these vessels, so they are called food vessels. Sometimes bodies were still cremated, and the burnt bones were placed within a food vessel or a larger pottery vessel called an urn.

On the Hill of Tara a small mound – the Mound of the Hostages – was partly excavated by Seán Ó Ríordáin, and after his death by Professor Ruaidhrí de Valera. Here the megalithic people had built a tomb and covered it first with a cairn of small stones and then with a layer of clay. In this clay covering, the later arrivals placed many cremated burials in urns and with food vessels. One body, of a youth, had not been burned, and was evidently of some importance, since the boy had been buried with a necklace of beads of bronze, amber and faience still in position around his neck. Faience is an artificial gemstone, a type of glass, bright blue in colour, which was manufactured in Egypt and the Near East about 1500 BC. Amber, a form of fossil resin, comes from the shore of the Baltic, and was then very fashionable – as it is today – in necklaces and other jewellery. These luxury goods – faience and amber – were being imported, probably in exchange for the gold and bronze objects Ireland was exporting at the time.

Though their tombs were not as elaborate as those of the earlier people, Bronze Age men built great circles of stone in which they held religious ceremonies. In a great circle at Grange, County Limerick – the largest in Ireland – fragments of broken beaker and food vessels were found near the base of the stones – souvenirs, perhaps, of some ritual feast. Another circle at Lough Gur has an inner and an outer ring of stones, and although we cannot tell what rites took place in them, these were the temples of the Bronze Age people.

About 800 BC, new ideas from various parts of Europe penetrated Ireland. Many new types of tool appeared, and more delicate work in wood and metal became possible. The style of warfare changed: close in-fighting with short heavy swords developed, and shields of bronze, leather or wood were used in defence. Farming was revolutionised by the introduction of simple ox-drawn ploughs; these could not turn the soil over in long furrows like the modern plough, but they could break up its surface, and so do away with a lot of hard spadework.

The result appears to have been a great increase in wealth, and chieftains were able to accumulate stocks of gold. Neck-ornaments or gorgets were cut out of sheet gold, and decorated with raised patterns. Bar gold was worked into penannular bracelets with expanded ends. Some gold ornaments were exported to England and beyond, and doubtless paid for luxury imports.

These Bronze Age people probably lived in simple settlements – single huts or groups of huts of wattle and daub surrounded by stockades in which the cattle could be kept safe. Or their homes may have been in clearings in the woodlands – log cabins surrounded by a wooden palisade like the homes of the American pioneers of a hundred years ago.

Another and more distinctive type of dwelling seems to have been coming into general use about this time. This is the crannóg or lake-dwelling, an artificial island laboriously constructed in the waters of a lake. The idea goes right back to neolithic times, and the type of dwelling was to remain in use until the medieval period. Whatever their type of dwelling, wealthy people lived in style, and cooked meat for special feasts in large bronze cauldrons hung over the fire.

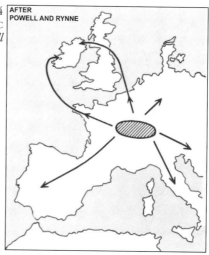

14

AFTER POWELL AND RYNNE

The expansion of the Celts, *c.* 400 BC
G.F. Mitchell

While Ireland was continuing to use bronze, another metal, iron, was coming into use in Europe. Iron ores are more common and therefore cheaper than copper ores, and iron for many purposes is superior to bronze. But the production of iron from its ores is more complicated, and technological difficulties slowed up its coming into common use. By about 600 BC, however, iron-using tribes led by wealthy chiefs were establishing themselves in central Europe. These people spoke a Celtic language, an ancestor or early relative of the Irish that is spoken today. They were a group of different peoples who were linked by a common language and by various characteristics in their appearance, dress and way of life, and were known to the Greeks as *Keltoi*, or Celts. Aided perhaps by their superior weapons, they spread west to Spain, east to Asia Minor and north to England and Ireland. There seem to have been two movements into Ireland – one to the western half, by people coming directly from the Continent, and a second to north-east Ireland by a group coming from northern Britain (Fig. 14). It is clear in any case that the Celts were established here by about 150 BC.

With the arrival of the Celts, Ireland entered on a new phase of her history. Apart from their ruined monuments and their blood – which probably still flows in our veins – little survives of the Stone Age hunters, the early farmers, the Bronze Age metalworkers and herdsmen who lived and died in Ireland for many hundreds of years. Their beliefs, their institutions, their traditions have passed away. But the Celtic immigrants were to dominate Ireland for more than a thousand years, and even today some remnants of their ways survive in the Irish-speaking households of the western seaboard. Theirs is the next part of the history of Ireland.

EARLY IRISH SOCIETY
1ST–9TH CENTURY
F. J. BYRNE

Already before the Christian era, Ireland was a Celtic country. The earliest waves of Celtic invaders may have arrived at the end of the Irish Bronze Age – in the sixth century BC. The Celts had long dominated central and western Europe, and for a brief period of glory they terrorised Italy and Greece. They sacked Rome in 390 BC, raided Delphi a century later, and founded the kingdom of Galatia far away in Asia Minor. In statues made by Greek artists who were impressed by their size and ferocity, we can almost recognise the very features of the chariot warriors of ancient Irish saga. The Celtic culture of the late Iron Age – from the fifth century BC on – is known as La Tène, after a site in Switzerland. La Tène culture probably reached Ireland in the second century BC. La Tène finds in Ireland include golden collars or torques – the typical ornament of the Celtic warrior – war trumpets and beautifully ornamented sword scabbards.

Such finds are concentrated in Ulster and Connacht – the very area where Irish saga tradition places the scene of the epic *Táin Bó Cuailgne* and other legends of the heroic age. The stories of Cú Chulainn and Conchobar Mac Nessa do reflect a historical situation. The Ulster capital of Emain Macha (Navan fort, near Armagh) is recorded as a city (*Isamnion*) on the map of Ireland drawn by Ptolemy of Alexandria in the second century AD. The way of life of the heroes in the *Táin* is exactly that of the Celts in Gaul, as described by the Greek philosopher Poseidonios in the first century BC. It is also very similar to that of the Homeric warriors in the *Iliad*. Still further east, the Sanskrit epic poem the *Mahabharata* depicts the same society of chariot-driving warriors in northern India some centuries earlier.

All these legends reflect historical phenomena, although they do not record strict history. The term 'Celtic' is primarily linguistic, and Celtic, like Greek and Sanskrit, is a branch of the Indo-European family of languages. So are Germanic, Latin, Slavonic and Persian. As the Indo-Europeans spread over Europe and parts of Asia in prehistoric times, they brought with them not only a language, but common religious beliefs and a common semi-barbaric structure of society.

The Irish language derives from a dialect called Q-Celtic. The Celts of Gaul and Britain spoke P-Celtic, the ancestor of Welsh and Breton. The P-

Celtic word for 'horse' was *epos*, whereas the Q-Celts said *equos*, which in Irish developed to *ech*, Modern Irish *each*. There is some evidence to suggest that the Q-Celts came from Spain. The latest Celtic invaders – those who introduced the La Tène culture – may well have been P-Celts from Britain. Cú Chulainn's boyhood name of Sétantae is identical with that of a British tribe, the *Setantii*, who lived on the Lancashire coast. The *Menapii* of Belgium appear on Ptolemy's map of Ireland in Wexford – later they are found in Ulster under the Q-Celtic form of their name as the *Fir Manach*.

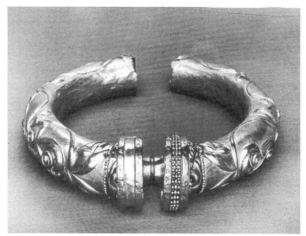

15   Gold collar from Broighter, County Derry, end of the 1st century BC
National Museum of Ireland

The earlier, non-Indo-European population, of course, survived under the Celtic overlordship. One group in particular, known to the P-Celts as *Pritani* (Welsh *Prydyn*) and to the Irish as *Cruithni*, survived into historical times as the Picts or 'painted people' of Scotland. The Cruithni were numerous in Ulster too, and the Loíges of Leinster and possibly the Ciarraige of Connacht and north Kerry belonged to the same people. But when Irish history properly begins, in the fifth century AD, all these peoples had become completely Celticised, sharing a common culture and a common Gaelic language. This language was introduced into Scotland by the Dál Riata of Antrim, who founded a powerful kingdom in Argyll. The movement of British Celts to Ireland was reversed in the fourth century, when the Irish began raiding Roman Britain. The Romans called them *Scotti* and the Britons *Gwyddyl*. The Irish borrowed this Welsh name for themselves as *Goídil* – Modern Irish *Gaoidhil*.

16   Hill of Tara, from the air

Bord Fáilte Éireann

These events marked the end of the heroic age. The great Ulster kingdom
of Emain Macha was destroyed by the Connachta, probably as late as 450 AD
– not 331, as you will find in most history books. In fact, when Armagh was
founded in 444 as the chief church in Ireland, Emain Macha may still have
been the most important political centre. Niall of the Nine Hostages, a prince
of the Connachta, seems to have won fame and power by successful raids on
Britain. From his brothers, Brión and Fiachra, descended the great ruling
families of Connacht. Niall's own descendants took the dynastic name of Uí
Néill. Three of his sons founded kingdoms in north-west Ulster. Others ruled
in the midlands, in Mide and Brega, and waged successful war against the
Laigin of Leinster. Around Emain Macha itself, the subject peoples seem to
have thrown off the yoke of the Ulaid and put themselves under the
protection of the Uí Néill. They formed a confederation of nine petty
kingdoms – a sort of satellite state called the Airgialla, 'the hostage givers' –
from whom Niall got his epithet of *Noígiallach*. The Ulaid themselves were
driven east of the Bann.

When documentary evidence becomes fuller in the seventh and eighth centuries, we see that Ireland has settled down to become an agricultural country, divided into mainly small kingdoms. These were at least 150 such *tuatha*, although the population of Ireland may have been less than half a million. The great warlords who had dominated the land with their chariots and hill-forts had gone. Heroic ages do not last long, but they are remembered forever. At this very time, the Old Irish Sagas were being composed by men who united native and Latin learning. Just as suburban Americans cherish the memory of the wild west, so Irish kings cast themselves in the role of Conall Cernach or Cú Chulainn. But the Irish nobleman was primarily a farmer. The battles which figure so prominently in the Annals rarely lasted longer than a summer's afternoon.

In this rural society there were no towns or villages. The only feature on the Irish landscape approximating to a town was the larger monastery. About the year 800, in his poetical calendar of saints Óengus, the Céile Dé, describes the scene:

> The strong fortress of Tara has perished with the death of her princes, with its quires of sages great Armagh lives on.
> The rath of Cruacha has vanished together with Ailill the victorious; fair above the kingdoms is the majesty in the city of Clonmacnoise.
> The proud fortress of Allen has perished with her boastful host; great is victorious Brigit, beautiful her crowded city.
> The fortress of Emain has faded away; only its stones survive; crowded Glendalough is the Rome of the Western world.[1]

The over-kings of the Uí Néill continued to call themselves 'kings of Tara', but they themselves lived more modestly in ring-forts or lake-dwellings such as the crannog at Lagore in County Meath, the home of the Uí Néill kings of South Brega.

The people lived in individual farms – the better homesteads were raths surrounded by an earthen rampart and stockade: the 'fairy forts' of the modern countryside. The king's house, according to the brehon laws, should have a double rampart, the outer ring being built by the forced labour of the king's lower-grade vassals – his *céili giallnai*. The king's most important functions were to lead his people in war and to preside over the *óenach*. This was an assembly held on regular occasions when the population of the *tuath* could meet to transact public and private business. There were also games and horse-racing – a survival from pagan funeral games, for the site of the *óenach* was normally an ancient tribal cemetery.

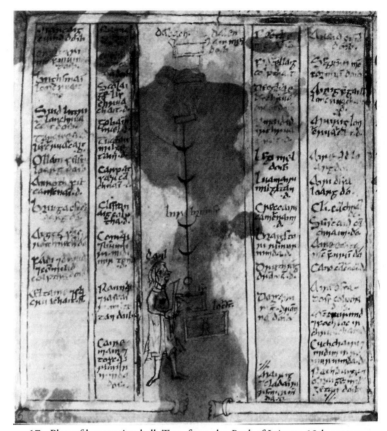

17   Plan of banqueting hall, Tara, from the *Book of Leinster*, 12th century

Trinity College, Dublin

In the twelfth century, the scribe of the *Book of Leinster* drew an imaginary sketch of the great banqueting hall of Tara as it was conceived to have been in the days of the legendary Cormac Mac Airt (Fig. 17). It shows in detail the official seating protocol, and lists the portion of meat to be served to each guest according to his rank. This picture is not completely unreal: the laws describe the seating arrangements in the less magnificent hall of a petty king in the eighth century. The door faces east, and beside it are the king's bodyguard of four mercenary soldiers:

> The personal surety for the king's base vassals west of these . . . Envoys are placed to the west of him; guest-companies after them; then poets; then harpers.[2]

18   Extract from the Brehon Laws in the *Book of Ballymote, c.* 1400
Royal Irish Academy

The Irish poets were not harpers. Even the bard, who was much inferior to the *filí*, was a member of the learned aristocracy and not a mere harper. The harper ranked as a freeman by virtue of his art, but other musicians, pipers, horn-players and jugglers were unfree. They were relegated to the corner near the door, beside the mercenaries.

19 Reconstruction of a crannóg by W. F. Wakeman
W. G. Wood-Martin, The Lake Dwellings of Ireland, *1886*

In the other half of the house, on the north, are a warrior and a champion guarding the door, each with his spear in front of him to prevent a disturbance of the banqueting hall. The king's noble clients west of these – they are the company who are in attendance on the king. The hostages are seated after them. A brehon after them. The king's wife west of him, and then the king.[3]

Hostages whose lives were forfeit were placed in chains in the corner farthest away from the door, under the king's watchful eye: they may have derived some consolation from being in the best position to hear the harper!

The giving of hostages or pledges, as well as the employment of elaborate forms of guarantee and suretyship, played a very large part in Irish life, both public and private. The king was not a judge, nor could he enact laws except in certain emergencies. The brehons were men learned in the difficult traditional law, which enshrined a very archaic Indo-European social system.

Early Irish law finds its closest parallel in traditional Hindu law. The brehons maintained that it represented the law of nature, so that Christianity might add to but not subtract from it. They even defended polygamy on the grounds that it was practised by the Old Testament patriarchs. In the manuscripts of the law schools, we find that the text of the law is written in large, clear letters, quite distinct from the explanatory notes and commentaries of a later date which usually surround it. Although the manuscripts are as late as the fifteenth or sixteenth century, the text is in difficult Old Irish of the eighth or even the seventh century and has been preserved unaltered and sacrosanct.

The laws teach us much about Irish society in the eighth century –

institutions such as fosterage of children, distraint of cattle to recover damages, ritual fasting as a method of asserting one's rights (this custom is also found in India). There are tracts on bee-keeping and on watermills, and tracts on marriage and the position of women.

The two pivotal institutions in Irish life were the *fine* or joint-family, which was the social unit, and the *tuath* or petty kingdom – the political unit. To translate these terms as 'clan' and 'tribe' respectively, as is sometimes done, is not very helpful and can be positively misleading. There was no organic connection between the two units. The *fine* was the family group and included all relations in the male line of descent for five generations. It corresponds to the Hindu 'joint-family', and in it was vested the ultimate ownership of family land, *fintiu*. If anyone died without immediate heirs, his property was distributed among his more distant relations in well-defined proportions. The individual as such had few or no legal rights – these were contingent on his membership of the *fine*.

The brehon lawyers drew up a very elaborate scheme of the different degrees of the relationship. The *geilfhine*, sometimes called *deirbfhine*, was the normal family group – basically the relationship between a man and his brothers – but it was extended over five generations to include his own children, his father's brothers, his grandfather's brothers, and even his great-grandfather and *his* brothers! Naturally, it was extremely unlikely that so many generations should be alive at the one time, but the lawyers had to provide for all possible contingencies. The next group, the *deirbfhine* or alternatively the *táebfhine*, brought in the first cousins for four generations; and the *iarfine* and *indfhine* the second and third cousins respectively.

The only term in general use outside of the law tracts is *deirbfhine*, though it is not always certain whether this refers to the first or second of the groups enumerated above. There was no system of primogeniture: land was shared equally between brothers; but the head of the senior line was the *cenn fine*, who represented the family in all its affairs. The *fine* were responsible for the misdeeds of their members and bore the duty of blood-vengeance if any member was slain. In practice they often accepted an *éraic* – a payment of blood-money from the slayer. If the latter had absconded, his fine were liable for the payment of the *éraic*. Women could not inherit land, but daughters might acquire a life interest in their father's land if they had no brothers.

In royal families, each member of the king's *deirbfhine* was theoretically a *rígdamnae* – eligible to be elected king. If one branch of the family monopolised the kingship for four generations, the others were in danger of falling outside the magic circle of the *deirbfhine* and of losing their royal status forever. To avoid this fate, they were often tempted to commit *fingal* – to slay their own kin. This was the worst crime in the Irish calendar, since there could be neither legal vengence nor compensation for it. To prevent such occurrences, a *tánaise ríg* or heir-apparent was usually elected during the king's lifetime. In practice, this would be the person who had most clients or vassals to support him. The ramifications of the *fine* make it easy to understand why Irish noble families were careful to preserve their genealogies – a function which was committed to the learned *senchaid*.

Irish society was rigidly stratified. Besides the unfree classes – slaves, labourers, workmen and the lower grades of entertainers – there were freemen and nobles. Rank depended on wealth as well as birth, and it was possible to rise or fall in status accordingly. Learning was also a qualification, for the *áes dána* or learned classes were equated in rank with the aristocracy, as were the Christian clergy. An *ollam* – a chief poet or brehon – was of equal status with a bishop or the king of a *tuath*. It was even possible for one of unfree status to acquire franchise by practising a skilled trade – smiths, physicians and harpers were classified as freemen. Hence the word *sáer* for a craftsman. Irish law had a maxim that a man was better than his birth: *Is ferr fer a chiniud*.

All freemen were landowners. The lawyers catalogued elaborate subdivisions of each class according to property qualifications. The *bóaire* or higher grade of freeman had to have land worth thrice seven *cumals* – that is to say, an amount equalling the value of sixty-three milch-cows. The Irish had a simple agrarian economy and did not use coined money. The basic unit of value was a *sét* (Modern Irish *séad*) – a young heifer. A higher unit was the *cumal* – a female slave, reckoned as equal to six *séts*. We find similar units in Homeric Greece, and even the Latin word for money, *pecunia*, comes from *pecus*, 'cattle'. The *cumal* and *sét* are not always to be understood in their literal sense, for they were equated with sums reckoned in shekels and ounces of silver, and we find the *cumal* used as a measure of land, as in this description of the *bóaire's* property. His house is described in detail:

All the furniture of his house is in its proper place –
    a cauldron with its spit and handles,
    a vat in which a measure of ale may be brewed,
    a cauldron for everyday use,
    small vessels: iron pots and kneading trough and wooden mugs, so that
    he has no need to borrow them;
    a washing trough and a bath,
    tubs, candlesticks, knives for cutting rushes;
    rope, an adze, an auger, a pair of wooden shears, an axe;
    the work-tools for every season – every one unborrowed;

a whetstone, a bill-hook, a hatchet, spears for slaughtering livestock;
a fire always alive, a candle on the candlestick without fail;
a full ploughing outfit with all its equipment . . .
There are two vessels in his house always:
a vessel of milk and a vessel of ale.
He is a man of three snouts:
the snout of a rooting boar that cleaves dishonour in every season,
the snout of a flitch of bacon on the hook,
the snout of a plough under the ground;
so that he is capable of receiving a king or a bishop or a scholar or a
brehon from the road, prepared for the arrival of any guest-company.
He owns seven houses:
a kiln, a barn, a mill (a share in it so that it grinds for him),
a house of twenty-seven feet,
an outhouse of seventeen feet,
a pig-stye, a pen for calves, a sheep-pen.
He has twenty cows, two bulls, six oxen, twenty pigs, twenty sheep, four
domestic boars, two sows, a saddle-horse, an enamelled bridle, sixteen
bushels of seed in the ground.
He has a bronze cauldron in which there is room for a boar.
He possesses a green in which there are always sheep without having to
change pasture.
He and his wife have four suits of clothes.[4]

The Greeks and Romans always spoke of the Celts as wearing trousers. But in Ireland only the lower classes seem to have worn them – they were tight-fitting and could be short or long. They were usually worn with a short jacket. But the aristocracy, both men and women, wore a voluminous cloak called a *brat* over a shirt or tunic – the *léine* – which varied in length. The *brat* was often secured with a beautiful brooch.

A man's status was expressed in very material terms by his *eneclann* or 'honour-price'. Damages due to him in a lawsuit were assessed according to this price. Furthermore, he was not able to make a legal contract for an amount worth more than this, nor was his evidence on oath valid in cases involving a larger amount.

The detailed inventory of the contents of an aristocrat's house in the same law-tract shows that it was basically the same as that of a prosperous commoner. The furnishings are more luxurious, of course: articles of yew-wood, bronze, silver and gold are mentioned. His hall had eight bed-cubicles arranged along the walls and furnished with mattresses, cushions and hides. Although there was little privacy anywhere in the Middle Ages, it is clear from old Irish texts that separate huts or houses within the *liss* or stockaded enclosure served the functions of separate rooms in a modern house. It is obvious that the nobleman too was a farmer:

> He has implements for every sort of farmwork, with a plough and its full
> legal equipment; he has two horses for harrowing . . .
> He is allowed to have pet animals:
> a deer-hound and horses, and a lap-dog for his wife.[5]

The element which really distinguished the aristocrat was *déis* – the possession of clients and vassals and the authority and influence which this entailed. Irish clientship was quite different from the feudal system of medieval Europe. The free or noble clients – the *sáer-chéili* – borrowed cattle from their lord with which to stock their own land. For this they paid a high rate of interest and accompanied the lord as part of his *dám* or retinue – the word *céile* in fact means companion. The so-called *dáerchéile* or *céile giallnai*, on the other hand, was not in fact 'unfree': he paid a lower rate of interest for his stock, but he also had to pay an annual food-rent and to perform certain menial services. He also had to provide free hospitality for the lord and his retinue during the *aimser chue* or 'coshering time' between New Year's Day and Shrovetide. Both forms of clientship were terminable on repayment of the original stock. A noble himself might be *céile* to another noble or to the king.

We are told of the *aire túise*, the highest grade of nobleman, that he was the *toísech* or chief of a large group of aristocratic kinsmen, a *cenél*:

> Twenty *séts* is his honour price: he swears in compurgation, he is bond,
> surety, guarantor, debtor or creditor and witness to that amount; he must
> be able to pay it when necessity arises, without having recourse to
> requisition or borrowing . . .
>
> So that he is of full assistance to the *tuath*, in representations, in oaths,
> in pledging, in giving hostages, in treaties across the border, on behalf of
> his kindred and in the house of a prince.
>
> He sustains legal agreements on behalf of his father and grandfather; he
> is able to enforce compensation by his own power; his oath overrides those
> of his inferiors in rank.[6]

It is easy to see that only through the patronage of such a person could the ordinary man hope to recover damages or debts due from a powerful neighbour. The nobles, for their part, were anxious to increase their political power by having as many clients as possible. Julius Caesar says that the

Helvetians were unable to convict Orgetorix of treason because he appeared in court surrounded by his clients and debtors (*clientes obaeratosque*). The elaborate nexus of mutual responsibilities entailed both by membership of a closely knit family group and by the relationship between client and patron in a small rural community ensured a reasonable measure of law and order in a society which had no police force, and where the state was not involved in most lawsuits, such as those for manslaughter or assault.

Relations between different *tuatha* were conducted on similar personal lines by the kings. Most *tuatha* were tribute-paying, under the suzerainty of a greater king. Certain so-called *sáer-tuatha* did not have to pay tribute, because their own king belonged to the same dynasty as the over-king. But all sub-kings, whether tributary or not, acknowledged their inferior status by receiving gifts – termed *tuarastal* or 'wages' – from the over-king. The latter did not normally interfere in the government of the subject *tuatha*. Irish law recognised three grades of kings: the *rí tuaithe*, king of a single *tuath*; the *ruire*, or over-king, also called *rí tuath*, king of several *tuatha*; and at the top the *rí ruirech* or *rí cóicid*, the king of a province.

If we look, for instance, at the kingdom of Ulaid as it was in the eighth century, we shall find that in County Down alone there were several *tuatha* or petty kingdoms: Bairrche in the Mourne Mountains; Leth Cathail, now the baronies of Lecale; In Dubthrian, now the barony of Dufferin; Uí Echach Arda in the Ards peninsula; Uí Derco Chéin around Belfast; Dál mBuinne east of Lough Neagh – and some others as well. All of these formed the over-kingdom of Dál Fiatach, now represented by the diocese of Down. Other over-kingdoms were Dál nAraidi and Dál Riata in the north, which together form the present diocese of Connor; Uí Echach Cobo, the diocese of Dromore; even Conaille Muirtheimne in the north of County Louth was an over-kingdom with two or three subject *tuatha*. Over all these stood the king of Ulster, *rí in Chóicid* – a position usually held by the king of Dál Fiatach, but sometimes by the king of Dál nAraidi or the king of Uí Echach Cobo.

Leinster presents a similar picture. The boundary between Laigin Tuathgabair and Laigin Desgabair is that between the dioceses of Kildare and Dublin–Glendalough on the one hand and Leighlin and Ferns on the other. The kingdom of Uí Failge comprised the baronies of Offaly in County Kildare together with that part of County Offaly which is in the diocese of Kildare. The kings of Uí Failge were related to the ruling Laigin dynasty and so were free from tribute. Not so the Loíges, whose chief territory lay in that part of County Laois which is in the diocese of Leighlin, though they had branches elsewhere in Leinster. It will be seen that the modern county boundaries have little relevance to early Irish history: part of County Offaly, for instance, was anciently in Munster, and still is in the diocese of Killaloe.

From the seventh century to the eleventh, the overlordship of all Leinster was held by the northern Laigin, the kingship alternating fairly regularly between three branches of the dynasty – the Uí Dúnchada near Dublin (Dolphin's Barn is a corruption of Dunphy's Cairn, *Carn Ua nDúnchada*), the Uí Fáelán around Naas, and the Uí Muiredaig near Mullaghmast. But in the eleventh and twelfth centuries their southern cousins, the Uí Chennselaig, were to emerge supreme under the leadership of the Mac Murchada family. The Leinster baronies often preserve the boundaries of ancient *tuatha*: for example, Uí Dróna (Idrone), Fotharta (the baronies of Forth in Carlow and Wexford) and Uí Bairrche (Slievemargy in Laois and Bargy in Wexford).

Our dioceses very often coincide with early Irish over-kingdoms. An example is Ossory, which has preserved the name as well as the territory of Osraige – a kingdom which vacillated in its allegiance between Munster and Leinster. Kilmore is the enlarged kingdom of Bréifne as it was in the twelfth century; Clonfert is Uí Maine and Kilmacduagh Uí Fiachrach Aidne. Even such relatively small kingdoms as Corcomruad and Corco Loígde obtained their own dioceses of Kilfenora and Ross.

The law-tracts do not recognise a high king of Ireland even as late as the eighth century. One text in fact calls the king of Cashel the greatest of kings. Nevertheless, as we have seen, in the fifth century Niall and his sons had upset the ancient division of Ireland into five fifths by setting up new kingdoms in the north and in the midlands. The Uí Néill over-king styled himself king of Tara. We know that Tara was an important site even in prehistoric times, but we do not know precisely at what date the ancestors of Niall gained control of it. Both the Ulaid and the Laigin seem to have had ancient claims to the title, and possibly it had a religious rather than a political significance. The *Feis Temro* or 'Feast of Tara' originally symbolised the marriage of the priest-king to Medb, who was really a goddess and not a human queen. This feast was last celebrated by King Diarmait Mac Cerbaill in the mid-sixth century. Diarmait was on good terms with Saint Ciáran of Clonmacnoise, according to tradition, but the legend of the cursing of Tara in his reign by Saint Ruadán of Lorrha shows that the church disapproved of his attachment to certain aspects of the pagan past. Saint Adamnán of Iona, however, in his *Life of Colum Cille*, describes Diarmait in high-flown terms as having been ordained by God as ruler of all Ireland. Adamnán was writing at the end of the seventh century. His contemporary, Muirchú, in his *Life of Patrick*, talks of Lóeguire son of Niall reigning in Tara, 'the capital of the Irish' (*caput Scottorum*), and gives him the title of *imperator*. These claims were not universally accepted.

20
Ireland in the 8th
century
F. J. Byrne

Scale in Miles
0 10 20 30 40

This map is not complete,
but confines itself to places
and kingdoms mentioned
in the text.

Dál
Riata

Ailech

Dál Naraide
(Cruithne) ULAID

Northern Uí Néill

IN FOCHLA

1   2
3
4

Emain
Macha

Uí Echach
Cobo
(Craithne)

Dál Fiatach

5

(Uí Briúin) AIRGIALLA
BREIFNE

Uí Fiachrach
Muaide

Conaille
Muirtheimne

6

Cruachu •

Uí Briúin
Aí

Ciarraige

CONNACHTA   MIDE   BREIGE

Uí Briúin
Séola

Uisneach •

Southern
Uí Néill

• Tara
• Lagore

7

Uí Maine

Uí Failge 8
• Ailend

Uí Fiachrach
Aidne

9 LAIGIN
TUATHGABAIR

Éoganacht
Árann

Corco
Mruad

Múscraige

Loígis

12

In Déis
(Dál Cáis)

OSRAIGE

10   11

LAIGIN
DESGABAIR
(Uí Cennselaig)

Éoganacht
Áine

Éoganacht
Caisil
• Cashel

Ciarraige
Luachra

Múscraige

Déisi
Muman

Éoganacht
Locha
Léin

MUMU

Éoganacht
Glendamnach

Múscraige
Éoganacht
Raithlinn

Corco

Loígde

1 Dál mBuinne   7 Uí Dúnchada
2 Uí Derco Chéin   8 Uí Fáeláin
3 Uí Echach Arda   9 Uí Muiredaig
4 In Dubthrian   10 Uí Dróna
5 Leth Cathail   11 Fotharta
6 Bairrche   12 Uí Bairrche

But the Uí Néill certainly presented a new phenomenon on the political scene. In particular, they demanded from Leinster the payment of a large cattle tribute, the *bóruma*. As the king of Leinster was technically a *rí cóicid*, he should not have had to pay tribute to anyone. The *bóruma* was never paid willingly, and many of the Uí Néill 'high kings' fell in battle in the attempt to levy it.

Meanwhile, Munster was ruled by the Eóganacht dynasty. This was divided into several groups with kingdoms planted strategically throughout Munster, dominating earlier peoples such as the Múscraige and the Corco Loígde. The king of any one of these groups was eligible to become king of Cashel. From the beginning, Cashel seems to have been a Christian centre, and several of its kings were also bishops or abbots. County Clare had been conquered from Connacht early in the fifth century, and the Eóganacht had colonised it with a subject people. These may have been related to the Déisi – at all events they were called In Déis, which simply means 'the vassals'. Later they were to emerge from obscurity under the name of Dál Cais.

At first the Eóganachta ignored the pretensions of the Uí Néill. But they became alarmed at their interference in Leinster. Cathal Mac Finguine in the eighth century and Feidlimid Mac Crimthainn in the ninth both challenged the Uí Néill supremacy. It was in the middle of the ninth century, however, during the crisis provoked by the Viking invasions, that Máel Sechnaill I, of the southern Uí Néill, first made the high kingship a reality. In 851 he secured the submission of the king of Ulaid, and a few years later brought the king of Osraige to heel. Then he invaded Munster and obtained hostages from the whole province. But the existence of the high kingship depended very much on the ability of the claimant. Among those who vindicated their claim was Flann Sinna, who erected the Cross of the Scriptures at Clonmacnoise in memory of his treaty with the king of Connacht. He also slew the scholarly king and bishop of Cashel, Cormac Mac Cuilennáin, at a battle in Leinster in 908. He was succeeded by Niall Glúndub, the ancestor of the O'Neills; Niall fell fighting the Dublin Norse near Islandbridge in 919 at the head of an army which was more representative of a national effort than that which fought under Brian at Clontarf a century later.

The absence of political unity makes the cultural unity of the country all the more remarkable. From the time of the earliest documents, we find a sophisticated and uniform language in use throughout Ireland. The *áes dána* or 'men of art' constituted the most important element of early Irish society. They included the *filid* – a word very inadequately translated as 'poets' – as well as the brehons and the historians and genealogists. They alone enjoyed franchise outside their own *tuatha* and travelled freely throughout Ireland. They were all originally Druids. Greek authors tell us of the importance of the Druids and poets among the Continental Celts, and Caesar says that the pupils of the Gaulish Druids had to learn by heart an immense number of verses. His account tallies closely with what we know of the Irish bardic schools as late as the seventeenth century. With the triumph of Christianity, the Druids as such disappeared. The poets gave up their more pagan and magical functions, but otherwise they and the other members of the learned caste continued to enjoy their full privileges.

The 'men of art' adapted the Latin alphabet to produce a native Irish literature, and in collaboration with the Christian monks tried to provide Ireland with a history as respectable and ancient as that of Babylon, Egypt, Greece and Rome. The result was the *Lebor Gabála*, which related the successive invasions of Ireland by Parthalón, Nemed, the Fir Bolg, the Tuatha Dé Danann and the Milesians. It is possible that these stories may preserve some genuine traditions: for instance, the Fir Bolg may be the Belgae – but in general the *Lebor Gabála* is an extremely artificial compilation. The Tuatha Dé Danann are in fact the Celtic gods worshipped by the pagan Irish. The church tolerated Celtic mythology if it was disguised as history.

The compromise arrived at between the church and the poets is reflected in the legend of the convention of Druim Cett in 575, where the poets were said to have been rescued from banishment by the intercession of Colum Cille. As a result, Ireland was in an almost unique position in the Middle Ages: here learning and literacy were not the preserve of the Christian clergy. As late as 1539, a formal treaty between Manus O'Donnell and O'Connor Sligo invokes the satire of the poets and excommunication by the clergy as penalties for its violation. And just as the Romans extirpated the Druids from Gaul and Britain, so too in the sixteenth century, when Gaelic society was on the verge of extinction, the Elizabethan pamphleteers reserved their most bitter venom for the 'lewd rhymers' – the poets who were the true bearers of the ancient Celtic tradition.

THE BEGINNINGS OF CHRISTIANITY
5TH AND 6TH CENTURIES
TOMÁS CARDINAL Ó FIAICH

Since the historian depends mainly on written documents for his knowledge of the past, Irish history properly speaking must begin with St Patrick, the author of the earliest documents known to have been written in Ireland. Indeed it is extremely doubtful whether our ancestors had any method of writing before his time except the ogham alphabet, a cumbersome system of representing letters by groups of short lines varying in number and position. The system sufficed for short inscriptions on tombstones and the like, but if a modern novel were to be written in it, it would require a surface over a mile in length. St Patrick wrote a Latin which was rugged and abrupt, with little of the grace and dignity of the classical language, but for all his shortcomings as a scholar, his writings provide us with our only contemporary narrative of the conversion of Ireland to Christianity.

There were certainly Christians in Ireland before St Patrick's arrival. Trade relations with Roman Britain and Gaul saw to that. Some scholars from Gaul may even have sought refuge in Ireland during the barbarian invasions of the empire. At any rate, Irish Christians were sufficiently numerous by 431 to justify the appointment of a bishop for them by Rome in that year.

What does St Patrick tell us about himself in his writings? A little about his family background and captivity. He was a native, he says, of Roman Britain, the son of Calpurnius of the village of Bannavem Taberniae; at the age of sixteen he was captured by Irish raiders along with thousands of others and spent six years in captivity in Ireland tending sheep in the woods and on the mountain. During this period he turned to God and to matters of religion, which he had neglected in his youth, and finally succeeded in making his escape. Back in Britain he was welcomed by his relatives as a long-lost son and they implored him to remain with them. He might have done so were it not for a vision which he recounts in his Confession with remarkable vividness half a century later:

And there I saw in the night the vision of a man whose name was Victoricus, coming as it were from Ireland, with countless letters. And he gave me one of them and I read the opening words of the letter, which were 'The voice of the Irish', and as I read the beginning of the letter I thought that at the same moment I heard their voice – they were those beside the Wood of Foclut, which is near the Western Sea – and thus did they cry out as with one mouth: 'We ask thee, boy, come and walk among us once more'.[1]

21
Ogham stone, Coolnagort, Dungloe,
County Kerry, 5th–8th century
Commissioners of Public Works in Ireland

St Patrick does not tell us where exactly he received his ecclesiastical training but in his old age he would write of his desire to go to Gaul to visit 'the saints of the Lord'; this suggests that he studied in Gaul. A seventh-century biography makes him a disciple of St Germanus of Auxerre, the site of whose monastery is still pointed out along the banks of the River Yonne. A stay on the island of Lérins, off the French Mediterranean coast, to which a primitive form of monasticism had spread from the Middle East, is also a possibility.

Without going beyond the saint's own words, we can learn many details of his missionary work in Ireland. He 'baptised thousands', 'ordained clerics everywhere', 'gave presents to the kings', 'was put in irons', 'lived in daily expectation of murder, treachery or captivity', 'journeyed everywhere in many dangers, even to the farthest regions beyond which there lived nobody' and rejoiced to see 'the flock of the Lord in Ireland growing splendidly with the greatest care and the sons and daughters of kings becoming monks and virgins of Christ'. It is probable that most of his missionary work took place north of a line running from Galway to Wexford. Most of the churches which later claimed St Patrick in person as their founder are situated in this half of the country. Of the twenty churchmen whose obituaries are entered in the annals in the generation after St Patrick's death, almost all are associated with the same area. And while paganism put up a stiff fight before being overthrown, Ireland was the only country in western Europe whose conversion produced no martyrs. Perhaps that was the reason why an Irish cleric, in the earliest sermon which has survived in the native tongue, elaborated his theory of the three kinds of martyrdom, white and green as well as red:

> Is í an bán-martra do dhuine, an tan scaras, as son Dé, re gach rud a charas.
> (This is white martyrdom to a man, when he renounces everything he loves for God; this is green martyrdom to him, when by fasting and labour he does penance.)[2]

The Irish monks had reason to know.

To fill in the details of his life left unrecorded by the saint himself – to give him an anchorage in time and place – has been the task of medieval biographers and modern scholars. Where was the elusive Bannavem Taberniae, his native village? Until the nineteenth century it was usually identified with Dumbarton on the Clyde. But an area so far north seemed inconsistent with Patrick's Roman citizenship, and this has induced modern scholars to seek his birthplace further south. The Severn valley, the island of Anglesey, and Ravenglass in Cumberland have all received strong support in recent times, but the question is still unresolved. Or again, where was the mysterious Wood of Foclut, whose people called Patrick back to Ireland? Faughill in north Mayo, Achill, Magherafelt in south Londonderry, Killultagh in south Antrim and Kilclief on Strangford Lough have all been advanced because of similarities in the Irish forms of their names. And where did the saint spend his years of captivity? Slemish and Croagh Patrick both have their advocates. Most disputed of all the questions connected with the saint at present is the problem of giving definite dates to his Irish mission. We are certain that it began in the second or third quarter of the fifth century and lasted about thirty years. But did the saint arrive in Ireland in 432 and die in 461, or did he arrive in Ireland in 456 and die about 490? The earlier dating fits better into the Continental background and the saint's associations with Auxerre. The later dating agrees better with the fact that some of the saint's disciples in Ireland survived until well into the sixth century. It is this problem of dating the saint's work in Ireland which has brought forward the theory of the two Patricks: a Roman missionary who came in the 430s, and a British missionary who arrived a generation later. But there we enter the region of textual criticism, which had better be left to the scholars. The saint who proclaimed himself 'the most unlearned of men' must surely be enjoying the battles of the scholars in pursuit of him.

22
Beginning of Saint Patrick's
Confession, in the *Book of
Armagh*, 9th century
Trinity College, Dublin

The system of church government which Patrick introduced to Ireland would naturally have been the episcopal one which he saw all around him in Britain and Gaul. The laws of a synod held before his death assume the existence of bishops with fixed sees, each exercising jurisdiction within his own diocese. But Patrick also introduced the monastic life into Ireland and wrote with gratitude of the great numbers of his new converts who embraced it – something then unusual in most parts of western Europe. The trend towards monasticism, which from the beginning had thus enjoyed an important but by no means predominant position within the Irish church, became more pronounced after the saint's death. Within a century, new monasteries had ousted many of the older Patrician foundations as the important centres of religion and learning, and ultimately Ireland became unique in western Christendom in having its most important churches ruled by a monastic hierarchy, many of whom were not bishops. Even Armagh, the church which was looked upon as in a special way Patrick's own, soon accommodated itself to the new system. Patrick's immediate successors there were bishops; before the end of the fifth century one of them, Cormac, was styled first abbot, and for the next two centuries the ruler of Armagh church was both bishop and abbot. The process was not completed till the eighth century, by which time the abbot of Armagh was no longer a bishop but had as a subordinate member of his community a bishop for the administration of those sacraments for which episcopal orders were necessary.

23   Sceilg Mhichíl from the air

Bord Fáilte Éireann

Whence came the impulse for this sixth-century flowering of monasticism? The tendency of the Irish temperament towards an ascetic way of life surely contributed to it, as did the strong and attractive personalities of the great monastic founders. But some of the impulse came from abroad, from Scotland and Wales. Ninian's foundation in Galloway, called *Candida Casa*, 'The White House', from the unusually bright appearance of its walls, was the training ground of St Enda, whose later monastery on the largest of the Aran

Islands was the school where many Irish abbots served their apprenticeship. But Aran's renown as a school of asceticism was soon eclipsed by the monastery of St Finnian and Clonard, who, under the influence of the Welsh reformers Cadoc and Gildas, placed a new emphasis on sacred study as part of the monastic life and thus attained the position which caused the martyrologies to name him 'the teacher of the saints of Ireland'. His twelve outstanding disciples at Clonard are linked together under the picturesque title of 'the twelve apostles of Ireland' and each became in turn an outstanding monastic founder in his own right – Colum Cille in Durrow, Derry and Iona, Ciáran in Clonmacnoise, Brendan in Clonfert, Molaisse in Devenish, Cainneach in Aghaboe and Mobhi in Glasnevin. Others, too, who had not been pupils of Finnian, followed the example of his disciples and thus arose a second wave of foundations during the sixth century which owed nothing to Clonard – Bangor, founded by Comgall; Moville, by Finnian; Glendalough, by Kevin; Tuam, by Jarlath; and Cork, by Fionnbar. Religious establishments for women were less numerous but no less celebrated; some of them, like St Brigid's foundation at Kildare and St Moninne's at Killeavy near Newry, went back to the end of the fifth century, while others, like St Ita's at Killeady, County Limerick, Caireach Deargan's at Cloonburren, County Roscommon, and St Safann's at Clauin Bronaigh in Meath, followed later. Indeed, St Brigid's foundation at Kildare was unique in sixth-century Ireland in being a double monastery for both men and women, each group following the same rule and using a common church, with the government of the whole community held jointly by the abbess and the bishop-abbot.

Monasteries established by the one founder tended to retain close ties with one another – such as Durrow, Derry, Iona and the others founded by St Colum Cille and his disciples. These groupings of monastic churches, no matter where they were situated, would have been somewhat on the lines of the present-day link-up of the various Franciscan or Dominican houses in Ireland in a single province under one provincial. The difference was that nowadays these groupings of the regular clergy exist side by side with groupings of the secular clergy into dioceses arranged on a geographical basis; in early Ireland the monastic groupings replaced dioceses altogether. Another peculiar feature of the early Irish monasteries was the tendency for many of them to choose their abbots as far as possible from the family to which the founder belonged. Thus, of the first twelve abbots of Iona, all except two belonged to the Cenél Connaill, from which Colum Cille himself was descended. This tendency undoubtedly helped to open the way for the later assumption of power in some of the large monasteries by local ruling families. Even from the beginning, however, Clonmacnoise was a notable exception to this rule.

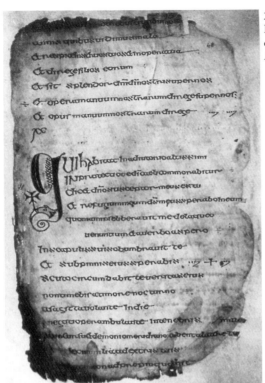

24
Page from the *Cathach*, late 6th century
Royal Irish Academy

A sixth-century Irish monastery must not be pictured like one of the great medieval monasteries on the Continent. It was much closer in appearance to the monastic settlements of the Nile valley or the island of Lérins than to later Monte Cassino or Clairvaux. Even the Latin word *monasterium*, when borrowed into Irish under the form *muintir*, was applied not to the buildings but to the community. For a modern equivalent, one could think of the army camps to be found in various parts of the country during the 1940s, each a collection of wooden huts for sleeping in, grouped around a few larger buildings used by the whole community. A modern holiday camp, with its rows of wooden chalets grouped around a few central halls, would be closer to it in appearance than a modern Mount Melleray.

From Adamnán's *Life of Colum Cille*, written in Iona in the seventh century, when some of those who had entered the monastery under the founder were still alive, we can reconstruct the authentic picture in great detail. Instead of a communal residence, the monks lived in individual cells constructed of wood or wattle, the abbot's cell slightly apart from the rest. In the west of Ireland, where wood was even then scarce, the cells were more usually constructed of stone; in any case, those are the only ones which have stood the test of time. Besides the cells of the monks, the monastic enclosure included within it the *church*, usually built of oak, with a stone altar, sacred vessels, relics and handbells for summoning the congregation (on the rare occasion when the church was of stone, this was of sufficient interest to be given a special name, the *damliag*, from which St Cianán's foundation at Duleek, County Meath, took its name); the *refectory*, with its long table, and adjoining it the *kitchen*, containing an open fire, cooking utensils, and a large cauldron of drinking water; the *library* and *scriptorium*, with manuscripts suspended in satchels by leather straps from the walls and an ample supply of writing materials – waxed tablets, parchment, quills and stylos, inkhorns and the rest. A workshop and forge were situated nearby, while outside the rampart came the cultivated lands and pastures belonging to the monastery, furnished with farm buildings and in addition a mill and limekiln.

'Pray daily, fast daily, study daily, work daily,' wrote Columbanus in his rule[3], and the monastic life became a round of divine worship, mortification, study and manual labour. With the exception of those brethren who worked on the farm, the monks assembled daily in the church for the various canonical hours. Sundays and saints' feast days were solemnised by rest from labour and the celebration of the Eucharist in addition to the divine office. Easter was the chief feast of the liturgical year, a time of joy after the austerities of Lent. Christmas was also a festival of joy, preceded by a period of preparation.

While the whole life of the monk and his retirement from the world was meant to be one great act of self-denial, additional mortification was imposed at fixed intervals. Every Wednesday and Friday throughout the year, except during the period from Easter to Pentecost, was observed as a fast day, when no food was taken till the late afternoon, unless when hospitality to a guest demanded relaxation of the rule. During Lent the fast was prolonged every day, except Sunday, till evening, when a light meal was allowed. The ordinary diet consisted of bread, milk, eggs and fish, but on Sundays and festivals and on the arrival of a guest, meat was probably permitted. The monks wore a white tunic underneath and over it a cape and hood of coarse, undyed wool. When working or travelling, they wore sandals. At night they slept in their habits. Their tonsure, unlike the Roman shaving of the crown of the head, took the peculiar Irish form of shaving the hair to the front of the head and allowing the hair at the back to grow long.

The principal subject of study was the sacred Scripture, much of which was committed to memory, especially the Psalms. Columbanus, a pupil of sixth-century Bangor, and Adamnán, a pupil of seventh-century Iona, show an extensive knowledge of Latin classical authors in their writings, especially of

Virgil and Horace, and pagan authors must be included among the liberal writings studied in Irish monasteries, as mentioned by the Venerable Bede. Lives of the fourth- and fifth-century Continental saints, such as Sulpicius Severus's *Life of St Martin of Tours* and Constantine's *Life of St Germanus*, found their way into the Irish monasteries at an early date and were used for reading to the community. Recent research has pointed to close cultural connections between Ireland and Spain in the sixth and seventh centuries: for instance, the writings of Isidore of Seville reached Ireland before being brought by Irish monks to central Europe.

25   Early Irish monastery

Liam de Paor

Copying of manuscripts formed an important part of the monastic occupations. The monastic scholar par excellence was the scribe, and Colum Cille and Baíthín, the first two abbots of Iona, laid the foundations of a scribal art which, with its later illuminative elements, formed one of the greatest glories of Irish monasticism. Of all the surviving manuscripts, however, only a handful go back to the period with which we are dealing – around the year 600. One is the *Cathach*, a fragmentary copy of the Psalms, traditionally looked upon as the copy made by Colum Cille in his own hand which led to the battle of Cúl Dreimhne and the saint's exile from Ireland. It is now preserved in the library of the Royal Irish Academy, Dublin, and shows the Irish style of writing before it was subjected to any seventh-century Continental influences. Another is a copy of the Four Gospels, arranged in the order Matthew, John, Luke, Mark, now in the library of Trinity College, which may have been written at Bobbio while Columbanus was still alive. Two other manuscripts of the same period from Bobbio are now in the Ambrosian Library, Milan, and a fourth Bobbio manuscript which was looked upon as having belonged to Columbanus himself is now in Turin. Showing none of the brilliant illumination of Irish manuscripts of a century or two later, they are still precious relics from the dawn of Irish Christianity.

The manual labour in which the early Irish monks engaged was primarily agricultural. Ploughing, sowing, harvesting and threshing are all mentioned as occupations of the sixth-century Iona monks. Others were engaged in making the various articles required for domestic use, and the need for sacred vessels of all kinds inspired an artistic approach to metalwork. Since fish formed such an important element in the diet, it is not surprising that the monks of Iona, as of all monasteries situated near the sea or the larger rivers, spent long hours in their boats. In common with all true fishermen, they liked to tell later of the 'big ones' which did not get away, and so Adamnán heard of the two huge salmon which Colum Cille's companions netted on the River Boyle in Roscommon more than a century before.

Some of the Irish monasteries seem to have had very large communities. Medieval sources refer to 3,000 monks of both Clonard and Bangor, but if this is not simply an exaggeration it must be taken to include all their daughter-houses as well. Upwards of a hundred would probably be the normal number during the sixth century in the larger monasteries: for instance, Columbanus had 200 monks divided among his three foundations in Gaul. By the early seventh century, when many English students flocked to Ireland, the numbers in some monasteries reached a few hundred. The great majority of the monks in each foundation were laymen and remained so, but a small number of the office-holders were in sacred orders. At the head of the community stood the abbot, who often nominated his own successor. He was assisted by the vice-abbot or prior, who looked after the material resources of the house, and by a group of the older brethren, called the seniores. One of these was usually in bishops' orders and one or two were ordained to the priesthood to celebrate Mass and administer the sacraments. Other posts in the monastery were those of scribe, cellarer, cook, guestmaster, miller, baker, smith, gardener, porter, and so on. Many monasteries had one or more anchorites, who secluded themselves from the rest of the community and lived lives of silence and prayer.

It is well known that Irish monastic discipline was strict, but a few instances from the rules of Columbanus will show just how severe it sometimes was. The smallest penalty, imposed for minor infringements of the rule, was the recitation of three psalms. Corporal punishment, inflicted on the hand with a leather strap, could vary from six to a hundred strokes. Periods of extra silence, fasting on bread and water, expulsion and exile were other penalties. The most severe, imposed by Columbanus for murder, was ten years' exile, of which some at least were to be spent on bread and water. Corporal punishment was nowhere prescribed in the Irish civil law and its introduction as a form of monastic chastisement is therefore all the more surprising. When the Irish monks went to the Continent, however, they found such punishment, together with the more extreme fasts and vigils, opposed by their Continental recruits and they ultimately abandoned it.

The great era of Irish monastic expansion abroad falls later than our period but already during the sixth century the pioneers of it had left Ireland. In its initial stages it had nothing of the character of the modern foreign missionary movement; in fact, it was not an organised movement at all. The motives uppermost in the minds of the *peregrini* were mortification and self-sacrifice – to renounce home and family like Abraham and seek a secluded spot where the ties of the world would not interfere with their pursuit of sanctity. Colum Cille's journey to Iona in 563 did not differ essentially, therefore, from Enda's journey to Aran a generation before. But once in Scotland, he found unlimited scope for his missionary zeal in the conversion of the Picts. Thus he became the prototype to later generations of the patriotic exile, thinking longingly in a foreign land of the little places at home he knew so well:

> Ionmhain Durmhagh is Doire,
> Ionmhain Rath-Bhoth go nglaine
>> Ionmhain Druim Thuama is mín meas,
>> Ionmhain Sord is Ceanannas.

> Da mba liom Alba uile
> Óthá a broinne go a bile,
>> Do b'fhearr liomsa áit toighe
>> Agam ar lár caomh-Dhoire.[4]

Colum Cille's mission inspired his namesake, Columbanus, to go further afield a generation later, and England, France, Belgium, Germany, Switzerland, Austria and Italy would soon re-echo to the tramp of Irish monks. Luxeuil, the greatest of Columbanus's foundations in France, was destined to influence directly or indirectly nearly a hundred other houses before the year 700. His journey from Luxeuil to Italy, like another Patrick or another Paul, was surely one of the great missionary voyages of history – twice across France, up the Rhine to Switzerland, across Lake Constance to Bregenz in Austria and southwards through the Alps and northern Italy until he founded his last monastery at Bobbio in 613.

26   Centres of Irish Christian influence in Europe, 6th–8th century

Liam de Paor

To stand by Columbanus's tomb in Bobbio is therefore to realise what the advent of Christianity meant to the Irish people. He was still proud of that people: 'We Irish, living at the edge of the world, followers of Saints Peter and Paul – there has never been a heretic or a schismatic among us.' He retained his individuality, that independence of spirit which had hurled anathemas at kings and queens and requested a pope not to allow 'the head of the church to be turned into its tail . . . for in Ireland it is not a man's position but his principles that count.'[5] He was still reluctant to give up his Irish method of calculating Easter or the episcopal exemption which the Irish monasteries enjoyed. To this native inheritance he added a mastery of Latin learning which few of his contemporaries could emulate, fashioning the new language into letters and sermons, poems and songs, even into a rowing chorus:

The tempests howl, the storms dismay,
But skill and strength can win the day,
    Heave, lads, and let the echoes ring;
For squalls and clouds will soon pass on
And victory lie with work well done
    Heave, lads, and let the echoes ring.[6]

The original Latin of this song is a far cry from the stumbling prose of St Patrick with which we began. It is a clear indication that the native and foreign elements in the Irish heritage are being welded into a new Christian culture and that Ireland, which received much from Europe since the arrival of St Patrick, has now also much to offer in return.

The Golden Age of Early Christian Ireland
7th and 8th Centuries
Kathleen Hughes

We have seen how Christianity came to Ireland, how church schools were set up and young clerics were given a Latin education. Irish scholars made rapid progress, for though Patrick in the fifth century was writing a very stumbling Latin, a century or more later Columbanus, Master of the Schools at Bangor in Ulster, could express himself fluently in Latin. Teachers in Irish ecclesiastical schools must have been hard at work during the fifth and sixth centuries. The boys learned Latin and studied the Scriptures, and the ablest of them could enjoy reading classical authors and could write excellent Latin verse.

But there were other schools in Ireland as well, schools of poets and of lawyers, which, for a considerable time, remained completely separate from the learning brought by the church. They had a long history and were honoured and respected by the people. The scholars educated in these secular schools formed a professional body, as closely knit as the clergy in Ireland today, and they contributed a great deal to the life of the country. They knew the law which governed men's actions; they could recite the genealogies (which were similar to one's birth certificate and title deeds today); they entertained and instructed people with their stories and histories. They told their traditions before men went into battle, to inspire them with reminders of the historic past; they praised the warriors' courage and prowess; they lamented those who were slain in war. These learned men of the pre-Christian period had to go through a long and severe training before they reached the top of their profession; but reading and writing were no part of it. Memory, not literacy, was the basis of their education, so that an Irish man of learning who could repeat, with complete accuracy, many complicated stories, whose sayings had grace, wit and fluency, could yet write down none of his fine tales or clever remarks.

The education provided in the church schools on the one hand and the schools of poets and lawyers on the other was completely different, not only in subject matter but in its whole method and approach. One of the most exciting and important historical facts of the seventh century is that these two quite separate worlds, the Latin and the Irish, began to borrow ideas and techniques from each other. For instance, by this time some of the poets and lawyers had not only learned to read and write, which must have been fairly easy, but had also begun to apply their new knowledge to the Irish language and to their own traditional body of learning. The old method of learning by memory in the secular schools did not cease, but rather some poets and lawyers were coming into closer contact with clergy of Latin education and were wanting to record their own learning in writing in the new manner. These two kinds of education, written Latin and oral Irish, *could* have remained completely distinct. When the Romans went to Celtic Britain, Latin schools were set up, but, as far as we know, British oral literature was not written down. Some people can remember Irish-speaking grandparents who learned to write English at school but who could not write Irish, though Irish was the language of their daily lives and they spoke it with grace and elegance. Some seventh-century Irish scholars applied the foreign methods of Latin scholarship to their own, and were sufficiently proud of it. One of the early Irish law tracts has a story telling how this came about. The hero is a man called Cenn Fáelad who was wounded in a battle fought in 636 and who was taken to Toomregán for nursing, to a house at the meeting of three streets between the houses of three professors:

And there were three schools in the place; a place of Latin learning, a school of Irish law and a school of Irish poetry. And everything that he would hear of the recitations of the three schools every day, he would have it by heart every night. And he fitted a pattern of poetry to these matters and wrote them on slates and tablets, and set them in a vellum book.[1]

We cannot be certain that things took place exactly like this, but something similar must have happened. So spoken learning came to be written down and permanently recorded.

The borrowing was not all in one direction. The bishops who had drawn up church laws in the fifth or sixth century had forbidden their converts to bring disputes before the secular law courts: Christians were not to appeal to the pagan brehons. But by the seventh and eighth centuries, church authorities and secular lawyers must have been on easy terms. By this time the brehons had been converted, and the clergy, by reason of their orders, had been given a position among the noble grades of society. When church leaders now drew up their ecclesiastical laws, they were influenced by the secular lawyers, and tried to phrase their own legislation in the Irish manner. They had to find, or make up, Latin words to describe Irish legal practices unknown to classical Roman law. By the seventh and eighth centuries, there must have been a considerable amount of friendly contact between ecclesiastical and secular lawyers.

Nor did the church cut herself off entirely from the Irish poets. Adamnán, writing his *Life of Colum Cille* at the end of the seventh century, tells us that when a poet visited the monastery of Iona he would usually be asked to entertain the monks by singing to them something of his own composition. Were the monks accustomed to hear in this way praises of former kings and heroes, perhaps the ancestors of their founder, and songs of battle? Monks and laymen were not cut off from each other. Monastic education was not reserved exclusively for those who were to enter religion but was also given to the sons of church tenants and to some laymen who in adult life would farm and raise families. So there must have been people in Ireland, educated in the church, who could read and write Latin but who knew and loved the old tales.

Many of these tales were of violence and bloodshed, not of peace and love. Listen to the boast of a pagan Ulster hero:

> I swear by that by which my people swear, since I took spear in my hand I have never been without slaying a Connachtman every day and plundering by fire every night, and I have never slept without a Connachtman's head beneath my knee.[2]

Churchmen could not well approve such conduct. Indeed, a seventh-century sermon urges self-sacrifice, not self-assertion. 'It is right,' says the preacher,

> that every one of us should suffer with his fellow in his hardship, and in his poverty and in his infirmity. We see from those wise words . . . that fellow-suffering is counted as a kind of cross.[3]

But even while some clerics, like this one, preached the true morality of Christ, others, writing the lives of the saints, were influenced by the generally accepted idea of what a hero should be like – brave, successful, hospitable, quick-witted. So although Patrick, on his own confession, was many times robbed, bound and in danger of death, his seventh-century biography shows him in triumph, worsting his pagan opponents, killing the king's Druid, cursing the king's host. Brigid is the perfect example of Irish hospitality: she can (by a miracle) milk her cows three times in one day to provide a meal for visitors; she can outwit a king (in the cause of charity) as well as any pagan hero could have done and with far more charm. The monastic scribes who wrote such saints' lives had been brought up on the Irish hero tales.

The church did not suppress the learning of the secular poets and storytellers, and ultimately much of this learning came to be recorded in writing and preserved in monastic libraries. Of course no man's learning, either Latin or Irish, will of itself get him into heaven. One scholar, writing a grammar book, put in a cautionary verse to this effect:

> Grammar, learning, glosses plain,
> Even philosophy is vain;
> Arithmetic and letters all
> In heaven's hall God shall disdain.[4]

Yet Irish, as well as Latin, could be used in the service of God. So someone wrote a grammar in the Irish tongue, and clerics used Irish in their schoolteaching. The division between the Latin and Irish worlds became less sharp in the seventh century than it had been when Christianity was first introduced. Laymen and clerics came together. Latin and Irish learning met and mingled; Christian artists used the designs of the earlier Irish craftsmen. Perhaps we can even see Christian and secular symbols alongside one another on the slab at Drumhallagh in County Donegal. In the lower arms of the cross are two bishops with their croziers. Above, in duplicate, is a figure with his thumb in his mouth, like the Irish hero Finn, who sucks his thumb to obtain knowledge.

27   Gallarus Oratory, County Kerry
Commissioners of Public Works in Ireland

28   Clonmacnoise from the air

Irish Press

The monasteries which housed the Latin schools followed Irish building techniques in their physical structure, although the Irish clergy must have been aware of Continental styles. The whole settlement was enclosed behind a ráth or cashel, like the monastery on Inishmurray, where the door and the stepped walling are very like those from secular forts. Inside were a number of cells, where the monks lived. This plan may be contrasted with that of a Continental Benedictine monastery in the early ninth century. Here the living quarters of the monks adjoined the church in a cloister, where the monks slept together in a common dormitory and ate together in a common refectory. Irish monks did not adopt this style of building, based on the Roman villa and courtyard. The early cells and churches were of wood, or of stone without mortar, each stone overlapping the one beneath on the inside, until at the top the roof could be joined with one stone. Chapels like this can still be seen: at Gallarus (Fig. 27) the mason fitted his stones together with such skill that the building stands complete and weatherproof to this day. Near the church was a graveyard, often with the tomb of a holy man beside the church entrance, and crosses stood within and around the monastic enclosure as the sacred sign which guarded its approaches.

In the seventh and eighth centuries, many of the monasteries which had been founded much earlier rose to positions of wealth and power. As one poet put it, writing in about 800:

> Little places taken
> First by twos and threes,
> Are like Rome reborn:
> Peopled sanctuaries.[5]

Such were the churches of Armagh, Clonmacnoise, Kildare, Glendalough and other places. Many of them had been founded near native forts, but the forts had declined, while the power of the churches had risen. The same poet tells us of the lost glory of King Ailill's chief fort of Connacht and the present splendour of Clonmacnoise, and of Glendalough's importance:

> Ailill the king is vanished
> Vanished Croghan's fort:
> Kings to Clonmacnoise now
> Come to pay their court.
>
> Navan town is shattered
> Ruins everywhere:
> Glendalough remains
> Half a world is there.[6]

Such monasteries were usually easily accessible, being on the main roads; they were cities, places of refuge, hostels, penitentiaries, schools and universities, as well as religious centres. Other monasteries, by contrast, were in remote and isolated places: Sceilg Mhichíl in the stormy Atlantic, or Kildreelig on Bolus Head, inside its stout rampart above the steep slope of the cliff edge. Men might retire to the desert to fast and pray. Some of our sources show us saints intent only upon God, with the lightest grasp upon material things, like St Brigid, who:

> loved not the world:
> she sat the perch of a bird on a cliff[7]

– the saint who has nothing and desires nothing but God. For Irish monastic life, in its enthusiasm and lack of uniformity, had its roots in the eastern desert, where monasticism began. But there was no standard norm. While some monks retired to forests or islands 'to be sitting awhile, praying to God in some place', others attended church councils, drew up laws, went on visitation, collected revenues or ran the schools. Such men were in constant touch with the world.

Masters of monastic schools were eager to have Latin books from the Continent. They welcomed new works and were looking for better texts of known authors. We know that books written in Spain were coming to Ireland in the seventh century, for some of the works of Isidore, Bishop of Seville, seem to have reached Ireland within a few decades of his death. Irishmen were also taking their own books to the Continent with them. St Columbanus founded monasteries at Luxeuil in Burgundy and Bobbio in north Italy. At both these monasteries, and at St Gall, founded by the disciple of Columbanus, there were very soon important libraries.

29
Page from the *Book of Durrow*, late 7th century
Trinity College, Dublin

Others beside Columbanus went to the Continent as 'pilgrims for Christ', in search of 'salvation and solitude'; they soon found themselves preaching the gospel and setting up communities. One of the most famous was St Fursey, buried at Péronne in north-eastern Gaul, a monastery where the monks loved

Patrick. Irishmen constantly stayed here, so it became known as Perona Scottorum ('Péronne of the Irish'). These houses supported scribes who copied books, and attracted men of learning. Scholars on pilgrimage took books out with them and brought books home in their luggage. For example, a service book from Bangor, probably written at the very end of the seventh century, found its way to Bobbio, we do not know for certain how, but most probably carried there by some monk in his book-satchel. Among the treasures of St Gall are books written and illuminated by Irish artists in a specifically Irish style. From about the middle of the seventh century until the Carolingian renaissance, art and learning in Gaul were at a low ebb, and some of the Irish foundations, with their active book production, stand out the more brilliantly in contrast with the general gloom. No doubt some Irish pilgrims, having visited their Continental brothers, went on as far as Jerusalem, for Adamnán, Abbot of Iona, who died in 704, wrote an account of the holy places on information supplied by a Gaul – though as far as we know he was never able to get there. The ninth-century copy of this book has plans which would have been of use to the tourist as well as of interest to the scholar in the library at home.

30   Ardagh Chalice, early 8th century
National Museum of Ireland

The fusion of Irish and Latin cultures is nowhere more clearly seen than in seventh- and eighth-century Irish art. In the pre-Christian period the patrons of Celtic art were the warrior aristocracy: it was for them that the smiths produced personal ornaments, weapons and horse-trappings. By the eighth century the church had become a great patron. A church might be small and dark, but its altar must have gleamed with bookcovers, reliquaries and altar-vessels. Many of these ornaments are in gilt-bronze, decorated with gold filigree arranged in intricate patterns, inlaid with enamel and precious stones, so that the surface has an exquisite variety of texture, yet at the same time the eye can easily grasp a coherent design. The seventh-century compiler of the *Life of Brigid* tells us that the church at Kildare contained two tombs, of St Brigid and Bishop Conláeth, placed to the right and left of the altar. 'These tombs,' he says, 'are richly decorated with gold and silver and many coloured precious stones; they have also pictorial representations in relief and in colours, and are surmounted by crowns of gold and silver.'[8] Once Irish smiths had made crowns for warriors; in the seventh century they were also turning their skill to glorifying Christ and his saints.

31
Athlone crucifixion plaque,
8th century
National Museum of Ireland

The pagan Irish artist had sometimes carved statues, which, to our eyes, seem grotesque and brutal lumps of stone. Yet in abstract design he had been a master. The Christian artist repeated the old motifs of curves and spirals: the scribe liked to decorate his books with them; the smith put them on his metalwork; the sculptor carved them on his crosses. But the Christian artist also needed to show Christ in human form, as a child in the Virgin's arms, as a man tempted as we are, as the Redeemer bearing the sins of the world yet triumphant over death. So new designs entered Irish art, sometimes influenced by types which came originally from the eastern end of the Mediterranean, sometimes by patterns from nearer home, copying the appearance of English jewellery.

Yet for all the foreign influence it received and adopted, Christian art continued to show its Celtic origins. Most people would agree that the *Book of Kells*, with its skilled execution and infinite variety, is one of the most perfect examples of such art. The Norman-Welshman, Gerald, saw a book like this at Kildare in the twelfth century. This is how he describes it:

32
Page from the *Book of Kells*,
c. 800: Arrest of Christ
Trinity College, Dublin

[It] contains the four Gospels . . . with almost as many drawings as pages, and all of them in marvellous colours. Here you can look upon the face of the divine majesty drawn in a miraculous way; here too upon the mystical representations of the Evangelists, now having six, now four, and now two wings. Here you will see the eagle; there the calf. Here the face of a man; there that of a lion. And there are almost innumerable other drawings. If you look at them carelessly and casually and not too closely, you may judge them to be mere daubs rather than careful compositions. You will see nothing subtle where everything is subtle. But if you take the trouble to look very closely, and penetrate with your eyes to the secret of the artistry, you will notice such intricacies, so delicate and subtle, so close together and well knitted, so involved and bound together, and so fresh still in their colourings that you will not hesitate to declare that all these things must have been the result of the work not of men but of angels.[9]

In the seventh and eighth centuries the old Celtic and the new Christian-Latin way of looking at things joined together. Because that happened, today we can study the Old Irish law tracts and enjoy the Old Irish tales; because of that, Irish artists gained a new vision, and yet interpreted the Christian message in their own individual style. So we have what is often called the Irish golden age. No doubt there was hardship – we know very little of what simple people thought – but on the whole Irish society must have been comparatively prosperous and there was much of beauty to be seen. The Irish did not keep all this to themselves. The English historian Bede tells us how St Aidan went from the monastery of Iona to convert the heathens of Northumbria. Monasteries and schools were set up in England and, for a time, some English students came to Ireland for further education. Speaking of these students, Bede tells us that the Irish welcomed them all kindly and, without asking for any payment, provided them with books and teachers. Irish monks took their own books to Northumbria and taught the scribe's art to their English pupils. While northern England had still been pagan, the Irish were already masters of a fine script. A psalter, known as the *Cathach* (Fig. 24), attributed to St Colum Cille, was written about 600, and it shows features which later became typical of Hiberno-Saxon manuscripts. In it the scribe provides headings with a series of decorated initials which diminish in size until they are brought into the body of the text. This was a favourite device of Irish scribes and can also be seen in manuscripts from Bobbio. It is used again, with much greater elaboration, in the *Book of Durrow*, which was written a generation or two later. Some modern scholars argue that this book was produced in Northumbria; others say it was written in Ireland or Iona.

But wherever it was produced, it was created under the direction of a man who had received an Irish training. If it was written in Northumbria, it demonstrates how much the Irish had taught their converts. Every good teacher learns from his pupils, and Irish illuminators had borrowed from the designs of English jewellers, perhaps even from the work of Pictish sculptors or from Roman remains still to be seen in Britain. But Irish masters left their stamp on English monasticism, so that even after 664 (when many Irishmen left Northumbria) their disciples continued to produce books which showed strong Irish influence, in marked contrast to the new styles in book decoration which were now coming into England from the Continent.

33   Funeral procession on base of North Cross, Ahenny, county Tipperary
Commissioners of Public Works in Ireland

We know a lot more about the Irish in England, because Bede, a great historian, wrote about them: on the Continent in the later seventh and eighth centuries we have to trace them through a series of less satisfactory clues. They helped to evangelise the pagan tribes of Germany, though their work was largely superseded by English missions. Irishmen on the Continent thought of and prayed for those at home. At Salzburg, where an Irishman named Fergil was abbot and bishop, the list of persons, living and dead, for whom the community undertook to pray includes the abbots of Iona, from Colum Cille, the founder, down to the fifteenth abbot, who was Fergil's contemporary. There are also Irish names written in the litany for Fergil's

German successor in the bishopric of Salzburg, saints whom Fergil himself had probably remembered in his prayers, among them the abbess of Clonbroney, who would have been middle-aged when Fergil was a boy. Fergil, and others less distinguished whose names are now forgotten, had an eagerness of mind and intellectual curiosity not common in the eighth century. The writings of seventh- and eighth-century Irishmen, often preserved in Continental libraries under false names, can still be identified by their style, idiom and special interests.

So the Irishman's love of learning, fostered by centuries of pagan tradition, combined itself with the art of writing and the Latin books brought by the Christians to Ireland. Irish artists learned to decorate with old patterns and new designs the manuscripts they wrote. Irish smiths turned their ancient skills to glorify the Christian church. Irishmen went out in pilgrimage, 'seeking salvation and solitude', but they also evangelised pagan peoples; they built up libraries on the Continent, wrote works of scholarship and helped to make ready for the flowering of learning which was to follow in ninth-century Gaul.

THE AGE OF THE VIKING WARS
9TH AND 10TH CENTURIES
LIAM DE PAOR

The noblest share of earth is the far western world
Whose name is written Scottia in the ancient books;
Rich in goods, in silver, jewels, cloth and gold,
Benign to the body in air and mellow soil.
With honey and with milk flow Ireland's lovely plains,
With silk and arms, abundant fruit, with art and men.

Worthy are the Irish to dwell in this their land,
A race of men renowned in war, in peace, in faith.[1]

These are lines from a Latin verse written by Donatus of Fiesole, an Irish bishop living in Italy in the ninth century. He was describing Ireland in her golden age – a land which had not been invaded since prehistoric times and which had been Christian for more than three centuries.

The eye of exile is fond, and Donatus perhaps paints too rosy a picture. All was not perfect in early Christian Ireland, and there are many signs that her monastic culture was already in decline by the end of the eighth century.

Yet the grandfather or great-grandfather of the poet could have known the artists who worked on such triumphs of the metalworker's craft as the Tara brooch or the Ardagh chalice. Donatus himself could have known the men who worked on the *Book of Kells*, the extraordinary masterpiece which marks the culmination of early Irish art. This book is unfinished – perhaps because of the disasters which befell many of the Irish monasteries at the end of the eighth century.

Some scholars believe that the *Book of Kells* was written and painted at the Irish foundation of St Colum Cille on the island of Iona off the Scottish coast. Iona is open to the sea on all sides and it was from the sea that, suddenly, disaster came. In 795, long, low ships, with patterned sails, appeared from the ocean and ran their prows up on the beach. From them came helmeted warriors, armed with heavy swords and iron spears, who ransacked the monastic village for valuables and slaves, taking as trinkets the jewelled shrines and ornaments of the altars. Raiders were back again in 802, and yet again in 806, when they murdered no fewer than sixty-eight of the monks. After this visitation the abbot, Cellach, moved to Ireland with the survivors, carrying with him the precious relics of Colum Cille. He was given land at Kells in the territory of the southern Uí Néill, where he founded a new monastery. One can imagine the *Book of Kells*, its ornamentation cruelly interrupted by the murderous raids, being carried back to the home country and housed with other valuables and relics in the building constructed at that time which is now known as Colum Cille's House at Kells. In gospel books as such the raiders had no interest, for they were illiterate, and pagans.

34 Viking ship, Gokstad, Norway, 9th century
Universitetetes Oldsaksamling, Oslo

The flight of Cellach and his monks was to be but one of many such flights in the coming years. In the very year of the first attack on Iona, raiders – probably indeed the same ships' crews – attacked Lambay off the Dublin coast, and for the next forty years or so the pagans from the sea struck again and again at the monasteries all around the shore of Ireland, even such lonely sanctuaries as the bleak Skellig, eight miles off the Kerry coast. Most of those who so fiercely attacked our shores came from the fjords of western Norway, sailing west to Shetland, then south to Orkney, along the Atlantic coast of

Scotland, and so to Ireland. From other parts of Scandinavia at this time raiding parties went out, not alone seafarers who could negotiate coasts and rivers in their ships, but horsemen as well, who would make long journeys overland. The Danes ravaged the Frisian coast and also eastern England, and tested the defences of Charlemagne's empire. The Swedes crossed the Baltic and penetrated deep into Russia. In time the Scandinavian ships were to appear off Cadiz and in the Mediterranean – even at the gates of the great imperial city of Byzantium itself.

What sort of people were the Vikings – to use the name by which the Scandinavian raiders are commonly called? They have received what is nowadays called a 'bad press', for most of the contemporary records of them come from the monasteries, which had good reason to fear and dislike them. In a violent time, their heathenism and their indifference to sanctuary struck horror into the monks. An Irish monk of the time, listening thankfully to the howling of a storm one night, wrote in the margin of his manuscript:

The wind is rough tonight
tossing the white-combed ocean;
I need not dread fierce Vikings
crossing the Irish sea.[2]

At home, these men were farmers and seamen, skilled in many crafts. Their way of life was not very different from that of the Irish of the period, except that they were still pagans, worshipping the old gods. Before the raids began, they had colonised the islands of Shetland and Orkney, where their settlements have been excavated. Here they lived a simple rural existence in farm villages like that at Jarlshof, where their longhouses have been found. Their technology was advanced and they had a keen eye for business and trade.

The Nordic peoples had developed great skills as carpenters and had gone through an intensive period of development in the design and construction of ships. They lavished great care and elaborate ornament on the vessels of kings and great leaders especially. One of these ships is described by a Saxon chronicler: 'with a golden beak and a purple sail furnished within a close fence of gilded shields'. Some of these have survived, for a dead Viking chief was buried in splendid style with his ships, his weapons and his goods, and such burials have been excavated. The Gokstad ship – a true Viking longship – shows well the low raking lines, the clinker construction of overlapping planks, and the curved prow which made these shallow-draught vessels seaworthy and yet suitable for inshore waters, estuaries and rivers. With the development of sails, which can be followed on Swedish stone-carvings, the Vikings were equipped for venturing out onto the dangerous and unknown Atlantic.

The invaders' courage and skill brought them not only on the southward course to Ireland, but also on the northward passage to the Faroes, Iceland, Greenland and even the foggy coasts of the North American Continent. Some went looking for new lands to colonise, for the Scandinavian populations were growing too big for the amount of farmland available at home. Others went to trade or to make what profit they could from piracy. New trading routes and merchant centres were coming into being in northern Europe, and these provided a stimulus for the Scandinavians, with their command of the waterways.

About the time of the earliest raids, the Vikings for the first time began to build towns – commercial centres such as Kaupang, Birka and Hedeby – at strategic points on the shipping routes. The towns were defended with earthen palisaded ramparts and wooden towers – traces of the ramparts still remain in Hedeby in Denmark and at other sites. Inside the ramparts were houses of timber or wattle-and-daub construction, and the size of the population no doubt fluctuated considerably, swelling for the winter and summer markets. The voyages, whether for trade or loot, or both, began to be organised on a larger scale, and fleets rather than single ships or small groups of ships plied the seaways. Such fleets appeared in Irish waters in 837, and with them the Norse attack changed its character.

There were sixty ships in the mouth of the River Boyne that year and sixty on the Liffey. Legendary history tells of one Turgesius who 'assumed the sovereignty of all the foreigners in Ireland', and records begin to tell of conflict between various Irish kings and the newcomers. The Norse were now trying to set up permanent bases in Ireland. The first was set up at the mouth of the Liffey, and from here large-scale expeditions were mounted deep into the interior of the country. Monasteries throughout the island were raided, but the chief Viking effort was probably directed at the seizure of land for settlement, following the pattern of ninth-century Viking activity elsewhere. The fleets rode at anchor on the Shannon lakes in the heart of Ireland.

The Norse apparently built their first fortified settlements in 841: one at Linn Duachaill (now Annagassan) on the Louth coast, the other at the Liffey mouth. The name 'longphort' which the Irish gave to these defended bases indicates that they began with the building of a stockade around the ships. The longphort on the Liffey was thereafter to play a central part in Irish history: this was the foundation of the city of Dublin.

Dublin indeed supplies us with a good deal of information about the Norse in Ireland at this time, for its ninth-century cemetery was accidentally discovered a hundred years ago when the railway cutting for the line from Kingsbridge was being made near Islandbridge. The Norse town itself would have been quite small – not much more than the present-day High Street. The *Thingmote*, or assembly place outside the town, was still there in the seventeenth century, when it was referred to as 'the fortified hill near the college'. The *Haugen* or 'burial-mounds' nearby gave their name to Hoggen Green, later known as College Green. The Haugen have long since been removed, but from the Islandbridge graves have come warriors' weapons: typical ninth-century Norwegian swords. These swords often had triangular pommels, sometimes with silver patterns hammered into the iron. There were also rarer and more costly Frankish swords, made by Continental armourers who signed their products, and iron spearheads, and specimens of that favourite Norse weapon, the iron axe. Some of the burials had a more pacific character, tools rather than weapons being buried with the dead – knives, hammers, forge-tongs and sickles. Women were buried wearing their distinctive Norse 'tortoise brooches' or with their household gear – linen smoothers and spindle whorls. One of the chief occupations of the Vikings is attested by a number of sets of folding bronze scales which were used by these first citizens of Dublin in striking their bargains.

35   Viking weapons, Norway, 9th century
Universitetets Oldsaksamling, Oslo

71

In the meantime, what of the Irish? What were they doing all these years and why did they not put up a better resistance to the invaders? It must be remembered that in ninth-century Ireland there was no one responsible for the defence of the island as a whole. There were many small kingdoms, and a traditional division of the island into two halves: Leth Cuinn, dominated by the Uí Néill of Tara, and Leth Moga, dominated by the Eóganachta of Cashel. At the time of their rise to power, centuries before, both of these paramount dynasties had taken lands from the Laigin, or Leinstermen. The Laigin had never fully acquiesced in the overlordship of either the Uí Néill or the Eóganachta, and their province in the south-east really formed a third, and crucially important, division of the country.

As the Norse crisis reached its peak, the Eóganachta and the Uí Néill began to come into conflict for the first time on a large scale. The career of Feidlimid mac Crimhthainn, king-bishop of Cashel, who challenged the kings of Tara and perhaps destroyed more churches than any of the Norse, is a symptom of the mounting anarchy in Irish affairs. He died in 847. From 850 onwards we have accounts in the annals of Irish alliances with Norse bands in the incessant warfare of the time, and we hear too of battles – often at sea – among the Norse themselves. A leader named Olaf founded a kingdom of Dublin, which remained a separate small state within the general Irish polity but with extensive overseas connections. The Norse were now drawn more and more into Irish affairs, playing their own parts in the complex and shifting alliances of the little kingdoms. From the confused welter of battles within kingdoms and battles between kingdoms in the second half of the ninth century, there did emerge a gradual strengthening of the power of the kings of Tara. The Vikings in the northern half of Ireland were gradually brought under control. Raids, sometimes on a large scale, continued, but the Norse policy of making fortified settlements was checked. Dublin remained a strong state. It played a large part in the affairs of the Vikings in Britain, since its rulers had dynastic interests in York. The Dublin Norse are frequently found allied with the Leinstermen or with the newly powerful south midland state of Osraige, under its king, Cerball.

As the ninth century drew towards its close there was a slackening of Norse activity in Ireland, while the conflict between the most powerful dynasties of the north and south came to a climax. Finally, in a great battle at Belach Mughna in Leinster, Flann Sinna, king of Tara, defeated Cormac mac Cuilennáin, king-bishop of Cashel, in 908. Cormac and many of the leaders of the Eóganachta were killed, and the power of the ancient Cashel dynasty began to suffer a decline from which it was never fully to recover.

What effect had all these raids and wars on Irish life and culture in the ninth century? Apart from the writings of annalists and chroniclers, we have an abundance of other kinds of evidence of the looting and destruction. Almost every Irish church of the time must have contained little silvered and enamelled caskets for holding relics. Most of those which still survive are finds from western Norway. Indeed the Irish archaeologist who visits the museums of Oslo, Bergen, Stavanger and Trondheim can fill his notebook with drawings of Irish metalwork found in the graves of Vikings who had returned to die at home with the loot of their expeditions to far-off Ireland. Often mountings or ornaments from reliquaries are found, reused to make brooches for the Vikings or their ladies. As a Scandinavian scholar puts it, 'It would be possible to reconstruct the Viking expeditions to Ireland on archaeological evidence alone, even if every literary record were lacking.'[3]

36
Irish enamelled bronze mounting from Viking grave, Myklebostad, Norway, 8th century
Bergen Museum – drawing, Liam de Paor

In Ireland itself, similar metal has been found from time to time – Irish-style metalwork used as harness mounts in a horse burial at Navan, pieces of metalwork of Irish manufacture reused as ornamental mounts for a set of Viking weights from the Islandbridge cemetery. From the contents of the Dublin graves one can easily picture the raiders riding back from the Irish midlands with enamelled and gilt trinkets, to be traded to the ships which had put in at the quayside from Norway or the Isles, perhaps in exchange for new Frankish swords.

Irish manuscripts at St Gall and other places on the Continent testify to another kind of movement of valuables out of Ireland: the books, carried off not as prey but for safe keeping by monks and scholars to the courts and monasteries of Europe. Some of the earliest examples now known of writing in the Irish language – usually explanatory notes on Latin books – have survived just because they were brought to the Continent in this manner. The number of manuscripts which were destroyed – 'drowned' as the chronicler picturesquely puts it, in lakes or sea – can never be calculated.

37   Round Tower and St Kevin's Church, Glendalough, built *c.* 900
Commissioners of Public Works in Ireland

If then we were to summarise the ninth century as a grim and barbarous period, we would have a good deal of evidence to support us. Yet it is easy to exaggerate the effect of marauding raids and small-scale wars and to forget that medieval chroniclers, like modern journalists, appreciated a good story and could find a ready market for sensationalism. Life went on. What is more surprising, we have much evidence for new developments in art and scholarship at this time. It is impossible to be precise about dates here, but it was in the time of the Viking wars that stone churches built with mortar began to replace wooden buildings in Ireland. Not many have survived the centuries, but we can in outline trace the development from timber prototypes to stone-roofed churches like St Kevin's at Glendalough. And in the same period of warfare and destruction, the building of the elegant bell-houses also began. The models for these were almost certainly early belfries in Italy, but a very distinctive Irish type was soon evolved which still adds grace to our landscapes. They were soon adapted to serve a secondary purpose as places of refuge, which is why in most of the round towers the doorway is raised some distance above the ground. From the top windows a small handbell rang out to tell the hours or to warn of sudden danger. All too often, however, as happened for example at Monasterboice, those who took refuge in a monastic belfry perished by fire together with the books and valuables they had with them, since the tower by its design served as an excellent chimney.

The development of stone sculpture throughout the Viking period in Ireland is more remarkable. The cross of Patrick and Columba at Kells was carved at this time, probably shortly after the community of Iona settled in Ireland. It is an early example of a series in which we can watch new schemes of figure-carving – mainly scenes from the Scriptures – being worked out throughout the century. The chief centre of the early figure-carving school was the valley of the River Barrow, especially at Castledermot and Moone. The carvings are influenced by the revival of art in the Carolingian empire, although there the work was chiefly in media other than stone. There is nothing in Europe of the time to compare with the elaborated schemes of imagery which were finally worked out by the Irish artists on great monuments like Muiredach's Cross at Monasterboice or on the Cross of the Scriptures at Clonmacnoise, erected early in the tenth century by the same Flann Sianna, king of Tara, who at the battle of Belach Mughna triumphed over Cormac mac Cuilennáin, king-bishop of Cashel. Cormac was renowned in Irish tradition as a patron of learning and a scholar in his own right. Scholarship too survived the early Viking wars, but a great deal of our evidence for it comes from the Continent.

Irishmen played a considerable part in the revival of learning in Europe under and after Charlemagne, and many of their writings have survived. Sedulius Scottus and Johannes Eriugena are only two of the eminent names of those who made their contribution in the main European tradition. At home, as we know from many sources, the process of fusion of the native and Latin traditions of literature and learning was carried on vigorously in the ninth and tenth centuries.

38
Muiredach's Cross,
Monasterboice, *c.* 923
*Commissioners of Public Works
in Ireland*

Ireland, however, was not to be allowed a very long breathing space for the pursuance of her cultural traditions. New large-scale Viking incursions began in the tenth century. In 914 a great fleet sailed into Waterford harbour and established a base there. From the new settlement of Waterford, the Scandinavians mounted expeditions deep into Munster. Some years later another Norse settlement was made at the head of the Shannon estuary – the beginning of the city of Limerick. Later chroniclers, looking back on this period, speak of 'immense floods and countless sea-vomitings of ships'[4] in Munster, but the chief development of the time was the emergence of trading towns. The most important of these was Dublin, apparently established on a new basis at this time near the ford which crossed the Liffey above its mouth.

Excavations at Wood Quay have shown that Dublin was a ramparted or walled town, in close contact from the tenth century onward with England, and certainly trading farther afield. A city of wooden streets and wooden houses and workshops, it soon became a major centre of crafts and manufacture as well as of commerce. Its products influenced the hinterland in many ways, as did those of Limerick and Waterford. The towns, especially Dublin and Limerick, changed the Irish economy and set in train new developments: the market had arrived.[5]

39
Detail from Muiredach's Cross,
Monasterboice: the arrest of
Christ
*Commissioners of Public Works
in Ireland*

While the rulers of Dublin and Waterford for a good part of the first half of the tenth century were occupied by their interests in York, in alliance with the Scots, until they were finally driven out by the English of Northumbria, the Norse met with steadily stiffening resistance in the northern half of the country: the quarrelsome kings were even from time to time impelled to patch up their own differences to deal with them. They did not found market towns in the north. In the south, Viking settlements, although small, were comparatively successful. The declining Eóganachta seemed unable or unwilling to hinder them.

In the second half of the tenth century a new, aggressive power emerged in Munster, through the expansion of a hitherto obscure petty kingdom of east Clare, Dál Cais, whose leader, Mathgamain, captured Cashel from the Eóganachta in 964. Shortly afterwards he defeated the Norse of Limerick at the battle of Sulchoid and sacked their city. The description of the sack of Limerick in the O'Brien tract *Cogad Gaedel re Gallaib* gives an impression of the wealth of a Viking port town:

They carried off the jewels and their best property, and their saddles beautiful and foreign, their gold and their silver; their beautifully woven cloth of all colours and of all kinds. The fort and the good town they reduced to a cloud of smoke and to red fire afterwards. The whole of the captives were collected on the hills of Saingel. Every one of them that was fit for war was killed, and every one that was fit for a slave was enslaved.[6]

Mathgamain himself was killed in 976 but his brother Brian Bóruma (otherwise Boru) within a few years brought first Limerick, then all of Munster, under his control. From Cashel he set about systematically building up power for himself.

In the meantime, the Norse of Dublin also suffered a disastrous defeat at the battle of Tara in 980. The victor was Máel Sechnaill son of Domnall, who became king of Tara in that year. In 981 he besieged and took the city of Dublin, carrying off a great prey from the Norse and imposing a heavy tribute on them.

The Norse from now on were reduced to playing subordinate roles in the renewed struggle for power between the rulers of the northern half and the southern half of Ireland. Máel Sechnaill, representing the ancient northern dynasty of the Uí Néill, showed considerable energy in this struggle, but Brian, representing the usurping southern dynasty of Dál Cais, showed the greater ability. He thought in terms which extended beyond the limited traditional Irish concept of kingship. The decisive event in the struggle was the battle of Glen Máma in 999, when Brian defeated the king of Leinster and the Dublin Norse, after which he plundered the city. Three years later Máel Sechnaill yielded to him at Tara, without a battle, and Brian became, in effect, king of Ireland, or, as he styled himself, 'emperor of the Irish'.

He still had, in the next twelve years, to suppress various dissident northern kings, but the most dogged resistance came from the kingdom of Leinster. Máel Mórda, king of Leinster, allied himself with the Dublin Norse again, and these in turn gathered in Viking allies from overseas for a final trial of strength at Clontarf in 1014. In the words of the Icelandic saga:

> Swordblades rang on Ireland's coast,
> Metal yelled as shield it sought,
> Spear-points in the well-armed host.
> I heard sword-blows many more;
> Sigurd fell in battle's blast,
> From his wounds there sprang hot gore.
> Brian fell, but won at last.[7]

Clontarf is conventionally taken as marking the end of the Viking wars. There were occasional Viking expeditions afterwards, but they were irrelevant to the dynastic wars which followed the death of Brian.

40   Viking ship in full sail

Liam de Paor

The Irish had learned from the Vikings. The mobility with ships and horsemen which had initially given the Norse an advantage had now become a feature of Irish warfare. The Vikings' superior weapons – the heavy swords, the iron spears, the helmets and mail – were now used by the Irish too. At Clontarf both sides fought with similar weapons. The Vikings in their towns were now largely Christian and were an established element in Ireland, influencing the Irish and being influenced by them. They were making silver brooches and other objects, of Irish type but with their own traditional patterns of ornament. Their styles of ornament in turn were being adapted by the Irish – who later were to embody Scandinavian animal-patterns in such works as the Cross of Cong and the carvings of Romanesque doorways.

Even before Clontarf, Dublin had begun to mint silver coins – the first ever in Ireland – and these continued to be issued until the time of the Norman invasion. In this we can see one of the most important effects of the Viking invasions on Ireland: their influence on the hitherto very simple economy of the country. With the establishment of the towns, Ireland ceased to be wholly rural, and the traffic of the ports opened her up to the outside world in a new way, as was to be shown by the important part the Norse towns played in the beginning of the church reforms of the eleventh and twelfth centuries.

The Norse left many permanent marks on Ireland. Words from their language were borrowed into Irish – especially words concerned with ships and trade. Norse words or forms also appear in many of our placenames (Wicklow, Waterford, Wexford, Leixlip, Lambay, and so on). The word Ireland itself is of Norse origin. In some placenames Irish words are used, but in a Norse construction, as in the modern names of the provinces, where *Lagins-tír*, for example (literally, 'the country of Lagin') has become Leinster. Other placenames, while purely Irish in vocabulary and form, refer to the presence of Viking colonies – Fingal in County Dublin is 'the country of the foreigners' and Baldoyle is 'the place of the dark foreigners', while a barony on Waterford harbour again preserves in its name the description *Gall-tír* – 'country of the foreigners'.

Perhaps the most enduring effect of the Vikings on Irish life was to shift the social and political centre of gravity once and for all from the midlands to the east coast – indeed, one might say to the Irish Sea.

Ireland in the Eleventh and Twelfth Centuries
c. 1000–1169
Brian Ó Cuív

In three notable ways the eleventh and twelfth centuries were an age of renaissance and progress in Ireland. Cultural activity and the arts, which had suffered a setback during the height of Viking power, came into their own again, revealing new and interesting trends. Religious reform, which was sorely needed after a period during which many abuses had crept in and moral standards had dropped, was not only undertaken but was carried through to the point where the church in Ireland, in full communion with the pope, had a basic diocesan organisation which could look to the pastoral care of its flock. In the political sphere the accession of Brian Bóruma (otherwise 'Boru') to the high kingship marked a break with the past. It paved the way for a strong central monarchy, and, in spite of considerable strife among the various dynasties, Ireland seemed to be moving in that direction when the Anglo-Norman invasion occurred and changed the course of history.

> Fearann cloidhimh críoch Bhanbha;
> bíodh slán cáich fá chomhardha
>   go bhfuil d'oighreacht ar Fhiadh bhFáil
>   acht foirneart gliadh dá gabháil.

(The land Ireland is sword land; let all men be challenged to show that there is any inheritance to Fiadh Fáil except of conquest by dint of battle.)

With those words of encouragement to a descendant of a Norman lord, a sixteenth-century poet[1] voices a thesis which had been put forward long before his time – that the Norman conquest of Ireland was justifiable on the grounds that there was no people from time immemorial who had taken Ireland otherwise than by force. Diplomacy required such reasoning, for the professional poets had to praise both Irish and Anglo-Irish chieftains. At any rate, if the poets had to choose between such a justification for the Norman invasion and that advanced by Henry II, king of England, they would undoubtedly have rejected Henry's case as being incompatible with the facts. For Henry had sought from Pope Adrian IV permission 'to enter the island of Ireland in order to subject its people to law and to root out from them the weeds of vice', 'to enlarge the boundaries of the church' and 'to proclaim the truths of the Christian religion to a rude and ignorant people'[2]. The poets, with their long tradition of native learning, knew how unfounded was the description 'rude and ignorant people'. They knew that in the very century in which Henry came to Ireland the leaders of their own profession had reorganised their craft and had laid the basis for a prescriptive grammar of Irish, the first such grammar of a western European language.[3] They knew of a revival of learning which had taken place in the eleventh and twelfth centuries in the great monastic schools and of which they had seen material evidence in the form of manuscripts in Irish and Latin. They knew that old artistic forms had been blended with new in the illumination of manuscripts and in the decorative metalwork of the period. And they knew of a great activity in church-building, during the course of which Romanesque and Gothic styles of architecture were introduced to Ireland.

In the monastic schools in the pre-invasion period, interest was no longer directed mainly towards Latin learning. Irish traditions had come into their own and we still have three remarkable manuscripts of the twelfth century which are clear evidence of this. One of them was compiled in the great monastery of Clonmacnoise about the year 1100, another probably somewhere in Leinster about the same time, and the third in the monastery of Terryglass in Tipperary between 1150 and 1200.[4] As we turn the pages of these manuscripts, we can picture a monk sitting in the writing-room copying pagan epic tales of the Ulster heroes such as *Táin Bó Cuailnge*, or the poem composed in praise of Colum Cille by the leader of the poetic profession at the end of the sixth century, or the genealogical lore by which the Irish kings and chieftains laid great store, or the Christian vision-text *Fís Adamnáin*, which is one of the forerunners of Dante's *Divine Comedy*. Much of this material was handed down from earlier times, and these manuscript compilations were now ensuring its safe transmission. We can hear the voice of the monk as he transcribes unceasingly:

> Is scíth mo chrob ón scríbainn;
>   ní dígainn mo glés géroll;
> sceithid mo phenn gulban caelda
>   dig ndaelda do dub glégorm.

> Sínim mo phenn mbec mbráenach
>   tar áenach lebar lígoll
> gan scor, fri selba ségann
>   dían scíth mo chrob ón scríbonn.

(My hand is weary with writing; my sharp great point is not thick; my slender-beaked pen jets forth a beetle-hued draught of bright blue ink.
I send my little dripping pen unceasingly over an assemblage of books of great beauty, to enrich the possessions of men of art, whence my hand is weary with writing.[5])

There are other manuscripts more restricted in scope, such as the two eleventh-century or early-twelfth-century copies of the *Book of Hymns*, of which one is in Trinity College, Dublin, and the other in the Franciscan House in Killiney. Here we see clear evidence of the survival of the art of illumination, and we are reminded of the Welshman Sulien, who came to study in Ireland in about 1045 and who apparently acquired not only a knowledge of our literature but also a familiarity with the techniques of illumination.[6]

41
Irish missal, 12th century, from Corpus Christi College, Oxford, now in the Bodleian Library
Oxford University Press

We think, too, of the new literature produced in these two centuries: tales and historical poems; lives of saints, sermons, biblical history and other religious texts, and fine devotional lyrics; 'The Vision of Mac Con Glinne', which is a wild goliardic satire on the monks of the time; and the Irish versions of the stories of Troy and Thebes, and 'The Civil War of the Romans'; and we recall that there, too, Irishmen were innovators, for not even the oldest French version of the Troy story is as old as ours.

When we turn to the surviving specimens of ornamental work in stone and metal, we get another glimpse of the versatility of Irish craftsmen and their readiness to adopt new patterns and techniques. Here on stone crosses, such as those of Kilfenora and Dysert O'Dea, there are artistic motifs for which a Scottish origin has been suggested. And on crosiers and reliquaries, and on the magnificent processional cross of Cong, which was commissioned by Toirdelbach Ua Conchobair, king of Connacht, in about 1123 to enshrine a relic of the True Cross, we see motifs which suggest Scandinavian influence, and we are reminded thereby of the Viking contribution to the making of Ireland in these centuries. For it has been pointed out that the gift of the Norsemen to Ireland was her own coastline, her seaport towns, the beginning of her civic communities, and her trade.

In ecclesiastical architecture the story is similarly one of development and innovation. A continuation of the tradition seen in the beehive huts of earlier times is shown in the stone-roofed churches such as those at Killaloe, Devenish and Kilmalkedar. In Cormac's chapel in Cashel, which was built by Cormac Mac Carthaig, king of Munster, and was consecrated in 1134 in the presence of the great assembly of dignitaries of the church and of royal persons, we have an exotic stone-roofed building which may owe something to German influence. Already the Romanesque style had been introduced, and it flourished throughout the twelfth century, producing such buildings as Saint Fingin's Church in Clonmacnoise and others whose magnificence we can guess at from what remains of them, such as the doorway of Clonfert Cathedral and the chancel arch at Tuam. The Gothic style, too, had appeared, and its influence was reflected in the transitional architecture which can be seen, for example, in Cistercian abbeys such as that at Boyle, which was probably commenced shortly after 1161 and not completed until 1218.

Cultural activity reflects the age and people to whom it belongs. On the basis of what we have seen, we would hardly concede that in the eleventh and twelfth centuries the Irish people were all rude and ignorant. But let us turn from this evidence and all that it tells us to what we know of the people of the time, and especially the rulers, through whose patronage so much of this cultural activity was made possible, and the churchmen, who secured the support of the kings, not only in this matter of culture and church-building but also in the more important matter of religious reform.

Our period opens with the accession of Brian Bóruma to the Irish high kingship. This was a break with a long tradition and provided an example which other provincial rulers were not slow to follow. The earlier tradition was that the king of Tara was the chief king in Ireland, and the Uí Néill of Meath and Ailech, from whom the Tara rulers were drawn, could look back upon a period of over 500 years during which their rule had rarely been seriously challenged. Even in Munster the Dál Cais, to whom Brian belonged, were a minor people whose rise to supreme power took place in little over half a century. Following the expansionist designs of his father, Cennétig, and of his brother, Mathgamain, Brian first established himself as king of Munster in the place of the traditional Eóganacht king of Cashel. Then he extended his power, until finally in 1002 his supremacy was acknowledged in the northern half of Ireland by Máel Sechnaill, king of Tara, who had been high king since 980.

42
Entry referring
to Brian Bóruma
in *Book of Armagh*
Trinity College, Dublin

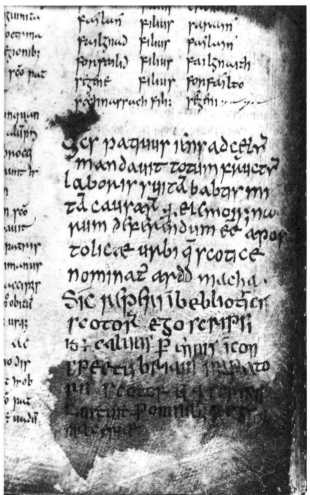

Not satisfied that the submission to him of the reigning high king demonstrated his own supreme authority, Brian made expeditions to the north in 1002 and 1005 in order to take hostages from the northern states. In the following years he made further expeditions to the north, took more hostages and thus showed himself to be undisputed king of Ireland. It was during his second expedition in 1005 that Brian visited Armagh, where he made an offering of twenty ounces of gold to the church and confirmed to the apostolic see of Saint Patrick the ecclesiastical supremacy over the whole of Ireland. The decision was recorded in Latin on a page of the ninth-century *Book of Armagh* in the presence of the high king by his scribe, who concluded the entry with the words (Fig. 42): '*Ego scripsi, id est Calvus perennis, in conspectu Briani imperatoris Scotorum et que scripsi finivit pro omnibus regibus Maceriae.*' ('I, Máel Suthain, have written this in the presence of Brian, emperor of the Irish, and what I have written he has determined for all the kings of Cashel.')[7]

With Brian, the Irish high-kingship became a reality. He was about sixty years of age when he attained it, and in the twelve years of his reign he consolidated his position in the political and military spheres, while at the same time, according to the twelfth-century text *Cogad Gaedel re Gallaib* ('The War of the Irish with the Foreigners'), initiating a rehabilitation of religious and learned institutions, as well as restoring communications by building bridges and roads. There may be exaggeration in this old account, but we have seen evidence of a renaissance in the eleventh and twelfth centuries and it would be less than just not to give some of the credit for this to Brian.

For most of us the name of Brian Bóruma calls to mind the Battle of Clontarf, which has always caught the imagination of the Irish people. The events which led to this battle were many, but fundamentally the issue involved was Brian's claim to rule all Ireland, including the Norse towns. So when the former high king Máel Sechnaill (otherwise Malachy) appealed to him for help against the Leinstermen and the Dublin Norse, Brian marched on Dublin. The result was the pitched battle on 23 April 1014 which we call 'the Battle of Clontarf' but which in Irish tradition is sometimes called 'Brian's battle'. It was, indeed, Brian's battle, for the support that he had from the other provinces on that Good Friday was relatively meagre, and, as we know, the men of North Leinster fought against him along with the Norsemen. The decisive victory lay with the Irish, and the final blow was given to Viking hopes of establishing their domination over Ireland as they were to do two years later in England under Canute. In Ireland they contented themselves henceforth with developing the towns which they had founded at Dublin, Wexford, Waterford, Cork and Limerick, and the eastern ports were to prove of great importance in the early years of the Norman invasion. The triumph at Clontarf was a sad one, for the losses on the Irish side included Brian himself, his eldest son Murchad and many other royal persons and nobles. Neither of Brian's other sons, Tadg and Donnchad, was powerful enough to take his father's place as king of Ireland, so it fell to the erstwhile king, Máel Sechnaill, to resume the rule of the whole country; he was now truly high king until his death in 1022.

Some idea of the political organisation of Ireland in the eleventh century is got when we consider that the country then consisted of between 100 and 200 kingdoms of varying size and importance together with the Norse towns. When we see the names of the more important local kingdoms, we recognise several which are familiar to us as barony or territorial names, such as Corcu Baiscinn, Corcu Duibne, Múscraige, Uí Echach of Munster, and another kingdom of the same name in Ulster which we know in the form 'Iveagh'. At a higher level Ireland was still a heptarchy of states – Munster, Leinster, Connacht, Meath, Ailech, Airgialla and Ulaid. As a result of Brian's successful intervention, the Uí Néill no longer shared solely among themselves the right of succession to the high kingship, which had now become a prize to be fought for by rival provincial kings. A new term appears in our records – rí co fresabra ('king with opposition'): this term was applied to a provincial king who aspired to the high kingship but did not gain the submission of all the other provinces – and few of the claimants can be rated higher than that. In fact, Airgialla and Ulaid did not count in the struggle for the high kingship, and even Meath was kept out of the running through the political manoeuvring of the other contestants.

Indeed, one of the noticeable features of the period, and one of the factors making for a lack of stability, is the interference of provincial kings in the affairs of other states or provinces. We see new political alignments, which led to the advancement of certain kingdoms and the decline of others. We note with surprise that among the kings of Dublin between 1070 and 1130 were two Leinster kings, two Munster kings and a Connacht king. Even more surprising is an annalistic statement that Domnall Ua Briain, a great-grandson of Brian Bóruma, took the kingship of the Hebrides in 1111. According to the chronicles of the kingdom of Man and the Isles, the people of Man had asked Muirchertach Ua Briain, then king of Ireland, to give them a ruler, and he sent them Domnall. All these dynastic movements were part of the political evolution of Ireland which was halted so completely by the Norman invasion.

Through our annalistic records we can trace events in this evolution during the century and a half from the death of Máel Sechnaill to the comings of the Normans in 1169. The picture that they give is one of violence, confusion and turmoil. We read of quarrels between kings and between chieftains, of the mutilation of rivals by blinding or in some other way, of military hostings, of burnings of dwellings and church buildings, of forays and battles, and of violent deaths. Yet in many ways conditions were not very different from what they had been in preceding centuries, nor was Ireland particularly unstable, compared with Wales or Scotland or England. In one respect, however, there was a remarkable development: the organisation of the church. It is worth considering this, in view of Henry's claim about the need to 'proclaim the truths of the Christian religion' to the Irish people of which he so fully convinced the pope that he was given in 1155 the authority he sought to invade Ireland.

43
Head of the crozier of the abbots of Clonmacnoise, late 11th century
National Museum of Ireland

It is well known that between the introduction of Christianity in the fifth century and the time of Brian Bóruma the church in Ireland had for the most part met the religious needs of the Irish people from within. Though in communion with Rome, it was to a large extent self-governing and self-renewing and, when circumstances required it, self-reforming. When we come to the eleventh century we find that many of the old monasteries founded by the early saints and their followers were still in existence and flourishing, and that they were spread throughout the country. Many of them, as we know, were centres of learning, but they were primarily religious centres, and we may suppose that from them and from others of which we know nothing the spiritual welfare of the people was looked after to some extent. Moreover, the *Schottenklöster* or 'Irish monasteries' of Ratisbon, Würzberg, Mainz and other places in Germany remind us that even in the eleventh century Ireland was sending missionary sons abroad, for those German foundations date from this later era, when John of Ireland, Marianus Scottus, Marianus of Ratisbon and others were preaching the gospel or leading lives of asceticism in Europe.

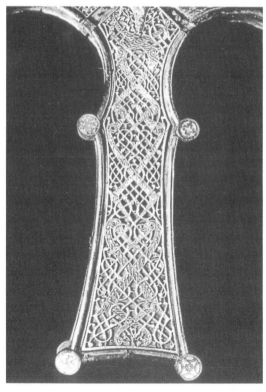

44
Cross of Cong, *c.* 1123, detail
National Museum of Ireland

We might suppose that, with numerous religious houses throughout Ireland and the missionary movement under way again, the moral well-being of the people was assured. Unfortunately this was not so, for after the long centuries of the Viking wars and consequent upheavals there was spiritual and moral laxity. Deeds of violence were frequent, even against priests and nuns and against church property. The sacraments were neglected, there was a reluctance to pay tithes, and the marriage laws of the church were disregarded. The laxity about marriage, it is true, may have been due to the brehon law, which differed from the rules of the church in this regard. However, there was clearly a need for a spiritual renewal, and with it reform of the church itself, for part of the trouble lay in the organisation of the church, which was monastic rather than diocesan – a feature which resulted in a lack of priests engaged in pastoral work. Another characteristic of the Irish church was that there was hereditary succession to certain church benefices and that these were frequently held by laymen. Of course, to a people accustomed to the principle of hereditary succession in other walks of life, including poetry, this would not have seemed strange.

45
Dysert O'Dea Cross, County
Clare, mid-12th century
Commissioners of Public Works
in Ireland

At any rate, reform was needed, and it came. Through the renewed contacts with western Europe, established by the latest wave of Irish missionaries, and also through Irish pilgrims who found their way to Rome, Irishmen at home became aware of the vast church reform which was taking place on the Continent. The fact that the Norse towns had become Christianised and from early in the eleventh century looked to Canterbury for episcopal consecration was an important factor. Among the earliest reformers were Máel Ísa Ua hAinmire, who was consecrated bishop of Waterford by

Saint Anselm of Canterbury in 1096, and Gilla Espaic, or Gilbert, who had been a monk with Anselm in Rouen and who was made bishop of Limerick about 1106 and was appointed papal legate. Gilla Espaic put forward a plan for a diocesan and parochial organisation for Ireland and a uniform liturgy. In the south, these reforming clerics had the support of Muirchertach Ua Briain, the high king. Armagh had already joined the movement in the person of Cellach Ua Sínaig, who inherited the position of abbot in 1105. Cellach was the seventh in a series of members of the Ua Sínaig family who held the position without taking holy orders, and several of whom were married[8], but before long he was consecrated as bishop while he was visiting Munster as 'comarba Pátraic, or 'heir of Patrick'. So now, for the first time in many years, Armagh, chief see of Ireland, was under the rule of an 'heir of Patrick' who was also a bishop, and Cellach was recognised as primate. In 1111 a national synod at Ráth Bresail, near Cashel, presided over by Cellach and the high king, divided Ireland into twenty-four sees, thus replacing the old monastic organisation.

46   Cistercian Abbey, Boyle, County Roscommon, 12th and early 13th century
Commissioners of Public Works in Ireland

Forty years were to pass before reorganisation was brought to a successful conclusion. In the meantime a younger man, Máel Maedóc, whom we know as Saint Malachy, had succeeded to Cellach, and it fell to him to conduct the necessary negotiations with the pope. On his journeys to Rome he stayed with Saint Bernard at Clairvaux, and he poured forth to Bernard his concern about the state of Ireland. He was so impressed with what he saw in Clairvaux that he introduced the Cistercians to Ireland, where their first settlement was begun at Mellifont in 1142 on land given by the king of Airgialla. On its completion in 1157 this fine abbey was consecrated in the presence of an assembly of bishops and kings. Among the royal gifts to the church on the occasion were 160 cows, sixty ounces of gold and a townland – all given by the high king – and sixty ounces of gold given by the king of Airgialla, as well as another sixty ounces given by the wife of Tighernán Ua Ruairc, who is better remembered today for her unfortunate escapade with Diarmait Mac Murchada, the king of Leinster. Though there had been Benedictines in Ireland early in the twelfth century, it was with the coming of the Cistercians that the era of the old Irish monasteries came to an end.

Saint Malachy died at Clairvaux in 1148 on his second journey to Rome, but his design for the Irish church bore fruit four years later when, at the Synod of Kells, Ireland was divided into thirty-six sees with four archbishoprics, and the *pallia* were distributed by the papal legate, Cardinal Paparo, to the archbishops of Armagh, Cashel, Dublin and Tuam. So in 1152 the legate could report to the pope that the church in Ireland now had the basic organisation to look to the pastoral care of its flock. The reports which led to Pope Adrian's strange grant to King Henry II three years later were either deliberately false or were based on a misunderstanding of the true state of affairs in Ireland.

47   Doorway of Clonfert Cathedral, County Galway, 12th century
Commissioners of Public Works in Ireland

Had the political evolution of Ireland towards a strong national monarchy proceeded as satisfactorily as the ecclesiastical reform, the *Laudabiliter* grant might never have been used by Henry II. Unfortunately the rivalry over the high-kingship did little to promote a sense of national unity. In fact, the position with regard to the kings of Ireland, whether 'full' or 'with opposition', in the period 1022–1169 is far from clear, and there are some periods for which no king is named – periods of 'joint rule', as they are called. However, we can compile from various sources, including the twelfth-century *Book of Leinster*, this list of kings for whom the supremacy was claimed:

> Donnchad, son of Brian Bóruma, of Munster
> Diarmait, son of Máel na mBó, of Leinster
> Toirdelbach Ua Briain of Munster
> Muirchertach Ua Briain of Munster
> Domnall Ua Lochlainn of Aileach
> Toirdelbach Ua Conchobair of Connacht
> Muirchertach Mac Lochlainn of Aileach
> Ruaidrí Ua Conchobair of Connacht

The list shows how things had changed. Only two of the eight kings are of the old stock, the Uí Néill; three are of the line of Brian; and Leinster and Connacht have now joined in the competition. For the first hundred years or so, the descendants of Brian Bóruma maintained fairly successfully their claim to supremacy. In the twelfth century the northern Uí Néill asserted themselves for two short periods. But the O'Connor star really appeared to be in the ascendant, for Toirdelbach Ua Conchobair was one of the most outstanding of all the kings since Brian Bóruma, and when his son Ruaidrí took the high kingship in 1166 it looked as if the O'Connors might succeed in establishing a feudal-style hereditary kingship which would be comparable to the dynasties in other countries. This dream was shattered, however, by the action of the king of Leinster, Diarmait Mac Murchada, or 'Diarmait of the foreigners', as he is called. It is perhaps significant that the Leinstermen always resented and resisted the central authority – that of Tara in prehistoric and early historic times, that of Brian Bóruma before the Battle of Clontarf, and now that of Ruaidrí Ua Conchobair. The matters at issue between Diarmait and Ruaidrí were not so vital, but they culminated in the banishment of Diarmait from Ireland. Another king might have accepted the judgement, and perhaps gone on a pilgrimage to Rome, where Brian Bóruma's son, Donnchad, had died in 1064 after being dethroned by his nephew. Instead Diarmait hied off to Bristol and thence to France, where he appealed to Henry II for aid to regain his kingdom of Leinster.

The resultant Norman landing in Wexford and all that followed form another chapter in the history of Ireland. It is sufficient at this point to say that, were it not for the unforeseeable consequences of Diarmait na nGall's action in seeking help abroad, the political evolution which, as we have seen, was a feature of the eleventh and twelfth centuries might have continued, to the point of producing a strong central native monarchy. As it was, the Gaelic hegemony in Ireland came to an end with Ruaidrí Ua Conchobair. The last entry in the *Book of Leinster* list of kings of Ireland from time immemorial is '*Ec in Ruadrí sin 'na ailithre i Cunga*' ('That Ruaidrí died as a pilgrim in Cong'). That was in 1198. Ruaidrí was buried in Clonmacnoise near the spot beside the high altar where his father, Toirdelbach Mór, had been buried in 1156. An epoch in our history had ended.

The Normans: Arrival and Settlement
1169–c. 1300
F. X. Martin

Ireland, more than most countries, cannot escape her past. The Norman settlement – over 800 years ago – has left an indelible mark on the face and character of the country, on its seaports, highways and bridges, its castles, churches and towns. The songs, the literature, the very faces of the people today pay tribute to those fearless Norman knights who came, saw and conquered, and settled in the country. No other event except the preaching of the gospel by Saint Patrick and his companions has so changed the destiny of Ireland.

And yet the coming of the Normans began as a casual, almost an accidental affair. If we compare it with the Norman invasion of England in 1066 the contrast is revealing. William the Conqueror planned and executed the invasion of England on a grand scale; recruits flocked to his banner from France, Germany and other parts of Europe. He had some claim to the English throne, and his fleet sailed from Normandy with the blessing of Pope Alexander II. His conquest of England was systematic, ruthless and complete.

The story of why the Normans came to Ireland begins as a personal drama, with two warrior kings, Dermot MacMurrough of Leinster and Tiernán O'Rourke of Breifne, pitted one against the other; it is a tale of raids and counter-raids, of bravery and brutality, of the abduction of O'Rourke's wife, Dervorgilla, of the undying resentment of O'Rourke, of the overthrow and exile of MacMurrough. And so the drama continued, but now as a one-man show, with MacMurrough pleading his case successively in England, France and Wales. And even when the Normans came – almost reluctantly, as we shall see – they rarely acted on an organised plan. Nevertheless, they came to stay.

Between 1156 and 1166 the struggle for political supremacy in Ireland lay between Murtough MacLochlainn of Ailech in the north, the most powerful king in Ireland, and Rory O'Connor, king of Connacht. MacMurrough supported Mac Lochlainn, and O'Rourke cast his lot with O'Connor. The struggle swayed forward and backward, from Ulster to Leinster, to Connacht and Munster, with endless campaigns, cattleraids, burnings and atrocities, so that, in the words of the annalist, 'Ireland was a trembling sod'[1].

O'Connor was content, once he had defeated MacMurrough, to take hostages from him and reduce his power to a small kingdom centred around Ferns in Wexford. But O'Rourke was implacable in his resolve to destroy MacMurrough. His burning resentment went back fourteen years, to his humiliation before all the men of Ireland in 1152 when his wife, Dervorgilla, had been abducted by MacMurrough. Yet she proved the old adage that a man chases a woman until she catches him, for according to both the Irish and Norman accounts it was she who arranged the abduction. An Irish historian, Keating, relates how she sent MacMurrough a message urging him to seize her:

> As to Dermot, when this message reached him he went quickly to meet the lady, accompanied by a detachment of mounted men, and when they reached where she was, he ordered that she be placed on horseback behind a rider, and upon this the woman wept and screamed in pretence, as if Dermot were carrying her off by force; and bringing her with him in this fashion, he returned to Leinster.[2]

48 Pembroke Castle, Pembrokeshire, 12th century: typical of the border society from which the Anglo-Norman invaders of Ireland came

Neither Dervorgilla nor Dermot could be accused of acting in the folly of youth – he was then aged forty-two and she was a ripe forty-four. O'Rourke recovered her the following year but he was determined to get even with MacMurrough, and now in 1166 he had his opportunity: MacMurrough's supporters and followers were melting away; his great ally, Mac Lochlainn of Ailech in the north, was dead; O'Rourke, O'Melaghlin and the north Leinster tribes were massing on his frontier; the Norsemen of Wexford were prepared to attack him in the rear. When Ferns was captured and his stone palace destroyed, he decided there was nothing for it but flight. He sailed away secretly with a few followers from Ireland in August 1166. He landed at Bristol, then the main port for commerce with Ireland, and thence went to France in search of Henry II, king of England. Dermot was determined to recover his inheritance in Ireland and was seeking allies.

King Henry was French rather than English. He was born in Normandy, reared in France, and spoke Norman French, not English; most of his life was passed on the Continent, and England was only part of his empire – the Angevin empire, which embraced England, Normandy, Anjou, Maine, Poitou and Aquitaine, with sovereign claims over Toulouse, Wales and Scotland.

He was a restless man, always on the move throughout his wide dominions, and Dermot, after travelling from city to city, deeper and deeper into the south of France, finally found him in a distant part of Aquitaine. Henry was already interested in Ireland; in 1155, when he had been but one short year on the throne, he considered an invasion of Ireland, but the project was postponed. His advisers sought the blessing of the papacy for a marauding expedition, just as William the Conqueror had when invading England a century earlier. In 1155 the pope was Adrian IV, the only Englishman ever to sit on the papal throne. It is fairly certain, though some historians have queried it, that he issued a bull *Laudabiliter* commissioning Henry to enter Ireland and set about its religious reform, but the king was too busy then to divert his forces to that mysterious and warlike island in the west.

In 1166, however, the problem became alive again when Dermot stood before him, an impressive figure and personality, as described by a contemporary, Gerald of Wales (Giraldus Cambrensis):

> Diarmait was tall and well built, a brave and warlike man among his people, whose voice was hoarse as a result of constantly having been in the din of battle. He preferred to be feared by all rather than loved. He treated his nobles harshly and brought to prominence men of humble rank. He was inimical towards his own people and hated by others. 'All men's hands were against him, and he was hostile to all men.'[3]

Dermot stated his case and made his offer:

Hear, noble King Henry,
Whence I was born, of what country.
Of Ireland I was born a lord,
In Ireland acknowledged king;
But wrongfully my own people
Have cast me out of my kingdom.
To you I come to make complaint, good sire,
In the presence of the barons of your empire.
Your liegeman I shall become
Henceforth all the days of my life,
On condition that you be my helper,
So that I do not lose everything,
You I shall acknowledge as sire and lord,
In the presence of your barons and earls.[4]

Henry, a man of boundless energy, high intelligence and rapid decision quickly summed up the situation: he himself was too busily engaged in his many territories to lead an expedition to Ireland but he had nothing to lose by encouraging this exiled king. He accepted Dermot's offer of fealty, promised to help him as soon as possible and loaded him with presents. More welcome to Dermot, however, was an open letter in which Henry invited his subjects, English, Norman, Welsh and Scots, to rally to Dermot's assistance. Dermot returned to Bristol but found that, even with the king's letter to his credit, there was no rush of recruits for an expedition to Ireland. He decided that the most likely place to find volunteers was across the Severn, along the Welsh border, where Normans were continually engaged in warfare with the native Welsh.

These Normans were French in speech and origin, restless members of the finest fighting stock in Europe. Many had intermarried with the Welsh nobility, but their children were without any special allegiance to England, Wales, or France. They were ruthless and cunning, experts as sailors and horsemen, builders of castles and churches, men with an instinct for discipline and order. They were tough, intelligent and land-hungry. Ireland, already famous in Welsh stories and legends, was beckoning to them across the water.

Dermot shrewdly sought an interview with one of the great Norman leaders in Wales, Richard FitzGilbert de Clare, the earl of Strigoil, better known as 'Strongbow'. Here was an experienced war-leader, descendant of a powerful Norman family, but now a discontented man, without wife, out of favour with Henry II, and therefore likely to seek fame and fortune in some new field such as Ireland. Strongbow was a hard bargainer. Eventually he agreed to lead an armed force to Ireland and restore Dermot to power, but on condition that Dermot give him his eldest daughter, Aoífe (Eva), in marriage, and the right of succession to the kingdom of Leinster.

49 Norman knights, from the Bayeux Tapestry, late 11th century
Vetusta monumenta, vi, 1819

Dermot then set off along the Welsh coast road to St David's, securing along the way and on his return journey promises of help from a number of Norman-Welsh knights whose names were to become part of Irish history – FitzHenry, Carew, FitzGerald, Barry. Before leaving Wales, he also visited Rhos in Pembrokeshire. Here he got promises of support from members of the vigorous Flemish colony which had come from Flanders sixty years previously. Their names were to figure prominently in the invasion of Ireland – Prendergast, Fleming, Roche, Cheevers, Synott.

Dermot could no longer restrain his impatience to return to Ireland and sailed back with a handful of Normans, Fleming and Welsh in 1167. He recovered his local power around Ferns, but O'Connor and O'Rourke attacked him once again and he submitted after a short fight. He even paid O'Rourke one hundred ounces of gold in reparation for the abduction of Dervorgilla. There the matter seemed to rest, but MacMurrough was only biding his time and sent urgent messages to Wales promising plunder, riches, and land for those who would come to his support.

> Gold and silver, I shall give them,
> A very ample pay.
> Whoever may wish for soil or sod,
> Richly shall I endow them.[5]

50   Norman foot soldiers, from the Bayeux Tapestry, late 11th century
Vetusta monumenta, vi, 1819

The first formidable contingents of invaders ran their flat ships in on the sandy beach at Bannow Bay early in May 1169, altogether, it is claimed, about 600 of them, led by Robert FitzStephen, Hervey de Montmorency and Maurice de Prendergast. There were mounted knights in mail, foot soldiers and archers on foot, 'the flower of the youth of Wales', with their deadly bows. Dermot promptly joined them with several hundred men, and the combined force marched on Wexford.

The Norsemen, the inhabitants of the town, sallied out to meet Dermot's army but received a shock when they discovered they were not dealing with a brave array of Irish warriors, lightly clad and armed with axes, swords, slings and javelins. Instead they were faced with serried ranks of foot soldiers and archers, flanked on either side by a squadron of horsemen, armed with long lances, kite-shaped shields, glittering helmets and coats of mail. Behind them massed Dermot's army, impatiently waiting for battle and the kill.

The Norsemen were driven back pell-mell into Wexford, and the next day the town capitulated. O'Connor and O'Rourke, alarmed at Dermot's activity, marched against him once again, but after some skirmishing near Ferns they came to terms. They were willing to recognise him as king of Leinster south of Dublin, and he was to rid himself of his foreign allies. O'Connor's main interest was to see that he himself was recognised as high king. Once MacMurrough had made his submission, O'Connor marched away, unaware of the danger from the Normans.

MacMurrough wrote urging Strongbow to hasten, assuring him that Ireland was there for the taking. Strongbow was now prepared to come in person, and as an advance guard he sent a daring young nobleman, Raymond

Carew, styled 'le Gros' ('the Fat'), one of the FitzGeralds, with ten knights and seventy archers. Raymond landed his men and horses at a rocky headland called Baginbun on the coast of Wexford, between Bannow Bay and the Hook. Here they threw up earthen ramparts, which are still to be seen. The attack came only too soon. An army, calculated in later Norman records, almost certainly with gross exaggeration, as 3,000 strong, of Norsemen from Waterford city and Gaelic Irish from the Decies, Ossory and Idrone, marched on the entrenched force of less than a hundred Normans and Flemings. The battle was short and decisive. An old jingle runs:

> At the creek of Baginbun
> Ireland was lost and won.

A herd of cattle collected by the Normans behind the ramparts was suddenly driven forth against the oncoming troops. This wild rush of horned beasts bore down on the foremost Norse and Irish, and while confusion reigned the Normans charged and overthrew their opponents. Seventy of the leading townsmen of Waterford were taken prisoner on the battlefield. No mercy was shown to them; their limbs were broken and their bodies thrown over the cliffs.

Before Waterford could recover from this disaster, worse befell it. On 23 August Strongbow and his army – said to have been 200 knights and 1,000 other troops – landed at Passage, near where the Rivers Suir and Barrow meet. He was joined by le Gros, and two days later the Normans swept on to the assault of Waterford. The Norse and the Irish within the walls now knew how merciless were the attackers and twice the Normans were beaten off, but the indomitable Raymond le Gros breached the walls at one weak point and led a fierce attack through the gap. Reginald's Tower, which still stands, witnessed some of the bloodiest fighting. When night fell the city was in the hands of the Normans.

Strongbow summoned MacMurrough, who came gladly, bringing his daughter, Aoife, to fulfil in part the bargain made in Wales two years previously. Popular tradition, and a well-known fresco in the precincts of the British House of Commons, depict the marriage taking place at the close of the battle, with the dead, the dying and flaming houses in the background. This is not historically accurate since MacMurrough did not arrive for at least some days after the battle. But it is symbolically true as the marriage was part of the Norman victory.

What manner of man was Strongbow, this new power in the land? Gerald of Wales described him:

He had reddish hair and freckles, grey eyes, a feminine face, a weak voice and a short neck, though in almost all other respects he was of a tall build. He was a generous and easy-going man. What he could not accomplish by deed he settled by the persuasiveness of his words . . . When he took up his position in the midst of battle, he stood firm as an immovable standard round which his men could regroup and take refuge. In war he remained steadfast and reliable in good fortune and bad alike. In adversity no feelings of despair caused him to waver, while lack of self-restraint did not make him run amok when successful.[6]

Strongbow was not impetuous, but he was daring. He and MacMurrough now proposed to march on Dublin, which was a semi-independent kingdom under the control of the Norsemen, with its Norse-Irish king Askulv. Dublin was in alliance with King Rory O'Connor, who hurried with his army to its defence; with him came another army led by MacMurrough's old enemy, O'Rourke of Breifne. O'Connor lay in wait at Clondalkin, on what was then the only main highway from Wexford to Dublin, and also sent bands of soldiers to guard two narrow defiles, one near the Wicklow coast, the other at Enniskerry. We must remember that Ireland was then covered with dense forests. MacMurrough outwitted O'Connor and O'Rourke, leading the Normans by a series of paths over the Wicklow and Dublin Mountains down by Rathfarnham and arriving in front of the city walls.

The Norsemen, nonplussed at the turn of events, began to sue for peace, utilising the archbishop of Dublin, St Laurence O'Toole, as their mediator. O'Connor and O'Rourke, indignant that the Norsemen were parleying with the Normans and MacMurrough, marched away in disgust. While negotiations were still proceeding, two young Norman knights, Raymond le Gros and Milo de Cogan, with a band of their followers suddenly burst into the city, cut down the guards and within a short time were masters of Dublin. Askulv and many of the Norsemen fled to their ships and sailed away to their kinsfolk in the Hebrides and the Isle of Man, vowing to return as avengers. Dublin fell to the Normans on 21 September 1170.

The Normans were only some months settled in the city when disaster threatened them from all sides. MacMurrough died about 1 May 1171, leaving Strongbow successor to a turbulent kingdom. The Leinster tribes revolted and rallied to support Murtough, nephew of Dermot MacMurrough. While Strongbow was visiting the dying MacMurrough at Ferns, an assault on Dublin by the Norsemen, led by Askulv, the deposed king of Dublin, tested the Norman fighting skill to the utmost. The Norsemen came in a fleet of ships from Norway, the Hebrides and the Isle of Man, carrying, it is claimed, a thousand men. Gerald of Wales described them:

They were warlike figures, clad in mail in every part of their body, after the Danish manner. Some wore long coats of mail, others iron plate skilfully knitted together, and they had round, red shields protected by iron round the edge. These men, whose iron will matched their armour, drew up their ranks and made an attack on the walls at the eastern gate.[7]

They advanced on foot in a solid phalanx against the eastern gate of Dublin, swinging that terrifying weapon, the broad battleaxe, but were met by a charge of Norman knights on horseback. The phalanx was broken in a fierce fight, and the Norsemen were cut down. Askulv was taken prisoner and tried in the hall of his own palace in Dublin, but any hope of mercy was extinguished by his proud defiance and open threats to his captors. He was beheaded there and then in the hall.

Strongbow returned to Dublin to meet a greater danger from the Gaelic Irish. Rory O'Connor arrived near Dublin with a large army, as did O'Carroll from Ulster, Murtough MacMurrough from southern Leinster, and the inevitable O'Rourke from Breifne. The sea approach was cut off by a fleet of thirty ships manned by Norsemen from the Isle of Man and the Hebrides.

The Gaelic Irish had no knowledge of siege warfare and therefore had to try to starve out the Normans. After two months thus beleaguered, the Normans grew desperate for want of food, and secretly decided to attack. Three companies, each of 200 men, under Strongbow, Raymond le Gros and Milo de Cogan, slipped out of the city, made a detour and then a sudden attack on Rory's camp at Castleknock. The attack was unexpected. O'Connor was bathing in the River Liffey with many of his men; over a hundred of them were killed, while O'Connor barely managed to escape. Many more of the Irish in the camp were slain and all their supplies were captured. This lightning victory ended the siege and established the Norman supremacy in arms over both Norse and Gaelic Irish.

Strongbow's worries were far from finished, however. The next threat came not from the Irish or Norse but from Strongbow's own royal master. Henry II had been quite willing to allow his subjects in Wales, the Normans and the Flemings, to gamble their lives and fortunes in a risky adventure to Ireland, but now that they had succeeded he had no intention of seeing a strong kingdom under Strongbow arising on England's flank. So he arrived at Waterford in October 1171 with a well-equipped army of knights, foot soldiers and archers. His journey up through the country was a triumphal process. The Normans, Irish and Norse all did homage to him. The bishops assembled at Cashel – St Laurence O'Toole, archbishop of Dublin, was one of them – and they likewise made submission to Henry II. Only the princes of Cenél Eógain and Cenél Connaill gave him no welcome; this was not due to any active hostility on their part but because those north-westerly parts of the country were too remote and too embroiled in their own disputes to interest themselves in the coming of the foreign king.

At this point it seemed as if a peaceful solution might be found for the Norman domination of Ireland. By the Treaty of Windsor in October 1175, Rory O'Connor pledged himself to recognise Henry II as his overlord and to collect annual tribute for him from all parts of Ireland, while Henry agreed to accept Rory as *ard-rí* ('high king') of the unconquered areas. The scheme broke down for two reasons. Rory was *ard-rí* in name only; he found it hard to enforce authority even in his own territory in Connacht. Secondly, Henry could not restrain his barons in Ireland from seizing more Irish land, and he himself made several grants of large areas without consulting Rory or the Irish kings.

The Norman conquest of the remainder of Ireland was never undertaken in a systematic fashion. The kings of England were too busily engaged in Continental wars to give any serious attention to Ireland, and it was left to the barons in Ireland to pursue it in a haphazard fashion. As a general rule the Normans contented themselves with the plains, the coasts and the riverways; they left the hill-country, the woods and the boglands to the native Irish.

Henry reserved to himself Dublin with its hinterland, and the coastal land from Bray down to Arklow; also Wexford, Waterford, and the adjoining district as far as Dungarvan. Most of Leinster was held by Strongbow as a vassal of the king, while the 'kingdom of Meath' was given to Hugh de Lacy as a counterbalance to Strongbow.

The organising of the kingdom of Meath was one of the notable achievements of the Normans. The kingdom included what are now the counties of Meath, Westmeath and Longford, with parts of Offaly and Cavan. This success was largely due to the masterly talents of Hugh de Lacy. He established his chief castles at Trim and Drogheda, and studded his territory with castles and manors as de Courcy was doing in Ulidia. The castles were occupied by his vassals and fellow-knights – the Plunketts, Nugents, Daltons, Barnewalls and others – while they attracted back the Gaelic Irish to till the land and herd the cattle.

The conquest of north-eastern Ulster was a remarkable adventure, and was the work of one daring Norman, John de Courcy. This tall, fair, muscular young knight was modest in private life but fierce in battle. Early in 1177 he collected about 300 soldiers from the discontented garrison at Dublin and Irish troops in addition. Under the eagle standard of the de Courcy family, they invaded Ulster and captured Downpatrick, the capital of Ulidia. The native king, MacDunlevy, gathered an army but was defeated. He retired, called upon Mac Lochlainn, the king of Cenél Eógain, and the two kings returned with a still greater army, a flock of clerics, two bishops and a collection of relics. This great Ulster rally was broken in battle in June 1177, and de Courcy became lord of Ulidia, which he ruled for twenty-seven fruitful years. Under his firm guidance, Norman genius left a permanent heritage in Ulster. Centres were established at Downpatrick, Dromore, Newry, Dundrum, Carlingford, Carrickfergus and Coleraine. But these were no mean garrisons: around each centre a town grew up, the surrounding countryside was tilled, and monks and canons regular built abbeys.

51   Carrickfergus Castle, County Antrim, early 13th century
Bord Fáilte Éireann

Despite the Treaty of Windsor, to which he had put his name in 1175, Henry II now began to sign away the lands which still belonged to the Gaelic Irish. To himself he reserved the city states of Cork and Limerick, but the MacCarthy 'kingdom of Cork' stretching from Mount Brandon in Kerry to Youghal was given to Robert FitzStephen and Milo de Cogan, while the O'Brien 'kingdom of Limerick', which embraced present-day north Kerry, Limerick, Clare and Tipperary, was granted to Philip de Braose. It will come as a surprise to many to find that Munster, under Norman influence, became one of the most French of places outside of France.

The Norman advance progressed steadily in the north, west and south. A castle was built at Coleraine and the advance began along the coast towards

Derry. Another castle at Clones brought a whole sweep of territory to the Normans. Fortresses at Roscrea, Clonmacnoise and Athlone brought the Normans to the Shannon. A line of fortresses sprang up along the coast from Cork to Bantry Bay, and across Kerry from Castlemaine to Killorglin and Killarney.

Perhaps the greatest demonstration of Norman arms was the conquest of Connacht. It was an act of treachery, since the O'Connors, kings of Connacht, had continued as faithful allies of the kings of England. But the young Norman-Irish barons – the de Burgos, the de Lacys, the FitzGeralds – could not be restrained. An impressive feudal array of Norman Ireland – knights with their foot soldiers, archers and retainers – crossed the Shannon in 1235 and bore down all before it. The army moved forward irresistibly, from Athlone to Boyle to Westport, brushing aside all opposition. What are now counties Roscommon and Leitrim were left to the Gaelic Irish, while the rest of the province was divided up among the Normans, the Welsh and the Flemings. Towns made their appearance in Connacht – Galway, Athenry, Dunmore, Ballinrobe and Loughrea. Galway and Athenry in particular became prosperous walled centres, but there were never sufficient Normans in Connacht for the province to become a feudalised area, as Leinster and large areas of Munster became.

By 1250 – within eighty years of the invasion – three-quarters of the country had been overrun by the Normans. Nobody has ever accused the Gaelic Irish of lack of courage, yet how can one account for the success of the Norman forces in Ireland? They were far less in numbers than the Irish, they were fighting far from their homes in England and Wales and they had little or no support from the king of England. It was each Norman for himself.

The Normans were not only a race of warriors, but those who came to Ireland were seasoned fighters against the Welsh, whose tactics and weapons were much the same as those of the Irish. The Normans advanced into battle on an organised plan, unlike the Irish, who bravely charged in disarray. The Normans, superior in their weapons – the long sword, the lance, the iron helmet, the hauberk of mail covering body, thighs and arms – contrasted with the Irish soldier carrying his axe and short sword, and clad in a linen tunic. Among the most feared groups of the invaders were the Welsh archers with their longbows; the Irish spear, javelin and sling-stones, hitherto so effective, were no match for the far-flying arrows of the Welsh. What Irish army could stand the shock first of a shower of deadly Welsh arrows, followed by a charge of armed Norman knights on horseback, completed by an onslaught from disciplined lines of Flemish foot soldiers?

Norman success did not end with victory on the field. Their fortresses ensured that they would hold the territory they conquered. Their first fortresses were not of stone. They began by building motes – they threw up a mound of earth, anything from twenty to forty feet in height, with very steep sides, and a flat space on the summit from thirty to a hundred feet across. Around the summit was a loop-holed wooden palisade crowned by a battlemented tower of wood. Around the base of the mote they dug a deep ditch; beyond the ditch was the enclosure or courtyard, where soldiers' quarters and workshops were built. This circular courtyard was ringed with an earthen rampart surmounted by a wooden palisade. Sometimes there was a further ditch dug and another rampart beyond that. Altogether the mote was a formidable obstacle for the Irish, and their only hope to overcome it was to make a surprise attack and set the wooden structures on fire. After 1200, the Normans, by then well established, began to substitute stone for wood, and their castles became in most cases impregnable against Irish attacks.

52   Motte and bailey, Tipperary Hills, County Tipperary, 12th century
Commissioners of Public Works in Ireland

It is too often assumed that the Normans brought only war and division to the country, but this is to look at the later centuries, when the Norman-Irish colony was in decline. Let us instead see what was accomplished by the Normans during the first century and a half of their time in Ireland.

The Normans were the first to give Ireland a centralised administration. Much of the credit for beginning this work must go to King John (1199–1216), a most exasperating and unfortunate monarch. Thanks to him, Dublin Castle was built and an active government established; coinage for Ireland was struck; the jury system was introduced. Sheriffs were appointed, and by 1260 there were, apart from Dublin, seven counties –

Louth, Waterford, Cork, Tipperary, Limerick, Kerry and Connacht; besides, there were the liberties of Meath, Wexford, Carlow, Kildare, Kilkenny and Ulster. The summoning of parliament in 1297 with elected representatives from each county and liberty was the first step on the long road to democracy.

It would be a mistake to think of Norman Ireland as engaged in continuous deadly warfare with the Gael. Once an area had been occupied by the Normans it gained peace and order, where previously there had been raids and counter-raids between warring factions of the great Gaelic families. It is true that war continued in the border areas between the Gael and the Gall, but that was no fiercer than the clash of arms within the Gaelic territories between different Gaelic families or various members of the same family. Contrast the organised 'land of peace' in Leinster, Meath and much of Munster with the turbulent condition of Connacht under the O'Connors.

This peace and order was not bought at the price of exterminating or expelling the ordinary Irishman from his land. In fact, the Normans strove hard to ensure that the Gaelic Irish would remain to herd cattle and till the soil, as they had been doing under their native chieftains. Now for the first time Ireland knew systematic agriculture and estate management. The only people to be displaced were the Gaelic nobility, as the Anglo-Saxon aristocracy had been in England, and this was not because of any anti-Gaelic policy but rather represented a struggle for power between two groups of aristocrats, the Norman and the Gaelic. The Normans undoubtedly came to conquer and transform, but also to adapt themselves to the country, as they had in England and Sicily. They were willing to consider the Gaelic chiefs as their social equals. Several of the great leaders were married to daughters of the native princes – Strongbow to Aoife, daughter of MacMurrough; de Courcy to Affreca, daughter of the king of Man; de Lacy to Rose, daughter of Rory O'Connor, the high king; William de Burgo to the daughter of Donal O'Brien, king of Thomond.

The towns were one of the lasting Norman gifts to the country. It is no exaggeration to state that the vast majority of the existing towns and villages in Ireland owe their origin to the Normans. Though the Norsemen established Dublin, Wexford, Waterford, Cork and Limerick, they made few permanent settlements inland. But wherever the Normans settled, a more, a manor or a castle was established, then a mill, workshops, houses for the officers, artisans and retainers, then a church, and very often a monastery or a friary. A regular market was held, and often an annual fair. And so gradually a town took shape. Sometimes, as at Athenry, New Ross and Drogheda, walls were built to enclose the town. The Gaelic Irish never took kindly to the towns, and for this reason the roll-calls of the towns list names which were almost invariably Norse, Norman, Welsh and English – Le Decer, Lawless, Keppok, Golding, Forster, Newton, Bodenham, Hollywood and the like – but you will rarely find the 'O's and 'Mac's among them.

53   Cistercian Abbey, Dunbrody, County Wexford, 13th century
Commissioners of Public Works in Ireland

The growth of towns meant the growth of trade, both inland and foreign. One clear proof of this is that the Normans were the first to make general use of coins in Ireland. The Irish kings had no mint of their own, and the Norse made very limited use of their silver coin. New Ross, near where the Rivers Nore and Barrow meet, is an example of how towns formed part of normal Norman life. It was founded early in the thirteenth century by William Marshal, son-in-law of Strongbow, as a port for his extensive estates in Leinster. A bridge spanned the river to the road leading to Marshal's principal castle at Kilkenny. The ruins of a church at Ross, in early English style, bear witness to the taste and piety of the townspeople. A poem written in Anglo-French to celebrate the enclosure of the town in 1265 shows that many trade guilds were already there, and a few years later we have abundant details of over 500 separate properties in the town. It was a flourishing town for the export of wool and hides, and we know that large quantities of wheat, cheese and other provisions went through Ross to the Norman armies in Wales. It became a rival of Waterford. In five years the customs duties on wool and hides alone brought a huge sum of money into the royal treasury.

The Norman invasion also produced a new wave of religious activity in the wake of Norman arms. The religious orders in particular benefited from Norman advance. For instance, the magnificent Cistercian abbeys of Dunbrody and Tintern in County Wexford; the extensive priories for canons regular of St Augustine at Kells, County Kilkenny, and Killagh, County Kerry; the Benedictine abbey at the Ards in Down. The Normans, who were always quick to seize on what was new, practical and progressive, also welcomed the friars to Ireland in the thirteenth century – Dominicans, Franciscans, Augustinians and Carmelites. These were the new religious orders, men dedicated to preaching, to popular religion, beloved of the people. Wherever the Normans went, clusters of friars followed; their churches and friaries sprang up throughout the Norman territories; they even penetrated ahead of the Normans into Gaelic territory, where they were also welcomed.

In France and England it was the Normans who built so many of those breathtaking medieval cathedrals – Beauvais and Rouen in France, Canterbury and Durham in England. Everything in Ireland was on a more modest scale, but here too it is to the Normans that we owe practically all our medieval cathedrals – St Patrick's in Dublin, St Mary's in Limerick, St Canice's in Kilkenny. Symbolically, Strongbow was buried in Christ Church Cathedral, Dublin, which he had helped to rebuild.

For a variety of reasons, the impetus of the Norman drive in Ireland had begun to slow down by the middle of the thirteenth century. The sparse Norman population outside of Leinster and parts of Munster, lack of male heirs for their principal ruling families, no direct supervision of Irish affairs by the kings of England, the absence of any organised plan to subjugate the country as a whole – all these took their toll. Besides, there was the drainage of men and supplies from Ireland to the wars in Scotland and Wales, as well as the fatal attraction which the wars against France on Continental soil were beginning to have on the kings of England. Equally important was a toughening of native Irish opposition to the Norman power, which manifested itself in a striking way in the Battles of Callan (1261) and Áth in Chip (1270).

By 1232 north Kerry was under Norman control, was ringed with castles and was functioning as a county under the sway principally of the FitzThomas branch of the Geraldine family. The MacCarthys, hemmed into the south-west extremity of Ireland, struck back against the increasing Norman pressure. FitzThomas summoned the feudal forces of Munster to his aid, and was also joined by an army under the king's justiciar, William de Dene. The Irish and colonial armies locked in a fierce battle at Callan, near Kenmare, in 1261, and the Norman-Irish were decisively overthrown.

FitzThomas, as well as his son and a host of followers, was killed in the fighting. Thereafter the Norman-Irish were restricted to the upper half of Kerry, while the MacCarthys and O'Sullivans held the south-west corner of Ireland as their own.

An equally momentous battle determined the fate of the north-western part of the country. The royal justiciar, Ralph d'Ufford, backed by the powerful Walter de Burgo, had regained control of Sligo, then Roscommon, and in 1270 these two leaders marched through Roscommon to Carrick-on-Shannon, 'and all the foreigners of Erin with them', say the Irish annals. They came to a bloody stop at the ford of Áth in Chip, where the Irish armies, led principally by Aedh O'Connor, displayed not only their customary courage but also unexpected military skill. The Norman-Irish were routed, leaving arms and suits of mail scattered on the field of battle; in the words of the annalist, 'no greater defeat had been given to the English in Ireland up to that time'. The gallowglasses, those magnificent fighters of Norse-Scottish stock, protected by mail and carrying their long axes, had come to join the forces of the O'Connors some years previously, and the Irish now had an effective answer to the Norman military superiority in battle.

No less important than these battles were two political events, signs of the change in the native Irish outlook. In 1258 Tadhg O'Brien, son of the king of Thomond, and Féilim O'Connor, son of the king of Connacht, marched to Caeluisce (Belleek) on the River Erne, and there acknowledged Brian O'Neill of Cenél Eógain as king of Ireland. The agreement was short-lived but it was a revolutionary step for the Irish kings to reach unity by free choice. Equally significant was the invitation in 1292–3 from a number of Irish chiefs to King Haakon of Norway, then with his fleet off the coast of Scotland, asking him to become their leader against the Normans. The invitation came to nothing, but Ireland was for the first time turning for help to other powers in Europe, a feature which was to become part of the pattern of Irish history.

The tragedy of the Norman invasion was not the conquest of Ireland – for that never took place – but its half-conquest. The Normans never came in sufficient numbers to complete the conquest, and the kings of England, on whom rested the responsibility for the peace and progress of Ireland, were either unwilling to assist their barons in Ireland or too distracted by dangers in England and wars on the Continent to turn their minds seriously to the Irish problem. If the conquest had been completed, as it had in Normandy, England and Sicily, a new nation would have emerged, combining the qualities of both people.

Instead, by 1300 there was a drawn battle, with the Normans controlling most of the country, but the tide was already beginning to turn against them. The Irish question had become part of the heritage of Ireland and England

54   Map of Ireland, *c.* 1150 – *c.*1250

Liam de Paor

THE MEDIEVAL ENGLISH COLONY
13TH AND 14TH CENTURIES
J. F. LYDON

It is found by the jury that, whereas William Bernard, on the Sunday after the Nativity of St John Baptist last, in the town of Newcastle of Lyons, was playing at ball with men of that town and the ball was struck in the direction of John McCorcan, who was standing near to watch the game, John ran towards the ball, which William was following in pursuit, and met him so swiftly that he wounded William in the upper part of his right leg with a knife which he, John, had upon him, which knife unfortunately without John's knowledge pierced its sheath and so injured William, to his damage of five shillings. And the jurors, being asked if John did this from ill-timed zeal or ran against William from malice aforethought, say that it was not so, but that it was for the purpose of playing that he ran towards him to hit the ball. Therefore it is considered that William recover against him his said damages.[1]

This was the judgement in a typical case which came before the court of the justiciar in Dublin in 1308. It is just the sort of case which might be heard in a district court today and it is a useful reminder of how much we owe to the settlers from England and Wales who colonised a large part of Ireland in the twelfth and thirteenth centuries. Our legal system and our courts of law are in large measure inherited from them. So too is our legislature (the Oireachtas), which is directly descended from the parliament that developed in medieval Ireland. Indeed the very idea of representation, by which the representatives elected by local communities (now our parliamentary constituencies) have the power collectively to bind through legislation the communities which elected them, is one of the great principles which we have inherited from medieval Ireland. Initially, parliament had been composed of the great secular and ecclesiastical lords. But gradually it became more representative of the whole community, with the election of delegates from the counties and towns, and of proctors (as they were called) from the lower diocesan clergy as well. Representatives of counties were elected to the parliament of 1297, of the towns in 1299, and of both in 1300. During the fourteenth century it became increasingly the practice to summon the commons to parliament, and before the end of the century they had established their right to be present. By then parliament had assumed the representative character it was to retain right down to the present day.

Our civil service and the system of administration through which it works, though greatly enlarged and much more complex, is still in essence a system devised in the thirteenth century. The medieval exchequer, presided over by the treasurer, with its higher officials and clerks, its complicated records (in Latin and French) and methods for keeping accounts, its control over state income and expenditure, is not completely dissimilar from the Irish exchequer as it exists today. Local government, too, shows many ties with the Middle Ages. While sheriffs have now disappeared, coroners survive. And the continued existence of mayors and corporations, town clerks and town councils, provides in many cases a direct link with a period when municipal authority was in its infancy in Ireland. The first list of freemen of Dublin comes from the last quarter of the twelfth century. The earliest Dublin charter, the first municipal charter in Ireland, was granted by Henry II as early as 1171–2, and on this was based the charters granted later by John after he became 'lord of Ireland'. These in turn were the models for other municipalities as they developed in Ireland.

55   Charter of Dublin, 1171/1172
Muniments Room, City Hall, Dublin

The part of Ireland which was colonised by settlers from England needed a code of law and a system of efficient central and local government if order was to be maintained and lawlessness suppressed. This was supplied in the thirteenth century, which was a great period of expansion and development in every sphere of life. Through the English colony, new links were forged with the world outside Ireland and new contacts were established with a European civilisation at the height of its development during what one writer has called 'the greatest of centuries'. The advent of the friars, and especially the Dominicans and Franciscans, brought a whole new world of learning to Ireland. Through the colony, the medieval papacy was brought into closer contact with the Irish than ever before. Because the early upper-class settlers spoke French and were products of a French-orientated civilisation, they brought with them a code of chivalry and a vision of courtly love which was to leave its mark on the Gaelic literature of the period. This can best be seen in the new form of Gaelic love poetry which was born – the *dánta grádha*, based on the *amour courtois*:

> There are two within this house tonight
> Whose looks of love betray their secret;
> Tho' lips may neither speak nor kiss,
> Eyes – pinpointed – are fiercely meeting.[2]

At the same time the English settlers were developing their own literature, of which very little has survived. But enough remains to show that Anglo-Irish poetry, probably because of a close contact with Gaelic poetry, could be surprisingly in advance of the English poetry of the day. For example, there is the famous poem of Friar Michael of Kildare, written in the early fourteenth century, called 'The Land of Cokaygne':

> Here there is a right fair abbey
> Both of white monks and of grey.
> Here are bowers and high halls,
> And of pasties are the walls
> Of flesh and fish and of rich meat,
> All the best that men may eat.
>
> Flour-cakes, the shingles all
> Of church and cloister, bower and hall,
> Pins there are of puddings rich,
> Meat that princes can bewitch.
> Men may sit and eat it long,
> All with right and not with wrong.[3]

56
The medieval court of exchequer, late 14th century, from the *Red Book of the Exchequer Facsimiles of the National Manuscripts of Ireland, iii,* 1879

In the towns the beginnings of drama can be discerned, with morality and miracle plays in places like Dublin and Kilkenny, performed by the local craft guilds – the carpenters, tailors, bakers and the rest.

The feudalised part of Ireland, then, the areas settled by the colonists, was part of a wider community – the feudal world of western Europe – and was benefiting from that contact. It was a land of manors and villages, with broad fields tilled in strips; a land of castles and small cottages, markets and fairs, parish churches, abbeys and friaries. Great progress was made everywhere in the arts of peace. Forest was cleared, and more land was ploughed as new methods of agriculture were introduced. Commercial life expanded and trade boomed. New walled towns, like Athenry and Nenagh, sprang up everywhere. Old ports were developed, such as Dublin and Waterford, or new ones created, like Drogheda, Galway and New Ross.

One of the most interesting survivals from the literature of this period, composed in Ireland, is a poem in French which describes in a long narrative how the town of New Ross was enclosed by walls in the thirteenth century. The citizens were afraid that, lacking walls, the town would be at the mercy of warring factions in the vicinity. And so, the poem tells us:

Commons both, and leading men,
Gathered in the council then,
What for safety to devise,
In shortest time and lowest price;
'Twas that around the town be thrown
Walls of mortar and of stone.

Masons and workmen were hired, to mark out and build walls.

Yet small advance these fellows made,
Though to labour they were paid.

So the town council met again and passed a law that all citizens must help in building the walls:

Vintners, drapers, merchants, all
Were to labour at the wall,
From the early morning time,
Till the day was in its prime.

Each day they came to labour, even the priests:

And the priests, when mass was chanted,
In the foss they dug and panted;
Quicker, harder, worked each brother,
Harder, far, than any other;
For both old and young did feel
Great and strong with holy zeal.

Finally, on Sunday, even the ladies arrived to join in the work:

Then on Sunday there came down
All the dames of that brave town;
Know, good labourers were they,
But their numbers none may say.
On the ramparts there were thrown
By their fair hands many a stone.
Who had there a gazer been,
Many a beauty might have seen.
In all the lands where I have been,
Such fair dames working I've not seen.[4]

And so the walls were completed, sufficiently strong to keep out the most determined enemy. Secure within, the town prospered and trade expanded.

57 Trim Castle, County Meath, early 13th century
Commissioners of Public Works in Ireland

The life of the town was very like that of similar towns in England, and this similarity was reflected in the buildings and art of the colony. The large parish church of St Mary's, New Ross, for example, perhaps the earliest fully Gothic church in Ireland, was built by William Marshal in what is known as the early English style. In the details of its ruined choir and transepts we can see the first transplantation to Ireland of the flourishing English Gothic of the time, which was to appear a little later in the design of the thirteenth-century cathedrals – like that of Cashel – of southern and eastern Ireland.

Great developments of this kind were taking place all over the colonised area. Everywhere one discerns progress. Everywhere, seemingly, stability reigned. In this 'quiett and welthie estate', as a sixteenth-century writer called it, the whole colony was to share. The records of the great lordship of Carlow show that the lord enjoyed a total revenue of about £450 from his lands there annually – at a time when the income of the Dublin exchequer was about £6,000. The great prosperity of the colony is also shown by the large sums of money which English kings like Henry III or his son Edward I were able to draw from the colony. It was this prosperity which made possible the lavish endowment of the church with land, and the building of abbeys and friaries which sprang up everywhere and whose magnificent ruins may still be seen in the Irish countryside.

58
St Mary's Church, New Ross,
County Wexford, 1220–35:
east window
*Commissioners of Public Works
in Ireland*

Prosperity meant leisure and the desire for education. Many of the Franciscan and Dominican houses had schools attached; so too had some of the cathedrals, like St Patrick's in Dublin. In 1320, the archbishop of Dublin, Alexander Biknor, founded a university in the city, though it did not outlast the troubled years which followed later in the century. For the most part, students preferred to go abroad to universities, like Paris, for example, and above all to the schools at Oxford. Probably the most famous of all these people was Richard FitzRalph, one of the great scholars of his time, who preached before the pope at Avignon, became chancellor of the University of Oxford and finally archbishop of Armagh. He was a well-known preacher and in a sermon that he preached on 25 March 1349, in the Carmelite church in Drogheda, he exhorted his people to put their trust in Mary, who would deliver them from their present distress. This distress was caused by the great plague which struck the country in the winter of 1348–9, the Black Death, which had already swept through Europe and in the process killed more than one third of the population. A Franciscan from Kilkenny, Friar Clyn, gives a vivid description of this plague and the ravages it caused in Ireland. According to him, the cities of Dublin and Drogheda were almost completely depopulated within a few weeks. In Kilkenny, he tells us, 'there was hardly a house in which only one had died, but as a rule man and wife with their children and all the family went the common way of death'. He expresses the shock and the horror the huge number of deaths caused and he recounts the common belief that the plague was going to sweep everyone away and bring the world to an end. He himself, an educated man, shared in this belief. The last words he wrote in his chronicle are poignant and moving:

> Among the dead expecting death's coming, I have set [these deeds] down in writing, truthfully as I have heard them and tested them; and lest the writing should perish with the writer and the work fail with the worker, I leave parchment to carry on the work, if perchance any man survives or any of the race of Adam may be able to escape this pestilence and continue the work I have begun.

Shortly after this, the chronicle stops suddenly and another hand added the words: 'it appears that the author died here'.[5] Friar Clyn himself fell victim to the plague.

The plague and its effects caused panic in the colony and created havoc among the settlers. Many fled from outlying districts to the towns, and from there back to England. Manors and villages were left deserted and fields untilled. The forest crept back into land which had been cleared. But this migration from Ireland and the decay of the colony was not only the result of the Black Death. It had been going on for some time as a result of a remarkable Gaelic revival which was threatening the colony everywhere. Already by the end of the thirteenth century a distinction was made between *terra pacis* and terra guerre, the 'land of peace' and the 'land of war'. By 1297 an Irish parliament found it necessary to legislate on how peace was to be maintained and on how war (when there was war) should be fought. We read of expeditions mounted against Gaelic Leinster, or against an O'Brien or a MacCarthy. There was, in fact, recurrent war. But it must be seen in its proper perspective. For most people in the colony, or for that matter in the Gaelic areas, the war was usually far away and never touched them. True, they might be expected to make a contribution towards the war effort, by providing money to finance it or food to feed the armies. And as always in time of war, there were financiers (usually Italians), merchants, shipowners and middlemen of all kinds who were only too ready to turn a war to profit. Indeed, it could be argued that the market towns, and especially the ports, prospered from the wars. And of course the landless knights, the gentlemen of leisure of the age, found employment in the wars. It would be hard, therefore, to argue that the wars that were fought in the thirteenth century were a very serious matter which vitally impaired the prosperity of the settlers or even severely retarded the development of the colony.

Nevertheless, one thing is quite clear. The Gaelic chieftains as a whole were never conquered or forced to come to terms. All over Ireland there were enclaves of independent Gaelic Irish, from which attacks could be mounted on the colony. Some of these, like the area controlled by MacCarthy of Desmond, were able to put up a successful resistance against the Anglo-Irish and beat them in open battle. The Battle of Callan in 1261, one of the first great Gaelic victories, virtually secured the future independence of the great lordship over which the MacCarthys ruled for the remainder of the Middle Ages. The O'Donnells of Donegal similarly consolidated their independence around the same time at the Battle of Credran (1257), when they halted Geraldine expansion into the north-west. Before the end of the thirteenth century, then, the tide had turned. The expansion of the colony was halted and gradually its frontiers were pushed back.

One of the most spectacular aspects of this Gaelic revival was the attempt to revive the old high-kingship. At a famous meeting at Caeluisce on the River Erne in 1258, the sons of the kings of Thomond and Connacht and the leading nobility met together and there, as the annalist puts it, 'gave supreme authority to Brian O'Neill'. But we must not make too much of this or think that there was a new national spirit, conspicuously absent in the past, now evident in Ireland. Brian O'Neill's closest neighbour in Ulster, O'Donnell of Donegal, refused to acknowledge the authority of O'Neill. And the man who was at this very time mounting the most successful resistance against the expanding colony, MacCarthy of Desmond, was not present at the meeting, nor, so far as we know, did he endorse the new sovereignty of O'Neill. In any event, the whole thing came to a sorry end afterwards, when Brian O'Neill was defeated and killed at the Battle of Downpatrick (1260). Three years later, in 1262–3, another abortive attempt to restore the high kingship resulted in an offer to King Haakon of Norway, but he died before he could land in Ireland. The most successful attempt at revival followed when in 1315, Edward Bruce, brother of King Robert of Scotland, was invited to Ireland and in 1316 was crowned high king. For three years, before he was killed at the Battle of Faughart in 1318, Bruce created havoc in the colony and rocked the settlement to its foundations. But notwithstanding this, he failed in the end, and with him the attempt to create a kingdom of Ireland and drive out the settlers ceased. From then on the Gaelic revival failed to find a national leader. Its impulse remained local down to the end of the Middle Ages; its success was measured in the innumerable battles fought by local chieftains or confederations of chieftains. So while everywhere the Gaelic recovery of lost territories was remarkable, there was never any serious attempt made to unite Gaelic Ireland or to bring about the downfall of the English government in Ireland and the end of the colony.

This great revival was manifested in other ways, not least by the new impulse given to Gaelic institutions and the Gaelic way of life. An expanding Gaelic area provided more patrons from the aristocracy for the poets, historians, lawyers and leeches. Many of the greatest books in Irish date from this period – great compilations like the *Leabhar Breac* or the *Yellow Book of Lecan* (with its curious imaginative drawing of the banqueting hall at Tara). These were essentially traditional in their content. Indeed, great volumes like the *Book of Ballymote* were almost one-volume libraries of Irish learning, story and verse, gathered together for the use of the leading Gaelic families. From this period of revival, too, come many of the commentaries on the old Irish law tracts, written by lawyers for the schools of law which they conducted, like the famous school of the Davorens in County Clare. And it is at this time too that the earliest medical treatises in Irish (mainly translations from Latin) were written down, or curiosities like the earliest astronomical treatise.

Without patrons, the poets and scholars of the period would have found it difficult to survive, and naturally enough they looked in the first place to the Gaelic noble families for this patronage. But it is clear that the Anglo-Irish nobility also patronised the Gaelic men of letters, even as early as the thirteenth century. And not only that, but some of them took to writing poetry in Irish themselves, occasionally displaying a skill which equalled that of the professionals. When Jenkin Savage died in 1374, the annalist records that 'he left poetry an orphan'. But the outstanding example without a doubt is the third earl of Desmond (d. 1398), a man who at one time was head of the English colony in Ireland, who also won fame for the quality of the poetry he composed in Irish. He is a perfect example of the process of cultural assimilation by which many of the settlers were to become, in the time-worn phrase, 'more Irish than the Irish themselves'. The fact is that, from the very beginning, many of the settlers married into Gaelic families. From Gaelic mothers and cousins they quickly picked up the Irish language, so that for many of them it became their first language. And from that it was but a short step to the adoption of Gaelic customs like fosterage.

Even by the end of the thirteenth century, the government in Dublin had become alarmed by the degree of assimilation which had already taken place. Its answer to the problem was a series of parliamentary enactments designed to keep the 'races' apart – what we in a race-conscious age would call a policy of apartheid. This legislation, some of it incidentally sent over from England, found its most famous expression in the statutes of the Kilkenny parliament of 1366. A great deal of nonsense has been written about these statutes in an attempt to show that they were anti-Irish in their purpose. But in fact the main target of the statutes and of similar legislation before and after was the

Anglo-Irish settlers in the land of peace. In spite of all the attempts of the government, however, the settlers were being swamped culturally in most parts of the country. Numerically inferior and lacking a real cultural tradition of their own, assimilation in some degree was inevitable. For some of them it meant being almost wholly absorbed by Gaelic Ireland. Here the classic example are the de Burghs, who became the Burkes of Connacht, almost indistinguishable in the eyes of the government from their Gaelic neighbours.

The Gaelic revival posed a more serious problem to the government in military terms. In the fourteenth century in particular, it proved impossible to maintain a sufficient defence against the resurgent Gaelic chieftains, even in regions dangerously close to Dublin, like Wicklow. With the help of the gallowglasses, who were mercenary soldiers from Scotland, and their own new-style armies and weapons, the Gaelic leaders were able to cancel out the military advantages which the settlers had enjoyed in the early days of the colony. In addition, it was soon discovered that the financial resources of the colony, greatly reduced by loss of territory to Gaelic Ireland and by the migration of settlers from Ireland, were not adequate to maintain an army large enough to carry on a regular and successful war against the Gaelic chieftains everywhere. In the end the colony was forced to fall back on help from England, which for a time was readily available. but England had her own problems to face in her wars with Scotland, and above all in the long struggle with France which we know as the Hundred Years' War (1338–1453). It was not easy to turn badly needed revenues aside to meet Irish requirements. But for most of the fourteenth century financial help was more or less readily made available to the Irish government, and expeditions were mounted in England to help to control the Gaelic revival. An outstanding example of this was the expedition of Edward III's son, Lionel, Duke of Clarence, in the 1360s. But none of these military interventions from England provided more than a temporary answer to the problem, and the Gaelic revival continued. England began to feel that this heavy financial outlay on Ireland was too much of a burden on her already overstrained financial resources. And the outlay was heavy, even by English standards. As long as the war with France continued, it proved increasingly difficult to find enough money for the Irish wars. Finally, before he died, Edward III decided that the time had come when the colony in Ireland must fend for itself and bear most of the cost of its own defence.

At the very end of the fourteenth century, however, peace with France and a truce with Scotland gave Richard II a wonderful opportunity to intervene decisively in Irish affairs. He did not hesitate, and in the autumn of 1394 he came himself, the first king to do so since 1210, at the head of a mighty army such as Ireland had never seen before. He waged a successful war in Leinster and forced the great Art MacMurrough to come to terms and promise to vacate Leinster altogether. Soon all the great Gaelic leaders came to the king and made their submissions in magnificent ceremonies and with great pomp. It looked as if at last the Gaelic revival had been checked, and the king sailed back to England confident that Ireland would present no problem in the future. Within a few months, however, war had broken out again. The king's own heir, Roger Mortimer, was killed in battle. Richard II came back, in terrible anger, in 1399. But by then the whole situation had changed. In Leinster Art MacMurrough had learnt a hard lesson and now proved impossible to pin down. And while the king was waging war in Leinster, his great enemy, Henry of Lancaster, landed in England and seized the throne. Richard II, it could be said, lost his throne in Ireland, and because of the Gaelic revival. And so he had to return to England suddenly, leaving the Irish problem unsolved. Never again in the Middle Ages did an English king come to Ireland. The colony continued to shrink as the Gaelic area continued to expand. The new Lancastrian dynasty in England, beset by a series of crises which it found difficult to overcome, had little time and less interest to spare for Ireland. It was left to go its own way, the Gaelic and Anglo-Irish elements learning to live together, until the original colony had shrunk to the Pale.

59
Meeting between Art
MacMurrough and the
Earl of Gloucester
June 1399,
from the British Museum,
Harleian MS 1319
*Facsimiles of the National
Manuscripts of Ireland, iii,*
1879

THE GAELIC RESURGENCE AND THE GERALDINE SUPREMACY
c. 1400–1534
ART COSGROVE

Richard II's expedition to Ireland in 1399 had failed to achieve a settlement of the country, and its most striking consequence was the overthrow of the king himself. For while Richard sought in vain to come to terms with Art MacMurrough amid the Leinster forests, Henry Bolingbroke, his rival for the English crown, had mustered the forces necessary to replace him as king of England and lord of Ireland. The responsibilities of that lordship lay lightly on Richard II's successors. No other monarch was to visit Ireland during the Middle Ages in an attempt to invest the title 'lord of Ireland' with practical significance. England's involvement in an expensive war against the French left her with neither the men nor the money to meet effectively the oft-repeated requests for assistance from the English colony. And from the mid-fifteenth century, England herself was gravely weakened by the struggle for the crown between the Lancastrian and Yorkist factions, known as the 'Wars of the Roses'.

In this situation, Ireland could not be completely ignored, for she became a factor of real importance in English politics, first by her espousal of the Yorkist cause, successful in 1461, and then, after 1485, by the threat she presented to the Tudor dynasty through her support of Yorkist pretenders. It became apparent that Ireland's fate might determine the course of English history; if she had contributed in 1399 to the overthrow of one king, she might now provide a starting point for the making of another. More particularly, there emerged the truth of the warning quaintly phrased by the author of the *Libelle of Englysche Polyce*, written about 1436:

> Nowe here beware and hertly take entente,
> As ye woll answere at the last jugemente . . .
> To kepen Yrelond, that it be not loste,
> For it is a boterasse and a poste
> Undre England, and Wales is another,
> God forbede but eche were other brothere,
> Of one ligeaunce dewe unto the kynge.[1]

Only when Ireland appeared as a threat to England's security was the English government prepared to attempt a reconquest of the country.

Inside Ireland, where the soldiers of the Gaelic chiefs were now a match for the colonists, the diminution of the land under English control, the attacks on the colony by the Gaelic Irish and the hibernicisation of the Anglo-Irish all continued with only sporadic interruptions throughout the fifteenth century.

In 1435 the Irish council requested the English king to consider:

> How that his land of Ireland is well nigh destroyed and inhabited with his enemies and rebels, in so much that there is not left in the nether parts of the counties of Dublin, Meath, Louth and Kildare, that join together, out of the subjection of the said enemies and rebels scarcely thirty miles in length and twenty miles in breadth, thereas a man may surely ride or go in the said counties to answer the king's writ and to do his commandments.[2]

And even the small area of the English Pale was beleaguered by attacks from the Gaelic Irish, so much so that the colony was constrained at one stage to request the king to complain to 'our . . . most holy father the pope . . . with a view to having a crusade against the said Irish enemies'[3]. To the English colonists the Gaelic Irish appeared little better than infidels or heretics!

But without financial support from England, the colony could do little to stem the Gaelic advance. Resort was had to 'black rents', bribes to the Gaelic chieftains, which brought a temporary cessation in their attacks, or else armies to fight the Gaelic Irish were supported by the local population, which was forced to find provisions for men and horses and quarters for the troops. This system of raising an army was known in Ireland by the term 'coign and livery'. Whether used by Gaelic or Anglo-Irish leaders or by English chief governors, it cast a heavy burden on those who sought to earn a peaceful living from the soil. Archbishop Swayne of Armagh summed up the evil effects of such a policy in 1428:

> All the lieutenants that have been in this country, when they come thither, their soldiers live on the husbandmen, not paying for horse-meat nor man-meat, and the lieutenant's purveyors take up all manner of victuals, i.e. corn, hay, beasts and poultry, and all other things needed for their household, and pay nothing therefore but tallies, so much so, as it is told to me, there is owing in this land by lieutenants and their soldiers within these few years £20,000.[4]

Outside the Pale area the country was divided into a patchwork of individual supremacies with varying degrees of loyalty to the English crown.

60
Clara Castle, County Kilkenny,: a typical tower-house of the late 15th century
Commissioners of Public Works in Ireland

The Gaelic chieftains conducted affairs inside their areas according to their laws and traditions, with little reference to the English administration. And straddling the country in a rough diagonal between Dublin and Cork were the three great Anglo-Irish lordships; the Butler earldom of Ormond and the Fitzgerald earldoms of Desmond and Kildare. And these earls, too, were caught up in the complex world of Gaelic Irish politics through their alliances with and antagonisms towards their Gaelic neighbours.

Into this situation there came as lieutenant in 1449 Richard, Duke of York. Thirty-seven years of age and a veteran of the war in France, the duke was seen as a possible focus of opposition to the weak and pietistic Henry VI as king of England. And his appointment to Ireland was designed to divert his attention from this role at a time when the pattern of the conflict between Lancaster and York was already taking shape.

Richard arrived at Howth in July 1449. Accompanying him was his wife Cecily Neville, whose renowned beauty had earned for her the title of the 'Rose of Raby'. The pair received an enthusiastic welcome. A Gaelic history records:

> He was received with great honour, and the earls of Ireland went into his house, as did also the Irish adjacent to Meath, and gave him as many beeves for the use of his kitchen as it pleased him to demand.[5]

Through his descent from the de Burgh and Mortimer families, the duke had hereditary claims to the earldom of Ulster and the lordships of Connacht, Trim and Laois. And he was accepted not only as a member of the Anglo-Irish aristocracy but also as an answer to the oft-repeated demands of the colony for the appointment as chief governor of a lord of noble birth from England. For the colony believed that:

> the people will more favour and obey [a lord of noble English birth] than any man of Irish birth, for men of the English realm keep better justice, execute your laws and favour more the common people there . . . better than ever did any man of that land or is ever like to do.[6]

61   Franciscan Abbey, Rosserk, County Mayo, mid-15th century
Commissioners of Public Works in Ireland

The Gaelic Irish, too, were impressed by this mighty prince from across the sea. So numerous were the submissions made to him by the Gaelic chieftains that a contemporary observer was brought to express the over-optimistic hope that 'ere twelve months come to an end, the wildest Irishman in Ireland shall be sworn English'[7].

In October 1449 a son, George, afterwards Duke of Clarence, was born to the duke and his wife; amid scenes of enthusiasm, he was baptised in Dublin with the earls of Ormond and Desmond as sponsors at his font. By the time of his departure from the country in August 1450, Richard had effectively forged the link between Ireland and the Yorkist cause which was to last for over forty years. And when the Yorkist forces were routed at Ludford Bridge in September 1459, it was to Ireland that the duke fled for refuge. Here he was received with open arms, and the Irish parliament took steps to legalise his position as chief governor of the country and to protect him against the charge of treason made by the English parliament. Therefore the Irish parliament declared in 1460 that Ireland was bound only by the laws accepted by its own parliament and that writs from England summoning residents of Ireland to answer charges outside this country were invalid.

Such measures were made necessary by the fact that, temporarily at least, England and Ireland differed in their allegiance; while the former still recognised the weak Henry VI, Ireland now supported the rebellious Duke of York. From Ireland the duke launched his attempt to secure the English throne. But he was killed at the Battle of Wakefield in December 1460, shortly after his departure from Ireland, and his Lancastrian enemies cut off his head and placed it, crowned derisively with a paper crown, on the walls of York. Despite this reverse, the Yorkist cause finally triumphed in England with the accession to the throne in March 1461 of the duke's son, Edward IV. And the possibility of a more lasting division between England and Ireland was thus averted.

Not that Ireland was without Lancastrian sympathisers. The Butlers of Ormond had not joined in the general sympathy for the Yorkist cause, and Sir John Butler attempted to revive Lancastrian hopes inside Ireland. But in 1462 his forces suffered a defeat at the hands of Thomas Fitzgerald, son of the seventh earl of Desmond, at the battle of Pilltown near Carrick-on-Suir. *The Annals of the Four Masters* record that 'there were 410 of the slain of his people interred, besides the number who were devoured by the dogs and birds of prey'. And among the spoils of victory taken by Desmond was a manuscript which was in part a copy of the great Irish codex known as *The Psalter of Cashel*.

That an earl of Desmond should interest himself in works in the Irish language was not surprising. The growing gaelicisation of the Desmond earls had been a feature of the previous hundred years. Gerald, the third earl of Desmond, on his death in 1398 was praised by *The Annals of Clonmacnoise* as a 'witty and ingenious composer of Irish poetry', and some of his verses survive in *The Book of Fermoy*. Thomas himself is described in a Gaelic source as:

> the most illustrious of his tribe in Ireland in his time for his comeliness and stature, for his hospitality and chivalry, his charity and humanity to the poor and the indigent of the Lord, his bounteousness in bestowing jewels and riches on the laity, the clergy and the poets.[8]

The victory at Pilltown had established this man as the most powerful lord inside Ireland. And in March 1463, when he had succeeded his father as eighth earl of Desmond, the Yorkist king, Edward IV, appointed him chief governor of the country, though he warned him at the same time against the adoption of Gaelic Irish law and customs. During the four years of his rule, Desmond, through his connections with Anglo-Irish and Gaelic Irish leaders, exercised authority over a much wider area than his immediate predecessors in the office.

The county of Cork was represented in parliament in 1463 for the first time in many years. In the same parliament, a relaxation was made in the laws against intercourse with the Gaelic Irish so that the citizens of Cork, Waterford, Limerick, and Youghal might legally trade with their Gaelic Irish neighbours.

Outside the Pale area, the towns, in general, remained English in language and sympathy long after the countryside around them had reverted to the Gaelic Irish. But they could not exist in isolation. As a statute of 1463 pointed out, 'the profit of every market, city and town in this land depends principally on the resort of Irish people bringing their merchandise to the said cities and towns'[9]. Nor was it easy for the towns to communicate with one another or with Dublin. Travelling by land in fifteenth-century Ireland was a difficult and hazardous business. The mayors of some towns were excused the duty of coming to Dublin to take the oath of allegiance to the crown because of the dangers presented by the journey. Attendances at parliament were depleted for the same reasons. And the journey from the Pale into the interior of the country became even more hazardous after the town of Castledermot fell to the Gaelic Irish. As was pointed out afterwards, the town:

> was one of the keys of Leinster for the king's liege people dwelling therein and thereabout and a safeguard and a good harbourage to the king's people that should pass from those parts and the east parts of Ulster, and from the counties of Louth, Meath, Dublin and Kildare to the parts of Munster ... [But] the said town was utterly destroyed by the said enemies and never recovered since, to the final destruction of all the parts thereabout.[10]

The towns that survived remained as walled enclaves of the English interest. Waterford, though captured by Sir John Butler in 1462, withstood a ten-day siege in 1495 when the Yorkist pretender Perkin Warbeck renewed his bid for support inside Ireland.

During Desmond's period of office, some attempt was made to provide a centre of higher education inside Ireland. In the absence of any local university, Anglo-Irish and Gaelic Irish students repaired to the English universities at Cambridge and Oxford. But many of these emigrants did not settle happily in this strange environment. And in 1422 the English parliament introduced legislation against those called 'wild Irishmen' who were accused of fomenting disturbances in Oxford. Limitations were placed on the entry of Irishmen into the university, and Irish scholars, forbidden to live in a hall of their own, were ordered to dwell among their English fellow students. Even at this stage, Irish emigrants did not easily integrate into English society. In Ireland, Desmond's project to set up in Drogheda a university 'in which may be made bachelors, masters and doctors in all sciences, as at Oxford' unfortunately came to nothing, but he did found at Youghal in 1464 a college dedicated to the Blessed Virgin which was modelled to some extent on All Souls, Oxford.

Desmond's close connections with the Gaelic Irish eventually incurred for him the hostility of the Pale residents led by the English bishop of Meath, William Sherwood. Desmond was accused of extorting coign and livery to support his forces, and at the time of his appointment the English king had warned him to repress 'the extortion and oppression of our true subjects there and especially that damnable and unlawful extortion and oppression used upon them called coign and livery'[11]. And in his campaign of 1466, when he was captured by his brother-in-law, O'Connor Faly of Offaly, he cannot have been readily distinguished from the Gaelic chieftains with whom he was allied or against whom he was fighting. These considerations led Edward IV to despatch to Ireland in 1467 Sir John Tiptoft, earl of Worcester, who was to replace Desmond as chief governor. Tiptoft was an English nobleman renowned for his scholarship and the cold ruthlessness he displayed towards his enemies. The use of summary methods of execution against the king's enemies earned for him the unenviable title of 'the butcher'. Shortly after his arrival in Ireland, both the earl of Desmond and his brother-in-law, the earl of Kildare, were accused of treason on the ground of their connections with the Gaelic Irish. When Desmond came to Drogheda to answer the charge, he was taken and beheaded on 14 February 1468.

The execution of Desmond is described with an air of shocked surprise in the Gaelic histories:

A great deed was done in Drogheda this year, to wit, the earl of Desmond . . . was beheaded. And the learned relate that there was not ever in Ireland a foreign youth that was better than he. And he was killed in treachery by a Saxon earl . . . [12]

The immediate reaction to the earl's execution was a rising of both Gaelic and Anglo-Irish lords with which Tiptoft had not the forces to cope. An agreement was therefore reached whereby Kildare was received back into favour on condition that he would make the Irishmen of Leinster to be at peace, according to his power. Subsequently Tiptoft returned to England, there himself to meet death during the brief Lancastrian restoration of 1470, when his execution had to be postponed for a day because of the mob which wished to lynch the infamous 'butcher'.

62   Carved figures from the cloiser of the Cistercian Abbey of
       Jerpoint, County Kilkenny, 15th century
                 Commissioners of Public Works in Ireland

The failure of Tiptoft's mission demonstrated the real difficulties involved in any attempted settlement of Ireland. To achieve a reconquest of the country demanded the expenditure of resources far beyond what any English king was prepared to spend. The only alternative, therefore, was to entrust the government of Ireland to Anglo-Irish lords like Desmond and Kildare who, through their close connection with the Gaelic Irish, could rule the country more effectively and less expensively than any man sent from England. But there was also the danger inherent in such a policy that an Anglo-Irish governor might use his position to enhance his own power independently of the English crown. One of the accusations made against the executed earl of Desmond, though never sustained, was that he had wished to make himself king of Ireland.

The alienation of the Desmond family and the eclipse of the house of Ormond paved the way for the rise of the Kildare earls, situated much nearer Dublin in their strong castle of Maynooth. And in 1478 there succeeded to the chief governorship Garrett More Fitzgerald, famous as 'the great earl'. The power of the great earl did not depend solely on his position as chief crown representative in Ireland. By his first marriage he had six daughters, all of whom 'married well'. And he thus established connections with a number of the chief families, Anglo-Irish and Gaelic Irish, in the land. A particularly close link was forged with the O'Neills of Tyrone, for the earl's sister Eleanor married Conn More O'Neill and their son, Conn Bacach O'Neill, earl of Tyrone, in turn married his cousin Alice, the earl's daughter.

In the tradition of the Fitzgeralds, the earl displayed an interest in both the languages and cultures of Ireland. The breadth of his interests can, to some extent, be gathered from his library, which contained works in Latin, French and Irish. And drawing to himself the loyalty of both Gaelic and Anglo-Irish, the earl came closer than anyone else to embodying a spirit representative of the whole of Ireland. Clearly he was a potential threat to English rule in Ireland. But in the event, he used his power not to make himself an independent ruler but to support the Yorkist cause, to which he remained attached.

Thus when the Lancastrian Tudor, Henry VII, succeeded to the English throne, Ireland was once again involved in Yorkist plots. In 1487 Lambert Simnel, the Yorkist pretender, was received in Ireland as the nephew of Edward IV, and on 24 May was crowned Edward IV of England in the presence of a large gathering of Irish nobles and prelates. And the earl's brother, Thomas Fitzgerald, accompanied the army which invaded England in support of the boy pretender and which was defeated at Stoke in June 1487. Simnel was captured and made a servant in the king's kitchen. Again in 1491 a second Yorkist pretender, Perkin Warbeck, was received in Cork as Prince Richard. Both the earls of Desmond and Kildare were implicated in the plot to place him on the English throne, though Warbeck departed from Ireland again in the spring of 1492.

Henry VII could not allow the continuance of the threat which Ireland now presented. Accordingly, in 1494 he sent over to Ireland Sir Edward Poynings, a capable soldier and administrator who had shared the king's exile and had been knighted after Henry's victory at Bosworth in 1485. Poynings was to reduce the country to 'whole and perfect obedience' and thus prevent Yorkist pretenders from again using Ireland as a base. If we can trust the testimony of the northern chief, O'Hanlon, the earl of Kildare also recognised Poynings' ability. For he warned O'Hanlon:

> Do not attempt anything against the deputy that you would not attempt against me myself, for he is a better man than I am, but enter into peace with him and give him your son as surety.[13]

63
King Henry VII, 1485–1509, by
an unknown Flemish artist
National Portrait Gallery, London

The acts of the parliament which Poynings summoned to Drogheda in December 1494 form the best-known legislation of the medieval Irish parliament.

The division between the four counties of the Pale (Louth, Meath, Dublin and Kildare) and the rest of the country was clearly recognised by the ordinance which required the inhabitants on the border of this area to build a double ditch six feet high to repel Gaelic Irish invaders. In a similar defensive vein it was laid down that the chief castles of the land – those of Dublin, Trim, Athlone, Wicklow, Greencastle and Carrickfergus – should have as constables men born in England.

The Statutes of Kilkenny in 1366 had attempted to proscribe the use of the Irish language, laws and customs. These were now confirmed, with the significant exception of the regulation forbidding the use of the Irish language. Clearly in the period since 1366 the use of the Irish language had become so widespread that any attempt to check the speaking of it was futile. As early as 1394 the most English of the Anglo-Irish magnates, the earl of Ormond, was able to act as interpreter in the dealings between Richard II and the Gaelic chiefs. Only the Pale area and some of the towns now retained the English language.

In general, the Kilkenny statutes had failed to check the Gaelic resurgence. Even in the matter of hairstyle and dress, Gaelic usages predominated and were again prohibited in 1537, when it was laid down:

> that no person or persons, the king's subjects within this land . . . shall be
> shorn or shaven above the ears, or use the wearing of hair upon their

heads, like unto long locks called 'glibes', or have or use any hair growing upon their upper lip, called or named a 'crommeal' . . .

At the same time, people were forbidden 'to wear any mantles, coat or hood made after the Irish fashion'[14].

The dress of the people in this period varied, as always, according to wealth or rank. The poorer inhabitants of the bogs and mountains usually went bareheaded, with little covering other than an Irish cloak. More prosperous men favoured a mantle of frieze or cloth and a wide linen tunic gathered into numerous pleats with wide-hanging sleeves, generally dyed saffron colour. On their heads were conical caps of frieze and their legs were encased in close-fitting hose called 'trews'. The women were fond of brightly coloured skirts, kilted, and embroidered with silk and many ornaments, while on their heads they wore a hood of folded linen. In this sphere, as in the case of language and law, the attempt of the English 'to teach us their ways' had not proved successful.

The standard of housing also varied. The tower houses were the typical dwellings of Anglo-Irish gentry and Gaelic chiefs at this time, and these impressive constructions of several storeys provided defence against the marauding raids of enemies as well as hospitality and entertainment for friends. On the other hand, observers reported to the pope from the dioceses of Ardagh and Clonmacnoise in 1516–17 that many of the Irish lived in fields and caves with their cattle and that the few houses that did exist were poor constructions of timber and straw.

The most celebrated enactment of the parliament of 1494 was that afterwards known as Poynings' Law down to its virtual repeal in 1782. Under its terms, parliament was to meet in Ireland only after royal permission had been granted and after the king and council in England had been informed of and had approved the measures which it was proposed to enact. Though variously interpreted in the three centuries that followed, its main purpose at the time was to prevent a chief governor from using parliament to the detriment of the king's interests, as Kildare had done when in 1487 he had caused it to give official recognition to a pretender to the English throne, Lambert Simnel.

Poynings' parliament had taken place against the background of a revolt provoked by the arrest of the Great Earl, whom Poynings suspected of treasonable alliance with the Gaelic Irish chiefs of the north. But he was restored to power by Henry VII in 1496 and remained in control of the country until his death in 1513. Though often termed 'the all-but-king of Ireland', he made no attempt to set himself up as the independent ruler of the country. Freed of his Yorkist sympathies, he remained loyal to the Tudor monarchy, though the power he exercised inside the country was amply demonstrated by his victory over the Clanrickard Burkes at the Battle of Knockdoe in 1504. Combining under him a large force of both Gaelic and Anglo-Irish leaders, Kildare crushed a similar confederation under Burke's leadership, thus ending a conflict which, according to some reports, was sparked off by Burke's ill-treatment of his wife, the earl's daughter, Eustacia. The Tudor kings, for their part, were content to have Ireland ruled for them by a loyal subject.

This policy of non-intervention from England was continued for some years after Garret Oge succeeded his father both as earl of Kildare and chief governor in 1513. But in 1519 the powerful Henry VIII decided to take a more active interest in Irish affairs. Kildare was summoned to London, and the Earl of Surrey, a nobleman respected for his ability both as soldier and statesman, was despatched to Ireland with a small force to reduce the land to good order and obedience.

Surrey found the task beyond his powers, and in 1521 he reported to the king his belief that Ireland could only be reduced by conquest and that this would require an army of 6,000 men supported by artillery and munitions from England. Fortresses would have to be built to control each section of the country that was successively occupied. And since military occupation alone could not endure unless accompanied by a large plan of colonisation, it would be necessary also to bring in English settlers to occupy Irish lands. But Henry VIII was not prepared to meet the cost of such a thorough policy, and Surrey was recalled in 1522.

Surrey had also been enjoined to bring about the unification and anglicisation of the Irish church. This was to be done under the authority of the English Cardinal Wolsey, who had risen from humble origins to become the king's chief adviser and the effective head of the English church. But this task, too, presented Surrey with insuperable obstacles.

The church in Ireland mirrored the divisions of secular society. The archdiocese of Armagh itself was split between the Pale residents of the south and the Gaelic Irish of the north, and the archbishop was able to exercise little jurisdiction over his flock 'among the Gaelic Irish', as he commonly lived not at Armagh but in his castle at Termonfeckin, County Louth. During the fifteenth century, English bishops appointed to dioceses in the Gaelic Irish area were usually absentees, and if they did reside in their dioceses were unable to understand either the language or traditions of their flocks. John Kite, an English official and a servant of Wolsey who was appointed to the archbishopric of Armagh, complained bitterly to his master about the 'barbarity' of both the Gaelic and the Anglo-Irish committed to his charge. In many other dioceses, the bishopric had become the preserve of particular

Gaelic Irish families and a number of bishops were of illegitimate birth. Preoccupied with secular and military affairs, prelates even neglected the repair of their churches. According to reports in 1516–17 the cathedrals of both Clonmacnoise and Ardagh were in ruins; in the latter, the writer relates:

> . . . hardly the walls are left. In it there is only one altar, exposed to the open air, on which Mass is celebrated by one priest only, and that rarely. There is no sacristy, bell-tower or bell, but only the bare requisites for the celebration of one Mass kept in a cupboard in the church.[15]

Another observer reported on the state of religion in the country in 1515:

> For there is no archbishop, nor bishop, abbot nor prior, parson nor vicar, nor any other person of the Church, high or low, great or small, English or Irish, that is accustomed to preach the word of God, saving the poor friars beggars . . . [16]

It was with justification that the friars beggars, the observant or reformed branches of the Franciscan, Dominican and Augustinian orders, were excepted from this general condemnation. The growth in the number of their houses throughout the country testifies to the strength of the movement. It was these men who, through constant preaching and administration of the sacraments, kept religion alive in Ireland during this period and stiffened Irish resistance to the religious innovations of Henry VIII when he broke with Rome after his marriage to Anne Boleyn in 1533.

In the same year, Garret Oge was summoned to England for the last time. When he departed in February 1534, he entrusted the government of the country to his eldest son, Thomas, Lord Offaly. On 11 June 1534 Offaly galloped into Dublin with a band of armed men each wearing a silken fringe on his jacket, the decoration which gave to Offaly the name 'Silken Thomas'. In the council chamber in St Mary's Abbey he flung down the sword of state and declared to the astonished councillors that he was no longer the king's deputy but his enemy.

Traditional accounts of the rebellion have tended to attribute it solely to the youthful impetuosity of Thomas himself. More recent research, however, suggests that Thomas acted with both the knowledge and approval of his father. The objective of the rebellion was to persuade the king that he could not afford to abandon his reliance on the Kildare earls in the government of Ireland. The demands put forward by Silken Thomas make this clear. He wanted a royal pardon for the rebellion and permission to hold the chief governorship of Ireland for life.[17]

64

Ireland, *c.* 1500, showing the Pale and the great lordships *after the map in* A History of Medieval Ireland, *1938*

Silken Thomas's revolt had not been inspired by his opposition to Henry VIII's religious policy, though he attempted to gain support for it on these grounds. But religion was to become the burning question in Ireland as elsewhere in Europe. And when a difference in religion was added to the differences already existing between England and Ireland in language, culture and tradition, the reconquest of the country, from England's point of view, became not just desirable but a pressing political necessity.

THE TUDOR CONQUEST
1534–1603
G. A. HAYES-McCOY

King Henry VIII, who succeeded to the throne of England in 1509 and became king of Ireland in 1541, occupies a position in time almost halfway between the Norman invasion and the cessation of British rule in the greater part of Ireland. Henry's arrogant and well-known figure is, however, as far as the history of the country is concerned, something more than a halfway mark.

His reign saw a new departure. Before it – particularly in the century before it – the English crown was powerless in most parts of Ireland, but Henry and his successors pushed their affairs so well that Henry's daughter Elizabeth was in due course able to pass on to her successor – that is, to James VI to Scotland, who became James I of England – something unique: the undisputed rule of the entire island. Between them, four sovereigns of the house of Tudor – Henry VIII, Edward VI, Mary and Elizabeth – completed the conquest of Ireland. Not only did they bring the whole country for the first time under the control of a central government, they ensured that that government would be an English one.

The principal motive which inspired the Irish undertakings of these sovereigns was self-protection. The first Tudor, Henry VII, had seized power in England, and he and his successors were determined to retain it. They feared that domestic rivals or foreign enemies might use Ireland as a base for operations against them. Irish recalcitrancy was, from their point of view, a danger which increased as the sixteenth century progressed and as they became more deeply involved in the European struggle for power and in the religious warfare of the age. Just as, towards the end of the century, the English were to aid the Dutch rebels against Spain, the Spaniards might – in fact, did – aid the Irish rebels against the English. If the Tudors were to continue to rule England, they must rule Ireland as well.

A further motive for the Tudor conquest of Ireland was provided by what later ages would call imperial expansion. England was jealous of the great power of Spain, and she became increasingly preoccupied with the necessity of extending her own dominion – and her trade – overseas. England's first steps to empire were taken within these islands. Ireland was the first field for English enterprise and colonisation. Sir Walter Raleigh, Sir Humphrey Gilbert, Ralph Lane – the leaders of the early English colonies in North

America – all gained their first experience in Ireland, and England learnt to establish herself beyond the Irish Sea before she leaped the Atlantic.

65
King Henry VIII, 1509–47,
after Holbein
National Portrait Gallery

Such consideration led in Henry VIII's time to the abandonment of the earlier English policy of keeping the Anglo-Irish and the Gaelic Irish apart. Soon, aggression took the place of defence. By 1534, Henry could dispense with much of the assistance of the Anglo-Irish lords upon which he and his predecessors had formerly relied and could undertake a more direct and more forceful control of Irish affairs. The power of the king's Irish council, which met in Dublin, increased steadily, and a new kind of English official, the forerunner of very many generations of skilled and loyal servants of the crown who were to manage Ireland for England, had begun to make its appearance.

The rebellion of Thomas Fitzgerald, the son of the ninth earl of Kildare, who was a leader of the Anglo-Irish and who is famous in our history as Silken Thomas, was quelled with ruthless severity. Sir William Skeffington, the king's representative, attacked the Fitzgerald stronghold of Maynooth Castle with his artillery. Guns were, of course, no novelty in the Ireland of that time, but Skeffington – for, as he said, 'the dread and example of others'[1] – used his weapons for a new purpose. When he had battered their fortifications and forced Silken Thomas's garrison to surrender, he gave the survivors 'the pardon of Maynooth' – that is, he executed them. It was an action without precedent in the Irish wars, which up to then, although they had been frequent, had not been bloody – and it was a foretaste of what was to come. The Tudor period in Irish history was one of violence. The rebellion completed the downfall of the house of Kildare; from that time forward, the viceroy was to be an Englishman – one whom few Irish lords could oppose – and until 1922 there was always to be an English army in Dublin.

Six years after the downfall of the Fitzgeralds, in 1541, Henry acquired a new crown. The Irish parliament declared him king of Ireland. If we except Edward Bruce, who was crowned in 1316 but never reigned, Henry was the first monarch to bear this title. He assumed it because it matched his Irish ambition better than the medieval title, lord of Ireland, which his royal predecessors had borne. And it was a natural step to take for one who had broken with Rome. Many people believed that the pope was the king of Ireland and that the lordship which the kings of England exercised was 'but a governance under the obedience of the same'[2]. Now they were disillusioned. Henry adopted a new symbol to suit his new authority. As his coinage shows, he introduced the harp as the emblem of Ireland.

66   Irish groat of Henry VIII

Nasional Museum of Ireland

Henry had neither the inclination nor the money (despite his new coinage) to continue the military offensive that had given him such a victory over the Leinster Fitzgeralds. Although his authority was much less in other places than it had been in rebellious Kildare, he soon abandoned Skeffington's spectacular methods and proposed to control Ireland by other means.

Outside the towns and the area of the English Pale, which was not 'above twenty miles in compass', Ireland was at that time largely inhabited by the two classes whom contemporary Englishmen called 'English rebels' and 'Irish enemies'. The 'rebels' were the Anglo-Irish lords who had fallen away from their allegiance and had adopted many of the ways of Gaelic life, that is, the Fitzgeralds of Desmond; the Roches, Barrys, Powers and others in Munster; the Butlers, Dillons, Tyrrells and many more in Leinster; the Burkes and others in Connacht; and a few families like the Savages in east Ulster. The 'Irish enemies' were more numerous. There were sixty or more Gaelic lords or captains, some of them descendants of the provincial kings of old, each of them a ruler of high or low degree and all of them independent of England – O'Neill, O'Donnell, Maguire, MacMahon, O'Reilly in Ulster; Kavanagh, O'Byrne, O'More, O'Connor in Leinster; MacCarthy, O'Brien, O'Sullivan in Munster; O'Connor and O'Kelly in Connacht – to name only the more notable of them.

The English had, up to this time, looked upon these Gaelic lords as inveterate enemies. They had done so because the system of society under which the Gaelic part of the Irish population lived – their traditions, institutions, laws and language – was still, although three centuries had elapsed since the Norman invasion, different from the English system. The Gaelic Irish had a cultural and institutional life of their own, a life that their ancestors had lived from time immemorial, and although they and the English lived side by side in Ireland they were, in fact, two different nations. In the centuries when the English had held the Gaelic Irish at arm's length, their interests had frequently conflicted to the point of enmity. Soon, when it became clear that the new policy of the Tudors would deny them their distinctiveness and would wipe out their independence, many of the Gaelic lords were to display an even greater enmity than before.

Yet Henry hoped to arrange the affairs of his new kingdom peaceably. He was well equipped for war, but he told his Irish lord deputy in 1520:

> We and our council think, and verily believe, that in case circumspect and politic ways be used, you shall bring the Irish lords to further obedience . . . which thing must as yet rather be practised by sober ways, politic drifts and amiable persuasions, founded in law and reason, rather than by rigorous dealing . . . or enforcement by strength or violence.[3]

Twenty years later – although in the meantime Lord Deputies Grey and St Leger had been demonstrating the government's strength by a series of expeditions (in reality they were raids) throughout Ireland – Henry was still recommending 'good and discreet persuasions'[4]. And his policy bore fruit. The earl of Desmond submitted to him on his knees; MacWilliam Burke of Galway humbly besought pardon; O'Brien submitted; Conn O'Neill, the greatest lord in Ulster, crossed to England and, speaking through an interpreter, thanked the king for his mercy and swore allegiance to him. These three were ennobled. Burke was made earl of Clanrickard, O'Brien earl of Thomond, and O'Neill earl of Tyrone. By the time of Henry's death in 1547, forty of the principal Gaelic and Anglo-Irish had made their peace and had undertaken to obey English law.

67   Irish warriors and peasants, by Albrecht Dürer, 1521
National Gallery of Ireland

Such of these lords as had been living according to the Irish system gave up their lands to the crown and received them back again as feudal fiefs. All agreed to abandon the old ways and, by learning English and ceasing to wear distinctively Irish garments, to establish uniformity of language and dress throughout the king's dominions. Henry's intention was to bring about a revolution. He wanted to substitute for the 'sundry sorts' of people who made up the Irish population – that is, the Anglo-Irish and Gaelic Irish – one class only, the king's subjects, all of whom would be anglicised. The agreements by which these alterations were promised or effected were, like so many treaties, entered into by independent powers, and, like treaties, many of them were made only to be broken. But no such wholesale changes – in particular no such inroads on the Gaelic system – had been contemplated before this in Ireland.

Nor was this policy of unification that was to bring about the destruction of the old Gaelic world Henry's only Irish legacy. He also introduced the Reformation. Henry clashed with the international Catholic Church because, in England, he was the self-willed ruler of a national state. The clash speedily became a breach. By 1534 Henry had abolished the English jurisdiction of the pope, had taken the pope's place by assuming the title 'supreme head on earth of the church of England' and had altered the succession to the throne so as to exclude the daughter of the queen whom – in defiance of the pope – he had divorced. Soon the English monasteries were dissolved. The attempt to repeat these changes in Ireland was part of the policy of anglicisation of the country. There was no popular resentment against the church in Ireland such as had become evident in England, and the new Protestantism can as yet have had few Irish followers, but it was necessary that Irish religious practice should, in the interest of Tudor absolutism, be made to conform with English practice. When the Irish parliament of 1536 passed – not without opposition – an act which made Henry 'the only supreme head on earth of the whole church of Ireland', their performance was justified by the statement that 'this land of Ireland is depending and belonging justly and rightfully to the imperial crown of England'[5].

The reformation was at first noticeable only in the towns and in the Pale, in which area, by the end of the reign, nearly all the religious houses had been dissolved. Things were different in the districts under Gaelic rule, where indeed the old church was separately organised. It was said as early as 1539 of the friars and other priests in Ulster that they:

> do preach daily that every man ought, for the salvation of his soul, fight and make war against our sovereign lord the king's majesty, and if any of them die in the quarrel his soul . . . shall go to Heaven, as the souls of SS Peter, Paul and others, who suffered death and martyrdom for God's sake.[6]

Ultimately the Reformation had little success in Ireland. Edward VI, who succeeded Henry VIII in 1547, attempted to introduce doctrinal changes. He was resisted. His successor, Mary, was a Catholic, and she officially restored the old religion. Queen Elizabeth I, the last of the Tudors, sought to establish a uniformity of Protestantism within her dominions. The resistance which Elizabeth encountered in Ireland was far greater than that which her father had met. The Irish parliament of 1560 – which, like all the parliaments of the century, represented only the more anglicised parts of the country – tried to make Ireland Protestant by legislation, but the religious conservatism of the people, the fact that the reformed religion was associated with an alien government, and the missionary efforts of the agents of the Counter-Reformation – the Jesuits and other priests who came to Ireland from the Continent – all combined to entrench Catholicism. The old religion, professed by Anglo-Irish and Gaelic Irish alike, soon disclosed itself as a force making for Irish unity, and for resistance to England. As time went on, it became increasingly clear that the established church was the church of the new English colony and of the official class.

Henry's successors, Edward, Mary and Elizabeth, continued their father's civil policy. Although the English determination to control Ireland increased as the century progressed, not even Elizabeth, who was the strongest of the Tudors, abandoned until the very end the hope of achieving her purpose by negotiation.

The first indication that negotiation might be inadequate came from Ulster. Conn O'Neill, who had agreed when he was made earl of Tyrone 'utterly to forsake' the name of O'Neill – that is, he agreed to become the subject of the new king of Ireland and renounced his claim to be an Irish king – died in 1559. The question was, who was to succeed him? If his son Matthew, the heir according to English law, succeeded, the Ulster part of Henry's settlement might have been preserved. But another son, Shane the Proud, claimed that he was the legitimate heir and that, according to the system upon which the O'Neill lordship and all the other Gaelic lordships rested, Conn had been a ruler only for life. Conn had had 'no estate in what he surrendered'; therefore, Shane held, the surrender and the grant of the earldom were of 'no value'[7].

It was a bold plea – all the more so in that Shane made it in the queen's court in London, where he went at Elizabeth's expense in 1562, accompanied by an escort of gallowglasses, or Scots-Irish mercenaries, 'armed with battleaxes, bareheaded, with flowing curls, yellow shirts dyed with saffron … large sleeves, short tunics and rough cloaks, whom the English followed with as much wonderment as if they had come from China or America'[8]. Strangely – but we must remember that the queen had hope of a compromise – Shane was 'sent home with honour'. He behaved as a king in Ulster for five more years and was in the end (1567) brought down not by the queen but by his neighbours, the O'Donnells and the Antrim Scots, whom he had 'yoked and spoiled at pleasure'. His head was placed on a spike over one of the gates of Dublin. By tolerating Shane, Queen Elizabeth had accepted, as far as Ulster was concerned, temporary reversal of the anglicisation project. She tolerated

Shane's successor, Turlough Luineach, in the same way. Turlough was no rebel; he cost the English nothing and was held in check by his rising rival, Hugh O'Neill. Hugh, the grandson of Conn, had been indoctrinated in England and it was hoped that he might eventually redeem the north.

68
Hugh O'Neill
H. Adami, La spada
d'Orione, *Rome, 1680*

Elsewhere, the queen was quite clearly gaining ground as the century advanced. The establishment in 1570 of presidencies in Munster and Connacht brought organised English government into the south and into the country beyond the Shannon; and by 1585, when almost all the modern countries had been defined, the queen largely controlled the provinces of Leinster, Munster and Connacht. Of these, Munster had proved the most difficult to subdue. The Munster lords resisted efforts to curtail their local authority. And they were led to take sides in defence of their religion in the ideological struggle which then split Europe, the struggle of Catholic against Protestant – a contest heightened in 1570 by the excommunication of the queen. Munster rebelled in 1579. Continental efforts to assist the rebels – in particular, a landing of Spaniards and Italians at Smerwick in 1580 – strengthened the English determination to crush them, and by 1583 the rebellion had been put down with great severity. It was followed by plantation, that is, by the dispossession of the rebellious landholders and their replacement by loyal English colonists. Plantation had already been tried in the midlands and the north, and it was the policy that was in the next century to transform Ulster and to set up the English colonies in America. Although the Munster plantation was not destined to be a success, Munster was quiet in 1585 when Connacht was taken in hand. Connacht presented little difficulty. The lords and great landholders of that province agreed to make a settlement which confirmed them in their estates, introduced money rents instead of the services and contributions in kind of the Irish system, and eventually abolished hereditary local jurisdiction.

So far, from the English point of view, all was well. It appeared that great progress had been made in the anglicisation of Ireland. The towns, none of which was of native origin, lent active support to the servants of the crown. When the survivors of the Spanish Armada came ashore after their shipwreck on the Irish coast in 1588, these enemies of England were almost everywhere treated as enemies by the Irish as well. And a significant effort in the progress of anglicisation was made when in 1592 Queen Elizabeth founded a university at Dublin. Ireland had diverged from the general pattern of medieval Europe in that all previous schemes to found a university had failed, and thus her first university (and the only one for 250 years) was inevitably identified with the Protestant establishment. Trinity College, Dublin, named after its prototype in Cambridge, and invested with all the powers of a university, was intended to be not only a centre of higher learning but also a pillar of the established church. It became a seat of learning, but it had no significant effect on the exodus of young Catholics to Continental seminaries for their higher education.

There was one outstanding exception in the record of Tudor success in Ireland. Ulster had been for long unaffected by the changes that were so noticeable elsewhere. But the northern lords were uneasy. They distrusted England. They remembered the attempts to poison Shane O'Neill, the massacre of the Scots in Rathlin, Bingham's breaches of faith in Connacht, the kidnapping of Hugh O'Donnell, the execution of O'Neill of Clandeboye, O'Rourke of Breifne, MacMahon of Monaghan – the list of acts of violence and treachery that Ulster attributed to the queen's agents lengthened as the century progressed. The Ulster lords looked uneasily upon arrangements that were made within their own bounds, in Monaghan, in 1591. Soon they were determined to make no more such arrangements and to keep out a president, sheriffs, provost marshals and English lawyers – men without sympathy who would, regardless of the consequences to the Gaelic communities, abolish all power that conflicted with the queen's.

The English conquistadores, for their part, accepted this challenge. Ulster was for them the recalcitrant Ireland, a possible point of entry for their Continental enemies, a bad example for the uneasily converted, the cajoled and the coerced of the other provinces. They believed that Hugh O'Neill would aid them and that Ulster, split by feuds, would never unite against them. If necessary, they would do by the strong hand in Ulster what had been done by negotiation in Connacht. They had no conception of the magnitude of their task; they did not foresee that they would have to fight as the English had never fought in Ireland before to prevent Ulster from undoing the Tudor conquest as a whole.

Some of the Ulster lords – in particular, Maguire – had been fighting to uphold their sovereignty and to keep the English out of Ulster since 1593. In 1595 Hugh O'Neill, earl of Tyrone, who had been assisting his more warlike neighbours for some time, openly joined them. From that moment until 1603, when Queen Elizabeth died, everything revolved round the issue of the Ulster war. It was the final contest which would decide the future of the Gaelic institutions and would complete – or make it impossible to complete – the Tudor conquest.

69
Armagh in ruins, *c.* 1600, *from a map by R. Bartlett* in *G. A. Hayes McCoy,* Ulster and Other Irish Maps, *c.* 1600, *1964*

The leading spirit, the man who was so largely responsible for the long series of Irish successes in the struggle, was Hugh O'Neill. This man, who had plotted successfully to overcome his rivals in Tyrone and who claimed (like Shane O'Neill) that he was overlord of the greater part of Ulster, was a courageous and cautious leader. Occasionally emotion overcame him, but ordinarily he was crafty, calculating and ambitious. He loved power, and the realisation that the queen would not tolerate his continued exercise of it was undoubtedly his chief motive in taking up arms. O'Neill knew that there could be no separate solution for Ulster, and consequently he tried to involve the whole country in the war. The English said that the Irish hoped 'to recover their ancient land and territories out of the Englishmen's hands'[9], to bring all Ireland under Gaelic rule and to make O'Neill the lieutenant of the pope and the king of Spain – England's ecclesiastical and civil enemies. O'Neill would probably have settled for less, perhaps for non-interference with the Gaelic lords, the employment of Irish men in offices of state and freedom for Catholicism. But both sides were driven to extremes. The aid of England's national enemy, Spain, became essential for O'Neill, and his acceptance of it increased what was, from the English viewpoint, his guilt. The old Tudor fear became a reality: Queen Elizabeth's enemies were using Ireland to injure England.

Until the end of 1601, when the Spaniards came, the Ulstermen remained on the defensive. They repulsed attacks in the two areas where it was possible to mount attacks against them: over the Blackwater north of Armagh and over the Erne at Ballyshannon. Their hope was to avoid any defeat – which would have broken up their confederacy – and to prolong the war. If they were still in the field when Elizabeth died, they might make better terms.

O'Neill fought in the traditional Irish way. He attacked moving columns of the English and laid ambushes, some of which developed – like Clontibret in 1595 – into battles. His soldiers were musketeers, cavalrymen and pikemen, like the English, and he did not lack firearms. He was an outstanding organiser and he perfected a system of native mercenaries called 'bonnachts' which provided him with a trained army of almost 10,000 men in 1601.

Until 1597, the English merely marched into the Irish territories and left garrisons in castles or roughly constructed forts. O'Neill's great victory at the Yellow Ford, north of Armagh, in 1598 made them more cautious. After that they tried simultaneous attacks on south-west and south-east Ulster, the entries to O'Donnell's country and to O'Neill's. When Lord Deputy Mountjoy, the best of their soldiers, came in 1600 they multiplied their garrisons and introduced a policy of frightfulness. They destroyed their enemy's corn in the fields, burnt houses and carried on the war through the winter. They used their sea power to make a landing behind O'Neill's back at Derry (1600).

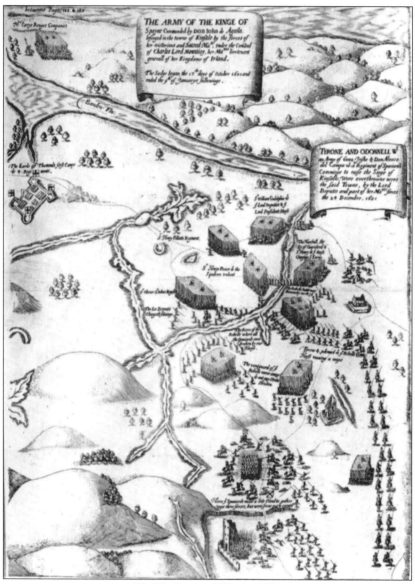

70   The Battle of Kinsale, 1601
Thomas Stafford, Pacata Hibernia, 1633

Still, the Ulstermen remained unsubdued, and when the Spaniards arrived in Kinsale O'Neill and O'Donnell marched south to join them. But this involved their assumption of the offensive, which was a new departure for them, and when they tried to cooperate with the besieged Spaniards at Kinsale their efforts met with disaster. Despite their years of military success, the Irish were unable to fight the kind of formal battle which their opponents – fully realising their own danger of being caught between the two fires – were quick to force upon them. When Mountjoy showed that he was going to attack them outside Kinsale, the Irish infantry tried to array themselves in the massive formations which had for so long brought victory to their Spanish allies in the great Continental battles of the age, but they had never fought in that way before. They were slow and inexpert in their movements, and, to increase their difficulties, their horsemen deserted them. Mountjoy's men came on. They overran the Irish piecemeal, one unwieldy division after another, and very soon all was over. O'Neill and his Ulster, Connacht and Munster allies were completely defeated. The Spaniards soon surrendered the town of Kinsale and, in due course, the hitherto unsubdued Ulster was overrun. The war ended with O'Neill's submission in 1603.

The Battle of Kinsale had decided everything. Mountjoy's victory meant the repulse of the Spanish invasion and the ultimate overthrow of O'Neill, O'Donnell and their companions. It meant also the downfall of the last of the Gaelic lordships and the end of the old Irish world. Queen Elizabeth was dead by the time of O'Neill's surrender at Mellifont (30 March 1603), but the policy of her house had succeeded. Ireland, despite the resistance of so many of her lords, was conquered.

The Colonisation of Ulster and the Rebellion of 1641
1603–60
Aidan Clarke

The history of Ireland in the first half of the seventeenth century was rich in event, and perhaps bewildering in the number and complexity of the interests involved. The Irish, the old English, the new English, the royalists, the parliamentarians and the Scots – each of them played their separate parts in the confusion of events. But what happened at that time can be summarised in a single brief sentence: the land of Ireland changed hands.

When the Treaty of Mellifont brought the Nine Years' War to an end, most of the land in every province was in the possession of Catholics – some of them the descendants of early English settlers, but most of them the native Irish themselves. By 1660, Catholics, whatever their origin, were allowed to own land only to the west of the River Shannon, in the province of Connacht and the county of Clare. Elsewhere, there were new landowners – Scots and English who had come to Ulster in the first decades of the century, and, in Leinster and Munster, more recent settlers who had arrived in the wake of Cromwell's armies in the 1650s.

The Tudor conquest of Ireland had arisen from the need to make a Protestant England safe in a Europe divided by religion, but that conquest was not complete. It was a measure of 'the great O'Neill's achievement that the Nine Years' War ended, not in the punishment of the defeated rebels, but in a negotiated settlement. O'Neill and O'Donnell – earls of Tyrone and Tyrconnell – were allowed to return to their lands and live among their people.

The war had changed many things. Ulster was dotted with forts and garrisons, and was no longer beyond the reach of English armies and English law. English authority extended, for the first time, over every part of Ireland, and the old Gaelic ways were withering. But O'Neill was still a force to be reckoned with, and the government had been glad enough to bring the war to a successful end, without insisting upon any compensation for its long and costly effort.

Circumstances quickly changed, however, and the opportunity to make a much more profitable use of victory soon presented itself. For O'Neill and many of his followers were unwilling to accept the new order of things – unable to settle down as ordinary landlords where they had lately been independent princes. After four resentful years of subjection to the English crown, O'Neill took ship, at Rathmullan in Lough Swilly (3 September 1607), and went into voluntary exile on the Continent. With him went O'Donnell and more than ninety of the leading men of Ulster.

The 'flight of the earls' left Ulster leaderless, and the government jubilant. There was no longer any need for caution or conciliation in Ulster. The exiles had left their people defenceless, and presented the government with an ideal opportunity to solve the problem of Ireland's chief trouble spot. The ideal solution had been known for generations. It was, in a word, plantation. The idea of plantation was straightforward. Land was the source of wealth and the basis of power. To take it from the Catholic Irish and give it to Protestant immigrants would at once weaken resistance to English rule and bring into being a Protestant community sufficiently numerous and sufficiently powerful to keep the peace in Ireland. If the Irish would not become Protestant, then Protestants must be brought to Ireland.

Under the Tudors, the idea had been experimented with only in the most half-hearted way, and the small groups of settlers 'planted' in Laois and Offaly in the 1550s and in Munster in the 1580s had made little difference to the balance of power in Ireland. What was planned in Ulster after the 'flight of the earls' was much more ambitious and far more systematic. In each county to be planted, the native Irish were to be segregated in defined areas, so that a network of new, entirely Protestant communities could be created. Preparations went ahead rapidly. Much of the land was confiscated in the six counties of Armagh, Cavan, Coleraine, Donegal, Fermanagh and Tyrone, and then granted out again in lots of from 1,000 to 2,000 acres at easy rents, on condition that those who received it should bring in Protestant tenants to cultivate the soil and build defences – a castle and a bawn – for the safety of the settlement. The region between the Rivers Foyle and Bann was treated as exceptional: for it the city of London was enlisted as collective 'undertaker', with special obligations (including the rebuilding of the ruined city of Derry) and special privileges. Hence Derry was renamed Londonderry, while the former county of Coleraine, augmented by territory that had hitherto been part of Tyrone, became the county of Londonderry.

In the years after 1609, the plantation gradually took shape. Settlers arrived in Ulster: many of them from England, many more from the lowlands of Scotland. With them they brought their own traditions, their own institutions and their own familiar way of life. They levelled the forests and devoted themselves to arable farming, rejecting the pastoral ways of the Irish. They built towns and villages of neat timber-framed houses and thatched or slated stone cottages, carefully sited and laid out as fortified frontier posts.

71   Donegal Castle: a Jacobean mansion added *c.* 1615 to an O'Donnell tower-house (15th–16th century) by the English 'servitor', Captain Basil Brooke, to whom the house and adjoining lands were granted under the plantation scheme

Bord Fáilte Éireann

They established markets and local industries, built churches and schools, and introduced the ordinary amenities of life to which they had been accustomed at home – and some, indeed, which were unusual, as in Moneymore in County Londonderry, where the residents were provided with a piped water supply. The changes which these numerous and socially diversified Protestant newcomers wrought in Ulster were dramatic and far-reaching. A whole new society was created, one which was not only entirely alien to the native traditions of the area, but also entirely different in character from every other part of Ireland. It was not just the Protestantism of the planters that made Ulster distinctive, but their whole way of life. Nonetheless, the colony did not go completely according to plan, for there were not enough settlers to exploit the resources of the province in full. The segregation plan was not carried out; the native Irish remained, as tenants and labourers, but were gradually forced by economic pressure to move to the worst lands. As a result, the supposedly Protestant area was riddled with native Irish Catholics – embittered and degraded, awaiting their chance to strike back.

In the years in which the plantation was being established, however, little attention was paid to the native Irish, and they, in their turn, remained relatively quiet. The government took it for granted that they were disloyal, and suspected that the chief among them were in constant communication with England's enemies on the Continent. In many cases, the government was right. Ireland had its place in the reckonings of Catholic European statesmen. When the Catholic archbishop of Armagh died in 1625, for instance, the choice of a new primate assumed an international significance: both France and Spain sponsored candidates. The candidate of Spain, which was at war with England and hoped to have the Irish as allies, was successful.

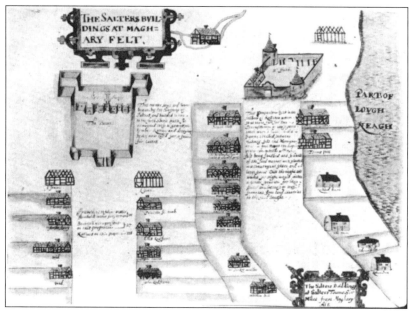

72   Magherafelt and Salterstown, County Derry, in 1622: plantation villages built by the Salters' Company of London, from Sir Thomas Phillips' survey
D. A. Chart, Londonderry and the London Companies, 1609–29, *1928*

But the significant link between Ireland and Europe was religious, not political. It was not Spain which was of first importance, but Rome, for these were the years of the Counter-Reformation – of the Catholic Church's drive to recover the ground that had been lost to Protestantism. At its most spectacular level, the Counter-Reformation was concerned with politics, but it also involved a sustained organisational effort to improve the routine administration of the church's affairs, and some of Rome's attention was devoted to making provision for the regular servicing of the church in Ireland. Arrangements were made to ensure a constant supply of clergy, to encourage the expansion of religious orders and to create educational facilities in Europe for young men from Ireland who wished to enter the priesthood. Throughout the early seventeenth century, this work of organisation and invigoration was steadily going on, and the position of the church in Ireland was being consolidated. Bishops were appointed to sees which had long been vacant, the religious orders – and the Franciscans in particular – recruited members widely and set up many new houses, and a steady stream of young men crossed to the Continent, to enter one or other of the twenty Irish colleges which prepared them for the Irish mission, or to become, like Luke Wadding, statesmen of the church and advisers to the papacy. This intimate and continuous contact with Continental Catholicism was the lifeline of the faith in Ireland.

Within Ireland itself, the government had quickly found that to defeat the Irish was not to defeat Catholicism – for there existed in Ireland a large and influential group which was, though Catholic in religion, English by descent, the group called the 'Old English'. They no longer, of course, controlled the government of Ireland, as they had in the past, but they still owned one third of the country's land, and they were still loyal to the English crown. But they were seriously disturbed by the fear that England no longer valued their allegiance, that the government tended to assume that all Catholics were disloyal and would no longer be prepared to distinguish between the native Irish and themselves. If this were so, then the government might be expected to accept remorselessly the first opportunity to deprive them of their land. For some years, political interest centred upon their attempts to persuade the government to renounce any such intention, and to allow an act of parliament to be passed giving them full security.

The government was not, in fact, disposed to trust them, but necessity compelled it to act as if it did. When Charles I came to the throne in 1625 and launched into a war against Spain, financial difficulties prompted him to grant concessions to the Old English in return for a large sum of money. In the 'Graces', which he granted in 1628, he promised them the guarantee which they had asked for – and in doing so, he seemed to be recognising that their position was indeed unique, and that they were entitled, though Catholic, to special consideration. But when the war came to an end, and the money was spent, his promise was broken, and the Graces repudiated.

It took skill and ruthlessness to weather the effect of this breach of faith. They were provided by a new lord deputy, Viscount Wentworth, who arrived in 1633 and set about the task of making Ireland self-supporting and rescuing its government from the local pressures which his predecessors had been unable to resist. Within six years, he had achieved his aims, building a strong, efficient and independent administration which fearlessly attacked the interests of every important group in Ireland.

73
King Charles I, 1625–49,
by Daniel Mytens, 1631
National Portrait Gallery, London

To the Old English it was his treatment of the Irish parliament that was the most ominous. Tradition had long accustomed them to regard that parliament as embodying their right to participate in the business of government from time to time, and to be consulted about matters of policy. The first breach in that tradition had come with the plantation in Ulster, which had naturally led to a considerable increase in the number of Protestant members of parliament. Nonetheless, when parliament met in 1613, the Old English were still sufficiently powerful to frustrate an attempt by the government to introduce anti-Catholic legislation. But the very fact that such an attempt was made revealed clearly that if the Old English were to maintain their position in Ireland, they must continue to control parliament. When Wentworth convened a parliament in 1634, however, it became evident that they had failed to do so. Wentworth exploited the occasion adroitly. By refusing to allow parliament to deal with any business other than that presented to it by the government, he made constructive opposition impossible. And by arranging for the election of a group of government officials, who held the balance of power in the House of Commons, he was able to play Catholic against Protestant to secure approval of a government policy which included the repudiation of the more important of the Graces. The Old English, who looked upon parliament as a means of protection against the government, discovered that in Wentworth's hands it had become another weapon against them.

74
Thomas Wentworth,
1st Earl of Strafford,
after Van Dyck
*National Portrait
Gallery,* London

It was this success in exploiting the Irish parliament that made it possible for the lord deputy to disregard local interests entirely in the following years. One quarter of Catholic land in Connacht was confiscated, and for the first time no distinction was made between the Irish and the Old English. Many of the planters in Ulster were penalised for failing to fulfil the conditions on which they had received their grants, and proceedings were taken against the Presbyterian practices which the Ulster Scots had brought with them from Scotland. The members of the Protestant establishment were cold-shouldered and deprived of the influence and the profits of government to which they had been accustomed. While Wentworth was in Ireland, there was no effective opposition to him, but as soon as he was called back to England in 1639, all those whom he had antagonised made common cause against him in the Irish parliament.

It was at this point that the turn of events in England began to have a decisive influence upon what happened in Ireland. Wentworth had been recalled because religious disagreements between the king of England and the Presbyterians in Scotland had ended in open war. In the summer of 1640, the Scots were victorious. When Charles asked the English parliament for help, it turned upon him and used his difficulties to demand a series of reforms which stripped him of much of his power.

At first, all this seemed very much to the advantage of discontented groups in Ireland. The Old English, the planters in Ulster, and many of the Protestants in other parts of Ireland joined together in the Irish parliament to destroy the inconveniently powerful system of government which Wentworth had created. Exception was taken to almost everything he had done in Ireland. Even his largely ineffectual attempts to promote economic enterprises were held against him, and he was alleged to have harmed Irish trade – though it seems clear that it was during his rule that the Irish economy fully recovered from the setbacks which it had suffered from the Elizabethan wars. The attack upon Wentworth was not confined to Ireland. The Irish parliament cooperated enthusiastically with the English parliament in preparing a charge of treason against him: together, they succeeded in bringing about his execution in 1641. At the same time, the Old English were able to use the king's troubles in England to persuade him to grant, once again, the Graces, and to agree to abandon the idea of planting Connacht.

Experience showed, however, that promises were not enough. The Old English were convinced that they could not safely continue to enjoy their property and their freedom of worship unless they could establish firmly their right to use the Irish parliament to protect themselves against future changes in government policy. They tried, therefore, to persuade Charles to allow parliament to play a more independent and influential role in the government of Ireland. Charles, however, who had already found it impossible to resist similar demands from the English parliament, was not prepared to agree to any reduction of his authority in Ireland, and the Old English were forced to rest content with his assurances of goodwill. But even while some in Ireland were doing their best to take advantage of the position in which the king's difficulties in England had placed him, others were beginning to realise that that weakness might prove very much to the disadvantage of Catholics in Ireland. For the English parliament was militantly and intolerantly Protestant, and so were its allies, the Scots. If either of the two should use their new power to take a hand in Irish affairs, there was every reason to believe that their policy would be to suppress the Catholic worship which Charles permitted, and to extend the area of plantation.

The fear that this would sooner or later happen was one of the motives which prompted some of the Irish, particularly in Ulster, to begin to think in terms of an armed rising. It was not the only reason. The Irish in Ulster had never reconciled themselves to English rule nor to the plantation: they had always hoped to recover the property and the social position which had been taken from them. In 1641, they saw their chance to profit from English divisions. Their plan was to seize Dublin Castle, capture the principal members of the government, and at the same time take possession of the chief strongholds in Ulster in a series of local risings.

If they had succeeded, they might very well have found themselves, overnight, in a position to dictate terms to the king and parliament of England. But they did not succeed. On 22 October, the eve of the day appointed, a drunken indiscretion led to the discovery of their plan. The key men were captured, and the attack on Dublin Castle never took place. But the local risings in Ulster went according to plan, and the movement spread rapidly and widely under the leadership of Sir Phelim O'Neill. O'Neill and his followers denied that they were rebels. They insisted that they had risen in arms to defend themselves and to protect the king from the English parliament. To attract support, O'Neill went to the trouble of forging instructions from Charles ordering the Ulstermen to rise in his defence. And each of his followers was required to take an oath of loyalty to the king.

75
Sir Phelim O'Neill: contemporary print
British Museum, Department of Prints and Drawings

At first, the Ulster Irish met with only local resistance. It was not until they had established themselves in control of most of Ulster and marched south into Leinster and Meath that they had their first engagement with government troops. At Julianstown Bridge, not far outside Drogheda, they defeated a small detachment marching to the relief of the town. Almost immediately afterwards, as they laid siege to Drogheda, they were joined by the Old English of the area, and the combined forces began to call themselves the 'Catholic Army'. The Old English made common cause with their Ulster fellow Catholics because they too were suspicious of the English parliament's intentions, because the government in Ireland had made it clear that it did not trust them and would not defend them, and because they were satisfied that the northern Irish remained loyal to the king. In the early months of

1642, the movement spread throughout Ireland and success seemed near. Then, reinforcements began to arrive from England and the government began to recover ground. By April, the northerners had been pushed back into Ulster, and many of those in arms were anxious for peace. But the government was not prepared to negotiate. It was determined to seize the chance to subdue Ireland once and for all. The English parliament, indeed, had already begun to borrow large sums of money on the security of the land which it expected to confiscate in Ireland.

It had become obvious that this was to be a fight to the finish. So, at the prompting of the clergy, arrangements were made to set up a central organisation to direct the war. It was agreed that a representative assembly should meet in Kilkenny in October 1642. By the time it met, the situation had changed in two important ways: the king and parliament of England had finally gone to war with one another, and exiles had begun to return from the Continent to lend a hand in Ireland, many of them experienced professional soldiers, among them Colonel Owen Roe O'Neill and Colonel Thomas Preston.

For some seven years thereafter the situation was extremely confused. The king maintained an army in Ireland under the command of the earl of Ormond, but the former's sole desire was to come to terms so that he could concentrate his resources upon the civil war against parliament in England, if possible with Irish help. The English parliament gradually built up an army in Ireland but made little effort to prosecute the war, since it regarded the defeat of the king in England as its first priority. The Scots also kept an army on foot in Ireland, but it was active only in defence of the planters in Ulster. The Confederate Catholics, as they called themselves, had adopted a hopeful motto – 'Ireland united for God, king and country' – but they were, nonetheless, divided. On the one hand were the Old English, who had little to gain and much to lose, and who were prepared to agree upon moderate terms with Charles. On the other hand were the Irish, led now by returned exiles and by an Italian papal nuncio, Archbishop Rinuccini. These men, knowing little of the circumstances in which the war had begun, and paying little attention to the danger of Charles being defeated by parliament, insisted upon seizing the chance to demand the full recognition of Catholicism and the restoration of confiscated lands to the Irish. No agreement proved possible, and the war dragged on, distinguished only by a masterly victory over the Scots won by O'Neill at Benburb on the Blackwater in 1646. It was not until the English civil war came to an end with the trial and execution of Charles in 1649 that events in Ireland took a decisive turn. The years of opportunity had been wasted in haggling and bargaining with Charles, while the really formidable enemy, the English parliament, had built up its strength.

When that parliament had disposed of Charles and abolished the monarchy in its own favour, it turned its attention to Ireland. Its ingrained distrust of Catholicism was inflamed by exaggerated reports of the brutality with which the Ulster planters had been treated in 1641. And when Oliver Cromwell landed at Dublin with a Puritan army in 1649, his mission was not only conquest but also revenge. The indiscriminate inhumanity with which that revenge was exacted upon the royalist garrison and many of the townspeople of Drogheda, and upon the defenders of Wexford, became indelibly impressed upon the folk memory of the Irish. So too did the severity of the settlement which followed the overcoming of Irish resistance. But that severity was not indiscriminate. Not many were executed for their part in the rebellion. Men in arms were treated leniently enough: they were allowed to emigrate to the Continent, and more than 30,000 took advantage of the opportunity. The poor were left undisturbed: a general pardon was issued, and they were able to resume their ordinary lives without fear of punishment. It was the wealth of the land of Ireland that the government of England was interested in. And it reserved its special fury for those who owned that land. It divided Catholic landowners in Ireland into two groups: those who had been guilty of involvement in the rebellion, and those who had not. The first were to lose all their estates, and all their property rights. The second were to be allowed to own a proportion of the amount of land which they had held. But it was not to be the same land. Ireland, also, was to be divided into two parts. The first part was to consist of Connacht and Clare, to which all who had established their innocence were to be transplanted and in which they were to receive the land to which they were entitled. The second part was to be the remaining twenty-six counties, in which confiscated land was used to pay the government's creditors – the adventurers who had lent money or provided supplies for the army, and the officers and soldiers who had served without adequate pay.

Though some of the ordinary soldiers did settle on the small pieces of land which they were given, most sold out their interest and returned to England. Those of the officers and adventurers who had received substantial grants were more apt to stay. In fact, arrangements made for the settlement under Cromwell of Irish land never approached the thoroughness intended by those who had planned the earlier plantation in Ulster. No organised attempt was made to establish Protestant communities, except in the towns. What was changed was the people who owned the land, not the people who lived and worked upon it. The Cromwellian settlement was not so much a plantation as a transference of the sources of wealth and power from Catholics to Protestants. What it created was not a Protestant community but a Protestant upper class.

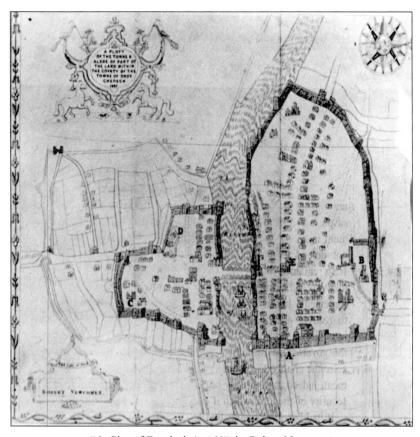

76 Plan of Drogheda in 1657, by Robert Newcomen

A good example of a medieval walled town – or rather pair of towns, as there were originally separate boroughs north and south of the river Boyne, each with its own walls and gates. The barbican of St Lawrence's Gate (A) is the most impressive remnant of the thirteenth-century fortifications. The Magdalene Tower (B) is part of a Dominican friary, where Richard II held court in 1395. A century later, Poynings held his famous parliament in the town. When Cromwell stormed Drogheda in 1649 he broke in at St Mary's churchyard (C) in the south-east corner. The steep height of the Millmount (D) was then seized and the defenders put to the sword. Another place of refuge, the steeple of St Peter's Church (E), was burned by Cromwell's orders, and a ruthless slaughter of garrison and townspeople followed.

John D'Alton, History of Drogheda, *1844*

Though dramatic changes were to come in the following years, when Charles I's son was restored to the English throne the newcomers managed to hold on to a great deal of what they had gained. And just as James I's plantation had permanently altered the character of Ulster, so Cromwell's settlement transformed the character of the landowning aristocracy of Ireland.

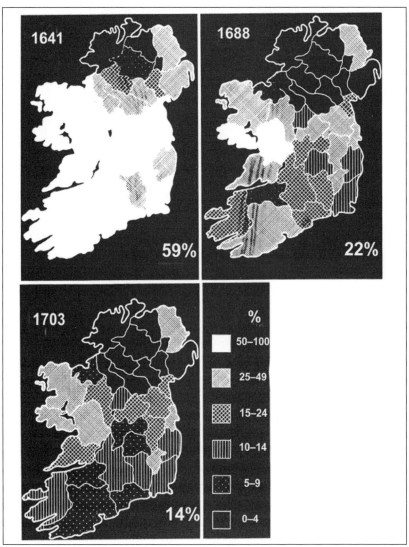

77   Maps, by J. G. Simms, showing the proportion of land owned by Catholics in Ireland according to counties, in 1641, 1688 and 1703. The effect of the Cromwellian confiscation, as modified at the Restoration, is indicated by the first and second maps, the effect of the Williamite confiscation by the second and third maps

13

The Restoration and the Jacobite War
1660–91
J. G. Simms

In 1660 the English Commonwealth collapsed and Charles II was called home. Catholics had fought for the royalist cause in Ireland and many of them had followed Charles into exile. They now looked forward to toleration of their faith and recovery of their lands. The king himself was sympathetic, but he had been recalled by the Commonwealth army, and it insisted that Cromwell's land settlement should be maintained. Charles made promises to both sides. Cromwellian soldiers and adventurers should keep what they had; Catholics should get back what they had lost for the sake of religion or support of the king. It was impossible to satisfy everyone. As Ormond, the lord lieutenant, remarked: 'there must be new discoveries of a new Ireland, for the old will not serve to satisfy these engagements'[1].

An act – the Act of Settlement – was passed by an all-Protestant parliament to give effect to the king's declaration. Innocents – the term was strictly defined – and a number of specially named royalists were to get their lands, and the Cromwellians were to be compensated with other lands of equal value. But such lands were not to be found, and it was necessary to pass a second act to explain the first one. This laid down that most Cromwellians should give up one third of their lands so that some Catholics could be restored. About 500 Catholics had been declared innocent before the court closed down. Most of them and a number of influential individuals, got back at least some of their former property. Many claimants were left unsatisfied, however, and the Gaelic Irish came off worst of all. Cromwellians resented having to give up even part of their estates, and recovery was a slow and troublesome business, even for those Catholics who recovered something. Many who failed to do so turned 'tory', took to the hills and woods, and raided the new settlers. Redmond O'Hanlon in Armagh and the three Brennans in Kilkenny were famous tories of this time.

When stock was taken of the Restoration settlement, Catholic landowners were better off than they had been under Cromwell, but they had recovered only a fraction of their original estates. In 1641, before the war began, they had owned about three-fifths of the land. At the end of the Restoration period they owned little more than one fifth. They resented the settlement as a breach of faith, and were ready to take the first chance of upsetting it. In later years, Dean Swift was to sum up their attitude:

The Catholics of Ireland . . . lost their estates for fighting in defence of their king. Those who cut off the father's head, forced the son to fly for his life and overturned the whole ancient frame of government . . . obtained grants of those very estates the Catholics lost in defence of the ancient constitution, and thus they gained by their rebellion what the Catholics lost by their loyalty.[2]

A Catholic bishop denounced the settlement as repugnant to God and nature. The poet Ó Bruadair lamented the purgatory of the men of Ireland and railed at the low breeding of the Cromwellians:

Roughs formed from the dregs of each base trade, who range themselves smugly in the houses of the noblest chiefs, as proud and genteel as if sons of gentlemen.[3]

78
James Butler, 1st Earl of Ormond
by Sir Peter Lely
National Gallery of Ireland

Religion was the other great question of the reign, and there were many ups and downs in the fortunes of the Catholic Church. Ormond was willing to grant toleration in return for an unquestioning acknowledgement of the state's authority and a denial of the pope's right to depose a king. He demanded that Catholics should sign a declaration to this effect – the remonstrance drawn up by the Franciscan Peter Walsh. But its terms were unacceptable to the church, and no concordat was reached. In practice the church was tolerated for much of the time, but there were often changes in the official attitude, and the hysteria of the 'popish plot' in England had its counterpart in Ireland. Archbishop Peter Talbot died in prison; Archbishop Oliver Plunkett was martyred on the scaffold.

The twenty-five years of Charles II's reign were in many ways a period of frustration and anxiety for Catholics, and of uneasy dominance for Protestants. But they were also a period of unusual peace and economic expansion in Ireland, in spite of restrictions imposed by English trading policy. The export of Irish cattle was banned, and Irish wool was reserved for England. But a flourishing butter and meat trade developed; Irish wool found a ready market in England and was often smuggled to the Continent. The population grew, and by the end of the reign Ireland had nearly two million inhabitants (three-quarters of them Catholic). Dublin was the second city in these islands and its population was estimated at over 60,000. Cork and Limerick were prosperous seaports. Protestants, besides owning most of the land, held a dominant position in administration and commerce. But there remained a nucleus of Catholic nobility and landed gentry, lawyers and traders who could form the basis for a Catholic revival if a favourable opportunity should arise.

That opportunity came in 1685, when Charles died and was succeeded by his Catholic brother, James II. Catholics in Ireland now hoped for a new deal: the alteration of the land settlement and the recognition of their church. But James was king of England: the land settlement and the established Church of Ireland were regarded as essential props of English rule, and James was committed to maintaining them. Protestants were anxious for the future, but took comfort from the king's assurances and from the appointment of his Protestant brother-in-law, Lord Clarendon, as lord lieutenant. Clarendon's first speech was a lifeline for Protestant landlords:

> I have the king's commands to declare upon all occasions that, whatever imaginary . . . apprehensions any men here may have had, his majesty hath no intention of altering the acts of settlement.[4]

But it was soon clear that the real power lay with Richard Talbot, brother of the dead archbishop; he had long been James's intimate and had shown himself an able and forceful advocate of Catholic claims. He was made earl of Tyrconnell and head of the Irish army, which he proceeded to reorganise by dismissing many Protestants and appointing Catholics instead. Clarendon was soon recalled and Tyrconnell took his place as viceroy. The appointment of the first Catholic viceroy for over a hundred years was welcomed by Irish Catholics and lampooned by an English Protestant:

> Ho, brother Teig, dost hear de decree,
> Dat we shall have a new deputy;
> Ho, by my soul, it is a Talbot,
> And he will cut all de English throat.[5]

79
Richard Talbot, Duke of Tyrconnell
National Portrait Gallery, London

Catholic judges and privy councillors were appointed, and more and more key posts in the administration were filled with Catholics. The Church of Ireland was not disestablished, but there was a marked unwillingness on the part of Catholics to pay dues to Protestant ministers. Church vacancies were left unfilled, and the income used to give subsidies to Catholic bishops.

Protestants took fright; merchants called in their stocks and pessimists left for England. Everything seemed to turn on the land settlement, and there was a growing demand by Catholics for its repeal. Judge Rice said he would drive a coach and six through the act of settlement. Counsellor Nagle in the famous Coventry letter argued that, if James died without a son, Catholics would have no security unless they were entrenched as landed proprietors: the settlement must be altered while the going was good. The Cromwellian mapmaker Sir William Petty and his friend Southwell compared the settlement to a ship in a stormy sea, and to St Sebastian shot through with arrows. Preparations were made for a parliament in which the Protestant monopoly of Charles II's reign would be replaced by an overwhelmingly Catholic membership. Town charters were revoked and the new corporations were mainly Catholic.

Two Catholic judges went over to England to get the king's approval to a bill for the alteration of the settlement. They were greeted by a London mob carrying potatoes stuck on poles and shouting 'Make way for the Irish ambassadors'. The parliament that Tyrconnell planned to hold threatened to bring about a reversal of the long-standing Protestant predominance in Ireland and to put a Catholic predominance in its place. The situation seemed ripe for a Catholic takeover, supported by the full weight of the government influence.

But revolution in England again frustrated the hopes of Irish Catholics. James II's policy of favouring his co-religionists had aroused the opposition of English Protestants, and the birth of a son to him gave the prospect of a continuing Catholic dynasty. In 1688 seven English notables invited William of Orange, husband of James's Protestant daughter, to invade England and drive out his father-in-law. The king's cause quickly collapsed in England, and he took refuge in the France of Louis XIV. But Tyrconnell held out for him in Ireland, and could count on the willing help of the Catholics, who saw in James the only hope for their land and religion. Protestants grew still more alarmed: migration assumed panic proportions, and the Ulster colonists prepared for armed resistance.

80   James II landing at Kinsale, 12 March 1689: contemporary Dutch print
National Gallery of Ireland

In March 1689 James landed at Kinsale with French money and arms. His chief interest in Ireland was as a stepping stone to the recovery of his throne, and he was unwilling to weaken the English hold on Ireland. The Irish were chiefly interested in James as a means of getting the land settlement altered and the position of the Catholic Church secured. James was forced to summon the parliament that a later generation was to call the 'patriot parliament' because it asserted its independence of the parliament of England. The declaratory act laid down the principle of the sovereignty of the 'king, lords and commons' of Ireland a century before Henry Grattan and the Volunteers. After much wrangling, the land settlement was reversed and the property of the Williamites as rebels was declared to be confiscated. Liberty of conscience was decreed; tithes were to be paid by Catholics to their priests, by Protestants to their ministers. Irish trade was to be freed from the restrictions of English law, and a ban was placed on the import of English coal.

The proceedings of the parliament represented, though not completely, the aspirations of the 'Old English' – Catholics of English stock – rather than those of the Gaelic Irish. Had James won the war, its legislation would have replaced a Protestant oligarchy with a Catholic oligarchy; it would not have undone the English conquest or restored Gaelic rule. James insisted on the maintenance of Poynings' Law to ensure Ireland's subordination to the English crown, and the Protestant Church of Ireland was not officially disestablished. Catholics were disillusioned by the king 'with his one shoe English and his one shoe Irish', who appeared bent on appeasing his Protestant subjects. The parliament was in any case ill timed, as its effectiveness depended on a Jacobite victory, and its debates distracted attention from the conduct of the war, which was the real business in hand.

The war that followed was a major crisis in our history. In Irish it is called *Cogadh an dá rí*, 'the war of the two kings', *Rí Séamus* and *Rí Liam*, but it was much more than that. It confirmed the change of kings in England and established a Protestant succession. But in the European context it was an important theatre of a war between France and a league of lesser powers – a league that crossed religious boundaries. The Holy Roman Emperor and the Catholic king of Spain were William's allies, and the pope himself was no friend to Louis XIV, the patron of James. Both sides fought with international armies, and Irish battles made headlines in several countries of Europe. In the Irish context the war was a struggle between Protestant and Catholic, the newer settlers and the older inhabitants. It was more closely balanced than any previous contest. Both sides were proud of their achievements and have enshrined them in their folklore. Catholic memories of Sarsfield and Limerick are matched by Protestant pride in Derry, Enniskillen and the Boyne.

The conflict began with the armed resistance of the Ulster colonists in Derry and Enniskillen. Derry endured the greater hardship and got the better publicity. They found a forceful leader in the Rev George Walker, whose diary of the three-month siege is a memorable record of courage and suffering. Derry was at the point of starvation when the relief ships broke through the boom and brought supplies to the beleaguered city. The Inniskillingers showed dash and military skill, and their victory at Newtownbutler was a major success. James's failure to reduce the north was fatal to his cause. His army retired and the way was clear for a Williamite landing under the veteran Marshal Schomberg.

The following year –1690 – the French sent 7,000 troops but demanded that as many Irish troops should be sent to France in their place. Soon afterwards William himself came over to Ireland. It was a risky step, for England was threatened by France and he did not have command of the sea. While he was in Ireland the French defeated the English and Dutch fleets at Beachy Head, and the way seemed clear for a French invasion of England – which, however, did not take place.

The two kings met at the Boyne, where James had drawn up his Irish and French troops on the southern bank. William had the larger army – about 36,000, as compared with James's 25,000. William's troops included Dutch, Danes, Germans and Huguenots, as well as British. He was not a great general, but showed himself a brave and reckless soldier. The day before the battle he was wounded by an Irish shot, and reports of his death got as far as Paris, where bells were rung and bonfires were lit. It was only a flesh wound, and with the phlegmatic remark 'it's well it came no nearer' he resumed his reconnoitring. The battle took place on 1 July by the old calendar (12 July new style), and its centre was the ford at Oldbridge about three miles above Drogheda. There was sharp fighting at the rover crossing, and William at the head of the Inniskillingers had a difficult passage. The Irish cavalry fought well, but at the end of the day James had fled, his army was in full retreat, and William was clearly the winner. In a military sense it was not a decisive victory; the Irish losses were small and their army lived to fight another day. But it was reported all over Europe, and it had a great psychological effect. *Te Deums* were sung in the Catholic cathedrals of Austria for the victory. Dublin and eastern Ireland fell to William, and the Jacobites made a disordered retreat to the Shannon. William thought that all resistance was over, and demanded unconditional surrender. Tyrconnell and the French took much the same view of the situation.

81   Patrick Sarsfield, Earl of Lucan
Franciscan House of Studies, Killiney, County Dublin

But the Irish had a spirited leader in Patrick Sarsfield, who inspired the defence of Limerick and contributed to it by blowing up William's siege train at Ballyneety (11 August 1690). The walls of Limerick were breached, but fiercely held, and William had to go back to England with half his work done. Tyrconnell and the French troops left for France. Sarsfield remained in effective command till the following year, when Tyrconnell returned and the French commander St Ruth arrived. French soldiers did not return, and for the rest of the war the Jacobite army was predominantly Irish.

The war dragged on into 1691, when Ginkel, the Dutch general, crossed the Shannon at Athlone, where the bridge was the scene of a desperate struggle. This was followed by 'Aughrim's dread disaster', the major battle of the war. St Ruth, the French commander, had chosen a strong position on the slopes of Kilcommodon hill. Ginkel's army floundered in the bog that separated the armies, and St Ruth called on his men to drive the enemy to the gates of Dublin. Then at a critical stage of the battle St Ruth was killed; a causeway through the bog was betrayed to Ginkel's men and confusion set in on the Irish side. Their losses were heavy, and Ginkel won an impressive victory.

82   The Battle of the Boyne, 1 July 1690, by Theodore Maas

National Library of Ireland

William was anxious to bring the war in Ireland to an end as soon as possible, so that he could transfer his army to the Continent, where it was badly needed for the defence of Holland. On his behalf, Ginkel had been bargaining with the Irish Catholics, offering toleration for their religion and security for their property in return for surrender. After Aughrim, Galway accepted the terms. The townsmen and the garrison were given guarantees for their property; priests and people were to be allowed the private practice of their religion.

Limerick was now the last place of importance to hold out. The Irish had little prospect of successful resistance, and their chief thoughts were of what bargain they could strike with Ginkel. The French officers urged them to hold on as long as possible, so as to keep William's army in Ireland for another campaigning season. They promised aid from France, but the Irish were disillusioned with Louis XIV, who had given them much less help than they had expected. They had no wish to be expended in the interests of French long-term strategy. Tyrconnell died and Sarsfield, who had in the year before been the mainstay of resistance, now thought it useless to go on. He decided to make terms with Ginkel, and after more than a week of bargaining, the Treaty of Limerick was signed (3 October 1691). It was agreed that as many of the Irish soldiers as wished should be given liberty and transport to go to France and fight on there. Sarsfield and some 14,000 others left Ireland, the forerunners of the 'wild geese' who in the eighteenth century made a name for themselves at Fontenoy and on many other European battlefields. Sarsfield himself had little longer to live; less than two years later he was fatally wounded at the Battle of Landen. But he had made a remarkable reputation, and his memory has been preserved in Irish songs and folklore.

For those that stayed behind, the Limerick terms seemed not ungenerous. Catholics were offered such rights of worship as they had enjoyed in Charles II's reign or were consistent with the laws of Ireland. Those who were in Limerick or other garrisons that resisted to the end were promised their property and the right to practice their professions. Sarsfield insisted that this guarantee should extend to those under the protection of the Irish in some counties of the west. Ginkel agreed, but when the treaty reached London the clause was missing, and a lengthy argument resulted in the Protestant Irish parliament refusing to ratify it.

The Treaty of Limerick was of great advantage to William, as it ended a troublesome sideshow in Ireland and allowed him to transfer his troops to Flanders, where he was hardpressed by the French. But his Protestant supporters in Ireland thought the terms of the treaty were foolishly generous, and their opposition resulted in the treaty giving Catholics much less than they expected. A number of individuals were allowed to keep their property, and the confiscation of land that followed the war was much less drastic than Cromwell's had been. Many were protected by the treaty, and the missing clause proved less important than Catholics had feared. There was confiscation of the property of those who had gone to France, of those who had died, and of some of those who had surrendered prematurely. The Catholic share of the land was in this way reduced to about one seventh. But all Catholics were soon subjected to new Penal Laws, and the century that followed was the classic age of Protestant ascendancy.

THE AGE OF THE PENAL LAWS
1691–1778
MAUREEN WALL

The Treaty of Limerick in 1691 marked the third great defeat for the Catholic cause in seventeenth-century Ireland. This time the victory seemed to be decisive, and the Irish parliament, now entirely Protestant, soon set about buttressing Protestant ascendancy in all walks of life. Members of the Church of Ireland were restored to their position as first-class citizens; Protestant nonconformists and Catholics were again made liable for payment of tithes to the established church, and a comprehensive series of new anti-Catholic measures was passed. These laws, like all Irish legislation since 1494, had the prior sanction of the king and his council in England; for the parliament in Dublin throughout the eighteenth century was but a colonial-type parliament, subordinate to the government in London. Moreover, in 1720 the right of the Westminster parliament to legislate for Ireland was formally declared by an act of that parliament (6 George I, c. 5). British policy for Ireland simply aimed at maintaining the connection between the countries and ensuring that Ireland should not compete with the mother country in matters of trade. For centuries, restrictions had been imposed on Irish trade by the Westminster parliament, and now in 1699 Ireland's export trade in manufactured woollen goods was virtually destroyed. It was useless for men like William Molyneux to challenge the right of that parliament to legislate for Ireland, for, however much Irish members of parliament might resent the fact that the kingdom of Ireland was being treated as a colony, they realised that they were an isolated minority, surrounded by a potentially hostile Catholic population and dependent on the military strength of the mother country for protection against invasion by a foreign foe or rebellion by the Catholic majority, in which they could lose everything.

To maintain the land settlement, therefore, and the Protestant settlement in church and state, the Irish parliament enacted what came to be called the 'popery code', which would, they believed, keep the Catholics in a state of permanent subjection. The Irish executive, headed by the lord lieutenant, was not controlled by the Dublin parliament. Thus the British government, while being a party to the making of anti-Catholic laws for Ireland, was also in a position to mitigate the severity of their enforcement, and so, by balancing one religious group against another, was able to use the age-old 'divide and rule' system to maintain its hold over the country.

It is important to remember that these laws were enacted against the background of a major European war in which Ireland had already been made the cat's-paw of the contending powers. Great numbers of Irish soldiers were in the army of Louis XIV of France, and might form the spearhead of an invasion force to which the Irish Catholic population would certainly rally to restore the Stuarts to the throne. These soldiers of fortune were the famous 'wild geese'. It is not surprising, therefore, that members of the all-Protestant parliament should have done everything in their power to retain for Protestants their privileged position. Ruling minorities have done the same before and since in many parts of the world. Of course, the persecution of Protestants in France, Spain and the Empire was cited to justify the savage laws now passed against Irish Catholics, but in these countries the members of the persecuted sect formed only a small minority, while Ireland was unique in western Europe in that the persecuted formed the majority of the population.

Ostensibly, the aim of the anti-Catholic laws was to eradicate the Catholic religion in Ireland, but in fact, apart from sporadic outbursts of persecution, the Penal Laws against religious worship were largely allowed to fall into desuetude from about 1716. Indeed, in the conditions prevailing in the eighteenth century their general enforcement would have proved an impossible task. The Penal Laws which were enforced, however, or which were automatic in their operation, were those which debarred Catholics from parliament, from holding any government office – high or low – from entering the legal profession and from holding commissions in the army and navy. This comprehensive exclusion was achieved by prescribing for all these officers and professions qualifying oaths, which no Catholic would take – oaths which contained such statements as the following:

> I do solemnly and sincerely, in the presence of God, profess, testify and declare that I do believe, that in the sacrament of the Lord's Supper there is not any transubstantiation of the elements of bread and wine into the body and blood of Christ, at or after the consecration thereof by any person whatsoever: and that the invocation, or adoration of the Virgin Mary, or any other saint, and the sacrifice of the Mass, as they are now used in the church of Rome, are superstitious and idolatrous . . . [1]

Great number of barristers and lawyers went over to the established church early in the century, including John Fitzgibbon, father of the future earl of Clare, chief architect of the Act of Union.

These qualifying oaths successfully closed all avenues of advancement to Catholics in public life, though they were free, to a great extent, to amass wealth in trade and industry. Protestant supremacy could never be completely secured, however, while Catholics retained any sizeable proportion of landed property. Even after the Williamite confiscation, Catholics still owned about 14 per cent of Irish land. A system was devised, by acts passed in 1704 and 1709, which forbade Catholics to buy land at all, or take leases for longer than thirty-one years, and which at the same time brought so many pressures, inducements and prohibitions to bear on Catholic landowners that by 1778 scarcely 5 per cent of Irish land was left in Catholic hands. In the meantime, for one reason or another most of the Catholic landlords – Viscount Fitzwilliam, Browne of the Neale, the Earl of Antrim, Martin of Ballinahinch, French of Monivea, Lord Kingsland, Lord Mountgarrett, Lord Dunsany and many others – had gone over to the established church, so that by 1778 Catholic proprietors owned but £60,000 a year of the total rental of Ireland, then calculated at £4,000,000.

83
An Irish cabin
Arthur Young,
Tour in Ireland, *1780*

At the other end of the scale was the mass of the Catholic peasantry, whose general condition of poverty and wretchedness was not due to the Penal Laws, and to whom it mattered little whether their landlords were Catholic or Protestant. As Catholics, their main grievance was the tithe payment to the established church, but in general the century witnessed a fall in their standard of living due largely to the rising population, which brought with it keen competition for farms and pushed up the already high rents. The trade restrictions and the lack of mineral wealth and of business initiative in the country condemned the bulk of the population to depend on agriculture for a livelihood, and to rely more and more on the potato for food. The great famine of the 1840s is proof that their condition continued to deteriorate long after most of the Penal Laws had been repealed.

Jonathan Swift, dean of St Patrick's, bitterly attacked the society which tolerated the terrible condition of the poor. In 1729 he published *A Modest Proposal*, a savage satire in which he offers for public consideration a scheme for killing off year-old children, whose flesh will make 'a most delicious, nourishing and wholesome food'. George Berkeley, Protestant bishop of Cloyne, also directed attention to the social and economic evils of Ireland in *The Querist*, first published in the 1730s. In it he asks hundreds of questions, for some of which answers have yet to be found:

> Whether there be any country in Christendom more capable of improvement than Ireland?
> Whether my countrymen are not readier at finding excuses than remedies?[2]

There is plenty of contemporary evidence of the wretched state of great numbers of the rural population at the time. For instance, Arthur Young, who toured Ireland in the 1770s, wrote:

> The cottages of the Irish, which are called cabbins, are the most miserable-looking hovels that can well be conceived . . . The furniture of the cabbins is as bad as the architecture; in very many consisting only of a pot for boiling their potatoes, a bit of a table, and one or two broken stools; beds are not found universally, the family lying on straw.[3]

It would of course be wrong to think of the life of the peasantry as one of unmitigated sadness and despair, though there were terrible visitations like the famine of 1741. But in normal times, when weather and harvests were good, they led a carefree enough life. The arts of the shanachie, singer, dancer and musician were widely cultivated and appreciated; and these people, though poor in the world's goods, had a rich treasury of folk culture, much of which has been preserved by their descendants even to our own day. The year saw a succession of religious feasts or pilgrimages to the well of the local saint. The pilgrimage to Lough Derg flourished, and the pilgrims brought home crosses (nowadays known as 'penal crosses') as souvenirs, inscribed with the date of their visit. Pilgrimages were, it is true, forbidden by law, but newspaper references and travellers' tales indicate that this fact cast no undue gloom over the proceedings. Indeed the chief opposition to them came from some of the Catholic bishops and clergy, who had been educated in the university cities of Europe and who viewed some of these native manifestations of piety with considerable disapproval and were, for instance, severe in their condemnation of festivities on May Day and of levity at wakes and patterns.

84
A wooden cross of the penal era
National Museum of Ireland

Although many bishops and hundreds of the regular clergy had left the country after the banishment act was passed in 1697, and had been forbidden to return under penalty of incurring death for high treason, about a thousand diocesan priests had been permitted to remain; and gradually, during the first two or three decades of the century, despite the savage laws on the statute book, the Catholic Church was reorganised and reformed. Before the middle of the century, the hierarchy had been restored to its full strength for the first time since the Reformation. Priests and bishops naturally fell under suspicion during periods of war between England and France, and when invasion threatened they were sometimes forced to go into hiding; but by and large, during peacetime, they went about their duties with little fear of molestation by the authorities so long as they inculcated, or tried to inculcate, in their flocks respect for their rulers and private property, and reminded them, as they so often did in published catechisms and sermons, that they must be subject to the temporal authority because all authority came from God. This was the only possible line for them to follow at the time, if they were to remain in the country with the connivance of the government. (Even after their position had been legalised in 1782, the Catholic clergy of Ireland did not dare to speak out against injustice by the ruling class until after the union of 1800, when bishops such as Doyle of Kildare and Leighlin, who denounced the peasants for their crimes against the property-owners, at the same time denounced those who were demanding rack rents, tithes and taxes from a poverty-stricken people.) Their admonitions to their flocks to obey the laws in the pre-1782 period, however, lost much of their force because the people knew that the bishops and many of the clergy were themselves breaking the law by their very presence in the country.

Not the least of the problems confronting bishops was the indiscipline of some of their clergy. Priests whom they censured sometimes denounced them to the civil authorities, and some became converts to the established church. The lament of Father Dominick O'Donnell's mother, said to have been composed when he became a Protestant clergyman in Donegal in 1739, is one of the best-known songs from the penal-law period:

> Crádh ort, a Dhoiminic Uí Dhomhnaill,
> Nach mairg ariamh a chonnaic thú;
> Bhí tú 'do shagart Dia Domhnaigh,
> 'S ar maidin Dia Luain 'do mhinistir.

> Pill, pill, a rúin ó,
> Pill, a rúin ó, is ná h-imthigh uaim;
> Pill ort, a chuid den tsaol mhór,
> Nó chan fheiceann tú 'n ghlóir mur' bpille tú.

> Thréig tusa Peadar is Pol,
> Thréig tú Eoin, 's an bunadh sin,
> Thréig tú bain-tiarna an domhain -
> Ó 'sí bhíos i gcónaí ag guí orainn.[4]

> (Woe to you, Dominick O'Donnell,
> Alas for anyone who ever saw you;
> On Sunday you a priest
> And on Monday morning a minister.

> Come back, come back, love,
> Come back, love, and do not leave me;
> Come back, my share of the world,
> For unless you come back you'll not see the eternal glory.

You abandoned Peter and Paul,
You abandoned John and their kindred,
You abandoned the queen of the universe –
Though it is she who is constantly praying for us.)

85 Catholic chapel, James's Gate, Dublin, built in 1738–49; with
minor alterations, including the addition of a bell, it remained
the parish church till 1853
reproduced from Catholic Emancipation Centenary Record, *ed.*
M. V. Ronan, 1929;
see also Nicholas Donnelly, Short Histories of Dublin Parishes,
pt lx, 1911, pp 230–32

Despite the Penal Laws, most of the cities and towns outside Ulster had their
Catholic chapels, and new ones were being erected from early in the century.
Only the places of worship of the established church could legally be dignified
by the name 'church', and all the old churches and monasteries and cathedrals,
which had escaped destruction at various times since the Reformation, and
indeed all the original church temporalities, were the property of the established
church. Many of the Dublin chapels were at first merely converted stables and
storehouses, but by the beginning of the second quarter of the century new
chapels were being built, almost all of them close together in the lanes and back
streets along the Liffey. These were St Mary's in Liffey Street, St Michan's in
Mary's Lane, St Paul's in Arran Quay, St James's in Watling Street, St Catherine's
in Dirty Lane, St Nicholas's in Francis Street, St Audoen's in Cook Street, St
Michael's in Rosemary Lane and St Andrew's in Hawkins Street, all in the charge
of the diocesan clergy. The religious orders had their chapels also. The Franciscan
chapel, at first in Cook Street, later moved to Merchant's Quay, where it was
popularly referred to as Adam and Eve's, from the sign of a nearby tavern. The
Dominicans were in Bridge Street, the Carmelites at Wormwood Gate and Ash

Street, the Augustinians in John's Lane, and the Capuchins in Church Street. The Dominican nuns were in Channel Row, the Poor Clares in King Street, the Carmelites at Arran Quay, and the Augustinians at Mullinahack.

86
Catholic chapel, Arles, County Leix; early 18th century
Francis Grose, Antiquities of Ireland, ii, 1795, *facing p. 34*

In rural Ireland chapels were often simple thatched structures, such as that at Arles in County Laois, but in many parts of the country, particularly in the north, it was often difficult to obtain sites for chapels from Protestant landlords. Moreover, some parishes were so large and scattered that they could not be served by one chapel, and Mass was often said in private houses and at Mass rocks in the open fields, or in 'scathlans' – little shelters where the priest and altar were at least partially protected from the elements. Sometimes too the people assembled for worship in the ruined shells of ancient abbeys such as Ballintubber and Graiguenamanagh. The harsh realities of conditions for Catholic worship in eighteenth-century Ireland are well illustrated by a story handed down in the family traditions of a prominent Fermanagh family. The story goes that Sir John Caldwell, the local squire in the period 1714–44:

> although a staunch Protestant, always treated the Roman Catholics with humanity and tenderness; in particular, one stormy day, when it rained very hard, he discovered a priest, with his congregation, at Mass under a hedge; and, instead of taking that opportunity of blaming them for thus meeting so near his house (and having the priest hung, as he might have done), he ordered his cows to be driven out of a neighbouring cow-house, and signified to the priest and people that they might there take shelter from the weather, and there finish their devotion in peace.[5]

87 Scene after open-air mass at a scathlan, Bunlin Bridge, County Donegal, 1867
Despite its date, this illustration may be taken as applicable to the period
surveyed in the present chapter

Sights and Scenes in Ireland, *1896*

Indeed, few of the Protestant propertied or professional class in Ireland
wished to see the masses of the people converted to Protestantism, since it was
to the material advantage of the ruling class to keep the privileged circle small.
Nor was there any display of missionary zeal on the part of the majority of the
bishops and clergy of the established church. Protestant nonconformists were
granted legal toleration of their religion in 1719, but they were still
compelled, like the Catholics, to pay tithes to the established church, and they
continued to be excluded from all offices under the crown. Their property
rights, however, were never withdrawn or restricted, as were those of
Catholics, and they continued to enjoy the right to carry arms, to vote in
elections and to sit in parliament. During the first three-quarters of the
century, the members of the established church could afford to discriminate
against Protestant nonconformists with impunity. There was no danger
whatever they might make common cause with the Catholics, and in the
event of invasion or rebellion they could be relied on to stake their lives and
property in defence of Protestantism and the English connection.

88
Charles O'Conor of
Belanagare
National Library of Ireland

Soon after the middle of the century, a Catholic party began to emerge from the ghetto into which they had been driven by the popery laws. Their spokesmen were Charles O'Conor of Belanagare, whose ancestors had been high kings before the Norman invasion, and John Curry, a Dublin doctor. These men, by their historical writings and pamphlets, sought first to disprove the charge, so often made by British historians, that the Gaelic Irish were a barbarous people, and the charge made by contemporary Protestant polemical writers that the Catholics were still only waiting for an opportunity to embark on a massacre of Protestants. These had for long been stock-in-trade arguments to justify the continuance of the popery laws. Curry and O'Conor, together with Thomas Wyse of the Manor of St John in Waterford, next sought to organise the rising Catholic middle class of the towns, who had largely escaped the net of the popery laws, into a delegate committee (founded in 1760) to act as a channel of communication between the Catholic population and the government, in an effort to secure some measure of relief from the Penal Laws. At the same time, Lords Trimlestown, Gormanston, Fingall and Kenmare, spokesmen of the now sadly depleted Catholic aristocracy, continued to regard themselves as hereditary leaders of Irish Catholics. These two groups differed on the question of leadership, but they were all agreed in accepting the English conquest and the Hanoverian succession, and there was none among them who wished for a Stuart restoration, still less for the re-emergence of a Gaelic state. The case they offered for consideration was that Catholic allegiance to the pope did not prevent their being loyal subjects of the king, that their record for seventy years had been one of unswerving loyalty to the established order, and that they deserved to be restored to some, at least, of the rights of which they had been deprived.

During the Seven Years' War (1756–63), the Catholics of Dublin and the other cities presented loyal addresses to king and parliament, insisting on their complete devotion to the British connection and their willingness to assist in repelling any attempt at invasion by a foreign power. In 1762, when England was confronted with a Catholic coalition of France, Austria and Spain, a scheme was under discussion between the Catholic leaders and the government for recruiting Irish Catholic regiments to fight in the army of England's ally, Portugal. But the members of the Irish parliament objected so violently to the arming of papists that the whole project was hastily dropped. Unfortunately, the proposal was immediately linked with an outbreak of agrarian violence in Munster. These Whiteboy activities in Munster were paralleled by similar agrarian disturbances among the Hearts of Oak and Hearts of Steel in Ulster, and were directly caused by grievances regarding enclosure of commonages, forced labour, unemployment, rack-rents and tithes – grievances for which they were refused redress in the law courts. Because he had expressed sympathy with the peasantry in their distress, Father Nicholas Sheehy was convicted on a trumped-up charge of murder, in the town of Clonmel in 1766, and was hanged, drawn and quartered. His grave in Shandraghan soon became a place of pilgrimage, and his death provided later generations of Whiteboys with a patron saint.

The proposal to enlist Catholic regiments, and an attempt to introduce a bill in parliament in 1762 to permit Catholics to take mortgages on land, awakened the fears, real or simulated, of many Protestants, and it suited the leaders of militant Protestant ascendancy to insist that the Whiteboy disturbances in Munster were a popish rebellion, fomented by the French. They called on influential Protestants to close their ranks and to defeat all efforts by Catholics, and by the administration, to alter in the smallest degree the system so wisely devised by their ancestors for their protection.

Had statutory reform of the tithe and the land system been carried through at this time, it might have considerably changed the course of Irish history. Instead, 1766 saw the introduction of the first act against the Whiteboys – one of the most significant events in the history of this country – for, although it was not apparent at the time, coercion as applied then, and during the subsequent 150 years, was an admission that Ireland was in a state of smothered war. Coercion served only to encourage in the masses of the rural population a spirit of non-cooperation with the ruling authorities, and a total lack of faith in legal methods and institutions as a means of redressing their wrongs. In spite of admonitions, denunciations and even excommunication by their own clergy, oath-bound secret societies continued to exist, and, particularly in times of distress, the people obeyed the local Whiteboy code instead of the law of the land.

It should not be forgotten that the Gaelic poets of the eighteenth century were the pamphleteers and journalists of the Gaelic-speaking multitude. Many a song was sung at a fair or in a tavern or around the firesides satirising a local convert, or a tithe proctor or land agent, or denouncing local injustice, or reminding the people of their national identity, and prophesying, rather unrealistically, a utopian future, with the Irish language and the Catholic religion high in favour again, when, with the aid of Louis of France, the Stuarts would return to the throne. These songs served to build up a public opinion of which the ruling class of the day, and even English-speaking well-to-do Catholics, were largely unaware. The Stuarts, for the most part, had never brought anything but disaster and disillusionment to Ireland, but to these simple country people, uninstructed in the realities of politics, any change, it seemed, was bound to be for the better, and they probably visualised the revolution, which they hoped would follow a Stuart return, in much the same way as an oppressed and exploited people today might think of communism as a panacea for all their ills.

From hundreds of such Jacobite songs one might perhaps choose 'Rosc Catha na Mumhan':

> D'aithníos féin gan bhréag ar fhuacht
> 'sar anaithe Thétis taobh le cuan,
> Ar chanadh na n-éan go séiseach suairc
> Go gcasfadh mo Shésar glé gan ghruaim.
> Measaim gur subhach don Mhumhain an fhuaim
> Is dá maireann go dubhach de chrú na mbuadh
> Torann na dtonn le sleasaibh na long
> Ag tarraingt go teann 'nár gceann ar cuaird.[6]

(I knew well by the cold and the stormy sea by the shore and by the tuneful and cheerful singing of the birds that my bright prince would return without sorrow. I think that for Munster and for our fine folk who are now dejected the noise of the waves against the sides of the ships drawing steadily near us is a joyful sound.)

Eventually, towards the end of the 1760s, when the hue and cry against the Whiteboys had died down, the Catholic upper and middle classes began to hope once again for some relaxation of the Penal Laws. At this time, a growing opposition group in the Irish parliament, led by such men as Henry Flood and the earl of Charlemont, was increasingly advocating resistance to British interference in Irish affairs. As a result, the British government tended to adopt a sympathetic attitude towards the Catholics as a counterpoise to the assertion of Irish Protestant nationalism and in order to restore the balance in the age-old game of 'divide and rule'. Some supporters of the administration, such as John Monk Mason and Sir Hercules Langrishe, sponsored bills in parliament in the years between 1762 and 1778 that would have enabled Catholics to take mortgages on land and to take leases for longer than thirty-one years, but the forces of militant Protestant ascendancy rallied their supporters each time to defeat these measures.

However, the War of American Independence brought about a new situation, and when France declared war on Britain in 1778 and rumours of invasion began to circulate once more, the British government decided to force the issue of Catholic relief, on the grounds that wartime strategy and the security of the empire demanded it. Not only was it deemed expedient to conciliate Catholics in case of invasion, but Catholic recruits were urgently needed for the army. The British government set a good example by passing a relief act for English Catholics early in 1778. Nevertheless, when Luke Gardiner introduced a bill in the Irish parliament permitting Catholics to take leases for 999 years and restoring full testamentary rights to Catholic landowners, it met with concerted and sustained opposition. In the end, after long and acrimonious debates, sometimes lasting far into the night, this first Catholic relief bill was steamrollered through the Irish parliament, because British statesmen believed that it was necessary for the safety of the empire at the time.

Those Protestants who had fought so long and so tenaciously to prevent any relaxation of the laws had always contended that once the popery code was relaxed in the smallest degree, it would be the signal for unlimited demands by the Catholics in the future. The prognostications were naturally proved correct. Catholic leaders regarded the act of 1778 as but a beginning, and the years from 1778 to 1829, or indeed until the beginning of the twentieth century, saw the emergence of a pattern now familiar in other countries: first the struggle for complete equality or for integration, as we would call it today, and when that failed, a struggle for political supremacy between the privileged minority on the one hand and the underprivileged majority on the other.

15

THE PROTESTANT NATION
1775–1800
R. B. McDOWELL

The War of American Independence profoundly and dramatically influenced Irish politics. There were significant resemblances between the position of Ireland and the North American colonies within the imperial framework. Each colony had a representative assembly, just as Ireland had its more venerable and decorative parliament. Yet the Westminster parliament claimed the right to legislate for both the colonies and Ireland alike. So when the American colonists defied the British parliament, they were fighting Ireland's battle. Many Irishmen appreciated this and openly sympathised with the colonists, their sympathy being intensified by the fact that many of the colonists were emigrants from Ireland, more especially from Ulster. But the government secured the support of the Irish parliament for its American policy, and as the war went on, military units maintained at Ireland's expense were sent overseas. The result was that when in 1778–9 France and Spain, taking advantage of their old rival's transatlantic difficulties, entered the war on the American side, Ireland, stripped of troops, lay open to invasion. Faced with this danger, Irishmen, or at any rate the Irish Protestants, sprang to arms. All over the country, groups of neighbours or public-spirited landlords formed volunteer corps. Volunteering soon became the fashion. The corps were numerous and splendidly uniformed. Reviews and parades were frequent. Gentlemen proudly used their volunteer rank, and Ireland soon abounded with captains and colonels. Volunteering not only provided an outlet for patriotism and opportunities for conviviality, but it also generated political activity. A corps easily became a debating society. And not only was political Ireland better organised than ever before but it soon became obvious that a drastic shift in power had taken place. Armed force – the ultimate arbitrator – was no longer controlled by the government but by the politically minded public.

All this coincided with a growing awareness of Ireland's grievances, commercial and constitutional. The dislocation of trade caused by the war strained a weak economy. By 1778, the commercial restrictions were being vigorously denounced as the source of Ireland's economic ills. The Volunteers paraded in Dublin with a cannon, having round its neck a placard with the words 'Free trade or this!' The British government, caught between British businessmen determined to maintain their privileges and angry Irishmen, fumbled, uncertain what was best to do. And when at last in 1779 it decided to conciliate Ireland by abolishing the commercial restrictions, it was too late to gain gratitude. By then a new agitation was gaining force – an agitation directed against the limitations on the powers of the Irish parliament imposed by Poynings' Law, and against the act of 1720 declaring the right of the British parliament to legislate for Ireland.

89   Volunteer parade in College Green, 4 November 1779, by Francis Wheatley
National Gallery of Ireland

This movement had a great and eloquent leader in Henry Grattan, who, after entering parliament in 1775, speedily established himself as a superb orator – nervous, high-flown, romantic. With generous enthusiasm, he demanded that Ireland should be granted its rightful status, that of an independent nation, though he always insisted that Ireland would remain linked to Great Britain by a common crown and by sharing a common political tradition. In a series of powerful speeches he expounded his case, but the government, retaining a majority in parliament by the use of patronage, successfully repulsed his attacks. Outside parliament, however, the situation was growing critical. In the autumn of 1781 Lord Cornwallis, at the head of a large British force, hemmed in at Yorktown, Virginia, by an American army and a French fleet, surrendered. Then in February 1782 delegates from a number of Ulster Volunteer corps gathered at Dungannon in the parish church and pledged their support to resolutions in favour of legislative independence. The old empire was crumbling with defeat in America, there was a loss of confidence, and in Ireland an absence of force. Shortly after the Dungannon meeting, Lord North, the British prime minister whose government had been struggling to maintain the old imperial system, was driven from office and the Whigs who took his place were anxious to conciliate Irish opinion by abolishing the restrictions on the Irish parliament. The declaratory act was repealed and in the following year the British parliament specifically renounced its claim to legislate for Ireland. And Poynings' act was so drastically modified that the only control over Irish legislation retained by the crown was the right to veto bills. Also it was agreed that Ireland should have an annual mutiny act and that the Irish judges should be irremovable except by deliberate parliamentary action.

90   The Custom House, Dublin, *c.* 1793, by James Malton
National Library of Ireland

Ireland was now in form an independent kingdom sharing a monarch with the neighbouring island. For the moment there was a great upsurge of satisfaction and pride. Signs of sovereignty appeared in many directions. An Irish post office separate from that of Great Britain was started, the Bank of Ireland was founded, the Custom House and the Four Courts were built. Rutland Square and Merrion Square were completed. The Dublin which Malton at this time depicted was undoubtedly and self-consciously a capital city.

The sense of national unity manifested itself in the removal of a number of religious, social and economic disabilities which in the past had been imposed on the Irish Catholics, though it should be quickly added that generosity was checked by caution. Only extreme liberals were prepared to allow Catholics a share in political power. There was also an optimistic feeling about the economic future. Agriculture, as the famous Arthur Young noted when he toured Ireland, was improving, though by rapidly advancing English standards there was plenty of room for further progress. Irish industry was expected to benefit from the availability of cheap labour and abundant water-power. The Irish parliament was ready to assist with tariffs and bounties, though keen protectionists sensed an unwillingness to go too far against English interests, and we still have a reminder of the economic optimism of the period in the great canals linking Dublin with the Shannon – impressive and extravagant eighteenth-century engineering feats.

91
James Caulfield, first Earl of Charlemont, by William Cuming
National Gallery of Ireland

It was soon seen, however, that constitutional forms did not correspond with political realities. Ireland was legally an independent country. But the king of Ireland was represented by a lord lieutenant nominated by the British government, and the lord lieutenant selected and controlled the Irish executive, which in turn controlled the patronage – peerages, places and pensions – that influenced the outlook of many MPs. Behind the façade of independence, the British government continued to exercise control over Irish affairs. There was an obvious remedy – to reform parliament so that it should more accurately mirror public opinion. And in the early eighties, liberals in England and Ireland were vigorously discussing schemes of reform. In Ireland the Volunteers took up the question, and after provincial conventions made up of delegates from different corps had agreed that the House of Commons must be made more representative, it was decided to hold a national Volunteer convention in Dublin which would prepare a plan and submit it to parliament to be turned into legislation. The delegates gathered at the Rotunda on 10 November 1783 under the chairmanship of Lord Charlemont, the general of the Volunteers, noted for his refined taste as a patron of architecture, in politics a very cautious Liberal. The most conspicuous of the delegates was Hervey, bishop of Derry and earl of Bristol, a magnificent prelate, a mighty builder of mansions, and at this time a strong radical. The most influential delegate was Henry Flood, a man with a strong political intellect and a severe oratorial style. Flood dominated the convention, and its plan of reform reflected his views. It was presented to the House of Commons but that body, refusing to be overawed by armed men, summarily rejected it. The MPs had gauged the situation correctly. The Volunteers were far too respectable and law-abiding to employ force against parliament. When what they believed was a reasonable plan was turned down, they had no idea what to do next. In fact, they went home quietly.

From then on, reformers were face to face with a major problem. What was to be done if a majority in parliament, determined not to lose their privileges and confident that the system in practice worked very well, simply refused to alter existing arrangements? At first, reformers seem to have believed that the pressure of public opinion, if it were mobilised and displayed to its fullest extent, might shame or frighten the House of Commons into reforming itself. And shortly after the Volunteer convention dissolved, the radicals of Dublin, led by Napper Tandy, an exuberant and at times absurd orator and a very shrewd political organiser, attempted to assemble a reform convention. It was to be made up of delegates from the counties and parliamentary boroughs who, having been chosen by the people, were to gather in Dublin and frame a plan of reform. It was a complete failure. Only a comparatively small number of delegates arrived (on 25 October 1784), and their deliberations attracted very little attention. In fact, Irish radicals were taught another lesson. In the absence of success, the momentum behind a movement can slacken as the public loses interest.

Indeed, during the mid-eighties Irish politics were remarkably placid. But it was the quiet that precedes a storm. Events in France – the meeting of the states general, a great representative assembly and the fall of the Bastille – were to start off a seismic political disturbance. It is impossible to sum up the significance of the French Revolution in a phrase. But it might be said that its driving ideas can best be expressed by the words liberty and equality. Liberty meant in the first place that the individual was protected against the arbitrary use of power by the government and in the second place that the nation – or at least those who were considered fit for the vote – should control the government. Equality meant that no section of the community should be legally privileged. Furthermore, all institutions were to be ruthlessly examined, judged by the criteria of liberty, equality and efficiency, and, if condemned, completely reshaped. It was the first time that a great European community had attempted to reconstruct the whole of its constitutional and administrative machinery. Of course many of the principles the French were enunciating were, it could be argued, the commonplaces of British and Irish political thinking. But whereas in the British Isles they were used to justify the revolution of 1688, in France they were being employed to open up a new era. The relics of the past were being swept away, and European men, or at least the middle classes, were taking control of their destiny. Liberals all over Europe were exhilarated at the prospect of reshaping society.

92
Theobald Wolfe Tone, *c.* 1792
National Library of Ireland

There were many links – commercial, cultural, religious and family – between Ireland and France, and the Irish newspapers provided abundant coverage of French happenings. And just at the very time the French Revolution was getting under way, Irish politics had for local reasons begun to stir. Six months before the states general met, George III, king of Great Britain and Ireland, went out of his mind. It was agreed that the regent of Britain and Ireland should be the Prince of Wales. But a great debate broke out over the method by which he should be installed in office. Grattan and his friends stressed that it should be made clear that the British regent did not automatically become regent of Ireland. The king's recovery put an end to the debate, but by then an Irish Whig or Liberal opposition led by Grattan, the Ponsonbys and Curran, a great advocate who could fuse indignation and humour in his speeches, had come into existence. It demanded not the reform but the 'purification' of parliament by the drastic scaling-down of the pension list and by limiting the number of office-holders permitted to sit in parliament. The Whigs denounced in scathing terms the government's methods of maintaining a majority.

At the same time, Grattan's fervent belief in the British connection was shown in the summer of 1790. There was a possibility of war between England and Spain when their claims clashed on the west coast of North America. Grattan emphasised that the interests of England and Ireland were inseparable. His attitude angered a young Protestant barrister, Theobald Wolfe Tone, who was beginning to take an interest in politics. He promptly published a pamphlet in which he argued that Ireland had no quarrel with Spain and that 'the good of the empire' was a specious phrase. About a year later he developed his views at greater length in his famous publication, An Argument on Behalf of the Catholics of Ireland. Tone argued that Ireland had 'no national government', its government being under British control, that the only way to counteract British influence over Irish affairs was by parliamentary reform, and that parliamentary reform could only be won if two underprivileged groups, the Irish Catholics and the Protestant radicals, cooperated in a reform programme that included Catholic emancipation.

Tone's views greatly impressed the Belfast liberals. Belfast, at this time a town of about 20,000 inhabitants, was pulsating with economic and political life. It was the centre of the linen trade, the importance of which was symbolised by the recently opened White Linen Hall, and Ritchie was about to open his new shipyard – a step that marked the beginning of a great industry. At the same time the inhabitants were intensely interested in voluntary organisations for charitable and educational purposes – the Belfast Society for the Promotion of Knowledge, for which Tone's friend, Thomas Russell, a dreaming soldier, was the first librarian; the governors of the Academy, who managed a successful grammar school; and the Belfast Charitable Society, which in the poorhouse took care of the sick poor and set sturdy beggars to work at spinning and weaving. The typical Belfastman of the period, a Presbyterian businessman, was bound to be critical of the ruling world of Episcopalian landlords and to suspect that his economic interests were being ignored.

Tone was invited to Belfast in the autumn of 1791. He was one of the few Irish politicians who found himself at home both in Belfast and Dublin, and during a fortnight of conversation and conviviality the Belfast Society of United Irishmen was founded (14 October). Immediately afterwards, Tone got in touch with Napper Tandy, that experienced municipal politician, and as a result of Tandy's efforts the Dublin Society of United Irishmen came into existence in November. These societies were middle-class debating societies which strove to mould public opinion. The Dublin society published numerous manifestos, including a plan of parliamentary reform which appeared in 1794. This plan suggested that Ireland should be divided into 300 parliamentary constituencies equal in population, and that every man should have a vote (one prominent member of the society considered it logical that women should have the vote too, but admitted that the idea was impractical).

How did the United Irishmen hope to secure reform? Apparently at first they still trusted to persuasion, to the pressure of public opinion. Volunteer corps and political clubs passed resolutions in favour of reform, and early in 1793 Ulster reformers held a representative convention at Dungannon, the delegates pledging their support to parliamentary reform. It was hoped that later a national convention could be held at Athlone. To radicals parliamentary reform was the first step towards a just and efficient administration of Ireland. They looked forward to the abolition of tithes, a reduction in government expenditure, lower taxation, the encouragement of trade and help for primary education.

But the pressure group which was successful during 1792 and 1793 was a Catholic body. In 1791 the Catholic committee began to stir itself. Strengthened by the loss of its more moderate members, who wished to leave the question of concessions to the government, the committee presented a petition to parliament asking for further relaxation of the Penal Laws. The result was the meagre Relief Act of 1792. When the Catholic question was being debated in the House of Commons, some MPs sneered at the committee's claim to represent the Catholics of Ireland. The committee, led by a number of energetic and successful Dublin businessmen, of whom the most prominent was John Keogh, reacted vigorously. They engaged Tone as their assistant secretary, thus both advertising their belief in toleration and obtaining a very efficient employee. And they decided to prove that they represented Catholic opinion by asking parish delegates to choose representatives from the counties and towns all over Ireland to meet in Dublin.

The Catholic convention assembled in Dublin in December 1792 and agreed to ask for the abolition of the remaining Penal Laws. A delegation was chosen to go to London to interview the prime minister, bypassing the Irish government. The lord lieutenant and his advisers were convinced that the Protestant ascendancy should not be tampered with at a time when the established order all over Europe was threatened. Concessions might set the country on a slippery slope. Fitzgibbon, the lord chancellor, a hard-headed, outspoken Conservative, was to argue that Catholic emancipation would lead to parliamentary reform and that a reformed parliament would break the connection with Great Britain – a connection which was essential to British safety and Irish social stability. In fact, his arguments almost completely reversed Tone's.

But the British government, facing the certainty of a war with revolutionary France, was desperately anxious to conciliate Irish opinion. And Burke, the great intellectual opponent of the revolution, was urgently eager to win over the Irish Catholics to the Conservative side by granting them the concessions to which they were morally entitled. The British government put pressure on the Irish government and the result was the Relief Act of 1793, which swept away most of the disabilities and gave the Catholics the vote. But Catholics were still excluded from parliament, from the judicial bench and from the higher offices of state. At the same time, the government agreed to some other concessions to Irish public opinion. Some pensioners and place-holders were excluded from the parliament. Cottages were exempted from the hearth tax: the powers of juries in libel cases were extended. But at the same time, Volunteering was suppressed, a paid home-defence force – the militia – under government control, was formed, and a convention act was passed forbidding assemblies to meet which claimed to represent a large section of Irish opinion.

By concession and repression, authority was preparing to meet a time of crisis. Abroad, Britain was now at war with France; at home, there was much agrarian discontent, directed against tithe and rent. And in Ulster, competition for land led to rural rioting between Catholics and Protestants, rioting culminating in the 'battle of the Diamond' and leading to the formation of the Orange Society (September 1795). The Whigs or Liberals led by Grattan were in favour of further concessions to the Catholics. Complete Catholic emancipation and a moderate parliamentary reform bill, stopping well short of manhood suffrage, would, they believed, satisfy the country at large. In January 1795, after a wartime coalition government had been formed in Great Britain, Fitzwilliam, a Whig and a friend of Grattan's, became lord lieutenant, and for the moment it looked as if the Irish Whigs would be in control. But Fitzwilliam was inexperienced and impetuous. The British government thought that in agreeing to complete Catholic emancipation he was exceeding his instructions. Fitzwilliam was recalled – a decisive disappointment to those who hoped to carry out reforms by constitutional methods.

Meanwhile, the radicals were growing impatient. Their impatience expressed itself in two forms. They began to organise themselves on military lines and tried to obtain help from revolutionary France. In the spring of 1794 William Jackson, a French agent, visited Dublin. Tone gave him a paper on Irish conditions which suggested that a French invasion would be welcomed. Jackson had brought with him to Ireland an old acquaintance, who steadily informed the government of his doings. In the event, Jackson was arrested and on being convicted of treason dramatically committed suicide in the dock on 30 April 1795.

Tone was in an awkward position since it was clear that he had had dealings with Jackson. But the legal evidence against him was thin and he was personally well liked by some influential Conservatives. So in the end he was permitted to emigrate to America. Using America as a stepping stone, he reached France at the beginning of 1796. There, speaking on behalf of the Irish radicals, he started to press for a French invasion, and in the summer his requests were reinforced by Arthur O'Connor, a young MP who had shocked the house by expressing radical views. Since the beginning of the war, the French had been considering an invasion of the British Isles, and Ireland was an obvious target. The very fact that it lay so far to the west rendered it easier for a French expedition to avoid the blockading squadrons. And if the French secured control of the Irish ports, it was clear that British trade would be seriously impeded and the whole west coast threatened. Moreover, as Tone especially emphasised, in Ireland the invader would meet with a friendly reception. In Paris he put the case forcibly to Carnot, 'the organiser of victory', and in December a French fleet carrying a force of 14,000 men, under the command of Hoche, one of the most brilliant of the young revolutionary generals, set out from Brest for Ireland. Everything went wrong for both the British and the French. The British fleet was badly placed and sluggishly led. The French, delayed by dockyard deficiencies, sailed as the winter storms set in. The fleet was scattered, Hoche's ship was carried far into the Atlantic, and the units which reached Bantry Bay, after tossing for some days in wild weather off the coast, failed to make a landing.

93   The parliament house and Trinity College, Dublin, *c.* 1793, by James Malton
National Library of Ireland

That the French should come so very near to success was most alarming to the Irish government, particularly as it was well aware that discontent at home was becoming effectively organised. In 1794, about a year after the war began, the Dublin Society of United Irishmen had been constrained by the authorities to suspend their meetings. Soon after, some of the middle-class reformers, acting along with urban working men and countrymen long accustomed to agrarian conspiracy, began to build up a widespread, secret, oath-bound society, pledged to obtain emancipation and reform. The organisation was based on innumerable small committees, which sent representatives to local committees, which sent their representatives to county committees, which in turn sent representatives to provincial committees, the system culminating in a national committee.

94   The Battle of Vinegar Hill, Enniscorthy, 21 June 1798: contemporary print
National Library of Ireland

The government took vigorous counter-measures. It encouraged the formation of yeomanry corps by Conservatives, eager to defend the existing order, suspended the habeas corpus act and passed an insurrection act which in a 'proclaimed district' imposed a curfew and gave the magistrates extensive powers to search for arms. And in 1797 Lake, a heavy-handed soldier, set to work by systematic raiding for arms to disarm Ulster. Soon, throughout Ireland, the desperate efforts of the government to check conspiracy produced a steady succession of incidents and outrages. The United Irishmen were determined to win Catholic emancipation, radical reform and independence.

The upholders of the existing order were equally determined to preserve law and order, maintain the connection with Great Britain and resist French aggression. Neither side was prepared to yield and each charged the other with being ultimately responsible for the unhappy condition of the country.

One practical consideration influenced the radicals. As time went on and their organisation was extended and improved, the danger grew that the government might regain the initiative and smash it. And the government had one valuable asset; its intelligence system. Early in 1797, Thomas Reynolds, who had a house in County Kildare, joined the United Irishmen. He was made a member of the Leinster provincial directory and shortly afterwards decided to supply the government with information. As a result, in March 1798 the Leinster directory of the United Irishmen, meeting at Oliver Bond's house in Bridge Street, Dublin, were all arrested. Lord Edward Fitzgerald, an experienced soldier and a fervent revolutionary, managed for some weeks to evade arrest but on 19 May his hiding place was discovered, and he was captured, mortally wounded. When, therefore, a few days later the United Irishmen rose in rebellion, their efforts were badly coordinated, and from a military point of view the rebellion was a series of isolated struggles. There was skirmishing in the counties round Dublin, which was firmly held by the authorities. In the south-east there was a widespread rising in the counties of Waterford and Wexford. Having secured control of their own counties, the rebels tried to drive west and north but were halted at New Ross and Arklow. Finally military columns converged on Vinegar Hill beside Enniscorthy, where the rebels had pitched their main camp, and after a fiercely fought engagement the United Irish force was dispersed. In the north there were risings in Antrim and Down. But Lake's operation in the previous year had seriously weakened the United Irishmen in Ulster. Moreover, the government forces kept control of the strategic centre of the area, Belfast. At Antrim the rebels under Henry Joy McCracken and at Ballynahinch under Henry Munro were decisively defeated.

A few days before the rebellion broke out, Napoleon sailed for Egypt, which he had decided should be the main French overseas objective. So with the forces available, only minor French expeditions could be sent to help the Irish rebels, and in fact these expeditions arrived after the rising had been suppressed. In August a small French force under Humbert landed at Killala and was joined by many Irishmen. Humbert's campaign was exciting but short. Having defeated a force of yeomanry and militia at Castlebar, he was surrounded by Cornwallis, the viceroy, at the head of a much larger force and was compelled to surrender at Ballinamuck in County Longford (8 September). A week or so after Humbert surrendered, another small French expedition set sail for the north of Ireland. Off Lough Swilly it was met by a superior British squadron and most of the French ships were captured (October). On board the flagship was Wolfe Tone, serving as a French officer. He was brought before a court martial in Dublin, found guilty and, before he could be executed, committed suicide (19 November).

95   Belfast from Cromac Wood, *c.* 1780
Note the shipping in the harbour, the rural setting of the town, and, in the background, Cave Hill with MacArt's Fort (where Tone and his friends spent a memorable day in May or June 1795)

Ulster Museum

The rebellion had one important consequence. It demonstrated unmistakably that Ireland presented an urgent political problem. To William Pitt, the British prime minister, Ireland constituted a challenge. Pitt had a powerful, creative intellect and was prepared to tackle a major question by producing a bold, long-term solution. In the eighties he had planned to make Great Britain and Ireland a great free trade area, but had been beaten by the suspicions and prejudice of vested interests. Now, in 1798, he decided on a union of the two parliaments – the British and the Irish. This, he argued, would ensure coordinated activity in an emergency, encourage British capitalists to invest in Ireland, thus raising Irish living standards, and, by transforming the position of Irish Protestants from that of a minority in Ireland into a majority in the United Kingdom, remove their fears of Catholic emancipation. Pitt's approach to politics might be described as mathematical. He found it hard to comprehend the importance of a force such as nationalism, in which emotional factors play a major part. When his proposal came before the Irish parliament, a body which always appreciated high-spirited rhetoric, a number of members, led by Grattan, emphasised with passionate intensity Ireland's separate identity among the nations, and asserted that Ireland possessed a national individuality which demanded political expression in the form of a separate parliament. After a strenuous and exciting debate in 1799, the government's proposal was rejected by a majority of five. The government then set to work to obtain a majority, partly by propaganda and persuasion, partly by trying to gratify the crudely personal objectives of many peers and MPs. By these methods it secured a majority for the union in both houses; the Act of Union was passed during the session of 1800 and on January 1801 Ireland became part of the United Kingdom.

96
Robert Emmet
National Library of Ireland

The enactment of the Union coincided with the end of the first phases of Anglo-French conflict, and within a few months of the act receiving the royal assent Cornwallis was in France negotiating a peace. But the Treaty of Amiens (27 March 1802) provided only a breathing space. By the summer of 1803 Great Britain and France were again at war, and the undismayed remnant of the United Irish leadership began to plan a new effort against the authority in Ireland. They again hoped to secure French help, but Napoleon was intent on a direct invasion of England, and the rising organised and led by Robert Emmet, a younger brother of one of the radical leaders of the nineties, ended in a scuffle in the streets of Dublin on the night of 23 July 1803. Emmet was captured, and after a trial in which he made a dramatic confession of his political faith, he was executed. Ireland settled down to a period of peace punctuated by agrarian disturbance and Catholic agitation.

The Age of Daniel O'Connell
1800–47
J. H. Whyte

This chapter covers roughly the first half of the nineteenth century, and we are calling it 'the age of Daniel O'Connell'. The title is appropriate because there is probably no other half-century of Irish history which is so dominated by the personality of one man. Daniel O'Connell, born in 1775, was the son of a small landlord in County Kerry. He was called to the bar in 1798 – being one of the first Catholics to enter the legal profession after Catholics were permitted to do so in 1792 – and rapidly became one of the most successful barristers in Ireland. He soon began to pursue a political career as well as practising at the bar, and from about 1814 until his death in 1847 he can be considered the most prominent politician in Ireland.

Before we embark on an examination of his career, however, a word should be said about the political situation in which he had to work. The Act of Union had been passed in 1800, and Ireland was now subject to the parliament at Westminster. The failure of the Union was not inevitable. Indeed there might have been great advantages for Ireland in being linked with what was then the richest country in the world. But the destiny of Ireland was now no longer decided by Irishmen. Of the 658 members of the House of Commons, only 100 represented Irish constituencies. Clearly, then, the success or failure of the union would depend on the attitudes taken to Irish problems by the MPs from Britain who formed the great majority.

For Irish problems existed in plenty. The most serious of these problems, we can see now on looking back, was the question of the land. The land of Ireland was simply not sufficient to feed all those who were trying to get a living off it. Population was increasing rapidly. This led to competition for land and drove up rents, thus reducing still further the people's resources. Things could have been better if farming methods had improved, but, except in Ulster, most farmers had no security of tenure, and they had learnt by experience that if they improved their holdings, the landlord was quite likely to put up the rent. And so the problem continued, getting worse year by year, until the famine of 1845–8, in the most terrible manner possible, reduced the population to more manageable proportions.

However, although on an objective view the land problem seems to have been the worst problem of early-nineteenth-century Ireland, it is fair to say that it was not the problem that most preoccupied politicians until the great famine made it impossible to ignore it. In earlier years, both British ministers and Irish politicians were more concerned with other, more immediate problems. Catholics and presbyterians resented paying tithes to the established church. Local government was controlled by small oligarchies in each borough. There was no provision for relief of the destitute. Many Irish industries were declining, under competition from large-scale industry in Britain.

97
Daniel O'Connell
National Library of Ireland

The most prominent issue of all, in the early years of the Union period, was the Catholic demand for full emancipation. Most of the Penal Laws had, it is true, been repealed in the 1780s and 1790s. Catholics could now maintain schools, join the professions and vote at parliamentary elections. But they were still debarred from all the more important offices in the state. They could not sit in parliament, and they could not be judges, or colonels in the army, or captains in the navy, or ministers in the government, or hold any except the most junior offices in the civil service. These restrictions naturally galled Catholics, all the more as Pitt had virtually promised, when he carried the union between Britain and Ireland in 1800, that it would be followed by complete emancipation for the Catholic body. But opposition from the king, and from Pitt's fellow ministers, proved too strong, and the plan was dropped.

O'Connell's long career was a packed and many-sided one, and we shall here be concerned with what were undoubtedly the two most important movements associated with it: the successful struggle for Catholic emancipation in the 1820s, and the unsuccessful struggle for repeal of the union with Britain in the 1840s.

In the first twenty years of the nineteenth century, the Catholic agitation for full emancipation was carried on by a coterie of landlords, merchants and professional men. They had no claim to speak for the mass of Irish Catholics, and they also quarrelled continually among themselves. So, although their doings took up plenty of space in the newspapers, it is not surprising that successive British governments found it unnecessary to take notice of them.

The real struggle for Catholic emancipation began with the forming of the Catholic Association by O'Connell in 1823. O'Connell had taken a prominent part in the ineffectual Catholic politics of the previous decade, and he had learnt from experience. There was an important difference between his association and previous attempts at Catholic organisation. The association was not confined to a clique of well-to-do Catholics. It aimed at a mass membership, which was to be secured in two ways.

Firstly, the association called in the aid of the Catholic clergy. The clergy had not played much part in the Catholic movement so far, but – distributed as they were all over the country, knowing their people, and trusted by them – they were splendidly placed to be the local leaders of the agitation. Secondly, and perhaps more important, the association inaugurated what was known as the 'Catholic rent'. This was a subscription of a penny a month – a sum so low that even the poorest could pay it. As a result, thousands joined the association, and it soon had a larger income from the pennies of the poor than previous Catholic bodies had ever obtained from the subscriptions of the rich. Just as important as the income brought in by the Catholic rent was its psychological effect. To pay a subscription to a movement increases one's interest in it, and now many thousands of Catholics, in all walks of life, were identified with the Catholic Association. Contemporary observers noticed the improved morale and corporate spirit of the Catholic body. As a Church of Ireland bishop, Dr Jebb of Limerick, noted:

> There is what we of this generation have never before witnessed, a complete union of the Roman Catholic body . . . In truth, an Irish revolution has, in great measure, been effected.[1]

It was not long before this new vitality in the Catholic body began to make itself felt. A general election was held in the summer of 1826. Catholics could not sit in parliament, but they had the vote, and in most of the Irish counties they formed a majority of the electorate. Most of these voters were tenant farmers, and hitherto they had generally voted for their landlords' nominees. In some counties this had meant that opponents of Catholic emancipation had been returned to parliament by a largely Catholic electorate. But a stop could be put to this if the Catholic Association could persuade these electors to vote according to their religion and not according to their landlords' wishes.

In the general election of 1826 this was done. In four counties – Waterford, Westmeath, Louth and Monaghan – sitting members who opposed the Catholic claims were turned out and replaced by new members who, though of course Protestants themselves, were supporters of Catholic emancipation. The victory was due to the organising power of O'Connell and the association. The Catholic rent provided the money. The local clergy canvassed the electors and led them to the polls. When some of the voters were victimised by their landlords after the election, the Catholic Association compensated them out of its funds. The association had only to perfect its organisation, and at the next general election it would be able to chase the opponents of Catholic emancipation out of almost every Irish county.

But before the next general election occurred, the association had won a still more spectacular and, as it proved, decisive triumph: the famous Clare election of 1828. In those days, MPs who were appointed to ministerial office were obliged to stand for re-election in their constituencies, and the election in this case was caused by the appointment of one of the MPs for Clare, Vesey Fitzgerald, to a post in the British Cabinet. Vesey Fitzgerald's position in Clare was a strong one. He had been the sitting member for the last ten years. He was a resident landlord, with, apparently, a good reputation among his tenants. He was himself friendly to Catholic emancipation. But he had taken office in a government opposed to the Catholic claims, and the Catholic Association was bound by resolution to oppose every member of such a government.

The association at first tried to find a friendly Protestant to stand as its candidate against Vesey Fitzgerald. But Fitzgerald was so strongly entrenched in Clare that it proved impossible to find an opponent. It was at this point that the idea was broached that O'Connell himself should oppose Fitzgerald. As a Catholic, O'Connell could not sit in parliament, but there was no law forbidding him to go forward as a candidate. O'Connell accordingly announced his candidature and went down to Clare. There, he was supported by the now well-tested electioneering machinery of the Catholic Association.

98 'Catholic petitioners, or symptoms of a peaceable appeal': cartoon of the Clare election, 1828, showing O'Connell at the head of a band of roughs

Radio Times Hulton Picture Library

The electors were canvassed by their priests and by officials of the association. When polling began, they were led to the booths in Ennis by their priests, in disciplined bands. Something of the atmosphere of disciplined enthusiasm can be caught even from the dry pages of contemporary newspapers. Here, for instance, is the account of one reporter:

Tuesday morning

Eight o'clock. Between 300 and 400 of John Ormsby Vandeleur's freeholders are now passing up the street to the Court House, preceded by colours, every man with a green leaf in his hand, and amidst the loudest cheering from the townspeople. They are western men from Kilrush, and brought in by their clergy to vote for O'Connell. Along the road the general cry of these men was – 'Here's Kilrush, high for O'Connell, high for our priest.' Mr O'Leary, the priest of Kilrush, came with them and the town is full of Catholic clergy. There are fifteen booths opened for polling.

Ten o'clock. Mr M'Inerney, the priest of Feakle, is just passed in at the head of a number of freeholders from that parish, carrying green boughs, and music before them.

Eleven o'clock. Another large body of men has passed in, preceded by a green silk flag, Shamrocks wreathed in gold – 'Scariff, and civil and religious liberty' in gold colours.

Mr O'Connell has been chaired to the Court House, and at the door implored the people to be true to their religion and their country.

Mr Maguire is moving about the streets and addressing every group of freeholders. The qualification oath is required, and magistrates are now administering it at the office of Mr Henry the sub-sheriff. This will retard the election if persevered in.

Twelve o'clock. Rev Mr Murphy of Corofin is come in with Mr Staunton Cahill, at the head of at least 500 men decorated with green branches and walking in ranks. Mr Murphy stood up in his gig, and was hailed with the loudest cheering.[2]

The organising skill of the Catholic Association had its inevitable effect. The gentry and the big farmers stood by Fitzgerald, but the small farmers deserted him almost en masse. O'Connell was elected by 2,057 votes against 982.

The British government at this time was headed by the Duke of Wellington, the great soldier of the Napoleonic Wars. The next most important member of the government was Sir Robert Peel, the home secretary. Both Wellington and Peel had been opposed to Catholic emancipation, but neither of them was completely inflexible on the matter. They recognised that the Clare election had produced a new situation. The excitement among Irish Catholics after their victory was so intense that there was no telling what might happen. Although O'Connell sincerely declared that he wished to win Catholic emancipation by peaceful means only, it was not certain that he could control his followers. And, with large numbers of Catholics in both the police and the army, the government could not count on the loyalty of the forces if a collision should occur.

There was another consideration which weighed with Wellington and Peel. Even if they wanted to pursue a policy of holding down the Catholics, they could not be sure that they would be supported by a majority in parliament. For there was already a strong body of opinion in parliament which felt that emancipation ought to be granted. A series of divisions in the 1820s had shown that the House of Commons was almost evenly divided on the question, with, as a rule, a slight majority in favour of emancipation. Only in the House of Lords was there a substantial majority against. Thus a policy of repression, while it might be supported in the House of Lords, would probably be defeated in the Commons.

To Wellington and Peel, these arguments were decisive. Though they did not like emancipation, no other course now seemed possible, and in the parliamentary session of 1829 they introduced a Catholic emancipation bill. Their arguments did not convince everybody, and a minority contested the bill to the end. But they carried with them enough peers and MPs to ensure a safe majority in both houses, and on 13 April 1829 the Catholic emancipation act became law. By its terms, all the important remaining restrictions on Catholics were removed. True, Catholics were still debarred from the lord lieutenancy of Ireland and from the lord chancellorships of England and Ireland. But they could be MPs, cabinet ministers, judges, generals and admirals. And even if the number of Catholics who could aspire to any of these positions was very small, the whole body gained in morale from the removal of the taint of inequality.

It was a great victory for O'Connell, and for the Catholic Association which he led. It seemed to show, also, the power of organised public opinion. Once the people of Ireland were sufficiently organised, it seemed, the British government must give way to their demands. There was no need to use violent means. There were, however, special advantages for O'Connell in this agitation. He was not facing resolute opponents. He was facing fairly moderate-minded ministers and a divided House of Commons. If the situation had been different, even the formidable organising power of the Catholic Association might have been insufficient to force a change.

The winning of Catholic emancipation left O'Connell as the hero of the great mass of the Irish people. His influence with them was higher than ever before, and he was the head of a small band of Irish members in the House of Commons. For twelve years after emancipation, he used his influence generally to support the English Liberal party. This, he felt, was in Ireland's best interest. The Liberals, he considered, were a good deal better than the Conservatives, and besides, he was able to win from them a steady trickle of reforms for Ireland. More people were given the vote, municipal government was cleaned up, the police was made into a more impartial force, and tithes were converted into a rent charge.

In 1841, however, the Liberals were defeated in a general election and the Conservatives returned to power. Their prime minister was Sir Robert Peel, the man who had so long opposed Catholic emancipation and who had in the end conceded it only when it was no longer possible to do anything else. O'Connell had always hoped some day to restore to Ireland her own parliament, and now that her enemies had returned to office there seemed no point in delaying his ambition any longer. He forthwith launched the second great agitation of his career – the campaign for repeal of the union between Ireland and Britain.

In this agitation, O'Connell could count on the sympathy of the bulk of the people of Ireland. Their instinctive national feeling, their admiration for him personally, and the programme of practical reforms which he promised once repeal was won – all these drew them to his side. He set about organising them in the same way as he had during the campaign for Catholic emancipation. He founded a Repeal Association (1840), which was run on the same lines as the Catholic Association had been. He collected a repeal rent, which realised much larger sums than the Catholic rent had ever done. He secured the help of most of the Catholic clergy, whom he was able to use as local organisers.

The most characteristic device of his campaign for repeal was the monster meeting. Mass meetings had been held during the Catholic emancipation campaign, but they now took place on a much greater scale. During 1843 – when the agitation had reached its climax – more than forty such meetings were held, each at a site selected so as to be central for the people of a large surrounding area. As demonstrations of the disciplined ardour of a people, these monster meetings surpassed even the Clare election of 1828. The attendance at them was enormous. At several it was estimated as being into the hundreds of thousands. No less impressive than the numbers were the earnestness and orderliness of the people. Some idea of the atmosphere of these meetings can be given by reading a contemporary description of one of the most successful, that at Tara (15 August 1843):

At nine o'clock in the morning a small train of private carriages containing O'Connell and a dozen friends set out from Merrion Square. They passed through some of the chief thoroughfares of Dublin, and the windows and pavements were already occupied by eager spectators. Carriages containing members of the corporation in their robes of office, and other notable citizens, fell in silently at various points, and in the suburbs a long line of vehicles, chiefly the famous Dublin jaunting cars, crowded with citizens, was waiting to join them, and the cortège became a procession. The route lay through a succession of hamlets, villages and towns, and in every hamlet, village or town the entire population was afoot in their holiday dress, and the houses were decorated with banners or evergreens. The local muster headed by its local band immediately took its place in the procession, on horseback or in vehicles. Wagons, capacious 'floats' brought from the city, and the country carts used in agriculture were all employed and were all found barely sufficient to accommodate the people. It was afterwards ascertained that toll was paid at Cabra, Phibsborough and Blanchardstown on 1,300 vehicles. The horsemen could not be strictly computed, but it was estimated that the number in attendance on O'Connell did not fall short of 10,000. Before the procession had arrived within a dozen miles of the historic hill, large crowds were discovered who had come from distant places during the night and bivouacked in the green pastures of Meath, under a genial August sky. A little later the repealers of Kells, Trim and Navan, the chief towns of Meath, joined the procession. They had more leisure and more inducement to aim at organisation, and they presented a striking appearance. Each town was preceded by its band in the national uniform of green and white, and by banners with suitable inscriptions. They were mustered by mounted marshals, distinguished by badges, horsemen four deep, footmen six deep, and the men of each parish marched, O'Connell afterwards declared, 'as if they were in battalions'. Three miles from the hill the vehicles had to be abandoned; from the immensity of the attendance there was space only for footmen. The abandoned vehicles were drawn up in line to wait the return of their occupants, and it is one of the wonders of this wonderful era that they were found at the day's close without appreciable loss or injury. Around the base of the hill the bands and banners were mustered. The bands amounted to forty, an equipment sufficient for an army; the banners were past counting.

The procession however was but a river discharging itself into an ocean. The whole district was covered with men. The population within a day's march began to arrive on foot shortly after daybreak, and continued to arrive, on all sides, and by every available approach, till noon. It was impossible from any one point to see the entire meeting; the hill rose almost perpendicular out of the level plain, and hill and plain were covered with a multitude 'countless as the bearded grain'. The number is supposed to have reached between 500,000 and 750,000 persons. It was ordinarily spoken of as a million, and was certainly a muster of men such as had never before assembled in one place in Ireland, in peace or war.[3]

What did O'Connell hope to gain by organising these tremendous meetings? The answer seems to be that he thought that the demonstration of the will of the Irish people would itself be enough to ensure the conversion of the British parliament to repeal. He put the point clearly when he launched the repeal agitation:

The actual mode of carrying the repeal must be to augment the numbers of the Repeal Association, until it comprises four-fifths of the inhabitants of Ireland . . .

When such a combination is complete, the parliament will naturally yield to the wishes and prayer of an entire nation. It is not in the nature of things that it should be otherwise.

Such a combination as I have spoken of was never yet resisted by any government, and never can. We arrived at a stage of society in which the peaceable combination of a people can easily render its wishes omnipotent.[4]

99   Repeal meeting at Tara, 15 August 1843
Illustrated London News, 26 August 1843

In support of this claim, he could point to his success in 1829. Catholic emancipation had been won by such means. There had been no need to fire a shot. The British government had given way as soon as it realised how powerful feeling in Ireland had become. But O'Connell seems to have overlooked vital differences between the situation of 1829 and that of 1843. In 1829, as we have seen, he already had much influential support on his side. About half the House of Commons, and a substantial minority even in the House of Lords, were already convinced of the wisdom of emancipation. It needed only the conversion of Wellington and Peel to turn this body of opinion into a decisive majority in both houses of parliament. In 1843, however, parliament was almost solidly opposed to repeal. In the House of Commons, O'Connell had only his own handful of supporters – about twenty members – while Liberals and Conservatives were united against him. In the House of Lords, he probably had no support at all. And not only were the numbers of his opponents much greater in 1843, but so was their determination. As we have seen, many of those English politicians who disliked Catholic emancipation were prepared to withdraw their opposition rather than face a war in Ireland. But on the question of repeal, they were ready to go to any lengths rather than yield. On 9 May 1843, the prime minister, Sir Robert Peel, made this clear in language about as emphatic as he could find:

> There is no influence, no power, no authority which the prerogatives of the crown and the existing law give to the government, which shall not be exercised for the purpose of maintaining the Union; the dissolution of which would involve not merely the repeal of an act of parliament but the dismemberment of this great empire . . . Deprecating as I do all war, but above all civil war, yet there is no alternative which I do not think preferable to the dismemberment of this empire.[5]

The last and biggest of the monster meetings was scheduled to be held on 8 October 1843, at Clontarf, the scene of Brian Boru's victory over the Norse on the outskirts of Dublin. A bare few hours before the meeting was due to begin, the government banned it. Parties were already on the move towards the meeting-place from distant districts. But O'Connell, true to his principle of always keeping within the law, complied with the government's order and called off the meeting.

This did not mean the end of the repeal agitation. The Repeal Association continued to meet. The repeal rent brought in almost as much in 1844 as it had in 1843. But O'Connell's retreat at Clontarf is generally, and rightly, seen as the turning point. For the government, by forbidding the meeting even at the risk of provoking bloodshed, had proved the falsity of O'Connell's basic assumption. It was not true that what he called 'the peaceable combination of a people' would necessarily prevail. After the failure of his monster meetings, O'Connell did not seem to know what to do next. Slowly the movement lost impetus, dissensions broke out in the Repeal Association, and long before O'Connell's death in 1847 it was clear that he had failed.

Has the repeal movement any permanent significance, then, in Irish history? The answer is that it undoubtedly has, but in ways rather different than those which O'Connell had anticipated. To the historian, the permanent effects of the repeal movement are to be found not in O'Connell's own activities but in those of a group of ardent politicians which his movement called into being – Young Ireland. This was the name given to a group of men, mostly in their twenties, who were associated with the *Nation*, a weekly newspaper founded in 1842 to assist O'Connell in his repeal campaign. Between them, this group worked out ideas that were to prove important in Irish politics for the rest of the nineteenth century and sometimes down to the present day.

100   Davy, Duffy and Dillon in the Phoenix Park, planning the
foundation of the *Nation*, 1842, by J. F. O'Hea
C. Gavan Duffy, Young Ireland, *2nd edition, 1896*

The most gifted of them was a Dublin Protestant barrister, Thomas Davis.
He did most to express the group's concept of Irish nationality as embracing
everyone who lived in Ireland, regardless of creed or origin. This idea did not
begin with Davis – it can be found in Tone and in O'Connell himself – but
it was expressed more fully and more generously by Davis than by anyone
before him.

Hardly less influential than Davis was the editor of the *Nation*, a Catholic
journalist from County Monaghan, Charles Gavan Duffy. He was responsible
for working out the tactical theory of how an Irish parliamentary party should
function in the House of Commons – the theory of remaining equally
independent of both English parties, and in particular of rejecting all
appointments from British governments of any colour. His ideas influenced,
in varying measure, all subsequent leaders of Irish parliamentary parties
during the period of the Union. A later recruit to the group was John Mitchel,
a unitarian solicitor from County Down. Mitchel was the one who most
explicitly made the case for complete separation from England, and who was
most ready to advocate the use of physical force. By doing so he revived a
tradition in Ireland that had subsided since the failure of the United Irishmen
but which remained continuously alive from his time, through the Fenians,
to the men of 1916.

A figure on the fringe of the group who deserves to be mentioned was
James Fintan Lalor. The crippled son of a farmer in County Laois, Lalor was
unknown personally to most of the Young Irelanders but he made his impact
by publishing letters in the *Nation* and other papers. He stressed the

importance of the land question. To him, national independence was an abstract idea which by itself would never fire the rural masses of Ireland. What mattered to them were the immediate evils of the land system – the high rents, the lack of security. The national question, he claimed, would never secure the full attention of the people of Ireland until it was linked with the land question. Parnell and Davitt were to operate on the same principle in 1879–82.

101   The affray at the widow McCormack's house on Boulagh Common, near Ballingarry, County Tipperary, 29 July 1848   *Illustrated London News, 12 August 1848*

In the short run, the Young Irelanders failed much more ignominiously than O'Connell himself. From being among his most devoted supporters, they became, after 1844, first his critics and then his opponents. Having broken away from him, they quarrelled among themselves, then plunged into an unplanned and completely unsuccessful insurrection in 1848, and nearly all ended up as either convicts or refugees.

But in the long run they were very far from failures, for they left behind them what they had written, and it is probably safe to say that no other group has had so great an influence on the thinking of later generations of Irishmen. More of the effects of this thinking will be seen in subsequent chapters. But it seems reasonable at this point to claim that the calling forth of this group was the greatest, if unintended, effect of O'Connell's repeal movement, just as the greatest effect of his leadership of the emancipation movement had been to arouse the political consciousness of the Irish Catholic masses.

17

THE GREAT FAMINE
1845–50
E. R. R. GREEN

The tempestuous course of Irish history in the nineteenth century often seems to resemble a mountain torrent in flood, where foam and swirling water hide the rock and boulders. The excitement of politics is like the rush and roar which so easily hold our attention. But what of the rocky channel which is the cause of all the turmoil? The fundamental conditions of economy and society are the channel down which the stream of history flows, and to write of one without the other is mere description without explanation.

Although there is no need to go any further back than the eighteenth century, there are a few general considerations which must first be taken into account. To begin with, there are certain limitations placed by nature on the economic potential of our country. We lack the mineral resources which are a guarantee of industrialisation, particularly the coal without which it was hardly possible in the nineteenth century. We do not lie at any of the great crossroads of international trade. Perhaps our greatest natural asset is the rich pasture produced by a mild and humid climate, but this favours a type of agriculture which provides only limited employment opportunities. Now, it is possible for societies as for individuals to achieve surprising success with limited resources, but we conspicuously lacked the kind of ordered and secure society which might have made this possible. A strong neighbour deprived us of independence at an early date but left the job of conquest no more than half finished. The energetic Tudor monarchs would probably have put this to rights except that their determination to be done with over-powerful noblemen coincided with a tragic schism in Christendom and precipitated a century and a half of dynastic and religious conflict.

This struggle ended with the failure of James II to regain his throne and was followed by nearly a century of peace – about the longest Ireland has ever known. The eighteenth century is a remarkable period in our history, far from well known and not at all easy for us to understand. It was not just a time of peace from exhaustion, as historians have often assumed. The country benefited from even a limited participation in Atlantic trade, as witnessed by the prosperity of the ports. Much was done to improve communications by the building of roads and canals. The linen industry was the conspicuous success in an industrial sector which became increasingly vigorous. Ireland too had retained her parliament, and it became important as a focus of patriotic sentiment.

Ireland was far from being the most distressful of European countries in the eighteenth century. On the contrary, her prospects for a time seemed on the whole rather bright. What went wrong, then? We can best find this out by subjecting the economy and society of eighteenth-century Ireland to a somewhat closer scrutiny. There were important weaknesses in both. The standard of life of the landlords was set in the main by their far richer brethren in England, which meant that too many of them were living beyond their means. In consequence, they cared little about what went on in their estates so long as they yielded the maximum money income. The tenants of such men could not hope to receive any help in investment or even to reap benefit from their own improvements.

As a result, irresponsibility at the peak of Irish society bred the same vice at the bottom. Commercial and industrial prosperity were threatened by the disparity between English and Irish resources of every kind – a threatening situation which was aggravated by the political subordination of one country to the other.

There were danger signals which might have been perceived and overcome but for the distortion of the Irish economy caused by the great war with France, a war which lasted over twenty years. The price of grain rose rapidly in wartime and more and more Irish grassland was broken up. A shift from pastoral to tillage farming created a demand for more labour as well. It was a situation which might have been exploited to their own advantage by tenant farmers and labourers but for the fact that the need for land was so great in a country with a rapidly increasing population. Ireland had been sparsely populated at the beginning of the eighteenth century, but conditions favoured a rise in numbers. To begin with, armies were no longer killing people or destroying their crops. Most important of all, the Irish people had assured themselves of abundant, healthy food by adopting a potato diet. Not only is the potato almost an ideal food, especially if supplemented by milk, but the produce in potatoes of a given area of ground is much greater than that for any grain crop.

Wartime emphasis on tillage completed the triumph of the potato. It enabled the farmer to produce grain purely as a cash crop and incidentally to offer a higher rent. Nor did he need money to pay labourers: they were satisfied with a patch of ground on which to grow potatoes. Those who were fortunate enough to possess sizeable leaseholds set up as landlords themselves by creating under-tenancies. Fathers subdivided their holdings to provide for sons. Landless men reclaimed the mountain and the bog, and colonised them.

Peace came in 1815, but there was no halting the forces released during the war. Although the economy was virtually stagnant, population continued to leap ahead. It was estimated that there were 5 million people in the country in 1800; by 1821 there were said to be over 6.5 million, and in 1841 there were over 8 million. Although not of a kind familiar to us now, Ireland after 1815 was faced with an unemployment problem on a gigantic scale. Emigration, both to Great Britain and to North America, developed steadily but the effect was barely visible. The figures of the 1841 census reveal the appalling insecurity of Ireland's vast population. Only 7 per cent of holdings were over thirty acres in size; 45 per cent were under five. In Connacht the holdings under five acres went as high as 64 per cent. Again, while Armagh was the most thickly populated Irish county, Mayo came second, and the most thinly populated counties were Meath and Kildare. Clearly, density of population and size of holdings bore little relation to the fertility of the soil.

Over two-thirds of the Irish people were dependent on agriculture for a livelihood in 1841, but the condition of the other third was far from enviable. The growing efficiency and scale of British industry struck hard at the small Irish manufacturer. In a United Kingdom there was no longer any use in invoking the aid of the government – not that protection could probably have done much in any case. Irish business was also severely hit by the policy of monetary deflation pursued by the authorities until the exchequers were amalgamated in 1826. The steamship and the railway had a similar effect to the removal of tariff protection by lowering transport and handling costs and striking at the livelihood of Irish manufacturers and wholesalers.

The survival of a vast impoverished population depended on the recurring fruitfulness of the potato and on that alone. The potato, too, is perishable and cannot be held in store to relieve scarcity like grain. In such circumstances, if anything were to happen to the potato harvest, disaster would occur on a scale which Ireland would be unable to control and for which the British government was unprepared. Dark and gloomy though the prospects of Ireland might have been, the disaster when it came was more sudden and complete than anyone could have imagined. There was a long spell of wet weather in July of 1845, which did no apparent harm to a promising potato crop. Then in August came news of a strange disease attacking the crop in the south of England. It was potato blight. The crop all along the eastern seaboard of the United States and Canada had been ravaged in 1842, but this was its first appearance in Europe. In September, blight was observed in Waterford and Wexford, and then spread rapidly until about half the country was affected.

102
Searching for potatoes
during the famine
Illustrated London News,
22 December 1849

Although partial potato failures were nothing new in Ireland, the authorities took prompt action. Sir Robert Peel, the prime minister, appointed a scientific commission to investigate the new disease. It unfortunately failed to discover that blight is actually a fungus growth and not a disease of the potato itself, and in consequence none of the suggested remedies were appropriate. Peel's relief measures on the other hand were prompt, skilful and on the whole successful. His immediate concern was to prevent soaring food prices in Ireland, and he accordingly purchased some £100,000 worth of Indian corn and meal in the United States early in November with which he hoped to be able to control the market. A relief commission was set up to cope with distress and the formation of local committees was encouraged. Local voluntary contributions were supplemented, usually to the extent of two-thirds, by government grants.

Relief works, of which the government paid half the cost, were also set up to provide employment, for it was proposed to sell food rather than give it away. The various schemes undertaken gave work to about 140,000 people at one time. The government also expended some £365,000 in 1845–6 and provided as much again in loans.

103
Charles Edward Trevelyan,
Assistant-secretary to the
Treasury, London, 1840–59
Hulton Picture Library

Peel decided against prohibition of exports of food from Ireland. Far more serious, in his mind, were the tariffs imposed on imported grain in the interests of the English farmer. Peel, therefore, took the momentous decision to repeal the corn laws, as they were called. Agricultural protection had been a burning issue in English politics for years, and had become symbolic of the struggle for power between the landed class and the businessmen. Peel persisted, although he knew that to do so was to bring down his government and to tear the Tories apart. A Whig government came in under Lord John Russell. The change boded ill for Ireland, for the Whigs were much more wedded to current beliefs about the economic system. These were the days when *laissez-faire* was the creed of intelligent and up-to-date people, all of whom were convinced that not only was it wrong for the government to meddle with economic laws but it was also futile to do so. Charles Trevelyan, who as permanent head of the treasury had been in control of relief, was very much in sympathy with these ideas. He could not have found a more congenial superior than the new chancellor of the exchequer, Charles Wood, a firm believer in economy and non-intervention. It was decided at once that in the event of a second failure of the potato crop, there would be no government buying: the supply of food was to be left exclusively to private enterprise.

104 A famine funeral
Illustrated London News, 13 February 1847

There was a second failure, in 1846, and this time it was complete. The prospect of an appalling disaster caused no modification in the government's plans. Relief was to be limited to public works. Nor was the government any longer to meet half the cost, which was to be borne entirely by the rates. The idea, of course, was to force the Irish landlords to bear the cost. The whole burden fell on the Irish board of works. Now winter set in – not a normal winter, but the harshest and longest in living memory. There was no food left, and panic began to seize the famished people. Hungry mobs roved the country, but above all they poured in on the relief works. The numbers employed leapt from 30,000 in September, to 150,000 in October, to 285,000 in November, and finally reached nearly half a million in December.

In the new year the government had to admit defeat; the board of works was spending nearly £30,000 a day and its staff had risen to over 11,500. The decision was taken in January 1847 to abandon public works and extend direct relief. It should be realised just how momentous this must have seemed to the English official mind. The basic principle of the great English poor-law reform of 1834 was that relief should be given only in workhouses, and it was orthodox belief that any departure from the rule resulted in population increasing faster than the means of subsistence. To begin with, an act was passed providing for the establishment of kitchens and the free distribution of soup. The most dramatic result of this measure was the expedition of Alexis Soyer, the famous chef of the London Reform Club, to set up his model kitchen, where soup could be made according to the same recipe as that which he had devised for the London poor.

105   Cork Society of Friends' soup kitchen. The man on the left is collecting tokens on a stick

Illustrated London News, 16 January 1847

Government relief measures were augmented by voluntary effort. Fund-raising groups were formed in Ireland, Britain, America and elsewhere; these groups provided the resources for feeding many of the worst sufferers, especially in Connacht. The Religious Society of Friends (Quakers) took a leading part in this work, and the reports of its agents from all over Ireland did much to inform public opinion in Britain on the nature of the catastrophe. One such report was from William Edward Forster, who was later to be chief secretary for Ireland.

The situation in Ireland had reached its worst by February 1847. Great gales blew and the country was covered in thick snow. Starving people crowded into the towns and flooded to the public works which the government was proposing to close. A fever epidemic now spread like wildfire through the country. What people called 'famine fever' was in fact two separate diseases, typhus and relapsing fever. Nor was this the only scourge. Dysentery was to be expected among people who had been eating raw turnips or seaweed or half-cooked Indian meal, and it too often led to the fatal bacillary dysentery, the 'bloody flux', which now also became epidemic. Scurvy became general among those who were forced to resort to Indian meal, which is lacking in vitamin C. 'Famine dropsy', or hunger oedema, to give it its proper name, was widespread, and resulted from starvation pure and simple. It is hardly relevant to ask how

Dún Aengus on Inis Mór in the Aran Islands, a huge semi-circular stone fortress that probably dates from the Iron Age (after 500 BC)

Shannon Development

Probably dating from the first century AD, this golden boat demonstrates native Irish craftsmanship in the pre-Christian era

National Museum of Ireland

The Annals of Ulster for the year AD 552 record that St Columba removed three relics, including a bell, from St Patrick's tomb. This iron bell, known as St Patrick's Bell, may be that which was buried with him

National Museum of Ireland

In the early Christian era, many monastic settlements in Ireland consisted of collections of beehive huts, some of which survive to this day. This example is from County Kerry.

Keewi Photography

Portrait of Christ, fol 32v, *The Book of Kells*
The eighth-century illuminated manuscript contains a text in Latin of the four gospels, with prefaces, summaries and canon tables

Trinity College, Dublin

The Marriage of Strongbow and Aoife by Daniel Maclise
The painting depicts the subjugation of the native Irish to the Normans in 1169–70
National Gallery of Ireland

King John's Castle, set on the Shannon at Limerick, was built around 1200 to fortify the city
and quell the Irish in the O'Brien kingdom of Thomond across the river
Shannon Development

Abraham Ortelius, *Theatrum Orbis Terrarum*, Antwerp, 1593.
This map of Ireland, drawn in 1573, indicates the territories of the major lords and chieftains and includes towns, ecclesiastical sites and castles. Relatively little detail is given of Ulster, which was still unconquered and unexplored by English surveyors.

National Library of Ireland

Oliver Cromwell
by Robert Walker

Cromwell's actions between 1649 and 1660 involved large-scale confiscation of land and the banishment of its former owners to the poorer parts of Ireland so that property and political power passed to the new colonists
courtesy of the National Portrait Gallery, London

The Irish House of Commons, 1780 by Francis Wheatley
The interior of the Irish parliament, which was made redundant by the Act of Union in 1801
Leeds Museums and Galleries (Lotherton Hall)

An Irish Volunteer Taking Liberty under His Protection
Jean Delatre, 1786.

The ideals of the French Revolution swept Ireland in the late eighteenth century, culminating in the doomed 1798 Rebellion
National Library of Ireland

O'Connell and His Contemporaries, The Clare Election, 1828 by Joseph Haverty
Daniel O'Connell, a Catholic barrister, opposed Catholic discrimination by standing for
parliament in 1828 and became a formidable and popular opponent to the Act of Union
National Gallery of Ireland

Charles Stewart Parnell,
Statesman
by Sydney Hall

The charismatic leader of the
Irish parliamentary party in
Westminster was revered by the
Irish people before his eventual
disgrace
National Gallery of Ireland

Economic Pressure by Seán Keating PRHA
In the nineteenth and twentieth century economic conditions and overpopulation brought
about enormous emigration from Ireland to more prosperous nations around the world
Courtesy of the Crawford Municipal Art Gallery, Cork

Letter from America by Jas. Brenan
Letters from the diaspora of Irish men and women were often their only contact with home
after emigration, as few could hope to return
Courtesy of the Crawford Municipal Art Gallery, Cork

The grim central hall in Kilmainham Jail, Dublin, where the 1916 rebels were held and executed after the Rising

Republican Court, 1921 by Seán Keating PRHA
During the war of independence and the civil war, ad hoc courts operated all over Ireland, dispensing justice and passing death sentences.

A Cumann na nGael election
poster from the general election
of 1932 or 1933. The party
sought to present itself as
upholding law and order and
associated Fianna Fáil, the
main opposition party, with the
use of force. Cumann na nGael
was defeated in both elections.
National Library of Ireland

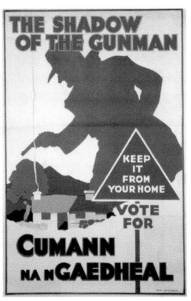

The Dockers (1934)
by Maurice MacGonigal

A depiction of social conditions
in Ireland under the newly
formed government. At the
Dublin docks, three 'button-
men' (workers who were hired
on a daily basis) wait for
employment.
*Courtesy of the Hugh Lane
Municipal Gallery of Modern Art*

Taoiseach Jack Lynch leads Ireland into Europe in 1973, ending Irish dependence on the British economy and providing new opportunities for the nation on the world stage

Colman Doyle

An Irish soldier on peacekeeping duty in Lebanon, where the Irish army has been operating since 1978. They will commence operations in Ethiopia–Eritrea in November 2001.

An Cosantóir

Women and children marching in support of republican hunger strikers in the Maze Prison. Ten of the hunger strikers died in 1981.

An Phoblacht

Annual parades are held by Orange lodges in Northern Ireland in celebration of unionist traditions

Pacemaker Press International Ltd

David Trimble, leader of the UUP, and John Hume, leader of the SDLP, received the Nobel Prize for Peace in 1996 in recognition of their work for peace in Northern Ireland

Pacemaker Press International Ltd

The political murals of Northern Ireland are world-famous. The Red Hand of Ulster, appropriated by the unionist tradition, here represents the paramilitary Ulster Volunteer Force.
Keewi Photography

A booming economy and liberalised society have wrought great changes in Ireland in the early part of the twenty-first century. In Dublin, old and new exist side by side.
Keewi Photography

The historical city of Galway has benefited from Ireland's increased prosperity but still maintains its individual charm
Keewi Photography

The then US President Bill Clinton visits Ireland at the end of his term of office in December 2000

The Irish Times

UK Prime Minister Tony Blair and Taoiseach Bertie Ahern, who both played an instrumental part in the architecture of the peace agreements in Northern Ireland

The Irish Times

Sonia O'Sullivan winning silver in the 5,000 metres at the 2000 Sydney Olympics
Sportsfile

Seamus Heaney, Ireland's foremost contemporary poet, received the Nobel Prize for Literature in 1995

Radio Telefís Éireann Stills Library

many died of starvation; there were many ways in which terrified and undernourished people exposed to the bitter winter and to infection in soup kitchens and workhouses or on public works could perish.

106   Emigrants leaving [Cork] for Liverpool on the *Nimrod* and the *Athlone*
Illustrated London News, 10 May 1851

People everywhere were now seized by a panic to get out of Ireland. Emigration was limited to the spring and summer, so that the effect of the partial failure of the potato crop in 1845 did little to increase the numbers that year. It was a different story in July and August of 1846, when universal failure brought the new spectacle of heavy autumn emigration. The poor cottiers went first, and then in the early weeks of 1847 the small farmers began to forsake the country in droves. Six thousand emigrants sailed from Liverpool alone in January. So great was the demand for passages that direct sailings began from Ireland. It was mainly from smaller Irish ports that the notorious 'coffin ships' sailed, old and overcrowded craft whose owners had been drawn into the traffic in the hope of high profits. Liverpool was the first city to be invaded by what was virtually an army of refugees. The population of the port at that time was about a quarter of a million, and in one January week in 1847 over 130,000 people had to be given poor relief. By June, it was reckoned that 300,000 destitute Irish people had landed in the town. A very high proportion of them, of course, soon sailed for North America, but a residue of the most poverty-stricken inevitably remained. More than 100,000 emigrants sailed for Canada in 1847 (the most economical way to the United States at that time being by this indirect route), of whom it is estimated that at least a fifth perished of privation and disease.

Meanwhile, the government, having set up the soup kitchens, proceeded to the next part of its plan for handling famine in Ireland. The Poor Law Extension Act of June 1847 proposed to dispose neatly of the whole problem by thrusting responsibility on the Irish poor law, thus leaving Ireland to bear the whole cost through the poor rates. The immediate sufferers were to be the Irish landlords, whom the Whigs blamed by and large for the disaster that had taken place. Inevitably, to reduce the burden of rates, the landlords became more determined in their efforts to evict pauper tenants. The process of clearance was helped by the 'quarter-acre clause' of the act, which excluded anyone who held more than one rood of ground from relief. An intolerable burden was placed on the Irish poor-law unions, whose workhouse accommodation was already grossly overcrowded. Even so, they managed to increase the maximum number of inmates from around 100,000 to 300,000 within four years. In 1849 the staggering number of 932,000 people were maintained in the workhouse for some period. There could hardly be more poignant evidence of the beggary to which Ireland had been reduced.

Black '47 had by no means seen the end of the famine. Blight struck less hard in the autumn of that year, and there was a return of confidence. In 1848, it returned with full virulence. But we know enough already of the horror of those years, and it is time to attempt a summing up of the consequences of the famine. To begin with, we need to be clear in our minds that this was primarily a disaster like a flood or earthquake. The blight was natural; no one can be held responsible for that. Conditions in Ireland which had placed thousands upon thousands of people in complete dependence on the potato are another matter. Yet the historian, if he is conscientious, will have an uneasy conscience about labelling particular classes or individuals as villains of the piece. The Irish landlords held the ultimate responsibility, but on the whole they were as much involved in disaster as their tenantry. The ministers of the crown who had to accept responsibility once the disaster occurred were callous, parsimonious and self-righteous. Yet these are the very qualities which Charles Dickens, for instance, found so distasteful in men of their class, and they were exhibited as much to the English as to the Irish poor.

The potato blight had destroyed the ramshackle economy which had grown up during the French wars. A staggering problem of unemployment was liquidated in the most terrible sense of that word. In 1851 the population was 6.5 million, 2 million less than the estimated population of 1845. Something like a million had succeeded in getting away and another million had perished. Yet if we turn to the agricultural statistics we find that, despite the loss, Irish production had increased rather than diminished. The area under cultivation had increased by over a million acres. The loss of population was paralleled by a decline in the number of holdings. Holdings of not more

107   A post-famine eviction scene
Illustrated London News, 16 December 1848

than five acres had fallen from 45 per cent of the total to just over 15 per cent. Holdings of over thirty acres were now 26 per cent instead of 7 per cent.

The pattern of modern Irish agriculture was beginning to emerge from the ruin caused by the potato blight – a family farm engaged in mixed tillage and livestock production, with the stock rather than grain increasingly providing cash income. The halt to subdivision, of necessity, brought fundamental social changes in Ireland as well. Gone were the days of early marriage and a countryside thronged with young people and children. For many, the price of holding together the family farm was to remain unmarried. For many others, there could be no staying in Ireland, and their energies went to the building of the United States or other new lands across the seas. Against the economic improvement must be set a worsening of political conditions. The resentment in Ireland against English handling of the famine crisis was deep and slow to heal. Worse still was the bitter hostility between landlord and tenant, which boiled over into a great agrarian conflict when falling farm prices caught the farmer in the late seventies. Change in such conditions was necessarily slow, and even today it might be argued that we still have much to do to repair the damage that the Irish economy suffered in the early nineteenth century and to heal the scars that the famine left on our society.

Fenianism, Home Rule and the Land War
1850–91
T. W. Moody

The forty-odd years between the famine and the fall of Parnell were dominated by two great questions: the land and national independence. The struggle of the tenant farmers for security in their holdings and the national struggle for independence each expressed itself in two ways, the one constitutional and parliamentary, the other revolutionary and conspiratorial. The constitutional tradition is represented in this period by Gavan Duffy's Irish Tenant League of the fifties and by Isaac Butt's home-rule movement of the seventies. The revolutionary tradition is represented by the sporadic violence of agrarian secret societies, by the Young Ireland rising of 1848, and above all by the Fenian movement of the sixties. Neither of the two methods of action proved effectual when used separately. But in 1879, in the face of an upsurge of agrarian distress that threatened to match that of the great famine, a common front between constitutional and revolutionary nationalists was achieved through the transcendent political genius of Charles Stewart Parnell and the passion for social justice of Michael Davitt.

The struggle for land and the struggle for independence became merged in a mass movement without precedent in Irish history. Two resounding successes were achieved – for the cause of the tenant farmers, in the so-called 'land war' of 1879–82, and for the cause of home rule, in 1886, when the British Liberal Party under the leadership of Gladstone acknowledged the justice and the necessity of giving Ireland self-government. Though the land question was far from being settled by 1882, though Gladstone's home-rule bill of 1886 was defeated in the House of Commons, and though the whole national movement was disrupted by the tragic fall of Parnell in 1890–1, the consequences of the 'new departure' of 1879 were to have a profound and lasting influence on the whole future of Ireland and of Anglo-Irish relations.

Post-famine Ireland was an exhausted, dispirited and divided country. In six years – 1845–51 – the population had been reduced by about 2 million. The upward trend of the preceding half-century was reversed. The population decline was accompanied by a gradual increase in the size of agricultural holdings and in gradually rising standards of rural living. But relations between landlords and tenants grew more embittered than ever as the tenants' demands for security grew more insistent and the efforts of landlords to get rid of unwanted tenants were redoubled. In the fifties the mass of the people, preoccupied with the struggle for survival, had neither the energy nor spirit to struggle for national independence. O'Connell's repeal movement had already collapsed before the great famine began. At the height of the famine, James Fintan Lalor had made a white-hot appeal to the tenant farmers to save themselves from starvation and at the same time to overthrow British authority by a general strike against rent. The message had fallen on deaf ears. The desperate attempt of the Young Irelanders in 1848 to win self-government by armed insurrection had begun and ended in the futile affray at Ballingarry. But if the spirit of resistance to British rule now burned very low, Ireland's population was more deeply divided than ever between the minority, largely Protestant, who supported the Union, and the majority, almost entirely Catholic, who were alienated from it.

To the majority of Irishmen the Union was now identified with hopes disappointed, grievances unremedied, liberties denied, with poverty, backwardness, and above all with the catastrophe of the great famine. On the other hand, a substantial minority regarded the Union as justified by its results and were determined at all costs to maintain it. They included the landowning aristocracy throughout Ireland and, in Ulster, a closely knit Protestant community composed of all social classes from landowners to factory workers. For unlike the rest of Ireland, the north-east experienced during the first half of the nineteenth century an industrial revolution that brought increasing prosperity to the region and transformed Belfast into a great centre of linen manufacture, shipbuilding and engineering. This industrial development, for which the capital was provided by Ulster Protestants, had its vital connections with industrial Britain and was a powerful vested interest on the side of the Union. In another way also, economic conditions in Ulster were exceptional: for in many areas, the tenant farmers enjoyed a degree of security in their holdings – the 'Ulster custom' – unknown anywhere else in Ireland.

So, then, the maintenance of the Union was regarded as a vital interest not only by Great Britain but also by an important element within Ireland itself. Yet the idea of a united, self-reliant and independent Irish nation was firmly established. On the eve of the great famine, the Young Ireland leader, Thomas Davis, had given classic expression to this idea: the Irish nation was a community in which Irishmen, whatever their creed or class or ancestry, were called upon to work together for the common good in mutual affection, mutual respect and political freedom. Davis's noble vision was to be cherished by every generation of Irish nationalists down to our own day, but was far removed from the realities of post-famine Ireland. It was in these circumstances that Charles Gavan Duffy, who had been one of Davis's closest colleagues, tried to reanimate the national spirit through the formation, in 1850, of an all-Ireland league of tenant farmers.

The aim of the Irish Tenant League was the 'three Fs' – fair rent, fixity of tenure, and freedom for the tenant to sell his interest in his holding – to be achieved through an independent Irish party in parliament. Such a party seemed to have emerged when, in the general election of 1852, about 40 professing supporters of tenant rights were returned to parliament out of a total Irish representation of 103. But the party quickly disintegrated. There were various reasons for its failure, but what most struck the public was the conduct of some of its leading Catholic members – Keogh, Sadleir and others – in advancing their own careers through the championship of Catholic interests, with complete disregard for the interests and principles of the Tenant League. Nicknamed 'the Irish Brigade', they are better known in Irish history as 'the pope's brass band'. The collapse of the league brought deep despondency and deep distrust of constitutional methods. The next phase of the national movement saw a fierce repudiation of constitutionalism and a fanatical reliance on physical force alone.

108 James Stephens   109 John O'Mahony
John Devoy, Recollections of an Irish Rebel, *1929*

The Irish Republican Brotherhood (IRB), or the Fenian organisation, was founded simultaneously in Dublin and New York in 1858 by a number of spirited men, nearly all of whom had been connected with the 1848 rising – James Stephens, John O'Mahony, Charles Kickham, John O'Leary, Thomas Clarke Luby and Michael Doheny. Jeremiah O'Donovan Rossa and his

Phoenix society of Skibbereen were the first notable recruits to the new movement. While fully accepting Thomas Davis's doctrine of Irish nationality, the Fenians believed that Britain would never concede independence except to physical force, and they therefore prepared by secret military organisation for an armed uprising, to be launched when Britain should be at a disadvantage. They concentrated on a single aim, independence, and insisted that the pursuit of any other aim, even reform of the land system, was a dangerous deviation. Yet, unlike previous revolutionary leaders, they made their converts almost entirely among working men – small farmers and labourers, clerks, shop assistants and artisans. By 1865 there were thousands of such men enrolled as Fenians and prepared for action, though numerically, Fenians never amounted to more than a small minority within the national movement.

110   John O'Leary   111   Thomas Clarke Luby
John Devoy, Recollections of an Irish Rebel, *1929*

The social composition of Fenianism, combined with its secret organisation, was the basis of the charge frequently made against Fenians, especially by the Catholic clergy, that they were communists. But a crucial fact about the Fenian movement is that its thinking was simply nationalist; it had no specific social programme for the Irish republic of its dreams. Nearly all its members were Catholics, but they firmly withstood the disapproval of their church and believed in complete separation of church and state. It differed from all previous national movements in that it drew its support not only from the Irish at home but also from the new Ireland that emigration had created in Britain and the USA. The special function of the American body was to aid the home organisation with arms and officers. Considerable numbers of US officers, trained in the American Civil War, came to Ireland in 1865 when that war ended; and it was only because, owing to a conflict of views among American Fenians, the promised arms did not also arrive that the rising intended for 1865 was postponed. If a rising had been launched in 1865, with relations between Britain and the USA distinctly strained, it would probably have been a serious, though hardly a successful, challenge to British rule. When a rising was at last attempted, in 1867, the government had the conspiracy well in hand and nearly all the Fenian leaders were in prison. The Fenian rising of 1867, like the Young Ireland rising of 1848, was no more than a gesture.

112   Charles Joseph Kickham   113   Jeremiah O'Donovan Rossa
John Devoy, Recollections of an Irish Rebel, *1929*

Fenianism seemed to have shot its bolt in 1867. But its spirit was not daunted by failure; new men arose to take the place of the imprisoned leaders, the secret organisation was quickly overhauled and improved, and a representative council was established to exercise the supreme authority hitherto vested in James Stephens. Thus reconstituted, the IRB settled down to the heartbreaking task of trying to keep itself in fighting condition until the day for action should come. It had to wait nearly fifty years, during which time the successes of constitutional nationalism seemed to have rendered Fenianism irrelevant as well as repugnant to the mainstream of Irish politics. In the eyes of unionists, Fenianism seemed to be a kind of disease that had infected the rabble of Ireland; but to those who understood it and those who believed in it, Fenianism was a flame, the 'phoenix flame', that went on burning, sometimes brightly, more often dimly, in the hearts of ordinary Irishmen. The IRB survived to take a leading part in 1916 in an insurrection of the kind it had aimed at in 1865.

114
John Devoy
John Devoy, Recollections of an
Irish Rebel, *1929*

The demonstration of national spirit afforded by the Fenians had profound effects both in Britain and Ireland. In Britain it reacted decisively on the mind of W. E. Gladstone, the greatest British statesman of the age, impelling him to embark upon a programme of 'justice to Ireland' to which he continued to give his best efforts for the rest of his life. His conscience had long been troubled on the subject of Ireland, but he confessed that it was the Fenian rising that had awakened him to a sense of 'the vast importance of the Irish question'[1]. His first administration (1868–74) marked a new era in the history of the Union both by the spirit in which he sought to solve Irish problems and by two great measures of reform. First, his Church Act of 1869 disestablished and disendowed the Anglican Church of Ireland, whose privileged position had been regarded as an unshakeable part of the Union itself. So far as law could do it, all religious denominations were placed on a footing of equality. The Church of Ireland was freed from its long connection with the state, and as a self-governing community entered, bitterly protesting, on a new, more challenging, but happier phase of its history. Second, Gladstone's Land Act of 1870 marked the first attempt of the British parliament to intervene in the land question on the side of the tenants. It proved ineffective for its purpose of protecting them against eviction, but it was the first step in that direction and as such was a landmark in British legislation. A third problem tackled by Gladstone was that of Catholic claims in the field of higher education, which Sir Robert Peel had tried, unsuccessfully, to satisfy by his institution of the Queen's Colleges in 1845. Gladstone's university bill of 1873 was a bold, ingenious and far-sighted scheme, centring on the concept of a great new University of Dublin, with many colleges and associated institutions throughout the country. In fact the bill antagonised the principal interests involved, both Catholic and Protestant, and its failure fatally weakened the government. The general election of 1874 resulted in the defeat of the Liberals and the return of the Conservatives to power under Disraeli. It was Disraeli who, in his last year of office, laid the foundation of a new university, the Royal University of Ireland, which, from 1880 to 1908, served as a working compromise between the claims of the Catholic hierarchy and the views of the British parliament.

While Gladstone was endeavouring to solve the Irish problem by reforms, a new effort to win independence by constitutional means was launched in Ireland. This was the home rule movement, founded in 1870 by Isaac Butt, the leading Irish barrister of the age, a man of large and colourful personality, a Protestant and formerly a unionist, who had been converted to nationalism by his experience of Irish suffering in the great famine and by the courage and integrity first of the Young Irelanders and then of the Fenians. The objective of the new movement – a subordinate parliament with control over Irish domestic affairs – fell far short of the independence sought by the Fenians. But that now seemed so remote a possibility that a number of influential Fenians, notably Patrick Egan and John O'Connor Power, chose to help Butt win an instalment of independence rather than to remain inactive indefinitely. So an essentially moderate and conservative movement, whose main support came from the Catholic middle classes, was started with the goodwill of extreme nationalists. For the Fenians this was a 'new departure', which soon led to deep division among them.

115
Isaac Butt, by John B. Yeats
National Gallery of Ireland

116
Charles Stewart Parnell
John Devoy, The Land of Éire, *1882*

In the general election of 1874 – the first to be fought under conditions of secret voting in accordance with the Ballot Act of 1872 – Butt's new party won more than half of all the Irish seats. For the next five years Butt advocated the home rule case in parliament with the utmost persuasiveness, patience and respect for the traditions of the House of Commons. But his claim to separate nationhood for Ireland was not taken seriously by either British party. Soon there arose within the Irish party a small group who held that Butt was quite wrong in trying to conciliate and convince the House of Commons. The right policy was to attack and exasperate both British parties by using the ancient procedure of the House of Commons for the purpose of obstructing its business. The pioneers of this policy of obstruction, Joseph Gillis Biggar and John O'Connor Power, both of them Fenians, were joined in 1875 by a newly elected MP, Charles Stewart Parnell, a young Protestant landowner from County Wicklow. He had inherited the seeds of Irish nationalism from both his Irish father and his American mother, who was of Irish descent. Though a poor speaker, he perfected the technique of obstruction and made himself the most-hated man in the House of Commons. This brought him into conflict with his leader, Butt, to whom the activities of the obstructionists were utterly obnoxious. A struggle for mastery between the elderly leader and the youthful new recruit began. By the middle of 1877 Parnell was obviously a rising, Butt a setting, star. Parnell had a matchless genius for leadership. His aloofness and self-restraint concealed a passionate nature of exceptional intensity and strength of purpose. Conservative in temperament and social outlook, pragmatic and clear-eyed in his approach to every problem, he concentrated his attention on achieving for Ireland the minimum of change that he judged necessary to solve the vital problems while always conveying an impression of dangerous and exciting extremism.

117
Michael Davitt, *c.* 1880
John Devoy, The Land of Éire, *1882*

In August 1876 the supreme council of the IRB formally condemned continued cooperation with the home rule movement, but the new policy continued to make converts among Fenians. The Fenian movement in America, as organised in the Clan na Gael, was showing keen interest in it and in Parnell's potentialities as a nationalist. Parnell welcomed Fenian support, and from 1877 onwards was never without it, but regarded any alliance with Fenians as unrealistic and likely only to hinder him in his chosen field.

This was Parnell's position when there entered into Irish politics a striking new personality, Michael Davitt, released from prison in December 1877 after seven years of penal servitude. The previous careers of Parnell and Davitt, who were both born in 1846 at the height of the famine, present a dramatic contrast. Parnell, the son of a country gentleman, was born in Avondale House, a comfortable country mansion in lovely surroundings in the heart of Wicklow. Until he entered parliament in 1874 he had lived an easy, affluent, aimless life, very much conforming to type. Davitt was the son of an evicted small tenant, exiled in 1850 from Mayo to Lancashire, where he spent a hard though not unhappy boyhood in the cotton town of Haslingden. At the age of nine he was working twelve hours a day in a cotton mill. He was just over eleven when in 1857 he lost his right arm in a machine he was minding. This led to four years of unexpected schooling and employment with the local postmaster. A life of comparative security seemed to be opening up when in 1865 Davitt threw himself into the Fenian movement. His Fenian activities earned him in 1870 a sentence of fifteen years' penal servitude, of which he served seven years, mainly in Dartmoor Prison. His release on ticket-of-leave in December 1877 was the outcome of a long and persistent agitation for amnesty for the Fenian prisoners, in which Butt, Parnell and others took a leading part. He emerged from prison a far more formidable enemy of Britain than when he went in. He was still a Fenian but critical of Fenian methods and Fenian dogmatism. Passionate and proud, he was also self-critical and self-disciplined. A Catholic who had been taught by a Wesleyan schoolmaster, he accepted religious diversity as a social fact and not a ground of estrangement among men. Hatred of British domination and of British landlordism in Ireland was in his blood, and yet, an Irishman reared in England, he rather liked the English and had an instinctive understanding of the English working man. Above all, he had a passion for social justice that transcended nationality.

Parnell and Davitt were quick to respect and to understand each other. Davitt wanted to get Parnell into the IRB and with his help to organise cooperation between Fenians and Parnellites. Parnell was interested but unconvinced. In 1878 Davitt went to America, where in collaboration with John Devoy, the dominant personality among American Fenians, he formulated a new policy for the national movement. The essence of this second 'new departure', which was endorsed by the Clan na Gael, was an alliance of revolutionary and constitutional nationalists on the two great issues of self-government and the land.

Both the supreme council of the IRB and Parnell refused to accept the new policy. But a rather different 'new departure' was launched by Davitt with spectacular success in 1879. This was his response to an economic crisis that, in the winter of 1878–9, threatened the rural population with a disaster comparable to that of the great famine. As the combined result of falling prices, crop failures and exceptionally wet weather, a multitude of small farmers were facing bankruptcy, starvation and eviction. Here was a crisis that dwarfed in importance all immediate political considerations, and Davitt threw all his energies into the task of promoting concerted action for self-defence among the tenant farmers. In April 1879, he joined with James Daly, editor of the *Connaught Telegraph*, and a number of local Fenians in organising a land meeting at Irishtown, in his native Mayo, that precipitated a general agitation in the west. It was clear to Davitt that the one man who could successfully lead the new movement was Parnell, who, after Butt's death in May 1879, was unquestionably marked out as the eventual leader of the home rule party. Parnell agreed to speak at the great land-meeting at Westport on 8 June, and there he gave a headline to the whole ensuing agitation: 'hold a firm grip of your homesteads and lands'[2]. Four months later, when Davitt founded the Irish National Land League to provide the agitation with a nationwide organisation, Parnell agreed to become its president.

The partnership of Parnell and Davitt in the Land League was essential to the success of the ensuing struggle – Parnell pre-eminent as the leader to whom all sections of national opinion rendered allegiance, Davitt the league's inspiring genius and principal organiser. The league combined in one great agrarian movement nationalists of all kinds, from moderate home-rulers to extreme republicans. The most combative element was provided by Fenians, though they acted without the approval of the IRB. The Clan na Gael gave the league timely financial help, which quickly broadened out into powerful backing from all sections of Irish nationalist opinion in America. The Catholic parish clergy were for the most part solidly behind the league, and so were a number of the Catholic bishops. In part the league served as a relief agency, augmenting the work of the voluntary relief-organisations through which, during the winter of 1879–80, the catastrophe of a second great famine was averted. But the league's essential task was to organise resistance to the landlords for the immediate purpose of preventing eviction and securing a reduction in rents, and for the ultimate purpose of transforming the tenant farmers into owners of their holdings. The so-called 'land war' of 1879–82 was the greatest mass movement of modern Ireland. An elaborate system of 'moral-force warfare' was developed: process-serving and evictions were made the occasion of great popular demonstrations; families evicted for non-payment of rent were sheltered and supported; an embargo was placed on evicted farms; persons involved in prosecutions because of their league activities were defended and the families of those sent to prison were cared for; and the terrible weapon of social ostracism, the boycott, was perfected as the ultimate sanction of the league against all persons who violated its code. For the first time, the tenant farmers as a class stood up to the landlords. The passions roused by the agitation inevitably erupted into violence and outrage, but it was just because the Land League was technically a lawful organisation that the government had so much difficulty in coming to grips with it.

In the midst of this upheaval a general election, held in April 1880, put an end to Disraeli's conservative administration and brought Gladstone back to office. In Ireland the election was fought on the land issue; and Parnell, with all the prestige that leadership of the land agitation gave him, won his first electoral triumph and became head of a militant Irish party in parliament. Gladstone entrusted the government of Ireland to one of his strongest and most dedicated colleagues, William Edward Forster, who accepted the chief secretaryship in a spirit of goodwill and conciliation towards Ireland. But his initial attempt to lessen tension by a temporary measure of protection for the tenants – the compensation-for-disturbance bill – was frustrated by the House of Lords in August, and he was left with no alternative but to enforce the existing land law against the tenants. So while he and Gladstone were preparing a new land bill, the land war became more embittered than before. The danger of famine was now past, but landlords redoubled their efforts to evict defaulting tenants. The ordinary law became paralysed, and the Land League assumed the functions of a rival government, whose courts – forerunners of the Sinn Féin courts set up in 1920 – wielded stronger sanctions than those of the state itself. It was during this phase of the land war that Captain Charles Boycott, of Lough Mask House, County Mayo, defied the league – and added a new word to the English language. In September 1880 he and his family were reduced to a state of isolation and helplessness from which they were rescued only by a relief expedition of fifty volunteer Orange labourers from Monaghan, protected by strong forces of troops. Some £350 worth of potatoes and other crops were thus harvested at a cost of over ten times their value.

118   Land League meeting at Kildare, 3 January 1881; Michael J. Boyton burning leases of the Duke of Leinster on a '98 pike
Illustrated London News, 8 January 1881

The government answered the Land League's challenge by obtaining exceptional powers of coercion from parliament and applying them with vigour and severity. Davitt was the first leader to be arrested (3 February). But at the same time Gladstone carried a new land act, based on the principle of the 'three Fs'. This transformed the landlord-tenant relationship and introduced a system of dual ownership. A special court was created to which tenants could apply to have a fair rent fixed for their holdings, and this judicial rent was to hold good for fifteen years. The full value of the act to the tenants was not at once appreciated. The Land League, insisting that peasant ownership and not the 'three Fs' was the only satisfactory principle of settlement, refused to call off the agitation. Gladstone retorted by arresting all the principal leaders – Parnell, Dillon, O'Brien, Brennan, Sexton and Kettle – and eventually suppressing the league itself (October 1881). The direction of the movement was taken over by an auxiliary body, the Ladies' Land League, initiated by Davitt before his arrest and headed by Anna Parnell, Charles's indomitable sister. But the ladies were not able to control the wilder elements in the agitation. The spectacle of Ireland being prey to irresponsible nobodies became as repugnant to Parnell as it was to Gladstone. Taking a realist view of the situation, Gladstone made peace with Parnell in the so-called Kilmainham Treaty of March 1882, by which the government agreed to make further concessions to the tenants, and Parnell agreed to call off the agitation. Forster, refusing to be a party to the agreement, resigned, the prisoners were released, the regime of coercion ceased, and Lord Frederick Cavendish was sent to Dublin as chief secretary to inaugurate a new and happier era. On the day of his arrival, 6 May, he and the undersecretary, T. H. Burke, were murdered in the Phoenix Park by members of a secret assassination club, the Invincibles. The deed threatened to destroy all the hopes raised by the Kilmainham treaty. It was followed by a ferocious new Coercion Act, but it did not prevent Gladstone from fulfilling Irish expectations with regard to the vital question of tenants' arrears, and it did not fundamentally alter Gladstone's attitude towards Parnell and Ireland.

The land war convinced British statesmen of both parties that the landlord system as it existed in Ireland was no longer defensible. Gladstone's remedy, the Land Act of 1881, progressively diminished the landlords' interest in the land. The fair rents fixed by the land court in the first three years showed an average reduction of nearly 20 per cent. Landlords began to feel that it would be better to sell out to their tenants on favourable terms than to share ownership with them. Dual ownership thus prepared the way for peasant proprietorship; and by a historical paradox, it was a Conservative Government that, in 1885, established, by the Ashbourne Act, the system of state-aided land purchase which, developed by many later acts – and especially the Wyndham Act of 1903 – did eventually abolish the old landlordism and turn Ireland into a land of owner-occupiers. This has been the greatest revolution in the history of modern Ireland, even though it was not the revolution that Davitt, the 'father of the Land League', had sought. 'The land for the people', the great watchword of the Land League, meant to the tenant farmers only one thing – that they themselves should become owners of their holdings. But from 1881 Davitt defined the phrase as meaning national ownership. From 1882 he never ceased to advocate this object as the only real solution to the land problem.

From the great famine to the land war, the idea of national independence had in practice meant little to the tenant farmers. But the land war was not merely an agrarian movement; it was also a great movement of national self-assertion. Parnell and Davitt had no doubt that the destruction of landlordism would lead to the overthrow of English power in Ireland. Parnell at Galway on 14 October 1880 made the characteristic statement: 'I would not have taken off my coat and gone to this work if I had not known that we were laying the foundation in this movement for the regeneration of our legislative independence.'[3] As soon as the agrarian crisis was over, Parnell withdrew from the agrarian agitation and steered the national movement firmly towards self-government, to be achieved by act of parliament. The Land League was replaced by a new organisation, the National League, dominated by the parliamentary party and providing it with effective electoral machinery. The discipline of the party was perfected and the whole national movement consolidated under Parnell's leadership in preparation for the next general election. That election, held in November–December 1885, was all the more significant because it was the first in British history to be fought on a comparatively democratic franchise. The result was a Liberal victory in Great Britain and an overwhelming Parnellite victory in Ireland, where pledge-bound home-rulers were returned for every seat outside eastern Ulster and Dublin University. To Gladstone, this result was decisive: in it he recognised 'the fixed desire of a nation, clearly and constitutionally expressed'[4]. In August 1885, after the defeat of his second administration, he became convinced that home rule was a just cause which he was called upon to champion, cost what it might. Thus in January 1886 he formed his third administration for the purpose of giving home rule to Ireland. He was then in his seventy-seventh year, the most dominating, most astounding, most dauntless figure in British politics.

Gladstone's home rule bill of 1886 contemplated a devolution of authority by the imperial parliament to an Irish parliament comparable with that which was to operate in Northern Ireland from 1921 to 1972. The intention of the bill, Gladstone declared, was to discharge a great historic debt of justice to Ireland, and in that spirit it was accepted in principle, while subjected to criticism in some of its details, by Parnell and his party, and by Irish nationalist opinion at home, in America, and in Australasia, as the basis of a lasting settlement. It involved British recognition of Ireland's claim to nationhood and British repudiation of the policy on which Ireland had been governed for centuries. It implied the application to Ireland of those traditions of British statesmanship that had fostered the growth of free institutions in Canada and other parts of the British Empire. That it was tabled at all was a triumph for Parnell's statesmanship and conclusive evidence of Gladstone's perception of the essential conservatism of Parnell. But to the Conservative Party, the bill was infamous – destructive of the unity of the empire, a betrayal of the loyalist and Protestant element in Ireland, a surrender to those who had proved by their duplicity and their crimes that they were unfit for self-government. The absence from the bill of any specific safeguards for Protestant interests in Ulster, such as a separate legislature, gave the opposition a valuable debating-point. Gladstone was aware of the Ulster problem but believed that the upper chamber of the proposed Irish legislature, which would be weighted in favour of social status and property, would adequately safeguard minority interests. Militant Orangeism counted for far less with him than the passionate insistence of the nationalists that (in Parnell's words):

> We want the energy, the patriotism, the talent, and works of every Irishman to make this great experiment . . . successful . . . We want . . . all creeds and all classes in Ireland. We cannot look upon a single Irishman as not belonging to us.[5]

The opposition of the Conservative Party could not have defeated the bill, but it was decisively augmented by a defection from the two extreme wings of the Liberal Party – Whigs under Lord Hartington on the right, radicals under Joseph Chamberlain on the left. The revolt of the aristocratic Whigs was predetermined by differences on social and imperial policy as well as over Ireland, but that of the radicals might conceivably have been avoided if Gladstone had handled Chamberlain differently – Chamberlain, who aspired to succeed him as leader of the party and to be the spearhead of social reform. The bill was defeated by a majority of thirty. If it had passed the Commons it would, of course, have been killed by the Lords, but in that case an appeal to the country could have been made under conditions more favourable than those under which Gladstone had to fight the general election of 1886 – the first to be fought in Great Britain on the issue of home rule. It resulted in a heavy defeat for Gladstone, which he accepted with magnificent courage and with no thought of abandoning the struggle.

This attempt, however unsuccessful, to carry home rule made 1886 a landmark in Anglo-Irish relations. It captured the imagination and won the admiration of Irishmen everywhere. It committed the large majority of the Liberal Party to home rule, and thus fundamentally altered the conditions of Irish and British politics. Nationalist Ireland could no longer regard Britain collectively as the national enemy, and the Irish were no longer, as they had been since 1880, an alien 'third force' in the British parliament. But the Liberal split proved irreparable. During the next twenty years the Liberals held office only once, for just under three years (1892-5). But that was not obvious in 1886, and Gladstone continued to the end of his public career (in 1894) to fight for home rule. He made remarkable progress in winning converts and considered, with good reason, that, if the next general election had occurred in the summer of 1890 instead of in 1892 (as it did), he would have had a handsome majority. His efforts were assisted by the egregious failure of the *Times* newspaper to ruin the reputation of the Parnellites, and with it that of the Liberals, by branding them with complicity in outrage and murder during and after the land war. A special commission of three high-court judges appointed to inquire into all the charges of the Times found that letters on which the most atrocious of them depended had been forged by a renegade nationalist, Richard Pigott. The judges' report produced a revulsion of feeling in Britain in Parnell's favour; but in less than a year all this advantage was wiped out by the revelation in the divorce court (November 1890) of Parnell's adultery with the wife of W. H. O'Shea, a former member of the home rule party.

The immediate reaction of British nonconformist opinion to the O'Shea case was violent hostility to Parnell's continued leadership of the Irish party. No section of British opinion had responded so ardently as the nonconformists to Gladstone's crusade for home rule as a great moral issue, and no single element was more vital to the existence of the Liberal Party than the nonconformists, especially since the secession of the Whig element. The party was thus threatened with a new and ruinous split. It was this political fact, and not any moral judgement on Parnell, that caused Gladstone to demand his temporary retirement from the leadership. Parnell's ferocious refusal to do so produced a bitter and demoralising split in the party he had largely created. His death a year later (on 6 October 1891), still desperately fighting for his leadership, did not end the split, which went on until 1900. Nevertheless, Gladstone succeeded in keeping the Liberal Party firm on the home rule issue, and when the general election of 1892 gave the Liberals a majority he formed his fourth and last administration for a renewed effort to carry home rule. His second home rule bill (1893) passed the House of Commons but was overwhelmingly defeated by the House of Lords. He was then eighty-four.

119   Gladstone introducing the Home Rule Bill in the House of Commons, 8 April
1886

Illustrated London News, 17 April 1886

Parnell's fall deprived the Irish party of a leader whose genius was irreplaceable, and seriously injured the home rule cause among the British public. It was all the more tragic because, in the supreme crisis of his life, Parnell abandoned the stern realism that had hitherto governed all his political conduct and allowed his passion and his pride to overmaster him. His refusal to contemplate even a temporary retirement forced an excruciating decision on a majority of his party.

Yet Parnell's achievement as a statesman, damaged though it was by his fall, was far from being undone; nor has it ever been undone. He brought Ireland's claims home to the British people as no Irish leader had ever succeeded in doing, and he is rightly remembered not by the actual extent of the self-government he was willing to accept from Britain but by the spirit of splendid defiance with which he voiced the Irish demand for independent nationhood. His superb leadership during the ten critical years created conditions that prepared the way for the final stages in the struggle for independence.

FROM PARNELL TO PEARSE
1891–1921
DONAL MCCARTNEY

The thirty years between the death of Parnell and the signing of the Anglo-Irish Treaty in 1921 flashed with more brilliance, and at the same time were riddled with more disappointment, than any comparable era in our history. At the beginning of the period, the Irish people seemed content that Ireland should remain part of the United Kingdom, retaining English institutions and the English language. In parliament, national demands went no further than a limited measure of control over domestic affairs and a continuation of the reform of the land system, enabling the tenant farmers to become owners of the land they worked. But in 1921 the demand was for a more definite break with England, and for a more distinct and separate national existence in politics, economics and culture. What follows is an attempt to account for the change that took place in the outlook of a generation.

In 1891 Parnell was dead. The forces which his leadership had held together in a great unified national movement had split apart, and the result was a decade of political division and ineffectiveness. The bitter years of the Parnellite split presented a sharp contrast with the days of Parnell's glory; and with the fall of Parnell the romantic hero, young men retreated from the party politics of home rule and fashioned their dreams in other activities. Small coteries turning away in disgust from the vicious political squabbling of the 1890s built for themselves so many separate little dreamworlds in a nationalistic Tír-na-nÓg, where poetry meant more than politics, and where ideals counted far more than votes.

One of these non-political movements emerging in what was called the Anglo-Irish literary revival was led by the poet William Butler Yeats. In Yeats's vision the poets, dramatists and writers would cater for the intellectual, as distinct from the material, needs of Ireland. For without an intellectual life of some kind, it was argued, the Irish could not long preserve their nationality. Yeats dreamed of the people cultivating a national literature that would be of the highest aesthetic quality. And in this movement he was assisted by a galaxy of literary talent – Lady Gregory, George Russell, Douglas Hyde, T. W. Rolleston, Standish O'Grady, J. M. Synge, George Moore, James Stephens and others. Between them they revived and romanticised the early legends and history of Ireland. And they sent into circulation the image of a new Irish hero, the legendary Cú Chulainn, famed for heroic feats, to replace a prosaic Grattan or O'Connell, the models of the home-rulers. The literary revivalists pictured Ireland as a poor old woman who would become a queen once more only when men became as chivalrous as Cú Chulainn and thought her worth dying for. This idea was dramatised by Yeats in *Cathleen Ní Houlihan*:

> It is a hard service they take that may help me. Many that are red-cheeked now will be pale-cheeked; many that have been free to walk the hills and the bogs and the rushes will be sent to walk hard streets in far countries; many a good plan will be broken; many that have gathered money will not stay to spend it; many a child will be born and there will be no father at the christening to give it a name. They that have red cheeks will have pale cheeks for my sake; and for all that they will think that they are well paid.

> They shall be remembered forever,
> They shall be alive forever,
> They shall be speaking forever,
> The people shall hear them forever.[1]

120 Douglas Hyde
Sarah Purser, R. H. A
National Gallery of Ireland

121 Eoin MacNeill
Cashman Collection
Radio Telefís Éireann

The nationalistic, and even separatist, impact of Yeats and his friends was profound, but it was limited and confined mainly to fellow poetic natures. However, what the literary revival lacked in popular appeal was supplied by the Gaelic League. The Gaelic League, founded by Douglas Hyde and Eoin MacNeill in 1893, had its own dream – at first to keep Irish alive where it was still spoken, and later, to restore Irish as the spoken language of the country. By giving up our native language and customs, said Hyde, we had thrown away the best claim we had upon the world's recognition of us as a separate nation. Therefore the task facing the present generation of Irishmen was the re-creation of a separate cultural Irish nation, and this could only be done by what Hyde called de-anglicisation – refusing to imitate the English in their language, literature, music, games, dress and ideas. Hyde argued that the practical steps taken by the Gaelic Athletic Association to revive the national games had done more good for Ireland in five years than all the talk for sixty. D. P. Moran vigorously developed Hyde's message. Every week in his influential paper, the *Leader*, Moran relentlessly propagated what he called the philosophy of Irish Ireland in well-written, pungent commentaries on passing events.

122   Eoghan O'Growney
Leabhar an t-Athair Eoghan:
The O'Growney Memorial Volume, *1904*

With such publicists as Hyde and Moran, workers like MacNeill and Pearse, and authors like O'Growney, Dinneen and An t-Athair Peadar, the Gaelic League caught hold of the popular imagination. It showed great potential as an adult-education-cum-entertainment movement with its language, history and dancing classes, its drama groups, its local *feiseanna* and the annual *oireachtas* and *ard-fheis*. The league became much more than a mere language or literary organisation. It propagated national self-reliance and self-respect, and campaigned against all forms of west-Britonism and *shoneenism*. The Gaelic League, in fact, became a well-organised, nationwide pressure group, and it could claim among its other achievements that it gave Irish a prominent place in every branch of education; closed the pubs on St Patrick's Day; turned that day into a national holiday; and promoted native industry by helping to organise industrial parades.

The Gaelic League appealed even to some unionists. Horace Plunkett, for example, then busily engaged in organising the cooperative movement in Irish agriculture, was impressed by the fact that in 1903 the number of Gaelic League branches, 600, had trebled in a couple of years; within a single year

Irish had been introduced to 1,300 national schools; the sale of its publications in a country which allegedly did not read stood at a quarter of a million for one year; its administrative expenses, collected by voluntary subscription, reached about £6,000 a year; and it was employing full-time some twenty-two people. The league, wrote Plunkett, was invigorating every department of Irish life and adding to the intellectual, social and moral improvement of the people.

Although it claimed to be non-political, the league had provided the best argument yet for the recognition of Ireland as a separate national entity. More than any other movement, the Gaelic League provided the atmosphere for the development in Ireland of the new-look nationalism then powerfully operating in Europe. According to this new nationalism, politically independent states should be raised up wherever there existed distinct cultural nations. The Gaelic League was demonstrating that Ireland was a cultural nation; therefore, went the argument, Ireland was entitled to become a nation-state.

Among the political groups coloured to a greater or lesser degree by the Gaelic League's philosophy were Sinn Féin, the IRB and Connolly's socialist movement. Sinn Féin owed its inspiration to Arthur Griffith, who, like so many other Dubliners, had remained stubbornly loyal to Parnell's memory. As in the case of Yeats and Hyde and their colleagues, Griffith, too, rejected the post-Parnellite politics of home rule. In the *United Irishman*, the paper which he edited from its foundation in 1899, Griffith first propounded his policy, which was in fact an extension of Parnell's obstruction tactics and an adaptation of the Land League's boycott – or, for that matter, the GAA's ban on foreign games, or the Gaelic League's policy of de-anglicisation – to the political situation. Griffith's articles were collected, and published in pamphlet form for the first time in 1904, under the title *The Resurrection of Hungary.*

The great attraction of the Sinn Féin policy – as it came to be called – was the sheer simplicity of its logic. Griffith held, as indeed did the leaders of the home rule party, that the Act of Union of 1800 was illegal. But Griffith drew from this the conclusion that the Irish MPs who since 1800 had sat in the Westminster parliament were thereby participating in an illegality and helping to perpetuate a crime. They should withdraw from the imperial parliament and, together with the elected representatives of the county councils and local authorities, set up at home in Ireland a Council of Three Hundred to take over the government of the country and to pursue a policy of political and economic self-sufficiency. This was the policy which had won the Hungarians their independence from Austria.

What is often overlooked is the fact that Griffith was himself a separatist, at least when he first formulated his policy, and was for a time a member of the IRB. When therefore he proposed that there should be a return to the constitutional position of Grattan's parliament with the crown as the personal link between Ireland and England, he did so because he held that in the circumstances the principle of a dual monarchy would win more widespread support in Ireland. Griffith's policy possessed a certain fascination for the members of separatist societies like Cumann na nGael and the National Council and Maud Gonne's *Inghinidhe na hEireann*, all of which had developed out of opposition to the royal visits of 1900 and 1903, as well as for the Belfast republicans who had founded the Dungannon Clubs. And these were welded together from 1908 to become the Sinn Féin organisation.

Sinn Féin had some success at local elections and started its own weekly paper. But although a young intellectual home ruler like T. M. Kettle could describe Griffith's policy as 'the largest idea contributed to Irish politics for a generation'[2], Sinn Féin won little sympathy from home rule supporters generally. Nevertheless, Sinn Féin felt confident enough to engage in a trial of strength with the Irish party in 1908. A young home-ruler, Charles J. Dolan, MP for North Leitrim, resigned his seat and offered himself for re-election as a Sinn Féin candidate. But the parliamentary party retained the seat by a two-to-one majority. Sinn Féin, however, although no match for the parliamentary party at the polls in the years when the prospects for home rule were brightening, continued to offer an alternative to parliamentarianism.

Between Sinn Féin and the IRB, there existed an affinity based on separatist tendencies in both, and cemented by close personal friendships. The big difference between the two was that while Sinn Féin stood by a policy of passive resistance and hoped by aiming at a dual monarchy to cast a net wide enough to catch most Irishmen, the IRB planned to establish an Irish republic by physical force. After the Parnellite split, the IRB, small in membership, suffered from its own internal divisions and did not consider rebellion feasible in the circumstances. But, like John Mitchel before them, men in the IRB dreamed of the outbreak of a war which would involve England and thereby provide Ireland with an opportunity:

> You that Mitchel's prayers have heard,
> 'Send war in our time, O Lord!'[3]

The growth of two armed camps in Europe, and the crowding of one diplomatic crisis on another, increased the possibility of a European war. A frail little man with an indomitable Fenian spirit which fifteen and a half years' imprisonment had not broken, and with a single idea in his head – to get the English out – was cheered by the prospect of a general war. To ensure that Ireland would be ready to seize its opportunity, Tom Clarke returned from exile in America. His small shop in Parnell Street became the nerve centre, and his closest friend, the handsome Seán Mac Diarmada, then the paid organiser of Sinn Féin, became the essential linkman in a revitalised IRB.

By 1910 the IRB was publishing its paper, *Irish Freedom*, managed by Mac Diarmada and edited by Hobson, with its motto taken from Wolfe Tone – 'to break the connection with England'. And soon eager young nationalists who, as Pearse put it, had been to school to the Gaelic League, like Pearse himself, MacDonagh, Plunkett and Ceannt, were being drawn into the IRB.

Independent of the IRB, another small group, of trade unionists and socialists, were dreaming of a somewhat different kind of revolution. Since the land war of the 1880s, a revolution had taken place in the ownership of the land of Ireland. For one of the effects of the land war was that, following a series of land acts, the unionist ascendancy landlords were replaced by small proprietors, for the most part Catholic and nationalist. The settlement of the land question, together with improved material conditions, left the farming classes reasonably well satisfied. In the larger towns, however, conditions were far from satisfactory. In 1911, although it was then held that there had been a 'manifest, material improvement' over the previous eleven years, Dublin had one of the most underfed, worst-housed, and badly paid populations in Europe. Twenty-one thousand families lived in single-room tenements. The death-rate at birth of 27.6 per 1,000 was higher than that of any other city in Europe (with Moscow second to Dublin). Pearse wrote in *Irish Freedom* (October 1913):

> I calculate that one-third of the people of Dublin are underfed; that half the children attending Irish primary schools are ill-nourished . . . I suppose there are 20,000 families in Dublin in whose domestic economy milk and butter are all but unknown; black tea and dry bread are their staple diet. There are many thousand fireless hearth-places in Dublin on the bitterest days of winter.[4]

Marx, Engels and Lenin, who had each kept a close eye on Ireland, had allowed for the fact that when the socialist revolution came to the world, overthrowing the existing social order, it might well be sparked off in this country. Events in Dublin in 1913 encouraged this belief among European socialists.

To improve the conditions of the working class, a fiery Jim Larkin, assisted by the more intellectual James Connolly, organised the Irish Transport and General Workers' Union. In August 1913 a showdown began between Larkin and the employers' leader, William Martin Murphy. Murphy organised some 400 employers into a federation and locked out the workers who were members of Larkin's union. By the end of September, 24,000 people were locked out. A bitter struggle, protracted over eight months, followed. Dublin witnessed massive rallies, baton charges by the police resulting in numerous injuries and a couple of deaths, riots, arrests, imprisonments, food-ships from English sympathisers, and sympathetic strikes.

123   Citizen Army on parade, 1914
Keogh Bros., Dublin

Neither side won, but the results were far-reaching. The spirit of militancy that had been aroused played a significant role in extending the revolutionary climate. The Citizen Army, which had been established to protect the strikers, continued in existence after the labour troubles had subsided, and was to play an important part in the rising of 1916. Connolly, who, as far back as 1896, had founded the Irish Socialist Republican Party, was all his life a nationalist as well as a socialist. In 1913, Connolly the socialist had called on the British working class to show solidarity with their brothers in Dublin and to stage a general sympathetic strike. But after some signs that this might be realised, Connolly was disappointed. For the future, he put his trust more and more in the establishment of a republic by the Irish workers themselves. 'The cause of labour,' he wrote, 'is the cause of Ireland, the cause of Ireland is the cause of labour.'[5] Besides, Tom Clarke, Pearse and *Irish Freedom* had given their backing to Larkin in 1913 and thus had increased the sympathy between the labour movement and the republicans.

Here, then, were a number of small dynamic groups – the literary movement, the Gaelic League, the GAA, Irish Ireland, Sinn Féin, the IRB and the labour movement – each concerned not so much with electoral or parliamentary success but devoted rather to some social, cultural or political ideal and together acting as a ferment in the mind of a generation. It was the interaction of these forces upon each other that was effecting the change in the mental climate of Ireland between 1891 and 1921.

124   Funeral of O'Donovan Rossa, Glasnevin, 1 August 1915
Cashman Collection, Radio Telefís Éireann

Pearse at Tone's graveside in 1913, and at O'Donovan Rossa's in 1915, is an excellent example of the synthesis of cultural and political separatist traditions then taking place in individuals. On these occasions, Pearse spoke as an IRB man, dressed in 1915 in the uniform of an Irish Volunteer, to honour Tone, the father of Irish republicanism, and Rossa, 'the unrepentant Fenian'. His opening paragraphs on Rossa were in Irish, showing the impact which the Gaelic League – 'the most revolutionary influence that has ever come into Ireland', as he called it – had on Pearse. And when in his oration at Tone's grave he spoke the passage about the sorrowful destiny of the heroes who turn their backs on the pleasant paths for Ireland's sake, he might well have been paraphrasing the words which Yeats had put into the mouth of Cathleen Ní Houlihan when she enticed the young man in the play to leave all things fair and follow her down the thorny path of history, or equally Pearse's words might have come from the lips of Cuchulainn defending the gap of the north as romanticised in the books of Standish O'Grady. Pearse admired both Tone and Rossa for reasons which would also have won the approval of the labour leader Connolly; running through these graveside orations was the defiant and self-reliant note of the Sinn Féin gospel. Thus were the ideals of the literary revival, of the Gaelic League, of the IRB, of Sinn Féin, of the Irish Volunteers and of Connolly's socialist republicans becoming part of the psychological make-up of a generation which Pearse represented.

What still made the loudest noise on the political surface, however, was home rule. The Liberal Party under Gladstone had introduced home rule bills in 1886 and 1893 which were defeated. With the unionists entrenched in office, and the Irish parliamentary party split, home rule did not become an issue again until 1906, when the Liberals returned to office and the prospects for home rule brightened. Meanwhile, the Irish party, reunited under Redmond since 1900, recaptured much of the support and respect which it had gained from the Irish electorate in the days of Parnell. Moreover, the reform of county government in 1898, which transferred control over local affairs from the landlord-dominated grand juries to popularly elected bodies – county councils, and rural and urban district councils – enabled nationalists to gain experience of local self-government which they looked forward to applying in an Irish parliament.

The general election of 1910, which made the Liberal government dependent on the support of the Irish party, brought home rule still nearer. For forty years home rule had embodied the hopes and aspirations of the vast majority of Irish nationalists. The Irish party could claim with some justification that nearly every major reform in Ireland during the past forty years was traceable to its efforts. And during these years there had been a massive commitment on the part of the Irish people to the parliamentary party. The decline in the fortunes of Sinn Féin, after losing the North Leitrim by-election, was only one indication of the greatly improved prospects of home rule, and of how close the parliamentary party was considered to have come towards achieving its main objective of a domestic parliament for Ireland. As Erskine Childers put it in 1911 in his book *The Framework of Home Rule:* 'If the Sinn Féin alternative meant anything at all, it meant complete separation, which Ireland does not want, and a final abandonment of constitutional methods.'[6]

In 1912 Pearse spoke from a home rule platform in Sackville Street. The home rule bill of that same year passed the Commons, and because of the Parliament Act of the previous year the House of Lords could not delay its coming into operation beyond 1914. In the interval, however, the unionists, basing their tactics on the fact of the existence of a stubborn Ulster aversion to home rule, mounted a violent agitation.

Edward Carson, a successful Dublin lawyer, aided and abetted by the leaders of the Conservative Party, led the opposition to home rule with considerable skill and courage. Two hundred and eighteen thousand pledged themselves to use 'all means' necessary to defeat home rule. The Ulster volunteers were established (January 1913) and armed by gun-running from Germany, and a provisional government was set up (September 1913) to take control of Ulster on the day that home rule became law. Carson declared: 'I am told it will be illegal. Of course it will. Drilling is illegal . . . the Volunteers are illegal and the government know they are illegal, and the government dare not interfere with them . . . Don't be afraid of illegalities'[7].

125   National Volunteers in training, 1913
Cashman Collection, Radio Telefís Éireann

The Orangemen felt assured of the full backing of the British Conservatives in whatever they might do, for Bonar Law, the leader of the party, had already publicly announced that he could imagine no length of resistance to which Ulster could go in which it would not have his support and that of the overwhelming majority of the British people.

Home rule had reached an impasse. Both Asquith, the prime minister, and Redmond, his Irish ally, thought it would be extremely unwise to make martyrs out of Carson and his supporters. Asquith calculated that merely by waiting he would see the unionists damage themselves politically by their unconstitutional antics. Asquith, who had not Gladstone's dedication, and Redmond, who was no Parnell, chose to fight the battle for home rule on the ground where they felt they could win – in parliament and by means of parliamentary majorities. Then, faced with Carson's intransigence, Asquith persuaded his fellow parliamentarian, Redmond, to retreat from his first position, which was home rule for all Ireland, and Redmond agreed reluctantly, and step by step, 'as the price of peace'.

Meantime, the voices off-centre of the stage grew louder in their criticism of the shilly-shallying about home rule. *Irish Freedom* declared that Carson was the only Irish MP with any backbone; and in imitation of what he had achieved in Ulster, the Irish Volunteers were founded in Dublin (November 1913).

The outbreak of war in 1914 put the question of home rule into cold storage, but the heat that had been generated over the past few years was not so readily turned off. In 1914 the country contained no less than five armies. First were the official forces, which, as the Curragh 'mutiny' had shown, could not be relied on to enforce a settlement of home rule for all Ireland. Then there were the private armies – the Ulster Volunteers, the Irish Volunteers, the Citizen Army and the IRB.

126
1916 Memorial: Statue of Cuchulainn by Oliver Sheppard in the General Post Office, Dublin
Bord Fáilte Éireann

The Irish Volunteers split when Redmond pledged support to England in the war for the defence of 'small nations'. For this he was severely criticised by the more advanced and sceptical nationalists. A contemporary jingle in Connolly's paper, the *Workers' Republic*, expressed their position:

Full steam ahead, John Redmond said
that everything was well chum;
home rule will come when we are dead
and buried out in Belgium.[8]

After the outbreak of the war the IRB, whose members held controlling positions in the Irish Volunteers, decided on an insurrection to take place before the ending of the war. They secured the cooperation of Connolly's Citizen Army which was also hoping for a rising. The outcome was the Easter rebellion of 1916.

It was not so much the rebellion of Easter week that completed the change in the attitude of the Irish people generally as its aftermath. Of the ninety rebels condemned to death for their part in the insurrection, fifteen, despite a mounting volume of protest, were executed, the first executions being on 3 May and the last ones ending on 12 May. The officials appeared to panic, martial law was imposed, and more people were arrested than had actually taken part in the rising. The pacifist, Sheehy Skeffington, although he had taken no part in the rising, was arrested and shot without trial. The government too, apart from the military, made more mistakes, and the threat of conscription hung over the country. The Irish parliamentary party blundered and lost the initiative. Everything that happened in the next few months played into the hands of Sinn Féin, which made the most of its opportunities.

127 Éamon de Valera addressing anti-conscription meeting at Ballaghadereen, 1918
Cashman Collection, Radio Telefís Éireann

128   Dáil Éireann, 1919
Radio Times Hulton Picture Library

1st row from left to right: L. Ginnell, M. Collins, C. Brugha, A. Griffith, É de Valera,
Count Plunkett, E. Mac Neill, W. T. Cosgrave, E. Blythe

2nd row: P. J. Maloney, T. McSwiney, R. Mulcahy, J. O'Doherty, J. Dolan, J. McGuinness,
P. O'Keefe, M. Staines, J. McGrath, B. Cusack, L. de Róiste, M. P. Colivet, Fr M.
O'Flanagan

3rd row: J. P. Ward, A. McCabe, D. Fitzgerald, J. Sweeney, R. J. Hayes, C. Collins, P. Ó Máille,
J. O'Mara, B. O'Higgins, J. A. Burke, K. O'Higgins

4th row: J. McDonagh, J. McEntee

5th row: P. Beasley, R. C. Barton, P. Galligan

6th row: P. Shanahan, S. Etchingham

(spelling of names as on back of photograph)

By the time of the general election in December 1918, the country had
moved unmistakably towards Sinn Féin. Sinn Féin won seventy-three seats,
the unionists twenty-six, and the parliamentary party a mere six. The defeat
of the parliamentary party took place in circumstances extremely
unfavourable to them. They had been geared to constitutionalism and in fact
committed to it under Redmond. Essentially they were a peacetime party, but
Ireland in 1918, and possibly since 1912, could hardly be described as at
peace. But their defeat in 1918 was not sudden, for their position was being
undermined for years past by Ireland's most able propagandists – Griffith in
his Sinn Féin papers, Moran in the *Leader*, Connolly in the *Workers' Republic*,
the IRB in *Irish Freedom*, and Hyde, who creamed off into the Gaelic League
some of the best talent in the country. The relentless criticism had a wearing-

away effect, and it proved decisive when the electorate was offered an alternative to parliamentarianism in the changed circumstances of 1918. Parnell had shown how forces in Ireland could be harnessed to support the Irish party in Westminster. But where Parnell was capable of making use of the Land League and even of the Fenians, the party without Parnell never gained the confidence of the Gaelic League, the IRB or Sinn Féin. It paid the penalty in 1918.

The victorious Sinn Féin constituted itself as Dáil Éireann, pledged itself to the Irish republic and proceeded to put into operation the policy of passive resistance which Arthur Griffith had outlined for it years before. Éamon de Valera, a senior surviving Volunteer officer, became head of the Dáil, with Arthur Griffith as his deputy and Michael Collins from the IRB as the ruthlessly efficient organiser of the military resistance which opposed British attempts to smash Sinn Féin.

The Anglo-Irish War from early 1919 to July 1921 – or the 'troubles' as the people euphemistically called it – seriously embittered Anglo-Irish relations. It was a struggle characterised by guerrilla warfare, ambushes, raids on police barracks, and planned assassinations on the one side; and reprisals, the shooting-up and burning-up of towns, executions and terrorising on the other, as the 'flying columns' of the Volunteers took on the Black and Tans and Auxiliaries of the British. Eventually public opinion in America and in Britain demanded a truce, which was arranged in July 1921. In December 1921, after months of negotiations, a treaty, which was essentially a compromise, was signed by the British and Irish representatives. The British conceded dominion status to the twenty-six counties, and the Irish negotiators brought back, not the republic, but 'freedom to achieve freedom'. Ironically, the unionists of Ulster who had most strenuously rejected home rule had been granted a measure of home rule by the Government of Ireland Act, 1920.

The unhappy legislative union established in 1800 between Ireland and Great Britain had been finally dissolved, but on terms none had visualised. The years 1891–1921 had been a crowded hour in Ireland's history. Solid achievement and improvement there had been in plenty. Larkin had built up trade unionism, William Martin Murphy a commercial empire, Cusack the GAA, MacNeill and Hyde the Gaelic League; while Redmond, Dillon, Devlin and their friends had brought the people within sight of the promised land of home rule. By a series of land purchase acts initiated before 1891 and continued throughout the period, the land question was well on the way to being solved in the interests of the tenants. By the Universities Act of 1908, establishing the National University of Ireland and the Queen's University of

Belfast, the university question of the nineteenth century was to a large extent solved, and the constituent colleges of the National University played a big part in the building of modern Ireland. Legislation had improved housing; old-age pensions had been granted; more money had been invested in education. A congested districts board, a department of agriculture, county councils and light railways had also been established during these years.

Yet there was also grave disappointment. Gladstone once said that men ought not to suffer disenchantment, since ideals in politics are never realised. In Ireland none of the dreams had been fulfilled. Not the Gaelic League's Irish-speaking nation, nor Yeats's literary-conscious people, nor the republic of the IRB, nor the workers' republic of Connolly, nor Griffith's economically self-sufficient dual monarchy, nor Redmond's home rule within an empire which the Irish helped to build, nor Carson's United Kingdom. Although all the dreams had to some extent been frustrated, the many dreamers had left their mark. With the signing of the treaty, however, the dreaming gave way to political realities.

Signatories of the Proclamation of
the Republic (24 April 1916)
by Seán O'Sullivan, R. H. A.
National Gallery of Ireland

129   Thomas James Clarke

130   James Connolly

131   Thomas MacDonagh

132 Seán Mac Diarmada

133 Patrick Henry Pearse

134 Éamonn Ceannt

135 Joseph Mary Plunkett

NORTHERN IRELAND: 1921–66
J. L. McCRACKEN

The vast majority of the Protestants in the north of Ireland were bitterly opposed to home rule. 'Home rule is Rome rule' was their slogan. They believed that under a Dublin parliament in which they would always be in a minority, their religion, their way of life and their economic interests would be endangered. And home rule aroused strong passions in Britain too, so that powerful elements there were ready to encourage and sustain the Ulstermen in their opposition. Gladstone's home rule bills of 1886 and 1893 were angrily received in Ulster: there was rioting in Belfast and the Orange order took on a new lease of life. Lord Randolph Churchill came to Belfast to 'play the Orange card', as he put it, and coined the rallying cry 'Ulster will fight; Ulster will be right'. By the time the third home rule bill was introduced in 1912, its opponents in Ulster were organised for resistance. An Ulster Unionist Council had been set up in 1905, a leader had been found in Sir Edward Carson, and the backing of the British Conservative Party had been secured. Bonar Law, the Conservative leader, vied with the Ulster Unionists in the violence of his language.

The Ulster Unionists did not confine themselves to words. A day of dedication was observed by Protestants throughout Ulster on 28 September 1912, when religious services were held and a solemn league and covenant was signed by over 218,000 men, who pledged themselves to use 'all means which may be found necessary to defeat the present conspiracy to set up a home rule parliament in Ireland'. An Ulster Volunteer Force was enrolled for political and military service against home rule, a provisional government was formed to take over the province on the day the home rule bill became law, and a consignment of arms was brought in from Germany – all this with the approval and often active assistance of sympathisers in Britain.

Even before this storm had reached its full intensity, the Liberal government had begun to seek a solution in compromise. A proposal that the Ulster counties might decide by plebiscite to be excluded from the operation of the home rule act for six years was rejected by the unionists. 'We do not want sentence of death, with a stay of execution for six years', said Carson.[1] Instead, at a conference at Buckingham Palace in July 1914, he demanded first the exclusion of the whole of Ulster and then of the present six counties. Redmond, the leader of the Irish parliamentary party, refused to accept either proposal, and the question of how long the exclusion should last was never discussed at all.

136   Sir Edward Carson addressing an anti-home rule meeting *c.* 1912
Public Record Office, Belfast

On the outbreak of the First World War, the home rule bill was passed, but the coming into force of home rule was postponed until the end of the war. Long before that, the situation was utterly changed by the 1916 rising and its aftermath. The home rule of the 1914 act which the unionists had rejected so violently fell far short of the demands of Sinn Féin. With a guerrilla war raging in the country, negotiations between the parties was impossible, so Lloyd George decided on an imposed settlement. The Government of Ireland Act, 1920, provided for the setting up of two governments and two parliaments in Ireland, one for the six counties which were to form Northern Ireland and the other for the rest of the country, which was to be called Southern Ireland. As well, Ireland was to have representatives in the British parliament, and a council of Ireland was to be constituted from members of the two Irish parliaments. Sinn Féin refused to have anything to do with the act and it was a dead letter so far as Southern Ireland was concerned. The Ulster Unionists also disliked it, but they decided to accept it as a preferable alternative to Dublin rule. Sir James Craig became prime minister and the Northern Ireland parliament was opened by King George V on 22 June 1921.

Northern Ireland had been brought into existence but its future was far from assured. The Anglo-Irish Treaty of December 1921, which ended the war of independence and set up the Irish Free State, applied to the whole of

Ireland, but Northern Ireland was given the choice of opting out of the agreement and retaining the status it had secured. This was done without delay. A more formidable threat to the new state was the campaign of violence and the sectarian strife which came near to plunging it into anarchy. In 1922, 232 people, including two unionist MPs, were killed, nearly 1,000 were wounded, and more than £3 million worth of property was destroyed. In combating this situation, the northern government relied in part on the British army, but it also established a regular armed police force and a special constabulary to form what Craig called 'a defence force against our enemies'[2]. Even after the restoration of law and order, the threat of the boundary commission still hung over Northern Ireland. The Anglo-Irish Treaty had stipulated that if Northern Ireland opted out of the Irish Free State, a boundary commission should be set up to fix the boundary between the two states. The Irish leaders were confident that the outcome would be the transfer of such large areas to the Free State that Northern Ireland would not be able to survive as a separate state. Craig was well aware of the danger and consequently he refused to cooperate. When the commission was set up in spite of him, he toured the border areas, reassuring his supporters with the pledge 'what we have we hold'. On the eve of the commission's reporting (7 November 1925), the *Morning Post* published a forecast of its findings which disclosed that only minor changes were contemplated and those mainly in favour of Northern Ireland. This precipitated a crisis which was resolved by a conference between the three prime ministers at which it was agreed to leave the border as it was. Craig returned to Belfast 'happy and contented'[3].

But the dilemma created by Lloyd George's solution was still unresolved. The act of 1920 set up a state in which about a third of the population was bitterly hostile. Some took part in the attempt to overthrow it by force; the rest, pinning their hopes on the boundary commission, adopted an attitude of non-cooperation. The nationalists who contested the first parliamentary election in Northern Ireland declared in their election manifesto: 'it is our fixed determination not to enter this north-east Ulster parliament'[4]. Though they changed their minds after the boundary issue was settled, they refused to act as the official opposition, and they were not organised as a party; Joe Devlin, the ablest of them, said he had no ambition to lead anyone. Since their aim was a united Ireland, since in other words they aimed not at the overthrow of the government but at the destruction of the state, they could not play the role of an opposition in the traditional parliamentary manner. Herein lay the dilemma which has vitiated political life in the North ever since. The nationalist attitude enabled the unionists to appropriate loyalty and good citizenship to themselves and to use the national flag as a party

137 Sir James Craig, later Viscount
Craigavon, Prime Minister of
Northern Ireland, 1921–40
Public Record Office, Belfast

138 Joseph Devlin, Ulster nationalist leader
Public Record Office, Belfast

139 John Miller Andrews, Prime Minister
of Northern Ireland, 1940–43
J. R. Bainbridge, Belfast

140 Sir Basil Brooke, later Viscount
Brookeborough, Prime Minister of
Northern Ireland, 1943–63
Leslie Stuart, Belfast

emblem. Since the nationalists drew their support exclusively from the Catholic part of the population, it led the Protestant unionists, or at least the rank and file of them, to identify Catholicism with hostility to the state. It justified, in unionist eyes, the arrangement of certain local government constituencies so as to prevent local government bodies falling into nationalist hands. It also detracted from the effectiveness of nationalist criticism of the government even on issues which had nothing to do with the constitutional question, and it encouraged irresponsibility, rashness and a narrow sectarian approach among some nationalists who could never hope to be other than a minority opposition, and who could never look forward to assuming office.

The situation in which the nationalists found themselves, and put themselves, also prevented the development of party organisation. Various attempts were made. In 1928 the National League was formed to achieve the national unity of Ireland, to demand justice for nationalists and to foster cooperation among all creeds and classes. In 1936 the Irish Union Association was established in Belfast by representatives of all the minorities to bridge the gulf between nationalists, republicans and Fianna Fáil supporters in the province. In the post-war period there was the anti-partition movement. But all these came to nothing. The truth was that, apart from the dissensions over methods within the anti-partition ranks, the incentive to organise was lacking. In some areas a nationalist was as certain of winning an election as a unionist was in others. No amount of party organisation was going to win votes outside of those areas. There was no floating vote on the constitutional issue.

The unionists, on the other hand, had every incentive to maintain an effective party machine. The unionist party was a broadly based one, including within its ranks people of all classes, many of whom, in a different political context, might have had Labour or Liberal affiliations. Although all the prime ministers were drawn from the landed gentry or large industrialist classes, working men and self-made men always featured amongst the leaders. But, while the government was always sensitive to backbench opinion, it frowned on any deviation from the orthodox unionist creed. This was evident in the period of consolidation which followed the crisis of the early years. In those years various pressure groups had caused embarrassment to the government. In 1925 the parliamentary secretary to the ministry of home affairs lost his seat to a representative of a dissident group called the 'unbought tenants'; the Protestant churches and the Orange order were agitating for an amendment to the education act of 1923; and the temperance reformers, strongly backed by sections of the Protestant clergy, were pressing for a measure of local option. The local optionists even put up candidates in opposition to official unionists in the general election of 1929. These and not the nationalists were the groups the prime minister had in mind when he decided to abolish proportional representation in parliamentary elections except for the university seats. In his opinion, 'there are really underlying everything two active, alert, vigorous parties in Ulster . . . one for the empire, the other for an all-Ireland parliament in Dublin'. Proportional representation clouded the issue.

> What I hold is, if the people of Ulster are ever going – and pray God they may not – into a Dublin parliament, I say let the people understand that they are voting to go into a Dublin parliament and not go in by any trick of a complicated system such as proportional representation.[5]

The abolition of proportional representation in 1929 made next to no difference to the nationalists; what it did was to prevent splinter groups of unionists from winning seats. From 1929, differences of opinion were usually thrashed out within the party circle, and when a dissident group like the progressive unionists went to the polls in 1938 they were ignominiously defeated. As things were, there was little place for the Labour party or for independents. Labour won three seats under PR in 1925; in 1965 they won two. As for the two major groups, their representation changed very little over the years. At the first general election in 1921, forty unionists, six nationalists and six republicans were returned; in 1965 the numbers were thirty-six unionists, nine nationalists, two Labour, and five others. The rigidity of the political situation in the North was shown in two other ways: the high number of uncontested seats at every general election and the stability of governments. Usually about 40 per cent of the members were returned without a contest and sometimes the percentage was over 60. As for the government, not only was there an unbroken period of unionist rule but there were very few changes of personnel. Lord Craigavon was prime minister from 1921 till his death in 1940. His successor, J. M. Andrews, held office only until 1943 but he had been a Cabinet minister since 1921. He was followed by Lord Brookeborough, who had been a minister for ten years. His spell of office lasted until 1963, when he was succeeded by Captain Terence O'Neill. Other ministers and ordinary members on both sides of the house served for long periods; in 1936, for example, 40 per cent of the members had been in the House of Commons since it came into existence fifteen years before. Northern Ireland was entitled to thirteen seats at Westminster and here too there was the same rigidity: normally all but two of these seats were held by unionists who consistently supported the Conservative Party.

Basically this situation developed out of the turmoil of the early years, but the course of events subsequently tended to perpetuate divisions and harden allegiances. As the unionist government found its feet, the 'step by step' policy of following British legislation began to take shape. The consolidation of the state was shown in such events as the establishment of an Inn of Court for Northern Ireland in 1926, the opening of the Law Courts Building in 1933, and above all the erection of Stormont. The foundation stone of the building, originally planned on an even grander scale, was laid in 1928. Its opening by the Prince of Wales in November 1932 was the occasion of a great unionist demonstration, but, as a protest against partition, the nationalist MPs took no part.

141   Shipbuilding at Belfast, October 1956. In the background: Belfast Lough, with White Head to the left

Central Office of Information, London

The thirties were years of persistent depression and unemployment in the North. The two great Ulster industries, linen and shipbuilding, were in decline, and agriculture was hard hit by the industrial depression at home and in Britain. The government's efforts to stimulate trade and industry had little effect. Unemployment rose from 13 per cent in 1927 to a peak of 28 per cent in 1931 and was still as high as 20 per cent on the outbreak of war. A by-product of this high unemployment was a resurgence of sectarian strife and a renewal of the campaign of violence. An attack on an Orange demonstration in 1931 set off a series of reprisals. There were disturbances in Belfast and elsewhere in 1932 and in succeeding years, culminating in serious rioting in Belfast in 1935, when a number of people were killed. The campaign of violence was carried on intermittently right into the forties, and provided justification, in unionist eyes, for the retention of the Special Powers Act. Originally passed as a temporary measure at the height of the 'troubles' in 1922, it was made permanent in 1933 and was invoked to deal with each successive outbreak.

Events in the rest of Ireland during these years also helped to keep alive the old issues in the North. The dismantling of the Anglo-Irish Treaty after 1932, the new Irish constitution of 1937, and the policy of raising the partition question on every possible occasion heartened the nationalists but confirmed the unionists in their resolve, as Craigavon said, that Ulster's position within the United Kingdom and the Empire must remain unchanged. Éire's neutrality in the war was the final proof of how far the paths of the two Irish governments had diverged.

To the North, the war brought a variety of new experiences. Although the British government turned down Craigavon's request that conscription should be applied to Northern Ireland, the people of the North shared the other wartime experiences of the British – high taxation, restrictions, rationing, and in Belfast severe air raids. Many Ulstermen joined the British forces. Thousands of British troops were trained in the province, new airfields were constructed, and Derry became an important naval base. In 1942 American troops began to arrive in the North. To de Valera's protest at their presence, Andrews replied that he had no right to interfere in Northern Ireland's affairs. With the development of wartime industries, an unwonted prosperity reigned. People from Éire came to work in the North, but they had to register and obtain permits, and the prime minister made it clear that they would not be allowed to remain and become voters: 'a unionist government must always be in power in Northern Ireland'.[6] There was movement in the other direction too: many people, among them unionist working men who had never before had the means or the inclination to do so, went south on holiday to escape from the rigours of wartime conditions. All these experiences were shared by unionists and nationalists, Protestants and Catholics alike.

After the war there was a growing emphasis on social and economic problems. Large-scale housing schemes were carried out, not only by local authorities but also by the Housing Trust, an organisation set up by the government in 1945. Legislation designed to aid existing industries and to attract new ones met with considerable success: world-famous firms like Courtaulds, du Pont, British Oxygen and Michelin Tyres established themselves in the province and thousands of new jobs were created. Under the stimulus of subsidies and development schemes, agriculture made great progress. The 'step by step' policy was maintained as the welfare state developed in Britain, with the result that the educational system, the health service, and unemployment and sickness benefit were far in advance of those available in the Republic. These post-war developments tended to underline the advantages of the link with Britain and the differences between north and south.

142 Terence O'Neill, Prime Minister of Northern Ireland, visits Seán Lemass, Taoiseach, 9 February 1965. With them are (left) Jack Lynch, Minister for Industry and Commerce, and (centre) Frank Aiken, Minister for External Affairs.

Lensmen Ltd, Dublin

On the other hand, economic necessity was responsible for a measure of cooperation between the two governments in the post-war era. In 1950 they agreed on a scheme for the drainage of the land around Upper and Lower Lough Erne and for the development of a hydroelectric generating station; in 1951 they assumed responsibility for the running of the Great Northern Railway; and in 1952 they set up the Foyle Fisheries Commission to administer the fisheries jointly acquired from the Honourable the Irish Society of London. These arrangements involved meetings between Cabinet ministers and civil servants from the two states.

But the old issues survived into the post-war age. Vigorous agitation against partition and the repeal of the External Relations Act in 1948 raised the constitutional question again. Unionist representations to the British government resulted in the passing of the Ireland Act in 1949, which provided that Northern Ireland should not cease to be part of the United Kingdom without the consent of its parliament. A new campaign of violence was carried on from 1956 to 1962. There were occasions when nationalist demonstrations were broken up by the police. Nationalists continued to complain of discrimination in the distribution of housing and jobs. Unionists used occasions like royal visits to reaffirm their loyalty to Britain. The two communities pursued their separate ways, with their different outlook and way of life. Yet both were sharing experiences which smoothed the way for some halting steps towards the better understanding for which a few individuals and groups had always worked. Increased prosperity, better housing, greater educational opportunities and the impact of TV form the background to such significant developments as the meeting between O'Neill and Lemass in January 1965, and the decision very shortly afterwards by Edward McAteer and his nationalist colleagues to accept the role of official opposition at Stormont. The possibilities of the new situation were summed up by O'Neill in these words:

> If a spirit of friendship can be established, then I believe that those sterile forces of hatred and violence which have flourished for so long will at last be crushed by the weight of public opinion.[7]

21

The Irish Free State and the Republic of Ireland, 1921–66
Patrick Lynch

A knowledge of contemporary history comes more often from political education than from historical education. The more recent the event, the more difficult it is to grasp its full historical significance and implications: the Civil War, for instance, aroused on both sides strong feelings which still influence opinions and make impartial judgements difficult.

Objectivity in history is probably unattainable. What follows tries, however, to chronicle with historical detachment a selection of the main events of the forty-five years 1921–66. It also seeks to explain the motives of a few of those responsible for these events, and, diffidently, makes some provisional historical judgements on them.

The Anglo-Irish War closed with the truce of 11 July 1921 and the dispatch of Sinn Féin representatives to London for negotiations with the British government. Initially Sinn Féin, led by Griffith and de Valera, were at one in arranging these negotiations. But the outcome of them, in the Anglo-Irish Treaty signed on 6 December 1921, divided Sinn Féin between those separatists who wanted the reality of an independence that would enable Ireland to look after its own affairs and those who wanted more, who opposed the treaty for a principle – the republic. There may have been disagreement as to what exactly the republic meant. Those who sought the republic, however, knew what it did not mean – it did not mean accepting a treaty which required an oath of allegiance to a British king.

On the side of the treaty were those led by Arthur Griffith. If the treaty failed to offer the full independence for which so many had fought, it did offer, Griffith suggested, a large measure of Irish control over Ireland's destinies. It offered what Michael Collins called the 'freedom to achieve freedom'[1], and when Griffith persuaded a majority of the Dáil to support the treaty, he declared that the treaty settlement had 'no more finality than that we are the final generation on the face of the earth'[2].

The treaty was approved by the Dáil by 64 votes to 57 (7 January 1922). British troops began to withdraw from Ireland by agreement, and Irish troops took over control. The provisional government announced the acceptance of the treaty to the people, and went to the country in a general election to seek support for its stand. De Valera – as president of the republic – and his followers opposed acceptance of the treaty, arguing that the people had no right to do wrong and that the Dáil had been persuaded to ratify the treaty against its better judgement. The result of a bitterly fought election (June 1922) endorsed the pro-treaty position: fifty-eight pro-treaty candidates were returned, thirty-six anti-treaty, seventeen Labour, and seventeen representing farmers, independents and others.

143
Arthur Griffith
Cashman Collection,
Radio Telefís Éireann

A civil war, which lasted until May 1923, ended in the defeat of those who, wishing to maintain the republic, had opposed the treaty. In the course of this war, Michael Collins was killed in an ambush (22 August 1922). The first head of the Irish Free State government, Arthur Griffith, had died ten days before, and was succeeded by William T. Cosgrave.

With the treaty, Britain believed with mistaken complacency that Ireland at last was taken out of British politics. This was partly because, despite the experience of 700 years, British statesmen had never really understood the Irish problem, and partly because the Irish problem was so complex and difficult. Looking back, one can only try to imagine what may have been in Griffith's mind when he accepted the treaty, knowing that it secured less than many Irishmen aspired to. Perhaps Griffith was influenced by the threats of the British prime minister, Lloyd George, as to the consequences of Ireland's rejecting the treaty. Perhaps he was influenced by Collins's belief that the Irish guerrilla campaign against vastly superior British forces was losing its momentum. The realistic Griffith must have been particularly concerned by the knowledge that the partition of part of Ulster from the rest of Ireland was already accomplished, and that no possible outcome of the negotiations between Sinn Féin and the British government could substantially alter this fact. Under the Government of Ireland Act, 1920, a separate parliament for six Ulster counties had come into existence. This was a parliament subordinate to Westminster, to which it sent thirteen representatives. The six counties were selected by Lloyd George as comprising the largest possible geographical area in which a majority of the population in favour of partition could reasonably be expected. This meant home rule of a kind for the partitioned area of Ulster. Griffith must have known ever since the enactment of the Government of Ireland Act that his separatist objective could not now be secured for the whole island. He probably decided to accept what could be secured by the treaty in the knowledge that only time, patience and endurance could obtain for the separated six counties the status and possibilities that the treaty offered to what was to be the Irish Free State.

144
Michael Collins, at the funeral of
Arthur Griffith, 12 August 1922
Walsh, Dublin

Irishmen, who, in the Anglo-Irish War, had held out for a republic, were not impressed by the dominion status which the treaty conferred. They would have preferred de Valera's proposal for external association with the British Empire, which would have left Ireland a republic in its internal affairs, yet retaining an association with the British Empire in its external dealing. Even this solution, however, would have had to contend with partition in Ulster.

A consideration which may have commended the treaty to some Irish people was the British hint that a boundary commission which was to be set up to determine the geographic limits of Northern Ireland might help to restore the territorial unity of Ireland by reducing Northern Ireland to an area so small as to be politically and economically unsustainable. This would be achieved by incorporating in the Irish Free State the areas in which nationalists were numerous. When, however, it did report, in 1925, the boundary commission contemplated making no change in the boundaries which existed in 1921. Its report was never published because a leakage of information to the *Morning Post* prompted the government of the Irish Free State to reach direct agreement with the British government.

The treaty gave a degree of autonomy to the Irish Free State that probably few Irishmen ever expected to see realised in their lifetime, even though some Irish naval bases were to be retained by Britain, and in certain circumstances, harbour and other facilities might be sought by Britain for defensive purposes. Griffith had set great store by the advantage and importance of fiscal and financial independence; these the treaty offered. The full possibilities of the dominion status conferred by the treaty were hardly foreseen, even by those who freely accepted the treaty. Many supporters of the treaty, for instance, had regretted that the Commonwealth tie should be a compulsory one. Over the next ten years, however, the Irish Free State was to play an increasingly active and significant part in the events leading to the Statute of Westminster in 1931. Such men as Desmond Fitzgerald, Patrick McGilligan and John A. Costello, working closely with the representatives of the Canadian government, were pioneers in transforming the remains of the old British Empire and reshaping the British Commonwealth by turning it into a free association of self-governing states.

De Valera and his party, Fianna Fáil, remained outside the Dáil until 1927. After the general election of that year, Fianna Fáil became the largest opposition party. De Valera lost the support, however, of republicans such as Seán MacBride and George Gilmore who refused to recognise the constitution or institutions of the Free State. In March 1932, Fianna Fáil secured seventy seats at a general election and de Valera formed his first government, with the support of the Labour Party. This crucial event consolidated the achievements of Irish political democracy in the Free State, for Cosgrave handed over office to men who a decade earlier had challenged the Free State's very existence. W. T. Cosgrave had been head of the government since 1922. De Valera was to remain in power for sixteen years, until 1948.

In 1930 the Irish Free State had been elected to the council of the League of Nations and de Valera was elected president of the council in 1932. The government formed in 1932 by the Fianna Fáil Party declared that it would pursue a republican policy, remove the oath of allegiance to the British crown from the Free State constitution and promote rapid industrialisation. Soon it began to withhold from Britain the land annuities and some other payments, amounting in all to about £5 million a year. The annuities were twice-yearly instalments payable by farmers in respect of the capital cost of buying out landlords. As the capital costs had been advanced by the British government, the Cosgrave government had collected the annuities from the farmers and forwarded them to London.

145
William Thomas Cosgrave,
President of the Executive Council
of the Irish Free State 1922–32,
on a visit to New York in 1928
Radio Times Hulton Picture Library

Britain retaliated by taxing imports of Irish cattle into Britain, and the Free State replied with duties on British goods. And so began the 'economic war', which persisted for over six years and which intensified the harmful effects on Ireland of the world economic depression of the 1930s. The farmers were the chief victims, yet by and large the electorate remained solidly behind de Valera. In 1938 the annuity dispute was settled by the payment to Britain of a capital sum of £10 million, and the treaty ports were handed over to the Irish government.

These events took place against a background of turbulence as Ireland, like other European countries at the time, was troubled by private armies – the

Irish Republican Army, which armed and drilled throughout the thirties, and the Army Comrades' Association, which, following the Continental fashion of the day, adopted a uniform from which its members were generally known as Blue Shirts.

146 Éamon de Valera, President of the Executive Council of the Irish Free State 1932–7, Taoiseach 1937–48, 1951–4, 1957–9, Uachtarán 1959–73
Taken on the occasion of a Radio Éireann broadcast on 'The nation's food requirements', 3 December 1941

Irish Press

Already in 1937 de Valera had introduced a new constitution to replace that which he regarded as imposed by the treaty. It declared Ireland to be a 'sovereign, independent, democratic state'. In the previous year, on the abdication of Edward VIII, the External Relations Act in effect made the state a republic, though the British monarch was recognised as an instrument for validating the accreditation of Irish diplomatic representatives to foreign countries. The new constitution was adopted by a plebiscite in 1937. In 1938 Dr Douglas Hyde became the first president under the new constitution.

Whether Ireland remained a member of the British Commonwealth or not after 1937 was still a matter of controversy. A test of membership might have been Irish attendance at Commonwealth conferences. From 1937, until the defeat of the Fianna Fáil government at a general election eleven years later, in 1948, however, Ireland was never represented at a Commonwealth conference. During most of these years, it is true, Britain was at war and Ireland was neutral, yet the British monarch remained a recognised Irish instrument under the External Relations Act.

Economically, the trade agreement of 1938 was very important. Irish goods were to be admitted free of customs duties to the British market, with the exception of quantitative regulation of agricultural produce. The Irish government guaranteed free admission to Ireland of certain classes of British goods yet retained the right to protect Irish industry, a very important concession to Seán Lemass, the dynamic minister for industry and commerce.

The war years were difficult for Ireland, but the people endured the hardships of unemployment, emigration and shortages of supplies as a small price to pay for the neutrality which the government under de Valera maintained with resolute determination. There can be little doubt that de Valera had the mass support of the Irish people behind him when he withstood the urgings of President Roosevelt to abandon neutrality and support the Allied cause. Very many Irish people – perhaps most – did, in fact, morally support the Allied cause against Nazi aggression, and many thousands of them served in the British forces as volunteers. But they also agreed with de Valera that an Ireland divided by a partition that was supported by Britain could not without stultifying itself and its aspirations join Britain in a campaign for democratic freedom and national self-determination. The government's policy was to maintain official neutrality and to seek, when it could, to preserve Irish men and women in Northern Ireland from being conscripted into the war effort. Its determination to limit the effects of the war and to identify the people in the South with those in the North was symbolically demonstrated when the government sent the fire brigades of Dublin and Dun Laoghaire to the help of Belfast on the night of a German fire-bomb raid on that city (15–16 April 1941). At the end of the war in Europe, the British prime minister, Winston Churchill, in his victory speech (13 May 1945) taunted Ireland for having remained aloof from the great struggle from which the Allies had just emerged. Rarely did any Irishman speak for so many of the Irish at home and in all parts of the world as did de Valera in his restrained and dignified reply to Churchill three days later.

The first post-war general election was held in 1948, and after sixteen years a majority of the electorate decided in favour of a change of government. Although Fianna Fáil was defeated, it remained the largest party. A government was formed, however, of a combination of parties, united not by a previously agreed common policy but in opposition to Fianna Fáil. The inter-party government, as it called itself, had the task of formulating a policy to which all its constituent groups could subscribe – Fine Gael, Clann na Poblachta, Labour, Clann na Talmhan and independents. Since the election had given a majority vote to no party and therefore endorsed none of the policies offered, it seemed that the people favoured merely change. In evolving this consensus, the new taoiseach, John A. Costello, had to face the fact that the treaty settlement to which his party, Fine Gael, had contributed so much had, since 1932, been dismantled step by step by de Valera's government in a succession of measures approved by the people. By 1948 the treaty was no longer an issue in Irish politics. And so the External Relations Act of 1936 was replaced in 1949 by an act which declared that the description of the state should be 'the Republic of Ireland'. The taoiseach recommended the Republic of Ireland Bill to the Dáil as a means of removing ambiguities in the constitutional position and of taking, as he said, the 'gun out of politics' in the twenty-six counties. The British government stated that it regarded the Republic of Ireland Act as bringing Ireland out of the Commonwealth. It had now been demonstrated that the dominion status conferred by the treaty did, in fact, confer the freedom to achieve freedom.

147   John Aloysius Costello, Taoiseach 1948–51, 1954–7
Taken at the first meeting of the first inter-party cabinet, 19 February 1948
Irish Press

In 1951 Costello's inter-party government broke up as a result of internal conflict following what was called the 'mother-and-child health scheme', sponsored by the minister for health, Dr Noël Browne, and condemned by the organised medical profession and the Catholic hierarchy. The inter-party government was replaced by a minority Fianna Fáil government under de Valera, supported by some independents. In 1954 there was a second inter-party government, with Fianna Fáil in opposition. This second inter-party government, again under Costello as taoiseach, continued to press forward with a heavy programme of capital investment, for the development of a country which in this respect had unavoidably been neglected in wartime. A balance-of-payments problem arose, however, because of excessive demands for imports of consumption goods in 1956, and the fiscal measures necessary to correct it, courageously introduced by Gerard Sweetman, so reduced the rate of economic growth that high unemployment and emigration followed. De Valera was returned to office again in 1957 and remained head of the government until, on the retirement of Seán T. O'Kelly, he became president of Ireland in 1959, when he was replaced as taoiseach by Seán Lemass.

Even now, it is too soon for an Irish historian to form more than a provisional judgement on the first decades of the Irish state. It would be too much to expect complete detachment from all those who took sides in the civil war, and even many of the next generation were influenced by the strong feelings aroused by it. It is certain, however, that William T. Cosgrave, president of the executive council, laid the foundations of efficient and honest administration, which enabled the country to recover in a surprisingly short time from the physical ravages of the Civil War. Indeed, most of his political opponents – those who opposed the treaty – would agree that Cosgrave and his colleagues in the first government of the Free State had a hard and thankless task and that they did very efficiently their duty as they saw it. Opponents of the treaty might argue that the first Free State government decided to do for the country, economically and socially, the same kind of thing that a British government might have done if the Free State had remained part of the United Kingdom. The new Irish civil service modelled itself consciously on what it deemed to be the virtues of the British civil service. Indeed, many of the new Irish civil servants had been transferred from the British service. After 1922, Merrion Street became Whitehall writ small. The Garda Siochána were built up as an example to the world of an unarmed police force. The national army was firmly and loyally under the control of the national government.

One wonders what might have happened had Griffith lived. It is true that the ten years from 1922 to 1932 were years of peace and progress in the Free

State, but the government's social and economic programme was a far cry from the glowing and heart-warming spontaneity of the democratic programme that General Richard Mulcahy had so eloquently proposed in the united Dáil Éireann on 21 January 1919. Unlike Griffith, not even the ablest members of Cosgrave's government had a completely coherent economic philosophy, in which both agricultural and industrial development equally fitted. Some of them – Ernest Blythe, Patrick Hogan and Patrick McGilligan – had immense analytical abilities, but they lacked faith in the possibility of really rapid industrial development without damaging the interests of the farmer. Griffith, on the other hand, had had deep ideological convictions on the economic significance of Sinn Féin, on the need for dynamic development of manufacturing industries, and on the use of tariffs. He would almost certainly have seen the first economic task of government as the achievement of an industrial revolution in the Free State of the kind that had been achieved earlier in north-eastern Ulster. The Irish agrarian revolution had already taken place under British rule, thanks to Davitt, Parnell and Dillon.

There had, of course, been tremendous difficulties facing the new government in 1922. First, the country had had to recover from the effects of the Civil War. Moreover, the Free State lacked an industrial tradition; the border had cut it off from the heavily industrialised areas around Belfast; industrial skills and training were scarce. In spite of these severe handicaps, there were very considerable achievements – the restoration of order after the Civil War, better marketing of agricultural produce, the Consolidating Land Act of 1923, the establishment of the sugar-beet industry, the setting up of the Agricultural Credit Corporation, the vast undertaking of the Shannon scheme. If Griffith had lived, however, it seems doubtful that he would have been satisfied with government action between 1922 and 1932 in using 'selective protection' as a means of carrying out its programme of industrialisation. The government's industrial policy reflected its lack of an industrialised economic ideology, as well as the influence of civil servants and economists whose background and training had closed their minds to most ideas outside the British liberal and laissez-faire tradition. It is, indeed, a nice historical irony, at which, as dialecticians, Marx and Engels would have smiled, that Griffith's protectionist policy for industrialisation had to await implementation until the advent to power of de Valera and Lemass after 1932.

Some of the principal economic advances of the first ten years after 1922 were due more to the imagination and initiative of individual ministers than to the advice of civil servants. The civil service saw its role as administering the system as it existed. Its intellectual climate was unlikely to promote a spirit of innovation, especially after the onset of the world economic depression in the early 1930s. The high quality and integrity of the civil service were consolidated by the government's creation of independent commissions for recruiting staff to both central and local public service. It was made abundantly and courageously clear by Cosgrave's government between 1922 and 1932 that self-government did not mean jobs at the expense of the taxpayer for postulants with political influence.

In economic policy, Fianna Fáil, when it came to power in 1932, showed itself prepared to pursue a vigorous programme of rapid industrialisation under Lemass, minister for industry and commerce, and willing to face the consequences for agriculture of the means employed to secure industrial development – tariffs which raised costs for the farmers. Like most members of the Cosgrave administration before him, Lemass had no doctrinaire economic position, but he was to commit himself to a course of state intervention in economic activity that gave a leftward direction, in practice, to his economic policies. Where private enterprise failed or was unable or unwilling to provide a necessary service, Lemass created a public enterprise. Aer Lingus, for instance, was created in 1936 to provide publicly owned air services, and in 1944 Córas Iompair Éireann took over surface transport services, which had run into difficulties under private ownership. Bord na Móna (1946) was one of the most successful creations. After 1932, Lemass became the architect of a new Irish industrial revolution. No Irish political party, not even the Labour Party, was socialist, yet public or state-sponsored enterprise played a large and crucial part in the economy.

After 1948, when the first inter-party government took office, economic policies were adopted which, in some cases, seemed even more radical than anything that Lemass had sponsored. The minister for finance, McGilligan, for instance, introduced the concept of the capital budget – the first explicit evidence of Keynesian influence in Irish public finance. Under successive governments since then, the state capital programme has grown progressively in significance. Lord Keynes, indeed, was seeming in practice to have more influence than Connolly on the Irish economy of the fifties and sixties.

When Fianna Fáil was returned at the general election of 1957 following the severe economic crisis of 1956, there was an unprecedented step in public administration. In 1958, T. K. Whitaker, secretary of the department of finance and head of the civil service, with the approval of the government published a survey entitled *Economic Development*, which was, in fact, a pointer towards the objectives at which he believed the country should aim if living standards were to be raised and unemployment and emigration reduced. Whitaker's prescription was, necessarily, a complicated one, which would be difficult to summarise and dangerous to simplify, but, by and large, he agreed that the country needed greatly increased capital investment, provided it was the right kind of investment, and by the right kind he meant productive investment that added to the wealth and welfare of the country and not merely redistributed existing wealth. Whitaker's report did not recommend economic planning as such, but the ends and means which he suggested could, in fact, best be achieved, or provided, by economic planning.

Based on Whitaker's report, the government approved and published its first *Programme for Economic Expansion*, towards the end of 1958. It is still contested whether that programme was, really, the cause of the remarkable economic recovery that occurred in the years after 1958 or whether its association with that recovery was fortuitous. In any event, growth during the years after 1958 increased by 4 per cent a year, in contrast to a growth rate of less than half that figure in the preceding years. Since *Economic Development* was published, the prestige of the civil service has been very high in Ireland in circles that earlier looked primarily to the politician for a lead in economic policy.

148   Harold Wilson, Prime Minister of Great Britain, and Seán Lemass, Taoiseach, signing the Anglo-Irish free-trade agreement at 10 Downing Street, 14 December 1965

Thomson Newspapers, London

In 1963–4 the government, under Lemass, introduced its *Second Programme for Economic Expansion*, to cover the seven years from 1964 to 1970. The government had now committed itself to all the trials and rewards that economic planning could produce in a free society. Perhaps, like Costello's government in 1956, Lemass in 1964 was trying to do too much too quickly, and so the country again ran into a balance-of-payments crisis in 1965. Yet despite the unpalatable measures necessary to correct these troubles, there remained hope that the aims of the Second Programme could be achieved by 1970 (see Chapter 22 below). In the meantime, the taoiseach, Lemass, had begun a series of meetings with Terence O'Neill, prime minister of Northern Ireland, which held the promise of closer and more constructive relations between the two parts of Ireland.

The year 1965 opened with a dramatic meeting between Lemass and O'Neill, and ended with a new Anglo-Irish trade agreement which offered hope of more mutually rewarding economic relations between Britain and Ireland than ever before. It now seemed possible that the next step would be for Ireland to join the European Economic Community (see Chapter 22 below). Closer economic relations with Britain were dictated by the logic of history and geography. For good or ill, Britain is our nearest neighbour. Most of our trade is with Britain. Most of our emigrants go there to work. Indeed, for many purposes, Britain and Ireland comprise a single market. To many people, an Anglo-Irish free-trade area had long seemed inevitable.

In the decades immediately after the treaty, in a mood of disillusion and frustration, it was to be expected, perhaps, that the emphasis should be on the more inward-looking aspects of our culture. In a heady spate of Puritanism, a riot of censorship banned novels by some of the greatest contemporary Irish writers, as well as the work of foreign artists of international repute. This, indeed, was a shameful fruit of political freedom. Yet, at the time, Irish literature of world renown was being created by James Joyce, William Butler Yeats, Seán O'Casey, Seán O'Faolain, Pádraic Ó Conaire and others. And, then, in the 1940s, the wonderful Brian Ó Nualláin, *alias* Myles na gCopaleen, *alias* Flann O'Brien, writing in Irish and English, came as a scourge of everything false and pretentious in Irish life and writing.

Nor did the treaty bring revolutionary developments in education. Primary schools, it is true, were required, in addition to their normal educational task, to help more effectively in the revival of Irish, and this responsibility has certainly placed a heavy burden on both pupils and teachers.

The state's financial support for education – primary, secondary, and university – was, however, far from generous over the years, but prospects for the future were much brighter. Vocational education, extended in the 1930s, achieved distinctive and valuable results, but only in the 1960s did it approach its potential in the context of the comprehensive schools. Internationally, perhaps, for Ireland the most significant educational or cultural event of the years since the treaty was the establishment, sponsored by de Valera, of the Dublin Institute for Advanced Studies (1940), which has attracted scholars of international distinction, among them Erwin Schroedinger, the theoretical physicist.

In 1960, a commission was appointed to inquire into, and report to the government on, all aspects of higher education. Its report was to herald a new approach to the whole subject (see Chapter 22 below).

Socially, too, there were great advances. The Irish Free State inherited in Dublin some of the worst slums on Europe. Even in 1966 a good part of Dublin still needed to be restored, but the slums in the old sense were gone and municipal standards were reasonably high throughout the country. The Irish trade union movement, whose growth had been retarded by internal dissension, was strong, numbering about 390,000 members. The movement was also impeded by partition, until in 1964 the Stormont government recognised the Irish Congress of Trade Unions as a negotiating body.

For many years, successive governments failed to find a satisfactory remedy for emigration, but in 1966, in spite of temporary economic difficulties, the signs were that it was possible to plan economic growth with a view to increasing living standards, improving social welfare and eliminating unnecessary emigration. As a nation, however, our greatest failure since the treaty was our failure to provide jobs at home for those who preferred not to emigrate.

Church and state clashed only once since the treaty – in 1951 on Dr Noël Browne's 'mother-and-child health scheme', which the Catholic hierarchy declared to be against Catholic social teaching on the rights of the family and of the church in education. Fifteen years later, in 1966, and after the pontificate of Pope John, it was difficult to imagine the issue of a means test being raised as an objection in principle to a medical service. Indeed, after Dr Browne had left office in 1951, a very similar health scheme was introduced by the new Fianna Fáil government, which satisfied the objections of the hierarchy.

In the twenty-one years since the Second World War, Ireland had achieved as conspicuous a place in the United Nations Organisation as she had earned in the League of Nations. In Geneva, in 1932, de Valera had made an appeal for justice and peace among nations that was tremendously reinforced by his moral standing as a political figure committed domestically to an apparently inflexible political doctrine. By his re-election in June 1966 as president of Ireland, he continued to remain a world political figure.

Since 1948, Liam Cosgrave first, and later Frank Aiken, led the Irish delegation to the annual general assemblies of the United Nations and indicated the part that a small nation might play in promoting the cause of international peace. The year which marked the golden jubilee of 1916 seemed particularly appropriate to remember the men of the Irish army who, under General Seán MacEoin, responded to the call of the United Nations to maintain order in the faraway republic of the Congo, and the other Irishmen who served in Cyprus. The men who declared the Irish republic in 1916 and those who supported it in arms, as well as the men and women who stood for the treaty and those who opposed it, would find common ground in saluting the Irish soldiers taking part in a peacekeeping force under the United Nations.

149
Irish soldier serving in United
Nations forces
John F. Kelly, R.H.A.

The Republic's economy was being rationalised in an empirical blend of private and public enterprise in preparation for entry to the European Economic Community. But the issue of *Planning a Just Society* by the main opposition party in 1965 was a reminder that economic growth, however essential, was not enough.

0 Scale in Miles 40
Boundaries of Provinces
Boundaries of Six Counties of Northern Ireland
DONEGAL
DERRY
ANTRIM
ULSTER
TYRONE
BELFAST
FERMANAGH
ARMAGH
DOWN
MONAGHAN
LEITRIM
SLIGO
MAYO
CAVAN
LOUTH
ROSCOMMON
LONGFORD
MEATH
CONNAUGHT
WESTMEATH
DUBLIN
DUBLIN
GALWAY
GALWAY
OFFALY
KILDARE
LEINSTER
LAOIS
WICKLOW
CLARE
CARLOW
KILKENNY
LIMERICK
WEXFORD
LIMERICK
TIPPERARY
MUNSTER
WATERFORD
CORK
KERRY
CORK

150 Map of Ireland, political

22

IRELAND: 1966–82

J. H. WHYTE

The leading feature of the period 1966–82 in both parts of Ireland was the unprecedented pace of change. In Northern Ireland, change was most obviously political, with turmoil succeeding decades of outward calm, but important social and economic changes occurred as well. In the Republic, change was above all economic and social. I shall discuss Northern Ireland first, since the crisis there affected the course of events in the Republic.[1]

Northern Ireland in 1966 seemed on the way to a brighter future. Economically, it was progressing. True, it suffered from high unemployment and from the steady contraction of its staple industries – linen, shipbuilding and agriculture. But its ministry of commerce was energetically attracting new industries and seemed to be making up for the decline of the old staples. Its greatest success was in man-made fibres: Northern Ireland became one of the main centres in Europe for this booming industry. Meanwhile, the ministry of development was pressing ahead with what was fashionably described as the 'infrastructure' – the framework of roads, utilities and housing which would make Northern Ireland attractive to the entrepreneur. The first piece of motorway anywhere in Ireland was opened between Belfast and Lisburn in 1962, and a new town (Craigavon), between Portadown and Lurgan, was founded in 1965. The growth rate in the period 1960–73 averaged 4 per cent *per annum*, which was higher than in the rest of the United Kingdom and equal to that of the Republic.

Politically, too, the atmosphere seemed to be improving. Ever since its foundation, Northern Ireland has been sharply divided between a Protestant majority and a Catholic minority. The ethnic boundary was maintained by a lack of intermarriage, by separate education and, in some places, by residential segregation. Political attitudes largely followed religious adherence, with Catholics generally favouring a united Ireland and Protestants supporting the maintenance of the link with Britain. Catholics complained bitterly of discrimination in jobs, housing, the enforcement of law and order, and the drawing of electoral boundaries. Protestants retorted that Catholics were disloyal to the state. But in 1963 a new prime minister, Captain Terence O'Neill, had come to office; he talked of building bridges between the communities. On the other side a Catholic leadership was emerging, which owed its education to the implanting in Northern Ireland of the British welfare state and which was more prepared than its predecessors to acquiesce in the constitutional status quo, provided Catholics received a fair deal within it. The IRA (Irish Republican Army), which as late as 1956–62 had tried to overthrow Northern Ireland by force, was in eclipse, and its leaders had taken to pursuing socio-economic issues. In the Republic, the taoiseach, Seán Lemass, had shown by his visit to Stormont in 1965 that he favoured better relations. The only sizeable group opposed to conciliation was to be found in the right wing of the Protestant community in Northern Ireland, where an eloquent agitator, Rev Ian Paisley, was gaining influence.

151
Ian Paisley
Radio Telefís Éireann, 1973

Thus the descent into turmoil was not inevitable. Despite the legacy of resentment and mistrust, the forces making for conciliation seemed as strong as those making for conflict, and even after the Troubles had begun, there was more than one point when it seemed possible that Northern Ireland might turn back towards peace. The story is best outlined in four periods: 1966–9, 1969–74, 1974–5, and 1975–82.

1966–9

A sign of the new mood of the Catholic community was the growth of the Northern Ireland Civil Rights Association, founded in 1967. This body, unlike previous organisations representing primarily the Catholic minority, did not challenge the existence of the Northern Ireland state but demanded merely the ending of abuses with it. From August 1968, marches and demonstrations in support of this objective were held in various towns. The police and the Protestant right wing, however, saw this development as a new attempt to undermine Northern Ireland – and as all the more dangerous because more insidious than an overt campaign against partition. Successive demonstrations were broken up by police and harassed by Protestant extremists. To describe the main confrontations – Derry (5 October 1968), Burntollet (4 January 1969), Derry and Belfast (12–15 August 1969) – would take up disproportionate space. Suffice it to say that by mid-August 1969 disorder had reached such a height that the police could no longer contain it, and the Northern Ireland government was obliged to request the British government to send in troops to restore order. The troops, whose arrival was taken in Catholic areas as a sign that the police had been defeated, were welcomed.

The Labour government then in office at Westminster had long been urging reform on the Northern Ireland government and had already obtained some concessions. It now insisted on the adoption of two packages of reforms (August and October 1969) which between them granted almost the whole of the Civil Rights Association's demands. The exclusively Protestant Special Constabulary was to be disbanded. Electoral boundaries were to be redrawn, housing administered by a non-partisan body, and safeguards introduced against discrimination in public employment. The reforms were bitterly resented on the Protestant right wing, and they aroused less gratitude among Catholics than they would have done if they had come a year earlier, before the disturbances. Nonetheless, they made an impact, and it seemed not impossible at the end of 1969 that Northern Ireland might find its way back to peace and stability.

152   James Chichester-Clark

Pacemaker Ltd, 1969

1969–74

The next eighteen months were touch and go. On the one hand, the forces making for confrontation were on the upsurge. The unionist right wing relentlessly criticised what it described as 'sell-out' by the Northern Ireland government, while at the other extreme the IRA prepared for a renewed campaign. But on the other hand, more moderate elements seemed to be in the ascendant in both Protestant and Catholic politics. The Northern Ireland government, under successive prime ministers (Captain O'Neill to April 1969, Major Chichester-Clark from April 1969 to March 1971, Brian Faulkner from March 1971), forged ahead with the reforms announced in 1969. On the Catholic side, a new party, the Social Democratic and Labour Party (SDLP), was founded in 1970, which, while its aims included a united Ireland by consent, put more stress on reform within Northern Ireland. If the reforms had been completed quickly, it might have been possible for the SDLP and the more moderate unionists to converge on some new consensus.

However, the reforms included a complicated restructuring of local government, which could not be completed until 1973. Meanwhile, the army, now strongly reinforced, had been involved in confrontations with Catholic rioters, and the initial goodwill earned by the troops in the Catholic areas of Belfast and Derry turned to hostility. Early in 1971, the IRA began its offensive. Soldiers and policemen were killed, and the number of bombings mounted month by month. The unionist government came under increasing pressure from Protestants for firm measures.

The obvious firm measure to take was internment – i.e. the holding without trial of suspected IRA members until the trouble was over. This had been successfully used in 1922, 1939 and 1956. In August 1971, Faulkner decided that the time had come to use it again. But the way it was employed on this occasion ensured that it would not achieve the same results as before. Firstly, the scale of the operation was unprecedented, with over 300 arrested (many of whom had to be quickly released when they were found to be innocent of IRA involvement). Secondly, internment was used exclusively against republicans, although extreme Protestants had done as much to provoke the crisis. Thirdly and most important, it soon became known that some of the internees had been grossly mistreated.

Internment, consequently, only increased the violence. Recruits flocked to the IRA. Many Catholics – not just republicans, but moderates like the supporters of the SDLP – went on rent and rate strike, or withdrew from public bodies. Demonstrations against internment were mounted. At one of these, in Derry on 30 January 1972, thirteen people were shot dead by the British army – the notorious 'Bloody Sunday'. This caused a wave of revulsion across nationalist Ireland, and the British embassy in Dublin was burnt down (2 February).

153
Brian Faulkner
Radio Telefís Éireann, 1969

However, the very seriousness of the situation increased the pressure for a settlement. At Westminster, where a Conservative government had been in power since June 1970, the unhappy consequences of Faulkner's policy were producing disenchantment with his regime. In March 1972 the British government suspended the Northern Ireland government and parliament, and introduced direct rule from Westminster. A new office in the British Cabinet was established, that of secretary of state for Northern Ireland, and a man with a gift for conciliation, William Whitelaw (later Lord Whitelaw), was appointed to it.

Direct rule did not produce any immediate improvement. Violence during the spring and summer of 1972 reached its highest level. The IRA, encouraged by success, redoubled its bombing campaign. Protestant private armies – the Ulster Defence Association and the Ulster Volunteer Force – emerged. Random murders of Catholics became frequent, in retaliation for murders by the IRA. A brief truce in June between the British army and the IRA collapsed in recrimination. However, the lowest point was reached when on 21 July 1972 ('Bloody Friday') the IRA overreached itself by letting off a chain of bombs in Belfast which killed 9 people and injured 130, and in the ensuing revulsion the army was able to re-establish itself in the Catholic areas of Belfast and Derry. After that, violence slowly declined.

Meanwhile, Whitelaw was coaxing the more moderate elements in both communities – Faulkner's unionists and the SDLP – towards agreement.

154 William Whitelaw

Pacemaker Ltd 1973

Unionists were mollified by repetitions of the guarantee that Northern Ireland would remain part of the United Kingdom as long as the majority of its inhabitants desired. The SDLP was promised a share in executive power, and the development of all-Ireland institutions. At an election for a new Northern Ireland Assembly, held in June 1973, Faulkner's unionists and the SDLP, with associated groups, gained a majority. In November 1973 they agreed, after tough bargaining, on the composition of a joint administration. In December 1973, in a conference at Sunningdale in Berkshire, the British and Irish governments, and members of the executive-designate, agreed to set up a Council of Ireland, with representatives from North and South to administer matters of common interest. On 1 January 1974 the new executive took office, with Faulkner at its head, and Gerry Fitt (later Lord Fitt), leader of the SDLP, as his deputy. Once again, it seemed as if Northern Ireland might be edging back from conflict towards consensus.

1974–5

It soon became clear, however, that support for the new executive was fragile. On the Catholic side, the IRA maintained its campaign in the weeks after the executive took office. On the Protestant side, Faulkner was repudiated by a majority of the unionist party and eventually set up a new party of his own. A general election for the Westminster parliament, held on 28 February 1974, produced victories for anti-Faulkner unionists in eleven out of twelve constituencies and indicated that three Protestant voters in four had voted for such candidates. Protestant opposition appeared to be directed not so much at power-sharing with the SDLP as at the proposed Council of Ireland, which was widely seen as a device to lure them towards a united Ireland.

155 Left to right: Oliver Napier, Liam Cosgrave, Edward Heath, Brian Faulkner and Gerry Fitt at the Sunningdale Conference

The Irish Times

On 14 May 1974, an organisation called the Ulster Workers Council announced a general strike against the Sunningdale agreement. Enjoying only limited support at first, it slowly gathered momentum until on 28 May Faulkner and his unionist colleagues on the executive decided that they no longer had sufficient support in the community to remain in office, and resigned. The executive forthwith collapsed. Opinions vary on how far its fall was inevitable. On the one hand, the strike could probably have been crushed if the police and army had moved against it decisively in the early stages. On the other hand, it seems likely that, even if the strike had been faced down, some other episode would have occurred that would have proved too much for the fragile unity of Protestant and Catholic.

The British government now tried another tack. Instead of pressurising Northern Ireland politicians into accepting a settlement, it left them to work one out for themselves. In May 1975 a convention of seventy-eight members was elected, in which politicians of all shades could seek to agree on the future government of Northern Ireland. Agreement in the convention seemed not impossible. By the end of August 1975, a unionist negotiating team led by William Craig – who had hitherto been seen as one of the most intransigent unionist politicians – was exploring with the SDLP the possibility of a compromise on 'voluntary coalition', which in effect meant that unionists would concede power-sharing for an experimental period, provided the SDLP put in abeyance their demand for a Council of Ireland.

1975–82

Once again, hopes of agreement were shattered. At the beginning of September 1975, Craig's proposed compromise with the SDLP was repudiated by his colleague, Rev Ian Paisley, and by the bulk of the unionists in the convention. A renewed outbreak by the IRA had something to do with the change, but the most important reason appears to have been a feeling among unionists that to concede even temporary power-sharing would be to yield too much to those whom they regarded as fundamentally opposed to the existence of the state. In the convention's report, completed in November 1975, the unionists insisted on the return of majority rule as it had existed before 1972, with only slightly more safeguards for minorities. The SDLP and moderate unionists refused to sign this report, which was forthwith rejected by the London government as failing to reflect an adequate measure of agreement between the communities.

From 1975, impasse reigned in Northern Ireland politics. At the end of 1975, internment, which had caused such bitterness when introduced in 1971, was brought to an end, but though violence declined in subsequent years, it did not cease. In 1976 the Peace People gave expression to the war-weariness of large sections of the population by organising giant demonstrations; but, though they gained massive short-term support, they were unable to articulate a programme, and faded into obscurity. In 1977, and again in 1979, British secretaries of state attempted to obtain agreement between the parties on a form of devolved government but were rebuffed with almost equal vehemence by the SDLP and the unionists. In 1981, ten republicans held in a Northern Ireland jail on terrorist offences died on hunger strike in pursuit of 'special status', the first and most notable being Bobby Sands. Though the British government faced down the strike, the courage shown by the strikers gained for the republican movement considerable sympathy, including electoral successes. In 1982 a new secretary of state, James Prior, made yet another attempt at securing agreement between the parties by his scheme of 'rolling devolution', and elections to a Northern Ireland Assembly were held in October. But the SDLP and republicans refused to take their seats, and Prior refused to devolve power to a unionist-dominated assembly.

156
James Prior
Pacemaker Ltd 1982

Stalemate seemed built into the situation. None of the parties was strong enough to impose its views; none was so weak that it felt impelled to alter them. The SDLP moved away from the search for a settlement within Northern Ireland and called for a united Ireland by consent, but it found no way of securing the consent which was so manifestly lacking. The IRA sought a united Ireland by coercion, but it was not powerful enough to make coercion effective and in attempting to do so only made unionists more intransigent. Most unionists sought to restore majority rule in Northern Ireland, but successive British governments rejected this demand because it would enable unionists once again to dominate the Catholic minority. Catholics felt no gratitude for this, because they felt that Britain could do much more to influence unionists towards accommodation.

Underneath the political stagnation of the late seventies and early eighties, however, important economic changes were taking place. This was not primarily a result of the violence, which reached its height in 1972, whereas the Northern Ireland economy continued to expand until 1973. From 1974 onwards, however, the economy was in decline. This was partly a result of the poor performance of the United Kingdom economy as a whole and partly because of a reduced readiness by the London government to direct aid towards the poorer regions of the United Kingdom. The violence also had an indirect effect, by discouraging investment. These factors combined to produce what has been described as the 'de-industrialisation' of Northern Ireland. During the period 1970–80, the share of the workforce employed in manufacturing fell from 32 to 23 per cent. Many of the largest factories in the region – especially in the man-made-fibre industry, which had once been so prosperous – shed workers or closed down altogether. Unemployment leapt to 20 per cent of insured workers in 1982. The picture would have been worse had not the service sector expanded as rapidly as manufacturing contracted: the proportion employed in services rose during the period 1970–80 from 41 to 54 per cent. Much of the increase was in the public sector, and was made possible only by subventions from the British exchequer. By the beginning of the eighties, for every three pounds of public money raised in Northern Ireland, five were spent there.

Accompanying these economic changes came an important social change: a slow alteration in the balance of the communities. A higher Catholic birth rate and reduced emigration meant that the Catholic proportion of the population was slowly rising, from 35 per cent in 1961 to somewhere approaching 40 per cent in 1981. Meanwhile, the de-industrialisation of Northern Ireland was hitting Protestants even harder than Catholics: the latter had always experienced a high unemployment rate, but now Protestant towns like Carrickfergus and Antrim had to face the closure of their largest employers. On the other hand, the growth of the service sector, with its multitude of white-collar jobs, gave opportunities to the increasing number of educated Catholics. Too much must not be read into these changes. In 1982 it remained true that the average Protestant was richer than the average Catholic. Nor did the economic and social changes of the previous few years have any visible impact on political attitudes. But they had long-term political implications: they made it harder for the kind of control that had existed before 1966 ever to be asserted again.

In the Republic, the period 1966–82 was on the whole one of rapidly increasing prosperity. True, there were sharp fluctuations. *The Second Programme for Economic Expansion* had to be abandoned before its completion date of 1970, and a more modest *Third Programme*, covering 1969–72, had to be abandoned also. The sharp slump of 1974–5, and the more long-lasting one which began in 1979, hit Ireland as much as the rest of the Western world. But the average rate of growth through the sixties and seventies was maintained at 4 per cent *per annum*.

There seem to have been two main reasons for this achievement. The first was the boost to agriculture given by entry into the European Community in January 1973. Irish farmers at once became eligible for the generous financial support available from the community, and their incomes rose dramatically, reaching a peak in 1978. The second was the performance of Irish industry. Down to the late fifties, Irish industry had consisted largely of small, often inefficient, units, producing mainly for a protected home market. The dismantling of tariff barriers made that kind of industry obsolete, and during the sixties and seventies the Industrial Development Authority made strenuous efforts to attract new firms, largely from abroad, which would have a good export market. The effort paid off, and Ireland became a centre for several industries with promising futures, such as electronics, chemicals and electrical goods. This development had the advantage of diversifying the Republic's export markets and making it less dependent on the British market, which was the most slowly growing of all developed countries.

With rapid economic change came rapid social change. The most striking development was demographic. After more than a century of decline, the population was rising again. From a low point of 2,818,000 at the census of 1961, it reached 3,440,000 at the census of 1981. Not only was the population larger, it was proportionately younger. In 1979 almost half of it was under twenty-five. While greater Dublin grew particularly fast, all parts of the country were affected: Leitrim was the only one of the twenty-six counties to experience a population decline in the decade 1971–81.

With social change came a change in values. The Republic in the mid-sixties seemed a country where traditional Catholic mores were still deeply entrenched. Books were banned for being indecent or obscene, the sale and import of contraceptives was illegal, divorce was unconstitutional, and abortion almost unheard-of. In subsequent years, this changed fast. The book censorship was eased as early as 1966, when thousands of titles were released from the list of banned books. The laws against contraceptives came under increasing attack, and in 1979 a measure was carried permitting their import and sale under certain restrictions. By the early eighties, pressure was beginning for a repeal of the constitutional ban on divorce. Abortion remained illegal, but thousands of Irish women went annually to England for abortions. The extent of marital breakdown was causing concern, and numbers of couples were living together without marrying. Homosexuals, who once did their best to avoid drawing public attention, formed a pressure group devoted to securing the repeal of their legal disabilities. To be sure, old customs did not collapse. The great majority of the population still went to church on Sundays, and the strength of long-established loyalties was shown by the enormous welcome given to Pope John Paul II when he visited Ireland in 1979. But the Irish value-system was becoming fragmented: part remaining traditionally Catholic, part influenced by ideas coming in from Britain, America and the Continent.

An active women's movement developed during the period. The difference it made to the economic position of women was limited. The Republic continued to have a lower proportion of working women than most countries in Europe, and much lower than Northern Ireland. But legal safeguards for women were improved. Legislation was passed to maintain equality of pay and of opportunity, and the tax structure was altered so as to treat working wives more generously.

Discussion of such issues was facilitated by developments in the mass media. Irish television had begun as recently as the end of 1961 but soon showed a willingness to tackle controversial questions. Irish newspapers became increasingly ready to publish investigative journalism, and Irish publishers offered a market for the findings of the first generation of Irish social scientists.

One area of particularly important change was education. The author of the preceding chapter in this volume, Professor Patrick Lynch, had an important part to play in this. He headed a research team whose report, published in 1966 under the title *Investment in Education*, unsentimentally analysed the deficiencies of the primary and second-level systems. A year later, the report of the Commission on Higher Education (1960–67) provided a matching survey of third-level problems. Spurred on by these and other influences, a succession of energetic ministers and civil servants pressed through a series of changes. New curricula were introduced at primary and post-primary level. Many small schools were replaced by larger and better-equipped units. The most sweeping changes took place at post-primary level, where existing schools were enlarged or amalgamated, new types of school introduced and, from 1967, education provided free for the vast majority of pupils. The free-education scheme proved popular beyond all expectation, and the number of pupils in post-primary schools shot up from 143,000 in 1965–6 to 301,000 in 1980–81. In higher education some of the central recommendations of the 1960–67 commission were put into effect, most notably by the setting up in 1968 of a permanent Higher Education Authority to advise the minister for education on the allocation of funds and generally to further the development of higher education. The universities were expanded, and supplemented by new institutions that emphasised vocational and technological subjects – national institutes for higher education and regional technical colleges. The Catholic hierarchy contributed to the new thinking on higher education – in 1970 it removed its long-standing 'ban' on the attendance of Catholics at Trinity College, and Trinity became an integral part of the national system of higher education.

Not all the changes in these sixteen years were favourable. Inflation remained at worrying levels. Though most people benefited from growing prosperity, there was an intractable pool of poverty, comprising 20 per cent or more of the population: some observers felt that the affluent majority were growing more callous towards their poorer neighbours. Crime increased sharply in Dublin, as did pollution in the countryside. There were complaints, in Dublin particularly, of poor postal, bus and telephone services, and of endless congestion. A worrying problem was the remorseless rise in population, which meant that more young people were entering the labour market than there were jobs to satisfy, so that unemployment remained high. For good or ill, however, there was no question that Ireland was being transformed, both economically and socially.

Politically, the pace of change was less breakneck than in society as a whole, but even there it was considerable. The sixteen years 1966–82 saw five taoisigh (prime ministers) and five changes in the party or parties in power, as against three taoisigh and three changes of party in the preceding sixteen years. The same three parties – Fianna Fáil, Fine Gael and Labour – dominated the scene, but they became more professional, better funded and more equipped to meet the era of television.

157
Jack Lynch
Radio Telefís Éireann, 1972

The period opened with Seán Lemass securely in office, having gained an overall majority in the general election of 1965. Suddenly, in November 1966, he announced his retirement, and a struggle for the leadership of Fianna Fáil ensued. The initial front-runners were two energetic young ministers, Charles Haughey and George Colley, but ultimately the party agreed on a somewhat older man, Jack Lynch, as a compromise candidate. Lynch, who owed his entry into politics to his prowess in Gaelic athletics, seemed at first a rather indecisive figure. Time was to show that he possessed more steel than appeared at first sight.

In October 1968, the Fianna Fáil government was defeated by almost 60 per cent to 40 per cent when it put to the electorate in a referendum a proposal to abolish proportional representation. It was widely expected that this heralded an electoral defeat, but when the next general election came, in June 1969, it produced a net gain of two seats for Fianna Fáil. Lynch's

158
Charles Haughey
Radio Telefís Éireann, 1973

position within the party was strengthened, which proved important when a few months later what became known as the 'arms crisis' burst upon it. In April 1970 customs officers at Dublin airport seized a consignment of arms which had been secretly imported from the Continent for use by republicans in the North. In May, Lynch dismissed two ministers, Charles Haughey and Neil Blaney, whom he believed to be implicated, and a third minister, Kevin Boland, resigned in protest against the taoiseach's action. Blaney and Haughey were arrested on charges of illegally importing arms; Blaney was discharged and Haughey acquitted. But Lynch weathered the storm. While Blaney and Boland left Fianna Fáil, only a handful of deputies followed them. Haughey remained in the party, although he was not restored to the front bench until 1975.

In February 1973, Lynch called a general election, which resulted in a defeat as unexpected as his victory in 1969 had been. Fianna Fáil actually gained votes in the election, but lost six seats, thus allowing a coalition of Fine Gael and Labour to take office. The crucial reason for the change was that Fine Gael and Labour made a pact before the election, and supporters of each party followed instructions to cast lower preferences in favour of the other. The new government was headed by Liam Cosgrave, son of the prime minister of 1922–32, as taoiseach.

The new government had to deal with the economic crisis of 1974–5 and with the intractable situation in Northern Ireland. Nonetheless, by-elections showed that the government was maintaining its support, and redrawing of constituency boundaries was generally expected to favour it when the next general election came. The election was held in June 1977. For the third time running, the electorate confounded the pundits. It returned Fianna Fáil with the largest majority ever obtained in an Irish general election – eighty-four seats, as against sixty-four for all others. An important factor was Fianna Fáil's election package, containing among other things a promise to abolish rates on private dwellings and road tax on smaller vehicles.

159
Liam Cosgrave
Radio Telefís Éireann, 1973

Following the election, Lynch once again became taoiseach. But his term was not an easy one. Some backbenchers disliked his relatively conciliatory attitude to the unionists and the British over Northern Ireland. In 1979 he had to face the revival of economic difficulties. Finally, in December of that year he unexpectedly resigned. A contest for the leadership ensued, with the same principal contenders as in 1966 – Charles Haughey and George Colley. This time no compromise figure emerged, and Haughey was elected by 44 votes to 38. He forthwith became taoiseach, but he had to contend with continued opposition to his leadership from within his party.

Haughey declared that he intended to make the solution of the Northern Ireland problem the main object of his premiership. But economic troubles and intra-party divisions kept breaking in. In June 1981 he called a general election, in the hope of strengthening his position. It had the opposite effect. No party was returned with a clear majority; independents and representatives of minor parties held the balance of power. A coalition of Fine Gael and Labour, this time under the leadership of Dr Garret FitzGerald, who had succeeded Cosgrave as leader of Fine Gael in 1977, took office.

160
Garret FitzGerald
Radio Telefís Éireann, 1978

FitzGerald saw the main problem facing his government as the economic crisis. Haughey, hoping that the depression which had set in in 1979 would be short, had maintained levels of public expenditure by borrowing the necessary funds, much of them from abroad. But the depression continued, and the country's external indebtedness increased by leaps and bounds. By the end of 1981 the total public-sector foreign debt reached £4.8 billion, or almost half the gross national product. In January 1982, in an attempt to reduce this enormous load, the government introduced a spectacularly severe budget. Its provisions went too far for one crucial independent deputy, and the government was defeated by a single vote.

A general election was held the following month (18 February 1982). Once again the results were indecisive, with independents and minor parties holding the balance of power. But Haughey was more successful than FitzGerald in winning them over, and he returned to office. His hold on power, however, proved precarious. Divisions within Fianna Fáil continued. A series of bizarre scandals touched several people close to Haughey. The recession bit deeper. Government revenue declined, the foreign debt rose even higher, and the government had to increase taxes yet further. In November a pivotal group (the Workers' Party, with three deputies) voted against Haughey on a motion of confidence, and he was obliged to resign. A general election followed – the third in eighteen months. It at last produced a clear result: Fine Gael and Labour between them had a clear majority over all other parties and groups. They negotiated a coalition and took office, with FitzGerald again as taoiseach.

So far in this chapter I have written about Northern Ireland and the Republic as if they had two distinct histories. This largely corresponds with the realities. However, there were some ways in which they shared a common experience, and I shall close by drawing attention to these aspects.

The most obvious of these was that, on 1 January 1973, both became part of the European Community: the Republic as a member state, Northern Ireland as part of the United Kingdom. The change did less to bring the two parts of Ireland together than some had expected. The increased support for agriculture available in the Community made much more difference to the Republic than to the North – partly because Northern Ireland agriculture had already been well subsidised under British rule, partly because the 'green pound' (the level at which agricultural subsidies were paid) was fixed by the respective national governments at a more favourable rate for farmers in the Republic than in the United Kingdom. Furthermore, when, in March 1979, the Community established a European Monetary System, the Republic joined it while the United Kingdom did not. This meant that the Republic's currency, instead of being tied to sterling as it had been since independence, was now linked to the currencies of Continental Europe. It soon fell in value as compared with British currency, the lowest point being reached in February 1981, when the Irish pound was worth only 73.38 pence sterling. This divergence benefited exporters from the Republic. But it meant that, for the first time, people crossing the border had to go to the trouble of changing their money into a different currency. In the short run, the Common Market had led to a more complete economic division of Ireland than had existed before.

However, in other respects the European Community brought some shared experiences. In June 1979 elections took place all over the Community for the European parliament, and the two parts of Ireland found themselves, for the first time since 1918, voting in the same election. Thereafter, members from the two parts of Ireland sat in the same parliament and found that, on non-political issues, unionist and nationalist did not inevitably vote in different lobbies.

A non-political force which affected both parts of Ireland was the ecumenical movement. Starting from small beginnings in the sixties, it became a substantial feature of Irish life in the seventies. Ecumenical conferences were held from 1964, and the Irish School of Ecumenics was founded in 1970. From 1968, the heads of the four main churches (Catholic, Church of Ireland, Presbyterian and Methodist) were meeting regularly, and on occasions issued joint statements. True, cordiality was less than complete. Catholic regulations on the upbringing of children in mixed marriages continued to give offence to Protestants. On the other side, two presbyterian moderators refused even to meet the Catholic primate. But on the whole, church leaders and theologians were speaking to each other more freely and frankly than ever before.

Another possible link between the two parts of Ireland opened up when, in

December 1980, the then taoiseach, Charles Haughey, secured from the British prime minister, Margaret Thatcher, an agreement that their respective civil servants should examine the 'totality of relationships' between the two islands. The strategy appeared to be that the British government might be induced to encourage closer relations between the two parts of Ireland, in return for the Republic's accepting some common institutions with the United Kingdom. An Anglo-Irish governmental council was set up in November 1981, with the prospect of an Anglo-Irish parliamentary council at some future date.

The rapprochement then came to an abrupt halt. There were a variety of reasons for this, of which the most important was the displeasure felt in

161   Haughey–Thatcher Meeting, 8 December 1980

Colman Doyle

Britain at the Irish government's refusal to support it in its dispute with Argentina over the Falkland Islands, which erupted in April 1982. But though no further progress was made, the agreements already reached were not repudiated. It remains to be seen whether the accords of 1980–81 were a dead end, or whether they were the beginnings of a framework in which a solution to Anglo-Irish problems could be found.

One thing remains clear: the period of 1966–82 was one of more rapid change than any preceding period of comparable length in Irish history.

23

IRELAND: 1982–94
RICHARD ENGLISH

In July 1982 UK Prime Minister Margaret Thatcher argued that 'no commitment exists for Her Majesty's Government to consult the Irish government on matters affecting Northern Ireland'. Yet the years under scrutiny in this chapter witnessed the development of formal structures by means of which such consultation became a significant part of Northern Irish political life. In elections for the new Northern Ireland Assembly, held in October 1982, Sinn Féin won 10.1 per cent of first-preference votes, while the Social Democratic and Labour Party (SDLP) gained 18.8 per cent. There was alarm in certain circles at the possibility that the IRA's political alter ego might come to displace the SDLP as the party representing the majority of Northern Irish nationalists – a prospect unacceptable both to Dublin and to London. Concern grew when Sinn Féin's Gerry Adams was elected as MP for West Belfast in the June 1983 UK general election, with his party winning 13.4 per cent of votes cast and the SDLP winning 17.9 per cent. In fact, there was little likelihood of Sinn Féin overtaking the SDLP among Northern nationalists, but there is no doubt that political developments were influenced by the perception that republicans were gaining ground in Northern Ireland.

The Irish government's establishment of a forum for debate among Ireland's constitutional parties provided the basis for a telling set of exchanges in relation to Northern Ireland. The New Ireland Forum, which first met in May 1983, comprised representatives from the main constitutional nationalist parties: Northern Ireland's SDLP and the Republic's Fianna Fáil, Fine Gael and Labour. Having received a large number of submissions, the Forum offered a final report which examined three options for Northern Ireland: that it become part of a unitary Irish state, part of a federal/confederal state, or be governed under a system of joint authority between Dublin and London. The last of these – according, at least, to the report – would involve giving 'equal validity to the two traditions in Northern Ireland'. This notion of equal validity was to become the leitmotif of much policy – Irish as well as British – in relation to the Northern Irish crisis during our period. Although British reactions to the Forum Report disappointed its architects, British governmental attitudes were shifting significantly in the direction of constitutional nationalist thinking. In November 1984 a joint communiqué, issued after a summit meeting between Margaret Thatcher and Irish Taoiseach

Garret FitzGerald, stated that 'the identities of both the majority and the minority communities in Northern Ireland should be recognised and respected and reflected in the structures and processes of Northern Ireland in ways acceptable to both communities'. Soon after this summit, there began the serious drafting of what was to become the 1985 Anglo-Irish Agreement. The Agreement, signed on 15 November, symbolised an attempt at a newly cooperative British–Irish approach to Northern Ireland. Endorsed (emphatically) by the House of Commons and (more narrowly) by the Dáil, the accord saw both governments 'affirm that any change in the status of Northern Ireland would only come about with the consent of a majority of the people of Northern Ireland', 'recognise that the present wish of a majority of the people of Northern Ireland is for no change in the status of Northern Ireland' and 'declare that if, in the future, a majority of the people of Northern Ireland clearly wish for and formally consent to the establishment of a united Ireland, they will introduce and support in the respective parliaments legislation to give effect to that wish'. Having sought to reassure unionists that Northern Ireland's place within the UK was secure as long as a majority there wanted it to remain so, the Agreement established a British–Irish Intergovernmental Conference which was to meet regularly and which would offer a framework within which matters relating to Northern Ireland could be discussed. This innovative development marked a dramatic change in the governance of the region; the permanent secretariat of civil servants (Northern and Southern) which underpinned the Conference served to emphasise the seriousness of the consultative role newly allotted to the Republic.

Both governments committed themselves, in the Agreement, to supporting the devolution of powers within Northern Ireland 'on a basis which would secure widespread acceptance throughout the community'. Indeed, the document stated that the Conference would 'concern itself with measures to recognise and accommodate the rights and identities of the two traditions in Northern Ireland', and the thinking behind the whole initiative relied on what might be termed a symmetrical approach. The two sides in Northern Ireland were to be accorded equal respect, validity and legitimacy, in the hope that it would be possible simultaneously to reassure unionists and mollify nationalists. Both Thatcher and FitzGerald – co-signatories to the document – have subsequently expressed disappointment with its impact, and it is important to note two particularly crucial points. First, the accord was implemented without the consent of the majority community in the region to which it referred. Unionist hostility to the Agreement was widespread and often fierce; moreover, while much of the heat has gone out of unionist hostility to the initiative, the Agreement is still perceived by many to be a step in a distinctly unwelcome direction. Thus, in February 1994, Democratic Unionist Party (DUP) leader Ian Paisley described the 1985 Agreement as a condominium 'in embryo', one that would eventually grow into a (dreaded) united Ireland. Second, those nationalists – such as Garret FitzGerald – who have argued for the achievement of Irish unity with unionist consent have failed to demonstrate either, first, signs that such consent is beginning to emerge or, second, an effective explanation of how or why it should do so. The Agreement's suggestion that a united Ireland would be forthcoming if unionist consent were to develop looks rather feeble when set against the fact that no such consent can reasonably be expected to emerge. But British and Irish policy toward the Northern crisis was founded on the belief that a symmetrical approach was indeed viable. Attempts to reassure unionists coexisted with claims that nationalist stock was rising. At the time of the Agreement, for example, Garret FitzGerald argued that 'Nationalists can now raise their heads knowing their position is, and is seen to be, on an equal footing with that of members of the unionist community.'

Those who wished to see the SDLP gaining strength at Sinn Féin's expense were encouraged by the results of the 1987 UK general election. The SDLP's share of the vote rose by 3.2 per cent, while Sinn Féin's share fell by 2 per cent. It is debatable how far this resulted directly from the Anglo-Irish Agreement, but it is clear that numerous difficulties were experienced by the republican movement during 1987. Sinn Féin's electoral disappointment was complemented by setbacks involving the Irish Republican Army (IRA). In May 1987 eight IRA men were killed during an attack on Loughgall Royal Ulster Constabulary (RUC) Station in County Armagh. In November of the same year an IRA bomb killed eleven people at a Remembrance Day ceremony in Enniskillen, County Fermanagh, and the IRA was drenched in a wave of popular and international revulsion. In March 1988 three IRA members on a mission in Gibraltar were killed by British soldiers in an episode which generated lasting controversy. The three were unarmed, and much debate ensued concerning the circumstances of their shooting.

While such incidents have a capacity to attract and sustain considerable attention, more significant developments were also under way. The 1989 Northern Ireland Fair Employment Act aimed both to protect individuals from discrimination and to address the problem of unequal employment opportunities in the region. The persistence of significantly different Catholic and Protestant rates of unemployment in Northern Ireland was considered a major political issue. In part this was because vociferous campaigners – particularly in the United States – had managed to build up considerable momentum in their agitation on the subject of Catholic disadvantage. Moreover, some observers held that religious disadvantage and/or discrimination lay at the root of Northern Ireland's political conflict. While the other grievances of the 1960s civil-rights movement had largely been met by the early 1970s, different employment levels – it was argued – remained a source of considerable tension between the two communities. The new legislation replaced the existing Fair Employment Agency with a (tougher) Fair Employment Commission, and it also made compulsory the monitoring of the composition of the workforce, in terms of perceived religion, in all but the smallest firms. The intention was both to identify areas of disadvantage and to implement action aimed at rectifying it.

Whatever the merits of such intention, the implementation of the project faced significant obstacles. Employment had become a politically charged topic in Northern Ireland, and the very qualities of consensus and equanimity required for the effective pursuit of the proposed project were precisely those whose absence had rendered the scheme urgent in the first place. Thus the government found itself criticised, on the one hand, for acting with insufficient resolution in redressing the imbalances in employment opportunity and, on the other, for exaggerating the importance of discrimination in producing Catholic disadvantage. Certainly, disadvantage and discrimination should not be blurred together, and both the question of economic location and that of the perilous state of the Northern Ireland economy as a whole presented severe problems for those endeavouring to rectify unequal job opportunities. Moreover, while some have argued that employment disadvantage helps to sustain the political conflict, it is also true that the political conflict renders more difficult the task of those trying to eradicate inequality in employment. In this sense, Northern Irish religious disadvantage in employment differs from some other forms of structural disadvantage. Racial or sexual imbalances in Britain, for example, are not complicated by the questions of political violence or state legitimacy relevant to Catholic–Protestant relations in Northern Ireland. Issues such as security-force membership or safety at work have proved particularly awkward in the Northern Irish context.

The May 1989 district council elections witnessed slight gains for the Ulster Unionist Party (UUP) and the SDLP, and setbacks for the DUP and Sinn Féin. Later in the year, Northern Ireland Secretary of State Peter Brooke suggested that the UK government would respond flexibly if the IRA abandoned violence and that the government might talk to Sinn Féin under such circumstances. In November 1990 Brooke declared that Britain had no 'strategic or economic interest' in Northern Ireland, and restated the government's preparedness to accept Irish unification in the (unlikely) event that consent to such a development should emerge. Earlier in 1990 Brooke had asserted that, in his view, enough common ground existed to make inter-party talks between the constitutional Northern Irish parties worthwhile. In what became known as the Brooke initiative, the Secretary of State aimed to build inter-party consensus in order that the 1985 Anglo-Irish Agreement could be transcended by arrangements which would be more broadly acceptable and (therefore) fruitful.

The process was to be three-stranded: strand one would involve the four Northern Ireland constitutional parties (UUP, SDLP, DUP, Alliance Party); strand two was to involve talks between Dublin and the Northern Irish parties; strand three was to address relations between Dublin and London. Predictably, there were numerous difficulties in implementing this schedule. There were, for example, problems concerning the venue for strand two, and concerning the question of who would chair this second strand of talks. Despite such obstacles, Peter Brooke claimed that the initial talks had indeed provided a useful foundation for further progress, and Patrick Mayhew (who became secretary of state for Northern Ireland in April 1992) continued the talks initiative.

Beginning formally on 29 April 1992, the Mayhew talks sequence moved swiftly, but the enormous differences which separated the various participants were made painfully apparent. There was, for example, a negative response from the other parties to the SDLP's proposal that Northern Ireland be governed by a six-person Commission (to comprise three people elected from Northern Ireland and three nominated, respectively, by the London government, the Dublin government and the European Community). Indeed, the talks became increasingly difficult as they grew more specific, and despite Patrick Mayhew's cautiously expressed optimism it appeared that the talks process had revealed the width of the gap separating the unionist and nationalist outlooks. The tension, during the talks, surrounding the Republic of Ireland's constitutional claim to the six counties of Northern Ireland reflected the basic divergence of opinion between unionists and nationalists over the legitimacy of partition. Again, while the UUP had conceded the principle that both power-sharing and some form of Irish dimension had a place in the government of Northern Ireland, the SDLP's more ambitious nationalist agenda meant that it was not possible to establish a deal on the basis of devolution plus a Dublin connection.

The April 1992 UK general election saw the SDLP vote increase and that of Sinn Féin decline. Sinn Féin's Gerry Adams lost his West Belfast seat to the SDLP's Joe Hendron – a significant and symbolic setback for the republican party – but the explosion of two bombs in the centre of London on 10 April signalled the continuing capacity of the IRA to pursue republican goals determinedly by brutal means. Loyalist violence, too, occasioned understandable concern. In 1992 republicans killed thirty-six people while loyalists killed thirty-nine, and the increasing levels of loyalist activity were complemented by friction between loyalists and the RUC. In the wake of the 1985 Anglo-Irish Agreement, there had developed considerable tension between loyalists and the police, the former perceiving the latter to be implementing Dublin-tainted rule. In the early 1990s such friction became, on occasions, more pronounced. In August 1992 the loyalist Ulster Defence Association (UDA) was banned by the government.

162
Gerry Adams
Sinn Féin

In the wake of the UDA proscription, some people wondered whether Sinn Féin should also have been outlawed. The republican party's relationship with the IRA made some observers feel that it too should be proscribed if moves were being taken against those involved with or supportive of terrorism. But the UK government's approach toward Sinn Féin at this time was one of attempting to coax it into the constitutional arena. If anything, the government was speaking in conciliatory rather than coercive tones when it addressed the republican movement. In a speech delivered in Coleraine in December 1992, for example, Patrick Mayhew asserted that

> There are leading Sinn Féin speakers who voice their wish for a peaceful solution and their desire to follow a constitutional path. Provided it is advocated constitutionally, there can be no proper reason for excluding any political objective from discussion. Certainly not the objective of an Ireland united through broad agreement fairly and freely achieved . . . In the event of a genuine and established cessation of violence, the whole range of responses that we have had to make to that violence could, and would, inevitably be looked at afresh.

163
John Hume
Cork Examiner

This message – that if republicans abandoned violence then the government would respond positively – formed the foundation of much British policy in this period. For his part, SDLP leader John Hume was also endeavouring to bring an end to republican violence and to bring Sinn Féin into constitutional politics. Having met and had discussions together, Hume and Sinn Féin President Gerry Adams issued, in April 1993, a joint statement in which they declared their acceptance 'that the Irish people as a whole have a right to national self-determination' and their view that the exercise of this right was 'a matter for agreement between the people of Ireland'.

When the UK Prime Minister (John Major) and the Republic of Ireland Taoiseach (Albert Reynolds) issued a Joint Declaration in December 1993, Hume considered that the conditions supposedly justifying republican violence had been rendered irrelevant. The Declaration, he argued, went through the reason traditionally offered by the IRA in an attempt to justify their violent campaign: 'It makes very clear that the British government has no selfish or strategic interest or economic interest in Ireland . . . And the second major reason given for the use of physical force is that (the British) are preventing the people of Ireland from exercising the right to self-determination and the Declaration is very clear on that.' Indeed, the December 1993 Joint Declaration did see the UK government agreeing 'that it is for the people of Ireland alone, by agreement between the two parts respectively, to exercise their right of self-determination on the basis of consent, freely and concurrently given, North and South, to bring about a united Ireland, if that is their wish.' While republicans might resent the document's acceptance of Northern Ireland's right to block such a development, there is no doubt that the Declaration did mark a significant concession to the language and framework of Irish nationalist argument.

The two governments' attempt to reconcile the competing aspirations of Ulster unionists and Irish nationalists, however, ran up against the same problem – that of starkly divergent assumptions – which had plagued the inter-party talks process. It remained difficult, for example, to see how one could reconcile unionist attachment to the UK with the statement of an IRA representative, published in the latter part of 1993, that 'The obstacle to peace in Ireland is the British presence and the partition of Ireland.' But the UK government's approach during the years covered in this chapter was one of trying simultaneously to reassure unionists and give concessions to nationalists. The 1985 Anglo-Irish Agreement and the 1993 Joint Declaration each, in their own way, reflected this policy. In November 1993 Secretary of State Mayhew set out the government's attitude in relation to Northern Ireland when he stated that

> The division which exists within the community – together with grievances which exist . . . in the social, the economic and constitutional fields – has led to inter-communal violence and terrorism, and it is the elimination of terrorism, from whatever quarter, that is the government's overriding objective. But the government believes that the underlying causes have to be addressed at the same time.

164   John Major
Cork Examiner

165   Albert Reynolds
Cork Examiner

In recent years the government's way of addressing the underlying causes of conflict has revolved around the notion of affording equal respect, legitimacy and validity to the two main traditions in the region: Protestant/unionist on the one hand, Catholic/nationalist on the other. In his Coleraine speech of December 1992, Patrick Mayhew declared: 'We are committed . . . to honouring our commitment to the wishes of a majority in Northern Ireland . . . The reality is that the identity of unionists is safeguarded in fact, and also in national and international law; it is also recognised as wholly legitimate by constitutional nationalists. But there is also the aspiration to a united Ireland, an aspiration that is no less legitimate.' This symmetrical approach to respective unionist and nationalist aspirations underpins recent UK government policy in Northern Ireland. In his preface to the 1993 Joint Declaration, Mayhew asserted that the document set out 'constitutional principles and political realities which safeguard the vital interests of both sides of the community in Northern Ireland'. In the declaration itself, the UK government stressed the need for 'full respect for the rights and identities of both traditions in Ireland'.

When considering the various responses to the Northern Ireland conflict – governmental and non-governmental – it is important to reflect on two central realities, and it might be appropriate to end the first section of this chapter with a brief mention of each. First, scholars have firmly established the regionally varied nature of political experience in Northern Ireland. As Professor John Whyte pointed out, 'Areas only a few miles from each other can differ enormously – in religious mix, in economic circumstances, in the level of violence, in political attitudes. This means that the nature and intensity of the conflict can vary widely.' This in turn underlines the basic reality of Northern Ireland's politics, namely that any single political arrangement is likely to leave a significant section of the population disaffected. Second, any discussion of Northern Ireland which fails to acknowledge certain economic realities will be bound to hinder, rather than advance, progress in the region. Northern Ireland exists on the periphery of a state whose post-war economic performance has been far from impressive. High levels of unemployment form a persistent part of the area's life and have contributed significantly to the pattern of recent political conflict. Moreover, the feebleness of Northern Ireland's economy must be taken fully into account when discussing possible political rearrangements or solutions. The British subvention to Northern Ireland, for example, is so large that it could not possibly be sustained by the Republic of Ireland. Economic arguments in favour of the continued union of Great Britain and Northern Ireland may not be the most emotionally charged defences of the unionist position, but they are certainly among the most persuasive.

As noted, the New Ireland Forum of 1983–4 examined three options for the future of Northern Ireland: that it become part of a unitary Irish state, part of a federal/confederal state, or be governed under a system of joint (Dublin–London) authority. The Fianna Fáil delegation to the Forum preferred the first of these options, and indeed the party's leader (Charles Haughey) argued that 'The only solution is as stated in the report: a unitary state with a new constitution.' This more nationalistic public stance was typical of Haughey's style of rhetoric and gesture. Leader of Fianna Fáil from 1979 to 1992, Haughey's career contained both rhetorical flourishes and pragmatic compromises in relation to the North. Indeed, the recent attitudes of the Republic's political parties towards the Northern Irish conflict have reflected considerable ambiguities. The central ambiguity is rooted in the double message of the state's 1937 constitution:

> Article 2: The national territory consists of the whole island of Ireland, its islands, and the territorial seas.
>
> Article 3: Pending the reintegration of the national territory and without prejudice to the right of parliament and government established by this constitution to exercise jurisdiction over the whole of that territory, the laws enacted by that parliament shall have the like area and extent of application as the laws of Saorstát Éireann and the like extra-territorial effect.

Similarly, political parties in the period under scrutiny in this chapter have tended to endorse the principle that (ideally) a united Ireland would be desirable, while simultaneously recognising that it is not practical in the foreseeable future to try to achieve such an arrangement. In this, the parties have echoed popular opinion. Thus, for example, when asked what were the main issues with which the parties should be concerned during the 1987 Republic of Ireland general election, only 3 per cent of respondents suggested that Northern Ireland should represent one of these issues. When asked in 1989 about the importance of a listed series of issues during the general election campaign of that year, 29 per cent of respondents said that Northern Ireland was very important. But this should be set against the fact that, when asked (unprompted) to list the main issues about which the electioneering parties should be concerned, Northern Ireland did not even feature as one of these issues. Thus the desire for a united Ireland is very much a low-level priority among the Republic's electorate.

The sequence of governments in the Republic during the 1980s saw Garret FitzGerald lead a Fine Gael–Labour coalition (1981–2), Charles Haughey head a Fianna Fáil administration (1982), FitzGerald return to power with a Fine Gael–Labour government (1982–7), and then Haughey lead first a Fianna Fáil team (1987–9) and then a coalition with the Progressive Democrats (1989–92). In 1981 Garret FitzGerald outlined his aim of rendering the Republic of Ireland more attractive to Northern Protestants. In what became known as his constitutional crusade, the Fine Gael leader set out to rid the state's constitution of features that might be unattractive to Ulster

Protestants. But the first of the major constitutional battles to be fought out via referendum during the 1980s did not fit into this pattern. FitzGerald himself has publicly referred not only to his own 'personal antipathy to abortion' but also to 'the opposition of the vast majority of people in Ireland, North and South, Catholic and Protestant, to abortion'. The 1981–3 campaign to insert a constitutional prohibition on abortion aimed to provide constitutional backing to the existing, restrictive abortion legislation. The Pro-Life Amendment Campaign (PLAC) argued the case for such a constitutional amendment on the grounds that it was necessary in order to prevent the future legalisation of abortion. In contrast, the Anti-Amendment Campaign (AAC) contested the issue, although the AAC was more loosely organised than PLAC. In September 1983 the referendum saw 67 per cent of those voting support the amendment (prohibiting the legalisation of abortion) and 33 per cent oppose it. The turnout was low, at 54 per cent.

More relevant to FitzGerald's liberalising crusade was the 1986 campaign to remove the constitutional ban on divorce. FitzGerald himself intended both that the proposed change would help North–South relations by rendering the Republic more pluralistic, and also that the citizens of the Republic themselves would benefit from the alteration. In April 1986 FitzGerald announced that the government would, the following month, introduce the wording of the Divorce Amendment Bill, and that in June a referendum on the issue would be held. At the end of April 1986 the Anti-Divorce Campaign (ADC) was launched. In contrast to the relative feebleness of the pro-divorce campaign, the ADC's approach was characterised by a well-coordinated efficiency. Locally, as well as nationally, the anti-divorce case was shrewdly put across, while a mixture of Catholic pulpit pressure and popular alarm about the (supposedly) possible effects which the introduction of divorce would have on property rights helped to push enough voters towards the anti-divorce stance. With a 60.5 per cent turnout, the June 1986 referendum saw 36.5 per cent vote in favour of the amendment, permitting the legalisation of divorce, and 63.5 per cent vote against.

The pattern which emerged from these two referendums is extremely complicated. Regional variation needs to be taken into account. For example, the five constituencies which produced a 'no' vote in the abortion referendum, and the six constituencies which produced a 'yes' vote in the divorce referendum, were all in Dublin. Again, the role of the Catholic Church raised intriguing political and historical questions. Catholic Church support for the anti-abortion amendment, and hostility to divorce, played a significant part in the two campaigns. Moreover, this raised the issue of the relationship between, on the one hand, the Republic's political and social ethos and, on the other, the expressed desire of the state's Irish nationalists for Irish unification. As noted, pro-abortion sentiment was hardly a central component of Ulster unionist politics but the divorce question was, perhaps, more relevant. After the rejection of the amendment permitting the legalisation of divorce, Garret FitzGerald observed that this result was 'something of a setback to the long-term prospect of the two parts of Ireland coming closer together politically'. Indeed, while it is hardly surprising that the ethos of so overwhelmingly Catholic a state should – to a significant degree – reflect Catholic thinking, the implications of this for irredentist nationalism were hardly encouraging. Professor Whyte shrewdly observed that, while Northern Protestants might agree with the Catholic bishops' argument that it is only natural for a majority ethos to prevail, such Protestants 'might conclude that, in that case, they would prefer to remain in their own state with its Protestant majority than join a state which would have a Catholic majority'. Attitudes on social issues in the Republic have, during the period under scrutiny in this chapter, been both complex and changing. The campaigns surrounding abortion and divorce have to be set against the increasing liberalisation, in recent years, of legislation relating to the availability of contraceptives. Moreover, in 1992 further referenda saw the electorate vote in favour of the right to travel outside the state for an abortion and of the right to information concerning the availability of abortion in other states. Again there was regional variation, with the vote against the right to travel and the right to information being highest in rural constituencies.

The general election of February 1987 resulted in Charles Haughey forming a minority Fianna Fáil government. The party increased its number of Dáil seats from seventy-five to eighty-one, while Fine Gael's share of seats fell from seventy to fifty-one. The Labour Party's share of first-preference votes fell from 9.4 per cent to 6.4 per cent, while its share of seats dropped from sixteen to twelve. A significant development was the emergence as an electoral force of the Progressive Democrats (PDs). Founded in 1985 by ex-Fianna Fáil Cabinet minister Desmond O'Malley – who had had a long-running feud with Charles Haughey – the PDs advocated the rationalisation and reform of the state apparatus, together with the limiting of the economic role of the state. In the 1987 election they secured 11.9 per cent of first-preference votes and obtained fourteen seats in the Dáil. A much less impressive debut was made by Sinn Féin, whose 1986 decision to break with abstentionism meant that they contested the February 1987 election with the intention of taking any Dáil seats which they might win. The party's performance, however, was dismal. Having put up twenty-seven candidates and fought vigorously during the campaign, Sinn Féin managed to secure only 1.9 per cent of first preference votes and failed to win a single seat.

It is important to note certain key points about the party-political system in the Republic during these years. The first concerns the position of (and relations between) Fianna Fáil's political rivals. From 1973 onwards, Fine Gael–Labour governments alternated with Fianna Fáil administrations: 1973–7, 1981–2, 1982–7, Fine Gael–Labour; 1977–81, 1982, 1987–9, Fianna Fáil. By 1987, however, divisions had deepened between Fine Gael and Labour. The former had shifted in the direction of fiscal rectitude, while the latter had seen its support suffer as a result of coalition. Moreover, the appearance of the PDs, together with the small but significant challenge posed on the left by the Workers' Party, meant that the non-Fianna Fáil parties represented a distinctly fragmented alternative. Second, the 1989 general election witnessed the end of what might be termed the Fianna Fáil-versus-the-rest model of Irish party politics. Traditionally, Fianna Fáil had stressed its distinctive capacity to form single-party government: since it had first taken office in 1932, Fianna Fáil had been the only party to govern without coalition partners. This (supposedly) brought greater stability, strength and efficiency and contrasted with the alliances which rival parties were forced to make in order to form governments. In 1989 the pattern changed. Fianna Fáil won seventy-seven seats, Fine Gael fifty-five, Labour fifteen, others nineteen, and Fianna Fáil went into coalition with the Progressive Democrats. Having followed the coalition path, Fianna Fáil took on a different role in the party system. In some ways, its position was strengthened. As the largest party, it represented the most powerful player in the coalition game: if a coalition had to be formed, then Fianna Fáil would find it easier to form the necessary deal than would any of its smaller rivals.

It has been argued that the 1989 election represented a turning point in the history of the Irish party system, and certainly Fianna Fáil's subsequent maintenance of governmental power by means of coalition (1989–92 with the PDs; 1993 onwards with Labour) would seem to support such a thesis. Grand claims were also made by some observers when Mary Robinson was elected president of the Republic in 1990. All previous presidents had been men and, with the exception of Douglas Hyde, all had been of Fianna Fáil pedigree. Robinson – who had a distinguished record in law and also in campaigning on human rights and minority issues – was nominated and supported as presidential candidate by the Labour Party, and also had the backing of (among others) the Workers' Party. During the summer of 1990 she followed an exacting schedule of countrywide campaigning, but the most dramatic feature of the presidential race involved the Fianna Fáil candidate, Brian Lenihan. In a television debate Lenihan denied that he had made a telephone call in 1982 to the then president, Patrick Hillery, in an attempt to pre-empt a dissolution of the Dáil. But in a taped interview with a research student Lenihan had already admitted that he *had* in fact made such a call. The tape being made available, Lenihan's credibility was significantly damaged, and this situation was only worsened by the fact that the Fianna Fáil candidate persisted in his denials.

166
Mary Robinson
Radio Telefís Éireann

Despite this setback, Lenihan attracted more first-preference votes than his two rivals, winning 44.1 per cent, against Robinson's 38.9 per cent, and Fine Gael's Austin Currie, who won 17 per cent. But the Currie transfers went overwhelmingly to Robinson, who was duly elected president with a second-count total of 52.8 per cent. Robinson's victory reflected a successful attempt to woo voters with what might be termed more progressive instincts. But while she became a highly visible president, too much significance should not be read into the election. The presidency is primarily a ceremonial office. Moreover, the supposed liberal triumph of 1990 was, in fact, part of a broader series of developments. Thus, for example, Fianna Fáil's first Presidential defeat mirrored the new vulnerability which recent electoral experience had exposed. It is also important that the extent of the progressive victory should not be overstated. Robinson's election certainly solidified the position of Labour Party leader Dick Spring. But when Labour achieved the impressive total of thirty-three seats in the 1992 general election, it was with Fianna Fáil that the party came to share governmental authority. As has been noted, recent changes in the Irish party system have not necessarily weakened the position of the previously dominant political party.

Of vital significance to any appreciation of this period of Irish history is the increasingly influential role played in Irish political life by the European Community (EC), and it might be appropriate to finish our chapter on this note. Most issues of domestic public policy now have a European dimension. In May 1987 Irish voters voted, by referendum, to permit the state to ratify the Single European Act, which reflected the desire for closer union between the EC's member states. The Treaty of Maastricht further developed the process of European union – union which was to involve economic, monetary, foreign, security and justice policies. In June 1992 a referendum saw Irish voters permit the ratification of this treaty. Indeed, the process of European integration is the essential context for understanding contemporary Irish politics. European law plays a vital role in influencing Irish political life, and European union increasingly determines the nature of the framework within which the Irish state must operate.

The June 1994 European elections saw the Republic's fifteen seats distributed as follows: Fianna Fáil 7, Fine Gael 4, Green Party 2, Labour Party 1, Independent 1. In Northern Ireland the European elections saw the three sitting members returned. The DUP's Ian Paisley topped the poll (163,246), closely followed by the SDLP's John Hume (161,992), with the UUP's Jim Nicholson (133,459) being elected on the strength of DUP transfers. Tellingly, Northern Ireland politicians offered widely divergent interpretations of these results. Paisley argued that, having topped the poll, he had received endorsement in his vehement opposition to the Downing Street Declaration; Hume argued that his vote, which had risen since the 1989 election, indicated popular support for the peace process (of which the Downing Street statement was a significant part); Nicholson suggested that his own increased vote pointed to a popular preference for the UUP's calmer strategy over the more confrontational style of the DUP. The IRA's declaration (on 31 August 1994) of a 'complete cessation of military operations' raised enormous hopes in relation to Northern Ireland, but the sharp divergence between unionist and nationalist aspirations remained.[1]

Ireland at the Turn of the Century: 1994–2001
Dermot Keogh

The final six years of the twentieth century and the first two years of the new millennium were characterised by a number of unforeseen and mainly positive developments in Ireland. Citizens of the Republic had lived for far too long with the dashed expectation that the country might offer higher living standards and economic security. It had failed to do so since the false dawn of the 1960s. In the century's twilight, a combination of domestic and international circumstances replaced earlier fatalism with a heady optimism. The economic turnaround was so swift that many in public life were arrogant enough to believe that they had personally been responsible for the reversal of national fortunes, and imprudent enough to think that the 'good times' would last forever.

I have isolated the following as the major developments of those years responsible for the economic 'miracle' of the self-styled 'Celtic Tiger' and the changing social ethos of the country:

- A restoration of political stability, lost during the early part of the 1990s
- Unprecedented levels of prosperity and high employment
- The continuation of large subsidy transfers to Dublin from Brussels
- The return of many Irish nationals who had emigrated during the 1980s
- Widespread recruitment of skilled and general labour from abroad to meet the demands of an expanding economy
- The arrival of unprecedented numbers of asylum-seekers and economic refugees, although numbers continued to be small by the standards of other European Union countries
- The decline of the institutional Catholic Church amid revelations of serious scandal
- Widespread allegations of bribery and corruption involving leading politicians and public officials
- Disclosure of a close affinity between the political sector and corporate Ireland
- Major developments in the establishment of a lasting peace and an end to political violence in Northern Ireland

The optimism and buoyancy of close-of-the-century Ireland would have been very difficult to predict in the late 1980s. However, change of a very radical nature occurred in the latter half of the twentieth century's final decade. The first area in need of examination is the process of restoring political stability.

The leader of the Labour Party, Dick Spring, surprised many by entering a coalition led by Albert Reynolds following the 1992 general election, as the aim of many Labour voters had been to get Fianna Fáil out of government. The architect of the agreement was Bertie Ahern, a negotiator and political fixer who had entered Dáil Éireann in 1977 and was perceived to have been a Haughey loyalist. The historic compromise between Fianna Fáil and Labour allegedly broke the mould in Irish politics at one level. The previous coalition, between the Progressive Democrats and Fianna Fáil, had ended in tears. Labour appeared to be under the impression in 1992 that, with its 33 seats, it could be the tail that wagged the dog. Despite the fact that the party was given major ministerial portfolios – finance and foreign affairs, for example – its leaders were very much mistaken if they hoped to launch Labour on the road to a historic political breakthrough. A projected tax amnesty in 1993 provoked a negative reaction among many of those who had voted for Labour, which effectively thwarted the onward march of that party. Apart from achieving significant progress towards peace in Northern Ireland, the Fianna Fáil–Labour coalition was more a historical blunder than a historic compromise. Labour failed to sup with a long spoon when in partnership with Fianna Fáil, and the party paid the electoral price. On 17 November 1994, Albert Reynolds resigned as Taoiseach amid controversy over the appointment as president of the High Court of the Attorney General, Harry Whelehan. The latter had been criticised for his handling of Father Brendan Smyth's extradition from Northern Ireland on charges of child sexual abuse. Whelehan also resigned as president of the High Court.[1] The government fell. However, for the first time in the history of the Irish state, the fall of a government was not followed by a general election.

Protracted discussions took place between the new leader of Fianna Fáil, Bertie Ahern, and Labour about the formation of a new coalition. This seemed the most likely outcome, and Ahern was poised to be the new Taoiseach. However, contrary to general expectations, Dick Spring chose to lead his party into government with a 'rainbow' coalition of Fine Gael and the Democratic Left. John Bruton, the leader of Fine Gael, became Taoiseach and Spring continued to hold the foreign-affairs portfolio. This proved to be a relatively effective partnership. Under its stewardship, the economic fortunes of the country continued to improve. The improvement was not sufficient, however, to dissuade the electorate from returning Fianna Fáil to power. The general election on 6 June 1997 saw Bertie Ahern emerge belatedly as Taoiseach in Fianna Fáil's coalition with the Progressive Democrats. Mary Harney became the new Tánaiste. Dick Spring stepped down as leader of the Labour Party on 5 November 1997, to be replaced by Ruairí Quinn. The latter had seen his party humiliatingly diminished in a general election where Labour was made to pay for its decision to enter government with Fianna Fáil. Aware that social democracy in Ireland would not make progress with a divided left, Quinn entered into merger talks with the Democratic Left party. The fusion of the two parties greatly strengthened the parliamentary performance of the Labour Party. Nevertheless, it created major tensions in constituencies where members of both parties had bitterly opposed each other, particularly over conflicting policy on Northern Ireland.

167
Mary Harney
© *RTÉ Stills Library*

Despite the significant ideological and personality differences between the two parties, the Fianna Fáil–Progressive Democrats coalition held firm during the last three years of the century. There were times when the Tánaiste, Mary Harney, and the Fianna Fáil Minister for Finance, Charlie McCreevy, appeared to have more in common on policy issues than the latter had with his own party. The appointment of Michael McDowell as Attorney General on 7 July 1999 further strengthened the national profile of the PDs. That position had become vacant upon the nomination of David Byrne as an European Commissioner, succeeding Pádraig Flynn.

Ireland was highly successful in making the state an attractive centre for the location of factories involved in the information-technology revolution. Most of the major names in the worldwide computer industry established factories in Ireland. A record exchequer surplus of over IR£1 billion was recorded on 6 April 1999, as sections of Irish society enjoyed levels of unprecedented affluence. The national telecommunications company, Telecom Éireann, was privatised on 6 July 1999. This event was designed to symbolise the healthy roar of the 'Celtic Tiger'. A slick and intensive publicity campaign tempted the citizens of the nation to become stakeholders in that new economic venture. Shares rose 20 per cent in the first week of trading and then dropped like a stone – to the great anger of the many first-time small investors who had unwisely invested hard-earned savings or borrowed in order to be part of that particular venture in the tiger economy. Their anger was compounded by the revelations in a succession of public tribunals about the former Fianna Fáil leader, Charles Haughey, a former Fianna Fáil Minister for Foreign Affairs, Ray Burke, and a Fianna Fáil backbencher, Liam Lawlor. It seemed that during the hard times in the 1980s those who had exhorted compliant taxpayers to tighten their belts had never had it so good.

President Mary Robinson, so much the symbol of the 'new' Ireland, came to the end of her term as President. She did not seek re-election. Instead, on 12 June 1997 she took up a position in Geneva as UN High Commissioner for Human Rights. According to traditional political logic, Albert Reynolds ought to have been the Fianna Fáil candidate for the presidency. Brian Lenihan had lost that election for Fianna Fáil in 1990 for the first time in the history of the office of the President. Determined to win in 1997, Bertie Ahern was fortunate enough to persuade the talented academic Mary McAleese to stand as the Fianna Fáil nominee. It was a wise choice, but it meant having to ensure that Albert Reynolds did not get the party nomination. Ahern, despite voting for Reynolds, secured a majority for his preferred candidate. Mary McAleese went on to win the presidential election by a handsome majority.

Leaving the issues of inter-party politics to one side, this was an inspired choice. Bringing a new dimension to the presidency, Mary McAleese has served with distinction in that office. President McAleese is an independent critical voice with her own unique style. She has come to symbolise something much deeper about the 'new' Ireland than what is conveyed in the shallow cliché: 'the Celtic Tiger'.

Much of the affluence experienced in Ireland in the 1990s was directly attributable to developments elsewhere. While some credit must be given to government strategy, the buoyant global economy provided the momentum for the Irish economic 'miracle'. Another factor that contributed to the Irish return to solvency has been underestimated: the movement towards peace in Northern Ireland.

168
Mary McAleese
© *RTÉ Stills Library*

In the 1990s the prize of peace in Northern Ireland had become a central policy goal for the Irish, British and US governments. The Taoiseach, Albert Reynolds, the British Prime Minister, John Major, and the US President, Bill Clinton, moved beyond the strategy of containment that had previously prevailed. They collectively saw peace as a realisable goal. Considerable foundations had been laid before Tony Blair's Labour Party came to power in the United Kingdom following the general election on 1 May 1997. Nevertheless, much credit for progress in the peace process must go to the new Northern Secretary, Mo Mowlam, who worked tirelessly and with refreshing candour until she was replaced by a more controversial appointee, Peter Mandelson.

William Jefferson Clinton was unique among US presidents, being the first to devote so much of his personal time and energy to finding a way forward in the resolution of Anglo-Irish problems. Senator George Mitchell, who became his close adviser in this area, wrote: 'He was the first American president to visit Northern Ireland while in office, the first to make ending the conflict there a high priority for the US government.'[2]

Clinton's interest in Ireland dated back to his time as a Rhodes scholar at Oxford University in the late 1960s. When campaigning for the Democratic nomination for President in 1992, the governor of Arkansas was accused of opportunism, as he had given priority to the Anglo-Irish issue. He told an influential audience in New York that, if elected to the White House, he would appoint a special peace envoy for Northern Ireland and grant the leader of Sinn Féin, Gerry Adams, a visa to enter the United States.[3]

As President, he did not immediately put the first suggestion into practice. He did, however, grant Adams a visa, on the advice of John Hume, who considered it essential for the future progress of peace that the Sinn Féin leader be allowed into the US to discuss developments freely with his followers. Hume was certain that the time was ripe for such a visit in early 1994.[4] This would follow protracted talks between Hume and Adams, which developed in intensity and depth throughout 1993.

As a backdrop to their discussions, on 23 October 1993 an IRA bomb killed nine people and injured 57, one of whom died later, in a fish-and-chip shop on the Shankill Road, Belfast. On 30 October, two members of the Ulster Freedom Fighters (UFF) entered the Rising Sun bar in Greysteel, County Derry, and went through the Hallowe'en crowd, shooting at will. Seven died in an attack which the UFF claimed was 'the continuation of our threats against the nationalist electorate that they would pay a heavy price for last Saturday's slaughter of nine Protestants.'[5] Talks, discussions and talks about talks continued amid the violence. There were unsuccessful inter-party talks in Northern Ireland, Irish government contacts with republicans, British government contact with Sinn Féin, and the Hume–Adams talks. The latter had first resulted in a statement on 24 April 1993 and then a further joint statement on 25 September 1993 which reported considerable progress on the creation of a peacr process.

On 15 December 1993, John Major and Albert Reynolds issued a joint declaration on Northern Ireland. The Downing Street Declaration (DSD), as it became known, is summarised below:

> The DSD, whose terms were negotiated not simply with nationalists and republicans but with unionists and loyalists, marked a decisive shift in the analysis of the conflict and in the political approach to it. It located the roots of the conflict in a historical process on the island of Ireland which primarily affected the people of Ireland, North and South (paragraphs 1, 2); it reaffirmed the British government's lack of 'selfish strategic or economic interest' in Northern Ireland and its intent to promote agreement on the island (paragraph 4); it affirmed a (revised) notion of national self-determination (paragraphs 4, 5) which was conjoined with an Irish acceptance of the need for consent of all significant groups to a constitutional settlement (paragraphs 5, 6, 7); and it pledged change in both parts of the island (paragraphs 6, 7, 9) in an attempt to undo the causes of conflict (paragraph 1).[6]

Here was a way forward. But there had been many historical 'turning points' before where Northern Ireland had failed to turn. It is in this context that the innovative role of Clinton and his advisers must be interpreted. Despite British opposition, Adams was given a forty-eight-hour visa at the end of January 1994. If the objective was to enhance his reputation as a political leader of stature, then it succeeded. The President, National Security Council and White House staff, as well as Irish-American interest groups and political heavyweights such as Ted Kennedy on Capitol Hill, impressed Adams the importance of the republican movement abandoning the use of political violence. With the assistance of further US support, an IRA ceasefire was brought into effect from midnight on 31 August 1994. On 13 October 1994 the Combined Loyalist Military Command (the Ulster Defence Association, the Ulster Freedom Fighters, the Ulster Volunteer Force and the Red Hand Commandos) also called a ceasefire.

The ceasefires provided the opportunity for both the British and Irish governments to enter into direct dialogue with Sinn Féin and the two loyalist parties with paramilitary links, the Progressive Unionist Party and the Ulster Democratic Party. Adams was given an unlimited visa to enter the US in September. He was allowed to travel throughout the country. Despite the outward triumphalism of the visit, Adams was there to convince his followers that the time had come to trade the armed struggle for the political process.

In February 1995, the British and Irish governments published *A New Framework for Agreement* (popularly known as the 'framework document') in an effort to sketch proposals for a constitutional and institutional settlement. The British Prime Minister, John Major, and the Taoiseach, John Bruton, sought to describe how an honourable accommodation might be reached without prejudice to the differing traditions. The framework document also applied the principles of the Downing Street Declaration by outlining proposals for constitutional change on both sides of the border, together with plans for new political structures within Northern Ireland, between the North and South, and between Great Britain and the Republic of Ireland. There was a further commitment in the area of mutual respect for human rights and a pledge to submit the outcome of talks with the parties to referenda in both the North and South. Adams was invited to participate in talks in Washington with government representatives. Sinn Féin was permitted to fund-raise in the United States, and Clinton invited Adams to the White House for celebrations on St Patrick's Day 1995. Two days before, the President was photographed shaking hands with the Sinn Féin leader.[7] On 29 March 1995 the British government announced that it was prepared to hold an exploratory dialogue with Sinn Féin.

A visit by John Major to Washington in April provided a public opportunity for Clinton to praise the courage of the British for having opened discussions with Sinn Féin. He also took the opportunity to mend bruised relations with London caused by the radical divergences in policy over Northern Ireland. But in the North, the British continued to insist that the IRA would have to decommission weapons before Sinn Féin would be allowed to participate in all-party talks. In June, while the IRA ceasefire continued to hold, Sinn Féin announced that they were no longer prepared to meet with British officials. There was strong unionist hostility to any normalisation of relations with Sinn Féin. Adams raised unionist ire in August 1995 when he told a Belfast rally: 'They [the IRA] haven't gone away, you know.' The previous month, Portadown had become the epicentre of street conflict. Orange marchers and nationalists confronted each other at the Catholic estates on the Garvaghy Road. The Reverend Ian Paisley of the Democratic Unionist Party and David Trimble of the Ulster Unionist Party marched together with their followers down the road and held hands aloft in triumph at the end, to the great delight of their followers. Catholic residents were obliged to stand by, humiliated, as they witnessed an act of Orange triumphalism. When the leader of the Ulster Unionist Party, James Molyneaux, resigned at the end of August 1995, Trimble was elected as his successor. His bravado on the Garvaghy Road had not done his popularity and standing in unionist circles any harm.

169
George Mitchell
© *The Irish Times*

The White House sought to sustain the momentum created by the ceasefires. Further initiatives in 1995 laid emphasis on inward investment to

Northern Ireland, to pave the way for economic recovery. Clinton had announced in late 1994 that the US contribution to the International Fund for Ireland was to be raised by $10 million to $30 million for 1996.[8] On 9 January 1995, seven days after he had retired as senator for Maine, George Mitchell was appointed special adviser to the President and to the Secretary of State on economic initiatives in Ireland. He made his first visit to Northern Ireland a month later and was struck by the symbolism of the Peace Line – a 30-foot-high wall, topped in some places with barbed wire, which separated the Catholic Falls area from the Protestant shankill area of Belfast, cutting through streets. 'It is one of the most depressing structures I've ever seen. To call it the Peace Line is a huge irony,' he wrote.[9] Few people did more in the years that followed to dismantle the divisions between communities in Northern Ireland. As he listened to people in Belfast discuss their problems, he became aware that he 'could just as well be in New York, Detroit, Johannesburg, Manila, or any other big city in the world'. He was told that there was a strong correlation between unemployment and violence and that, without jobs in the inner cities, there would never be a durable peace. While he recognised that the dispute in Northern Ireland was 'not purely or even primarily economic in origin and nature', he saw that it was necessary to address the issue of jobs and prosperity.[10] A tangible sign of US willingness to give economic support to the peace process was the organisation of a trade and investment conference in Washington in May to which hundreds of US and Northern Ireland business people came, together with the major political leaders.

The Forum for Peace and Reconciliation was established by the Irish government and held its first meeting in Dublin Castle on 28 October 1994. Boycotted by the unionists, it was attended by almost all the other major political parties on the island with the exception of the Democratic Left. The body helped to extend further the dialogue between rival groups on the island while it also commissioned a number of useful studies.[11] However, with Trimble now the leader of the Ulster Unionist Party, there did not appear to be any prospect of a breakthrough.

With determined efforts being made by the Irish and US governments to sustain the IRA ceasefire, Clinton visited Ireland and the Britain between 29 November and 1 December 1995. After talks in London with John Major and an address to the Houses of Parliament, on 30 November he travelled to Belfast, where he spoke with evident conviction to employees and guests at the Mackie Metal Plant about being

proud to support Northern Ireland. You have given America a very great deal. Irish Protestant and Irish Catholic together have added to America's strength. From our battle for independence down to the present day, the Irish have not only fought in our wars; they have built our nation, and we owe you a very great debt.

But he warned that there would be those who would oppose the peace process:

The greatest struggle you face is between those who, deep down inside, are inclined to be peacemakers, and those who, deep down inside, cannot yet embrace the cause of peace. Between those who are in the ship of peace and those who are trying to sink it, old habits die hard.

Clinton assured his audience that the United States would stand with those who took risks for peace, in Northern Ireland and around the world. He pledged that Washington would do all it could, through the International Fund for Ireland and in many other ways, to ease the load of those on the path to peace. Later that evening he went to a civic reception in front of the city hall and attended a concert where local boy Van Morrison sang to the tens of thousands who came to express their support for peace. A further hopeful augury had been the announcement on 5 October 1995 that Seamus Heaney, a Derryman, had won the Nobel Prize for Literature.

Senator George Mitchell had been persuaded by President Clinton to chair the newly established International Body on Decommissioning of Weapons. The British government remained very nervous about the initiative but agreed to support it, nominating the recently retired Chief of the Canadian Defence Forces, General John de Chastelain, to the new body. The Irish government proposed the former Prime Minister of Finland, Harri Holkeri, to sit on the commission. Its report was published on 23 January 1996. It urged all parties in peace negotiations to commit themselves to six principles underpinning democracy and non-violence. These included the total and verifiable decommissioning of all paramilitary weapons. The Mitchell report proposed that the parties should consider a proposal whereby decommissioning might occur during negotiations.[12]

There was little time for celebration. On Friday 9 February 1996, the IRA ended its ceasefire by exploding a massive bomb at 7.00 p.m. in Canary Wharf in London's Docklands. Weighing about 1,000 pounds, it was concealed within a specially designed compartment in a lorry. Two local workers died in the blast, which was responsible for millions of pounds' worth of damage to the financial-services sector. The IRA, in a statement, demanded 'an inclusive negotiated settlement' and accused the British government of 'bad faith' and the unionists of 'squandering this unprecedented opportunity to resolve the conflict.' On 15 June, a one-and-a-half-ton bomb in a van destroyed Manchester city centre. There was further violence on the Garvaghy Road near Drumcree during the summer months. In October, the IRA exploded two bombs inside British army barracks in Northern Ireland.

Mitchell and his two colleagues continued with the task of attempting to secure progress through inclusive talks. But movement was slow. Dependent upon Unionist votes to sustain its majority in the Commons, the Tory government dragged its feet on Northern Ireland. Elections to a forum in Northern Ireland in May 1996 saw Sinn Féin take 15.5 per cent of the vote, a very strong performance given that the Sinn Féin leadership had stated that they would not take their seats. The talks continued, but little progress could be made without the presence of Sinn Féin. In 1997, the IRA caused disruption on British motorways by phoning bomb threats to the police. The Aintree Grand National was also prevented from being run, using the same tactics. The victory of the Labour Party in the British election in May 1997 helped to shift the alignment of political forces in Northern Ireland, as Tony Blair's party won by a landslide. Unionist MPs no longer held the balance of power in the Commons. The new Northern Secretary, Mo Mowlam, laid less emphasis on decommissioning than her Conservative predecessors. Her personal commitment and political adroitness helped lay the foundation for radical change.

Yet the violence continued. The IRA killed two policemen in Lurgan. Twenty-one people died in sectarian attacks in 1997. Loyalists were responsible for thirteen of those deaths. Portadown's Garvaghy Road was again the scene of violence as the Orange parade was forced through with the help of the police and the British army. In the light of the continuing violence, it came as a major surprise when the IRA announced a resumption of its ceasefire on 20 July 1997. Sinn Féin was admitted to the peace talks on 9 September. The British Prime Minister, on a visit to Belfast, enraged many unionists by shaking hands with Gerry Adams. Blair repeated the handshake inside 10 Downing Street at a later date.

On 12 January 1998, the two governments published propositions on 'heads of agreement'. This had been the work of a round of intensive negotiations that had begun on 24 September 1997 between Dublin and London, between Belfast and Dublin, and within Northern Ireland. Under the Taoiseach, Bertie Ahern, the Irish negotiating team included the Minister for Foreign Affairs, David Andrews, and the Progressive Democrat Minister of State at the Department of Foreign Affairs, Liz O'Donnell. The proposition helped to focus the negotiations. Mitchell set a deadline of midnight on 9 April 1998 for completion of the agreement. There were frenetic last-minute discussions involving Tony Blair, Bertie Ahern and the leaders of the Northern parties. On Good Friday, 10 April, final agreement was secured at a plenary session of the talks. A new British–Irish agreement was signed, with both governments pledging that Dublin and London would give effect to its provisions. In referenda on 22 May 1998, the people of Ireland, North and South, endorsed the agreement. For the first time since 1918, all the people on the island voted together to decide their political future.[13] In the South, the electorate also voted to amend Articles 2 and 3 of the Constitution. This was an act of faith in the peace process.

The Good Friday Agreement (popularly referred to as 'the Belfast Agreement') was divided into eleven sections. It began with a declaration of support and commitment to a range of principles, including non-violence and partnership, equality and mutual respect. The governments set out their shared views on constitutional issues, based on the principles of consent and self-determination as set down in the Downing Street Declaration of 1993. This was followed by provisions for the setting up of a new assembly in Northern Ireland, a North–South council and a British–Irish council. New and enhanced provisions with regard to rights and equality of opportunity formed the next section, followed by a commitment by all parties to work in good faith and to use any influence they had to achieve decommissioning of weapons within two years of approval of the agreement. Under the heading of security, there was provision for the normalisation of security arrangements and practices. A programme for the rapid release of prisoners was outlined, and the final section discussed the agreement's validation and review.

Elections took place on 25 June 1998 to the new Northern Ireland Assembly. When the body met on 1 July, David Trimble was elected as First Minister designate and Séamus Mallon of the SDLP as Deputy First Minister designate. When the Assembly was formed in December 1999, Sinn Féin held two ministries. The political and administrative talent now on display simply underscored the squandered years since the introduction of direct rule in the early 1970s. The gun, the bomb and the bullet had deprived generations in Northern Ireland of an opportunity to participate in the normal business of government. The violence had had a negative impact on the economic and social development of the island as a whole since the 1960s.

In the year of the Good Friday Agreement – 1998 – fifty-five people died in violence in Northern Ireland. Three Catholic brothers, aged between eight and ten, died on 12 July when loyalists petrol-bombed their home in a predominantly Protestant area of Ballymoney. On 15 August – a traditional Catholic holiday – twenty-eight people were killed in a car-bomb blast in Omagh. The attack also claimed another victim, who died a few days later. A republican splinter group, the Real IRA, had placed a 500-pound bomb in a parked car in a crowded shopping street on a sunny summer Saturday. It was one of the worst outrages of the Troubles. A fortnight after the explosion, President Clinton, accompanied by his wife and daughter, joined Tony Blair and his wife on a visit to meet about 700 of the injured and their relatives. A plaque was unveiled which read: 'In remembrance of the men, women and children who died in the terrorist bombing, August 15, 1998. May their memory serve to foster peace and reconciliation.'[14]

President Clinton returned to Ireland at the end of the year. In Dublin Bertie Ahern told him that while many people had been involved in the peace process, 'it would not have been possible without you.' On 13 December Bill Clinton spoke to an audience of over 8,000 people in Belfast. He said: 'I believe in the peace you are building. I believe there can be no turning back.'

The scandal of corruption in public life was a continuing theme in the 1990s. Most Irish people viewed with disbelief the revelations that emerged about the governance of the Irish state. In 1994, the Finance Bill provided that Irish tax exiles were to be permitted to spend six months in the country each year while retaining their non-residence status. The same year the shocked citizen read about a 'passports for sale' scheme, about which the populace had been told nothing. A foreigner making a million-pound investment in the country was entitled, under the official scheme, to apply for an Irish passport. In one case, a passport was granted to a Saudi family who had invested in a pet-food firm owned by some members of Albert Reynolds' family. The scheme was legal but many feared that beneficiaries would be unworthy. It was even more problematical because the holder of an Irish passport was also a citizen of the European Union, with all the residency rights that that bestowed in each of the member states.

An insight into Irish society has been provided by testimony given before a number of public tribunals which sat through the 1990s. The work of several of those tribunals continued in 2001.

In May 1991, the Oireachtas set up a tribunal of inquiry into the beef-processing industry. The terms of reference of what became known as the Beef Tribunal were to inquire into allegations regarding illegal activities, fraud and malpractice in the beef-processing industry, which had been referred to in Dáil Éireann and in an ITV television programme transmitted on 13 May 1991. By the time Mr Justice Liam Hamilton reported on 29 July 1994, the country had been given an insight into the sometimes bizarre operations of the industry and into its relationship with the Department of Agriculture and the Department of Industry and Commerce. The report also cast light on government decisions in relation to the beef industry. Its revelations have been summarised as follows:

> There had been, for three years, a sustained and intense relationship between a government and a company . . . In the course of that relationship the government broke the law and asked few questions of the company . . . The company was, at the same time, abusing public funds on a large scale and contriving to cheat the public of taxes . . . The public still faced potential liabilities of up to £200 million, liabilities which it had unknowingly incurred without any benefit in order to help a private company in Ireland and a violent dictator in Iraq.[15]

The powers of the Beef Tribunal had been limited by a nervous government. When the next tribunal was established, it was in a position to act with greater freedom. The McCracken Tribunal was set up by the rainbow coalition under John Bruton in early 1997 to investigate alleged payments by supermarket millionaire Ben Dunne to Charles Haughey and to the former Fine Gael minister Michael Lowry. Mr Justice Brian McCracken of the High Court presided over hearings that produced sensational testimony. Ben Dunne was centre stage. His evidence was extraordinary. On one occasion, it emerged, Dunne dropped in on Haughey in 1991 on his way from playing golf. It was about a week after Haughey had seen off a vote of no confidence in his leadership within the Fianna Fáil Party. Sensing that the Taoiseach was depressed, Ben Dunne said, he took out of his pocket three bank drafts to the value of £210,000. No name had been inserted on the drafts. Dunne said, 'Look, that is something for yourself.' Haughey allegedly replied, 'Thank you, big fellow.' The McCracken report, published on 15 July 1997, concluded:

> The Tribunal considers it quite unacceptable that Mr Charles Haughey, or indeed any member of the Oireachtas, should receive personal gifts of this nature, particularly from prominent businessmen within the state. It is even more unacceptable that Mr Charles Haughey's whole lifestyle should be dependent upon such gifts, as would appear to be the case. If such gifts were to be permissible, the potential for bribery and corruption would be enormous.

McCracken referred the papers to the Director of Public Prosecutions. The tribunal findings were a devastating blow for Haughey, but worse was to follow.

The Moriarty Tribunal was established in September 1997. Under Mr Justice Michael Moriarty, the tribunal is investigating payments to Charles Haughey and Michael Lowry. It is also charged to investigate whether any political decision made by either of those men while in office might have benefited a person or a company making a payment. The Moriarty Tribunal is also investigating Ansbacher deposits (off-shore accounts), but only to ascertain if any politician received money from such an account and who was responsible for making the payment. In May 2000, the Moriarty Tribunal estimated that Haughey had been in receipt of £8.6 million from leading businessmen between 1979 and 1996. The revelations continued throughout 2001.

170
Charles Haughey
© *The Irish Times*

The Flood Tribunal was established by the Oireachtas in October 1997. Under the chairmanship of Mr Justice Feargus Flood, it was set up to investigate the planning background to a parcel of 726 acres in north County Dublin. It was alleged that the former Minister for Foreign Affairs, Ray Burke, received a payment of £80,000 from Joseph Murphy Structural Engineering. Burke admitted getting £30,000. The terms of reference of the tribunal were extended in June 1998 following a disclosure that another £30,000 had been paid to Burke by Rennicks Manufacturing Ltd. The Flood Tribunal was also given the power to investigate all illegal payments to politicians in the context of the planning process. In April 2000, two builders gave testimony that they had given donations to Burke and Fianna Fáil over a fifteen-year period but did not know how the money had been divided between them.

The Fianna Fáil Dublin West TD, Liam Lawlor, was another person who appeared before the Flood Tribunal. He resigned from the Fianna Fáil parliamentary party in June 2000. Fined and briefly imprisoned for failure to comply with the tribunal in January 2001, he continued to have dealings with it throughout the year. He remained a member of Dáil Éireann in August 2001 while facing a second jail sentence.

Frank Dunlop, a public-relations consultant and former Fianna Fáil press officer, caused a sensation when he told the Flood Tribunal that he had given £112,000 in 1991 to fifteen Dublin city councillors before they voted on a controversial planning application for a major shopping centre. He claimed that he had made payments of £180,000 to thirty-eight politicians on behalf of a property developer.

These, and revelations like them, continue in 2001 to rock Irish democracy to its very core.

On 24 November 1995, a referendum in the South resulted in a narrow majority in favour of the introduction of divorce. That measure had been opposed vigorously by the leadership of the Catholic Church, but many lay Catholics reluctantly took the view that divorce was a social necessity if the issues of marriage breakdown and inheritance were to be addressed. For the three-year period to 31 July 2000, 26,472 divorces were granted in Ireland.

The troubled and divisive issue of abortion still awaited legislation in 2001. In the 1990s, roughly 5,000 Irish women went abroad annually – mainly to England – to have abortions. Exact figures relating to this issue are not available. On 25 November 1992 – the day of the general election – a referendum was held on constitutional amendments on the right to travel, the right to information and the right to have an abortion. Voters accepted the first two and rejected the third. In 2000 an all-party committee in the Oireachtas studied the issue, and its findings were reported later that year to government. There was no easy answer. Abortion continues to divide Irish opinion and any future debate is likely to be every bit as acrimonious as was the case in the referenda of 1983 and 1992.

In the 1990s, the clerical Catholic Church was forced to confront a number of scandals of varying degrees of severity. High-profile paternity suits ensured that the private lives of the Bishop of Galway, Eamonn Casey, and well-known priest Father Michael Cleary were splashed all over the front pages of Irish newspapers. Serious allegations were also made against state-funded and religious-run orphanages and industrial schools. Many of the allegations related to events going back to the 1940s and 1950s. Two television programmes set the framework for the public discussion on this area. *Dear Daughter* was broadcast on RTÉ on 28 February 1996. In it, Christine Buckley told the story of her time in St Vincent's Industrial School Goldenbridge, Dublin, run by the Sisters of Mercy. Her account was an indictment of the manner in which that school allegedly operated. But the coverage in the programme was neither comprehensive nor definitive, and it raised many questions. On 9 May 1996 allegations of abuse were made against the Sisters of Charity orphanage at Madonna House in Dublin. A report documented some fifteen cases. In April and May 1999, RTÉ broadcast Mary Raftery's three-part documentary entitled *States of Fear* on the history of the industrial-school system in Ireland. The reaction to the programmes was extensive and intensive, in the newspapers and on radio. It was followed by a number of books on the subject.[16]

However, taken as a whole, these commentaries do not constitute a reliable history of the industrial-school system in Ireland. That may emerge from the findings of the commission to inquire into childhood abuse set up by the government in May 1999, when the Taoiseach apologised to the victims of childhood abuse on behalf of the state and its citizens 'for our collective failure to intervene, to detect their pain, to come to their rescue'.

The Catholic Church experienced a falling-off in attendance at weekly Mass and the sacraments during the 1990s, but the place of religion in the lives of Irish people ought not to be determined by the health of the institutional church. In the summer of 2001, the relics of Saint Thérèse of Lisieux were taken in solemn procession around Ireland, North and South.

171   The relics of Saint Thérèse of Lisieux arrive in Ireland
© *The Irish Times*

The popular response was overwhelming. Tens of thousands of people – young and old – came out to participate in all-night vigils. The suggestion that Ireland was a post-Christian society in 2001 was contradicted by the phenomenon of the response to Saint Thérèse's relics, the high turnout at the pilgrimages to Croagh Patrick and Lough Derg, and the packed cathedral during the annual Galway Novena of Prayers. Ireland remained a country of contrasts and contradictions.

The 1990s saw the election of two women Presidents of Ireland in succession. Seven years after the victory of Mary Robinson, the race for the presidency in 1997 was between four women and one man, and resulted in the election of Mary McAleese. The fact that all the major political parties considered it expedient to choose a woman candidate was a measure of the extent to which Irish women had shown their determination to challenge the bastions of patriarchy in that society. The Oireachtas was one such bastion. In the 1990s women were elected in greater numbers than ever before in the history of the state. Yet the numbers in Dáil Éireann and the Seanad remain far from achieving gender parity. Ireland has a very long way to go before it reaches the 50 per cent female representation to be found in Scandinavian countries, but by 2001 no Taoiseach would form a Cabinet that did not include women in ministries of major importance.

Governments in the 1990s promoted policies of gender equality. The Oireachtas was not a shining light of achievement in that regard. Neither was the civil service, although there was progress. Although women found it difficult to secure positions as secretaries general of government departments, they were more strongly represented in the upper echelons of the civil service than had been the case in the early 1990s. The Department of Foreign Affairs had the best record in this regard: here, women were more strongly represented at all levels than they were in other departments, and women were appointed as ambassadors to a number of postings, including Austria, Argentina and the United Nations.

In business and the professions, the 'Celtic Tiger' provided opportunities for many women entrepreneurs to come to the fore. However, a certain 'rugby-club culture' continued to permeate the upper levels of Irish business, and this proved difficult to combat.

The Catholic Church was to be the most recalcitrant of institutions in Ireland on issues relating to gender equality. The Church of Ireland permitted the ordination of women priests in the 1990s – an issue that continued to divide that church. But the innately conservative majority of the Irish hierarchy, on instructions from the Holy See, remained as impenetrable as a brick wall on the question of the ordination of women. The Irish Catholic Church, despite the influence of many dynamic female religious, remains a redoubt of chauvinistic attitudes. But the combined strength of laywomen and nuns, supported by many males, has served as a strong lobby for change. Since most of those who regularly attend Mass and the sacraments in Ireland are women, the failure of the leadership of the Catholic Church to listen and learn has cost the institution dearly.

Organised women's networks have grown in stature, in part owing to the referenda on abortion and divorce in the 1980s and 1990s. The 'women's vote' has become an important force that political parties ignore at their peril. In the field of education, women attend universities and third-level colleges in increasing numbers, forming the majority in arts faculties. However, although universities are obliged by new legislation to introduce greater gender equality, the number of women professors and senior lecturers in Irish third-level colleges remains pathetically small. Women have made more of an impact in the upper echelons of the trade-union movement than in any other Irish institution. The professions, such as medicine and law, have made some advances in recent years. But the numbers of women judges and consultants, although growing, are quite small. Irish women are, in contrast, very well represented in the arts in general, both as artists and in management.

As women departed from their traditional roles, prejudice and poor prospects dogged the newest members of Irish society: the asylum-seekers and refugees whose arrival has been one of the most obvious results of the economic boom.

The growing economy made Ireland an attractive destination for those from more disadvantaged areas in Europe and Africa. Immigration to Ireland had been minimal in the twentieth century, limited to small numbers of displaced people – from Jews fleeing Russian pogroms in the early part of the century to Hungarians, Chileans, Vietnamese and Bosnians abandoning their countries for a more peaceful life in Ireland later in the century. Since 1991, however, people of more than a hundred different nationalities have applied for refuge in Ireland.[17]

In 2001, the Department of Justice recorded that 3,887 people had claimed asylum in the state up to the end of May.[18] The numbers had grown exponentially during the latter part of the 1990s. The Department of Justice received 39 applications for asylum in 1992, 91 in 1993, 362 in 1994, 424 in 1995, 3,883 in 1997 and 4,626 in 1998. According to the 2001 figures for the period up to May, the 3,887 applications showed a drop of 763 on the same period for the previous year. Nigerians accounted for 1,392 of those claims, while Romanians made 499 applications. In 1998, 40 per cent of applicants came from Nigeria and 22 per cent from Romania, with Algeria, Libya, Angola and Congo together making up 15 per cent. In 1999, Romania headed the list of applicants with 1,678, followed by Nigeria with 1,155, then 459 from Poland, 219 from Kenya, 206 from Algeria, 197 from Moldova and 175 from Congo/Zaire. There were 141 applications from Slovakia, 125 from Angola and 113 from Russia.[19] In 2000, the Irish government signed an agreement with Nigeria to help deport unsuccessful asylum-seekers. Only about one out of ten Nigerian asylum-seekers have succeeded in gaining refugee status.

The figures for the period between 1992 and 17 November 2000, prior to the implementation of the 1996 Refugee Act (as amended), showed that 749 people, or 8 per cent of applicants, had been granted refugee status. Another category showed that 6,976, or 68 per cent, had been refused refugee status substantively. Another recording category of the Department of Justice showed that 2,467, or 24 per cent, had been refused refugee status under manifestly unfounded procedure. That curiously named category is usually an accelerated procedure. The total number of decisions taken in the period was 10,192. The recommendations of the Refugee Applications Commissioner between 20 November 2000 and 31 May 2001 were as follows: granted refugee status, 118, or 6.5 per cent; refused refugee status substantively, 1,119, or 61.3 per cent; refused refugee status under manifestly unfounded procedure, 589, or 32.2 per cent. That recorded the number of decisions taken as 1,826.

The Irish government introduced tough measures to tighten up security at Irish ports and airports. Asylum claims made at the port of Rosslare in 2001 until the end of May represented 0.6 per cent of all 3,887 applications – a sharp contrast to the previous year, when asylum applications at the port accounted for 13.4 per cent of all claims, according to an *Irish Times* report. 'More than two-thirds of asylum seekers this year made their claim at the offices of the Refugee Applications Commissioner in Dublin's Lower Mount Street. A further quarter made their claim at Dublin Airport, with less than 1 per cent at the ports of Dublin and Dún Laoghaire and Shannon Airport,' claimed the same report.[20] The Minister for Justice, John O'Donoghue, said in the Dáil in February 2001 that people who might have been trying to enter Ireland to seek asylum had been turned back at Cherbourg due to the new controls. He also said that such people could claim asylum in France or the state through which they entered EU territory.

The Cherbourg measures drew strong criticism from spokespeople for church organisations, who claimed that the measures constituted 'pre-emptive 'exclusion' of asylum seekers. Amnesty International, according to *The Irish Times*, expressed concern that the state was making access to its territory – and therefore asylum procedures – more difficult. There were fears that the tightening up of regulations might push more and more asylum-seekers into the arms of unscrupulous traffickers.

However stringent the entry measures, thousands of people from eastern Europe and Africa will continue to reach Irish shores in the first decade of the twenty-first century. These, together with the tens of thousands of migrant workers encouraged to come to work in the booming economy, present Ireland with the challenge of adapting its relatively homogeneous society to the reality of multiculturalism. This process has brought, and continues to bring, its own tensions. The slogan 'Ireland for the Irish' may be heard more and more often at election time as populists seek to exploit ambivalent feelings towards the 'outsider' and manipulate fears about 'foreigners' for votes. A 'little Ireland' mentality has a dangerous resonance for those who seek greater tolerance in Irish society.

The media have a very important role to play in the dissemination of positive images of Ireland's inexorable move towards becoming a multiracial and multicultural society. But misleading headlines and sensationalised reporting are perpetuating a myth of the country being overwhelmed by 'foreigners'. A lead story in the *Irish Independent* on 3 July 2001 reported that 'immigrants are flocking into Ireland at the rate of 2,000 a week, official figures reveal. If present trends continue, we could have an influx of almost 100,000 adults – more than the population of Limerick – this year alone.' In writing the headline for the piece, the sub-editor confused a possibility with a fact: 'Immigrant influx will hit 100,000 this year'. Such inaccuracy feeds the flames of prejudice.

The change in Ireland's economic circumstances was mirrored by an apparent change in attitudes towards Europe: on 7 June 2001 the electorate voted to reject the Treaty of Nice in a referendum.

The treaty had been negotiated over a ten-month period by fifteen countries in an effort to set out the arrangements for a union of twenty-seven member states, in preparation for the forthcoming enlargement of the European Union. Fears of threats to Ireland's power in Europe, of diminished national self-determination and of the erosion of Irish neutrality drove the 'No' campaign.

Only 34.79 per cent of eligible voters took part, but 54 per cent voted no. An editorial in *The Irish Times*, entitled 'Defeat for Complacency', sought to capture the essence of the outcome, arguing that: 'This is a decisive result, which must be accepted and respected by the government and the campaign protagonists. It is also a regrettable one, both in substance and in terms of democratic procedure.'[21]

In terms of democratic procedure, the debate on the future of Europe did not take place. The Fianna Fáil–Progressive Democrat government's 'Yes' campaign was thwarted from the outset by divisions within the coalition. The Tánaiste, Mary Harney, had accused her EU partners in *The Irish Times* in September 2000 of being 'wedded to an outmoded philosophy of high taxation and heavy regulation which condemns millions of their people to unemployment'. The Tánaiste and the Minister for Arts, Heritage, Gaeltacht and the Islands, Síle de Valera (a granddaughter of Éamon de Valera), preferred to downplay the European influence on Ireland and emphasise the strong links between Ireland and the US.

172   The 500-euro note; one of a set introduced in January 2002
European Central Bank

By the end of the referendum campaign, the Minister for Finance, Charlie McCreevy, had openly broken with the Taoiseach on Ireland's future attitude towards the EU. He had defied the European Union's budgetary policy guidelines earlier in the year. A formal reprimand from the European Commission and Council of Ministers left him quite unrepentant. 'I hope everyone wears the green jersey on this and stands together to defend our economic success,' Harney said in defence of her friend and ministerial colleague on national radio.

All the major political parties favoured Nice in June 2001, but the mismanaged campaign and the government's failure to gauge the mood of the electorate resulted in an embarrassing, unprecedented revolt against Europe. Humiliated at home and abroad, the government announced the establishment of a Forum on Europe to stimulate informed debate on an increasingly vexatious topic. It was expected that the electorate would be asked to respond to a second referendum on the same issue in 2002.

Responding to global trends, the Irish economy in mid-2001 was beginning to show signs of slowing down. There were redundancies in the traditional industries of textiles and steel manufacture, but there were also growing job losses in the information-technology sector. The national tourist industry had been severely hit by an outbreak of foot-and-mouth disease in the United Kingdom, which led to restrictions on movements and the cancellation of major events including the annual St Patrick's Day parade in Dublin. This crisis created further pressure on an economy already feeling the effects of the slowdown in the United States.

Despite these signs and the warnings from the European Union about inflationary pressures, Irish people had never had it so good. Unemployment figures were low and demand for skilled workers high, leading to immigration and its attendant problems.

Tribunals abounded in Ireland in 2001, demonstrating the capacity of the state to confront the abuses of the past and introduce measures to rectify faults within various institutions. The committee system in Dáil Éireann, too, demonstrated its potential to adjust to meet the new challenge of achieving greater openness in the political decision-making process. A determined effort was being made to address the need for radical reform of parliament, government institutions and the health service.

Reform of the health service, however, proved the most intractable issue. The Minister for Health, Mícheál Martin, had money to rebuild the service, but struggled against the usual obstacles of greed and vested interests. His plan to provide a free GP service to citizens over the age of seventy was enlightened. It helped challenge the fundamental injustice of a two-tier system – one for public patients and one for the privately insured.

Education, too, presented a challenge for the reformers, as it had been undercapitalised for decades at all levels. The 1990s saw an opportunity to initiate change, but it was feared that in the event of a decline in the national economy the cash would not be there to provide the necessary investment. Secondary teachers displayed a new-found militancy and their industrial action in 2001 seemed for a time to threaten the viability of the Leaving Certificate examination.

There was the further concern that Ireland had not made the best use of regional and structural funds from the European Union. After nearly thirty years in the EU, the Irish transport infrastructure was among the worst in the Union. The rail service, with the exception of the Dublin–Belfast line, was sub-standard, and the road system lacked extended stretches of motorway. Meanwhile, travel within the capital city by car or bus was often difficult. One major innovation in public transport in Dublin was LUAS, a rapid rail system due to begin service in 2004. Other cities were not so favoured.

In the world of literature and the arts, Ireland was enjoying a renaissance in 2001. The Nobel laureate Seamus Heaney was the foremost figure in literature, but novelists such as John Banville, poets like Eavan Boland, Paul Durcan and John Montague, and dramatists of the calibre of Brian Friel ensured that Ireland's literary fame continued. In art, music and the cinema, Irish men and women were internationally successful.

The wealth of the country encouraged its flourishing intellectual life, denoting Ireland's new confidence. Yet a gulf was widening between the rich and the poor, as the welfare culture declined in favour of what seemed to be almost a Thatcherite, stratified society. This would be a challenge for the future.

Ireland in 2001 was in a strong position to deal with the unpredictable and the unknown. The problems of the island were likely to prove manageable, provided a shaky peace process continued to hold, the international economy remained fundamentally sound and political leaders remembered – to paraphrase Professor Patrick Lynch in his contribution to this volume – that economic growth, however essential in the planning of a just society, is not enough.

NOTES

CHAPTER 3 (pp 25–40)

1 Prologue to *Félire Óengusso*; see Whitley Stokes, *On the Calendar of Oengus* (1880), pp xviii ff.
2 *Crith Gablach*, ed. D. A. Binchy (1941), p. 23, § 46; cf. Eoin MacNeill, in *Proceedings of the Royal Irish Academy*, 26 C 16 (1923), pp 305 ff.
3 Ibid.
4 Ibid., pp 7 ff, § 14, 15.
5 Ibid., p. 16, § 27.
6 Ibid.

CHAPTER 4 (pp 41–53)

1 *The Works of St Patrick*, translated by Ludwig Bieler (1953), p. 28.
2 Whitley Stokes and J. Strachan (ed.), *Thesaurus Palaeohibernicus*, ii (1903), p. 247 (spelling modernised).
3 *Sancti Columbani Opera*, ed. G. S. M. Walker (1957), pp 122 ff.
4 *Betha Colaim Chille*, ed. A. O'Kelleher and G. Schoepperle (1918), p. 294.
5 *Sancti Columbani Opera*, pp 46–9.
6 Ibid., p. 190, 11 4–9; English rendering by Tomás Ó Fiaich.

CHAPTER 5 (pp54–66)

1 *Ancient Laws of Ireland*, iii, 88.
2 R. Thurneysen (ed.), *Scéla Mucce Meic Datho* (Medieval and Modern Irish series, vi), pp 15-16.
3 *Thesaurus Palaeohibernicus*, ii, 246.
4 G. Calder (ed.), *Auraicept na n-Éces* (1917), p. 6, translated by Robin Flower, in *The Irish Tradition* (1947), p. 45.
5 W. Stokes (ed.), *Félire Óengusso* (1905), p. 26, translated by Frank O'Connor, in *Kings, Lords and Commons* (London, 1962), p. 4.
6 *Félire Óengusso* (1905), p. 25, translated by Frank O'Connor, ibid, p. 3.
7 *Thesaurus Palaeohibernicus* ii, 327.
8 Migne, *Patrologia Latina*, lxxii, col. 789.
9 J. J. O'Meara (ed.), Giraldus Cambrensis Topographia Hibernie, in *Proceedings of the Royal Irish Academy*, 52 C 4, pp 151–2 (1940; translated by J. J. O'Meara in *The History and Topography of Ireland by Gerald of Wales* (Penguin Books, 1982), p. 84.

CHAPTER 6 (pp 67–80)

1 From Latin verses by Donatus, bishop of Fiesole, in *Monumenta Germaniae Historica*, Poet. *Lat. Aevi Carol.*, iii (1890), pp 691–2, translated by Liam de Paor.
2 Poem in margin of St Gall Priscian, in *Thesaurus Palaeohibernicus*, ii, 290, translated by Liam de Paor.
3 Johs. Bøe, 'An Ornamented Bronze Object Found in a Norwegian Grave' in *Bergens Museums Aarbok*, 1924–5, Hist.-Antikv. Raekke, no. 4, p. 34.
4 *Cogadh Gaedhel re Gallaibh*, translated by J. H. Todd (1867), p. 41.
5 P. F. Wallace, 'Anglo-Norman Dublin: Continuity and Change' in Donnchadh Ó Corráin (ed.), *Irish Antiquity* (Cork), 1981), pp 247–67; 'The Origins of Dublin' in B. G. Scott (ed.), *Studies in Early Ireland: Essays in Honour of M. V. Duignan* (Belfast, 1982), pp 129–43.

6 *Cogadh Gaedhel re Gallaibh*, p. 79.

7 From Njal's Saga, translated by Holger Arbnam, in *The Vikings* (1961), p. 72.

CHAPTER 7 (pp 81–94)

1 *The Bardic Poems of Tadhg Dall Ó Huiginn* (Irish Texts Society, vol. xxi), ed. Eleanor Knott, poem 17.

2 Edmund Curtis and R. B. McDowell (ed.), *Irish Historical Documents 1172–1922*, p. 17.

3 For some account of this grammatical material see Osborn Bergin, 'The Native Irish Grammarian' in *Proceedings of the British Academy*, xxiv; Brian Ó Cuív, 'Linguistic Terminology in the Mediaeval Irish Bardic Tracts' in *Transactions of the Philological Society* (1965), and *The Linguistic Training of the Mediaeval Irish Poet* (1973).

4 The three manuscripts are (i) *Lebor na hUidre*, now in the Royal Irish Academy, Dublin, (ii) Rawlinson B. 502, now in the Bodleian Library, Oxford, (iii) *Lebor na hUachongbála*, commonly known as the *Book of Leinster*, now in part in Trinity College, Dublin, and in part in the Franciscan Library in Dún Mhuire, Killiney, County Dublin. It has been argued recently by Professor Pádraig Ó Riain (in *Éigse*, xvii, 161–76) that the main part of the Rawlinson MS is the codex which was known as *Lebor Glinne Dá Loch*, or *Book of Glendalough*.

5 *Early Irish Lyrics*, ed. G. Murphy (1956), pp 70–71.

6 *Book of Armagh*, f. 16 rº. See fig. 42.

7 The hereditary nature of *comarbas Pátraic* between the tenth and twelfth centuries can be seen from the following genealogical table in which members of the Uí Shínaig family are shown. The names of those who held the office of *comarba Pátraic* and of two members who contested the abbacy in the time of St Malachy are printed in italics and the dates of tenure of office added in brackets:

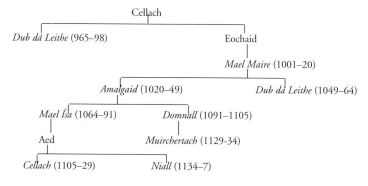

CHAPTER 8 (pp 95–112)

1 *Annals of the Four Masters*, ed. John O'Donovan, 1145, 1171.

2 Geoffrey Keating, *Foras Feasa ar Éirinn*, ed. David Comyn and P. S. Dineen, iii, 318 (319).

3 Giraldus Cambrensis, *Expugnatio Hibernica, the Conquest of Ireland*, ed. A. B. Scott and F. X. Martin (1974), p. 41.

4 *The Song of Dermot and the Earl*, ed. G. H. Orpen (1892), pp 22–5.

5 Ibid., p. 34–5.

6 Giraldus Cambrensis, as above, pp 87, 89.

7 Ibid., p. 77.

Professor Martin wishes to express in a special way his gratitude to Dr Jocelyn Otway-Ruthven, of Trinity College, Dublin, who read this chapter in its final draft and made candid comments and corrections.

CHAPTER 9 (pp 113–124)

1 *Calendar of the Justiciary Rolls, Ireland 1308–14*, p. 103.

2 Seán Ó Tuama, 'The New Love Poetry' in Brian Ó Cuív (ed.), *Seven Centuries of Irish Learning* (1961), p. 111.

3 Kathleen Hoagland, *1000 Years of Irish Poetry* (1953), p. 313.

4 J. T. Gilbert, *Facsimiles of the National Manuscripts of Ireland* (1884), pp 98–100.
5 Aubrey Gwynn, 'The Black Death in Ireland' in *Studies*, March 1935, pp 27–8.

CHAPTER 10 (pp 125—138)

1 *The Libelle of Englyshe Polycye*, ed. G. F. Warner (1926), p. 36.
2 Cited by H. G. Richardson and G. O. Sayles, *The Irish Parliament in the Middle Ages* (1952), p. 180, n. 40.
3 *Statute Rolls of the Parliament of Ireland, Henry VI*, p. 567.
4 *Register of John Swayne*, ed. D. A. Chart (1935), p. 108.
5 *Annals of the Four Masters*, ed. John O'Donovan, iv, 965.
6 *Statute Rolls of the Parliament of Ireland, Henry VI*, p. 50.
7 Edmund Curtis, 'The Viceroyalty of Richard, Duke of York' in *Journal of the Royal Society of Antiquaries of Ireland*, lxii (1932), p. 166.
8 *Annals of the Four Masters*, iv, 1051–3.
9 *Statute Rolls of the Parliament of Ireland, 1st to 12th years Edward IV*, p. 139.
10 Margaret Griffith, 'The Talbot–Ormond Struggle for Control of the Anglo-Irish Government, 1414–47' in *Irish Historical Studies*, ii, no. 8 (Sept. 1941), p. 396.
11 P.R.O., Council and Privy Seal Warrants, E 28/89, 30 Mar., 3 Edward IV.
12 *Annals of Ulster*, iii, 219–21.
13 G. O. Sayles, 'The Vindication of the Earl of Kildare from Treason, 1496' in *Irish Historical Studies*, vii, no. 25 (Mar. 1950), p. 43.
14 Constantia Maxwell (ed.) *Irish History from Contemporary Sources* (1923), p. 113.
15 *Vetera Monumenta Hibernorum et Scotorum Historiam Illustrantia*, 1216–1547, ed. Augustine Theiner (Rome, 1864), p. 521.
16 *State Papers, Henry VIII, Ireland*, ii, 15.
17 See Art Cosgrove, *Late Medieval Ireland, 1370–1541* (Dublin, 1981), pp 116–20.

CHAPTER 11 (pp 139–151)

1 Skeffington and the Irish council to Henry VIII, 26 Mar. 1535 (*State Papers, Henry VIII, Ireland*, ii, 236 ff).
2 'A certain information for our sovereign lord's commissioners in Ireland, 1537' (ibid., ii, 480).
3 Henry VIII to Surrey, 1520 (ibid., ii, 52 ff).
4 Henry VIII to lord deputy and Irish council, 1541 (ibid., iii, 332 ff).
5 28 Henry VIII c. 5 (*Irish Statutes* (1786), i, 90).
6 Statement of Thomas Lynch of Galway (*State Papers, Henry VIII, Ireland*, iii, 141).
7 William Camden, *Annals* (1615), p. 78.
8 Ibid.
9 Lord justice and Irish council to privy council, 5 Nov. 1597 (*Calendar of State Papers, Ireland, 1596–7*, p. 436).

CHAPTER 12 (pp 152–164)

1 Sir John Davies to Earl of Salisbury, 12 Sept. 1607 (*Calendar of State Papers, Ireland, 1606–8*, p. 237).

CHAPTER 13 (pp 165–175)

1 Thomas Carte, *Life of Ormonde* (1736), ii, 140.
2 Jonathan Swift, *Works*, ed. T. Scott (1910), iv. 94.
3 *Poems of David Ó Bruadair*, ed. J. C. MacErlean (1917), iii, 15.
4 *Clarendon Correspondence*, ed. S. W. Singer (1828), ii, 475.
5 'Lilliburlero' in T. C. Croker, *Historical Songs of Ireland* (1841), pp 66–7.

CHAPTER 14 (pp 176–189)

1 3 William and Mary, c. 2.

2 George Berkeley, *The Querist*, in *The Works of George Berkeley, Bishop of Cloyne*, ed. A. A. Luce and T. E. Jessop, vi (1953), p. 128.
3 Arthur Young, *A Tour of Ireland* (1780), ii, pt 2, pp 35, 36.
4 *Dánta Diadha Uladh*, ed. Énri Ó Muirgheasa (1936), pp 281–3.
5 John Burke, *A General and Heraldic Dictionary of the Peerage and Baronetage of the British Empire* (1828), p. 89.
6 *Amhráin Phiarais Mhic Gearailt*, ed. Risteard Ó Foghludha (1905), p. 23.

CHAPTER 16 (pp 204–217)

1 Quoted in J. A. Reynolds, *The Catholic Emancipation Crisis in Ireland* (1954), p. 22.
2 *Dublin Evening Post*, 3 July 1828.
3 C. Gavan Duffy, *Young Ireland* (1880), pp 344–7.
4 *First Series of Reports of the Loyal National Repeal Association of Ireland* (1840), pp viii–ix.
5 Duffy, op. cit., p. 217.

CHAPTER 18 (pp 228–244)

1 Lord Eversley, *Gladstone and Ireland* (1912), p/ 18.
2 *Freeman's Journal*, 9 June 1879, quoted in Michael Davitt, *The Fall of Feudalism in Ireland*, p. 154.
3 R. Barry O'Brien, *Life of Charles Stewart Parnell* (1898), i, 240.
4 John Morley, *Life of William Ewart Gladstone* (1903), iii, 240.
5 *Speech by Mr Charles Stewart Parnell in the House of Commons, on the motion for the second reading of the bill for the future government of Ireland, 7 June 1886*, p. 13.

CHAPTER 19 (pp 245–261)

1 W. B. Yeats, *Nine One-Act Plays* (1937), p. 36.
2 T. M. Kettle, 'Would the Hungarian Policy Work?' in *New Ireland Review*, Feb. 1905.
3 W. B. Yeats, 'Under Ben Bulben' (1938) in *Collected Poems* (1961), p. 398.
4 P. H. Pearse, *Political Writings and Speeches* (1922), pp 177–8.
5 *The Workers' Republic*, 6 Nov. 1915.
6 Erskine Childers, *The Framework of Home Rule* (1911), p. 168.
7 Dorothy Macardle, *The Irish Republic* (new ed., 1951), pp 89–90; see also Ian Colvin, *Life of Lord Carson*, ii (1934), 206.
8 *The Workers' Republic*, 6 Nov. 1915.

CHAPTER 20 (pp 262–271)

1 Ian Colvin, *Life of Lord Carson*, ii (1934), p. 298.
2 *Commons in NI*, ii, 603.
3 *Belfast News Letter*, 7 Dec. 1925.
4 St John Ervine, *Craigavon* (1949), p. 416.
5 *Hansard NI (commons)*, viii, 2272.
6 *Annual Register, 1942*, p. 98.
7 *Hansard NI (commons)*, lix, 15.

CHAPTER 21 (pp 272–287)

1 Treaty debates, 19 Dec. 1921, p. 32.
2 Ibid., 7 Jan. 1922, p. 337.

CHAPTER 22 (pp 288–305)

1 For the vast literature on this subject, see *A Social Science Bibliography of Northern Ireland, 1945–83*, compiled by Bill Rolston, Mike Tomlinson, Liam O'Dowd, Bob Miller and Jim Smyth. Belfast 1983.

CHAPTER 23 (pp 306–320)

1 For excellent surveys of the scholarship relevant to recent Irish politics and history, see J. Whyte, *Interpreting Northern Ireland* (Oxford, Clarendon, 1990) and J. Coakley and M. Gallagher (eds.), *Politics in the Republic of Ireland* (Dublin, Folens, 1993 edn.).

CHAPTER 24 (pp 321–344)

1 On 22 April 1997, Brendan Smyth was found guilty in a Dublin court on 74 charges of indecent and sexual assault.

2 Senator George Mitchell, *Making Peace – The Inside Story of the Making of the Good Friday Agreement* (Heinemann, London, 1999), p. 26.

3 Andrew J. Wilson, Irish America and the Ulster Conflict *1968–1995* (Blackstaff Press, Belfast, 1995), p. 293

4 Interview with John Hume, University College Cork, 1995

5 David McKittrick, Seamus Kelters, Brian Feeney and Chris Thornton, *Lost Lives – The Stories of the Men, Women and Children Who Died as a Result of the Northern Troubles* (Mainstream, Edinburgh and London, 1999), p. 1336.

6 Joseph Ruane and Jennifer Todd (eds.), *After the Good Friday Agreement – Analysing Political Change in Northern Ireland* (University College Dublin Press, Dublin, 1999), pp 6–7.

7 Wilson, op. cit., pp 298–299.

8 Ibid, p. 300.

9 Mitchell, op. cit. pp 10–11.

10 Ibid, pp 10–12

11 I was commissioned by the forum to make a study of the role of the Catholic Church in the development of the Irish state. See *Building Trust in Ireland – Studies Commissioned by the Forum for Peace and Reconciliation* (Blackstaff Press, Belfast, 1996), pp 89–213.

12 Mitchell, op. cit., pp 33ff

13 Irish Department of Foreign Affairs information leaflet, 'Northern Ireland Peace Process – The Making of the Good Friday Agreement of 1998'.

14 Rosemary Nelson, a prominent solicitor, was murdered on 15 March 1999; a bomb was placed under her car in Lurgan, County Armagh.

15 Fintan O'Toole, *Meanwhile Back at the Ranch – The Politics of Irish Beef* (Vintage, 1995), London pp 281–2. The book is a condensed account of the events and the Beef Tribunal that is very critical of the manner in which the government sought to protect itself throughout the hearings.

16 Based on *States of Fear*, Mary Raftery and Eoin O'Sullivan published *Suffer the Little Children: The Inside Story of Ireland's Industrial Schools* in 1999. In 1998, Susan McKay's *Sophia's Choice* was published. The following year, Bernadette Fahy wrote *Freedom of Angels: Surviving Goldenbridge Orphanage*.

17 Paul Cullen, *Refugees and Asylum-Seekers in Ireland* (Cork University Press, Cork, 2000), p. 17.

18 *The Irish Times*, 11 June 2001.

19 Cullen, op. cit. p. 17.

20 *The Irish Times*, 11 June 2001; The article continues: 'The number of people seeking asylum at Rosslare has dropped dramatically this year. Only twenty-four people claimed asylum at the County Wexford port in the first five months of the year, compared to 514 for the same period last year, according to statistics from the Office of the Refugee Applications Commissioner. The drop in asylum applications at Rosslare follows document controls introduced last November by Irish Ferries staff in the French port of Cherbourg. Acting on garda advice, staff have started preventing immigrants with false or inadequate documentation from boarding at Cherbourg.'

21 *The Irish Times*, 9 June 2001.

A Bibliography of Irish History

The following is a bibliography of published works in English or Irish on the history of Ireland. Most of them were written in the twentiety century. A new section, Bibliographical Addenda, brings the bibliography up to date. For further bibliographical information, consult 'Writings in Irish History', published annually in *Irish Historical Studies*. With some exceptions it does not include source material, printed or in manuscript, but the reader who seeks for guidance to this vast field is referred to section XV below.

The arrangement within most sections is broadly according to chronological order of subject.

Works in section I relate to more than one of the periods covered by sections IV–XII. Section II comprises works ranging widely over Irish history. Works in section XIII relate to all the periods covered by sections VI–X. Some works that cross period divisions appear in more than one section.

I GENERAL HISTORY OF IRELAND

SOURCE COLLECTIONS

Edmund Curtis and R. B. McDowell (ed.). *Irish Historical Documents, 1172–1922*. London, 1943; reprint, 1968.

Constantia Maxwell (ed.). *Irish History from Contemporary Sources, 1509–1610*. London, 1923.

James Carty (ed.). *Ireland from the Flight of the Earls to Grattan's Parliament, 1607–1782*. Dublin, 1949.

James Carty (ed.). *Ireland from Grattan's Parliament to the Great Famine, 1783–1850*. Dublin, 1939.

James Carty (ed.). *Ireland from the Great Famine to the Treaty, 1851–1921*. Dublin, 1951.

Basil Chubb (ed.). *A Source Book of Irish Government*. Dublin, 1964.

GENERAL WORKS

Edmund Curtis. *A History of Ireland*. London, 1936; 6th edition, 1950.

Sean O'Faolain. *The Irish*. Penguin Books, 1937; new edition, 1978.

J. C. Beckett. *A Short History of Ireland*. London, 1952; 6th edition, 1979; reprint. 1981.

Brian Inglis. *The Story of Ireland*. London, 1956; 2nd edition, 1965.

Robert Kee. *Ireland: A History*. London, 1980.

Eoin MacNeill. *Phases of Irish History*. Dublin, 1919.

Edmund Curtis. *A History of Medieval Ireland, from 1086 to 1513*. London, 1923; 2nd edition, 1938; reprint, 1968.

A. J. Otway-Ruthven. *A History of Medieval Ireland*. With an introduction (on Ireland before the coming of the Normans) by Kathleen Hughes. London, 1968; reprint 1980.

Extended review by F. X. Martin, in *Studia Hibernica*, no. 14 (1974), pp 143–60.

J. C. Beckett. *The Making of Modern Ireland, 1603–1923*. London, 1966; paperback edition, 1969; new edition, 1981.

J. C. Beckett. *Confrontations: Studies in Irish History*. London, 1972.

F. G. James. *Ireland in the Empire, 1688–1770*. Cambridge (Mass.), 1973.

W. O'Connor Morris. *Ireland, 1798–1898*. London, 1898.

P. S. O'Hegarty. *A History of Ireland under the Union, 1801–1922*. London, 1952.

Oliver MacDonagh. *Ireland, the Union and its Aftermath*. London, 1977. (First published as *Ireland*, Englewood Cliffs (N.J.), 1968.)

F. S. L. Lyons, *Ireland Since the Famine*. London, 1971; revised edition, 1973.

F. S. L. Lyons. *Culture and Anarchy in Ireland, 1890–1939*. Oxford, 1974.

Dorothy Macardle. *The Irish Republic: A Documented Chronicle of the Anglo-Irish Conflict*. Preface by Éamon de Valera, London, 1937; 4th edition, Dublin, 1951; American edition, New York, 1965.

The Gill History of Ireland. Edited by J. F. Lydon and Margaret MacCurtain. 11 vols. Dublin, 1972–5.

The Helicon History of Ireland. Edited by Art Cosgrove and Elma Collins. To be completed in 10 vols. Dublin, 1981–.

A New History of Ireland. Edited by T. W. Moody, F. X. Martin and F. J. Byrne. To be completed in 10 vols. Oxford, 1976–. (A cooperative history, under the auspices of the Royal Irish Academy).

II GENERAL WORKS IN SPECIAL FIELDS

THE CELTS

T. G. E. Powell. *The Celts*. London, 1958

Joseph Raftery (ed.). *The Celts*. Cork, 1964.

Myles Dillon and Nora K. Chadwick. *The Celtic Realms*. London, 1967; 2nd edition, 1972.

Proinsias Mac Cana. *Celtic Mythology*. London, 1970.

ECONOMIC AND SOCIAL HISTORY

D. A. Chart. *The Economic History of Ireland*. Dublin, 1920.

Charles Doherty. 'Exchange and Trade in Early Medieval Ireland' in *Journal of the Royal Society of Antiquaries of Ireland*, cx (1980), pp 67–89.

M. D. O'Sullivan. *Italian Merchant Bankers in Ireland in the Thirteenth Century*. London, 1962.

Jacques Bernard. 'The Maritime Intercourse between Bordeaux and Ireland, *c.* 1450–*c.* 1520' in *Irish Economic and Social History*, vii (1980), pp 7–21.

A. K. Longfield. *Anglo-Irish Trade in the Sixteenth Century*. London, 1929.

George O'Brien. *The Economic History of Ireland in the Seventeenth Century*. Dublin and London, 1918.

George O'Brien. *The Economic History of Ireland in the Eighteenth Century*. Dublin, 1918.

George O'Brien. *The Economic History of Ireland from the Union to the Famine*. London, 1921.

A. E. Murray. *A History of the Commercial and Financial Relations between England and Ireland from the Period of the Restoration*. London, 1903.

L. M. Cullen. *The Emergence of Modern Ireland, 1600–1900*. London, 1981.

L. M. Cullen and T. C. Smout (ed.). *Comparative Aspects of Scottish and Irish Economic and Social History, 1600–1900*. Edinburgh, 1977.

L. M. Cullen and François Furet (ed.). *Ireland and France, Seventeenth to Twentieth Centuries: Towards a Comparative Study of Social History*. Paris, 1980.

L. M. Cullen. *An Economic History of Ireland since 1660*. London, 1972.

L. M. Cullen. *Anglo-Irish Trade, 1660–1800*. Manchester, 1968.

L. M. Cullen and Paul Butel (ed.). *Négoce et Industrie en France et en Irlande aux XVIIIe et XIXe Siècles*. Paris, 1980.

L. M. Cullen (ed.). *The Formation of the Irish Economy*. Cork, 1969.

K. B. Nowlan (ed.). *Travel and Transport in Ireland*. Dublin and New York, 1973.

R. N. Salaman. *The History and Social Influence of the Potato*. Cambridge, 1949; reprint, 1970.

K. H. Connell. 'The Potato in Ireland' in *Past & Present*, no. 23 (Nov. 1962), pp 57–71.

Conrad Gill. *The Rise of the Irish Linen Industry*. Oxford, 1925; reprint, 1964.

Patrick Lynch and John Vaizey. *Guinness's Brewery in the Irish Economy, 1759–1876*. Cambridge, 1966.

E. B. McGuire. *Irish Whiskey: A History of Distilling, the Spirit Trade and Excise Controls in Ireland*. Dublin, 1973.

Michael Drake. 'Marriage and Population Growth in Ireland, 1750–1845' in *Economic History Review*, xvi, no. 2 (Dec. 1963), pp 301–13.

R. D. C. Black. *Economic Thought and the Irish Question, 1817–1870*. Cambridge, 1960.

Elizabeth R. Hooker. *Readjustments of Agricultural Tenure in Ireland*. Chapel Hill, (N.C.), 1938.

David O'Mahony. *The Irish Economy*. Cork, 1962; 2nd edition, 1967.

James Meenan. *The Irish Economy Since 1922*. Liverpool, 1970.

Commission of Inquiry into Banking, Currency and Credit (1934–1938), reports. Dublin, Stationery Office, (1938). (P. 2628)

Maurice Moynihan. *Currency and Central Banking in Ireland, 1922–1960*. Dublin, 1975.

Economic Development. Dublin, Stationery Office, 1958. (Pr. 4803)

Science and Irish Economic Development: Report of the Research and Technology Team Appointed by the Minister for Industry and Commerce in November 1963 (in association with OECD). 2 vols. Dublin, Stationery Office, 1966. (Pr. 8975, Pr. 9093)

N. J. Gibson and J. E. Spencer (ed.). *Economic Activity in Ireland: A Study of Two Open Economies*. Dublin 1977.

Barry Moore, John Rhodes, and Roger Tarling. 'Industrial Policy and Economic Development: The Experience of Northern Ireland and the Republic of Ireland' in *Cambridge Journal of Economics*, ii (1978).

K. A. Kennedy and B. R. Dowling. *Economic Growth in Ireland: The Experience Since 1947*. Dublin, 1975.

B. R. Dowling and J. Durkan (ed.). *Irish Economic Policy: A Review of Major Issues*. Dublin, 1978.

J. W. O'Hagan (ed.). *The Economy of Ireland: Policy and Performance*. 3rd edition. Dublin, 1981.

L. M. Cullen. *Life in Ireland*. London and New York, 1968.

Constantia Maxwell. *The Stranger in Ireland*. London, 1954.

Constantia Maxwell. *Country and Town in Ireland under the Georges*. London, 1940; new edition, Dundalk, 1949.

S. J. Connolly. *Priests and People in Pre-famine Ireland, 1780–1845*. Dublin, 1982.

L. M. Cullen. *Six Generations: Life and Work in Ireland from 1790*. Cork, 1970.

R. B. McDowell (ed.). *Social Life in Ireland, 1800–45*. Dublin, 1957.

K. H. Connell. *Irish Peasant Society: Four Historical Essays*. Oxford, 1968.

Terence Brown. *Ireland: A Social and Cultural History, 1922–1979*. Fontana Paperbacks, 1981.

TOWNS

R. A. Butlin (ed.). *The Development of the Irish Town*. London and Totowa (N.J.), 1977.

David Harkness and Mary O'Dowd (ed.) *The Town in Ireland*. Belfast, 1981.

H. B. Clarke. *Dublin, c. 840–c. 1560: The Medieval Town in the Modern City*. Dublin, 1978.

A. P. Smyth. *Scandinavian York and Dublin*. Vol. i, Dublin, 1975; vol. ii, 1981.

National Museum of Ireland. *Viking and Medieval Dublin*. Dublin, 1973.

P. F. Wallace. 'Dublin's Waterfront at Wood Quay: 900–1317' in G. Milne and B. Hobley (ed.), *Waterfront Archaeology in Britain and Northern Europe* (Council for British Archaeology, Research report no. 41, London, 1981), pp 109–18.

P. F. Wallace. 'Anglo-Norman Dublin: Continuity and Change' in D. Ó Corráin (ed.), *Irish Antiquity* (Cork, 1981), pp 247–67.

P. F. Wallace. 'The Origins of Dublin' in B. G. Scott (ed.), *Studies on Early Ireland: Essays in Honour of M. V. Duignan* (Belfast, 1982), pp 129–43.

P. F. Wallace. 'Carpentry in Ireland, AD 900–1300: The Wood Quay Evidence' in S. McGrain (ed.), *Woodworking Techniques before AD 1500* (British Archaeological Reports, International Series no. 129, Oxford, 1982), pp 263–99.

John Ryan. 'Pre-Norman Dublin' in *Journal of the Royal Society of Antiquaries of Ireland*, lxxix (1949), pp 64–83.

M. D. O'Sullivan. *Old Galway: The History of a Norman Colony in Ireland*. Cambridge, 1942.

William O'Sullivan. *The Economic History of Cork City from the Earliest Times to the Act of Union*. Dublin and Cork, 1937.

J. F. Lydon. 'The City of Waterford in the Later Middle Ages' in *Decies*, xii (1979), pp 9–15.

Gearóid Mac Niocaill. *Na Buirgéisi, XII–XV Aois*. I vol, in 2, Dublin, 1964.

Gearóid Mac Niocaill. 'Socio-economic Problems of the Late Medieval Town' in David Harkness and Mary O'Dowd (ed.), *The Town in Ireland* (Belfast, 1981), pp 7–21.

M. J. Craig. *Dublin, 1660–1860*. London, 1952.

J. G. Simms. 'Dublin in 1685' in *Irish Historical Studies*, xiv, no. 55 (Mar. 1965), pp 212–26.

Constantia Maxwell. *Dublin under the Georges*, 1714–1830. London, 1936; 2nd edition, London and Dublin: 1946; revised edition, London, 1956.

LAW, GOVERNMENT AND PARLIAMENT

Eoin MacNeill. *Early Irish Laws and Institutions*. Dublin, 1935.

Eoin MacNeill. 'Ancient Irish Law: The Law of Status and Franchise' in *Proceedings of the Royal Irish Academy*, 36C 16 (1923).

D. A. Binchy. *Crith Gablach*. Dublin, 1941.

D. A. Binchy. *The Linguistic and Historical Value of the Irish Law Tracts* (Sir John Rhys memorial lecture). London, British Academy, 1943.

Liam Ó Buachalla. 'Some researches in Ancient Irish Law' in *Journal of the Cork Historical and Archaeological Society*, lii (1947), pp 41–54, 135–48; liii (1948), pp 1–18.

Bryan Murphy. 'The Status of the Native Irish after 1331' in *Irish Jurist*, ii (1967), pp 116–38.

G. J. Hand. *English Law in Ireland, 1200–1324*. Cambridge, 1967.

A. G. Donaldson. *Some Comparative Aspects of Irish Law*. Durham (N.C.), 1957.

H. G. Richardson and G. O. Sayles. *The Irish Parliament in the Middle Ages*. Philadelphia, 1952; new impression, 1966.

H. G. Richardson and G. O. Sayles. *Parliament in Medieval Ireland*. Dublin Historical Association, 1964.

Brian Farrell (ed.). *The Irish Parliamentary Tradition*. Dublin, 1977.

D. B Quinn. 'The Early Interpretation of Poynings' Law' in *Irish Historical Studies*, ii no. 7 (Mar. 1941), pp 141–54.

R. Dudley Edwards and T. W. Moody, 'The History of Poynings' Law, 1494–1615' in *Irish Historical Studies*, ii, no. 8 (Sept. 1941), pp 415–24.

T. W. Moody. 'The Irish Parliament under Elizabeth and James I: A General Survey', in *Proceedings of the Royal Irish Academy*, 45 C 6 (1939), pp 41–81.

V. W. Treadwell. 'The Irish Parliament of 1569–71' in *Proceedings of the Royal Irish Academy*, 65 C 4 (1966), pp 55–89.

Aidan Clarke. 'The History of Poynings' Law, 1615–41' in *Irish Historical Studies*, xx, no. 80 (Sept. 1977), pp 384–417.

J. L. McCracken. *The Irish Parliament in the Eighteenth Century*. Dublin Historical Association, 1971.

V. W. Treadwell. 'The Irish Customs Administration in the Sixteenth Century' in *Irish Historical Studies*, xx, no. 80 (Sept. 1977), pp 384–417.

T. J. Kiernan. *History of the Financial Administration of Ireland to 1817*. London, 1930.

R. B. McDowell. *The Irish Administration, 1801–1914*. London, 1964.

J. H. Whyte. 'The Influence of the Catholic Clergy on Elections in Nineteenth-Century Ireland' in *English Historical Review*, lxxv, no. 295 (Apr. 1960).

Peter Jupp. 'Irish Parliamentary Elections and the Influence of the Catholic Vote, 1801–20' in *Historical Journal*, x (1967), pp 183–96.

Brian Walker. 'The Irish Electorate, 1806–1915' in *Irish Historical Studies*, xviii, no. 71 (Mar. 1973), pp 183–96.

Nicholas Mansergh. *The Irish Free State: Its Government and Politics*. London, 1934.

D. N. Haire. 'In Aid of the Civil Power, 1868–90' in F. S. L. Lyons and R. A. J. Hawkins (ed.), *Ireland Under the Union* (Oxford, 1980), pp 115–48.

Brian Farrell. *The Founding of Dáil Éireann: Parliament and Nation Building*. Dublin, 1971.

J. L. McCracken. *Representative Government in Ireland: A Study of Dáil Éireann, 1919–1948*. London, 1958.

Donal O'Sullivan. *The Irish Free State and its Senate*. London, 1940.

F. B. Chubb. *The Government and Politics of Ireland*. With a historical introduction by David Thornley. Stanford and London, 1970; paperback edition, 1974; 2nd edition, 1982.

R. K. Carty. *Party and Parish Pump: Electoral Politics in Ireland*. Waterloo, Ontario, 1981.

Ronan Fanning. *The Irish Department of Finance, 1922–58*. Dublin, 1978.

Seán Reámonn. *History of the Revenue Commissioners*. Dublin, 1981.

THE CHURCHES

Kathleen Hughes. *The Church in Early Irish Society*. Cambridge, 1966.

P. J. Corish (ed.). *A History of Irish Catholicism*. Dublin, 1967–72. (An incomplete series of brief studies by various authors issued in sixteen separate fascicles)

N. K. Chadwick. *The Age of the Saints in the Early Celtic Church*. London, 1961.

D. D. C. Pochin Mould. *The Irish Saints*. Dublin, 1964.

John Ryan. *Irish Monasticism: Origins and Early Development*. Dublin, 1934; reprint, Shannon 1972, with new introduction.

J. A. Watt. *The Church in Medieval Ireland*. Dublin, 1972.

J. A. Watt. *The Church and the Two Nations in Medieval Ireland*. Cambridge, 1970.

Kathleen Hughes and Anne Hamlin. *The Modern Traveller to the Medieval Irish Church*. London, 1977.

Aubrey Gwynn and R. N. Hadcock. *Medieval Religious Houses: Ireland*. London, 1970.

Aubrey Gwynn. 'The Twelfth and Thirteenth Centuries' in Aubrey Gwynn and D. F. Gleeson, *A History of the Diocese of Killaloe* (Dublin 1962, pp 135–291). (An account of the general reform movement in the church)

F. X. Martin. 'The Irish Friars and the Observant Movement in the Fifteenth Century' in *Proceedings of the Irish Catholic Historical Committee*, 1960, pp 10–16.

F. X. Martin. 'The Irish Augustinian Reform Movement in the Fifteenth Century' in J. A. Watt, J. B. Morrall and F. X. Martin (ed.), *Medieval Studies Presented to Aubrey Gwynn* (Dublin, 1961), pp 230–64.

Aubrey Gwynn. *The Medieval Province of Armagh, 1470–1545*. Dundalk, 1946.

Aubrey Gwynn. 'Ireland and the English Nation at the Council of Constance' in *Proceedings of the Royal Irish Academy*, 45 C 8 (1940), pp 183–233.

Canice Mooney. 'The Irish Church in the Sixteenth Century' in *Irish Ecclesiastical Record*, xcix (1963) pp 102–113.

Brendan Bradshaw. *The Dissolution of the Religious Orders in Ireland under Henry VIII*. Cambridge, 1974.

F. X. Martin. 'Confusion Abounding: Bernard O'Higgins, O.S.A., Bishop of Elphin, 1542–1561' in Art Cosgrove and Donal McCartney (ed.), *Studies in Irish History Presented to R. Dudley Edwards* (Dublin, 1979), pp 38–84.

F. X. Martin. *Friar Nugent: A Study of Francis Lavalin Nugent (1569–1635), Agent of the Counter-Reformation*. Rome and London, 1962.

D. F. Cregan. 'The Social and Cultural Background of a Counter-Reformation Episcopate, 1618–60' in Art Cosgrove and Donal McCartney (ed.), *Studies in Irish History Presented to R. Dudley Edwards* (Dublin 1979), pp 85–117.

James McCaffrey. *History of the Catholic Church in the Nineteenth Century*. 2 vols. Dublin, 1909.

P. J. Corish. 'Gallicanism at Maynooth: Archbishop Cullen and the Royal Visitation of 1853' in Art

Cosgrove and Donal McCartney (ed.), *Studies in Irish History Presented to R. Dudley Edwards* (Dublin 1979), pp 176–89.

Emmet Larkin. *The Making of the Roman Catholic Church in Ireland, 1850–1860*. Chapel Hill, (N. C.), 1980.

Emmet Larkin. *The Roman Catholic Church and the Creation of the Modern Irish State, 1878–86*. Philadelphia and Dublin, 1975.

Emmet Larkin. *The Roman Catholic Church and the Plan of Campaign in Ireland, 1886–8*. Cork, 1978.

Emmet Larkin. *The Roman Catholic Church in Ireland and the Fall of Parnell, 1886–1891*. Liverpool, 1979.

W. A. Phillips (ed.) *The History of the Church of Ireland*. 3 vols. Oxford, 1933–4.

D. H. Akenson. *The Church of Ireland: Ecclesiastical Reform and Revolution, 1800–1885*. New Haven and London, 1971.

T. J. Johnston, J. L. Robinson and K. W. Jackson. *A History of the Church of Ireland*. Dublin, 1953.

Kenneth Milne. *The Church of Ireland: A History*. Dublin, 1966.

R. B. McDowell. *The Church of Ireland, 1869–1969*. London, 1978.

Michael Hurley. *Irish Anglicanism, 1869–1969: Essays on the Role of Anglicanism in Irish Life Presented to the Church of Ireland, on the Occasion of the Centenary of its Disestablishment, by a Group of Methodist, Presbyterian, Quaker and Roman Catholic Scholars*. Dublin, 1970.

J. S. Reid. *History of the Presbyterian Church in Ireland*. Edited by W. D. Killen. 3 vols. Belfast, 1867.

J. M. Barkley. *A Short History of the Presbyterian Church in Ireland*. Belfast, 1959.

J. L. M. Haire (ed.). *Challenge and Conflict: Essays in Irish Presbyterian History and Doctrine*. Belfast, 1981.

C. H. Crookshank. *History of Methodism in Ireland*. 3 vols. Belfast, 1885–8.

R. L. Cole. *History of Methodism in Ireland 1860–1960*. London, 1960.

Isabel Grubb. *Quakers in Ireland, 1654–1900*. London, 1927.

Louis Hyman. *The Jews of Ireland*. Shannon, 1972.

EDUCATION

N. D. Atkinson. *Irish Education: A History of Educational Institutions*. Dublin, 1969.

D. H. Akenson. *The Irish Education Experiment: The National System of Education in the Nineteenth Century*. London and Toronto, 1970

Mary Daly. 'The Development of the National School System, 1831–40' in Art Cosgrove and Donal McCartney (ed.), *Studies in Irish History Presented to R. Dudley Edwards* (Dublin 1979), pp 150–63.

D. H. Akenson. *A Mirror to Kathleen's Face: Education in Independent Ireland, 1922–1960*. Montreal and London, 1975.

John Coolahan. *Irish Education: Its History and Structure*. Dublin, 1981.

Constantia Maxwell. *A History of Trinity College, Dublin, 1591–1892*. Dublin, 1946.

K. C. Bailey. *A History of Trinity College, Dublin, 1892–1945*. Dublin, 1947.

R. B. McDowell and D. A. Webb. *Trinity College, Dublin, 1592–1952: An Academic History*. Cambridge, 1982.

John Healy, *Maynooth College, 1798–1895*. Dublin, 1895.

T. W. Moody. 'The Irish University Question of the Nineteenth Century' in *History*, xliii, no. 148 (1958), pp 90–109.

T. W. Moody and J. C. Beckett. *Queen's, Belfast, 1845–1949: The History of a University*. 2 vols. London, 1959.

Robert Allen. *The Presbyterian College, Belfast, 1853–1953*. Belfast, 1954.

Fergal McGrath. *Newman's University: Idea and Reality*. Dublin, 1951.

Michael Tierney (ed.). *Struggle with Fortune: A Miscellany for the Centenary of the Catholic University of Ireland, 1854–1954*. Dublin, 1954.

Fathers of the Society of Jesus. *A Page of Irish History: Story of University College, Dublin, 1883–1909*. Dublin, 1930.

Report of the Council of Education: (1) The Function of the Primary School; (2) The Curriculum to be Pursued in the Primary School. Dublin, Stationery Office, (1954). (Pr. 2583)

Report of the Council of Education: The Curriculum of the Secondary School. Dublin, Stationery Office, (1962). (Pr. 5996)

The Restoration of the Irish Language. Dublin, Stationery Office, 1965. (Pr. 8061)

Investment in Education. Report of the Survey Team Appointed by the Minister for Education in October 1962. 2 vols. Dublin, Stationery Office, 1965. (Pr. 8311), 1966 (Pr. 8527)

Commission on Higher Education (1960–67), Presentation and Summary of Report. Dublin, Stationery Office, 1967. (Pr. 9326)

Commission on Higher Education (1960–67), report. 2 vols. Dublin, Stationery Office, 1967. (Pr. 9389, Pr. 9588)

Higher Education Authority, First Report 1968–9. Dublin, Stationery Office, (1969). (The first of a continuing series)

LANGUAGE, LITERATURE AND LEARNING

Brian Ó Cuív (ed.). *A View of the Irish Language*. Dublin, 1969.

David Green. *The Irish Language*. Dublin, 1966.

Douglas Hyde. *A Literary History of Ireland from the Earliest Times to the Present Day*. London, 1899; new edition, with an introduction by Brian Ó Cuív, London and New York, 1967.

A. de Blacám. *Gaelic Literature Surveyed*. Dublin and Cork, 1933.

K. H. Jackson. *The Oldest Irish Tradition*. Cambridge, 1964.

Myles Dillon (ed.). *Irish Sagas*. Dublin, 1959; reprint with new introduction, 1968

Myles Dillon. *Early Irish Literature*. Chicago, 1948.

Myles Dillon. *The Cycles of the Kings*. Oxford, 1946.

Eleanor Knott and Gerard Murphy. *Early Irish Literature*. Chicago, 1948.

Liam de Paor. *Great Books of Ireland*. Dublin, 1967.

James Carney. *Early Irish Poetry*. Cork, 1965.

Frank O'Connor. *Kings, Lords and Commons: An Anthology from the Irish*. Translated by Frank O'Connor. London, 1961; reprint, 1962.

Frank O'Connor. *The Backward Look: A Survey of Irish Literature*. London, 1967.

Proinsias Mac Cana. *Literature in Irish*. Dublin, 1980.

Proinsias Mac Cana. *The Learned Tales of Medieval Ireland*. Dublin, 1981.

Brian Ó Cuív (ed.). *Seven Centuries of Irish Learning, 1000–1700*. Dublin, 1961.

Robin Flower. *The Irish Tradition*. Oxford, 1947.

Roger McHugh and Maurice Harmon. *Short History of Anglo-Irish Literature from its Origins to the Present Day*. Dublin, 1982.

St John D. Seymour. *Anglo-Irish Literature, 1200–1582*. Cambridge, 1929.

Thomas MacDonagh. *Literature in Ireland: Studies in Irish and Anglo-Irish Literature*. Dublin, 1916.

Sean Ó Tuama (ed.). *The Gaelic League Idea*. Cork and Dublin, 1971.

Malcolm Brown. *The Politics of Irish Literature from Thomas Davis to W. B. Yeats*. London, 1972.

Peter Costello. *The Heart Grown Brutal: The Irish Revolution in Literature from Parnell to the Death of Yeats*. Dublin, 1977.

Benedict Kiely. *Modern Irish Fiction: A Critique*. Dublin, 1950.

T. J. B. Flanagan. *Irish Novelists, 1800–1850*. New York, 1959.

Robert Farren. *The Course of Irish Verse*. London, 1948.

W. B. Stanford. *Ireland and the Classical Tradition*. Dublin and Totowa (N.J.), 1976.

J. J. O'Meara. *Eriugena*. Cork, 1963.

Katherine Walsh. *A Fourteenth-Century Scholar and Primate: Richard FitzRalph in Oxford, Avignon and Armagh*. Oxford, 1981.

K. T. Hoppen. *The Common Scientist in the Seventeenth Century: A Study of the Dublin Philosophical Society, 1683–1708*. London, 1970.

J. G. Simms. *William Molyneux of Dublin*. Edited by P. H. Kelly. Blackrock (County Dublin), 1982.

THE THEATRE

W. S. Clark. *The Early Irish Stage: The Beginnings to 1720*. Oxford, 1955.

W. S. Clark. *The Irish Stage in the County Towns, 1720–1800*. Oxford, 1965.

Micheál Mac Liammóir. *Theatre in Ireland*. Dublin, 1950.

Robert O'Driscoll. *Theatre and Nationalism in Twentieth Century Ireland*. London, 1971.

Lennox Robinson (ed.). *The Irish Theatre: Lectures Delivered during the Abbey Theatre Festival Held in Dublin in August 1938*. London, 1939.

Hugh Hunt. *The Abbey: Ireland's National Theatre, 1904–79*. Dublin, 1979.

THE VISUAL ARTS AND MUSIC

Peter Harbison, Homan Potterton and Jeanne Sheehy. *Irish Art and Architecture from Pre-history to the Present*. London, 1978.

Françoise Henry. *Early Christian Irish Art*. Dublin, 1954.

Françoise Henry. *Irish Art in the Early Christian Period (to 800 AD)*. London, 1940; revised edition, 1965.

Françoise Henry. *Irish Art during the Viking Invasions (800–1020 AD)*. London, 1967.

Françoise Henry. *Irish Art in the Romanesque Period (1020–1170 AD)*. London, 1970.

Françoise Henry and G. L. Marsh-Micheli. 'A Century of Irish Illumination (1070–1170)' in *Proceedings of the Royal Irish Academy*, 62 C 5 (1962).

G. F. Mitchell and others. *Treasures of Early Irish Art, 1500 BC to 1500 AD, from the Collections of the National Museum of Ireland, Royal Irish Academy, [and] Trinity College, Dublin*. New York: Metropolitan Museum of Art, 1977.

R. A. Stalley. *Architecture in Ireland, 1150–1350*. Dublin, 1971.

H. G. Leask. *Irish Churches and Monastic Buildings*. 3 vols. Dundalk, 1955, 1958, 1960.

John Hunt. *Irish Medieval Figure Sculpture, 1200–1600*. 2 vols. Dublin, 1974.

M. J. Craig. *Dublin, 1660–1860*. London, 1952; reprint, 1980.

M. J. Craig. *The Architecture of Ireland from the Earliest Times to 1880*. Dublin, 1982.

Anne Crookshank and the Knight of Glin. *The Painters of Ireland, c. 1660–1920*. London, 1978.

Anne Crookshank. *Irish Art from 1600 to the Present Day*. Dublin, 1979.

Jeanne Sheehy. *The Rediscovery of Ireland's Past: The Celtic Revival, 1830–1930*. London, 1980.

Records of Eighteenth-Century Domestic Architecture and Decoration in Ireland. 5 vols. Dublin, Georgian Society, 1909–13.

Brian Boydell (ed.). *Four Centuries of Music in Ireland*. London, 1979.

Donal O'Sullivan. *Irish Folk Music, Song and Dance*. Dublin, 1952; revised reprint, 1961, 1969.

Donal O'Sullivan. *Songs of the Irish*. Dublin, 1967; reprint, Cork, 1981.

Donal O'Sullivan. *Carolan: The Life, Times and Music of an Irish Harper*. 2 vols. London, 1958.

NATIONALISM

T. W. Moody (ed.). *Nationality and the Pursuit of National Independence*. Belfast, 1978.

J. G. Simms. *Colonial Nationalism, 1698–1776*. Dublin, 1976.

Emil Strauss. *Irish Nationalism and British Democracy*. London, 1951.

Robert Kee. *The Green Flag: A History of Irish Nationalism*. London, 1972.

A. C. Hepburn (ed.). *The Conflict of Nationality in Modern Ireland*. London, 1980.

T. W. Moody (ed.). *The Fenian Movement*. Cork, 1968; reprint, Dublin and Cork, 1978.

Erhard Rumpf and A. C. Hepburn. *Nationalism and Socialism in Twentieth-century Ireland*. Liverpool, 1977.

Tom Garvin. *The Evolution of Irish Nationalist Politics*. Dublin, 1981.

L. M. Cullen. 'The Cultural Basis of Modern Irish Nationalism' in Rosalind Mitchison (ed.), *The Roots of Nationalism: Studies in Northern Europe* (Edinburgh, 1980).

UNIONISM

Hugh Shearman. *Not an Inch: A Study of Northern Ireland and Lord Craigavon*. London, 1942.

Patrick Buckland. *Irish Unionism 1: The Anglo-Irish and the New Ireland, 1885–1922*. Dublin and New York, 1972.

Patrick Buckland. *Irish Unionism 2: Ulster Unionism and the Origins of Northern Ireland, 1886–1922*. Dublin and New York, 1973.

Patrick Buckland (ed.). *Irish Unionism, 1885–1923: A Documentary History*. Belfast, 1973.

Patrick Buckland. *Irish Unionism, 1885–1922*. London, Historical Association, 1973.

Peter Gibbon. *The Origins of Ulster Unionism: The Formation of Popular Protestant Politics and Ideology in Nineteenth-century Ireland*. Manchester, 1975.

Sybil Gribbon. 'The Social Origins of Ulster Unionism' in *Irish Economic and Social History*, iv (1977), pp 66–72. (A review article on the preceding)

D. C. Savage. 'The Origins of the Ulster Unionist Party, 1885–6' in *Irish Historical Studies*, xii, no. 47 (Mar. 1961), pp 185–208.

J. F. Harbinson. *The Ulster Unionist Party, 1882–1973: Its Development and Organisation*. Belfast. 1973.

THE LAND QUESTION

W. F. T. Butler. *Confiscation in Irish History*. Dublin, 1917; 2nd edition, 1918.

J. P. Prendergast. *The Cromwellian Settlement of Ireland*. London, 1865; revised edition, 1870; 3rd edition, 1922.

Margaret MacCurtain. 'Rural Society in Post-Cromwellian Ireland' in Art Cosgrove and Donal McCartney (ed.), *Studies in Irish History Presented to R. Dudley Edwards* (Dublin, 1979) pp 118–36.

J. G. Simms. *The Williamite Confiscation in Ireland, 1690–1703*. London, 1956.

David Large. 'The Wealth of the Greater Irish Landowners, 1750–1815' in *Irish Historical Studies*, xv, no. 57 (Mar. 1966), pp 21–47.

J. E. Pomfret. *The Struggle for Land in Ireland, 1800–1923*. Princeton, 1930.

Brian O'Neill. *The War for the Land in Ireland*. With an introduction by Peadar O'Donnell. New York, 1933.

J. S. Donnelly Jr. *The Land and the People of Nineteenth-century Cork: The Rural Economy and the Land Question*. London and Boston, 1975.

W. E. Vaughan. 'Landlord and Tenant Relations between the Famine and the Land War, 1850–75' in L. M. Cullen and T. C. Smout (ed.), *Comparative Aspects of Scottish and Irish Economic and Social History, 1600–1900* (Edinburgh, 1971), pp 216–26.

W. E. Vaughan. 'An Assessment of the Economic Performance of the Irish Landlords, 1851–81' in F. S. L. Lyons and R. A. J. Hawkins (ed.), *Ireland under the Union* (Oxford, 1980), pp 173–99.

E. D. Steele. *Irish Land and British Politics: Tenant Right and Nationality, 1865–1870*. Cambridge, 1974.

Barbara L. Solow. *The Land Question in the Irish Economy, 1870–1903*. Cambridge (Mass.), 1971.

N. D. Palmer. *The Irish Land League Crisis*. New Haven, 1940.

Paul Bew. *Land and the National Question*. Dublin, 1978.

S. D. Clark. *Social Origins of the Irish Land War*. Princeton, 1979.

H. E. Socolofsky. *Landlord William Scully*. Lawrence (Kansas), 1979.

T. W. Moody. *Davitt and Irish Revolution, 1846–82*. Oxford, 1981.

THE LABOUR MOVEMENT

James Connolly. *Labour in Ireland*. Introduction by Robert Lynd. Dublin, 1917. New edition, introduction by Cathal O'Shannon, Dublin, 1960. (Comprises 'Labour in Irish History' and 'The Reconquest of Ireland')

W. P. Ryan. *The Irish Labour Movement, from the Twenties to Our Own Day*, Dublin and London, 1919.

T. W. Moody. 'Michael Davitt and the British Labour Movement, 1882–1908' in *Transactions of the Royal Historical Society*, 5th series, iii (1953), pp 53–76.

J. D. Clarkson. *Labour and Nationalism in Ireland*. New York, 1925; reprint, 1970.

J. W. Boyle (ed.). *Leaders and Workers*. Cork, 1965.

Charles McCarthy. *Trade Unions in Ireland, 1894–1960*. Dublin, 1977.

Charles McCarthy. *The Decade of Upheaval: The Irish Trade Unions in the Nineteen Sixties*. Dublin, 1973.

C. D. Greaves. *The Life and Times of James Connolly*. London, 1961.

Emmet Larkin. *James Connolly, Irish Labour Leader, 1876–1947*. London, 1965.

J. A. Gaughan. *Thomas Johnson, 1872–1963*. Dublin, 1980.

Dermot Keogh. *The Making of the Irish Working Class: The Dublin Trade Union Movement and Labour Leadership, 1880–1914*. Belfast, 1981.

IRISH EMIGRATION AND THE IRISH ABROAD

Sylvia L. Thrupp. 'A Survey of the Alien Population of England in 1440' in *Speculum*, xxxii (1957), pp 262–72.

John Denvir. *The Irish in Britain from the Earliest Times to the Fall and Death of Parnell*. London, 1894.

J. A. Jackson. *The Irish in Britain*. London, 1963.

M. A. G. Ó Tuathaigh. 'The Irish in Nineteenth-century Britain' in *Transactions of the Royal Historical Society*, 5th series, xxxi (1981), pp 149–73.

Fergus D'Arcy. 'The Irish in Nineteenth-century Britain: Reflections on their Role and Experience' in *Irish History Workshop*, i (1981), pp 3–12.

Barbara Kerr. 'Irish Seasonal Migration to Great Britain, 1800–38' in *Irish Historical Studies*, iii, no. 12 (Sept. 1943), pp 365–80.

James E. Handley. *The Irish in Scotland, 1798–1845*. Cork, 1943.

James E. Handley. *The Irish in Modern Scotland*. Cork, 1947.

D. N. Doyle and Owen Dudley Edwards. *America and Ireland, 1776–1976*. Westport (Conn.), 1979.

D. N. Doyle. *Ireland, Irishmen and Revolutionary America, 1760–1820*. Dublin and Cork, 1981.

W. F. Adams. *Ireland and Irish Emigration to the New World from 1815 to the Famine*. New Haven, 1932.

S. H. Cousens. 'Emigration and Demographic Change in Ireland, 1851–61' in *Economic History Review*, xiv, no. 2 (Dec. 1961), pp 275–88.

Arnold Schrier. *Ireland and the American Emigration, 1870–1900*. Minneapolis, 1958.

T. N. Brown. *Irish-American Nationalism, 1870–1890*. Philadelphia and New York, 1966.

T. W. Moody. 'Irish-American Nationalism' in *Irish Historical Studies*, xv, no. 60 (Sept. 1967), pp 438–45. (A review article on the preceding)

K. A. Miller, with Bruce Boling and D. N. Doyle. 'Emigrants and Exiles: Irish Cultures and Irish Emigration to North America, 1790–1922' in *Irish Historical Studies*, xxii, no. 86 (Sept. 1980), pp 97–125.

Cormac Ó Gráda. 'Some Aspects of Nineteenth-century Irish Emigration' in L. M. Cullen and T. C. Smout (ed.), *Comparative Aspects of Scottish and Irish Economic and Social History, 1600–1900* (Edinburgh, [1972]), pp 65–71.

David Fitzpatrick. 'Irish Emigration in the Late Nineteenth Century' in *Irish Historical Studies*, xxii, no. 86 (Sept. 1980), pp 126–43.

Carl Wittke. *The Irish in America*. Baton Rouge (Louisiana), 1950.

George Potter. *To the Golden Door: The Story of the Irish in Ireland and America*. Boston, 1960.

W. V. Shannon. *The American Irish*. New York, 1963.

Commission on Emigration and other Population Problems, 1948–1954, reports. Dublin, Stationery Office, 1954. (Pr. 2541)

OTHER SUBJECTS

K. W. Nichols. 'The Irish Genealogies: Their Value and Defects' in *Irish Genealogist*, v (1975), pp 256–61.

Gearóid Mac Niocaill. *The Medieval Irish Annals*. Dublin Historical Association, 1975.

Michael Dolley. *Medieval Anglo-Irish Coins*. London, 1972.

G. A. Hayes-McCoy. *The Irish at War*. Cork, 1964.

G. A. Hayes-McCoy. *Irish Battles*. London, 1969.

Katharine Simms. 'Warfare in the Medieval Gaelic Lordships' in *Irish Sword*, xii (1976), pp 98–108.

R. E. Glasscock and T. E. McNeill. 'Mottes in Ireland: A Draft List' in *Bulletin of the Group for the Study of Irish Historical Settlement*, iii (1972), pp 27–51.

Terence Barry. *Medieval Moated Sites of S.E. Ireland: Counties Carlow, Kilkenny, Tipperary and Wexford*. Oxford, 1977.

Kevin Danaher. 'Irish Tower Houses and their Regional Distribution' in *Bealoideas*, xlv–xlvii (1977–9), pp158–63.

H. G. Leask. *Irish Castles and Castellated Houses*. Dundalk, 1941.

Hugh Shearman. *Anglo-Irish Relations*. London, 1948.

J. C. Beckett. *The Anglo-Irish Tradition*. London, 1976.

P. J. O'Farrell. *Ireland's English Question: Anglo-Irish Relations, 1534–1970*. London, 1971.

P. J. O'Farrell. *England and Ireland Since 1800*. London, 1975.

C. Cruise O'Brien. *States of Ireland*. London, 1972.

Elizabeth Malcolm. 'Temperance and Irish Nationalism' in F. S. L. Lyons and R. A. J. Hawkins (ed.), *Ireland Under the Union* (Oxford, 1980), pp 69–114.

H. F. Kearney. 'Fr Mathew: Apostle of Modernisation' in Art Cosgrove and Donal McCartney (ed.), *Studies in Irish History Presented to R. Dudley Edwards* (Dublin, 1979), pp 164–75.

Margaret MacCurtain and Donncha Ó Corráin (ed.) *Women in Irish Society: The Historical Dimension*. Dublin, 1978.

L. P. Curtis. *Anglo-Saxons and Celts: A study of Anti-Irish Prejudice in Victorian Britain*. Bridgeport (Conn.), 1968.

L. P. Curtis. *Apes and Angels: The Irishman in Victorian Caricature*. Washington D.C., 1971.

Katharine Simms. 'The Legal Position of Irishwomen in the Late Middle Ages' in *Irish Jurist*, v (1975), pp 96–111.

Marcus de Búrca (Bourke). *The GAA: A History*. Dublin, 1980.

N. P. Canny. 'The Formation of the Irish Mind: Religion, Politics and Gaelic Irish literature, 1580–1750' in *Past & Present*, no. 95 (May 1982), pp 91–116.

Maurice Gorham. *Forty Years of Irish Broadcasting*. Dublin, 1967.

Gay Byrne. *To Whom It May Concern: Ten Years of the Late Late Show*. Dublin, 1972.

Broadcasting Review Committee, report 1974. Dublin, Stationery Office, 1974. (Pr. 3827)

III HISTORICAL GEOGRAPHY OF IRELAND

T. W. Freeman. *Ireland: A General and Regional Geography*. London, 1950; 4th edition, 1972.

A. R. Orme. (The World's Landscapes, 4) *Ireland*. London, 1970.

G. F. Mitchell. *The Irish Landscape*. London, 1976.

F. H. A. Aalen. *Man and the Landscape in Ireland.* London, 1978.

E. E. Evans. *The Personality of Ireland: Habitat, Heritage and History.* Cambridge, 1973.

Nicholas Stephens and R. E. Glasscock (ed.). *Irish Geographical Studies in Honour of E. Estyn Evans.* Belfast, 1970.

E. E. Evans. *Irish Folkways.* London, 1957.

M. W. Heslinga. *The Irish Border as a Cultural Divide.* Assen, 1962; reprint, 1971.

Eileen McCracken. *The Irish Woods Since Tudor Times: Their Distribution and Exploitation.* Newton Abbot, 1971.

W. J. Smyth. 'The Western Isle of Ireland and the Eastern Seaboard of America – England's First Frontiers' in *Irish Geography*, xi (1978), pp 1–22.

T. W. Freeman. *Pre-famine Ireland: A Study in Historical Geography.* Manchester, 1957.

T. Jones Hughes. 'Society and Settlement in Nineteenth-century Ireland' in *Irish Geography*, v (1965), pp 79–96.

Ruth Dudley Edwards. *An Atlas of Irish History.* London, 1973; 2nd edition, London, 1981.

J. H. Andrews. *Irish Maps.* Dublin, 1978.

J. H. Andrews. *A Paper Landscape: The Ordnance Survey in Ireland.* Oxford, 1975.

R. N. Hadcock. *Map of Monastic Ireland, Scale 1:625,000.* Dublin, Ordnance Survey, 1960; 2nd edition, 1964.

Atlas of Ireland, Prepared under the Direction of the Irish National Committee for Geography. Dublin, Royal Irish Academy, 1979.

IV PREHISTORIC IRELAND

S. P. O Riordáin. *Antiquities of the Irish Countryside.* Cork, 1942; 5th edition, revised by Ruaidhri de Valera, London. 1979.

Joseph Raftery. *Prehistoric Ireland.* London, 1951.

P. C. Woodman. *The Mesolithic in Ireland.* Oxford, 1978.

Michael Herity and George Eogan. *Ireland in Prehistory.* London, 1977.

Peter Harbison. *Guide to the National Monuments of Ireland.* Dublin, 1970: 2nd revised edition, 1979.

V IRELAND FROM THE FIRST TO THE TWELFTH CENTURY

J. F. Kenney. *Sources for the Early History of Ireland: Ecclesiastical.* New York, 1929; reprint, New York, 1966, with preface by Ludwig Bieler.

E. R. Norman and J. K. S. St Joseph. *The Early Development of Irish Society: The Evidence of Aerial Photography.* Cambridge, 1969.

Myles Dillon (ed.). *Early Irish Society.* Dublin, 1954.

Eoin MacNeill. *Celtic Ireland.* Dublin and London, 1921; 2nd edition, with introduction and notes by Donncha Ó Corráin, Dublin, 1981.

Cecile O'Rahilly (ed.). *Táin bó Cúailnge, from the Book of Leinster.* Dublin, 1967.

Cecile O'Rahilly (ed.). *Táin bó Cúailnge, Recension I.* Dublin, 1976.

T. F. O'Rahilly. *Early Irish History and Mythology.* Dublin, 1946.

Kathleen Hughes. *Early Christian Ireland: Introduction to the Sources.* London, 1972.

Máire and Liam de Paor. *Early Christian Ireland.* London, 1958.

Libri Sancti Patricii: The Latin Writings of St Patrick. Edited and translated by Newport J. D. White. Dublin, 1905.

Libri Epistolarum Sancti Patricii Episcopi. Edited by Ludwig Bieler. 2 vols. Dublin, 1952.

The Works of St Patrick; St Secundinus, Hymn on St Patrick. Edited and translated by Ludwig Bieler. Westminster (Maryland) and London, 1953.

J. B. Bury. *The Life of St Patrick and His Place in History.* London, 1905.

Eoin MacNeill. *Saint Patrick.* London, 1934; new edition, edited by John Ryan, with other Patrician writings by MacNeill, and a bibliography of Patrician literature by F. X. Martin. Dublin and London, 1964.

T. F. O'Rahilly. *The Two Patricks.* Dublin, 1942; reprint, 1957.

Ludwig Bieler. *The Life and Legend of Saint Patrick: Problems of Modern Scholarship.* Dublin, 1949.

John Ryan (ed.). *Saint Patrick.* Dublin, 1958.

James Carney. *The Problem of Saint Patrick.* Dublin, 1961.

D. A. Binchy. 'Patrick and His Biographers, Ancient and Modern' in *Studia Hibernica*, 2 (1962).

R. P. C. Hanson. *Saint Patrick, His Origins and Career*. Oxford, 1968.

'Muirchú's Life of Patrick'. Translated by N. J. D. White, in *St Patrick, his Writings and Life*. (London, 1920).

Adomnan's *Life of Columba*. Edited and translated by A. O. and M. O. Anderson. London, 1961.

Frank MacManus. *Saint Columban*. Dublin, 1963.

Liam de Paor. 'A Survey of Sceilg Mhichíl' in the *Journal of the Royal Society of Antiquaries of Ireland*, lxxxv (1955).

Ludwig Bieler. *Ireland, Harbinger of the Middle Ages*. London, 1963.

D. Whitelock, R. McKitterick and D. Dumville. *Ireland in Early Medieval Europe*. Cambridge, 1982.

Donncha Ó Corráin. *Ireland Before the Normans*. Dublin, 1972.

F. J. Byrne. *Irish Kings and High-kings*. London, 1973.

Martin MacNamara. *The Apocrypha in the Irish Church*. Dublin, 1975.

Brian Ó Cuív. *The Impact of the Scandinavian Invasions on the Celtic-speaking Peoples, c. 800–1100 AD*. Dublin, 1975.

A. P. Smyth. *Scandinavian Kings in the British Isles, 850–880*. Oxford, 1977.

Johannes Brondsted. *The Vikings*. London, 1960.

Gwyn Jones. *A History of the Vikings*. Oxford, 1968.

James Graham-Campbell. *The Vikings*. London, 1980.

P. H. Sawyer. *The Age of the Vikings*. 2nd edition. London, 1971.

P. G. Foote and D. M. Wilson. *The Viking Achievement*. London, 1970.

Michael Dolley. *Viking Coins of the Danelaw and of Dublin*. London, 1965.

A. B. Scott. *Malachy*. Dublin, 1976.

VI MEDIEVAL IRELAND

J. F. O'Doherty. 'St Laurence O'Toole and the Anglo-Norman Invasion' in *Irish Ecclesiastical Record I* (1937), pp 449–77; li (1938), pp 131–46.

J. F. O'Doherty. 'The Anglo-Norman Invasion, 1167–71' in *Irish Historical Studies*, i, no. 2 (Sept. 1938), pp 154–7.

G. H. Orpen. *Ireland Under the Normans, 1169–1333*. 4 vols. Oxford, 1911–20; reprint, 1968.

G. H. Orpen. 'Ireland to 1315' in *Cambridge Medieval History*, vii (1932), pp 527–47.

G. H. Orpen. 'The Effects of Norman Rule in Ireland, 1169–1333' in *American Historical Review*, xix (1913–14), pp 245–56.

R. Dudley Edwards. 'Anglo-Norman Relations with Connacht, 1169–1229' in *Irish Historical Studies*, i, no. 2 (Sept. 1938), pp 135–53.

W. L. Warren. *Henry II*. London, 1973. (Section on Ireland, pp 187–206)

W. L. Warren. 'John in Ireland, 1185' in John Bossy and Peter Jupp (ed.), *Essays Presented to Michael Roberts* (Belfast, 1976), pp 11–23.

W. L. Warren. 'King John and Ireland' in J. F. Lydon (ed.), *England and Ireland in the Later Middle Ages* (Dublin, 1981), pp 26–42.

Michael Richter. 'The First Century of Anglo-Irish Relations' in *History*, lix (1974), pp 194–210.

M. P. Sheehy. 'The Bull *Laudabiliter*: A Problem in Medieval Diplomatique and History' in the *Journal of the Galway Archaeological and Historical Society*, xxix (1960–61), pp 45–70.

Giraldus Cambrensis. *Expugnatio Hibernica, The Conquest of Ireland*. Edited, with translation, by A. B. Scott and F. X. Martin. Dublin, 1978.

Gerald of Wales. *The History and Topography of Ireland*. Edited, with translation, by John J. O'Meara. London, 1978.

F. X. Martin. *No Hero in the House: Diarmait Mac Murchada and the Coming of the Normans to Ireland*. Dublin, 1977. (O'Donnell Lecture, 1975)

Michael Dolley. *Anglo-Norman Ireland, c. 1100–1318*. Dublin, 1972.

K. W. Nicholls. *Gaelic and Gaelicised Ireland in the Middle Ages*. Dublin, 1972.

J. F. Lydon. *The Lordship of Ireland in the Middle Ages*. Dublin, 1972.

J. F. Lydon. *Ireland in the Later Middle Ages*. Dublin, 1973.

Robin Frame. *Colonial Ireland, 1169–1369*. Dublin, 1981.

Brian Graham. 'The towns of medieval Ireland' in R. A. Butlin (ed.) *The Development of the Irish Town*. (London and Totowa (N.J.), 1977), pp 28–60.

Robin Frame. *English Lordship in Ireland, 1318–1361*. Oxford, 1982.

Barry W. O'Dwyer. *The Conspiracy of Mellifont, 1216–1231*. Dublin Historical Association, 1970.

Robin Frame. 'The Bruces in Ireland, 1315–18' in *Irish Historical Studies*, xlx, no. 73 (Mar. 1974), pp 3–37.

J. F. Lydon. 'The Bruce Invasion of Ireland' in *Historical Studies*, iv, edited by G. A. Hayes-McCoy (London, 1963), pp 111–25.

Robin Frame. 'Power and Society in the Lordship of Ireland, 1272–1377' in *Past & Present*, no. 76 (1977), pp 3–33.

J. F. Lydon. 'The Problem of the Frontier in Medieval Ireland' in *Topic: A Journal of the Liberal Arts* (Washington, Pa.), no. 13 (spring 1967), pp 5–22.

C. A. Empey. 'The Butler Lordship' in *Butler Society Journal*, i (1971), pp 174–87

Bryan Murphy. 'The Status of the Native Irish after 1331' in *Irish Jurist*, ii (1967), pp 116–38.

Aubrey Gwynn. 'The Black Death in Ireland' in *Studies*, xxiv (1935), pp 558–72.

Art Cosgrove. *Late Medieval Ireland, 1370–1541*. Dublin, 1981.

Art Cosgrove. 'The Execution of the Earl of Desmond, 1468' in *Journal of the Kerry Archaeological and Historical Society*, viii (1975), pp 11–27.

Art Cosgrove. 'Hiberniores ipsis Hibernicis' in Art Cosgrove and Donal McCartney (ed.) *Studies in Irish History Presented to R. Dudley Edwards* (Dublin, 1979), pp 1–14.

C. A. Empey and Katharine Simms. 'The Ordinances of the White Earl and the Problem of Coign in the Later Middle Ages' in *Proceedings of the Royal Irish Academy*, 75 C 8 (1975), pp 161–87.

A. J. Otway-Ruthven. 'The Character of Norman Settlement in Ireland' in J. L. McCracken (ed.), *Historical Studies*, v (London, 1965), pp 75–84.

A. J. Otway-Ruthven. 'Knight Service in Ireland' in the *Journal of the Royal Society of Antiquaries of Ireland*, lxxxix (1959), pp 1–15.

A. J. Otway-Ruthven. 'The Organisation of Anglo-Irish Agriculture in the Middle Ages' in the *Journal of the Royal Society of Antiquaries of Ireland*, lxxxi (1951), pp 1–13.

J. F. Lydon. 'Richard II's Expeditions to Ireland' in the *Journal of the Royal Society of Antiquaries of Ireland*, xciii (1963), pp 135–49.

R. J. Mitchell. *John Tiptoft*. London, 1938.

Donough Bryan. *The Great Earl of Kildare*. Dublin, 1933.

G. O. Sayles. 'The Vindication of the Earl of Kildare from Treason, 1496' in *Irish Historical Studies*, vii, no. 25 (Mar. 1950), pp 39–47.

Agnes Conway. *Henry VII's Relations with Scotland and Ireland*. Cambridge, 1932.

Steven Ellis. 'Henry VII and Ireland, 1491–6' in J. F. Lydon (ed.), *Ireland in the Later Middle Ages* (Dublin, 1981), pp 237–54.

VII IRELAND IN THE SIXTEENTH CENTURY

T. W. Moody, F. X. Martin and F. J. Byrne (ed.). *Early Modern Ireland, 1534–1691*. Oxford, 1976. (*A New History of Ireland*, vol. iii)

Margaret MacCurtain. *Tudor and Stuart Ireland*. Dublin, 1972.

Richard Bagwell. *Ireland Under the Tudors*. 3 vols. London, 1885–90; reprint, 1963.

Philip Wilson. *The Beginnings of Modern Ireland*. Dublin and London, 1912.

James Hogan. *Ireland in the European System*. London, 1920.

R. Dudley Edwards. *Church and State in Tudor Ireland*. Dublin, 1935.

Brendan Bradshaw. *The Irish Constitutional Revolution of the Sixteenth Century*. Cambridge, 1979.

D. B. Quinn. 'Henry VIII and Ireland, 1509–34' in *Irish Historical Studies*, xii, no. 48 (Sept. 1961), pp 318–44.

W. F. T. Butler. *Gleanings from Irish History*. London, 1925.

David Mathew. *The Celtic Peoples and Renaissance Europe*. London, 1933.

G. A. Hayes-McCoy. 'Gaelic Society in Ireland in the Late Sixteenth Century' in *Historical Studies*, iv, edited by G. A. Hayes-McCoy (London, 1963), pp 45–61.

Steven Ellis. 'Tudor Policy and the Kildare Ascendancy in the Lordship of Ireland' in *Irish Historical Studies*, xx, no. 79 (Mar. 1977), pp 235–71.

Steven Ellis. 'The Kildare Rebellion and the Early Henrician Reformation' in the *Historical Journal*, xix (1976), pp 807–30

Brendan Bradshaw. 'Cromwellian Reforms and the Origins of the Kildare Rebellion', in *Transactions of the Royal Historical Society*, xxvii (1977), pp 69–93.

Stephen Ellis. 'Thomas Cromwell and Ireland, 1532–40' in *Historical Journal*, xxiii (1980).

James Hogan. 'Shane O'Neill Comes to the Court of Elizabeth' in Séamas Pender (ed.) *Féilscríbhinn Torna: Essays and Studies Presented to Professor Tadhg Ua Donnchadha* (Cork, 1947), pp 154–70.

N. P Canny. *The Elizabethan Conquest of Ireland: A Pattern Established, 1565–1576.* Hassocks, 1976.

N. P. Canny. *The Upstart Earl: A Study of the Social and Mental Life of Richard Boyle, First Earl of Cork, 1566–1643.* Cambridge, 1982.

Captain Cuellar's Adventures in Connaught and Ulster, 1588. Edited by Hugh Allingham. London, 1897.

R. E. Hardy. *Survivors of the Armada.* London, 1966.

Cyril Falls. *Elizabeth's Irish Wars.* London, 1950.

G. A. Hayes-McCoy. 'Strategy and Tactics in Irish Warfare, 1593–1601' in *Irish Historical Studies*, ii, no. 7 (Mar. 1941) pp 255–79.

G. A. Hayes-McCoy. 'The Army of Ulster, 1593–1601' in the *Irish Sword*, i (1949–53), pp 105–17.

G. A. Hayes-McCoy. 'The Tide of Victory and Defeat: I The Battle of Clontibret, 1595; II The Battle of Kinsale, 1601', in *Studies*, xxxviii (1949), pp 158–68, 307–17.

J. J. Silke. 'Spain and the Invasion of Ireland, 1601–2' in *Irish Historical Studies*, xiv, no. 56 (Sept. 1965), pp 295–312.

D. B. Quinn. *The Elizabethans and the Irish.* Ithaca (New York), 1966.

Edmund Spenser. *A View of the Present State of Ireland* (1596). Edited by W. L. Renwick. Oxford, 1934; reissue, 1970.

VIII IRELAND IN THE SEVENTEENTH CENTURY

T. W. Moody, F. X. Martin and F. J. Byrne (ed.). *A New History of Ireland*, vol iii, *Early Modern Ireland, 1534–1691.* Oxford, 1976.

Margaret MacCurtain. *Tudor and Stuart Ireland.* Dublin, 1972.

Richard Bagwell. *Ireland Under the Stuarts.* 3 vols. London, 1909–16; reprint, 1963.

George O'Brien. *The Economic History of Ireland in the Seventeenth Century.* Dublin and London, 1919.

P. J. Corish. *The Catholic Community in the Seventeenth and Eighteenth Centuries.* Dublin, 1981.

N. P. Canny. *The Upstart Earl: a Study of the Social and Mental Life of Richard Boyle, First Earl of Cork, 1566–1643.* Cambridge, 1982.

N. P. Canny. 'The Flight of the Earls, 1607' in *Irish Historical Studies*, xvii, no. 67 (Mar. 1971), pp 380–99.

Sir John Davies. *A Discovery of the True Causes Why Ireland was Never Entirely Subdued Until His Majesty's Happy Reign.* London, l612; facsimile reprint, Shannon, 1969.

George Hill. *An Historical Account of the Plantation in Ulster, 1608–20.* Belfast, 1877; reprint, Shannon, 1970.

T. W. Moody. *The Londonderry Plantation, 1600–1641: The City of London and the Plantation in Ulster.* Belfast, 1939.

Aidan Clarke. *The Old English in Ireland, 1625–42.* London, 1966.

Aidan Clarke. *The Graces, 1625–41.* Dublin Historical Association, 1968.

H. F. Kearney. *Strafford in Ireland, 1633–41.* Manchester, 1959.

Aidan Clarke. 'The Genesis of the Ulster Rising of 1641' in Peter Roebuck (ed.), *Plantation to Partition* (Belfast, 1981), pp 29–45.

St J. D. Seymour. *The Puritans in Ireland, 1647–61.* Oxford, 1921; reprint, 1969.

Aidan Clarke. 'Ireland and the General Crisis' in *Past & Present*, no. 48 (1970), pp 79–99.

C. P. Meehan. *The Confederation of Kilkenny.* Dublin, 1905.

J. C. Beckett. 'The Confederation of Kilkenny Reviewed' in M. Roberts (ed.), *Historical Studies*, ii (London, 1959), pp 29–41.

David Stevenson. *Scottish Covenanters and Irish Confederates: Scottish-Irish Relations in the Mid-Seventeenth Century.* Belfast, 1981.

T. C. Barnard. *Cromwellian Ireland: English Government and Reform in Ireland, 1649–1660.* Oxford, 1975.

J. P. Prendergast. *The Cromwellian Settlement of Ireland.* London, 1865; revised edition, 1870; 3rd edition, 1922.

Edward MacLysaght. *Irish Life in the Seventeenth Century After Cromwell.* Dublin and Cork, 1939; 2nd edition, Cork, 1950; reprint, Shannon, 1969.

W. E. H. Lecky. *History of Ireland in the Eighteenth Century.* Vol. i. London, 1892.

J. G. Simms. *Jacobite Ireland, 1685–91.* London and Toronto, 1969.

J. C. Beckett. *Protestant Dissent in Ireland, 1687–1780.* London, 1948.

Thomas Davis. *The Patriot Parliament of 1689.* Edited by C. Gavan Duffy. London, 1893.

J. G. Simms. *The Williamite Confiscation in Ireland, 1690–1703.* London, 1958.

J. G. Simms. *The Treaty of Limerick*. Dublin Historical Association, 1961; reprinted, 1965.

J. G. Simms. *The Jacobite Parliament of 1689*. Dublin Historical Association, 1966.

IX IRELAND IN THE EIGHTEENTH CENTURY

J. A. Froude. *The English in Ireland in the Eighteenth Century*. 3 vols. London, 1872–4; 2nd edition, 1881.

W. E. H. Lecky. *History of Ireland in the Eighteenth Century*. 5 vols. London, 1892.

W. E. H. Lecky. *The Leaders of Public Opinion in Ireland*. 2nd edition, London, 1871. (Studies of Swift, Flood, Grattan and O'Connell)

E. M. Johnston. *Ireland in the Eighteenth Century*. Dublin, 1974.

Thomas Bartlett and D. W. Hayton (ed.). *Penal Era and Golden Age: Essays in Irish History, 1690–1800*. Belfast, 1979.

R. B. McDowell. *Ireland in the Age of Imperialism and Revolution, 1760–1800*. Oxford, 1979.

George O'Brien. *The Economic History of Ireland in the Eighteenth Century*. Dublin, 1918.

L. M. Cullen. 'Problems in the Interpretation and Revision of Eighteenth-century Irish Economic History' in *Transactions of the Royal Historical Society*, 5th series, xvii (1967), pp 1–22.

H. F. Kearney 'The Political Background to English Mercantilism, 1695–1700' in *Economic History Review*, xi (1959), pp 484–96.

Patrick Kelly. 'The Irish Woollen Export Prohibition Act of 1699: Kearney Revisited' in *Irish Economic and Social History*, vii (1980), pp 22–43.

L. M. Cullen. 'The Smuggling Trade in Ireland in the Eighteenth Century' in *Proceedings of the Royal Irish Academy*, 67 C 5 (1969), pp 149–75.

Daniel Corkery. *The Hidden Ireland: A Study of Gaelic Munster in the Eighteenth Century*. Dublin, 1925; 4th impression, 1956.

L. M. Cullen. 'The Hidden Ireland: Reassessment of a Concept' in *Studia Hibernica*, no. 9 (1969), pp 7–47.

Oliver W. Ferguson. *Jonathan Swift and Ireland*. Urbana (Illinois), 1962.

Jonathan Swift. *The Drapier's Letters to the People of Ireland against Receiving Wood's Halfpence (1724)*. Edited by Herbert Davis. Oxford, 1935; reprint, 1965.

George Berkeley. *The Querist*. Dublin, 1735 (Best edition in *The Works of George Berkeley, Bishop of Cloyne*, ed. A. A. Luce and T. E. Jessop, vi (London, 1953))

Michael Drake. 'The Irish Demographic Crisis of 1740–41' in *Historical Studies*, vi, edited by T. W. Moody (London, 1968), pp 101–24.

J. G. Simms. 'Connacht in the Eighteenth Century' in *Irish Historical Studies*, xi, no. 42 (Sept. 1958), pp 116–33.

J. C. Beckett. *Protestant Dissent in Ireland, 1687–1780*. London, 1948.

Maureen Wall. *The Penal Laws, 1691–1760*. Dublin Historical Association, 1961.

Maureen Wall. 'The Catholics of the Towns and the Quarterage Dispute in Eighteenth-century Ireland' in *Irish Historical Studies*, viii, no. 30 (Sept. 1952), pp 91–114.

Maureen Wall. 'The Rise of a Catholic Middle Class in Eighteenth-century Ireland' in *Irish Historical Studies*, xi, no. 42 (Sept. 1958), pp 91–115.

Maureen Wall. 'Catholic Loyalty to King and Pope in Eighteenth-century Ireland' in *Proceedings of the Irish Catholic Historical Committee* (1960), pp 17–24.

Thomas Wall. *The Sign of Dr Hay's Head*. Dublin, 1958.

R. B. McDowell. *Irish Public Opinion, 1750–1800*. London, 1944.

J. S. Donnelly Jr. 'The Whiteboy Movement, 1761–8' in *Irish Historical Studies*, xxi, no. 80 (Mar. 1978), pp 20–54.

J. S. Donnelly Jr. 'The Rightboy Movement, 1785–8' in *Studia Hibernica*, nos 17–18 (1977–8), pp 120–202.

Arthur Young. *A Tour in Ireland. . . Made in the Years 1776, 1777 and 1778, and Brought Down to the End of 1779*. London, 1780; edited by A. W. Hutton. 2 vols, 1892; reprint, Shannon, 1970.

Maurice R. O'Connell. *Irish Politics and Social Conflict in the Age of the American Revolution*. Philadelphia, 1965.

J. C. Beckett. 'Anglo-Irish Constitutional Relations in the Later Eighteenth Century' in *Irish Historical Studies*, xiv, no. 53 (Mar. 1963), pp 20–38.

Edith M. Johnston. *Great Britain and Ireland, 1760–1800: A Study in Political Administration*. Edinburgh, 1963.

A. P. W. Malcolmson. *John Foster: The Politics of the Anglo-Irish Ascendancy*. Oxford, 1978.

Patrick Rogers. *The Volunteers and Catholic Emancipation, 1778–93.* London, 1934.

R. R. Madden. *The United Irishmen, Their Lives and Times.* 7 vols. London, 1842–6; revised edition, 4 vols. 1857–60.

Rosamund Jacob. *The Rise of the United Irishmen, 1791–4.* London, 1937.

Robert Dunlop. *Henry Grattan.* London, 1889.

W. E. H. Lecky. *Leaders of Public Opinion in Ireland.* 3rd edition. Vol. I: *Flood and Grattan,* London, 1903.

Stephen Gwynn. *Henry Grattan and His Times.* London, 1939.

Theobald Wolfe Tone. *Life of Theobald Wolfe Tone . . . Written by Himself and Continued by his Son.* Edited by W. T. W. Tone. 2 vols. Washington, 1826. (A new edition of Tone's writings, including much new material, is in preparation by T. W. Moody and R. B. McDowell.)

Frank MacDermot. *Theobald Wolfe Tone: A Biographical Study.* London, 1939; new edition, Tralee, 1968.

D. A. Chart. (ed.). *The Drennan Letters 1776–1819.* Belfast, 1931.

Hereward Senior. *Orangeism in Ireland and Britain, 1795–1836.* London and Toronto, 1966.

E. H. Stuart Jones. *An Invasion that Failed: the French Expedition to Ireland, 1796.* Oxford, 1950.

Charles Dickson. *The Wexford Rising in 1798: Its Causes and Course.* Tralee, 1955.

Charles Dickson. *Revolt in the North: Antrim and Down in 1798.* Dublin and London, 1960.

Thomas Pakenham. *The Year of Liberty: The Story of the Great Irish Rebellion of 1798.* London, 1969.

Richard Hayes. *The Last Invasion of Ireland: When Connacht Rose.* Dublin, 1937; 2nd edition, 1939.

G. C. Bolton. *The Passing of the Irish Act of Union.* London. 1966.

X IRELAND, 1800–50

M. A. G. Ó Tuathaigh. *Ireland before the Famine, 1798–1848.* Dublin, 1972.

S. J. Connolly. *Priests and People in Pre-famine Ireland, 1780–1845.* Dublin, 1982.

D. A. Chart. *Ireland from the Union to Catholic Emancipation.* London, 1910.

R. B. McDowell. *Public Opinion and Government Policy in Ireland, 1801–1846.* London, 1952.

R. B. McDowell (ed.). *Social Life in Ireland, 1800–45.* Dublin, 1957.

Desmond Bowen. *The Protestant Crusade in Ireland, 1800–70: A Study of Protestant-Catholic Relations between the Act of Union and Disestablishment.* Dublin and Montreal, 1978.

R. W. Postgate. *Robert Emmet.* London, 1931.

Leon Ó Broin. *The Unfortunate Mr Robert Emmet.* Dublin and London, 1958.

Galen Broeker. *Rural Disorder and Police Reform in Ireland, 1812–36.* London and Toronto, 1970.

Ian Dalton. *Protestant Society and Politics in Cork, 1812–1844.* Cork, 1981.

James A. Reynolds. *The Catholic Emancipation Crisis in Ireland, 1823–29.* New Haven, 1954.

M. A. G. Ó Tuathaigh. *Thomas Drummond and the Government of Ireland, 1835–41.* The O'Donnell lecture delivered at University College, Galway, on 15 December 1977. Dublin: National University of Ireland.

K. B. Nowlan. *The Politics of Repeal: A Study in the Relations between Great Britain and Ireland, 1841–50.* London, 1965.

D. A. Kerr. *Peel, Priests and Politics: Sir Robert Peel's Administration and the Roman Catholic Church in Ireland, 1841–1846.* Oxford, 1982.

W. E. H. Lecky. *Leaders of Public Opinion in Ireland.* 3rd edition. Vol. II: *Daniel O'Connell.* London, 1903.

Robert Dunlop. *Daniel O'Connell and the Revival of National Life in Ireland.* New York and London, 1908.

Sean O'Faolain. *King of the Beggars.* London, 1938.

Michael Tierney (ed.). *Daniel O'Connell: Nine Centenary Essays.* Dublin, 1949.

Angus Macintyre. *The Liberator: Daniel O'Connell and the Irish Party, 1830–47.* London, 1965.

L. J. McCaffrey. *Daniel O'Connell and the Repeal Year.* Lexington (Kentucky), 1966.

Rachel O'Higgins. 'Irish Trade Unions and Politics, 1830–50' in *Historical Journal,* iv (1961), pp 208–17.

F. A. D'Arcy. 'The Artisans of Dublin and Daniel O'Connell, 1830–47: An Unquiet Liaison' in *Irish Historical Studies,* xvii, no. 66 (Sept. 1970), pp 221–43.

Jacqueline Hill. 'The Protestant Response to Repeal: the Case of the Dublin Working Class' in F. S. L. Lyons and R. A. J. Hawkins (ed.), *Ireland under the Union* (Oxford, 1980), pp 35–68.

J. H. Whyte. 'Daniel O'Connell and the Repeal Party' in *Irish Historical Studies,* xi, no. 44 (Sept. 1959), pp 297–316.

David Large. 'The House of Lords and Ireland in the Age of Peel, 1832–50' in *Irish Historical Studies,* ix, no. 36 (Sept. 1955), pp 367–9.

365

Randall Clarke. 'The Relations between O'Connell and the Young Irelanders' in *Irish Historical Studies*, iii, no. 44 (Sept. 1959), pp 297–315.

J. F. Broderick. *The Holy See and the Irish Movement for the Repeal of the Union with England, 1829–47.* Rome, 1951.

Charles Gavan Duffy. *Young Ireland: A Fragment of Irish History, 1840–50.* (Ends in 1845 with the death of Davis. A revised edition (London, 2 vols, 1896) has the same title except that the terminal dates are given (correctly) as 1840–1845.)

Charles Gavan Duffy. *Four Years of Irish History, 1845–1849: A Sequel to 'Young Ireland'.* London, 1883.

Charles Gavan Duffy. *Thomas Davis: The Memoirs of an Irish Patriot, 1840–1846.* London, 1890.

T. W. Moody. *Thomas Davis, 1814–1845.* Dublin, 1945.

T. W. Moody. 'Thomas Davis and the Irish Nation' in *Hermathena*, ciii (1966), pp 5–31. (Includes a bibliography of Davis's writings and of writings on Davis.)

K. B. Nowlan. *Charles Gavan Duffy.* Dublin, 1964.

Denis Gwynn. *Young Ireland and 1848.* Cork, 1949.

C. E. Trevelyan. *The Irish Crisis.* London, 1848.

Transactions of the Central Relief Committee of the Society of Friends during the Famine in Ireland in 1846 and 1847. Dublin, 1852.

John O'Rourke. *The History of the Great Irish Famine of 1847, with Notices of Earlier Famines.* Dublin, 1875.

W. P. O'Brien. *The Great Famine in Ireland and a Retrospect of the Fifty Years 1845–95.* London, 1896.

R. Dudley Edwards and T. D. Williams (ed.). *The Great Famine: Studies in Irish History, 1845–1852.* Dublin, 1956; reprint, with introduction by E. R. R. Green, New York, 1976.

Cecil Woodham-Smith. *The Great Hunger: Ireland 1845–9.* London, 1962.

S. H. Cousens. 'The Regional Variation in Mortality during the Great Irish Famine' in *Proceedings of the Royal Irish Academy*, 63 C 3 (1963), pp 127–49.

XI IRELAND, 1850–1921

F. S. L. Lyons. *Ireland Since the Famine.* London, 1971; revised edition, 1973. (Full, classified bibliography)

Joseph Lee. *The Modernisation of Irish Society, 1848–1918.* Dublin, 1973.

Nicholas Mansergh. *The Irish Question, 1840–1921.* London, 1948; new edition, 1965.

J. H. Whyte. *The Independent Irish Party, 1850–59.* Oxford, 1958.

Charles Gavan Duffy. *The League of North and South.* London, 1886.

T. K. Hoppen. 'National Politics and Local Realities in Mid-Nineteenth-Century Ireland' in Art Cosgrove and Donal McCartney (ed.)., *Studies in Irish History Presented to R. Dudley Edwards* (Dublin, 1979), pp 190–227.

S. H. Cousens. 'The Regional Variations in Population Changes in Ireland, 1861–1881' in *Economic History Review*, xvii, no. 2 (Dec. 1964), pp 301–21.

T. N. Brown. *Irish-American Nationalism, 1870–1890.* Philadelphia and New York, 1966.

Desmond Ryan. *The Phoenix Flame: A Study of Fenianism and John Devoy.* London, 1937.

T. W. Moody (ed.). *The Fenian Movement.* Cork, 1968; reprint, Dublin and Cork, 1978.

John O'Leary. *Recollections of Fenians and Fenianism.* 2 vols. London, 1896; reprint, Shannon, 1969.

John Devoy. *Recollections of an Irish Rebel . . .* New York, 1929; reprint, Shannon, 1969.

William O'Brien and Desmond Ryan (ed.). *Devoy's Post Bag, 1871–1928.* 2 vols. Dublin, 1948, 1953.

Mark Ryan. *Fenian Memories.* Dublin, 1945.

Leon Ó Broin. *Fenian Fever: An Anglo-Irish Dilemma.* London, 1971.

Leon Ó Broin. *Revolutionary Underground: The Story of the Irish Republican Brotherhood, 1858–1924.* Dublin, 1976.

Marcus Bourke. *John O'Leary: A Study in Irish Separatism.* Tralee., 1967.

Desmond Ryan. *The Fenian Chief: A Biography of James Stephens.* (Edited by Patrick Lynch and Owen Dudley Edwards.) Dublin and Sydney, 1967.

R. V. Comerford. *Charles J. Kickham: A Study in Irish Nationalism and Literature.* Portmarnock, 1979.

R. V. Comerford. 'Anglo-French Tension and the Origins of Fenianism' in F. S. L. Lyons and R. A. J. Hawkins (ed.), *Ireland under the Union* (Oxford, 1980), pp 149–72.

R. V. Comerford. 'Patriotism as Pastime: The appeal of Fenianism in the mid-1860s' in *Irish Historical Studies*, xxii, no. 87 (Mar. 1981), pp 239–50.

Mark Tierney. *Croke of Cashel: The Life of Archbishop Thomas William Croke, 1823–1902.* Dublin, 1976.

E. R. Norman. *The Catholic Church and Ireland in the Age of Rebellion, 1859–73.* London, 1965.

Lord Eversley. *Gladstone and Ireland: The Irish Policy of Parliament, 1850–94.* London, 1912.

J. L. Hammond. *Gladstone and the Irish Nation.* London, 1938; new impression, with introduction by M. R. D. Foot, 1964.

E. D. Steele. 'Gladstone and Ireland' in *Irish Historical Studies,* xvii, no. 65 (Mar. 1970), pp 58–88.

J. K. Vincent. 'Gladstone and Ireland' in *Proceedings of the British Academy,* lxii (1977), pp 193–238.

Michael MacDonagh. *The Home Rule Movement.* Dublin, 1920.

T. P. O'Connor. *The Parnell Movement.* London, 1886; new edition, 1887.

T. de V. White. *The Road of Excess* (A biography of Isaac Butt). Dublin, 1946.

D. A. Thornley. *Isaac Butt and Home Rule.* London, 1964.

R. B. O'Brien. *The Life of Charles Stewart Parnell, 1846–1891.* 2 vols. London, 1898.

Henry Harrison. *Parnell Vindicated: The Lifting of the Veil.* London, 1931.

M. M. O'Hara. *Chief and Tribune: Parnell and Davitt.* Dublin and London, 1919.

Leon Ó Broin. *Parnell: Beathaisnéis.* Dublin, 1937.

C. Cruise O'Brien. *Parnell and His Party, 1880–90.* Oxford, 1957; corrected impression, 1964.

F. S. L. Lyons. *Charles Stewart Parnell.* London, 1977; paperback edition, 1978.

F. S. L. Lyons. *The Fall of Parnell, 1890–91.* London, 1960.

F. Sheehy Skeffington. *Michael Davitt: Revolutionary, Agitator and Labour Leader.* London, 1908: reprint, with introduction by F. S. L. Lyons, 1967.

T. W. Moody. *Davitt and Irish Revolution, 1846–82.* Oxford, 1981.

Michael Davitt. *The Fall of Feudalism in Ireland, or the Story of the Land League Revolution.* London and New York, 1904.

N. D. Palmer. *The Irish Land League Crisis.* New Haven, 1940.

T. W. Moody. 'Michael Davitt and the British Labour Movement, 1882–1906' in *Transactions of the Royal Historical Society,* 5th series, iii (1953), pp 53–76.

F. S. L. Lyons. *John Dillon: A Biography.* London, 1968.

J. V. O'Brien. *William O'Brien and the Course of Irish Politics, 1881–1918.* Berkeley (Cal.), 1976.

L. P. Curtis. *Coercion and Conciliation in Ireland, 1880–92.* Princeton and London, 1963.

K. R. M. Short. *The Dynamite War: Irish-American Bombers in Victorian Britain.* Dublin, 1971.

C. J. Woods. 'Ireland and Anglo-papal Relations, 1880–85' in *Irish Historical Studies,* xviii, no. 69 (Mar. 1972), pp 29–60.

Richard Hawkins. 'Gladstone, Forster and the Release of Parnell, 1882–8' in *Irish Historical Studies,* xvi, no. 63 (Sept. 1969), pp 417–45.

Tom Corfe. *The Phoenix Park Murders: Conflict, Compromise and Tragedy in Ireland, 1879–1882.* London, 1968.

W. F. Mandle. 'The IRB and the Beginnings of the Gaelic Athletic Association' in *Irish Historical Studies,* xx, no. 80 (Sept. 1977), pp 418–38.

A. B. Cooke and J. R. Vincent. *The Governing Passion: Cabinet Government and Party Politics in Britain, 1885–86.* Brighton, 1974.

Alan O'Day. *The English Face of Irish Nationalism: Parnellite Involvement in British Politics, 1880–86.* Dublin, 1977.

F. S. L. Lyons. *The Irish Parliamentary Party, 1890–1901.* London, 1951.

C. Cruise O'Brien (ed.). *The Shaping of Modern Ireland* (1891–1916). London, 1960.

Catherine B. Shannon. 'The Ulster Liberal Unionists and Local Government Reform, 1885–98' in *Irish Historical Studies,* xviii, no. 71 (Mar. 1973), pp 307–23.

C. J. Woods. 'The General Election of 1892: The Catholic Clergy and the Defeat of the Parnellites' in F. S. L. Lyons and K. A. J. Hawkins (ed.), *Ireland Under the Union* (Oxford, 1980), pp 149–72.

D. W. Miller. *Church, State and Nation in Ireland, 1898–1921.* Dublin, 1973.

A. J. Ward. *Ireland and Anglo-American Relations, 1899–1921.* London, 1969.

R. M. Henry. *The Evolution of Sinn Féin.* Dublin, 1920.

J. J. Horgan. *Parnell to Pearse.* Dublin, 1948.

Denis Gwynn. *The Life of John Redmond.* London, 1932.

Padraic Colum. *Arthur Griffith.* Dublin, 1959.

Seán Ó Lúing. *Art Ó Gríofa.* Dublin, 1953.

R. P. Davis. *Arthur Griffith and Non-violent Sinn Féin.* Dublin, 1974.

R. P. Davis. *Arthur Griffith.* Dublin Historical Association, 1976.

W. Alison Phillips. *The Revolution in Ireland, 1906–1923.* 2nd edition, 1926.

Leon Ó Broin. *The Chief Secretary: Augustine Birrell in Ireland.* London, 1969.

W. B. Stanford and R. B. McDowell. *Mahaffy: A Biography of an Anglo-Irishman.* London, 1971.

Brian Inglis. *Roger Casement*. London, 1973.

Pádraic H. Pearse. *Political Writings and Speeches*. Dublin, 1922; reprint, 1958.

Pádraic H. Pearse. *Plays, Stories, Poems*. Dublin, 1917; reprint, 1952.

Ruth Dudley Edwards. *Patrick Pearse: The Triumph of Failure*. London, 1977.

James Connolly. *Socialism and Nationalism*. Introduction and notes by Desmond Ryan. Dublin, 1948

James Connolly. *The Workers' Republic*. Introduction by William McMullen. Dublin, 1951.

James Connolly. *Labour and Easter Week*. Introduction by William O'Brien. Dublin, 1949

C. D. Greaves. *The Life and Times of James Connolly*. London, 1961.

Proinsias Mac an Bheatha. *Tart na Córa – Séamus Ó Congaile, a Shaol agus a Shaothar*. Dublin, 1963.

Emmet Larkin. *James Larkin, Irish Labour Leader, 1876–1947*. London, 1965.

A. P. Ryan. *Mutiny at the Curragh*. London, 1956.

James Fergusson. *The Curragh Incident*. London, 1963.

F. X. Martin (ed.). *The Irish Volunteers, 1913–15: Recollections and Documents*. Dublin, 1963.

F. X. Martin (ed.). *The Howth Gun-running and the Kilcoole Gun-running, 1914: Recollections and Documents*. Dublin, 1964.

Diarmuid Lynch. *The IRB and the 1916 Rising*. Edited by F. O'Donoghue, Cork, 1957.

Desmond Ryan. *The Rising: The Complete Story of Easter Week*. Dublin, 1949; 3rd edition, 1957.

Owen Dudley Edwards and Fergus Pyle (ed.). *1916: The Easter Rising*. London, 1968.

K. B. Nowlan (ed.). *The Making of 1916: Studies in the History of the Rising*. Dublin, 1969.

J. Bowyer Bell. *The Secret Army: A History of the IRA, 1916–1979*. London, 1970; 3rd edition, Dublin, 1979.

T. P. Coogan. *The IRA*. London, 1970; 2nd edition, Glasgow, 1980.

Leon Ó Broin. *Dublin Castle and the 1916 Rising: The Story of Sir Matthew Nathan*. Dublin, 1966.

F. X. Martin (ed.). *Leaders and Men of the Easter Rising: Dublin 1916*. London and Ithaca, 1967.

F. X. Martin. '1916 – Myth, Fact and Mystery' in *Studia Hibernica*, 1967 [1968], pp 7–126. Review article of published literature, 1916–66, on the Easter Rising.

T. D. Williams (ed.). *The Irish Struggle, 1916–1926*. London, 1966.

Edgar Holt. *Protest in Arms: The Irish Troubles, 1916–23*. London. 1960.

F. X. Martin (ed.). 'Eoin MacNeill on the 1916 Rising' in *Irish Historical Studies*, xii, no. 37 (Mar. 1961), pp 226–71.

F. X. Martin and F. J. Byrne (ed.). *The Scholar Revolutionary: Eoin Mac Neill, 1867–1945, and the Making of the New Ireland*. Shannon, 1973.

Michael Tierney. *Eoin Mac Neill: Scholar and Man of Action, 1867–1945*. Edited by F. X. Martin. Oxford, 1980.

Margery Forester. *Michael Collins –The Lost Leader*. London, 1971.

F. X. Martin (ed.). *1916 and University College, Dublin*. Dublin, 1966.

Florence O'Donoghue. *No Other Law: The Story of Liam Lynch and the Irish Republican Army., 1916–1923*. Dublin, 1954.

Tomás Ó Néill and Pádraig Ó Fiannachta. *De Valera*. 2 vols. Dublin, 1968.

Frank Pakenham and T. P. O'Neill. *Éamon de Valera*. London, 1970.

C. D. Greaves. *Liam Mellows and the Irish Revolution*. London, 1971.

Andrew Boyle. *The Riddle of Erskine Childers*. London, 1977.

Thomas Jones. *Whitehall Diary: iii, Ireland, 1918–25*. Edited by Keith Middlemas. London, 1971.

Charles Townshend. *The British Campaign in Ireland, 1919–1921*. London, 1969.

D. G. Boyce. *Englishmen and Irish Troubles: British Public Opinion and the Making of Irish Policy, 1918–22*. London, 1972.

Frank Pakenham. *Peace by Ordeal*. London, 1955; new edition, 1962.

David Fitzpatrick. *Politics and Irish Life, 1913–21: Provincial Experience of War and Revolution*. Dublin, 1977.

XII IRELAND, 1921–82

John A. Murphy. *Ireland in the Twentieth Century*. Dublin, 1975.

T. P. Coogan. *Ireland Since the Rising*. London, 1966.

Denis Gwynn. *The Irish Free State, 1922–7*. London, 1928.

J. M. Curran. *The Birth of the Irish Free State, 1921–1923*. Alabama, 1980.

Terence Brown. *Ireland: A Social and Cultural Hisrory, 1922–79*. Fontana Paperbacks, 1981.

George O'Brien. *The Four Green Fields*. Dublin, 1936.

Peadar O'Donnell. *There Will Be Another Day*. Dublin, 1963.
T. D. Williams (ed.). *The Irish Struggle, 1916–26*. London, 1966.
Francis MacManus (ed.). *The Years of the Great Test, 1926–39*. Cork, 1967.
K. B. Nowlan and T. D. Williams (ed.). *Ireland in the War Years and After, 1939–51*. Dublin, 1969.
J. T. Carroll. *Ireland in the War Years*. Newton Abbot, 1975.
J. J. Lee (ed.). *Ireland, 1945–70*. Dublin, 1979.
Sáorstát Éireann, Irish Free State, Official Handbook. Dublin, 1932.
T. de V. White. *Kevin O'Higgins*. London, 1948.
Mary C. Bromage. *De Valera and the March of a Nation*. London, 1956.
Tomás Ó Néill and Pádraig Ó Fiannachta. *De Valera*. 2 vols. Dublin, 1968.
Lord Longford and T. P. O'Neill. *Éamon de Valera*. Dublin and London, 1970.
John Bowman. *De Valera and the Ulster Question, 1917–1973*. Oxford, 1982.
D. W. Harkness. *The Restless Dominion: The Irish Free State and the British Commonwealth of Nations, 1921–31*. London and Dublin, 1969.
G. J. Hand (ed.). *Report of the Irish Boundary Commission, 1925*. Shannon, 1969.
Nicholas Mansergh. *Survey of British Commonwealth Affairs: Problems of External Policy, 1931–39*. London, 1952.
Nicholas Mansergh. *Survey of British Commonwealth Affairs: Problems of Wartime Cooperation and Post-War Change, 1939–52*. London, 1958.
J. Bowyer Bell. *The Secret Army: A History of the IRA, 1916–79*. London. 1970; 3rd edition, Dublin, 1979.
T. P. Coogan. *The IRA*. London, 1970; 2nd edition, Glasgow, 1980.
Calton Younger. *Ireland's Civil War*. London, 1968.
Maurice Manning. *The Blueshirts*. Dublin, 1971.
J. H. Whyte. *Church and State in Modern Ireland, 1923–1970*. Dublin, 1971; 2nd edition, 1980.
Patrick Keatinge. *A Place Among the Nations: Issues of Irish Foreign Policy*. Dublin, 1978.
D. R. O'Connor Lysaght. *The Republic of Ireland*. Cork, 1970.
Jack White. *Minority Report: The Anatomy of the Southern Irish Protestant*. Dublin, 1975.
Frank Litton (ed.). *Unequal Achievement: The Irish Experience, 1957–1982*. Dublin, 1982.
T. Ryle Dwyer. *Michael Collins and the Treaty*. Dublin and Cork, 1981.
T. Ryle Dwyer. *De Valera's Darkest Hour: In Search of National Independence, 1919–1932*. Dublin and Cork, 1982.
T. Ryle Dwyer. *De Valera's Finest Hour: In Search of National Independence, 1932–1959*. Dublin and Cork, 1982.
Kevin Boland. *The Rise and Decline of Fianna Fáil*. Dublin and Cork, 1982.

XII IRELAND, 1983–2001

D. H. Akenson. *The Irish Diaspora: A Primer*. Belfast, 1993.
J. Augusteijn (ed.). *Ireland in the 1930s: New Perspectives*. Dublin, 1999.
J. Bardon. *A History of Ulster*. Belfast, 1992.
R. Barrington. *Health, Medicine and Politics in Ireland, 1900–1970*. Dublin, 1987.
P. Bew, E. Hazelkorn and H. Patterson. *The Dynamics of Irish Politics*. London, 1989.
A. Bielenberg (ed.). *The Irish Diaspora*. London, 2000.
P. Bishop and E. Mallie. *The Provisional IRA*. London, 1987.
D. G. Boyce and A. O'Day (eds). *Modern Irish History: Revisionism and the Revisionist Controversy*. London, 1996.
D. G. Boyce. *Nationalism in Ireland*. London, 1982, 1995.
C. Brady (ed.). *Interpreting Irish History: The Debate on Historical Revisionism*. Dublin, 1994.
T. Brown. *Ireland: A Social and Cultural History 1922–1985*. London, 1985.
S. J. Connolly (ed.). *The Oxford Companion to Irish History*. Oxford, 1998.
T. P. Coogan. *Michael Collins*. London, 1990.
T. P. Coogan. *De Valera: Long Fellow, Long Shadow*. London, 1993.
T. P. Coogan. *Wherever Green is Worn: The Irish Diaspora*. London, 2001.
J. Cooney. *John Charles McQuaid: Ruler of Catholic Ireland*. Dublin, 1999.
M. E. Daly. *Social and Economic History of Ireland Since 1800*. Dublin, 1981.
R. Dunphy. *The Making of Fianna Fáil Power in Ireland, 1923–48*. Oxford, 1995.
R. English. *Radicals and the Republic: Social Republicanism in the Irish Free State 1925–1937*. Oxford, 1994.
B. Fallon. *An Age of Innocence: Irish Culture 1930–1960*. Dublin, 1998.

R. Fanning. *Independent Ireland*. Dublin, 1983.

R. Fanning et al. (eds). *Documents on Irish Foreign Policy*, Vol. 1, 1919–22 and Vol. 2, 1922–6. Dublin, 1998 and 2000.

R. Fisk. *In Time of War: Ireland, Ulster and the Price of Neutrality*. London, 1983.

D. Fitzpatrick. *The Two Irelands 1912–1939*. Oxford, 1998.

R. Foster. *Modern Ireland 1600–1972*. London, 1998.

T. Garvin. *Nationalist Revolutionaries in Ireland*. Oxford, 1987.

T. Garvin. *1922: The Birth of Irish Democracy*. Dublin, 1996.

B. Girvin and G. Roberts (eds). *Ireland and the Second World War: Politics, Society and Remembrance*. Dublin, 2000.

B. Girvin. *Between Two Worlds: Politics and Economy in Contemporary Ireland*. Dublin, 1989.

P. Hart. *The IRA and Its Enemies: Violence and Community in Cork 1916–23*. Oxford, 1998.

A. Hayes and D. Urquhart (eds). *The Irish Women's History Reader*. London, 2001.

T. Hennessey. *A History of Northern Ireland, 1920–1996*. Basingstoke, 1997.

T. Hennessey. *Dividing Ireland: World War One and Partition*. London, 1998.

M. Hopkinson. *Green Against Green: The Irish Civil War*. Dublin, 1988.

K. T. Hoppen. *Ireland Since 1800: Conflict and Conformity*. London, 1989.

J. Horgan. *Seán Lemass: Enigmatic Patriot*. Dublin, 1997.

J. Horgan. *Noel Browne: Passionate Outsider*. Dublin, 2000.

J. Horgan. *Irish Media: A Critical History Since 1922*. London, 2001.

A. Jackson. *Ireland, 1798–1998: Politics and War*. Oxford, 1999.

K. Jeffery. *Ireland and the Great War*. Cambridge, 2000.

M. Kennedy. *Ireland and the League of Nations, 1923–1946*. Dublin, 1996.

M. Kennedy and J. Skelly (eds). *Irish Foreign Policy, 1919–1966*. Dublin, 2000.

D. Keogh. *Ireland and Europe 1919–1989*. Cork and Dublin, 1989.

D. Keogh. *Twentieth Century Ireland: Nation and State*. Dublin, 1994.

D. Keogh. *Ireland and the Vatican: The Politics and Diplomacy of Church and State*. Cork, 1995.

D. Keogh. *Jews in Twentieth-Century Ireland*. Cork, 1998.

J. J. Lee. *Ireland 1912–85: Politics and Society*. Cambridge, 1989.

F. McGarry. *Irish Politics and the Spanish Civil War*. Cork, 1999.

D. McMahon. *Republicans and Imperialists: Anglo-Irish Relations in the 1930s*. New Haven, 1984.

M. Milotte. *Communism in Modern Ireland*. Dublin, 1984

A. Mitchell and P Ó Snodaigh (eds). *Irish Political Documents 1916–1949*. Dublin, 1985.

P. Murray. *Oracles of God: The Roman Catholic Church and Irish Politics, 1922–37*. Dublin, 2000.

N. Ní Donnchadha and T. Dorgan (eds). *Revising the Rising*. Derry, 1991.

E. O'Connor. *A Labour History of Ireland 1824–1960*. Dublin, 1992.

S. Ó Buachalla. *Education Policy in Twentieth Century Ireland*. Dublin, 1988.

J. P. O'Carroll and J. A. Murphy (eds). *De Valera and His Times*. Cork, 1983.

D. Ó Drisceoil. *Censorship in Ireland 1939–45: Neutrality, Politics and Society*. Cork, 1996.

C. Ó Grada. *Ireland: A New Economic History 1780–1939*. Oxford, 1994.

C. O'Halloran. *Partition and the Limits of Irish Nationalism*. Dublin, 1987.

E. O'Halpin. *The Decline of the Union: British Government in Ireland, 1892–1920*. Dublin, 1987.

E. O'Halpin. *Defending Ireland: The Irish State and Its Enemies Since 1922*. Oxford, 1999.

H. Patterson. *The Politics of Illusion: A Political History of the IRA*. London, 1997.

J. Regan. *The Irish Counter-Revolution 1921–36*. Dublin, 1999.

T. Salmon. *Unneutral Ireland: An Ambivalent and Unique Security Policy*. Oxford, 1989.

R. Savage. *Irish Television: The Political and Social Origins*. Cork, 1996.

F. Tobin. *The Best of Decades: Ireland in the 1960s*. Dublin,1984.

C. Townshend. *Ireland in the Twentieth Century*. London, 1998.

M. Ward. *Unmanageable Revolutionaries: Women and Irish Nationalism*. Dingle, 1983.

K. Woodman. *Media Control in Ireland 1923–1983*. Galway, 1986.

XIV ULSTER HISTORY

T. E. McNeill. *Anglo-Norman Ulster: The History and Archaeology of an Irish Barony, 1177–1400*. Edinburgh, 1980.

Katharine Simms. 'The Archbishops of Armagh and the O'Neills, 1347–1471' in *Irish Historical Studies*, xix, no. 73 (Mar. 1974).

Katharine Simms. '"The King's Friend": O'Neill, the Crown and the Earldom of Ulster' in J. F. Lydon (ed.), *England and Ireland in the Later Middle Ages* (Dublin, 1981), pp 214–36.

George Hill. *An Historical Account of the MacDonnells of Antrim.* Belfast, 1873; reprint, 1976.

George Hill. *An Historical Account of the Plantation in Ulster . . . 1608–20.* Belfast, 1877; reprint, Shannon, 1970.

Cyril Falls. *The Birth of Ulster.* London, 1936.

T. W. Moody. *The Londonderry Plantation, 1609–41: The City of London and the Plantation in Ulster.* Belfast, 1939.

T. W. Moody (ed.). 'The Revised Articles of the Ulster Plantation, 1610' in *Bulletin of the Institute of Historical Research*, xii, no. 36 (Feb. 1935), pp 178–83.

T. W. Moody. 'The Treatment of the Native Population under the Scheme for the Plantation in Ulster' in *Irish Historical Studies*, i, no. 1 (Mar. 1938), pp 59–63.

J. B. Woodburn. *The Ulster Scot: His History and Religion.* London, 1915.

M. Perceval Maxwell. *The Scottish Migration to Ulster in the Reign of James I.* London, 1973.

C. D. Milligan. *History of the Siege of Londonderry.* Belfast, 1951.

J. G. Simms. *The Siege of Derry.* Dublin, 1966.

Peter Roebuck (ed.). *Plantation to Partition: Essays in Ulster History in Honour of J. L. McCracken.* Belfast, 1981.

R. J. Dickson. *Ulster Emigration to Colonial America, 1718–1775.* London, 1966.

E. R. R. Green (ed.). *Essays in Scotch-Irish History.* London, 1969.

Mary McNeill. *The Life and Times of Mary Ann McCracken, 1770–1866: a Belfast Panorama.* Dublin, 1960.

Finlay Holmes. *Henry Cooke.* Belfast, 1982.

Peter Jupp. 'County Down Elections, 1783–1831' in *Irish Historical Studies*, xviii, no. 70 (Sept. 1972), pp 177–206.

Desmond Murphy. *Derry, Donegal, and Modern Ulster, 1790–1921.* Londonderry, 1981.

D. H. Akenson. *Between Two Revolutions: Islandmagee, County Antrim, 1798–1920.* Ontario, 1979.

T. W. Moody and J. C. Beckett (ed.). *Ulster Since 1800: A Political and Economic Survey.* London, 1955; reprint, with corrections, 1957.

T. W. Moody and J. C. Beckett (ed.). *Ulster Since 1800: A Social Survey.* London, 1957; reprint, with corrections, 1958.

E. R. R. Green. *The Lagan Valley, 1800–1850: A Local History of the Industrial Revolution.* London, 1949.

W. E. Coe. *The Engineering Industry of the North of Ireland.* Newton Abbot, 1969

J. A. McCutcheon. *The Industrial Archaeology of Northern Ireland.* Belfast, 1980.

R. W. Kirkpatrick. 'Origins and Development of the Land War in Mid-Ulster, 1879–85' in F. S. L. Lyons and R. A. J. Hawkins (ed.), *Ireland Under the Union* (Oxford, 1980), pp 201–36.

R. F. Foster. 'To the Northern Counties Station: Lord Randolph Churchill and the Prelude to the Orange Card' in F. S. L. Lyons and R. A. J. Hawkins (ed.), *Ireland Under the Union* (Oxford, 1980), pp 237–88.

Patrick Buckland. *Irish Unionism 2: Ulster Unionism and the Origins of Northern Ireland, 1886–1922.* Dublin and New York, 1973.

A. T. Q. Stewart. *The Ulster Crisis.* London, 1967; reprint, 1979.

Liam de Paor. *Divided Ulster.* London, 1970.

Hugh Shearman. *Not an Inch: A Study of Northern Ireland and Lord Craigavon.* London, 1942.

T. W. Moody. *The Ulster Question, 1603–1973.* Dublin and Cork, 1974. (Extensive bibliography)

A. T. Q. Stewart. *The Narrow Ground: Aspects of Ulster, 1609–1969.* London, 1977.

D. W. Miller. *Queen's Rebels: Ulster Loyalism in Historical Perspective.* Dublin and New York, 1978.

St John Ervine. *Craigavon: Ulsterman.* London, 1949.

Edward Marjoribanks and Ian Colvin. *Life of Lord Carson.* 3 vols. London, 1932, 1934, 1936.

A. T. Q. Stewart. *Edward Carson.* Dublin, 1981.

John Bowman. *De Valera and the Ulster Question, 1917–1973.* Oxford, 1982.

Hugh Shearman. *Northern Ireland, 1921–1971.* Belfast, 1971. (Many valuable illustrations)

Patrick Buckland. *A History of Northern Ireland.* Dublin, 1981.

R. J. McNeill. *Ulster's Stand for Union.* London, 1922.

W. S. Armour. *Armour of Ballymoney.* London, 1934.

Denis Gwynn. *The History of Partition, 1912–1925.* Dublin, 1950.

J. W. Blake. *Northern Ireland in the Second World War.* Belfast, 1956.

Nicholas Mansergh. *The Government of Northern Ireland.* London, 1936.

Thomas Wilson (ed.). *Ulster under Home Rule: A Study of the Political and Economic Problems of Northern Ireland*. London, 1955.

R. J. Lawrence. *The Government of Northern Ireland: Public Finance and Public Services, 1921–1964*. Oxford, 1965.

K. S. Isles and N. Cuthbert. *An Economic Survey of Northern Ireland*. Belfast, 1957.

D. P. Barritt and C. F. Carter. *The Northern Ireland Problem: A Study in Group Relations*. London, 1962; 2nd edition, 1972.

Sydney Elliott. *Northern Ireland Parliamentary Election Results, 1921–71*. Chichester, 1973.

Paul Bew, Peter Gibbon, and Henry Patterson. *The State in Northern Ireland, 1921–72*. Manchester, 1979.

D. H. Akenson. *Education and Enmity: The Control of Schooling in Northern Ireland, 1920–1950*. Newton Abbot and New York, 1973.

Michael Farrell. *Northern Ireland: The Orange State*. London, 1976.

Liam O'Dowd, Bill Rolston, and Mike Tomlinson. *Northern Ireland between Civil Rights and Civil War*. London, 1980.

Derek Birrell and Alan Murie. *Policy and Government in Northern Ireland: Lessons of Devolution*. Dublin, 1980.

Richard Rose. *Governing Without Consensus: An Irish Perspective*. London, 1971.

Paul Arthur. *Government and Politics in Northern Ireland*. London, 1980.

Patrick Buckland. *The Factory of Grievances: Devolved Government in Northern Ireland, 1921–39*. Dublin, 1979.

Martin Wallace. *British Government in Northern Ireland from Devolution to Direct Rule*. Newton Abbot, 1982.

David Watt (ed.). *The Constitution of Northern Ireland: Problems and Prospects*. London, 1981.

Rosemary Harris. *Prejudice and Tolerance in Ulster*. Manchester, 1972.

David Boulton. *The UVF, 1966–73: An Anatomy of Loyalist Rebellion*. Dublin, 1973.

John Darby. *Conflict in Northern Ireland: The Development of a Polarised Community*. Dublin, 1976.

Terence O'Neill. *Ulster at the Crossroads*. London, 1969.

Terence O'Neill. *Autobiography*. London, 1972.

Brian Faulkner. *Memoirs of a Statesman*. Edited by John Houston. London, 1978.

Sunday Times Insight Team. *Ulster*. 2nd edition. London, 1972.

Ian MacAllister. *The Northern Ireland Social Democratic and Labour Party*. London, 1977.

Robert Fisk. *The Point of No Return: The Strike which Broke the British in Ulster*. London, 1975.

Dervla Murphy. *A Place Apart*. London, 1978.

Bob Kowthorn. 'Northern Ireland: an Economy in Crisis' in *Cambridge Journal of Economics*, v, (1981).

J. M. Mogey. *Rural Life in Northern Ireland: Five Regional Studies*. London, 1917.

Hugh Shearman. *Ulster*. London, 1949.

Lord Longford and Anne Hardy. *Ulster*. London, 1981.

J. C. Beckett and R. E. Glasscock (ed.). *Belfast: Origin and Growth of an Industrial City*. London, 1967.

Jonathan Bardon. *Belfast: An Illustrated History*. With picture research by Henry V. Bell. Belfast, 1982; reprint, with corrections, 1983.

Ian Budge and Cornelius O'Leary. *Belfast: Approach to Crisis, a Study of Belfast Politics, 1613–1970*. London, 1973.

Henry Patterson. *Class Conflict and Sectarianism: the Protestant Working Class and the Belfast Labour Movement, 1868–1920*. Belfast, 1980.

Gilbert Camblin. *The Town in Ulster*. London, 1951.

C. E. B. Brett. *Buildings of Belfast, 1700–1914*. London, 1967.

Alistair Rowan. *The Buildings of Ireland: North-west Ulster: The Counties of Londonderry, Donegal, Fermanagh and Tyrone*. Harmondsworth, 1979.

Emrys Jones. *A Social Geography of Belfast*. London, 1960.

Richard Deutsch and Vivien Magowan. *Northern Ireland, 1968–73: A Chronology of Events*. Vol. i: 1968–71; vol. ii: 1972–73. Belfast, 1973, 1974 (includes valuable bibliography and appendices)

Richard Deutsch. *Northern Ireland, 1921–1974: A Select Bibliography*. New York and London, 1975.

XV BIOGRAPHICAL AND OTHER WORKS OF REFERENCE

T. W. Moody, F. X. Martin and F. J. Byrne (ed.). *A New History of Ireland*. Vol. viii: *A Chronology of Irish History to 1976*. Oxford, 1982.

Alfred Webb. *Compendium of Irish Biography* ... Dublin, 1878.

J. S. Clone. *A Concise Dictionary of Irish Biography*, Dublin, 1928, 2nd edition, [1937].

Henry Boylan. *A Dictionary of Irish Biography*. Dublin, 1878.

Edward MacLysaght. *Irish Families: Their Names, Arms and Origins*. Dublin, 1957.

Edward MacLysaght. *More Irish Families*. Galway and Dublin, 1960.

Edward MacLysaght. *Supplement to Irish Families*. Dublin, 1964.

Edward MacLysaght. *Guide to Irish Families*. Dublin, 1963.

Dictionary of National Biography. Edited by Leslie Stephen and Sidney Lee. 66 vols. London, 1885–1901. Reprinted with corrections, 22 vols, 1908–9.(The main dictionary to 1900; continued from 1901 in decadal volumes. Contains innumerable Irish biographies.)

Concise Dictionary of National Biography. 2 vols: (1) to 1900 (corrected impression, London, 1959); (2) 1901–1970 (1982).

Dictionary of American Biography. Edited by Allen Johnson and Dumas Malone. 20 vols. New York and London, 1928–37. (Contains many Irish-American biographies.)

John Lodge. *Peerage of Ireland*. Revised edition, by Mervyn Archdall. 7 vols. Dublin, 1789.

G.E.C. *Complete Peerage of England, Scotland, Ireland, Great Britain and the United Kingdom* . . . Edited by Vicary Gibbs and others. 13 vols. London, 1910–59.

Aubrey Gwynn and R. N. Hadcock. *Medieval Religious Houses*. London, 1970.

F. E. Ball. *The Judges in Ireland, 1121–1921*. 2 vols. London, 1926.

Thom's Irish Almanac and Official Directory for the Year 1844 (etc.). Dublin, 1844 (etc.).

Ulster Year Book, 1926 (etc.). Belfast, HM Stationery Office, 1926 (etc.).

Samuel Lewis. *A Topographical Dictionary of Ireland*. 2 vols. and Atlas. London, 1837.

Census of Ireland, 1901: General Topographical Index. Dublin, HM Stationery Office, 1904 (Cd 2071).

Brian Cleeve (ed.). *Dictionary of Irish Writers*. 3 vols. Cork, 1967, 1969, 1971.

D. J. Hickey and J. E. Doherty. *A Dictionary of Irish History Since 1800*. Dublin, 1980.

W. E. Vaughan and A. J. Fitzpatrick. *Irish Historical Statistics: Population, 1821–1971*. Dublin, 1978. (New History of Ireland Ancillary Publications II)

B. M. Walker. *Parliamentary Election Results in Ireland, 1801–1922*. Dublin, 1978. (New History of Ireland Ancillary Publications IV)

Lord Killanin and M. V. Duignan. *Shell Guide to Ireland*. London, 1962.

Department of Foreign Affairs. *Facts About Ireland*. 5th edition. Dublin, 1981.

XVI BIBLIOGRAPHIES, SERIAL PUBLICATIONS AND FESTSCHRIFTS

BIBLIOGRAPHIES

Edith M. Johnston. *Irish History: A Select Bibliography*. London Historical Association, 1969; revised reprint, 1972.

J. F. Kenney. *The Sources for the Early History of Ireland: Ecclesiastical*. New York, 1929; reprint, New York, 1966, with preface by Ludwig Bieler.

P. W. A. Asplin. *Medieval Ireland, c. 1170–1498: A Bibliography of Secondary Works*. Dublin, 1971.

For the period 1485–1914 a bibliography of Irish history is provided by the Irish sections of the Royal Historical Society's *Bibliography of British History, 1485–1603* (2nd edition, London, 1959); — 1603–1714 (1928); — 1714–89 (1951); — 1789–1851(1977); — 1851–1914 (1976).

James Carty. *Bibliography of Irish History, 1870–1911*. Dublin, 1940.

James Carty. *Bibliography of Irish History, 1911–21*. Dublin, 1936.

Writings on Irish history, 1936–78. A bibliography of current publications, published annually in *Irish Historical Studies* from 1938 to 1979.

Select bibliography of publications in Irish economic and social history published in 1973 (etc.). Published annually in *Irish Economic and Social History* since 1974.

Royal Historical Society. *Annual Bibliography of British and Irish History: Publications of 1975* (etc.). Edited by G. R. Elton. Hassocks, 1976–.

T. W. Moody (ed.). *Irish Historiography, 1936–70*. Dublin, 1971.

J. J. Lee (ed.). *Irish Historiography, 1970–79*. Cork, 1980.

Irish Manuscripts Commission, Catalogue of Publications Issued and in Preparation, 1928–1966. Dublin, Stationery Office, 1966.

A Guide to the Reports on Collections of Manuscripts. . . Issued by the Royal Commissioners for Historical Manuscripts. Part I – *Topographical (Index)*. London, Stationery Office, 1914.

Guide to the Reports of the Royal Commission on Historical Manuscripts, 1870–1911. Part II – *Index of Persons*. 2 vols. London, Stationery Office, 1935, 1938.

R. J. Hayes (ed.). *Sources for the History of Irish Civilisation: Articles in Irish Periodicals.* 9 vols. Boston (Mass.), 1970.

K. J. Hayes (ed.). *Manuscript Sources for the History of Irish Civilisation.* 11 vols. Boston (Mass.), 1966; *Supplement.* 3 vols. 1979.

A. R. Eager. *A Guide to Irish Bibliographical Material: A Bibliography of Irish Bibliographies and Sources of Information.* London, 1963; 2nd edition, 1980.

PERIODICALS

Irish Historical Studies (Dublin, 1938–; biannual).
Historical Studies: Papers Read Before the Irish Conference of Historians (London, 1958–).
Irish Economic and Social History (1974; annual).
Proceedings of the Royal Irish Academy, section C (Dublin, 1836–).
Journal of the Royal Society of Antiquaries of Ireland (Dublin, 1892).
Studia Hibernica (Dublin, 1961–; annual).
Proceedings of the Irish Catholic Historical Committee (Dublin, 1955–; annual).
The *Irish Sword* (Dublin, 1949–; biannual).
Ulster Journal of Archaeology (Belfast, 1853–62; 1895–1911; 1938–; annual).
Dublin Historical Record (Dublin, 1938).
Journal of the Cork Historical and Archaeological Society (Cork, 1892–).
Journal of the Galway Historical and Archaeological Society (Galway 1904–).
Journal of the County Louth Archaeological Society (Dundalk, 1904–).
Studies (Dublin, 1912–; quarterly).
Irish Ecclesiastical Record (Dublin, 1864–1968; monthly).
Ulster Genealogical & Historical Guild Newsletter (Belfast, 1978).

SERIES

Studies in Irish History. Edited by T. W. Moody and others. First series, vols i–vii, London, 1944–56; second series, vols i–x, 1960–75.

New History of Ireland Ancillary Publications. Edited by T. W. Moody, F. X. Martin and F. J. Byrne. Dublin, 1971–.

Dublin Historical Association. Irish history series. Dundalk, 1961–.

Dublin Historical Association. Medieval Irish history series. Dundalk, 1964–.

Irish Life and Culture: a series of pamphlets issued by the Cultural Relations Committee of Ireland. Dublin, 1950–.

The Thomas Davis Lectures. A continuing programme of half-hour talks, mainly on Irish history, culture and social life, broadcast annually by Radio Telefís Éireann from 1953. Many Thomas Davis series have been published in book form, especially as paperbacks; a complete list for 1953–67 by F. X. Martin is in *Irish Historical Studies,* xv, no. 59 (Mar. 1967). Most of the published Thomas Davis series are included in sections II–XII above.

Insights into Irish History. Edited by L. M. Cullen. Dublin, 1971–.

The O'Donnell Lectures. An annual series of lectures on Irish history, given in rotation at the colleges of the National University of Ireland. Dublin: National University of Ireland, 1957–.

Public Record Office of Northern Ireland. Education Facsimiles. Belfast, HM Stationery Office, 1969–. (Packs of twenty loose documents with general introduction, notes and illustrations)

National Library of Ireland. Facsimile Documents. Dublin, Coordinating Committee for Educational Services based on the institutions of science and art, 1976–. (Packs of loose documents, on similar plan to preceding)

FESTSCHRIFTS

John Ryan (ed.). *Féil-sgríbhinn Eóin Mhic Néill: Essays and Studies presented to Eoin Mac Neill.* Dublin, 1940.

H. A. Cronne, T. W. Moody and D. B. Quinn (ed.). *Essays in British and Irish History in Honour of James Eadie Todd.* London, 1949.

J. A. Watt, J. B. Morrall and F. X. Martin (ed.). *Medieval Studies Presented to Aubrey Gwynn, S.J.* Dublin, 1961.

John Bossy and Peter Jupp (ed.). *Essays Presented to Michael Roberts, Sometime Professor of Modern History in the Queen's University of Belfast.* Belfast, 1976.

K. R. Andrews, N. P. Canny and P. E. H. Haire (ed.). *The Westward Enterprise: English Activities in Ireland, the Atlantic and America, 1480–1650.* Liverpool, 1978. (Essays in honour of D. B. Quinn)

Art Cosgrove and Donal McCartney (ed.). *Studies in Irish History presented to R. Dudley Edwards.* Dublin, 1979.

Thomas Bartlett and D. W. Hayton (ed.). *Penal Era and Golden Age, 1690–1800.* Belfast, 1979. ('A tribute to J. C. Beckett')

F. S. L. Lyons and R. A. J. Hawkins (ed.). *Ireland Under the Union, Varieties of Tension: Essays in Honour of T. W. Moody.* Oxford, 1980.

J. F. Lydon (ed.). *England and Ireland in the Later Middle Ages: Essays in Honour of Jocelyn Otway-Ruthven.* Dublin, 1981.

Peter Roebuck (ed.). *Plantation to Partition: Essays in Ulster History in Honour of J. L. McCracken.* Belfast, 1981.

J. M. Goldstrom and L. A. Clarkson (ed.). *Irish Population, Economy and Society: Essays in Honour of the Late K. H. Connell.* Oxford, 1981.

XVI BIBLIOGRAPHICAL ADDENDA

I GENERAL HISTORY OF IRELAND
David Edwards

SOURCE COLLECTIONS

B. Donovan and D. Edwards. *British Sources for Irish History, 1485–1641.* Dublin, 1997.

GENERAL WORKS

S. Duffy. *A Concise History of Ireland.* Dublin, 2000, 2001.

S. Duffy (ed.). *Atlas of Irish History.* Dublin, 1994.

J. Lydon. *The Making of Ireland.* London, 1998.

II GENERAL WORKS IN SPECIAL FIELDS
David Edwards

LAW, GOVERNMENT AND PARLIAMENT

L. J. Arnold. 'The Irish Court of Claims of 1663' in *Irish Historical Studies,* xxiv, no. 96 (Nov. 1985), pp 417–30.

T. C. Barnard. 'Lawyers and the law in later seventeenth-century Ireland', in *Irish Historical Studies,* xxviii, no. 111 (May 1993), pp 256–82.

P. Bonsall. *The Irish RMs: The Resident Magistrates in the British Administration in Ireland.* Dublin, 1997.

J. G. Crawford. 'The origins of the Court of Castle Chamber: A Star Chamber jurisdiction in Ireland', in *American Journal of Legal History* xxiv (1980).

J. G. Crawford. *Anglicising the Government of Ireland: The Irish Privy Council and the Expansion of Tudor Rule, 1556–78.* Blackrock, 1993.

D. Edwards. 'Beyond Reform: Martial Law and the Tudor Reconquest of Ireland', *History Ireland,* v, no. 2 (Summer 1997), pp 16–21.

S. Ellis. 'Privy seals of chief governors in Ireland, 1392–1560', in *Bulletin of the Institute of Historical Research,* 51 (1978).

S. Ellis. 'Parliament and community in Yorkist and Tudor Ireland', in A. Cosgrove and J. I. McGuire (eds.), *Parliament & Community: Historical Studies XIV.* Belfast, 1983.

R. Frame. 'Commissions of the peace in Ireland, 1302–1461', in *Analecta Hibernica* XXXV (1992).

N. Garnham. 'The trials of James Cotter and Henry, Baron Barry of Santry: two case studies in the administration of criminal justice in early eighteenth-century Ireland', in *Irish Historical Studies,* xxxi, no. 123 (May 1999), pp 328–42.

B. Griffin. *The Bulkies: Police and Crime in Belfast, 1800–1865.* Dublin, 1997.

A. R. Hart. *A History of the King's Sergeants at Law in Ireland.* Dublin, 2000.

J. Herlihy. *The Royal Irish Constabulary: A Short History and Genealogical Guide.* Dublin, 1997.

L. Irwin. 'The Irish Presidency Courts, 1569–1672', in *Irish Jurist* 12 (1977).

C. Kenny. *King's Inns and the Kingdom of Ireland: The Irish 'Inns of Court', 1541–1800.* Dublin, 1992.

C. Kenny. 'The exclusion of Catholics from the legal profession in Ireland, 1537–1829', in *Irish Historical Studies,* xxv, no. 100 (Nov. 1987), pp 337–57.

W. J. Lowe. 'The Constabulary agitation of 1882', in *Irish Historical Studies*, xxxi, no. 121 (May 1998), pp 37–59.

J. Lydon (ed.), *Law and Disorder in Nineteenth-Century Ireland: The Dublin Parliament of 1297*. Dublin, 1997.

A. J. Sheehan, 'Irish revenues and English subventions, 1559–1622', in *Proceedings of the Royal Irish Academy,* 90 C (1990), pp 35–65.

V. Treadwell, 'Sir John Perrot and the Irish parliament of 1585–6', in *Proceedings of the Royal Irish Academy*, 85 C (1985), pp 259–308.

THE CHURCHES

K. Bottigheimer. 'The failure of the Reformation in Ireland: *Une question bien posée*', in *Journal of Ecclesiastical History*, 36 (1985).

B. Bradshaw. 'The Edwardian Reformation in Ireland', in *Archivium Hibernicum*, 34 (1976–7).

B. Bradshaw. 'Sword, word and strategy in the Reformation in Ireland', in *Historical Journal*, 21 (1985).

B. Bradshaw. 'The Reformation in the cities: Cork, Limerick and Galway, 1534–1603', in J. Bradley (ed.), *Settlement and Society in Medieval Ireland*, Kilkenny, 1988. pp 445–76.

N. Canny. 'Why the Reformation failed in Ireland: *Une question mal posée*', in *Journal of Ecclesiastical History*, 30 (1979).

A Clarke. 'Varieties of uniformity: the first century of the Church of Ireland', in W. J. Shiels and D. Wood (ed.), *The Churches, Ireland and the Irish: Studies in Church History 35* (Oxford 1989), pp 105–22.

S. Ellis. 'Economic problems of the church: Why the Reformation failed in Ireland', in *Journal of Ecclesiastical History*, 41 (1990).

A. Ford. *The Protestant Reformation in Ireland, 1590–1641*. Frankfurt, 1985; repr. Dublin, 1997.

A. Ford, J. McGuire and K. Milne (eds). *As by Law Established: The Church of Ireland Since the Reformation*. Dublin,1995.

A. Ford. 'The Reformation in Kilmore before 1641', in R. Gillespie (ed.), *Cavan: Essays on the History of an Irish County.* Dublin, 1995.

A. Forrestal. *The Catholic Synods in Ireland, 1600–90*. Dublin, 1998.

J. Murray, A. Ford, J. I. McGuire, S. J. Connolly, F. O'Ferrall and K. Milne. 'The Church of Ireland: a critical bibliography, 1536–1992', in *Irish Historical Studies* xxviii, no. 112 (Nov. 1993), pp 345–84.

K. Herlihy (ed.). *Irish Dissent* series. Dublin, 1995– .

P. Fagan. *Catholics in a Protestant Country: The Papist Constituency in Eighteenth-Century Dublin*. Dublin, 1998.

R. Gillespie. *Devoted People: Belief and Religion in Early Modern Ireland*. Manchester, 1997.

R. Gillespie. 'The Presbyterian Revolution in Ulster, 1660–1690', in W. J. Shiels and D. Wood (ed.), *The Churches, Ireland and the Irish: Studies in Church History 35*. Oxford, 1989.

H. A. Jefferies. *Priests and Prelates of Armagh in the Age of Reformations, 1518–58*. Dublin, 1997.

H. A. Jefferies. 'The diocese of Dromore on the eve of the Tudor Reformation', in L. Proudfoot (ed.), *Down: History & Society* (Dublin, 1997), pp 123–40.

C. Lennon. *The Lords of Dublin in the Age of Reformation*. Blackrock, 1989.

C. Lennon. 'The chantries in the Irish Reformation: The case of St Anne's Guild, Dublin, 1550–1630', in R. V. Comerford et al (eds.), *Religion, Conflict and Coexistence* (Dublin, 1990), pp 6–25.

C. Lennon. *An Irish Prisoner of Conscience of the Tudor Era: Richard Creagh, Archbishop of Armagh.* Dublin, 1999.

M. Mac Craith. 'The Gaelic reaction to the Reformation', in S. G. Ellis and S. Barber (eds.), *Conquest & Union: Fashioning a British State, 1485–1725* (London, 1995).

J. D. Neville. 'Irish Presbyterians under the restored Stuart monarchy', *Eire/Ireland* 16/2 (1981), pp 29–42.

T. Ó hAnnracháin. 'Rebels and confederates: The stance of the Irish clergy in the 1640s', in J. Young (ed.), *Celtic Dimensions of the British Civil Wars* (Edinburgh 1997), pp 96–115.

M. A. Valante. 'Reassessing the Irish "monastic town"', in *Irish Historical Studies* xxxi, no. 121 (May 1998), pp 1–18.

H. C. Walshe, 'Enforcing the Elizabethan settlement: The vicissitudes of Hugh Brady, Bishop of Meath, 1563–84', in *Irish Historical Studies* xxvi, no. 104 (Nov. 1989).

M. J. Westerkamp, *Triumph of the Laity: Scots-Irish Piety and the Great Awakening, 1625–1760*. Oxford, 1988.

OTHER SUBJECTS

T. Bartlett and K. Jeffery (eds.). *A Military History of Ireland*. Cambridge, 1996.

J. Burke, 'The New Model Army and the problems of siege warfare, 1648–51', in *Irish Historical Studies* xxvii, no. 105 (May 1990), pp 1–29.

III HISTORICAL GEOGRAPHY OF IRELAND
David Edwards

F. H. A. Aalen, K. Whelan and M. Stout (eds.), *Atlas of the Irish Rural Landscape*. Cork, 1997.

P. J. Duffy, D. Edwards and E. FitzPatrick (eds.). *Gaelic Ireland, c. 1250–c. 1650: Land, Lordship and Settlement*. Dublin, 2001.

P. J. Duffy. 'The territorial organisation of Gaelic landownership and its transformation in County Monaghan, 1591–1640', in *Irish Geography*, 14 (1981).

P. J. Duffy. 'Patterns of landownership in Gaelic Monaghan in the late sixteenth century', *Clogher Record* 10/3 (1981), pp 304–22.

IV EARLY MEDIEVAL IRELAND
Damian Bracken

REFERENCE AND GUIDES TO THE SOURCES

J. J. G. Alexander. *Insular Manuscripts, Sixth to Ninth Century*. London, 1978.

F. J. Byrne. 'Seventh-century documents', *Irish Ecclesiastical Record* 108 (1967), pp 164–82.

G. Henderson. *From Durrow to Kells: The Insular Gospel-Books, 650–800*. London, 1987.

K. Hughes. *Early Christian Ireland: Introduction to the Sources*. London, 1972.

J. F. Kenney. 'The Sources for the Early History of Ireland: Ecclesiastical', in W. T. H. Jackson (ed.) *Records of Civilization: Sources and Studies 9*. New York, 1929; repr. Dublin, 1979.

M. Lapidge and R. Sharpe. *A Bibliography of Celtic-Latin Literature 400–1200, Royal Irish Academy Dictionary of Medieval Latin from Celtic Sources Ancillary Publications 1*. Dublin, 1985.

G. Mac Niocaill. *The Medieval Irish Annals*. Dublin, 1975.

R. Sharpe. *Medieval Irish Saints' Lives*. Oxford, 1991.

A. P. Smyth. 'The earliest Irish annals: Their first contemporary entries and the earliest centres of recording', *Proceedings of the Royal Irish Academy* 72 (C) (1972), pp 1–48.

GENERAL HISTORIES OF EARLY MEDIEVAL IRELAND

F. J. Byrne. *Irish Kings and High-Kings*. London, 1973.

T. M. Charles-Edwards. *Early Christian Ireland*. Cambridge, 2000.

J. Lydon. *The Making of Ireland*. London, 1998.

E. Mac Neill. *Phases of Irish History*. Dublin, 1919.

G. Mac Niocaill. *Ireland Before the Vikings*. Dublin, 1972.

H. Mythum. *The Origins of Early Christian Ireland*. London, 1992.

D. Ó Corráin. *Ireland Before the Normans*. Dublin, 1972.

D. Ó Corráin. 'Prehistoric and early Christian Ireland', in R. F. Foster (ed.) *The Oxford Illustrated History of Ireland*. Oxford, 1989.

D. Ó Cróinín. *Early Medieval Ireland: 400–1200*. London, 1996.

A. P. Smyth. *Celtic Leinster*. Blackrock, 1982.

CULTURE

B. Bischoff. *Latin Palaeography: Antiquity and the Middle Ages*. Tr. D. Ó Cróinín and D. Ganz. Cambridge, 1990.

D. Bracken. 'Rationalism and the Bible in seventh–century Ireland', in A. M. Luiselli Fadda and É. Ó Carragáin (ed.) *Le Isole Brittaniche e Rome in Età Romanobarbarica, Biblioteca di cultura Romanobarbarica I*. Rome, 1998.

J. Carey. *The Irish National Origin-legend: Synthetic Pseudohistory*. Cambridge, 1994.

J. Carney. *Studies in Irish Literature and History*. Dublin, 1955.

C. Donahue. 'Beowulf, Ireland and the natural good', *Traditio* 7 (1949–51), pp 263–77.

M. Esposito. *Latin Learning in Medieval Ireland*. Ed. M. Lapidge. London, 1988.

P. Grosjean. 'Sur quelques exégètes irlandais du VIIe siècle', *Sacris Erudiri* 7 (1955), pp 67–98.

A. Harvey. 'Early literacy in Ireland: The evidence from ogam', *Cambridge Medieval Celtic Studies* 14 (1987) 1–15.

A. Harvey. 'Latin literacy and Celtic vernaculars around the year 500', in C. J. Byrne, M. Harry and P. Ó

Siadhail (eds.) *Celtic Languages and Celtic Peoples: Proceedings of the Second American Congress of Celtic Studies.* Halifax, 1992.

D. R. Howlett. *The Celtic Latin Tradition of Biblical Style.* Blackrock, 1995.

V. Law. 'The Insular Latin Grammarians', in *Studies in Celtic History 3.* Woodbridge, 1988.

V. Law. *Wisdom, Authority and Grammar in the Seventh Century: Decoding Virgilius Maro Grammaticus.* Cambridge, 1995.

D. MacManus. 'A chronology of Latin loan-words in early Irish', *Ériu* 34 (1983), 21–69

D. MacManus. *A Guide to Ogam: Maynooth Monographs 4.* Maynooth, 1991.

D. MacManus. 'Linguarum diuersitas: Latin and the vernaculars in early medieval Britain', *Peritia* 3 (1984), pp 151–88.

D. MacManus. 'The so-called Cothrige and Pátraic strata of Latin loan-words in early Irish,' in P. Ní Chatháin and M. Richter (ed.) *Irland und Europa: Die Kirche im Frühmittelalter* (Stuttgart, 1984).

E. Mac Neill. 'Beginnings of Latin culture in Ireland', *Studies* 20 (1931) (2 articles).

K. McCone. *Pagan Past and Christian Present, Maynooth Monographs 3.* Maynooth, 1990.

F. McGrath. *Education in Ancient and Medieval Ireland.* Blackrock, 1979.

P. Ní Chatháin and M. Richter (ed.). *Ireland and Christendom: The Bible and the Missions.* Stuttgart, 1987.

P. Ní Chatháin and M. Richter (ed.). *Ireland and Christendom: The Early Church.* Stuttgart, 1984.

F. O'Mahony (ed.). *The Book of Kells: Proceedings of a Conference at Trinity College Dublin 1992.* Dublin, 1994.

J. J. O'Meara and B. Naumann (ed.). *Latin Script and Letters: AD 400–900: Festschrift Presented to Ludwig Bieler on the Occasion of his Seventieth Birthday.* Leiden, 1976.

J. Stevenson. 'The beginnings of literacy in Ireland', in *Proceedings of the Royal Irish Academy* (C) 89 (1989), pp 127–65.

CHRISTIANISATION AND THE CHURCH

A. O. Anderson and M. O. Anderson. *Adomnán's Life of Columba.* London, 1961.

L. Bieler. *Studies on the Life and Legend of St Patrick*, ed. R. Sharpe. London, 1986.

D. A. Binchy. 'Patrick and his biographers: Ancient and modern', *Studia Hibernica* 2 (1962), pp 7–173.

L. Bitel. *Isle of the Saints: Monastic Settlement and Christian Community in Early Ireland.* London, 1990.

J. Blair and R. Sharpe. *Pastoral Care Before the Parish.* Leicester, 1992.

T. M. Charles-Edwards. 'Palladius, Prosper and Leo the Great: Mission and Primatial Authority', in D. N. Dumville, *Saint Patrick, AD 493–1933*, Woodbridge, 1993.

P. J. Corish. *The Christian Mission.* Dublin, 1972.

W. Davies. 'The myth of the Celtic church', in N. Edwards and A. Lane (eds.), *The Early Church in Wales and the West* (Oxford, 1992).

L. de Paor. *St Patrick's World.* Blackrock, 1993.

C. Etchingham. 'Bishops in the early Irish church: A reassessment', *Studia Hibernica* 28 (1994), pp 35–62.

C. Etchingham. *Church Organisation in Ireland, AD 650–1000.* Naas, 1999.

C. Etchingham. 'The early Irish church: Some observations on pastoral care and dues', *Ériu* 42 (1991), pp 99–118.

A. Firey. 'Cross-examining the witness: Recent research in Celtic monastic history', in *Monastic Studies* 14 (1983), pp 31–49.

L. Gougaud. *Christianity in Celtic Lands.* London, 1932.

E. J. Gwynn. *The Irish Church in the Eleventh and Twelfth Centuries.* Blackrock, 1992.

R. P. C. Hanson. *St Patrick: His Origins and Career.* Oxford, 1968.

M. Herbert. *Iona, Kells and Derry: The History and Hagiography of the Monastic 'Familia' of Columba.* Oxford, 1988.

K. Hughes. *The Church in Early Irish Society.* London, 1966.

A. Mac Shamhráin. *Church and Polity in Pre-Norman Ireland: The Case of Glendalough.* Maynooth, 1996.

D. Ó Corráin. 'The Early Irish Churches: Some Aspects of Organisation', in Ó Corráin (ed.) *Irish Antiquity* (Cork, 1983).

P. O'Dwyer. *The Céli Dé.* Dublin, 1981.

T. O'Loughlin. *Celtic Theology: Humanity, World and God in Early Irish Writings.* New York, London, 2000.

P. Ó Riain. *Corpus Genealogiarum Sanctorum Hiberniae.* Dublin, 1985.

J. Ryan. *Irish Monasticism: Origins and Early Development.* London, 1931.

R. Sharpe. 'Armagh and Rome in the seventh century', in P. Ní Chatháin and M. Richter (eds.), *Ireland and Christendom: The Bible and the Missions* (Stuttgart, 1987).

R. Sharpe. 'Some problems concerning the organization of the Church in early medieval Ireland', *Peritia* 3 (1984), pp 230–70.

R. Sharpe. 'St Patrick and the See of Armagh', *Cambridge Medieval Celtic Studies 4* (1982), pp 33–59.

SOCIETY AND INSTITUTIONS

KINGSHIP AND DYNASTIC HISTORY

E. Bhreathnach. 'Temoria: Caput Scotorum?', *Ériu* 47 (1996), pp 67–88.

D. A. Binchy. *Celtic and Anglo-Saxon Kingship*. Oxford, 1970.

D. A. Binchy. 'The Fair of Tailtiu and the Feast of Tara', *Ériu* 18 (1958) pp 113–38.

F. J. Byrne. *The Rise of the Uí Néill and the High-kingship of Ireland*. Dublin, 1969.

F. J. Byrne 'Tribes and tribalism in early Ireland', *Ériu* 21 (1971), pp 128–64.

T. M. Charles-Edwards. 'Early medieval kingships in the British Isles', in S. Bassett (ed.) *The Origins of Anglo-Saxon Kingdoms* (London, 1989).

T. M. Charles-Edwards. 'The heir-apparent in Irish and Welsh law', *Celtica* 9 (1971), pp 180–90.

D. Corráin. 'Nationality and kingship in pre-Norman Ireland', in T. W. Moody (ed.) *Nationality and the Pursuit of National Independence* (Belfast, 1978).

S. T. Driscoll and M. R. Nieke (ed.). *Power and Politics in Early Medieval Britain and Ireland* (Edinburgh, 1988).

D. N. Dumville. 'Kingship, genealogies and regnal lists', in P. H. Sawyer and I. N. Wood (eds.), *Early Medieval Kingship* (Leeds, 1977).

M. J. Enright. 'Iona, Tara and Soisson: The origin of the royal anointing ritual', in H. Belting et al. (ed.) *Arbeiten zur Frühmittelalterforschung* 17 (Berlin, 1985).

M. Gerriets. 'Kingship and exchange in pre-Viking Ireland', *Cambridge Medieval Celtic Studies* 13 (1987) pp 39–72.

M. Gerriets. 'The king as judge in early Ireland', *Celtica* 20 (1988), pp 1–24.

B. Jaski. *Early Irish Kingship and Succession*. Dublin, 2000.

G. MacNiocall. 'The "heir designate" in early medieval Ireland', *Irish Jurist* 3 (1968), pp 326–29.

D. Ó Corráin. 'Irish regnal succession', *Studia Hibernica* 11 (1971), pp 7–39.

P. Wormwald. 'Celtic and Anglo-Saxon kingship: Some further thoughts', in P. Szarmach (ed.) *Sources of Anglo-Saxon Culture* (Kalamazoo, 1986).

FAMILY STRUCTURE

R. Baumgarten. 'The kindred metaphors in Bechbretha and Coibnes Uisci Thairidne', *Peritia* 4 (1985), pp 307–27.

T. M. Charles-Edwards. *Early Irish and Welsh Kinship*. Oxford, 1993.

A. Cosgrove (ed.). *Marriage in Ireland*. Dublin, 1985.

M. Dillon. *Early Irish Society*. Dublin, 1954.

B. Jaski. 'Marriage laws in Ireland and on the Continent in the early Middle Ages', in C. E. Meek and M. K. Simms (eds.), *'The Fragility of her Sex?' Medieval Irish Women in their European Context*. (Blackrock, 1996).

T. Ó Cathasaigh. 'The sister's son in early Irish literature', *Peritia* 5 (1986), pp 128–60.

D. Ó Corráin. 'Women in early Irish society', in Ó Corráin and M. MacCurtain (eds.) *Women in Irish Society: The Historical Dimension*. Dublin, 1978.

M. O'Dowd et al. (eds.). *Chattel, Servant or Citizen? Women's Status in Church, State and Society.* Belfast, 1995.

N. Patterson. *Cattle-lords and Clansmen: The Social Structure of Early Ireland*. Notre Dame, 1994.

N. Patterson. 'Patrilineal kinship in early Irish society: The evidence from the Irish law texts', *Bulletin of the Board of Celtic Studies* 37 (1990), pp 133–65.

K. Simms. 'The legal position of Irishwomen in the later Middle Ages', *Irish Jurist* 10 (1979), pp 96–111.

LAW (CANON AND VERNACULAR)

D. A. Binchy. 'Ancient Irish law', *Irish Jurist* 1 (1966), pp 84–92.

D. A. Binchy. 'Bretha Cróilge, sick-maintenance in Irish law', *Ériu* 12 (1934–38), pp 1–134.

D. A. Binchy. 'Bretha Nemed', *Ériu* 17 (1955), pp 4–6.

D. A. Binchy. 'Irish history and Irish law II', *Studia Hibernica* 16 (1976), pp 7–45.

D. A. Binchy. 'The date and provenance of Uraicecht Becc', *Ériu* 18 (1958), pp 44–54.

D. A. Binchy. 'The linguistic and historical value of the Irish law tracts', *Proceedings of the British Academy* 29 (1943), pp 195–227.

D. A. Binchy. 'The pseudo-historical prologue to the *Senchus Már*', *Studies* 11 (1922), pp 15–28.

D. Bracken. 'Immortality and capital punishment: patristic concepts in Irish law', *Peritia* 9 (1995), pp 167–86.

D. Bracken. 'Latin passages in Irish vernacular law: notes on sources', *Peritia* 9 (1995), pp 187–96.

L. Breatnach. 'Canon law and secular law in early Ireland: The significance of Bretha Nemed', *Peritia* 3 (1984), pp 439–59.

L. Breatnach. 'The ecclesiastical element in the Old Irish legal tract Cáin Fhuithirbe', *Peritia* 5 (1986,) pp 36–52.

J. Carey. 'An edition of the pseudo-historical prologue to the *Senchas Már*', *Ériu* 45 (1994), pp 1–32.

J. Carey. 'The two laws in Dubthach's judgement', *Cambridge Medieval Celtic Studies 19* (1990), pp 1–18.

T. M. Charles-Edwards. 'A contract between king and people in early medieval Ireland? Críth Gablach on kingship', *Peritia* 8 (1994) pp 107–19.

T. M. Charles-Edwards, M. E. Owen and D. B. Walters (eds.). *Lawyers and Laymen.* Cardiff, 1986.

F. Kelly. *A Guide to Early Irish Law.* Early Irish Law Series 3, Dublin, 1988.

E. Mac Neill. *Early Irish Laws and Institutions.* Dublin, 1935.

E. Mac Neill. 'Ireland and Wales in the History of Jurisprudence', *Studies* 16 (1927), pp 245–58, 605–15, repr. in D. Jenkins (ed.), *Celtic Law Papers* (Brussels 1973), pp 173–92.

E. Mac Neill. 'Ancient Irish law: The law of status or franchise', *Proceedings of the Royal Irish Academy* (C) 36 (1921–24), pp 265–316.

G. Mac Niocaill. 'Christian influences on early Irish law', in P. Ní Chatháin and M. Richter (eds.) *Irland und Europa: Die Kirche im Frühmittelalter.* (Stuttgart, 1984).

K. McCone. 'Dubthach maccu Lugair and a matter of life and death in the pseudo-historical prologue to the *Senchas Már*', *Peritia* 5 (1986) pp 1–35.

N. McLeod. *Early Irish Contract Law.* Sydney Series in Celtic Studies 1, Sydney, 1992.

M. Ní Dhonnchadha. 'The guarantor list of Cáin Adomnáin, 697', *Peritia* 1 (1982), pp 178–215.

D. Ó Corráin. 'Irish law and canon law', in P. Ní Chatháin and M. Richter (eds.), *Ireland and Christendom: The Early Church* (Stuttgart, 1984).

D. Ó Corráin. 'Irish vernacular law and the Old Testament', in P. Ní Chatháin and M. Richter (eds.) *Ireland and Christendom: The Bible and the Missions* (Stuttgart, 1987).

D. Ó Corráin, L. Breatnach and A. Breen. 'The laws of the Irish', *Peritia* 3 (1984), pp 382–438.

H. Pryce. 'Early Irish canons and medieval Welsh law', *Peritia* 5 (1986), pp 107–27.

M. P. Sheehy. 'Some influences of ancient Irish law on the *Collectio Canonum Hibernensis*', in S. Kutter (ed.), *Proceedings of the Third International Congress of Medieval Canon Law* (Vatican, 1971).

M. P. Sheehy. 'The *Collectio Canonum Hibernensis* – A Celtic phenomenon', in H. Lowe (ed.), *Die Iren und Europa im Frühmittelalter* (Stuttgart, 1982).

R. Thurneysen. 'Aus dem irischen Recht I–V', *Zeitschrift für Celtische Philologie* 14–18 (1923–30), *passim*.

ECONOMY AND SETTLEMENT

J. Bradley (ed.). *Settlement and Society in Medieval Ireland: Studies Presented to Francis Xavier Martin, OSA.* Kilkenny, 1988.

C. Doherty. 'Exchange and trade in early medieval Ireland', *Journal of the Royal Society of Antiquaries of Ireland* 110 (1980), pp 67–89.

C. Doherty. 'Some aspects of hagiography as a source for Irish economic history', *Peritia* 1 (1982), pp 300–28.

C. Doherty. 'The monastic town in early medieval Ireland', in *The Comparative History of Urban Origins in Non-Roman Europe* (Oxford, 1985).

M. Gerriets. 'Economy and society: Clientship according to the Irish laws', *Cambridge Medieval Celtic Studies* 6 (1983), pp 43–61.

M. Gerriets. 'Money in early Ireland according to the Irish laws', *Comparative Studies in Society and History* 27 (1985), pp 323–39.

B. G. Graham. 'Early medieval Ireland: Settlement as an indicator of social and economic transformation, *c.* 500–1100', in B. J. Graham and L. J. Proudfoot (eds.), *An Historical Geography of Ireland* (London, 1993).

F. Kelly. *Early Irish Farming.* Dublin, 1997.

IRELAND AND EUROPE
IRELAND AND THE CONTINENT

C. Bammel. 'Insular manuscripts of Origen in the Carolingian Empire', in G. Londorf and D. N. Dumville (eds.), *France and the British Isles in the Middle Ages and Renaissance* (Woodbridge, 1991).

L. Bieler. *Ireland and the Culture of Early Medieval Europe.* London, 1987.

B. Bischoff. 'Turning–points in the history of Latin exegesis in the early Irish church: AD 650–800', in M. McNamara (ed.) *Biblical Studies – The Medieval Irish Contribution, Proceedings of the Irish Biblical Association* 1. (Dublin, 1976).

P. A. Breatnach. 'The origins of the Irish monastic tradition at Ratisbon (Regensburg)', *Celtica* 13 (1980), pp 58–77.

M. Brennan. *A Guide to Eriugenian Studies: A Survey of Publications 1930–1987.* Fribourg, 1989.

M. Cappuyns. *Jean Scot Érigène: Sa Vie, Son Œuvre, Sa Pensée.* Paris, 1933.

H. B. Clarke and M. Brennan (eds.). *Columbanus and Merovingian Monasticism.* British Archaeological Records, International Series 113, Oxford, 1981.

J. J. Contreni. 'The Irish contribution to the European classroom', in D. Ellis Evans, J. G. Griffith and E. M. Rope (eds.), *Proceedings of the Seventh International Congress of Celtic Studies* (Oxford, 1983).

D. N. Dumville. 'Ireland, Brittany and England: Transmission and Use of the *Collectio Canonum Hibernensis*', in C. Laurent and H. Davis (ed.), *Irlande et Bretagne, vingt siècles d'histoire: Actes du colloque de Rennes* (29 – 31 Mars 1993) (Rennes, 1994).

M. Esposito. *Irish Books and Learning in Medieval Europe*, ed. M. Lapidge. London, 1990.

P. Fournier. 'De l'influence de la collection irlandaise sur la formation des collections canoniques', *Nouvelle Revue Historique de Droit Français et Étranger* 23 (1899), pp 27–78.

P. Grosjean. 'Vigile de Salzbourg en Irlande', *Analecta Bollandiana* 78 (1960), pp 92–123.

A. Gwynn. 'The continuity of the Irish tradition at Würzburg', *Herbipolis Jubilans, Würzburger Diözesangeschichtsblätter.* Würzburg, 1952.

M. Herren. 'On the earliest Irish acquaintance with Isidore of Seville', in E. James (ed.) *Visigothic Spain: New Approaches.* (Oxford, 1982).

J. N. Hillgarth. 'Ireland and Spain in the seventh century', *Peritia* 3 (1984), pp 1–16.

J. N. Hillgarth. 'The East, Visigothic Spain and the Irish', *Studia Patristica* 4 (1961), pp 442–56.

J. N. Hillgarth. 'Visigothic Spain and early Christian Ireland', *Proceedings of the Royal Irish Academy* 62 (1863), pp 167–94.

L. Holtz. *Donat et la Tradition de l'Enseignement Grammatical. Étude sur l'Ars Donati et sa Diffusion (IVᵉ–IXᵉ siècle) et Édition Critique.* Paris, 1981.

E. James. 'Ireland and western Gaul in the Merovingian period', in D. Whitelock, R. McKitterick and D. Dumville (eds.), *Ireland in Early Medieval Europe.* Cambridge, 1982.

M. Lapidge (ed.). *Columbanus: Studies on the Latin Writings.* Woodbridge, 1997.

C. Laurent and H. Davis (ed.). *Irland et Bretagne: Vingt Siècles d'Histoire.* Rennes, 1994.

C. H. Lawrence. *Medieval Monasticism: Forms of Religious Life in Western Europe in the Middle Ages.* London, 1984.

H. Löwe. *Die Iren und Europa.* 2 vols. Stuttgart, 1982.

Janet L. Nelson. 'Queens as Jezebels: the careers of Brunhild and Bathild in Merovingian history', in Derek Baker (ed.), *Medieval Women* (Oxford, 1978).

P. Ní Chatháin and M. Richter (eds.) *Ireland and Christendom: The Bible and the Missions.* Stuttgart, 1987.

P. Ní Chatháin and M. Richter (eds.) *Ireland and Europe: The Early Church.* Stuttgart, 1984.

P. Ní Chatháin and M. Richter (eds.). *Ireland and Europe in the Early Middle Ages: Learning and Literature.* Stuttgart, 1996.

D. Ó Cróinín. 'Merovingian politics and insular calligraphy: The historical background to the Book of Durrow and related manuscripts', in M. Ryan (ed.), *Ireland and Insular Art AD 500–1200* (Dublin, 1987).

D. Ó Cróinín. 'Rath Melsigi, Willibrord, and the earliest Echternach manuscripts', *Peritia* 3, (1984) pp 17–49.

J. M. Picard (ed.). *Aquitaine and Ireland in the Middle Ages.* Dublin, 1995.

J. M. Picard (ed.). *Ireland and Northern France AD 600–850.* Dublin, 1991.

R. E. Reynolds. 'Canon law collections in early ninth-century Salzburg', in S. Kuttner and K. Pennington (eds.), *Proceedings of the Fifth International Congress on Medieval Canon Law.* (Vatican, 1980).

M. Richter. *Ireland and Her Neighbours in the Seventh Century.* Dublin, 1999.

J. W. Smit. *Studies on the Language and Style of Columba the Younger (Columbanus).* Amsterdam, 1971.

C. Stancliffe. 'Red, white and blue martyrdom', in D. Whitelock, R. McKitterick and D. N. Dumville (eds.), *Ireland in Early Medieval Europe: Studies in Memory of Kathleen Hughes* (Cambridge, 1982).

L. Traube. 'Perrona Scottorum', *Sitzungsberichte der Philos.-Philos. und Histor. Classe der Kaiserliche Bayerische Akademie der Wissenschaften* (1900), pp 469–537.

M. Walsh and D. Ó Cróinín. *Cummian's Letter 'De Controuersia Paschali' and the 'De Ratione Conputandi'*. Toronto, 1988.

H. Zimmer. *The Celtic Church in Britain and Ireland* (tr. A. Meyer). London, 1902.

IRELAND AND BRITAIN

M. O. Anderson. 'Dalriada and the creation of the kingdom of the Scots', in D. Whitelock, R. McKitterick and D. Dumville (eds.), *Ireland in Early Medieval Europe* (Cambridge, 1982).

J. Bannerman. *Studies in the History of Dalriada*. Edinburgh, 1974.

J. Bannerman. 'The Dál Riata and Northern Ireland', in J. Carney and D. Greene (eds.), *Celtic Studies: Essays in Memory of Angus Matheson* (London, 1968).

D. Bullough. 'Columba, Adomnán and the achievement of Iona', *Scottish Historical Review* 43 (1964), pp 111–30; 44 (1965), pp 17–33.

J. Campbell. 'The debt of the early English Church to Ireland', in P. Ní Chatháin and M. Richter (eds.), *Ireland and Christendom: The Bible and the Missions* (Stuttgart, 1987).

T. M. Charles-Edwards. 'Bede, the Irish and the Britons', *Celtica* 15 (1983), pp 42–52.

T. O. Clancy and G. Márkus. *Iona: The Earliest Poetry of a Celtic Monastery*. Edinburgh, 1995.

M. Herbert. *Iona, Kells and Derry: The History and Hagiography of the Monastic 'Familia' of Columba*. Oxford, 1988.

C. Ireland. 'Aldfrith of Northumbria and the learning of a sapiens', in K. A. Klar et al. (eds.), *A Celtic Florilegium: Studies in Memory of Brendan Ó Hehir* (Lawrence MA, 1996).

M. McNamara. 'Ireland and Northumbria as illustrated by a Vatican manuscript', *Thought* 54 (1979), pp 274–90.

H. Moisl. 'The Bernician royal dynasty and the Irish in the seventh century', *Peritia* 2 (1983), pp 103–26.

T. O'Loughlin. 'Adomnán the illustrious' in *Innes Review* 66 (1995), pp 1–14.

J. Ryan. 'Ecclesiastical relations between Ireland and England in the seventh and eighth centuries', *Journal of the Cork Historical and Archaeological Society* 43 (1938), pp 109–12.

D. Whitelock. 'Bishop Ecgred, Pehtred and Niall', in D. Whitelock, R. McKitterick and D. Dumville (eds.), *Ireland in Early Medieval Europe* (Cambridge, 1982).

C. D. Wright. 'The Irish "enumerative style" in Old English homiletic literature, especially Vercelli Homily IX', *Cambridge Medieval Celtic Studies* 18 (1989), pp 27–74.

V MEDIEVAL IRELAND
David Edwards

T. B. Barry, R. Frame & K. Simms (eds.). *Colony and Frontier in Medieval Ireland*. London, 1995.

J. Bradley (ed.). *Settlement and Society in Medieval Ireland*. Kilkenny, 1988.

R. R. Davies. *Domination and Conquest: The Experience of Ireland, Scotland and Wales, 1100–1300*. Cambridge, 1990.

P. J. Duffy, D. Edwards and E. FitzPatrick (eds.). *Gaelic Ireland, c. 1250–c. 1650: Land, Lordship and Settlement*. Dublin, 2001.

S. Duffy. *Ireland in the Middle Ages*. Dublin, 1997.

R. Frame. *The Political Development of the British Isles, 1100–1400*. Oxford, 1990.

B. Smith (ed.). *Britain and Ireland, 900–1300*. Cambridge, 1999.

S. Duffy. 'Irishmen and islesmen in the kingdoms of Dublin and Man, 1052–1171', *Ériu* 43 (1992).

S. Duffy. 'The Bruce brothers and the Irish Sea world, 1306–29', in *Cambridge Medieval Celtic Studies* 21 (1991), pp 55–86.

A. A. M. Duncan. 'The Scots' invasion of Ireland, 1315', in R. R. Davies (ed.), *The British Isles, 1100–1500: Comparisons, Contrasts and Connections*. Edinburgh, 1988.

S. G. Ellis. '"More Irish than the Irish themselves"? The Anglo-Irish in Tudor Ireland', in *History Ireland* 7/1 (Spring 1999), pp 22–6.

M. T. Flanagan. *Irish Society, Anglo-Norman Settlers, Angevin Kingship: Interactions in Ireland in the Late Twelfth Century*. (Oxford 1989).

R. Frame. 'King Henry III and Ireland: The shaping of a peripheral lordship', in P. R. Coss and S. D. Lloyd (eds.), *Thirteenth-Century England IV*. Woodbridge, 1992.

R. Frame. '"Les Engleys nées en Irlande": The English political identity in medieval Ireland', in *Transactions of the Royal Historical Society* sixth series, 3 (1993).

R. Frame. 'Military Service in the lordship of Ireland 1290–1360: Institutions and society on the Anglo-Gaelic frontier', in R. Bartlett and A. Mackay (eds.), *Medieval Frontier Societies* (Oxford 1989; repr. 1996), pp 101–26.

J. Gillingham. 'The English invasion of Ireland', in B. Bradshaw, A. Hadfield and W. Maley (eds.), *Representing Ireland: Literature and the Origins of Conflict, 1534–1660* (Cambridge, 1993), pp 24–42.

B. Hudson, 'William the Conqueror and Ireland', in *Irish Historical Studies* xxix, no. 114 (Nov. 1994), pp 145–58.

S. Kingston, 'Trans-insular lordship in the fifteenth century', in T. M. Devine and J. F. McMillan (eds.), *Celebrating Columba: Irish–Scottish Connections, 597–1997*. Edinburgh, 1999.

J. Lydon (ed.). *England and Ireland in the Later Middle Ages*. Dublin, 1982.

J. Lydon (ed.). *The English in Medieval Ireland*. Dublin, 1984.

J. Lydon. 'Ireland and the English crown, 1171–1541', in *Irish Historical Studies*, xxix, no. 115 (May 1995), pp 281–94.

K. L. Maund. *Ireland, Wales and England in the Eleventh Century*. Woodbridge, 1991.

K. W. Nicholls. 'Anglo-French Ireland and after', in *Peritia* 1 (1982).

K. W. Nicholls. 'Worlds apart? The Ellis two-nation theory on late-medieval Ireland', *History Ireland*, 7/2 (Summer 1999), pp 22–6.

C. Ó Cleirigh. 'The O'Connor Faly lordship of Offaly, 1395–1513', in *Proceedings of the Royal Irish Academy* 96 (1996), pp 87–102.

K. Simms. 'Guesting and feasting in Gaelic Ireland', in *Journal of the Royal Society of Antiquaries of Ireland* 108 (1978), pp 67–100.

K. Simms. *From Kings to Warlords: The Changing Political Structure of Gaelic Ireland in the Later Middle Ages*. Dublin, 1987; repr. Woodbridge, 2000.

K. Simms. 'Bards and Barons: The Anglo-Irish Aristocracy and the Native Culture', in R. Bartlett and A. Mackay (eds.), *Medieval Frontier Societies* (Oxford 1989; repr. 1996), pp 177–198.

B. Smith. 'A county community in early fourteenth-century Ireland: The case of Louth', *English Historical Review*, 107 (1993).

B. Smith. 'The de Pitchford family in thirteenth-century Ireland', in *Studia Hibernica* 27 (1993).

VI IRELAND IN THE SIXTEENTH CENTURY
David Edwards

Sixteenth-century Ireland is currently well served by two fine general surveys: Colm Lennon, *Sixteenth-Century Ireland: The Incomplete Conquest* (Dublin, 1994), and Steven G. Ellis, *Ireland in the Age of the Tudors, 1447–1603: English Expansion and the End of Gaelic Rule* (London, 1998). Also useful is the early part of Nicholas Canny, *From Reformation to Restoration: Ireland, 1534–1660* (Dublin, 1987). Those interested in the collapse of the Gaelic social order and the re-emergence of English colonial dominance should consult Ciaran Brady and Raymond Gillespie (eds.), *Natives & Newcomers: The Making of Irish Colonial Society, 1534–1641* (Dublin, 1986), and Patrick J. Duffy, David Edwards and Elizabeth FitzPatrick (eds.), *Gaelic Ireland, c. 1250–c. 1650: Land, Lordship and Settlement* (Dublin, 2001). The ideological struggle between English and Irish, conqueror and conquered, is best approached by Hiram Morgan (ed.) *Political Ideology in Ireland, 1541–1641* (Dublin, 1999), and Brendan Bradshaw, Andrew Hadfield & Willy Maley (eds.), *Representing Ireland: Literature and the Origins of Conflict, 1534–1660* (Cambridge, 1993).

B. Bradshaw. 'Edmund Spenser on justice and mercy', in T. J. Dunne (ed.), *The Writer as Witness: Historical Studies XVI* (Cork 1985), pp 76–89.

B. Bradshaw. 'Robe and sword in the conquest of Ireland', in C. Cross, D. Loades and J. J. Scarisbrick (eds.), *Law and Government Under the Tudors*. Cambridge, 1988.

B. Bradshaw. 'The Tudor Reformation and revolution in Wales and Ireland: The origins of the British problem', in B. Bradshaw and J. Morrill (eds.), *The British Problem, c. 1534–1707: State Formation in the Atlantic Archipelago* (London, 1996).

C. Brady. 'Faction and the origins of the Desmond rebellion of 1579', *Irish Historical Studies* (1981).

C. Brady. 'Conservative subversives: The community of the Pale and the Dublin administration, 1556–86', in P. J. Corish (ed.), *Radicals, Rebels and Establishments: Historical Studies XV* (Belfast, 1985), pp 11–32.

C. Brady. 'Spenser's Irish crisis: humanism and experience in the 1590s', in *Past & Present*, no. 111 (1986).

C. Brady. 'Sixteenth-century Ulster and the failure of Tudor reform', in C. Brady, M. O'Dowd and B. Walker (eds.), *Ulster: An Illustrated History* (London, 1989), pp 77–102.

C. Brady. 'The decline of the Irish kingdom', in M. Greengrass (ed.) *Conquest & Coalescence: The Shaping of the State in Early Modern Europe* (London, 1991).

C. Brady. *The Chief Governors: The Rise and Fall of Reform Government in Tudor Ireland, 1536–88.* Cambridge, 1994.

C. Brady. *Shane O'Neill.* Dundalk, 1996.

C. Brady. 'Comparable histories? Tudor reform in Wales and Ireland', in S. G. Ellis and S. Barber (eds.), *Conquest and Union: Fashioning a British State, 1485–1725* (London, 1995).

N. Canny. *The Formation of the Old English Elite in Ireland* (O'Donnell lecture, Galway, 1974). Dublin, 1975.

N. Canny. 'Edmund Spenser and the development of an Anglo-Irish identity', in *The Yearbook of English Studies*, 13 (1983).

V. Carey. 'The end of the Gaelic political order: The O'More lordship of Laois, 1536–1603', in P. G. Lane and W. Nolan (ed.), *Laois: History and Society* (Dublin 1999), pp 213–48.

V. Carey. 'John Derricke's *Image of Irelande*, Sir Henry Sidney, and the massacre at Mullaghmast, 1578', *Irish Historical Studies*, xxxi, no. 123 (May 1999), pp 305–27.

P. Coughlan (ed.). *Spenser and Ireland.* Cork, 1989.

B. Cunningham. 'The composition of Connaught in the lordships of Clanricard and Thomond, 1577–1641', in *Irish Historical Studies* xxiv (1984).

J. E. A. Dawson. 'Two kingdoms or three? Ireland in Anglo-Scottish relations in the middle of the sixteenth century', in R. A. Mason (ed.) *Scotland and England, 1286–1815* (Edinburgh, 1987).

D. Edwards. 'The Butler revolt of 1569', *Irish Historical Studies*, xxviii, no. 111 (May 1993), pp 228–55.

D. Edwards. 'Ideology and experience: Spenser's *View* and martial law in Ireland', in H. Morgan (ed.), *Political Ideology in Ireland* (1999), pp 127–57.

D. Edwards. 'In Tyrone's shadow: Feagh McHugh O'Byrne, forgotten leader of the Nine Years War', in C. O'Brien (ed.), *Feagh McHugh O'Byrne* (1998), pp 212–48.

D. Edwards. 'The MacGiollapadraigs (Fitzpatricks) of Upper Ossory, 1532–1641', in P. G. Lane and W. Nolan (ed.), *Laois: History and Society* (Dublin 1999).

S. G. Ellis. *The Pale and the Far North: Government and Society in Two Early Tudor Borderlands.* Galway, 1988.

S. G. Ellis. *Tudor Frontiers and Noble Power: The Making of the British State.* Oxford, 1995.

F. Fitzsimons. 'The lordship of O'Connor Faly, 1520–70', in W. Nolan and T. P. O'Neill (eds.) *Offaly: History and Society* (Dublin, 1998), pp 207–35.

R. J. Hunter. 'The end of O'Donnell power', in W. Nolan, L. Ronayne and M. Dunlevy (eds.), *Donegal: History and Society* (Dublin, 1995), pp 229–65.

L. McCorristine. *The Revolt of Silken Thomas: A Challenge to Henry VIII.* Dublin, 1987.

J. J. N. McGurk. *The Elizabethan Conquest of Ireland: The 1590s Crisis.* Manchester, 1997.

H. Morgan. 'The end of Gaelic Ulster: a thematic interpretation of events between 1534 and 1610', in *Irish Historical Studies*, xxvi, no. 101 (May 1988), pp 8–32.

H. Morgan. *Tyrone's Rebellion: The Outbreak of the Nine Years War in Tudor Ireland.* Woodbridge, 1993; repr. 1998.

H. Morgan. 'The Fall of Sir John Perrot', in J. Guy (ed.), *The Reign of Elizabeth I: Court and Culture in the Last Decade* (Cambridge 1996).

H. Morgan. 'British policies before the British state', in B. Bradshaw and J. Morrill (eds.), *The British Problem, c. 1534–1707.* London, 1996.

J. Murray. 'Archbishop Alen, Tudor reform and the Kildare rebellion', in *Proceedings of the Royal Irish Academy* 89 C (1989), pp 1–16.

K. W. Nicholls. *Land, Law and Society in Sixteenth-Century Ireland.* Dublin, 1976.

C. O'Brien (ed.). *Feagh McHugh O'Byrne: The Wicklow Firebrand.* Rathdrum, 1998.

M. Ó Siuchrú. 'Foreign involvement in the revolt of Silken Thomas, 1534–5', in *Proceedings of the Royal Irish Academy* 96 C (1996), pp 49–62.

P. J. Pivernous. 'Sir Warham St Leger and the first Munster plantation', *Eire/Ireland* 14/2 (1979), pp 16–36.

D. Potter. 'French intrigue in Ireland during the reign of Henri II, 1547–59', in *International History Review* 5 (1983).

A. J. Sheehan. 'Official reaction to the native land claims in the plantation of Munster', in *Irish Historical Studies* 23 (1982–3).

A. J. Sheehan. 'The overthrow of the plantation of Munster in October 1598', in *Irish Sword*, 15 (1982–3).

A. J. Sheehan. 'The killing of the earl of Desmond, November 1583', in *Cork Historical and Archaeological Scociety Journal* 88 (1983).

H. C. Walshe. 'The rebellion of William Nugent, 1581', in R. V. Comerford et al (eds.), *Religion, Conflict and Coexistence* (1990), pp 26–52.

VII IRELAND IN THE SEVENTEENTH CENTURY
David Edwards

There is no satisfactory general survey of seventeenth-century Ireland. The latter part of Nicholas Canny, *From Reformation to Restoration: Ireland, 1534–1660* (Dublin, 1987) is insightful, but should be augmented by the chapters written by Aidan Clarke, Patrick Corish and J. G. Simms in T. W. Moody, F.X. Martin and F. J. Byrne (eds.), *A New History of Ireland, iii: Early Modern Ireland, 1534–1691* (Oxford, 1976). For the later seventeenth century, see the relevant chapters of David Dickson, *New Foundations: Ireland 1660–1800*, second edition (Dublin, 2000).

J. Agnew. *Belfast Merchant Families in the Seventeenth Century*. Dublin, 1996.

L. J. Arnold. *The Restoration Land Settlement in County Dublin, 1660–1688*. Dublin, 1993.

T. C. Barnard and J. Fenlon (ed.). *The Dukes of Ormonde, 1610–1745*. Woodbridge, 2000.

T. C. Barnard. *Cromwellian Ireland: English Government and Reform in Ireland, 1649–1660*. Oxford, 1975; repr. 2000.

T. C. Barnard. 'Crises of identity among Irish Protestants, 1641–1685', *Past & Present* 127 (1990), pp 39–83.

T. C. Barnard, 'Land and the limits of loyalty: The second Earl of Cork and first Earl of Burlington, 1612–98', in T. C. Barnard and J. Clark (eds.), *Lord Burlington: Architecture, Art and Life* (London 1995).

T. C. Barnard. 'The political, material and mental culture of the Cork settlers, c. 1650–1700', in P. O'Flanagan and C. G. Buttimer (eds.), *Cork: History and Society* (Dublin 1993).

T. C. Barnard. 'Scotland and Ireland in the later Stewart monarchy', in S. G. Ellis and S. Barber (eds), *Conquest and Union: Fashioning a British State, 1485–1725* (London, 1995).

T. C. Barnard. 'New opportunities for British settlement: Ireland, 1650–1700', in N. Canny (ed.), *Origins of Empire* (Oxford, 1998), pp 309–27.

K. Bottigheimer, *English Money and Irish Land: The Adventurers in the Cromwellian Settlement of Ireland*. Oxford, 1971.

K. Bottigheimer. 'Civil war in Ireland: The reality in Munster', *Emory University Quarterly* 22 (Spring 1966), pp 46–56.

K. Bottigheimer. 'The Restoration land settlement in Ireland: A structural view', in *Irish Historical Studies* 18 (1972).

W. F. T. Butler. *Confiscations in Irish History*. Dublin, 1917.

N. Canny. 'In defence of the constitution? The nature of Irish revolt in the seventeenth century', in L. M. Cullen and L. Bergeron (eds.), *Culture et Pratiques Politiques en France et en Irlande, 16th–18th Siècle* (Paris, 1990), pp 23–40.

N. Canny. 'The attempted anglicisation of Ireland in the seventeenth century: an exemplar of "British History"', in R. G. Asch (ed.), *Three Nations – A Common History? England, Scotland, Ireland and British History, c. 1600–1920* (Bochum, 1993).

N. Canny. 'Irish, Scottish & Welsh responses to centralisation, c. 1530–c. 1640: A comparative perspective', in A. Grant and K. J. Stringer (eds.), *Uniting the Kingdom? The Making of British History* (London, 1995).

J.Casway. *Owen Roe O'Neill and the Struggle for Catholic Ireland*. Philadelphia, 1984.

J. Casway. 'The last lords of Leitrim', *Breifne* 7/26 (1988), pp 556–74.

A. Clarke. 'Colonial constitutional attitudes in Ireland, 1640–60', in *Proceedings of the Royal Irish Academy* 90 C (1990), pp 357–75.

A. Clarke. 'The 1641 Depositions', in P. Fox (ed.), *Treasures of the Library of TCD* (Dublin, 1986), pp 111–22.

S. J. Connolly. *Religion, Law and Power: The Making of Protestant Ireland, 1660–1760* (Oxford, 1992).

B. Cunningham. *The World of Geoffrey Keating*. Dublin, 2001.

R. Gillespie. *Conspiracy: Ulster Plots and Plotters in 1615*. Belfast, 1987.

R. Gillespie. 'Continuity and change: Ulster in the seventeenth century', in C. Brady, M. O'Dowd and B. Walker (eds.), *Ulster: An Illustrated History* (London, 1989), pp 104–33.

R. Gillespie. 'The transformation of the borderlands, 1600–1700', in R. Gillespie and H. O'Sullivan (eds.), *The Borderlands: Essays on the History of the Ulster–Leinster Border* (Belfast, 1989), pp 75–92.

R. Gillespie. 'The Irish Protestants and James II, 1688–90', in *Irish Historical Studies* xxviii, no. 110 (Nov. 1992), pp 124–33.

R. Gillespie (ed.). *Settlement and Survival on an Ulster Estate: The Brownlow Leasebook, 1667–1711*. Belfast, 1988.

F. W. Harris. 'The rebellion of Sir Cahir O'Doherty and its legal aftermath', *Irish Jurist* 15 (1980), pp 298–325.

F. W. Harris. 'The state of the realm: English military, political and diplomatic responses to the flight of the earls, 1607–8', *Irish Sword* 14 (1980–1), pp 47–64.

D. W. Hayton. 'From barbarian to burlesque: English images of the Irish, *c.* 1660–1750', *Irish Economic and Social History* 15 (1988), pp 5–31.

G. H. Jones. 'The Irish fright of 1688: Real violence and imagined massacre', in *Bulletin of the Institute of Historical Research* 55/132 (1982), pp 148–53.

J. Kelly. 'The origins of the Act of Union: An examination of unionist opinion in Britain and Ireland, 1650–1800', *Irish Historical Studies* 25 (1987), pp 236–63.

P. Kelly. '"A light to the blind": The voice of the dispossessed elite after the defeat at Limerick', *Irish Historical Studies* xxiv, no. 96 (Nov. 1985), pp 431–62.

W. Kelly. 'James Butler, twelfth Earl of Ormond, the Irish government and the Bishops' Wars, 1638–40', in J. Young (ed.), *Celtic Dimensions of the British Civil Wars* (Edinburgh, 1997), pp 35–52.

P. Little. '"Blood and friendship": The Earl of Essex's efforts to protect the Earl of Clanricarde's interests, 1641–6', *English Historical Review* 112/448 (Sept. 1997), pp 927–41.

M. MacCarthy Morrogh. *The Munster Plantation: English Migration to Ireland, 1583–1641*. Oxford, 1986.

J. McCavitt. *Sir Arthur Chichester, Lord Deputy of Ireland, 1605–1616*. Belfast, 1998.

J. McCavitt. 'The Flight of the Earls, 1607', in *Irish Historical Studies* xxix, no. 114 (Nov. 1994), pp 159–73.

B. Mac Cuarta (ed.). *Ulster 1641: Aspects of the Rising*. Belfast, 1993.

B. Mac Cuarta. 'A planter's interaction with Gaelic culture: Sir Matthew De Renzi, 1577–1634', in *Irish Economic and Social History* 20 (1993), pp 1–17.

J. I. McGuire. 'The Church of Ireland and the Glorious Revolution of 1688', A. Cosgrove and D. MacCartney (eds.), *Studies in Irish History* (Dublin, 1979), pp 137–49.

J. I. McGuire. 'The Dublin Convention, the Protestant community and the emergence of an ecclesiastical settlement in 1660', in A. Cosgrove and J. I. McGuire (eds.), *Parliament and Community: Historical Studies* XIV (Belfast, 1983), pp 121–46.

J. I. McGuire. 'Why was Ormond dismissed in 1692?', *Irish Historical Studies* xviii (1973), pp 295–312.

J. F. Merritt (ed.). *The Political World of Thomas Wentworth, Earl of Strafford, 1621–1641*. Cambridge, 1996.

J. Miller. 'The Earl of Tyrconnell and James II's Irish policy, 1685–88', *Historical Journal* 20/4 (1977), pp 803–23.

J. Morrill. 'Three kingdoms and one commonwealth? The enigma of mid-seventeenth-century Britain and Ireland', in A. Grant and K. J. Stringer (eds.), *Uniting the Kingdom? The Making of British History* (London, 1995).

E. Ó Ciardha. 'Tories and moss-troopers in Scotland and Ireland in the Interregnum', in J. Young (ed.), *Celtic Dimensions of the British Civil Wars* (Edinburgh, 1997), pp 141–63.

J. Ohlmeyer. *Civil War and Restoration in the Three Stuart Kingdoms: The Career of Randall MacDonell, Marquis of Antrim, 1609–1683*. Cambridge, 1993.

J. Ohlmeyer. '"Civilizing of those rude partes": Colonisation within Britain and Ireland, 1580s–1640s', in N. Canny (ed.), *Origins of Empire* (Oxford, 1998), pp 124–47.

J. Ohlmeyer. *Ireland from Independence to Occupation: 1641–1660*. Cambridge, 1995.

J. Ohlmeyer. 'The wars of religion, 1603–60', in T. Bartlett and K. Jeffrey (eds.), *A Military History of Ireland* (Cambridge, 1996), pp 160–87.

M. Ó Siuchrú. *Confederate Ireland, 1642–49*. Dublin, 1999.

M. Ó Siuchrú (ed.). *Kingdoms in Crisis*. Dublin, 2001.

H. Pawlisch. *Sir John Davies and the Conquest of Ireland: A Study in Legal Imperialism*. Cambridge, 1985.

M. Perceval-Maxwell. *The Outbreak of the Irish Rebellion of 1641*. Dublin, 1994.

M. Perceval-Maxwell. 'Ireland and Scotland 1638–1648', in J. Morrill (ed.), *The Scottish National Covenant in its British Context* (Edinburgh, 1991), pp 193–211.

A. J. Sheehan. 'The recusancy revolt of 1603', *Archivium Hibernicum* 38 (1983), pp 3–13.

D. Stevenson. *Scottish Covenanters and Irish Confederates: Scottish–Irish Relations in the Mid-Seventeenth Century*. Belfast, 1981.

J. Smyth. 'The communities of Ireland and the British state, 1660–1707', in B. Bradshaw and J. Morrill (eds.), *The British Problem, c. 1534–1707: State Formation in the Atlantic Archipelago* (London, 1996).

V. Treadwell. *Buckingham and Ireland: A Study in Anglo-Irish Politics*. Dublin, 1998.

M. K. Walsh. *Destruction by Peace: Hugh O'Neill after Kinsale*. Monaghan, 1986.

J. Scott Wheeler. *Cromwell in Ireland*. Dublin, 1999.

VIII IRELAND IN THE EIGHTEENTH CENTURY
Daire Keogh

By far the best general survey of eighteenth-century Ireland is David Dickson, *New Foundations; Ireland 1660–1800*, second edition (Dublin, 2000). More specialized readers might begin with T. W. Moody and W. E. Vaughan (eds.), *A New History of Ireland, IV: Eighteenth-Century Ireland, 1691–1800* (Oxford, 1986).

J. Agnew (ed.). *The Drennan–McTier Letters*. 3 vols. Dublin, 1999.

T. Bartlett. *The Fall and Rise of the Irish Nation: The Catholic Question 1690–1830*. Dublin, 1992.

T. Bartlett. 'Ireland and the British Empire', in P. J. Marshall (ed.), *The Oxford History of the British Empire, II: The Eighteenth Century*. Oxford, 1998.

T. Bartlett (ed.). *Life of Theobald Wolfe Tone: Memoirs, Journals and Political Writings Compiled and Arranged by William T. W. Tone*. Dublin, 1998.

J. Brady. *Catholics and Catholicism in the Eighteenth-Century Press*. Maynooth, 1965.

R. E. Burns. *Irish Parliamentary Politics in the Eighteenth Century*. 2 vols. Washington, 1989–90.

A. Carpenter (ed.). *Verse in English from Eighteenth-Century Ireland*. Cork, 1998.

L. Chambers. *Rebellion in Kildare in 1790–1803*. Dublin, 1998.

S. J. Connolly. *Religion, Law and Power: The Making of Protestant Ireland 1660–1760*. Oxford, 1992.

P. Corish. *The Catholic Community in the Seventeenth and Eighteenth Centuries*. Dublin, 1981.

D. Corkery. *The Hidden Ireland: A Study of Gaelic Munster in the Eighteenth Century*. Dublin, 1925.

M. Craig. *Dublin 1660–1860: A Social and Architectural History*. London, 1952.

C. Cruise O'Brien. *The Great Melody: A Thematic Biography of Edmund Burke*. London, 1992.

L. M. Cullen. *An Economic History of Ireland since 1660*. London, 1972.

L. M. Cullen. *Anglo-Irish Trade 1660–1800*. Manchester, 1968.

N. Curtin. *The United Irishmen: Popular Politics in Ulster and Dublin 1790–98*. Oxford, 1994.

D. Dickson (ed.). *The Gorgeous Mask: Dublin, 1700–1850*. Dublin, 1987.

D. Dickson, D. Keogh and K. Whelan (eds.). *The United Irishmen: Republicanism, Radicalism and Rebellion*. Dublin, 1993.

M. Elliott. *Wolfe Tone: Prophet of Irish Independence*. New Haven, 1989.

P. Fagan (ed.). *Ireland in the Stuart Papers*. Dublin, 1995.

R. F. Foster. *Modern Ireland 1600–1972*. London, 1988.

J. A. Froude. *The English in Ireland in the Eighteenth Century*. 3 vols. London, 1872.

D. Gahan. *The People's Rising: Wexford 1798*. Dublin, 1995.

N. Garnham. *The Courts, Crime and Criminal Law in Ireland 1692–1760*. Dublin, 1996.

H. Gough and D. Dickson (eds.). *Ireland and the French Revolution*. Dublin, 1990.

K. Herlihy. *The Politics of Irish Dissent*. Dublin, 1997.

F. G. James. *Ireland in the Empire, 1688–1770*. Cambridge, Mass., 1973.

E. M. Johnston. *Ireland in the Eighteenth Century*. Dublin, 1974.

A. Kavanaugh. *John Fitzgibbon, Earl of Clare*. Dublin, 1997.

J. Kelly. 'The origins of the Act of Union: an examination of unionist opinion in Britain and Ireland 1650–1800' in *Irish Historical Studies* xxv (1985–6), pp 236–63.

J. Kelly. *Prelude to Union: Anglo-Irish Politics in the 1780s*. Cork, 1992.

J. Kelly. *Henry Flood: Parties and Politics in Eighteenth-century Ireland*. Dublin, 1998.

D. Keogh. *The French Disease: The Catholic Church and Irish Radicalism 1790–1800*. Dublin, 1993.

D. Keogh and N. Furlong (eds.). *The Women of 1798*. Dublin, 1998.

D. Keogh and K. Whelan (eds.). *Acts of Union*. Dublin, 2001.

W. E. H. Lecky. *History of Ireland in the Eighteenth Century*. 5 vols. London, 1892.

C. D. A. Leighton. *Catholicism in a Protestant Kingdom: A Study of the Irish Ancien Regime*. Dublin, 1994.

I. McBride. *Scripture Politics: Ulster Presbyterianism and Irish Radicalism in the Late Eighteenth Century*. Oxford, 1998.

M. MacCurtain and M. O'Dowd (eds.). *Women in Early Modern Ireland*. Edinburgh, 1991.

R. B. McDowell. *Ireland in the Age of Imperialism and Revolution 1760–1801*. Oxford, 1979.

P. McNally. *Patriots and Undertakers: Parliamentary Politics in Early Hanoverian Ireland*. Dublin, 1997.

W. A. Maguire (ed.). *Kings in Conflict: The Revolutionary War in Ireland and Its Aftermath 1689–1750*. Belfast, 1990.

A. P. W. Malcomson. *John Foster: The Politics of the Anglo-Irish Ascendancy*. Oxford, 1978.

A. P. W. Malcomson (ed.). *Eighteenth-century Irish Official Papers in Great Britain: Private Collections*. 2 vols. Belfast, 1973–90.

K. Milne, *The Irish Charter Schools 1730–1830*. Dublin, 1997.

T. W. Moody, R. B. McDowell and C. J. Woods (eds.). *The Writings of Theobald Wolfe Tone*. 3 vols. Oxford, 1999–.

I. Murphy. *The Diocese of Killaloe in the Eighteenth Century*. Dublin, 1991.

G. O'Brien (ed.). *Politics, Parliament, People: Essays in Eighteenth-Century Irish History*. Dublin, 1989.

B. Ó Buachalla. *Aisling Ghéar: Na Stíobhartaigh agus an t-Aos Léinn 1603–1788*. Dublin, 1996.

N. Ó Ciosáin. *Print and Popular Culture in Ireland, 1750–1800*. London, 1997.

R. O'Donnell. *The Rebellion in Wicklow 1798*. Dublin, 1998.

T. Power. *Land, Politics and Society in Eighteenth-Century Tipperary*. Oxford, 1993.

C. Pórtéir (ed.). *The Great Irish Rebellion of 1798*. Dublin, 1998.

J. Smyth. *The Men of No Property: Irish Radicals and Popular Politics in the Late Eighteenth Century*. Dublin, 1992.

A. T. Q. Stewart. *A Deeper Silence: The Hidden Origins of the United Irishmen*. London, 1993.

L. Swords. *A Hidden Church: The Diocese of Achonry 1689–1818*. Dublin, 1997.

M. Wall, Gerard O'Brien (ed.). *Catholic Ireland in the Eighteenth Century*. Dublin, 1989.

K. Whelan, *The Tree of Liberty: Radicalism, Catholicism and the Construction of Irish Identity*. Cork, 1996.

C. J. Woods (ed.). *Journals and Memoirs of Thomas Russell, 1791–95*. Dublin, 1991.

IX IRELAND IN THE NINETEENTH CENTURY
Laurence M. Geary

Jane Barnes. *Irish Industrial Schools, 1868–1908*. Dublin, 1989.

Michael Beames. *Peasants and Power: The Whiteboy Movement and Their Control in Pre-Famine Ireland*. Brighton, 1983.

John Belchem. 'Republican spirit and military science: the "Irish brigade" and Irish-American nationalism in 1848', *Irish Historical Studies* xxix, no. 115 (May 1995), pp 44–64.

George L. Bernstein. 'Liberals, the Irish Famine and the role of the state', *Irish Historical Studies* xxix, no. 116 (Nov. 1995), pp 513–536.

Paul Bew. *C. S. Parnell*. Dublin, 1980.

Paul Bew. *Conflict and Conciliation in Ireland*. Oxford, 1987.

Paul Bew. *Ideology and the Irish question: Ulster Unionism and Irish Nationalism 1912–1916*. Oxford, 1994.

Paul Bew. 'A vision to the dispossessed? Popular piety and revolutionary politics in the Irish land war, 1879–82', in Judith Devlin and Ronan Fanning (eds.), *Religion and Rebellion: Historical Studies* xx. Dublin, 1997, pp 137–151.

Andy Bielenberg and David Johnson. 'The production and consumption of tobacco in Ireland, 1800–1914', *Irish Economic and Social History*, xxv (1998), pp 1–21.

Evelyn Bolster. *A History of the Diocese of Cork: The Episcopate of William Delany, 1847–1886*. Cork, 1993.

Kenneth D. Brown. 'Life after death: a preliminary survey of the Irish Presbyterian ministry in the nineteenth century', *Irish Economic and Social History*, 22 (1995), pp 49–63.

Angela Bourke. *The Burning of Bridget Cleary*. London, 1999.

Austin Bourke. *'The Visitation of God'? The Potato and the Great Irish Famine*. Dublin, 1993.

Joanna Bourke. 'Women and poultry in Ireland', *Irish Historical Studies*, 25, no. 99 (May 1987), pp 293–310.

Joanna Bourke. 'The best of all home rulers: the economic power of women in Ireland, 1800–1914', *Irish Economic and Social History*, 18 (1991), pp 34–47.

Joanna Bourke. *Husbandry to Housewifery: Women, Economic Change and Housework in Ireland, 1890–1914*. Oxford, 1993.

D. G. Boyce (ed.) *The Revolution in Ireland, 1879–1923*. London/Dublin, 1988.

D. G. Boyce. *The Irish Question and British Politics, 1868–1986*. London, 1988.

D. G. Boyce. *Nineteenth-century Ireland: The Search for Stability*. Dublin, 1990.

D. G. Boyce. *Ireland, 1828–1923: From Ascendancy to Democracy*. Oxford, 1992.

D. G. Boyce and Alan O'Day (eds.). *Parnell in Perspective*. London, 1991.

Kenneth D. Brown. 'Life after death: A preliminary survey of the Irish Presbyterian ministry in the nineteenth century', in *Irish Economic and Social History*, xxii (1995), pp 49–63.

Stewart J. Brown and David W. Miller (eds.), *Piety and Power in Ireland, 1760–1960. Essays in Honour of Emmet Larkin*. Belfast, 2000.

A. D. Buckley. 'On the club': Friendly societies in Ireland', *Irish Economic and Social History*, 14 (1987), pp 39–58.

David N. Buckley. *James Fintan Lalor: Radical*. Cork, 1990.

Philip Bull. 'The United Irish League and the reunion of the Irish Parliamentary Party, 1898–1900', *Irish Historical Studies*, xxvi, no. 101 (May 1988), pp 51–78.

Philip Bull. 'The significance of the nationalist response to the Irish Land Act of 1903', *Irish Historical Studies*, xxviii, no. 111 (May 1993), pp 283–305.

Philip Bull. *Land, Politics and Nationalism: A Study of the Irish Land Question*. Dublin, 1996.

Helen Burke. *The People and the Poor Law in Nineteenth-century Ireland*. Dublin, 1987.

Mary Rose Callaghan. *Kitty O'Shea: A Life of Katherine Parnell*. London, 1989.

Mary Campbell. *Lady Morgan: The Life and Times of Sydney Owenson*. London, 1988.

Ronald D. Cassell. *Medical Charities, Medical Politics: The Irish Dispensary System and the Poor Law, 1836–1872*. London, 1997.

Samuel Clark and James S. Donnelly, Jr (eds.). *Irish Peasants: Violence and Political Unrest, 1780–1914*. Manchester, 1983.

Caitriona Clear. *Nuns in Nineteenth-century Ireland*. Dublin, 1987.

B. M. Coldrey. *Faith and Fatherland: The Christian Brothers and the Development of Irish Nationalism, 1838–1921*. Dublin, 1988.

Paul Connell. *Parson, Priest and Master: National Education in County Meath, 1824–1841*. Dublin, 1995.

S. J. Connolly. *Religion and Society in Nineteenth-century Ireland*. Dundalk, 1985.

Des Cowman and Donald Brady (eds.). *The Famine in Waterford, 1845–1850: Teacht na Bprátaí Dubha*. Dublin, no date.

E. Margaret Crawford (ed.). *Famine, the Irish Experience, 900–1900: Subsistence Crises and Famines in Ireland*. Edinburgh, 1989.

E. Margaret Crawford. *The Hungry Stream: Essays on Famine and Emigration*. Belfast, 1997.

John Crawford. *St Catherine's Parish, Dublin, 1840–1900: Portrait of a Church of Ireland Community*. Dublin, 1996.

Virginia Crossman. 'Emergency legislation and agrarian disorder in Ireland, 1821–41', *Irish Historical Studies*, xxvii, no. 108 (Nov. 1991), pp 309–323.

Virginia Crossman. *Local Government in Nineteenth-century Ireland*. Belfast, 1994.

Virginia Crossman. *Politics, Law and Order in Nineteenth-century Ireland*. Dublin, 1996.

Fintan Cullen. *Visual Politics: The Representation of Ireland, 1750–1930*. Cork, 1997.

Mary Cullen. 'How radical was Irish feminism between 1860 and 1920?' in P. J. Corish (ed.), *Radicals, Rebels and Establishments: Historical Studies 15* (Belfast, 1985), pp 185–201.

Kieran Anthony Daly. *Catholic Church Music in Ireland, 1878–1903: The Cecilian Reform Movement*. Dublin, 1995.

Mary E. Daly. *Dublin, the Deposed Capital: A Social and Economic History, 1860–1914*. Cork, 1985.

Mary E. Daly. *The Famine in Ireland*. Dublin, 1986.

Mary E. Daly. *The Spirit of Earnest Inquiry: The Statistical and Social Inquiry Society of Ireland, 1847–1997*. Dublin, 1997.

Richard Davis. *The Young Ireland Movement*. Dublin, 1987.

Peter Denman. '"The red livery of shame": The campaign against army recruitment in Ireland, 1899–1914', *Irish Historical Studies*, xxix, no. 114 (Nov. 1994), pp 208–233.

James S. Donnelly Jr and Kerby A. Miller (eds.). *Irish Popular Culture, 1650–1850*. Dublin, 1998.

James S. Donnelly Jr. *The Great Irish Potato Famine*. London, 2001.

Tom Dunne. *Maria Edgeworth and the Colonial Mind*. Cork, 1984.

Brian Fallon. *Irish Art, 1830–1990*. Belfast, 1994.

W. L. Feingold. *The Revolt of the Tenantry: The Transformation of Local Government in Ireland, 1872–86*. Boston, 1984.

David Fitzpatrick. *Irish Emigration, 1801–1921*. Dublin, 1984.

David Fitzpatrick. 'Unrest in rural Ireland', *Irish Economic and Social History*, xii (1985), pp 98–105.

David Fitzpatrick. *Ireland and the First World War*. Dublin, 1986.

David Fitzpatrick. *Oceans of Consolation: Personal Accounts of Irish Migration to Australia.* Cork, 1994.

Tadhg Foley and Sean Ryder (eds.). *Ideology and Ireland in the Nineteenth Century.* Dublin, 1998.

R. F. Foster. *Paddy and Mr Punch: Connections in Irish and English History.* London, 1993.

Andrew Gailey. *Ireland and the Death of Kindness: The Experience of Constructive Unionism, 1890–1905.* Cork, 1987.

Tom Garvin. 'Priests and Patriots: Irish Separatism and Fear of the Modern, 1890–1914', Irish Historical Studies xxv, no. 97 (May 1986) pp 67–81.

Frank Geary. 'Regional industrial structure and labour force decline in Ireland between 1841 and 1851', *Irish Historical Studies,* xxx, no. 118 (Nov. 1996), pp 167–194.

Laurence M. Geary. *The Plan of Campaign, 1886–1891.* Cork, 1986.

Laurence M. Geary. 'John Mandeville and the Irish Crimes Act of 1887', *Irish Historical Studies,* xxv, no. 9 (May 1987).

Laurence M. Geary (ed.). *Rebellion and Remembrance in Modern Ireland.* Dublin, 2001.

Laurence M. Geary. 'The whole country was in motion': Mendicancy and vagrancy in pre-Famine Ireland', in Jacqueline Hill and Colm Lennon (eds.), *Luxury and Austerity: Historical Studies 21.* (Dublin, 1999).

Maurice Goldring. *Faith of Our Fathers: The Formation of Irish Nationalist Ideology, 1890–1920.* Dublin, 1982.

B. J. Graham and Susan Hood. 'Town tenant protest in late nineteenth- and early twentieth-century Ireland', *Irish Economic and Social History,* xxi (1994), pp 39–57.

Peter Gray. *The Irish Famine.* London, 1995.

Peter Gray. *Famine, Land and Politics: British Government and Irish Society, 1843–1850.* Dublin, 1999.

Peter Gray. 'National humiliation and the Great Hunger: Fast and famine in 1847', *Irish Historical Studies,* xxxii, no. 126 (Nov. 2000), pp 193–216.

Timothy W. Guinnane. *The Vanishing Irish: Households, Migration and the Rural Economy in Ireland, 1850–1914.* Princeton, 1997.

Brian Harvey. 'Changing fortunes on the Aran Islands in the 1890s', *Irish Historical Studies,* xxvii, no. 107 (May 1991), pp 237–249.

Mona Hearn. *Below Stairs: Domestic Service Remembered in Dublin and Beyond, 1880–1922.* Dublin, 1933.

Dana Hearne (ed.). *Anna Parnell's Tale of a Great Sham.* Dublin, 1986.

A. C. Hepburn. 'Work, class and religion in Belfast, 1871–1911', *Irish Economic and Social History,* x (1983), pp 33–50.

Janice Holmes and Diane Urquhart (eds.). *Coming into the Light: The Work, Politics and Religion of Women in Ulster, 1840–1940.* Belfast, 1994.

K. T. Hoppen. *Elections, Politics and Society in Ireland, 1832–85.* Oxford, 1984.

K. T. Hoppen. *Ireland Since 1800: Conflict and Conformity.* London, 1989.

John Hutchinson. *The Dynamics of Cultural Nationalism: The Gaelic Revival and the Creation of the Irish Nation State.* London, 1987.

Eugene Hynes. 'Nineteenth-century Irish Catholicism, farmers' ideology and national religion: explorations in cultural explanation', in Roger O'Toole (ed.), *Sociological Studies in Roman Catholicism: Historical and Contemporary Perspectives* (Lewiston, 1990), pp 45–69.

Alvin Jackson. *The Ulster Party: Irish Unionists in the House of Commons, 1884–1911.* Oxford, 1989.

Alvin Jackson. 'The failure of unionism in Dublin, 1900', *Irish Historical Studies* xxvi, no. 104 (Nov. 1989), pp 377–395.

Alvin Jackson. *Colonel Edward Saunderson: Land and Loyalty in Victorian Ireland.* Oxford, 1995.

Greta Jones and Elizabeth Malcolm (eds.). *Medicine, Disease and the State in Ireland, 1650–1940.* Cork, 1999.

David Seth Jones. *Graziers, Land Reform and Political Conflict in Ireland.* Washington, 1995.

Alison Jordan. *Who Cared? Charity in Victorian and Edwardian Belfast.* Belfast, 1992.

Donald E. Jordan. *Land and Popular Politics in Ireland: County Mayo from the Plantation to the Land War.* Cambridge, 1994.

Peter J. Jupp and Stephen A. Royle. 'The social geography of Cork city elections, 1801–1830', *Irish Historical Studies,* xxix, no. 113 (May 1994), pp 13–43.

Margaret Kelleher. *The Feminization of Famine: Expressions of the Inexpressible?* Cork, 1997.

Margaret Kelleher and James H. Murphy (eds.). *Gender Perspectives in Nineteenth-century Ireland: Public and Private Spheres.* Dublin, 1997.

John Kendle. *Ireland and the Federal Solution: The Debate over the United Kingdom Constitution, 1870–1921.* Kingston/Montreal, 1989.

Liam Kennedy, Paul S. Ell, E. M. Crawford and L. A. Clarkson (eds.). *Mapping the Great Irish Famine: A Survey of the Famine Decades*. Dublin, 1999.

Donal A. Kerr. '*A Nation of Beggars'? Priests, People and Politics in Famine Ireland, 1846–1852*. Oxford, 1994.

Donal A. Kerr. *The Catholic Church and the Famine*. Dublin, 1998.

Colm Kerrigan. 'The social impact of the Irish temperance movement, 1839–45', *Irish Economic and Social History*, xiv (1987), pp 20–38.

Colm Kerrigan. *Father Mathew and the Irish Temperance Movement, 1838–1849*. Cork, 1992.

Christine Kinealy. *This Great Calamity: The Irish Famine, 1845–52*. Dublin, 1994.

Carla King. *Michael Davitt*. Dublin, 1999.

Noel Kissane. *The Irish Famine: A Documentary History*. Dublin, 1995.

Emmet Larkin. *The Roman Catholic Church and the Home Rule Movement in Ireland, 1870–1874*. Chapel Hill, 1990.

Emmet Larkin. *The Roman Catholic Church and the Emergence of the Modern Irish Political System, 1874–8*. Dublin, 1996.

Marie-Louise Legg. *Newspapers and Nationalism: The Irish Provincial Press, 1850–1892*. Dublin, 1999.

Leon Litvack and Glenn Hooper (eds.). *Ireland in the Nineteenth Century: Regional Identity*. Dublin, 2000.

David Lloyd. *Nationalism and Minor Literature: James Clarence Mangan and the Emergence of Irish Cultural Nationalism*. Berkeley, 1987.

James Loughlin. 'The Irish Protestant Home Rule Association and nationalist politics, 1886–93', *Irish Historical Studies*, xxiv, no. 95 (May 1985), pp 341–60.

James Loughlin. *Gladstone, Home Rule and the Ulster Question, 1882–1893*. Dublin, 1986.

W. J. Lowe and E. L. Malcolm. 'The domestication of the Royal Irish Constabulary, 1836–1922', *Irish Economic and Social History*, xix (1992), pp 27–48.

W. C. Lubenow. *Parliamentary Politics and the Home Rule Crisis: The British House of Commons in 1886*. Oxford, 1988.

Maria Luddy and Cliona Murphy (eds.). *Women Surviving: Studies in Irish Women's History in the Nineteenth and Twentieth Centuries*. Dublin, 1990.

Maria Luddy. *Women and Philanthropy in Nineteenth-century Ireland*. Cambridge, 1995.

Gerard J. Lyne. *The Lansdowne Estate in Kerry under W. S. Trench, 1849–1872*. Dublin, 2001.

J. B. Lyons. *The Enigma of Tom Kettle: Irish Patriot, Essayist, Poet, British Soldier, 1880–1916*. Dublin, 1983.

Lawrence W. McBride (ed.). *Images, Icons and the Irish Nationalist Imagination*. Dublin, 1999.

Donal McCartney. *The Dawning of Democracy: Ireland, 1800–1870*. Dublin, 1987.

Donal McCartney. *Parnell: The Politics of Power*. Dublin, 1991.

Donal McCartney. *W. E. H. Lecky: Historian and Politician, 1838–1903*. Dublin, 1994.

D. P. McCracken. 'The management of a mid-Victorian Irish iron-ore mine: Glenravel, County Antrim, 1866–1887', *Irish Economic and Social History*, xi (1984), pp 60–72.

Donal P. McCracken. 'Irish settlement and identity in South Africa before 1910', *Irish Historical Studies*, xxviii, no. 110 (Nov. 1992), pp 134–149.

Oliver MacDonagh. *The Hereditary Bondsman: Daniel O'Connell, 1775–1829*. London, 1988.

Oliver MacDonagh. *The Emancipist: Daniel O'Connell, 1830–47*. London, 1989.

Thomas McGrath. *Politics, Interdenominational Relations and Education in the Public Ministry of Bishop James Doyle of Kildare and Leighlin, 1786–1834*. Dublin, 1998.

Thomas McGrath. *Religious Renewal and Reform in the Pastoral Ministry of Bishop James Doyle of Kildare and Leighlin, 1786–1834*. Dublin, 1998.

Jane McL. Côté. *Fanny and Anna Parnell: Ireland's Patriot Sisters*. Dublin, 1991.

Ambrose Macaulay. *William Crolly, Archbishop of Armagh, 1835–1849*. Dublin, 1994.

Mary Peckham Magray. *The Transforming Power of the Nuns: Women, Religion and Cultural Change in Ireland, 1750–1900*. New York, 1998.

Martin Maguire. 'A socio-economic analysis of the Dublin Protestant working class, 1870–1926', *Irish Economic and Social History*, xx (1993), pp 35–61.

Martin Maguire. 'The organisation and activism of Dublin's Protestant working class, 1883–1935', *Irish Historical Studies*, xxix, no. 113 (May 1994), pp 65–87.

Elizabeth Malcolm. *'Ireland Sober, Ireland Free': Drink and Temperance in Nineteenth-century Ireland*. Dublin, 1986.

Elizabeth Malcolm. 'Troops of largely diseased women': VD, the contagious diseases acts, and moral policing in late-nineteenth-century Ireland', *Irish Economic and Social History*, xxvi (1999), pp 1–14.

Elizabeth Malcolm. '"The reign of terror in Carlow": the politics of policing Ireland in the late 1830s', *Irish Historical Studies*, xxxii, no. 125 (May 2000), pp 59–74.

John Mannion. 'Migration and upward mobility: the Meagher family in Ireland and Newfoundland, 1780–1830', *Irish Economic and Social History*, xv (1988), pp 54–70.

Patrick Maume. 'Parnell and the IRB oath', *Irish Historical Studies*, xxix, no. 115 (May 1995), pp 363–370.

Patrick Maume. *The Long Gestation: Irish Nationalist Life, 1891–1918*. Dublin, 1999.

Joy Melville. *Mother of Oscar: The Life of Francesca Wilde*. London, 1994.

David W. Miller. 'Irish Presbyterians and the Great Famine', in Hill and Lennon (eds.), *Luxury and Austerity* (Dublin, 1999), pp 165–181.

John Molony. *A Soul Came Into Ireland: Thomas Davis, A Biography*. Dublin, 1995.

Joel Mokyr. *Why Ireland Starved: A Quantitative and Analytical History of the Irish Economy, 1800–1850*. London, 1983.

Gerard Moran. *A Radical Priest in Mayo: Father Patrick Lavelle, The Rise and Fall of an Irish Nationalist, 1825–86*. Dublin, 1994.

Gerard Moran. 'James Daly and the rise and fall of the Land League in the west of Ireland, 1879–82', *Irish Historical Studies*, xxix, no. 114 (Nov. 1994).

Chris Morash (ed.). *The Hungry Voice: The Poetry of the Irish Famine*. Dublin, 1989.

Chris Morash. *Writing the Irish Famine*. Oxford, 1995.

Chris Morash and Richard Hayes (eds.). *'Fearful Realities': New Perspectives on the Famine*. Dublin, 1996.

Ignatius Murphy. *The Diocese of Killaloe, 1800–1850*. Dublin, 1992.

Ignatius Murphy. *The Diocese of Killaloe, 1850–1904*. Dublin, 1995.

James H. Murphy. 'The role of Vincentian parish missions and the "Irish Counter Reformation" of the mid-nineteenth century', *Irish Historical Studies*, xxxiii, no. 94 (Nov. 1984), pp 152–171.

James H. Murphy. *Catholic Fiction and Social Reality in Ireland, 1873–1922*. Westport, Connecticut, 1997.

A. C. Murray. 'Agrarian violence and nationalism in nineteenth-century Ireland: the myth of ribbonism', *Irish Economic and Social History*, xiii (1986), pp 56–73.

Frank Neal. 'Lancashire, the famine Irish and the poor laws: a study in crisis management', *Irish Economic and Social History*, xxii (1995), pp 26–48.

Frank Neal. *Black '47: Britain and the Famine Irish*. Basingstoke, 1998.

Janet Nolan. *Ourselves Alone: Women's Emigration from Ireland, 1885–1920*. Lexington, 1989.

Gerard O'Brien. 'The new poor law in pre-Famine Ireland: A case history', *Irish Economic and Social History*, xii (1985), pp 33–49.

Brendan O'Cathaoir. *John Blake Dillon, Young Irelander*. Dublin, 1990.

Breandán Ó Conaire (ed.). *The Famine Lectures. Comhdháil an Chraoibhín*. Boyle, 2001.

Maurice R. O'Connell (ed.). *Daniel O'Connell: Political Pioneer*. Dublin, 1991.

Emmet O'Connor. 'Active sabotage in industrial conflict, 1917–23', *Irish Economic and Social History*, xii (1985), pp 50–62.

John O'Connor. *The Workhouses of Ireland: The Fate of Ireland's Poor*. Dublin, 1995.

Alan O'Day. *Parnell and the First Home Rule Episode, 1884–87*. Dublin, 1986.

Alan O'Day (ed.). *Reactions to Irish Nationalism*. London, 1987.

Alan O'Day and John Stephenson (eds.). *Irish Historical Documents Since 1800*. Dublin, 1992.

Alan O'Day. *Irish Home Rule, 1867–1921*. Manchester, 1998.

Fergus O'Ferrall. *Catholic Emancipation: Daniel O'Connell and the Birth of Irish Democracy, 1820–1830*. Dublin, 1985.

Cormac Ó Gráda. *Ireland Before and After the Famine: Explorations in Economic History, 1800–1925*. Manchester, 1988.

Cormac Ó Gráda. *The Great Irish Famine*. Dublin, 1989.

Cormac Ó Gráda. 'The heights of Clonmel prisoners, 1845–9: Some dietary implications', *Irish Economic and Social History*, 18 (1991), pp 24–33.

Cormac Ó Gráda. *Ireland: A New Economic History, 1780–1939*. Oxford, 1994.

Cormac Ó Gráda. *An Drochshaol: Béaloideas agus Amhráin*. Baile Atha Cliath, 1994.

Cormac Ó Gráda (ed.). *Famine 150: Commemorative Lecture Series*. Dublin, 1997.

Cormac Ó Gráda. *Black '47 and Beyond: The Great Irish Famine in History, Economy and Memory*. Princeton, 1999.

Niamh O'Sullivan. *Aloysius O'Kelly: Re-orientations: Painting, Politics and Popular Culture*. Dublin, 1999.

Patrick O'Sullivan. *The Irish Worldwide: History, Heritage, Identity*, vols 1–6. London, 1992–7.

Gary Owens. '"A moral insurrection": Faction fighters, public demonstrations and the O'Connellite campaign, 1828', *Irish Historical Studies*, xxx, no. 120 (1997), pp 513–41.

Rosemary Cullen Owens. *Smashing Times: The History of the Irish Suffrage Movement, 1890–1922*. Dublin, 1984.

Senia Paseta. *Before the Revolution: Nationalism, Social Change and Ireland's Catholic Elite, 1879–1922*. Cork, 1999.

Senia Paseta. 'Nationalist responses to two royal visits to Ireland, 1900 and 1903', *Irish Historical Society*, xxxi, no. 124 (Nov. 1999), pp 488–504.

Edward Pearce. *Lines of Most Resistance: The Lords, the Tories and Ireland, 1886–1914*. London, 1999.

Cathal Póirtéir. *The Great Irish Famine*. Cork, 1995.

Lindsay Proudfoot. 'The management of a great estate: Patronage, income and expenditure on the Duke of Devonshire's Irish property, c. 1816–1891, *Irish Economic and Social History*, xiii (1986), pp 32–55.

Lindsay Proudfoot. 'Landlord motivation and urban improvement on the Duke of Devonshire's Irish estates, c. 1792–1832', *Irish Economic and Social History*, xviii, (1991) pp 5–23.

Lindsay Proudfoot. *Urban Patronage and Social Authority: The Management of the Duke of Devonshire's Towns in Ireland, 1764–1891*. Washington, 1995.

Jacinta Prunty. *Dublin Slums, 1800–1925: A Study in Urban Geography*. Dublin, 1998.

Jacinta Prunty. *Margaret Aylward, 1810–1889: Lady of Charity, Sister of Faith*. Dublin, 1999.

Oliver P. Rafferty. *The Church, the State and the Fenian Threat, 1861–75*. Houndsmills, 1999.

R. M. Rhodes. *Women and the Family in Post-Famine Ireland*. Connecticut, 1991.

Joseph Robins. *The Miasma: Epidemic and Panic in Nineteenth-century Ireland*. Dublin, 1995.

S. A. Royle. 'Irish famine relief in the early nineteenth century: The 1822 famine on the Aran Islands', *Irish Economic and Social History*, xi (1984), pp 44–59.

Robert Scally. *The End of Hidden Ireland: Rebellion, Famine and Emigration*. Oxford, 1995.

Pauline Scanlan. *The Irish Nurse: A Study of Nursing in Ireland, History and Education, 1718–1981*. Manorhamilton, 1991.

Ellen Shannon-Mangan. *James Clarence Mangan: A Biography*. Dublin, 1996.

Robert Sloan. 'O'Connell's Liberal rivals in 1843', *Irish Historical Studies*, xxx, no. 117 (May 1996), pp 47–65.

Alfred P. Smyth. *Faith, Famine and Fatherland in the Irish Midlands: Perceptions of a Priest and Historian, Anthony Cogan, 1826–1872*. Dublin, 1992.

Shin-ichi Takagami. 'The Fenian rising in Dublin, March 1867', *Irish Historical Studies*, xxix, no. 115 (May 1995), pp 340–362.

Akihiro Takei. 'The first Irish linen mills', *Irish Economic and Social History*, xxi (1994), pp 28–38.

Janet K. TeBrake. 'Irish peasant women in revolt: The Land League years', *Irish Historical Studies*, 27, no. 109 (May 1992), pp 63–80.

Francis Thompson. 'Attitudes to reform: Political parties in Ulster and the Irish Land Bill of 1881', *Irish Historical Studies*, xxiv, no. 95 (May 1985), pp 327–40.

Charles Townshend. *Political Violence in Ireland: Government and Resistance Since 1848*. Oxford, 1983.

Michael Turner. 'Livestock in the agrarian economy of Counties Antrim and Down from 1803 to the Famine', *Irish Economic and Social History*, xi (1984), pp 19-43.

Michael Turner. *After the Famine: Irish Agriculture, 1850–1914*. Cambridge, 1996.

W. E. Vaughan. *Landlords and Tenants in Ireland, 1848–1904*. Dublin, 1984.

W. E. Vaughan (ed.). *New History of Ireland*, Vol. v: *Ireland Under the Union, 1: 1801–1870*. Oxford, 1989.

W. E. Vaughan. *Landlords and Tenants in Mid-Victorian Ireland*. Oxford, 1994.

W. E. Vaughan. *New History of Ireland*, Vol. vi: *Ireland Under the Union, 2: 1870–1921*. Oxford, 1996.

B. M. Walker. *Ulster Politics: The Formative Years, 1868–86*. Belfast, 1989.

Trevor West. *Horace Plunkett: Cooperation and Politics: An Irish Biography*. Gerrards Cross, 1986.

M. J. Winstanley. *Ireland and the Land Question, 1800–1922*. London, 1984.

Audrey Woods. *Dublin Outsiders: A History of the Mendicity Institution, 1818–1998*. Dublin, 1998.

Tom Yager. 'Mass eviction in the Mullet peninsula during and after the great famine', *Irish Economic and Social History*, xxiii (1996), pp 22–44.

X Twentieth-century Irish History
Donal Ó Drisceoil

D. H. Akenson. *The Irish Diaspora: A Primer*. Belfast, 1993.

J. Bardon. *A History of Ulster*. Belfast, 1992.

R. Barrington. *Health, Medicine and Politics in Ireland, 1900–1970*. Dublin, 1987.

P. Bew, E. Hazelkorn and H. Patterson. *The Dynamics of Irish Politics*. London, 1989.

A. Bielenberg (ed.). *The Irish Diaspora.* London, 2000.

P. Bishop and E. Mallie. *The Provisional IRA.* London, 1987.

D. G. Boyce and A. O'Day (eds.). *Modern Irish History: Revisionism and the Revisionist Controversy.* London, 1996.

D. G. Boyce. *Nationalism in Ireland.* London, 1982, 1995.

C. Brady (ed.). *Interpreting Irish History: The Debate on Historical Revisionism.* Dublin, 1994.

T. Brown. *Ireland: A Social and Cultural History 1922–1985.* London, 1985.

S. J. Connolly (ed.). *The Oxford Companion to Irish History.* Oxford, 1998.

T. P. Coogan. *Michael Collins.* London, 1990.

T. P. Coogan. *De Valera: Long Fellow, Long Shadow.* London, 1993.

T. P. Coogan. *Wherever Green is Worn: The Irish Diaspora.* London, 2001.

J. Cooney. *John Charles McQuaid: Ruler of Catholic Ireland.* Dublin, 1999.

M. E. Daly. *Social and Economic History of Ireland since 1800.* Dublin, 1981.

R. Dunphy. *The Making of Fianna Fail Power in Ireland, 1923–48.* Oxford, 1995.

R. English. *Radicals and the Republic: Socialist Republicanism in the Irish Free State 1925–1937.* Oxford, 1994.

B. Fallon. *An Age of Innocence: Irish Culture 1930–1960.* Dublin, 1998.

R. Fanning. *Independent Ireland.* Dublin, 1983.

R. Fanning et al (eds.). *Documents on Irish Foreign Policy, Vol 1, 1919–22* and *Vol 2, 1922–6.* Dublin, 1998 and 2000.

R. Fisk. *In Time of War: Ireland, Ulster and the Price of Neutrality.* London, 1983.

D. Fitzpatrick. *The Two Irelands 1912–1939.* Oxford, 1998.

R. Foster. *Modern Ireland 1600–1972.* London, 1998.

T. Garvin. *Nationalist Revolutionaries in Ireland.* Oxford, 1987.

T. Garvin. *1922: The Birth of Irish Democracy.* Dublin, 1996.

B. Girvin and G. Roberts (eds.). *Ireland and the Second World War: Politics, Society and Remembrance.* Dublin, 2000.

B. Girvin. *Between Two Worlds: Politics and Economy in Contemporary Ireland.* Dublin, 1989.

P. Hart. *The IRA and its Enemies: Violence and Community in Cork 1916–23.* Oxford, 1998.

A. Hayes and D. Urquhart (eds.). *The Irish Women's History Reader.* London, 2001.

T. Hennessey. *A History of Northern Ireland, 1920–1996.* Basingstoke, 1997.

T. Hennessey. *Dividing Ireland: World War One and Partition.* London, 1998.

M. Hopkinson. *Green Against Green: The Irish Civil War.* Dublin, 1988.

K. T. Hoppen. *Ireland Since 1800: Conflict and Conformity.* London, 1989.

J. Horgan. *Seán Lemass: Enigmatic Patriot.* Dublin, 1997.

J. Horgan. *Noel Browne: Passionate Outsider.* Dublin, 2000.

J. Horgan. *Irish Media: A Critical History since 1922.* London, 2001.

A. Jackson. *Ireland, 1798–1998: Politics and War.* Oxford, 1999.

K. Jeffery. *Ireland and the Great War.* Cambridge, 2000.

M. Kennedy. *Ireland and the League of Nations, 1923–1946.* Dublin, 1996.

M. Kennedy and J. Skelly (eds.). *Irish Foreign Policy, 1919–1966.* Dublin, 2000.

D. Keogh. *Ireland and Europe 1919–1989.* Cork and Dublin, 1989.

D. Keogh. *Twentieth-Century Ireland: Nation and State.* Dublin, 1994.

D. Keogh. *Ireland and the Vatican: The Politics and Diplomacy of Church and State.* Cork, 1995.

D. Keogh. *Jews in Twentieth-Century Ireland.* Cork, 1998.

M. Laffan. *The Resurrection of Ireland: The Sinn Féin Party, 1916–1923.* Cambridge, 1999.

J. J. Lee. *Ireland 1912–85: Politics and Society.* Cambridge, 1989.

F. McGarry. *Irish Politics and the Spanish Civil War.* Cork, 1999.

D. McMahon. *Republicans and Imperialists: Anglo-Irish Relations in the 1930s.* New Haven, 1984.

M. Milotte. *Communism in Modern Ireland.* Dublin, 1984.

A. Mitchell and P. Ó Snodaigh (eds.). *Irish Political Documents 1916–1949.* Dublin, 1985.

P. Murray. *Oracles of God: The Roman Catholic Church and Irish Politics, 1922–37.* Dublin, 2000.

N. Ní Dhonnchadha and T. Dorgan (eds.). *Revising the Rising.* Derry, 1991.

E. O'Connor. *A Labour History of Ireland 1824–1960.* Dublin, 1992.

S. Ó Buachalla. *Education Policy in Twentieth-Century Ireland.* Dublin, 1988.

J. P. O'Carroll and J. A. Murphy (eds.). *De Valera and his Times.* Cork, 1983.

D. Ó Drisceoil. *Censorship in Ireland 1939–45: Neutrality, Politics and Society.* Cork, 1996.

C. Ó Grada. *A Rocky Road: The Irish Economy Since the 1920s.* Manchester, 1997.

C. O'Halloran. *Partition and the Limits of Irish Nationalism*. Dublin, 1987.

E. O'Halpin. *The Decline of the Union: British Government in Ireland, 1892–1920*. Dublin, 1987.

E. O'Halpin. *Defending Ireland: The Irish State and Its Enemies Since 1922*. Oxford, 1999.

H. Patterson. *The Politics of Illusion: A Political History of the IRA*. London, 1997.

J. Regan. *The Irish Counter-Revolution 1921–36*. Dublin, 1999.

T. Salmon. *Unneutral Ireland: An Ambivalent and Unique Security Policy*. Oxford, 1989.

R. Savage. *Irish Television: The Political and Social Origins*. Cork, 1996.

F. Tobin. *The Best of Decades: Ireland in the 1960s*. Dublin, 1984.

C. Townshend. *Ireland in the Twentieth Century*. London, 1998.

M. Ward. *Unmanageable Revolutionaries: Women and Irish Nationalism*. Dingle, 1983.

K. Woodman, *Media Control in Ireland 1923–1983*. Galway, 1986.

A CHRONOLOGY OF IRISH HISTORY

We are grateful to the Oxford University Press for generous permission to draw upon *A New History of Ireland, vol. viii: A Chronology of Irish History, to 1976* (Oxford, 1982).

A hyphen between dates (e.g. 742–8) signifies a period or process; a solidus (e.g. 1161/2) signifies alternative dates for a specific event or events; a saltire (e.g. 1145x1151) signifies the period within which a specific event, which cannot be more precisely dated, occurred.

Dates between 1582 and 1752 are given according to Old Style for the day and the month but according to New Style for the year. The following abbreviations are used:

a.	*ante* (before)
c.	*circa* (about)
Con.	Conservative party
d.	died
DUP	Democratic Unionist Party
DL	Democratic Left
FF	Fianna Fáil Party
FG	Fine Gael Party
GB	Great Britain
GP	Green Party
IRA	Irish Republican Army
IRB	Irish Republican Brotherhood
Lab.	Labour Party
Lib.	Liberal Party
NI	Northern Ireland
NILP	Northern Ireland Labour Party
NUI	National University of Ireland
PIRA	Provisional IRA
PM	Prime Minister
RUC	Royal Ulster Constabulary
RTÉ	Radio Telefís Éireann
SDLP	Social Democratic and Labour Party
TCD	Trinity College Dublin
UCC	University College Cork
UCD	University College Dublin
UCG	University College Galway
UDA	Ulster Defence Association
UDR	Ulster Defence Regiment
UK	United Kingdom

2,000,000–30,000 BC	Pleistocene period: intense cold of great ice age. Topography of Ireland much as today; sea level fluctuating.
3000 BC	Sea level stabilised: building of megalithic tombs begins.
2500 BC	Radiocarbon dating for building of passage grave at Newgrange (County Meath); wheat cultivated at Newgrange.
1800 BC	Tin (probably from Cornwall) alloyed with copper to make bronze; gold worked.
1200 BC	Later phase of Bronze Age; gold ornaments very numerous; many new types of object, including weapons and ornaments, made under influences from northern Europe.
680 BC	Radiocarbon dating for first circular inhabitation enclosure at Emain Machae (Navan fort, near Armagh).
500 BC	Iron metallurgy in Ireland, though Bronze Age economy still in evidence.

200 BC	Bronze and iron objects: sculpture in stone and wood; Turoe stone.
AD 1–500	Building of crannogs, hill forts and ring forts continues; earliest examples of La Tène-influenced art-styles in Ireland.
c. 130–80	*Ptolemy's Geography*; includes detailed map of Ireland with identifiable names of rivers, towns and tribes.
297–c. 450	Irish raids on Roman Britain.
431	Palladius sent as first bishop to Irish Christians by Pope Celestine; *Annals of Ulster* begin.
432	Traditional date of St Patrick's mission.
c. 445–53	Probable floruit of Niall Noígiallach, founder of Uí Néill dynasty.
a.c. 490	St Éndae founds earliest Irish monastery at Aran.
493	Traditional date for death of St Patrick (Wed. 17 Mar).
c. 500–700	Archaic Old Irish linguistic period.
520–c. 620	Efflorescence of early Irish monasticism.
524/6	Death of St Brigit of Kildare (1 Feb.).
546	Derry founded by St Colum Cille (Columba).
547/8	Clonmacnoise founded by St Ciarán.
c. 550	Beginnings of monastic Hiberno-Latin writing: hymns and penitentials.
c. 550– c. 600	Earliest Irish text committed to writing.
563	Iona founded by St Colum Cille (Pentecost Sunday, 13 May).
575	Convention of Druim Cett (County Derry).
c .580– c. 680	Latin literature flourishes in Ireland: works of Latin grammar and biblical exegesis.
c. 590	St Columanus begins Irish mission on Continent: founds Annegray, Luxueil and Fontaines.
a. 597	The *Cathach Psalter*: earliest Irish MS, allegedly written by St Colum Cille, now in Royal Irish Academy, Dublin.
615	Death of St Columbanus at Bobbio (Sun. 23 Nov.).
622	Death of St Cóemgen (Kevin) of Glendalough (3 June).
635–51	St Aidan's mission from Iona to Northumbria: founds Lindisfarne.
649–50	Death of St Fursu in France (16 Jan.); buried at Péronne (Peronna Scottorum, Picardy) by founder, Erchinoald, mayor of the palace in Neustria.
c. 650–750	High achievement in Irish metal-working; stone sculpture: Ossory group of high crosses; classical period of Old Irish laws.
664	Synod of Whitby: Roman Easter accepted in Northumbria; Colmán, bishop of Lindisfarne, and his adherents retire to Ireland; found Inishbofin (668).
c. 668–730	Gradual transition from tribalism to dynastic polity in Ireland.
670–c. 690	Armagh seeks to establish its primacy; Muirchú and Tírechán write hagiographical works on St Patrick.
680x691	Antiphony of Bangor written.
689	Martyrdom of St Kilian at Würzburg (8 July).
c. 692x697	Adomnán's *Vita Columbae*.
698–700	Three years of famine and pestilence; cannibalism rumoured.
c. 700–750	Moylough belt shrine; Tara brooch; Ardagh chalice.
c. 700– c.900	Classical Old Irish linguistic period.
710x725	Compilations of Irish canon law (*Collectio Hibernensis*) by Cú Chuimne of Iona and Rubin Mac Connad of Dairinis (Molana Island, near Youghal).
716	Iona accepts Roman Easter.
720	Othmar founds monastery of St Gallen, Switzerland.
c. 740	Compilation of *Senchas Már*, Irish legal corpus.
	Ending of Iona chronicle; compilation of annals continued in Ireland; earliest genealogical corpus for whole of Ireland compiled.
742–8	St Boniface clashes with St Vergilius and other Irish missionaries in Germany.
c. 750–800	*St Gall Gospels* and *Book of Kells* illuminated.
c. 750–75	Composition of *Irish World Chronicle* at Bangor.
c. 770– c. 840	Céle Dé (Culdee) reform movement within Irish church.
795	First Viking raids on Ireland.
c. 800	*Félire Óengusso*, martyrology in Old Irish verse, by Óengus mac Óengobann 'the Culdee'; Stowe Missal written.

802	Iona raided by Vikings.
806	Iona raided by Vikings; chief relics removed to Kells.
807–13	Vikings raid western seaboard.
823	Bangor raided by Vikings: bishops and scholars killed.
824	Bangor again raided by Vikings; Skellig raided by Vikings.
825	Dícuil's geography, *De Mensura Orbis Terrarum* written at Frankish court; Dúngal teaches at Pavia.
837–76	Intense Viking activity in Ireland: semi-permanent bases established.
841	Permanent Norse encampment (*longphort*) at Annagassen, County Louth, and at Dublin (nucleus of later kingdom of Dublin).
845	Viking leader Turgéis drowned by Maél Sechnaill mac Máele Ruanaid, king of Mide. Johannes Scottus Eriugena joins royal school at Laon.
848–58	Sedulius Scottus at Liège.
853	Olaf (Amlaíb) 'son of king of Laithlind' assumes sovereignty over Norse kingdom of Dublin.
861–2	Áed Findliath, king of Ailech, allies with Dublin Norse against high king.
876–916	'Forty years peace': relative respite from Viking attacks on Ireland.
900–c. 911	Hiberno-Norse infiltration of Cumberland, Lancashire and Cheshire.
900–c.1050	Early Middle Irish linguistic period.
	Decline of Latin learning; elaboration of Irish native traditions; *dindshenchas* poetry Secularisation of monastic schools.
908	Flann Sinna, king of Tara, defeats Cormac mac Cuilennáin, king-bishop of Cashel, at Belach Mughna, County Carlow.
c.909x916	Flann's cross (Cross of Scriptures) erected at Clonmacnoise.
914	Large Viking fleet establishes base at Waterford.
916–19	Reign of High King Niall Glúndub.
916–37	Renewed Viking activity in Ireland.
920–52	Dublin kings strike coins at York.
921–6/7	Sitric, grandson of Ivar, king of Dublin, reigns in York.
	Godfrid, grandson of Ivar, rules in Dublin.
922	Foundation of Norse town of Limerick.
a. 924	Muiredach's cross at Monasterboice.
964	Rise of Dál Cais: Mathgamain mac Cennétig seizes kingship of Cashel.
c. 970–80	St Catroe of Armagh founds monastery at Metz.
975	Death of Cináed ua hArtacáin, 'chief poet of Ireland'.
	Monastery of St Martin's at Cologne assigned to Irish monks.
978	Brian Borúma mac Cennétig defeats Máel Muad mac Brain and becomes king of Munster.
980	Máel Sechnaill II mac Domnaill, king of Mide, defeats Olaf Cuarán, king of Dublin, and Hebridean Norse, at battle of Tara, and succeeds to high-kingship on death of Domnall Ua Néill at Armagh.
981, 989	Máel Sechnaill II captures Dublin.
995	Máel Sechnaill II captures Dublin for third time; seizes ring of Thor and sword of Carlus.
999	Brian Bóruma defeats Máel Mórda, king of Leinster, and Sitric Silkbeard at Glen Máma (near Saggart, County Dublin).
1000	Brian Bóruma captures Dublin (Jan.) and burns Wood of Thor; Sitric Silkbeard submits.
1002	Máel Sechnaill II acknowledges Brian Bóruma as high king of Ireland.
1005	Brian Bóruma visits Armagh: leaves twenty ounces of gold on altar and confirms primacy of Armagh (entry by his secretary Máel Suthain in *Book of Armagh*).
1006	Brian Bóruma claims hostages from north: undisputed high king of Ireland.
1014	Battle of Clontarf (23 Apr., Good Friday): Munster forces under Brian Bóruma defeat and kill Máel Mórda, king of Leinster, and Jarl Sigurd of Orkney, with much slaughter on both sides; Brian killed (buried at Armagh).
	Máel Sechnaill II resumes high-kingship; continues till his death in 1022.
1022–72	High-kingship in abeyance.
1028	Sitric Silkbeard, king of Dublin, and Flannacán, king of Brega, go on pilgrimage to Rome.

*c.*1028x1036	Christ Church Cathedral founded by Sitric and Dúnán, first bishop of Dublin.
1049	Irish monk, Aaron of Cologne, consecrated archbishop of Cracow (d. 1060).
c. 1050–*c.* 1200	Late Middle Irish linguistic period: reworking of traditional sagas; elaboration of pseudo-historical tracts; new recensions of genealogical tracts.
1066	Irish missionary bishop, Johannes, martyred in Mecklenburg.
1068	Sons of Harold Godwinson attack Bristol with Irish fleet.
1074	Death of Dúnán, first bishop of Dublin (6 May); Patricius (Gilla Pátraic) consecrated by Lanfranc; Lanfranc's letters to Toirrdelbach Ua Briain and Gofraid, king of Dublin, urging ecclesiastical reforms.
1075	Church of St Peter at Regensburg granted to Marianus Scottus II and Irish pilgrims.
c. 1090–1120	Flowering of Irish Romanesque metalwork.
1092	Manuscript of *Annals of Inisfallen* written; continued by various hands until fourteenth century.
c. 1100	Gerald of Windsor, castellan of Pembroke, marries Nest, daughter of Rhys ap Tewdwr.
1101	First Synod of Cashel: Muirchertach Ua Briain grants Cashel to church; Máel Ísu Ua hAinmere bishop of Cashel (and papal legate?).
1102	Muirchertach Ua Briain marries one daughter to Sigurd, king of Man, son of Magnus Bareleg, king of Norway, and another to Arnulf of Montgomery, who sends Gerald of Windsor as his envoy to Ireland.
	St Anselm, archbishop of Canterbury, writes to Muirchertach Ua Briain urging ecclesiastical reforms.
*c.*1107	Gilla Espuic of Limerick corresponds with St Anselm; composes *De Statu Ecclesiae.*
1111	Synod of Ráith Bressail: diocesan organisations of Irish church planned.
	Domnall Ua Briain assumes kingship of Hebrides.
1120	Óenach Tailten revived by Toirrdelbach Ua Conchobair.
1124	Round tower at Clonmacnoise finished by Gilla Críst Ua Máel Eóin and Toirrdelbach Ua Conchobair.
1124–7	St Malachy bishop of Down and Connor and abbot of Bangor.
1127–34	Building of Cormac's chapel at Cashel.
1127–1226	Irish Romanesque architecture and sculpture flourish.
1130	Compilation of Leinster codex, Rawlinson B 502: earliest Irish genealogical manuscript extant.
1132	St Malachy consecrated archbishop of Armagh.
1134	Cormac's chapel at Cashel consecrated.
1137	Conchobar Ua Briain and Diarmait Mac Murchada with 200 ships from Dublin and Wexford lay siege to Waterford; Ua Briain submits to Mac Murchada in return for overlordship of Desmond.
1139	St Malachy visits Rome to ask Innocent II for two pallia; visits St Bernard at Clairvaux.
1142	First Irish Cistercian house founded at Mellifont.
1145x1151	St Bernard of Clairvaux writes to Diarmait Mac Murchada 'king of Ireland' admitting him to membership of Cistercian confraternity.
1151	Battle of Móin Mór (in north County Cork): Toirrdelbach Ua Briain, king of Munster, defeated by Toirrdelbach Ua Conchobair and Diarmait Mac Murchada: 7,000 Munstermen killed.
1152	Synod of Kells convened (6 Mar.); later transferred to Mellifont: Cardinal Paparo brings four pallia and completes diocesan organisation of Irish church; departs (24 Mar.).
	Diarmait Mac Murchada abducts Dervorgilla, wife of Tigernán Ua Ruairc.
1155	Proposal for invasion of Ireland by Henry II discussed at Council of Winchester but rejected (29 Sept.).
1155–6	John of Salisbury visits Pope Adrian IV at Rome (Nov.–July); obtains papal privilege (bill *Laudabiliter?*) approving projected conquest of Ireland by Henry II.
1162	Synod of Clain, in presence of Diarmait Mac Murchada and Gilla Meic Liac: primacy of Armagh reaffirmed; ordinance that only alumni of Armagh should be recognised as *fir léigind* (lectors) in Irish churches.
	Lorcán Ua Tuathail consecrated archbishop of Dublin by Gilla Meic Liac, archbishop of Armagh.
	Diarmait Mac Murchada gains complete control over Dublin.
1166	Tigernán Ua Ruairc marches to Ferns: destroys castle of Diarmait Mac Murchada;

	Ruaidrí Ua Conchobair banishes Mac Murchada from Ireland (1 Aug.); Mac Murchada flees to Bristol.
1167	Mac Murchada returns from Wales with small force of Flemings under Richard fitz Godebert of Rhos; recovers kingdom of Uí Chenneslaig (Aug.).
1169	Robert fitz Stephen, Hervey de Montmorency and Maurice de Prendergast land at Bannow Bay, County Wexford (May).
	Wexford captured by Diarmait Mac Murchada, assisted by Normans.
1170	Richard de Clare (Strongbow), earl of Strigoil, lands near Wexford (23 Aug.); captures the city, and marries Aífe, daughter of Mac Murchada (25 Aug.).
	Dublin captured by Mac Murchada and Norman allies (21 Sept); custody given to Miles de Cogan (1 Oct.).
1171	Mac Murchada dies at Ferns (c. 1 May); succeeded by his son-in-law, Strongbow.
	Henry II lands at Crook, near Waterford (17 Oct.).
	Henry II at Dublin; submission of kings of north Leinster, Bréifne, Áirgialla and Ulster (11 Nov.).
1171–2	Second synod of Cashel in session (winter).
1171/2	Henry II grants charter to Dublin.
1172	Meath (Ua Máel Sechlainn kingdom of Mide) granted to Hugh de Lacy by Henry II (c. 1 Apr.).
	Pope Alexander III writes to Irish kings enjoining fealty to Henry II (20 Sept.).
1174	Death of Flann Ua Gormáin, 'arch-lector of Armagh and of all Ireland' (since 1154; had studied in France and England for twenty-one years.)
c. 1174	Henry II grants charter to Dublin, conceding free-trading rights throughout his dominions.
1175	Treaty of Windsor between Henry II and Ruaidrí Ua Conchobair (6 Oct.).
1177	John de Courcy invades Ulster and captures Downpatrick; builds castle (c. 1 Feb.).
	Council of Oxford: John, ten-year-old son of Henry II, designated 'Lord of Ireland' (May).
c. 1179	Irish monks of Schottenklöster at Vienna take control of German monastery at Kiev (Russia).
c. 1180	John de Courcy marries Affreca, daughter of Godred, king of Man; Hugh de Lacy marries daughter of Ruairdrí Ua Conchobair.
1180x1190	Carrickfergus castle built by de Courcy.
1183	First visit to Ireland of Gerald of Wales (Feb.).
1185	Pope Lucius III orders annual convocation of abbots of Irish Benedictine monasteries in Germany to be held at Regensburg.
	John, lord of Ireland, lands at Waterford (25 Apr.); leaves Ireland (17 Dec.).
c. 1188	Gerald of Wales completes *Expugnation Hibernica*.
c. 1200	Standardisation of classical Modern Irish grammar and of poetic diction and metre by bardic schools.
c. 1200–c. 1650	Classical Modern Irish linguistic period.
1204	Dublin Castle established as centre of royal administration.
1207	First national coinage, carrying symbol of the harp.
1210	King John lands at Waterford (20 June).
	Carrickfergus captured by John; the de Lacys flee; Maud de Braose and her son William captured (28 July).
1213	Philip II Augustus prepares to invade England; William Marshal leads '500' Anglo-Irish barons to England in support of John.
1215	Schottenklöster formally organised as 'national' order under abbot of St Jakob at Regensburg.
1216–27	The 'conspiracy of Mellifont' by Irish Cistercians.
1216	Magna Carta issued for Ireland (12 Nov.; transmitted Feb. 1217).
1217	Royal mandate against promotion of Irishmen to cathedral benefices (14 Jan.; repudiation of mandate by Honorius II, 1220).
1224	First Irish Dominican foundations, at Dublin and Drogheda.
c. 1224–30	First Irish Franciscan foundations, at Youghal and Cork.
1226	Abbot of Clairvaux appointed by general chapter to reform Irish Cistercian houses.
1227	All Connacht granted as fief to Richard de Burgh (21 May).

1237–8	Encastellation of Connacht by Anglo-Irish.
c. 1239	Thomas Aquinas, pupil of Peter of Ireland, (professor of philosophy at University of Naples).
a. 1247	Connacht shired.
1250	Pope revokes ordinance of certain Irish prelates excluding Irishmen from Irish canonries (24 Sept.).
1251	Mint opened at Dublin (Oct.; over £43,000 coined before closure, 1254).
1252	'Irish riot' at Oxford University; written agreement of peace (similarly in 1267 and 1274).
1257	Battle of Credran (County Sligo): Fitz Gerald advance northwards halted by O'Donnells.
1258	At Caeluisce (County Sligo): Fitz Gerald advance northwards halted by O'Donnells.
1259	Áed Ó Conchobair marries daughter of Dubgall Mac Sumarlaide, who brings dowry of 160 *gallóclaig.*
1260	Battle of Downpatrick (16 May): Brian O'Neill defeated and killed by justiciar.
1261	Battle of Callan (near Kenmare): Fíngen Mac Carthaig defeats justiciar (William of Dene); numerous castles destroyed.
1262–3	Irish kings offer high-kingship to Haakon IV, king of Norway, for support in expelling English from Ireland.
1264	Parliament at Castledermot (18 June).
1265	Norman-French poem composed on building of defences at New Ross.
1270	Battle of Áth in Chip (near Carrick-on-Shannon): Walter de Burgh defeated by Áed Ó Conchobair; his brother William Óc killed.
1280	Anglo-Irish magnates directed to assemble for purposes of examining Irish petition for English law.
1297	Parliament at Dublin: liberties and counties represented; beginning of widespread representation.
1299	Parliament at Dublin (20–27 Jan; 3 May): towns represented.
1300	Parliament at Dublin (24 Apr.): counties and towns represented.
1301	Large Irish army serves with Edward I in Scotland, under command of justiciar (Wogan).
1310	Parliament at Kilkenny: statute against reception of Irishmen as members of Anglo-Irish religious houses (9 Feb.).
1311	Papal permit for establishment of university (*studium generale*) at Dublin (see 1320).
1315	Edward Bruce lands at Larne (26 May); captures Dundalk and is inaugurated as 'high king' (29 June).
1315–17	Famine in western Europe, including Ireland.
1316	Edward Bruce crowned king of Ireland near Dundalk (*c.* 1 May).
1316–31	Friar James, OFM, of Ireland, accompanies Odoric de Pordenone as far as China.
1318	Battle of Faughart: Edward Bruce defeated and killed by John de Bermingham (14 Oct.).
1320	Parliament at Dublin: approval for foundation of university at Dublin (27 Apr. see 1311, 1465).
1323	Dame Alice Kyteler convicted of heresy by Richard Ledred (Leatherhead), bishop of Ossory (2 July).
c. 1325	*Book of Kildare* compiled: collection of literary and religious pieces, in Latin, English and Norman-French.
c. 1327/8	Petition from 'divers men of Ireland' to Edward III that English law be available to Irishmen without special charter.
c. 1330	Manuscript collection of poems and other literary compositions in Hiberno-English, Norman-French and Latin compiled (BL, Harl.MS913)
1331	Ordinances for conduct of Irish government: include decree that there should be one law (*una et eadem lex*) for Irish and Anglo-Irish, except for betaghs.
1337–44	Richard FitzRalph at papal court, Avignon.
1348	Black Death appears at Howth and Drogheda (early Aug.).
1351	'Nodlaig na Garma': convention of poets and men of learning held by Uilliam Buidhe Ó Ceallaigh; Godfraidh Fionn Ó Dálaigh's poem 'Filidh Éireann go haointeach' (Christmas).

1366	Parliament at Kilkenny: 'statute of Kilkenny' promulgated (19 Feb.).
1378x1392/4	*Book of Uí Mhaine* written for Muircheartach Ó Ceallaigh, bishop of Clonfert.
1394	Richard II arrives at Waterford (2 Oct.).
1395	Irish kings submit to Richard II (Jan.–Apr.); Richard returns to England (15 May).
1399	Richard II again in Ireland (1 June–27 July).
1409–10	League of mendicant friars in Ireland against attacks of John Whitehead at Oxford.
1416–18	*Great Book of Lecan* compiled by Giolla Íosa Mór Mac Fir Bhisigh with assistance of Murchadh Riabhach Ó Cuíndlis and Ádhamh Ó Cuirnín.
1422	Further proclamation for expulsion of Irishmen and Irish students from England.
1423	Observant priory (OSA) established at Banada, County Sligo; first house of friars observant movement in Ireland.
1431	Polyphonic choir established at St Patrick's Cathedral, Dublin.
1435	Ordinance prohibiting Irish poets and musicians from being in Anglo-Irish areas (1 Apr.).
1445	Uilliam Ó Raghallaigh becomes first Irish-born provincial of Franciscans in Ireland.
1446	Royal charter to guild of barbers and surgeons at Dublin (18 Oct.).
	First known use of term 'Pale' to denote area under Dublin control.
1449	Richard, duke of York, arrives in Ireland as lieutenant; returns to England (22 Aug.).
1459	Yorkists defeated at Ludford Bridge (12 Oct.); duke of York takes refuge in Ireland.
1460	Parliament at Drogheda: duke of York confirmed as lieutenant by Anglo-Irish in opposition to Ormond; declaration that only acts of Irish parliament should bind Ireland (8 Feb.).
	Yorkists defeated at battle of Wakefield; duke of York killed (30 Dec.).
1461	Henry VI deposed (4 Mar.); replaced by Edward IV, son of Richard, duke of York; Lancastrians defeated at Towton (29 Mar.).
1462	Battle of Pilltown, County Kilkenny: Ormond's supporters defeated by Thomas Fitzgerald, son of seventh earl of Desmond.
1463	Thomas Fitzgerald succeeds his father as eighth earl of Desmond; appointed lord deputy by Edward IV (1 Apr.).
1465	Desmond's project to set up a university at Drogheda.
1468	Tiptoft holds parliament at Drogheda: earls of Desmond and Kildare and Edward Plunkett attainted; Desmond executed (4 Feb.).
1478–1513	Supremacy of Gerald or Garret Fitzgerald, eighth earl of Kildare (Gearóid Mór, 'the great earl').
1485	Battle of Bosworth: Richard III defeated and killed; succeeded by Lancastrian Henry VII.
1487	Lambert Simnel crowed king of England as Edward VI at Christ Church, Dublin (24 May).
	First recorded use of firearms in Ireland, by troops of Aodh Ruadh Ó Domhnaill.
1491	Perkin Warbeck (claiming to be Richard, son of Edward IV) lands at Cork (Nov.).
1494–5	Sir Edward Poynings lord deputy.
1494	Parliament at Drogheda: 'Poynings' Law' enacted (1 Dec., see 1782).
1495	Waterford besieged by supporter of Perkin Warbeck (July).
1499–1506	Maurice O'Fihely, OFM, Conv., of Tuam edits works of Duns Scotus (printed at Venice).
c. 1500	*Book of Lismore* written for Finghín Mac Carthaigh Riabhach.
1504	Battle of Knockdoe, near Galway: earl of Kildare with Ó Domhnaill and English of Pale defeat Clanricard and Ó Briain (19 Aug.).
1513	Garret More, eighth earl of Kildare, dies of gunshot wounds; succeeded as ninth earl and lord deputy by his son Garret Oge.
1519	Kildare summoned to London (12 Jan.)
1520	Thomas Howard, earl of Surrey, appointed lord lieutenant (10 Mar.) and sent to Ireland with 500 troops (23 May).
	Henry VIII directs Surrey to subdue Irish lords 'rather . . . by sober ways . . . and amiable persuasion, founded in law and reason, than by . . . strength or violence' (Sept. ?).
1521	Surrey submits plan for reconquest to Henry VIII (30 June).
	Henry VIII sends livery of knighthood to Conn Bacach Ó Néill.
1529	Gonzalo Fernandez, chaplain of Charles V, arrives in Ireland to treat with earl of Desmond (24 Feb.).

1532	Garret, ninth earl of Kildare (Gearóid Óg) appointed deputy; James Butler, son of earl of Ossory, treasurer; George Cromer, archbishop of Armagh, chancellor (5 July).
1533	Henry VIII marries Anne, daughter of Sir Thomas Boleyn, earl of Wiltshire and Ormond (25 Jan.).
1534	Kildare leaves for England; his son, Thomas, Lord Offaly ('Silken Thomas'), appointed as his deputy (Feb.).
	Revolt of Silken Thomas (June).
1535	Surrender of Silken Thomas (Aug.).
1536	'Reformation parliament' in Dublin (1–3 May): Silken Thomas and others attainted; royal supremacy enacted.
1537	Execution of Silken Thomas and his five uncles in London (3 Feb.).
	Acts of parliament (Oct.–Dec.): against authority of pope; for suppression of monasteries.
1538	Brian O'Connor of Offaly submits to Lord Deputy Grey: gives undertakings containing germ of 'surrender and regrant' policy (6 Mar.).
1539	Dissolution of monasteries within the Pale begins.
	O'Neill and O'Donnell routed by Lord Deputy Grey at Bellahoe, on Meath–Monaghan border (Aug.).
1540–43	Lord Deputy St Leger's pacification: introduction of 'surrender and regrant'.
1541	Henry VIII declared 'king of Ireland' by act of Irish parliament (18 June).
1542	First Jesuit mission to Ireland (Feb.–Mar.).
	Conn O'Neill created earl of Tyrone, with succession to his illegitimate son, Matthew, created baron of Dungannon (1 Oct.).
1547–53	Edwardian Reformation in Ireland.
1549	First English Act of Uniformity prescribes the use of the Book of Common Prayer (14 Mar.).
	English Book of Common Prayer ordered to be used in Ireland (9 June).
1550–7	Plantation in Laois and Offaly.
1552	Second English Act of Uniformity prescribing use of second Book of Common Prayer (14 Apr.).
1553–8	Marian reaction in Ireland: restoration of papal authority.
1555	Bull of Pope Paul IV making Ireland a kingdom.
1558	Matthew, baron of Dungannon, killed by order of Shane O'Neill.
1559	Shane O'Neill succeeds Conn as The O'Neill (*a.* 17 July).
1560	Elizabeth's first Irish parliament (11/12 Jan.–1 Feb.) restores royal supremacy and prescribes use of second English Book of Common Prayer (with amendments).
1561–7	Rebellion of Shane O'Neill.
1561	Shane O'Neill proclaimed a traitor (8 June).
1562	Shane O'Neill submits to Elizabeth at Whitehall (6 Jan,); returns to Ireland (26 May); again in rebellion (Nov.).
	Brian O'Neill, second baron of Dungannon, killed by Turlough Luineach O'Neill, tanist to Shane O'Neill (12 Apr.); Brian's brother taken to England.
1564	Shane O'Neill campaigns against MacDonnells of Antrim (Sept.)
1565	Shane O'Neill defeats MacDonnells at Glenshesk (2 May).
1566	Shane O'Neill burns Armagh cathedral (Aug.).
1567	Shane O'Neill defeated by O'Donnell at Farsetmore, near Letterkenny (8 May); takes refuge with MacDonnells, and killed by them at Cushendun, County Antrim (2 June).
1568	Hugh O'Neill recognised as baron of Dungannon (1 Mar.).
1568–73	First Desmond rebellion.
1569	Act for the attainder of Shane O'Neill (11 Mar.).
	Sir Edward Fitton appointed president of Connacht (1 June).
1570	Pope Pius V excommunicates Queen Elizabeth by bull *Regnans in Excelsis* (25 Feb.).
	Sir John Perrot appointed president of Munster (13 Dec.).
1571	First printing in the Irish language in Dublin (June).
1573–6	Earl of Essex's attempt to set up colony in Antrim.
1575	Massacre on Rathlin Island by Essex's soldiers (26 July).
1579	Sir Nicholas Malby appointed president of Connacht (31 Mar.).
1579–83	Second Desmond rebellion.

1580	Revolt in Leinster headed by Viscount Baltinglass and Fiach MacHugh O'Byrne (July); government force defeated by O'Byrne in Glenmalure (25 Aug.).
	Papal force at Smerwick massacred by government force under Lord Deputy Grey (10 Nov.).
1582	Bull of Pope Gregory XIII for reform of calendar: 4 Oct. 1582 to be followed by 15 Oct.; year to begin on 1 Jan. (24 Feb.; see 1751).
1584	Hugh O'Neill, baron of Dungannon, made tanist to Turlough Luineach O'Neill (Mar.).
	Dermot O'Hurley, archbishop of Cashel, hanged in Dublin (20 June).
1585	Parliament in Dublin (26 Apr.–25 May): Baltinglass attainted; Hugh O'Neill takes seat in House of Lords as earl of Tyrone.
	Commissioners make agreements with Connacht landowners – 'composition of Connacht' (July–Oct.).
1585	Scheme for plantation in Munster (Dec.).
1586	Parliament in Dublin (26 Apr.–14 May): Desmond and his supporters attainted.
	Agreement made by Lord Deputy Perrot with Sorley Boy MacDonnell and his nephew Angus: greater part of the Route (region in north Antrim extending south-east of Coleraine to Ballymoney and east to Dunluce) granted to Sorley Boy; the Glens (east Antrim from Ballycastle to Larne) granted to Angus (18 June).
1587	Hugh O'Neill granted patent conferring title of earl of Tyrone.
1588	About twenty-five ships of Spanish armada wrecked off Irish coasts (Sept.).
1590	Foundation of first Irish college, Alcalá, on the Continent.
1591	Earl of Tyrone marries Mabel Bagenal, sister of Sir Henry Bagenal, marshal of the army (3 Aug.).
	Hugh Roe O'Donnell (kidnapped by government at Rathmullen, Sept. 1587) escapes from Dublin Castle (26 Dec.).
1592	Charter incorporating Trinity College Dublin (3 Mar.).
1595–1603	Rebellion of Hugh O'Neill, earl of Tyrone.
1595	Earl of Tyrone defeats Bagenal's force at Clontibret, County Monaghan (13 June).
	Turlough Luineach dies (Sept.); succeeded as The O'Neill by earl of Tyrone.
1596	Fiach MacHugh O'Byrne revolts (Sept.; killed May 1597).
1598	Bagenal defeated by Tyrone at the Yellow Ford, between Armagh and Blackwater (14 Aug.).
	Munster plantation attacked by súgán earl of Desmond (Oct.).
1599	Phelim MacFeagh O'Byrne routs English force at Deputy's Pass, near Wicklow (29 May).
	Sir Conyers Clifford, president of Connacht, killed in engagement with Hugh Roe O'Donnell in Curlew Mountains, County Roscommon (5 Aug.).
1600	Tyrone campaigns in Munster (Feb.–Mar.).
	Expedition to Lough Foyle under Sir Henry Docwra lands at Culmore (15 May) and establishes strong position at Derry.
1601	Spanish army under Don Juan del Águila to support Tyrone lands at Kinsale (Sept.); invested by government forces under Lord Deputy Mountjoy (26 Oct.); Tyrone and O'Donnell, attempting to cooperate with the besieged, are heavily defeated by Mountjoy (24 Dec.).
	O'Donnell leaves Ireland for Spain (27 Dec.); Tyrone withdraws to Ulster.
1602	Águila surrenders Kinsale to Mountjoy.
	Tyrone's principal vassal, Donal O'Cahan, submits to Docwra (27 July).
	Hugh Roe O'Donnell dies at Simancas (Aug.).
	O'Neill inaugural chair at Tullahogue, County Tyrone, destroyed by Mountjoy (Sept.).
	Rory O'Donnell, brother and successor of Hugh Roe, submits to Mountjoy (Dec.).
1603	Death of Elizabeth and accession of James I (24 Mar.).
	Surrender of Tyrone at Mellifont (30 Mar.).
	First assizes held in Donegal; first sheriffs appointed for Donegal and Tyrone.
	Rory O'Donnell, brother of Hugh Roe, created earl of Tyrconnell (29 Sept.).
1605	Proclamation declaring all persons in the realm to be the free, natural and immediate subjects of king and not subjects of any lord or chief (11 Mar.).
1606	Irish custom of gavelkind declared illegal by royal judges (Jan./Feb.).

	Foundation of St Anthony's Franciscan College, Louvain.
1607	Earls of Tyrone and Tyrconnell and others secretly sail from Lough Swilly – 'flight of the earls' (4 Sept.).
	Fugitive earls and their associates charged with high treason, and their lands declared forfeited (Dec.).
1608	Tanistry declared illegal by court of king's bench (Jan./Feb.).
	Revolt of Sir Cahir O'Doherty, of Inishowen (Apr.–July).
1608–10	Preparations for plantations in six escheated counties in Ulster: Donegal, Coleraine, Tyrone, Armagh, Fermanagh and Cavan.
1610	Agreement between crown and city of London for plantion of city of Derry, town of Coleraine, county of Coleraine and barony of Loughinsholin, County Tyrone (28 Jan.).
	Settlers from England and Scotland begin to arrive in Ulster.
1612	Cornelius O'Devany, OFM, bishop of Down and Connor, convicted of treason (Jan.) and hanged in Dublin (Feb.).
	Dungannon incorporated (27 Nov.) – first of forty new boroughs, many in Ulster, incorporated between Nov. 1612 and May 1613.
1613	Charter incorporating Derry as city of Londonderry, creating new county of Londonderry, incorporating Irish Society of London and granting to it most of temporal land in County Londonderry (29 Mar.; see 1635).
1613–5	James I's Irish Parliament.
1621	Authorisation for plantations in parts of Leitrim, King's County, Queen's County and Westmeath (20 Jan.).
1625	England at war with Spain.
1626	Charles I offers concessions ('graces') to his Irish subjects in return for grants to maintain an expanded army (22 Sept.).
1627	England at war with France.
1628	Charles issues 'graces' in return for promise of £40,000 a year for three years.
1632	Compilation of *The Annals of the Four Masters* by Michael O'Clery and others, begins at Donegal (completed 10 Aug. 1636).
1633	Viscount Wentworth (created earl of Strafford, 12 Jan. 1640) lord deputy (July).
1634–5	Charles I's first Irish parliament.
1635	City of London and Irish Society found guilty of mismanagement and neglect of Londonderry plantation; sentenced to fine of £70,000 and forfeiture of Londonderry property, etc. (28 Jan.; see 1657).
1635–6	Wentworth prepares for a plantation in Connacht.
1640	Charles I's second Irish parliament meets (16 Mar.).
1641	Bill for the attainder of earl of Strafford passed by English House of Commons (21 Apr.; Strafford executed 12 May).
	Rising begins in Ulster (22 Oct.).
	Government forces defeated at Julianstown Bridge, near Drogheda, by Ulster rebels (29 Nov.).
	Meeting at Knockcrofty, near Drogheda, between Ulster Irish and Old English (Dec.) leads to alliance between them.
1642	Scottish army under Robert Munro lands at Carrickfergus (15 Apr.).
	First regularly constituted presbytery in Ireland meets at Carrickfergus (10 June.).
	Owen Roe O'Neill arrives in Ulster (8/9 July).
	Civil war begins in England (22 Aug.).
	Catholic confederacy ('Confederation of Kilkenny') instituted (Oct.).
1643	Cessation of hostilities between royalists and confederates (15 Sept.).
1645	End of Civil War in England; last pitched battle at Langport, Somerset (10 July).
	Secret 'Glamorgan treaty' between king and confederates (25 Aug.).
	Archbishop Giovanni Rinuccini, papal envoy to confederates, arrives at Kenmare, County Kerry (12 Oct.).
	Second secret 'Glamorgan treaty' (20 Dec.).
1646	'Ormond peace' with confederates (28 Mar.).
	Monro defeated at Benburb, County Tyrone, by Owen Roe O'Neill (5 June).
	Rinuccini and O'Neill repudiate 'Ormond peace' (Aug.–Sept.).
1647	Ormond surrender Dublin to parliamentary forces under Col. Michael Jones (July).

	Jones defeats confederates at Dungan's Hill, near Trim (8 Aug.).
1648	Second Civil War in England (May–Aug.); Scots defeated by Cromwell at Preston, Lancashire. (17 Aug.).
	Open breach between O'Neill and confederate council (Sept.).
1649	Second 'Ormond peace' with confederates (17 Jan.).
	Execution of Charles I (30 Jan.).
	Departure of Rinuccini from Ireland (23 Feb.).
	Jones defeats Ormond at Rathmines (2 Aug.).
	Cromwell arrives in Dublin as commander-in-chief (15 Aug.).
	Cromwell takes Drogheda by storm: massacre of garrison (about 2,600) and townspeople (11 Sept.).
	Cromwell takes Wexford: second massacre (about 2,000) (11 Oct.).
	New Ross surrenders to Cromwell (19 Oct.).
	Owen Roe O'Neill dies at Cloughoughter, County Cavan (6 Nov.).
1650	Cromwellian conquest completed (Jan.–May).
1652	Act for the settlement of Ireland (12 Aug.).
1652–3	Cromwellian land-confiscation.
1653	'Barebones' parliament (4 July–12 Dec.), in which Ireland and Scotland are represented by six and five members respectively.
1654	First Protectorate parliament meets (3 Sept.); Ireland represented by thirty members.
1657	Charter of Cromwell restoring Londonderry property etc. to city of London (see 1635, 1662).
1658	Death of Cromwell (3 Sept.).
1660	Restoration of monarchy in England (Feb.–May); Charles II proclaimed king in Dublin (14 May).
	Navigation Act, for controlling England's external trade (13 Sept.); treats England and Ireland as an economic unit.
1660–65	Restoration land settlement (Act of Settlement, 1662; Court of Claims, 1662–3; Act of Explanation, 1665).
1661–6	Charles II's Irish parliament.
1662	Charter of Charles II replacing Cromwell's charter of Londonderry (10 Apr.; see 1657).
1662–9	Ormond lord lieutenant.
1663	England act restricts Irish trade with colonies and importation of Irish cattle into England (27 July).
1666	English act prohibits importation of Irish cattle into England (18 Jan.).
1671	Second English Navigation Act prohibits direct importation from colonies to Ireland (22 Apr.); act expires in 1681 (18 Jan.) but is renewed in 1685 (2 July).
1672	First grant of *regium donum* to presbyterian ministers (*c.* Oct.).
1677–85	Ormond again lord lieutenant.
1678–81	'Popish plot'.
1681	Execution of Archbishop Oliver Plunkett in London (1 July).
1685	Death of Charles II and accession of James II (6 Feb.).
1687	Richard Talbot, earl of Tyrconnell, lord deputy (Feb.).
1688	Derry and Enniskillen defy James II (Dec.).
1689	James II arrives at Kinsale (12 Mar.).
	Siege of Derry (18 Apr.–28 July).
	James II's Irish parliament (7 May–18 July).
	Defenders of Enniskillen defeat Jacobite force at Newtownbutler, County Fermanagh (31 July).
1690	William III lands at Carrickfergus (14 June); defeats James II at Oldbridge on River Boyne (1 July); departure of James II to France.
	First siege of Limerick (9–30 Aug.).
	Jacobite force under Patrick Sarsfield destroys Williamite baggage train at Ballyneety (11 Aug.).
1691	Williamite victory at Aughrim (12 July).
	Second siege of Limerick (Sept.–Oct.).

Treaty of Limerick (3 Oct.) marks end of war: Irish army allowed to go to France and continue in James II's service; Catholics promised the religious privileges they enjoyed in Charles II's reign.

First recorded meeting of Presbyterian General Synod of Ulster (at Antrim, 30 Sept.).

Catholics effectively excluded from parliament and public office in Ireland by act of English parliament (24 Dec.).

1691–1703	Williamite land confiscation.
1693	Death of Patrick Sarsfield, after Battle of Landen (23 July).
1695–1709	Penal legislation against Catholics.
1698	William Molyneux's tract, *The Case of Ireland's Being Bound by Acts of Parliament in England Stated*, published in Dublin (Apr.).
1699	English act restricting export of Irish woollens (26 Jan.).
1700	Subsidy authorised to Louis Crommelin for establishing a linen industry (14 Feb.).
1701	James II dies at St Germains (6 Sept.); his son recognised by Louis XIV as James III.
1702	William III dies (8 Mar.); succeeded by Anne.
1704	Sacramental test for public office, applicable to both Catholics and Protestant Dissenters (4 Mar.).
1705	English act permits direct export of Irish linen to American colonies (14 Mar.).
1707	Union of English and Scottish parliaments takes effect (1 May).
1709	Irish House of Lords expresses hope that Irish union with England will follow union of England and Scotland (9 May).
1710	Board of trustees for linen manufacture established (28 Aug.).
1713	Jonathan Swift installed as dean of St Patrick's Cathedral, Dublin (13 June).
1714	Anne dies (1 Aug.); succeeded by George I, first of Hanoverian line.
1715	Jacobite rising in Scotland under earl of Mar (Sept.–Nov.).
1718	Beginning of extensive migration of Ulster Scots to American colonies (June–July).
1719	Toleration Act for Protestant Dissenters (2 Nov.).
1720	British act (6 George I, *c.* 5) declaring right of British parliament to legislate for Ireland and denying appellate jurisdiction of Irish House of Lords (7 Apr.).
1722	Patent to William Wood to coin copper halfpence for circulation in Ireland (12 July).
1724	First of Swift's 'Drapier's Letters' (Feb./Mar.; 2nd letter, 6 Aug.; 3rd letter, 5 Sept.; 4th letter, 'To the whole people of Ireland', 22 Oct.; 5th letter, 31 Dec.).
1726	Abraham Shackleton, Quaker, opens school at Ballitore, County Kildare (1 Mar.; continues as headmaster till 1756; Edmund Burke a pupil, 1741–3).
	Non-subscribing Presbyterians separate from main Presbyterian body to form presbytery of Antrim (June).
1727	George I dies (11 June); succeeded by George II.
1729	Foundation stone laid of Edward Lovet Pearce's new parliament building in College Green (3 Feb.; parliament meets there for first time 5 Oct. 1731).
	New wave of emigration of Ulster Scots to American colonies.
1731	Dublin Society for Improving Husbandry, etc. formed (25 June; 'Royal Dublin Society', 19 June 1820).
1736	House of Commons condemns tithe of agistment on pasturage for dry and barren cattle (18 Mar.).
1737	First number of *Belfast News Letter* (1 Sept.).
1739	British act removing duties on import of Irish woollen yarn into GB (14 June).
1739–41	Severe weather, bad harvest, fever and famine.
1742	Handel's *Messiah* performed for first time in Music Hall, Fishamble Street, Dublin (13 Apr.; first performance in Cork, 6 Dec. 1744).
1745	Jacobite rising under 'Young Pretender' begins in Scotland (July; Jacobite victory at Prestonpans, 21 Sept.; defeat at Culloden, 16 Apr. 1746).
	Earl of Chesterfield lord lieutenant (31 Aug.; till Mar. 1746).
1751	British act for reform of calendar (22 May; see above, 1582; takes effect on 2 Sept. 1752, next following day becoming 14 Sept.).
	Irish parliament authorises application of revenue surplus to reduction of national debt (19 Dec.); dispute between House of Commons and government.
1752	Building of west front of Trinity College begins (completed, 1759).
1753	Renewed dispute between House of Commons and government over revenue surplus.

1757	Lying-in hospital (known as Rotunda from 1767) opened in Dublin (8 Dec.).
1758	'Wide street commissioners' for Dublin appointed by Irish parliament (29 Apr.).
	British act permitting the importation of salted beef, pork and butter from Ireland (20 June).
1759	British act removing restrictions on import of Irish cattle into GB (5 Apr.).
	Henry Flood enters parliament (21 Nov.); becomes leader of opposition.
	Rioting in Dublin on rumour of legislative union with GB (3 Dec.).
1760	François Thurot enters Belfast Lough with three French ships and takes Carrickfergus (21 Feb.; withdraws 26 Feb.).
	Origin in Dublin of Catholic Committee on initiative of Dr John Curry, Charles O'Conor and Thomas Wyse (c. 31 Mar.).
	George II dies (25 Oct.); succeeded by George III.
1761	Beginning of Whiteboy movement in Munster (c. Oct.–Dec.).
1763	Oakboy or Hearts of Oak disturbances begin in Ulster.
	First number of *Freeman's Journal* (10 Sept.; last number, 19 Dec. 1924).
1764	Rotunda concert hall built (see 1757).
1766	Father Nicholas Sheehy, convicted of inciting Whiteboys to murder, executed at Clonmel (15 Mar.).
	Tumultuous Risings Act, against Whiteboys (7 June).
1767–72	Lord Townsend lord lieutenant.
1768	Octennial Act, limiting life of parliament to eight years (16 Feb.).
1769	Steelboy or Hearts of Steel disturbances in Ulster (July).
1768–9	Money bill dispute between House of Commons and government.
1771	Benjamin Franklin in Ireland (5 Sept.–c. 23 Oct.); attends meeting of House of Commons (10 Oct.).
1772	Act to repress Steelboy disturbances in five Ulster counties (28 Mar.; repealed in 1774).
	'Bogland Act' enables Catholics to take bog reclamation leases of sixty-one years (2 June).
1773	First performance, at Covent Garden Theatre, London, of Oliver Goldsmith's *She Stoops to Conquer* (15 Mar.).
1774	Act enabling Catholics to testify their allegiance to king (2 June).
1775	First performance, at Covent Garden Theatre, London, of R. B. Sheridan's *The Rivals* (17 Jan.).
1775–83	War of American Independence.
1775	Henry Flood appointed vice-treasurer (27 Oct.), abandoning parliamentary opposition.
	Henry Grattan's maiden speech in House of Commons (15 Dec.); takes Flood's place as leader of opposition.
1776	New anti-Whiteboy act (Apr.; made perpetual in 1800).
	Arthur Young begins tour of Ireland (20 June; continued in 1777 and 1778; his *Tour of Ireland* published in 1780).
	American Declaration of Independence (4 July).
1778	Volunteer movement begins with enrolling of company in Belfast (17 Mar.).
	John Paul Jones, American privateer, twice raids Belfast Lough (Apr.).
	Gardiner's first Catholic Relief Act, enabling Catholics to take leases for 999 years and to inherit in same way as Protestants (14 Aug.).
1779	Belfast Charitable Society decides to set up cotton manufacturing in Poorhouse (19 May).
	Volunteers, parading on College Green, demand removal of restrictions on Irish trade (4 Nov.).
1780	British act allows Ireland to trade with British colonies on equal terms with GB (24 Feb.).
	Grattan in House of Commons moves resolutions in favour of legislative independence (19 Apr.).
	Relief Act repeals sacramental test for Protestant Dissenters (2 May; see 1704).
	Mutiny Act (Aug.) (perpetual; see 1782).
	John Beresford appointed chief commissioner of revenue (16 Dec.).

1781	British force under Cornwallis surrenders to Washington at Yorktown (Va): virtual end of War of American independence.
	First stone of James Gandon's Custom House, Dublin, laid (8 Aug.; opened, 7 Nov. 1791).
1782	Habeas Corpus Act (12 Feb.).
	Ulster Volunteer convention at Dungannon adopts resolutions in favour of legislative and judicial independence and relaxation of Penal Laws (15 Feb.).
	Grattan again moves for an address to king declaring Ireland's right to legislative independence (22 Feb.).
	Grattan for third time moves declaration of rights, which is carried unanimously by both houses of parliament (16 Apr.).
	Gardiner's second Catholic Relief Act allowing Catholics to acquire land, except in parliamentary boroughs, and removing other disabilities, including various restrictions on Catholic clergy and Catholic worship (4 May).
	Act validating marriages by Presbyterian ministers (4 May).
	Act establishing Bank of Ireland (4 May; bank opens 25 June 1783).
	House of Commons votes £50,000 to purchase lands to be settled on Grattan (31 May).
	British act repealing Declaratory Act of 1720, and thereby conceding parliamentary independence (21 June).
	Poynings' Law (see 1494) amended: all bills approved by both houses of parliament to be transmitted unaltered to London – Yelverton's Act (27 July).
	Act for securing the independence of the judiciary – Forbes's Act (27 July).
	Gardiner's third Catholic Relief Act, allowing Catholics to be teachers and to act as guardians (27 July).
	Mutiny Act (annual; see 1780) (July).
1783	British Renunciation Act acknowledging exclusive right of Irish parliament to legislate for Ireland and exclusive jurisdiction of Irish courts (17 Apr.).
	Second Volunteer convention at Dungannon to prepare for parliamentary reform (8 Sept.).
	National Volunteer convention on parliamentary reform, at Rotunda, Dublin (10 Nov.–2 Dec.).
	Volunteers' parliamentary reform bill rejected by House of Commons by 157 to 77 (19 Nov).
	William Pitt PM of GB (19 Dec.).
1784	Act regulating corn trade – Foster's Corn Law (14 May).
	Opening of St Mary's Catholic Chapel, Belfast, attended by First Belfast Volunteer Company (30 May).
	Formation of Peep o'Day Boys (Protestant) and Defenders (Catholic) arising out of dispute (4 July) at Markethill, County Armagh.
	Radical reform congress in William Street, Dublin (25–7 Oct,; second session, 20 Jan.–4 Feb. 1785; third session, 20–30 Apr.).
1785	Pitt's proposals for regulating trade between GB and Ireland introduced in Irish House of Commons by Thomas Orde, chief secretary (7 Feb.; scheme abandoned, Aug.).
	First meeting of Irish Academy (3 May; title changed to Royal Irish Academy by charter, 28 Jan. 1786).
	Renewed disturbances of Whiteboys, now called Rightboys, in Munster (Sept.).
1786	First stone of James Gandon's Four Courts laid (3 Mar.; first sitting of judges there, 3 Nov. 1796).
	Belfast Academy opened (1 May; becomes Belfast Royal Academy, 1887).
1788	George III becomes insane (5 Nov.; regency crisis; king declared to have recovered, 10 Mar. 1789).
1789	John Fitzgibbon (earl of Clare, 12 June 1795) appointed lord chancellor.
	Meeting of States General at Versailles (5 May) opens the way to revolution in France.
	Whig Club formed in Dublin (26 June).
	Fall of Bastille in Paris (14 July).
1790	Northern Whig Club formed in Belfast (28 Feb.).
	Edmund Burke's *Reflections on the Revolution in France* published (1 Nov.).

1791	Thomas Paine's *Rights of Man*, pt 1. published (13 Mar.; pt 2, 1792).
	Demonstrations in Dublin, Belfast and elsewhere commemorating fall of Bastille (14 July).
	Wolfe Tone's *Argument on Behalf of the Catholics of Ireland* (*c.* 22 Aug.).
	Tone's first visit to Belfast (Oct.): Society of United Irishmen founded (14 Oct.).
	First meeting of Dublin Society of United Irishmen (9 Nov.).
	Viscount Kenmare and sixty-seven others secede from Catholic Committee, in which John Keogh is now dominant (27 Dec.).
1792	First number of *Northern Star*, organ of Belfast United Irishmen (4 Jan.); editor, Samuel Neilson.
	Langrishe's Catholic Relief Act, allowing Catholics to practise as solicitors and barristers (18 Apr.) and repealing laws against intermarriage of Protestants and Catholics.
	Gathering of Irish harpers in Belfast (11–14 July).
	Wolfe Tone appointed agent and assistant secretary of Catholic Committee (25 July).
	Catholic convention in Tailor's Hall, Dublin (3–8 Dec.).
	Catholic delegates, accompanied by Tone, travel from Dublin to London via Belfast to present petition to king (Dec.).
1793	Execution of Louis XVI in Paris (21 Jan.).
	France declares war on GB (1 Feb.).
	Convention of Ulster Volunteers at Dungannon (15–16 Feb); proclamation suppressing them (11 Mar.).
	Hobart's Catholic Relief Act, giving Catholics the parliamentary franchise and removing most of their remaining disabilities, but leaving them excluded from parliament, judgeships and the higher public offices (9 Apr.).
	Act establishing militia, at strength of 14,948 (9 Apr.; strength increased to 21,660 in 1795).
	Convention Act, prohibiting any assembly, other than parliament, chosen to represent the people (16 Aug.).
	Opening of St Patrick's College, Carlow, the first Catholic college for higher studies in Ireland (1 Oct.).
1794	United Irishmen's plan of parliamentary reform published (15 Feb.).
	Rev. William Jackson, agent of French revolutionary government, arrested in Dublin (28 Apr.).
	Dublin Society of United Irishmen suppressed (23 May).
1795	Fitzwilliam's viceroyalty (Jan.–Mar.): disaster for Catholic expectations.
	Suicide of William Jackson (30 Apr.).
	Act providing for establishing Catholic seminary at Maynooth (5 June; Royal College of St Patrick opened, *c.* 1 Oct.).
	Tone embarks at Belfast for America (13 June).
	'Battle of the Diamond', near Loughgall, County Armagh, between Peep o'Day Boys and Defenders (21 Sept.) leads to foundation of Orange Society.
1796	Tone arrives in France from USA (1 Feb.).
	Insurrection Act (24 Mar.).
	Habeas Corpus Suspension Act (26 Oct.; continued to 1 June 1799).
	Act regulating new yeomanry corps (9 Nov.).
	French invasion fleet, with Tone on board, in Bantry Bay (22–7 Dec.).
1797	Bank of Ireland suspends gold payments (26 Feb.).
	General Gerard Lake begins disarming of Ulster (13 Mar.).
	William Orr, United Irishman, hanged at Carrickfergus (14 Oct.).
1798	Leaders of Leinster directory of United Irishmen arrested (12 Mar.).
	Arrest of Lord Edward Fitzgerald (19 May; dies from wound 4 June).
	United Irish rising in Leinster (May–June): insurgents initially successful in County Wexford but defeated at Tara (26 May), Curragh (29 May), New Ross (5 June), Arklow (9 June) and Vinegar Hill, near Enniscorthy (21 June); massacre of Protestants at Scullabogue, County Wexford (5 June).
	United Irish rising in Ulster (June): insurgents defeated at Antrim (7 June) and Ballynahinch (13 June).

French force under General Humbert in Connacht (Aug.–Sept.): defeats government forces at Castlebar (27 Aug.); surrenders to Cornwallis, lord lieutenant, at Ballinamuck (8 Sept.).

French squadron under Admiral Bompart, with Tone on board, defeated outside Lough Swilly (12–20 Oct.); Tone captured at Buncrana (3 Nov.).

Tone convicted of high treason by court martial in Dublin and sentenced to be hanged (10 Nov.); cuts his throat (12 Nov.) and dies in provost marshal's prison, Dublin Barracks (19 Nov.).

1799	Last session of Irish parliament (15 Jan.–2 Aug.): Pitt in British House of Commons advocates parliamentary union of GB and Ireland (31 Jan.); Irish House of Commons passes Union proposals (5–6 Feb.); Union bulls introduced in Irish House of Commons (21 May); and in British (17 June); British Act of Union (2 July); Irish act 1 Aug.).

Orange lodges pass resolutions against Union (Feb.–Mar.).

1801	Union of Great Britain and Ireland begins (1 Jan.).
1802	Peace of Amiens between Britain and France (27 Mar.).
1803	Renewed war between GB and France (18 May).

Rising of Robert Emmet in Dublin (23 July); Emmet convicted of high treason (19 Sept.) and executed (20 Sept.).

Thomas Russell convicted at Downpatrick of high treason (20 Oct.); executed (21 Oct.).

Michael Dwyer, in revolt in Wicklow since 1798, surrenders to government (14 Dec.).

1808	Work on site in Sackville Street for monument to Viscount Nelson begins (30 Jan.).

Controversy over proposed royal veto on appointments to Catholic bishoprics (May–Sept.); veto proposals rejected by bishops (14–15 Sept.); rise of Daniel O'Connell.

Christian Brothers, lay teaching order, founded by Edmund Rice at Waterford (Aug.).

1811	Kildare Place Society founded to conduct non-denominational schools (2 Dec.).
1813	Catholic Relief Bill introduced by Grattan in UK House of Commons (30 Apr.; defeated by 251 to 247, 24 May).
1814	Belfast Academical Institution opened (1 Feb.; 'Royal' prefixed to title, 1831).
1815	Napoleon defeated at Waterloo (18 June); end of war with France.
1816	Failure of potato crop causes famine, aggravated by typhus epidemic (Aug.–Oct.).
1817	Typhus epidemic widespread (continues till Dec. 1819, causes some 50,000 deaths).

Exchequers of GB and Ireland amalgamated as from 5 Jan., under Consolidated Fund Act (1 July 1816).

Foundation stone of Wellington obelisk in Phoenix Park laid (17 June; completed 1820).

1820	Grattan dies in London.
1821	George IV visits Ireland (12 Aug.–3 Sept.): Dunleary Harbour renamed Kingstown.

Failure of potato crop (Sept.–Nov.).

1822	Fever follows famine in west of Ireland (June; continues till Dec.).
1823	Catholic Association founded in Dublin (12 May).
1826	Irish currency assimilated with British as from 5 Jan., under Currency Act of 27 June 1825.

Act providing for uniform valuation of lands and tenements for purpose of local taxation (26 May; Richard Griffith later appointed commissioner of valuation).

Fever epidemic and collapse of textile industry in Dublin, Belfast, Cork and other towns (c. July).

General election (June–July): O'Connell successfully mobilises Catholic electors for Villiers Stuart against Lord George Beresford in County Waterford; sitting MPs similarly defeated in counties Westmeath, Louth and Monaghan by supporters of Catholic emancipation.

1828	O'Connell returned MP in by-election in Clare (24 June), defeating Vesey Fitzgerald by 2,057 votes to 982.
1829	Relief Act enabling Catholics to enter parliament, belong to any corporation, and hold higher offices in state – 'Catholic emancipation' (13 Apr.).

Act raising county franchise from 40s. to £10 freehold (13 Apr.).

	O'Connell returned unopposed for Clare (30 July; enters parliament (4 Feb. 1830) after taking new oath of allegiance).
	Non-subscribing Presbyterians withdraw from synod of Ulster (Aug.–Sept.; they form the Remonstrant Synod of Ulster, 25 May 1830).
1830	George IV dies (26 June); succeeded by William IV.
1831	'Tithe war' begins: 120 police move into Graiguenamanagh, County Kilkenny, to seize cattle in payment of the tithe (3 Mar.); 'tithe massacre' at Newtownbarry, County Wexford (18 June); twelve police killed serving processes at Carrickshock, County Kilkenny (14 Dec.).
	Scheme of primary education instituted (Nov.).
1832	Asiatic cholera appears in Belfast and Dublin (Jan.; spreads throughout Ireland and continues till 1833).
	Parliamentary Reform Act (7 Aug.): Irish seats increased from 100 to 105 and £10 franchise introduced in boroughs; electorate increased to 1.2 per cent of population.
1833	Church Temporalities Act (14 Aug.) abolishes ten bishoprics and provides for appointment of ecclesiastical commissioners.
	Tithe Arrears Act (29 Aug.).
1834	Repeal of Union debated in House of Commons on motion of O'Connell (22–30 Apr.).
	National bank founded under O'Connell's auspices in London (21 June).
	Opening of Dublin–Kingstown railway, the first in Ireland (17 Dec.).
1835	'Lichfield House compact' between whigs, radicals and O'Connellites (Feb.–Mar.).
	First and second reports of select committee of House of Commons on Orangeism presented to House (20 July).; followed by two other reports (presented on 6 Aug. and 7 Sept.).
	Thomas Drummond under-secretary (25 July 1835); dies in office (15 Apr. 1840).
	Association of Non-subscribing Presbyterians formed by combination of Remonstrant Synod, Presbytery of Antrim, and Synod of Munster.
1836	Grand Orange Lodge of Ireland decides to dissolve (14 Apr.).
	Act amalgamating county constabulary and peace preservation force into centralised police force under inspector general (20 May; 'Royal Irish Constabulary' from 1867).
1837	William IV dies (20 June); succeeded by Victoria.
1838	Father Theobald Mathew, OFM Cap., with support of William Martin, a Quaker, founds total abstinence movement at Cork (10 Apr.).
	Poor Relief Act (31 July) extends English poor law system to Ireland: elected boards of guardians, responsible to a poor law commission, set up to administer a workhouse system.
	Act converting tithe into a rent charge (15 Aug.).
1839	The 'big wind' (6–7 Jan.).
1840	O'Connell forms National Association (15 Apr.; renamed Loyal National Repeal Association, 16 July).
	General Synod of Ulster and Secession Synod combine to form General Assembly of the Presbyterian Church of Ireland (10 July).
	Municipal Reform Act (10 Aug.).
1841	Thomas Davis joins Repeal Association (17 Apr.).
	Defeat of whig ministry; Sir Robert Peel PM (20 Aug.).
	O'Connell elected lord mayor of Dublin (1 Nov.; till 1 Nov. 1842).
1842	Father Mathew's total abstinence crusade at its peak (Jan.); 3 million pledged adherents.
	First number of *Nation* – the weekly founded by Young Ireland group – Thomas Davis, Charles Gavan Duffy and John Blake Dillon.
1843	Repeal debate in Dublin corporation, Butt leading the case against O'Connell (28 Feb.–2 Mar.).
	Monster repeal meetings at Trim (9 Mar.) and Hill of Tara (15 Aug.).
	Meeting announced by O'Connell for 8 Oct. at Clontarf proscribed by government (1 Oct.); O'Connell cancels meeting.
	O'Connell charged with conspiracy (14 Oct.).

Devon Commission into state of law and practice relating to occupation of land appointed (20 Nov.; reports 14 Feb. 1845, recommending compensation for improvements and minor reforms).

1844   O'Connell and others found guilty (Jan.–Feb.); O'Connell sentenced to one year's imprisonment, etc. (30 May); judgement reversed by House of Lords (4 Sept.).

Act to establish board of charitable donations and bequests (9 Aug.).

1845   Earl of Rosse's telescope at Birr Castle comes into operation (15 Feb.) – the largest in the world; (dismantled, 1908).

Dispute between O'Connell and Young Ireland over Queen's Colleges scheme (May).

Act providing for capital grant to Maynooth College of £30,000 and increasing annual grant from £8,928 to £26,360 (30 June).

Queen's Colleges Act (31 July; see 1849).

Arrival of potato blight in Ireland reported in press (9 Sept.).

Thomas Davis dies in Dublin (16 Sept.).

Peel orders purchase in USA of £100,000 of Indian corn for Ireland (c. 9–10 Nov.).

Relief committee appointed by government (18 Nov.).

1846   Act authorising public works to relieve distress (5 Mar.).

Act authorising county relief works (5 Mar.).

Peel's act in effect repealing Corn Laws (26 June).

Peel replaced as PM by Lord John Russell (30 June).

Breach between O'Connell and Young Ireland over principle of physical force (28 July).

Complete destruction of potato crop (Aug.–Sept.).

Central Relief Committee of Society of Friends set up (13 Nov.).

1847   Irish Confederation formed (13 Jan.).

Soup kitchens system established; famine at its height (Feb.).

O'Connell dies at Genoa (15 May; funeral in Dublin, 5 Aug.).

Poor Relief Act (8 June), empowering boards of guardians to grant outdoor relief, but persons holding above one-quarter acre of land are excluded from benefit.

First collection of agricultural statistics, undertaken by constabulary (c. June).

Potato harvest good but small; corn harvest good (July).

John Mitchel breaks away from *Nation* (Dec.; starts militant *United Irishman*, 12 Feb. 1848).

1848   Revolution in Paris (22–4 Feb.); Louis-Philippe abdicates.

Treason-felony Act (22 Apr.).

Mitchel convicted under Treason-felony Act and sentenced to fifteen years' transportation (26–7 May).

Last number of *United Irishman* (27 May); first number of John Martin's *Irish Felon* (24 June) includes first three articles by James Fintan Lalor on linking repeal to land question.

General failure of potato crop (July–Sept.).

Fifth and last number of *Irish Felon* (22 July).

Young Ireland rising in Munster under William Smith O'Brien and others (July–Aug.); engagement between confederates and police near Ballinagarry, County Tipperary (29 July).

O'Brien, Thomas Francis Meagher, Terence Bellew McManus and Patrick O'Donohoe convicted of high treason and sentenced to death (7–9 Oct.; sentences commuted to transportation for life, 5 June 1849).

Cholera reappears (Nov.; continues into 1849).

1849   William Crolly, Catholic archbishop of Armagh, dies of cholera at Drogheda (6 Apr.).

Potato blight reappears (May).

Sectarian affray at Dolly's Brae, near Castlewellan, County Down (12 July).

Encumbered Estates Act providing for creation of Encumbered Estates Court (28 July).

Queen Victoria and Prince Albert in Ireland (3–12 Aug.).

Queen's Colleges at Belfast, Cork and Galway opened to students (Oct.).

1850   Paul Cullen, Catholic archbishop of Armagh (24 Feb. translated to Dublin 3 May 1852; archbishop of Dublin, 1852–78).

Tenant right conference in Dublin (6–9 Aug.), concluding in formation of Irish Tenant League.

National synod of Catholic bishops at Thurles: one of its statutes declares Queen's Colleges to be fraught with 'grave and intrinsic dangers' to Catholics (22 Aug.–10 Sept.).

Charter founding the Queen's University in Ireland (3 Sept.)

1851 Ecclesiastical Titles Act (1 Aug.), prohibiting assumption in UK of territorial titles by Catholic bishops.

Catholic Defence Association of Great Britain and Ireland formed (19 Aug.) – the 'Irish Brigade'.

1852 General election (July): about forty MPs returned in Tenant League interest.

Conference of Tenant League in Dublin: policy of independent opposition in parliament adopted (8–9 Sept.)

William Keogh and John Sadleir, members of independent Irish party, accept office in Aberdeen's ministry (19 Dec.).

1853 Act extending income tax to Ireland (28 June).

Queen Victoria and Prince Albert visit Dublin (29 Aug.–4 Sept.).

Assembly's College, Belfast, opened for theological training of Presbyterian clergy (5 Dec.).

Robert Hickson opens yard at Queen's Island, Belfast, for building iron ships (Edward J. Harland becomes manager, Dec. 1854).

1854 Act making provision for establishment of National Gallery in Dublin (10 Aug.).

Catholic University of Ireland opened (3 Nov.); J. H. Newman first rector.

1855 Emmet Monument Association formed in New York by Micheal Doheny and John O'Mahony to work for Irish independence (c. Feb.).

Cecilia Street School of Medicine opened as part of Catholic University (2 Nov.).

Gavan Duffy emigrates to Australia (6 Nov.).

1856 James Stephens, former Young Irelander, returns to Ireland from exile in France (Jan.).

Suicide of John Sadleir (17 Feb.).

Phoenix Society formed at Skibbereen by Jeremiah O'Donovan (later called O'Donovan Rossa).

1857 Sectarian rioting in Belfast (13–19 July, Sept.).

1858 Secret organisation, later known as IRB (Irish Republican Brotherhood), founded in Dublin by James Stephens (17 Mar.; parallel body, Fenian Brotherhood, founded in New York by John O'Mahony, Apr. 1859).

Act providing for creation of General Medical Council to maintain standards in medical education and for registration of medical practitioners in UK (2 Aug.).

Edward Harland buys Robert Hickson's shipyard at Belfast (see 1853) and takes into partnership Gustav Wilhelm Wolff (firm assumes name Harland & Wolff, 1 Jan. 1862).

1859 First number of *The Irish Times* (29 Mar.).

Independent Irish party splits (31 Mar); break-up of Tenant League.

Evangelical revival in Ulster; reaches its height with mass prayer-meeting in Botanic Gardens, Belfast (29 June).

1860 Series of excessively cold and wet seasons begins (Jan.; lasts till 1862, followed by droughts in 1863 and 1864); severe agricultural depression.

Napier's Land Act (28 Aug.).

Deasy's Land Act (28 Aug.).

Partry (County Mayo) evictions.

1861 John George Adair evicts forty-seven tenants on his estate at Derryveagh, County Donegal (8–10 Apr.).

American Civil War begins (12 Apr.; ends, 26 Apr. 1865).

Funeral of Terence Bellew McManus in Dublin (10 Nov.).

1862 Poor Relief Act (7 Aug.), extending provisions for outdoor relief and abolishing 'quarter acre' restriction of 1847 act.

1863 First number of *Irish People*, Fenian weekly (28 Nov.): Thomas Clarke Luby, proprietor; O'Donovan Rossa, manager; John O'Leary, editor.

1864 Laying of foundation stone of O'Connell Monument in Dublin (8 Aug.) leads to two weeks of sectarian rioting in Belfast.

Stephens declares 1865 to be the date for the Fenian insurrection (c. Aug.).

1865	Dublin International Exhibition opened in Earlsfort Terrace (9 May).
	Police raid offices of *Irish People* (15 Sept.); Rossa, Luby and O'Leary arrested; last number of paper, 16 Sept.
	Magee College, Londonderry, opened as combined arts and Presbyterian theological college (10 Oct.).
	Stephens arrested (11 Nov.); rescued from Richmond prison, Dublin (24 Nov.).
1866	Habeas corpus suspended (17 Feb.; suspension continued till 1869).
	Fenian council of war rejects Devoy's plan for an immediate rising (20–21 Feb.) Devoy arrested (23 Feb.).
	Fenian raids on Canada (Apr.–June)
	Archbishop Cullen created cardinal (22 June): first Irishman to achieve this rank.
	Stephens deposed as head centre of Fenian Brotherhood (17 Dec.)
1867	Abortive Fenian attempt to seize Chester Castle (11 Feb.).
	Fenian rising in counties of Kerry, Dublin, Cork, Limerick, Tipperary and Clare (Feb.–Mar.).
	United Brotherhood or Clan na Gael founded at New York by Jerome J. Collins (20 June).
	Act providing for establishment of Public Record Office at Four Courts, Dublin (12 Aug.).
	IRB convention at Manchester appoints Col. Thomas J. Kelly to succeed Stephens (17 Aug.).
	Rescue of Kelly and Capt. Timothy Deasy in Manchester (18 Sept.).
	Execution of Allen, Larkin and O'Brien at Manchester (23 Nov.).
	Clerkenwell explosion (13 Dec.).
1868	Irish Parliamentary Reform Act (13 July): borough franchise reduced from £8 to £4 rated occupiership; lodger franchise introduced.
	General election (Nov.): liberal victory, Gladstone PM (3 Dec.).
	Thomas O'Hagan (Lord O'Hagan, 14 June 1870) lord chancellor of Ireland (18 Dec.); first Catholic to hold this office since reign of James II.
1869	Release of forty Fenian prisoners, including Charles Joseph Kickham (Mar.).
	Amnesty Association formed in Dublin (June).
	Act disestablishing and disendowing Church of Ireland (26 July; act takes effect 1 Jan. 1871).
1870	First chapter of Kickham's *Knocknagow* published in New York *Emerald* and Dublin *Shamrock* (Mar.; whole work published in book form; Dublin, June 1873).
	Home rule movement launched by Isaac Butt in Dublin (19 May).
	Michael Davitt sentenced to fifteen years' penal servitude (18 July).
	Gladstone's first Land Act (1 Aug.).
1871	Release of thirty-three Fenian prisoners, including Devoy, Rossa, O'Leary and Luby (Jan.).
	'Westmeath Act' allowing detention without trial for agrarian offences (16 June).
	Fenian invasion of Canada (5 Oct.).
1872	Ballot Act introduces secret voting (18 July).
	Sectarian rioting in Belfast (15–20 Aug.).
1873	Home Rule Confederation of Great Britain founded at Manchester (Feb.).
	Gladstone's university bill defeated (12 Mar.).
	Home Rule conference at Rotunda, Dublin (18–21 Nov.): Home Rule League founded.
1874	General election: fifty-nine professing home rulers returned (Feb.); Gladstone resigns; Conservative ministry under Disraeli (20 Feb.).
	Butt's motion on home rule defeated in House of Commons by 458 to 61 (30 June–2 July).
1875	John Mitchel elected MP for Tipperary (16 Feb.); barred from taking his seat; re-elected (12 Mar.); dies (20 Mar.).
	Parnell retuned to parliament as member for Meath (19 Apr.).
	O'Connell centenary celebrations (5–7 Aug.).
	National synod of bishops at Maynooth (30 Aug.–20 Sept.): renews condemnation of Queen's Colleges (see 1850) and applies it to Trinity College (see 1970).

1876	'Skirmishing fund' instituted at New York by O'Donovan Rossa (Mar.).
	Catalpa rescue of six Fenian convicts from Western Australia (17–18 Apr.).
	Seventh annual convention of Clan na Gael in Philadelphia decides to form joint revolutionary directory with IRB (8–15 Aug.).
	Supreme council of IRB resolves to withdraw all support from home rule movement (20 Aug.).
1877	Parnell, Joseph Gillis Biggar, Frank Hugh O'Donnell and other Irish 'obstructives' prolong sitting of House of Commons for over twenty-four hours (31 July–1 Aug.)
	Parnell elected president of Home Rule Confederation of Great Britain in place of Butt (28 Aug.).
	First of three years of bad harvests and agricultural depression (culminating in major economic crisis in 1879).
	Davitt released from Dartmoor (19 Dec.).
1878	Earl of Leitrim murdered near Mildford, County Donegal (2 Apr.).
	Intermediate Education Act (16 Aug.).
	Davitt on lecturing tour in America (Sept.–Dec.): he and Devoy propose 'new departure' for Fenian movement.
	'New departure' announced by Fenian leaders in New York (27 Oct.).
1879	Supreme council of IRB, at Paris, rejects 'new departure' proposals presented by Davitt and Devoy (Jan.).
	Land agitation launched with meeting at Irishtown, County Mayo (20 Apr.).
	Isaac Butt dies (3 May).
	Parnell at Westport land meeting (8 June): 'hold a firm grip of your homesteads and lands'.
	Repeal of Convention Act of 1793 (21 July).
	Land League of Mayo founded at Castlebar (16 Aug.).
	Irish National Land League founded in Dublin (21 Oct.).
	Duchess of Marlborough's fund for relief of distress opened (Dec.).
1879–82	The 'land war'.
1880	Mansion House fund for relief of distress opened (Jan.).
	Parnell addresses US House of Representatives on situation in Ireland (2 Feb.).
	Parnell launches Irish National Land League of the United States (11 Mar.).
	General election (Mar.–Apr.): triumph for Parnell and Land League; Gladstone again PM (23 Apr.); William Edward Forster chief secretary for Ireland (Apr.).
	Charter founding Royal University of Ireland (27 Apr.).
	Parnell elected chairman of Irish parliamentary party (17 May).
	'Boycotting' of Capt. Charles C. Boycott, of Lough Mask House, County Mayo (25 Sept.–26 Nov.).
	Viscount Mountmorres murdered near Clonbur, County Galway (25 Sept.).
	Parnell's speech at Galway (24 Oct.).
	Ladies Land League of New York founded by Fanny Parnell (15 Oct.).
	Trial of Parnell and others for conspiracy begins in court of queen's bench (28 Dec.; ends 25 Jan. in disagreement of jury).
1881	Ladies' committee under Anna Parnell set up by Land League (26 Jan.) – origin of Ladies' Irish National Land League.
	Davitt rearrested in Dublin (3 Feb.).
	Protection of Person and Property Act (2 Mar.).
	Peace Preservation Act (21 Mar.).
	Land League of Great Britain founded in London (25 Mar.).
	First number of *United Ireland*, weekly organ of Parnellites (13 Aug.), edited by William O'Brien.
	Second Gladstone Land Act (22 Aug.): '3 Fs' legalised.
	Arrest of Parnell (13 Oct.) and other Land League leaders.
	No-rent manifesto (18 Oct.).
	New land court opened at 24 Upper Merrion Street, Dublin (20 Oct.).
	Land League proclaimed as an unlawful association (20 Oct.).
1882	Queen's University in Ireland dissolved (3 Feb.).
	'Kilmainham Treaty' (Apr.) accepted by Cabinet (2 May); Forster resigns.

Parnell, John Dillon and James J. O'Kelly released from Kilmainham (2 May); Davitt from Portland (6 May).

Lord Frederick Cavendish, new chief secretary, and Thomas Henry Burke, under-secretary, murdered in Phoenix Park (6 May; trial and execution of Invincibles, Apr.–June 1883).

Davitt at Liverpool advocates land nationalisation in preference to peasant proprietorship as principle of land settlement (6 June).

New Coercion Act (12 July).

Arrears of Rent Act (18 Aug.).

Labourers' Cottages and Allotments Act (18 Aug.).

Irish National League founded in Dublin, in succession to Land League (17 Oct.).

1883   Irish National League of America founded in Philadelphia in succession to American Land League (25–7 Apr.).

Letter of Roman Congregation of Propaganda 'De Parnellio' to Irish bishops and clergy forbidding them to take part in collection for Parnell tribute (11 May; Parnell receives cheque for over £37,000 at public meeting in Rotunda, 11 Dec.).

1884   Dynamite campaign in GB: Thomas James Clarke and three others sentenced to life imprisonment (June).

Gaelic Athletic Association founded at Thurles (1 Nov.).

Bill to redistribute parliamentary seats introduced by Gladstone (1 Dec.).

Franchise Act (6 Dec.) gives vote to householders: immense increase in Irish rural electorate.

1885   Chamberlain's first draft of central board scheme (5 Jan.).

Parnell's 'ne plus ultra' speech at Cork (21 Jan.).

Irish Loyal and Patriotic Union founded to defend Union of Great Britain and Ireland (1 May).

Chamberlain's central board scheme rejected by Cabinet (9 May).

Defeat of Gladstone's second ministry (23 June); Salisbury PM.

Act redistributing parliamentary seats (25 June).

Ashbourne Act, providing for land purchase with advance by state of entire purchase money (14 Aug.).

Labourers Act (14 Aug.).

Parnell's manifesto to Irish voters in GB calling on them to vote against Liberals in forthcoming general election (21 Nov.).

General election (23 Nov.–19 Dec.): Parnell wins eighty-five seats and holds balance between Liberals and Conservatives.

Gladstone's conversion to home rule announced prematurely by his son (17 Dec.).

1886   Salisbury's government defeated (27 Jan.); Gladstone forms his third administration (1 Feb.).

Gladstone introduces home rule bill in House of Commons (8 Apr.).

Rioting in Belfast (4–10 June, 7 July–19 Sept.).

Home rule bill defeated in House of Commons by 341 to 311, some ninety-three liberals voting with the majority (8 June).

General election (July): Gladstone defeated; Salisbury ministry formed (25 July).

'Plan of Campaign' announced in United Ireland (23 Oct.).

1887   Arthur James Balfour chief secretary (Mar.; till Aug. 1892).

'Parnellism and crime' articles published in the Times (Mar.–Dec.).

Mgr Persico, papal envoy to Ireland (7 July–24 Oct.).

New Coercion Act (19 July).

'Mitchelstown massacre' (9 Sept.).

Radicals and nationalists demonstrating in Trafalgar Square, London, against imprisonment of William O'Brien clash with police and troops: over one hundred casualties – 'Bloody Sunday' (13 Nov.).

1888   Roman circular condemning Plan of Campaign (20 Apr.). and boycotting (20 Apr.).

Parnell addresses the Eighty Club in London on Plan of Campaign and Roman circular (8 May).

Special commission appointed to investigate charges against Parnell and others (13 Aug.).

1889	Pigott forgeries exposed before special commission (20–22 Feb.).
	Parnell and Gladstone at Hawarden (8–19 Dec.: discussion on home rule).
	O'Shea files petition for divorce, citing Parnell as co-respondent (24 Dec.).
1890	Report of special commission (13 Feb.): Parnell and associates exonerated from most serious charges, including complicity in Phoenix Park murders (13 Feb.).
	Opening of Science and Art Museum and of National Library of Ireland (29 Aug.).
	First number in London of Davitt's weekly *Labour World* (26 Sept; continues till 30 May 1891).
	Hearing of O'Shea divorce suit (15, 17 Nov.); verdict against Mrs O'Shea and Parnell (17 Nov.).
	Parnell re-elected chairman of Irish parliamentary party (25 Nov.).
	Publication of Gladstone's letter to Morley urging Parnell's resignation (25 Nov.).
	Parnell's manifesto to the Irish people published (29 Nov.).
	Debates in Committee Room 15 on Parnell's leadership: majority decide against him (1–6 Dec.).
1891	Irish National Federation, organisation of anti-Parnellites, inaugurated in Dublin (10 Mar.).
	Conference in Dublin decides to form Irish Labour League (24 Mar.).
	O'Shea's divorce decree made absolute (June); Parnell marries Katharine O'Shea at Steyning, Sussex (25 June).
	Balfour Act extends facilities for land purchase and establishes congested districts board (5 Aug.).
	Death of Parnell in Brighton (6 Oct.); funeral in Dublin (11 Oct).
	John Redmond leader of Parnellites (Dec.).
1892	Ulster convention in Belfast (17 June): 12,000 delegates resolve to have nothing to do with any home rule parliament.
	General election (July): fourth Gladstone ministry formed (Aug.).
	Belfast Labour Party formed (29 Sept.): first labour party in Ireland.
1893	Gladstone introduces second home rule bill (13 Feb.).
	Report of evicted tenants commission (25 Feb.).
	Disturbances in Belfast (21–2 Apr.) as a result of second reading of home rule bill.
	Foundation of Gaelic League (31 July).
	Home rule bill passes House of Commons (2 Sept.); defeated in House of Lords (9 Sept.).
	Trade Union Congress meets in Belfast (5–9 Sept.).
1894	Resignation of Gladstone (3 Mar.); Rosebery PM.
	Irish Agricultural Organisation Society formed by Horace Plunkett (28 Apr.).
	First Irish Trade Union Congress (27–8 Apr.).
	Childers commission appointed to inquire into financial relations between GB and Ireland (26 May; final report, 5 Sept. 1896)
	Alfred Webb, home rule MP for West Waterford, elected president Indian National Congress (26 Dec.).
1895	Rosebery ministry (Lib.) defeated (11 June); Salisbury (Con.) PM (25 June).
	General election (July); defeat of Liberals.
1896	Dillon elected chairman of anti-Parnellites (18 Feb.)
	Irish Socialist Republican Party formed in Dublin (29 May); secretary James Connolly.
	Irish race convention in Dublin (1–3 Sept.)
1898	William O'Brien launches United Irish League at Westport to agitate for dividing up grazing lands among small farmers (23 Jan.).
	Ancient Order of Hibernians (Board of Erin) unites with AOH of America at Trenton, New Jersey (27 June–1 July).
	Local government act provides for creation of elected county and district councils (12 Aug.).
	First number of Connolly's *Workers' Republic* (13 Aug.).
	T. J. Clarke released from Portland (29 Sept.).
	Davitt (MP since 1892) withdraws from parliament to protest against Boer War (25 Oct.).
	Queen Victoria in Ireland (3–26 Sept.).

1899	Irish Literary Theatre founded (May).
	First number of Arthur Griffith's *United Irishman* (4 Mar.).
	First number of *An Claidheamh Soluis*, official organ of Gaelic League (18 Mar.).
1900	Redmond elected leader of reunited Irish parliamentary party (6 Feb.).
	First number of D. P. Moran's the *Leader* (1 Sept.).
	Cumman na nGaedheal founded by Griffith (30 Sept.).
1901	Queen Victoria dies (22 Jan.); succeeded by Edward VII.
	Robertson commission on university education appointed (1 July; final report 28 Feb. 1903).
	United Irish League of America formed at New York (4 Dec.).
1902	Ancient Order of Hibernians achieves unity in Ireland under Board of Erin (4 Mar.).
	Arthur James Balfour (Con.) succeeds Salisbury as PM (12 July).
	Emergence of Ulster branch of Irish Literary Theatre (Nov.; renamed Ulster Literary Theatre 1904).
	Dunraven land conference (20 Dec.; report, 3 June 1903).
1903	Irish Literary Theatre becomes Irish National Theatre Society (1 Feb.).
	Independent Orange Order formed in Belfast (11 June).
	Edward VII in Ireland (21 July–1 Aug.).
	Wyndham Land Act (14 Aug.).
1904	First instalment of Griffith's *The Resurrection of Hungary* in *United Irishman* (2 Jan.).
	Annie Fredericks Horniman adapts disused Mechanics' Institute, Abbey Street, Dublin, as a theatre and offers it rent-free to the National Theatre Society (Apr.). First performance in Abbey Theatre, 27 Dec.
1905	Ulster Unionist Council formed (Mar.).
	First Dungannon Club formed by Bulmer Hobson in Belfast (8 Mar.).
	Magheramorne manifesto of Independent Orange Order (13 July); author Robert Lindsay Crawford.
	Scheme of devolution proposed in manifesto of Dunraven's Irish Reform Association (26 Aug.).
	Sinn Féin policy proposed by Griffith (28 Nov.).
	Resignation of Balfour; Liberal administration formed by Sir Henry Campbell-Bannerman (5 Dec.).
1906	General election: victory for Liberals (Jan.).
	First number of *Sinn Féin* edited by Griffith (5 May).
	Fry Commission to inquire into Trinity College, Dublin (2 June; reports, 31 Aug., 12 Jan. 1907).
	Dudley Commission on congestion in Ireland (20 July; reports, 14 Nov., 5 May 1908).
	Peace Preservation Act of 1881 expires (31 Dec.): controls on possession and importation of arms relaxed.
1907	Sinn Féin League inaugurated through amalgamation of Dungannon Club with Cumann na nGaedheal (21 Apr.).
	Irish International Exhibition opens at Ballsbridge, Dublin (4 May; ends, 9 Nov.).
	Irish council bill (May–June).
	Theft of state jewels from Dublin Castle discovered (6 July).
	Mutiny of police in Belfast (24 July).
	Pius X issues '*Ne temere*' decree on mixed marriages (2 Aug.).
	Evicted Tenants Act (28 Aug.).
	Sinn Féin League amalgamates with National Council (5 Sept.; name 'Sinn Féin' adopted Sept. 1908).
1908	C. J. Dolan defeated as Sinn Féin candidate for North Leitrim (21 Feb.).
	Herbert Henry Asquith PM (8 Apr.).
	Irish Universities Act, providing for institution of National University of Ireland and the Queen's University of Belfast (1 Aug.).
	Old Age Pensions Act (1 Aug.).
	Patrick Pearse opens St Enda's School for Boys (8 Sept.).
	Irish Transport and General Workers' Union formed; James Larkin general secretary (29 Dec.).
1909	David Lloyd George introduces 'people's budget' (29 Apr.).

	Fianna Éireann, headed by Countess Markievicz, formed by Bulmer Hobson (16 Aug.) Birrell's Land Act (3 Dec.) gives powers of compulsory purchase to congested districts board.
1910	General election (Jan.–Feb.): Irish party hold balance.
	Sir Edward Carson elected chairman of Irish Unionist Party (21 Feb.)
	Edward VII dies (6 May): succeeded by George V.
	James Connolly's *Labour in Irish History* first published in book form in Dublin (Nov.).
	First number of IRB monthly, *Irish Freedom*, edited by Patrick McCartan (Nov.; suppressed Dec. 1914)
	General election (Dec.): Irish party again hold balance.
1911	George V in Dublin and neighbourhood (7–12 July).
	Parliament act (18 Aug.).
1912	Winston Churchill visits Belfast (8 Feb.) and with Redmond addresses large crowd on home rule in Celtic Park.
	Andrew Bonar Law at demonstration at Balmoral, Belfast, pledges support of Belfast unionists for Ulster resistance to home rule (9 Apr.).
	Titanic, White Star line, built in Belfast by Harland and Wolff, sinks on maiden voyage to New York (14–15 Apr.).
	Solemn League and Covenant subscribed in Ulster (28 Sept.).
1913	Third home rule bill passes House of Commons by 267 to 257 (16 Jan.); bill defeated in House of Lords by 326 to 69 (30 Jan.).
	Ulster Volunteer Force formally established (31 Jan.).
	Home rule bill again passes House of Commons (7 July) and is again defeated in House of Lords (15 July).
	Conflict in Dublin between workers, led by James Larkin, and employers, led by William Martin Murphy (30 Aug.–1 Sept.).
	Lockout of workers by Employers' Federation begins (2 Sept.; some 25,000 workers locked out by 22 Sept.; lockout continues till Feb. 1914).
	Provisional government of Ulster, backed by Ulster Volunteer Force, provided for (24 Sept.).
	Æ's open letter 'To the Masters of Dublin' published in the *Irish Times* (7 Oct.).
	Irish Citizen Army founded (19 Nov.).
	Irish Volunteers founded (25 Nov.).
1914	The 'Curragh incident' (20 Mar.).
	Cumman na mBan founded as women's counterpart to Irish Volunteers (2 Apr.).
	Ulster Volunteers' gun-running at Larne, Bangor, and Donaghadee (24–5 Apr.)
	Home rule bill passes House of Commons for third time (25 May).
	James Joyce's *Dubliners* published (15 June).
	Murder of Archduke Franz Ferdinand at Sarajevo (28 June).
	Buckingham Palace conference (21–24 July).
	Austrian ultimatum to Serbia (23 July).
	Howth gun-running (26 July).
	Kilcoole gun-running (1–2 Aug.).
	Britain declares war on Germany (4 Aug.).
	Supreme council of IRB decides on insurrection before end of war (Sept.).
	Third home rule bill receives royal assent but its operation is suspended (18 Sept.).
	Redmond, at Woodenbridge, County Wicklow, appeals to Irish Volunteers to serve 'not only in Ireland itself but wherever the firing line extends, in defence of right, of freedom and religion in this war' (20 Sept.); MacNeill and other members of original committee of Volunteers repudiate Redmond's leadership (24 Sept.).
1915	*Lusitania* sunk off Old Head of Kinsale (7 May).
	Coalition ministry formed under Lloyd George; includes Bonar Law and Carson (25 May).
	Pearse's oration at funeral of O'Donovan Rossa (1 Aug.).
1916	The *Aud* arrives in Tralee Bay (20 Apr.).
	Casement lands at Banna Strand (21 Apr.).
	Easter Rising begins in Dublin (24 Apr.).

Francis Sheehy-Skeffington and two others murdered by Capt. J. C. Bowen-Colthurst (26 Apr.).

Pearse orders surrender (29 Apr.)

Execution of fifteen leaders of rising (3–12 May).

Casement hanged (3 Aug.).

Lloyd George PM of coalition government (7 Dec.; continues till Oct. 1922).

1917   Count Plunkett elected as Sinn Féin candidate for North Roscommon (5 Feb.).

Revolution in Russia (8–15 Mar.); abdication of Tsar Nicholas II (15 Mar.) (O. S. 23 Feb.–2 Mar.).

Éamon de Valera elected as Sinn Féin candidate for East Clare (10 July).

Irish convention meets in Trinity College Dublin (25 July; last meeting 5 Apr. 1918).

1918   Report of Irish convention published (12 Apr.).

One-day general strike (except in Ulster) against conscription (23 Apr.).

Mail boat *Leinster* sunk by German submarine between Kingstown and Holyhead; some 500 drowned (10 Oct.).

End of First World War (11 Nov.).

Act entitling women to sit and vote in House of Commons (21 Nov.).

General election (14–28 Dec.): Sinn Féin 73, home-rulers 6, unionists 25, independent unionists 6. Countess Markievicz, Sinn Féin MP, first woman elected to House of Commons.

1919   War of Independence begins with ambush at Soloheadbeg, County Tipperary (21 Jan.; ends July 1921).

Sinn Féin representatives meet in Dublin as Dáil Éireann (21 Jan.).

Dáil Éireann adopts provisional constitution and declaration of independence (21 Jan.).

De Valera elected president of Dáil Éireann (1 Apr.).

Dáil resolves that Irish Volunteers must swear allegiance to Irish Republic and to Dáil (20 Aug.; Volunteers become known as IRA).

1920   First enrolments of 'Black and Tans' (2 Jan.).

Disturbances in Derry (Apr., May, June).

Disturbances in Belfast, expulsions of Catholics from shipyards and engineering works (21–4 July).

More disturbances in Belfast (22–3 Aug.): some thirty deaths; curfew imposed.

Black and Tan raid on Balbriggan, County Dublin (20 Sept.).

Terence MacSwiney, lord mayor of Cork, dies in Brixton prison on seventy-fourth day of hunger strike (25 Oct.).

'Bloody Sunday' (21 Nov.): fourteen suspected secret service agents shot dead in Dublin by IRA groups; Black and Tans fire on crowd at Gaelic football match in Croke Park, killing twelve.

Cork sacked by Black and Tans (11–12 Dec.).

Government of Ireland Act (23 Dec.), providing for subordinate parliaments and administrations at Dublin and Belfast.

1921   Carson resigns as leader of Ulster Unionists (4 Feb.); Sir James Craig elected by Ulster Unionist Council in his place.

General election to parliaments of Southern Ireland and Northern Ireland (May); all candidates nominated for Southern Ireland parliament (Sinn Féin 124, independents 4) returned unopposed; in Northern Ireland elections 40 unionists, 6 nationalists, 6 Sinn Féin returned.

Custom House, Dublin, destroyed by IRA (25 May).

House of Commons of Northern Ireland meets (7 June): Cabinet appointed under Sir James Craig (Viscount Craigavon, 1927) as PM (continues till 24 Nov. 1940).

Northern Ireland parliament opened by George V (22 June).

Truce between IRA and British army in Ireland (9 July).

Sinn Féin MPs elected to Southern Ireland parliament meet in Mansion House, Dublin, as second Dáil Éireann (16 Aug.; see 21 Jan. 1919).

Anglo-Irish Treaty signed in London (6 Dec.); involves split in Sinn Féin.

Election of Éamon de Valera as chancellor of the National University of Ireland (Dec.).

1922   Treaty approved by Dáil Éireann by 64 to 57 (7 Jan.).

Violence in Belfast; many killed (12–15 Feb., 20–22 May).

Special Powers Act, Northern Ireland (7 Apr.; made permanent 1933).

IRA declared illegal organisation by Northern Ireland government (23 May).

Northern Ireland Act, establishing Royal Ulster Constabulary (31 May).

General election for Dáil Éireann (16 June): pro-treaty majority.

Field Marshal Sir Henry Wilson assassinated in London by IRA (22 June).

Civil War begins (28 June; Four Courts destroyed 30 June).

Death of Arthur Griffith (12 Aug.).

Michael Collins killed at Béal na Bláth, County Cork (22 Aug.).

William Thomas Cosgrave elected head of provisional government by Dáil (9 Sept.): president of executive council and minister for finance (6 Dec.; continues till Mar. 1932).

Constitution of Irish Free State bill approved by Dáil (25 Oct.).

Erskine Childers convicted by military court of unlawful possession of revolver (17 Nov.; shot 24 Nov.).

First of seventy-seven executions of Irregulars by shooting (17 Nov.; last 2 May 1923).

Irish Free State Constitution Act (UK) (5 Dec.), ratifies constitution as approved by Dáil, and Anglo-Irish treaty.

1923	First meeting of United Council of Christian Churches and Religious Communions, combining representatives of Church of Ireland, Presbyterian church, and Methodist church (23 Jan.; see 1966).

Cumann na nGaedheal founded by Cosgrave as party of supporters of treaty (Mar.); in government till Mar. 1932.

End of Civil War (May).

Boyne Obelisk (memorial of battle of 1690) blown up by persons unknown (31 May).

Education Act (Northern Ireland) providing for non-denominational schools under local authority (22 June).

Irish Free State Act to establish Garda Siochána (Civic Guard) (8 Aug.).

Hogan Act, to provide for completion of land purchase in Irish Free State (9 Aug.).

Irish Free State admitted to League of Nations (10 Sept.).

1924	Opening of Belfast station (2BE) of BBC (15 Sept.).

First meeting, in London, of Boundary Commission (6 Nov.).

1925	Northern Ireland Land Act to complete land purchase in Northern Ireland (28 May).

Irish Free State act authorising Shannon hydroelectric scheme (4 July).

Morning Post publishes forecast of Boundary Commission's report (7 Nov.; report, not published till 1969, confirms prediction).

Agreement between governments of UK, Irish Free State and Northern Ireland revoking powers of Boundary Commission and maintaining existing boundary of Northern Ireland (3 Dec.).

1926	Irish Free State broadcasting station (2RN) opened in Dublin (1 Jan.).

Fianna Fáil Party launched by de Valera in Dublin (16 May).

1927	Irish Free State Act providing for establishment of Agricultural Credit Corporation (28 May).

Kevin O'Higgins, Irish Free State minister for justice, assassinated (10 July).

Irish Free State general election (9 June): Fianna Fáil largest opposition party; de Valera and Fianna Fáil enter Dáil (11 Aug.).

1928	Irish Manuscripts Commission appointed (10 Oct.); Eoin MacNeill chairman (till 1945).
1929	Proportional representation in parliamentary elections abolished in Northern Ireland (16 Apr.).
1930	First censorship board in Irish Free State appointed (12 Feb.).

Irish Free State elected to council of League of Nations (17 Sept.).

1931	An Óige (Irish Youth Hostels Association) inaugurated (7 May).

First number of *Irish Press*, founded by de Valera (5 Sept.).

Statute of Westminster (11 Dec.).

1932	Army Comrades Association formed (9 Feb.; renamed National Guard 20 July 1933).

General election in Irish Free State (16 Feb.): Cosgrave (see 1922) succeeded by de Valera (FF) as president of executive council (9 Mar.; continues till 1948).

Payment of land annuities to British government withheld by de Valera (30 June); 'economic war' with Britain begins (July; continues till 1938).

De Valera makes inaugural speech as chairman of League of Nations assembly at Geneva (26 Sept.).

Strikes, marches and riots in Belfast in protest against unemployment (4–13 Oct.).

Northern Ireland parliament buildings at Stormont, Belfast, formally opened by Prince of Wales (16 Nov.).

1933   O'Duffy dismissed as chief commissioner of Gárda Siochána (22 Feb.).

Army Comrades Association adopts blue shirt and black beret as distinctive dress (24 Mar.); association, under leadership of General Eoin O'Duffy adopts name National Guard (20 July).

National Guard proclaimed unlawful association (22 Aug.).

United Irish Party (later known as Fine Gael) launched under presidency of O'Duffy (2 Sept.).

1934   O'Duffy resigns from Fine Gael Party (21 Sept.).

Anglo-Irish 'cattle and coal' agreement (21 Dec.).

1935   Disturbances in Belfast (6–9 May, 12 July).

1936   George V dies (20 Jan.); succeeded by Edward VIII.

Irish Free State Act abolishing senate (29 May; restored 29 Dec. 1937).

IRA declared illegal in Irish Free State (18 June).

Irish Free State Act providing for formation of Aer Lingus as national airline (14 Aug.).

O'Duffy and followers leave Ireland for Spain to fight for Franco rebels as 'Irish brigade' (20 Nov.; return on 22 June 1937).

Edward VIII abdicates (11 Dec.); succeeded by George VI; Irish Free State Constitutional Amendment Act removing from constitution all reference to crown and governor general (11 Dec.); External Relations Act giving effect to abdication and recognising crown for purposes of external relations (12 Dec.).

Left-wing Irish unit led by Frank Ryan joins government forces in Spain (16 Dec.).

1937   New constitution approved by Dáil (14 June); referendum gives favourable majority of 685,105 to 526,945 (1 July).

George VI in Northern Ireland (28–9 July).

New constitution of Éire comes into effect (29 Dec.).

1938   Anglo-Irish agreement on 'treaty ports', finance and trade (25 Apr.); act of Dáil gives effect to agreement (16 May).

Douglas Hyde, first president of Éire, inaugurated (25 June; continues till June 1945).

New movement for better understanding between North and South announced (23 Dec.; becomes Irish Association for Cultural, Economic and Social Relations).

1939   First of series of IRA bomb attacks in England(16 Jan.; ends, Mar. 1940).

Offences against the State Act, Éire (14 June).

IRA bomb explosion in Coventry (25 Aug.) kills five, wounds seventy.

Second World War begins with German invasion of Poland (1 Sept.); de Valera announces government's intention to remain neutral (2 Sept.); Northern Ireland belligerent as part of UK.

Britain and France declare war on Germany (3 Sept.).

IRA raid on Magazine Fort, Phoenix Park (23 Dec.).

1940   Two emergency bills against IRA passed by Oireachtas (3 Jan.).

Act providing for Dublin Institute for Advanced Studies (19 June).

German aircraft bomb creamery at Campile, County Wexford (26 Aug.).

Viscount Craigavon, PM of Northern Ireland, dies (24 Nov.); succeeded by J. M. Andrews (continues till 20 Apr. 1943).

1941   German bombs dropped in Counties Carlow, Dublin, Kildare, Louth, Meath, Wexford and Wicklow (1–3 Jan.).

German air raids on Belfast (15–16 Apr.): over 700 killed and over 400 seriously wounded; Dublin and Dun Laoghaire fire brigades sent to assistance of Belfast.

German bombs on North Strand, Dublin: thirty-four killed, ninety injured, 300 houses destroyed or damaged (31 May).

1942   American troops arrive in Northern Ireland (Jan.); protest by de Valera.

Federated Union of Employers formed in Dublin (25 Mar.).

	IRA attacks on RUC in Dungannon (3 Apr.) and in Belfast (5 Apr.).
	Act establishing Central Bank in Dublin as currency authority, replacing Currency Commission (4 Nov.).
1943	Arts Council established in Northern Ireland (1 Feb.).
	J. M. Andrews resigns as PM of Northern Ireland (28 Apr.); succeeded by Sir Basil Brooke (Viscount Brookeborough, 4 July; continues till 25 Mar. 1963).
	Comhdháil Náisiúnta na Gaeilge, coordinating body for Irish-language organisations, formed (26 Oct.).
1944	Córas Iompair Éireann, Irish transport company, set up (8 Dec.).
1945	Act providing for Northern Ireland Housing Trust (6 Feb.).
	Congress of Irish Trade Unions formed (25 Apr.).
	'VE day' (8 May): end of war in Europe.
	Churchill's victory speech (13 May); de Valera's reply (16 May).
	Seán T. O'Kelly elected president of Éire (16 June) in succession to Douglas Hyde (see 1939, 1952).
1946	Turf Development Act, Éire, establishing Bord na Mona (1 June).
	Clann na Poblachta founded under Seán MacBride (6 July).
	Ireland's application for admission to United Nations (July–Aug.; see 1955).
	Act establishing Institute for Industrial Research and Standards in Dublin (27 Aug.).
	Act provides for setting-up of Labour Court in Dublin.
1947	Education act, Northern Ireland (27 Nov.).
	Health Act, Éire (13 Aug.): RC bishops express disapproval of some clauses, especially those concerning mother-and-child services.
1948	General election in Éire (4 Feb.): de Valera (see 1932) succeeded by John A. Costello (FG) as taoiseach, heading inter-party government (18 Feb.; continues till May 1951) (See 1951).
	Health Services Act, Northern Ireland (4 Feb.).
	Organisation for European Economic Development instituted (16 Apr.); Éire and UK members.
	An Taisce, national trust for planning and conservation in Republic, established (15 July; recognised as statutory body by ministerial regulation, 7 Sept. 1964).
	Ulster Transport Authority established (10 Aug.).
	Costello announces government's intention to repeal External Relations Act (7 Sept.).
	Judgment in High Court, Dublin, against Foyle and Bann Fisheries Ltd concerning fishing in Clonleigh, County Donegal (13 Oct.; Belfast and Dublin governments agree on joint control of Foyle fisheries, 9 July 1950; and see 1952).
	Republic of Ireland Act (21 Dec.) repeals External Relations Act, 1936, and provides for declaration of republic.
1949	North Atlantic Treaty against armed aggression signed in Washington by USA, Canada, GB, France and other states (4 Apr.).
	Éire formally declared a republic (18 Apr.).
	Convention signed in London by ten European states, including Ireland and UK, establishing Council of Europe, with seat at Strasbourg (5 May).
	Ireland Act, UK (2 June), declares that Republic of Ireland is not part of British dominions, but that it is not to be regarded as a foreign country, and that Northern Ireland shall not cease to be part of UK without consent of Northern Ireland parliament.
1950	Holy Year begins (1 Jan.).
	Act of Oireachtas implementing agreement between Dublin and Belfast governments for Erne drainage and electricity scheme (13 June; corresponding act by Northern Ireland parliament, 27 June).
	Judgment of Supreme Court, Dublin, in Tilson case (5 Aug.).
	Industrial Development Authority Act, Ireland established (20 Dec.).
	Bank strike in Republic (23 Dec.; continues till 16 Feb. 1951).
1951	Agreement between governments of Ireland and Northern Ireland on running of Great Northern Railway (9 Jan.).
	Dr Noel Browne, minister for health, resigns over 'mother-and-child' scheme (11 Apr.).
	Arts Council founded in Republic of Ireland (8 May).

General election in Republic of Ireland (30 May): Costello (see 1948) succeeded by de Valera (FF) as taoiseach (continues till June 1954) (See 1948, 1954).

Abbey Theatre, Dublin, destroyed by fire (18 July; see 1966).

1952 Social Welfare Act for coordinated system of social insurance in Republic (14 June).

Seán T. O'Kelly (see 1945) president for second term (25 June; till June 1959)

Act providing for legal adoption in Republic (13 Dec.).

Joint commission on Foyle fisheries set up by governments of Republic and Northern Ireland

1953 Comhairle Radio Éireann, appointed by Erskine Childers, minister for posts and telegraphs, with non-statutory control over broadcasting, takes office, with Maurice Gorham as director of broadcasting (1 Jan.; see 1960).

Car ferry *Princess Victoria* sinks off County Down coast (31 Jan.).

Gael-linn, financed by football pools, for promotion of Irish language, established (3 May).

Library of Alfred Chester Beatty (mining engineer, art collector, and philanthropist) containing his unique collection of oriental manuscripts, pictures, etc., officially opened at Shrewsbury Road, Dublin (8 Aug.; see 1968).

First of Thomas Davis Lectures, a continuing series, broadcast by Radio Éireann (27 Sept.).

1954 General election in Republic (18 May): de Valera (see 1951) succeeded by Costello (FG) as taoiseach, heading second inter-party government (2 June; continues till Mar. 1957) (See 1951,1957).

IRA raid on Gough Military Barracks, Armagh (12 June).

Bank officials in Republic begin working short hours (4 Dec.), leading to closure of banks till 23 Mar. 1955. (see 1950, 1966).

1955 First regular television service in Northern Ireland begins transmission from Divis (21 July).

Saor Uladh, a breakaway from IRA, attack police barracks at Rosslea, County Fermanagh (26 Nov.).

Republic admitted to United Nations Organisation (14 Dec.).

1956 Balance of payments crisis in Republic.

T.K. Whitaker appointed secretary to Republic's department of finance (30 May).

Maura Lyons, fifteen-year-old Catholic, disappears from her home in Belfast after becoming converted to Protestantism through preaching of Rev Ian Paisley (23 Oct.; reappears at Paisley's home, 10 May 1957, and is placed in remand centre; petition to make her a ward of court granted by Lord MacDermott, lord chief justice, 20 May 1957).

IRA campaign in Northern Ireland begins with attacks on border customs posts by Saor Uladh (11 Nov.; continues till Feb. 1962).

Ronnie Delaney wins gold medal at Olympic Games, Melbourne, Australia (1 Dec.).

1957 General election in Republic (5 Mar.): Costello (see 1954) succeeded by de Valera (FF) as taoiseach (20 Mar.; continues till June 1959) (See 1961).

Treaty of Rome instituting European Economic Community signed by France, West Germany, Italy, Belgium, Holland and Luxembourg (25 Mar.).

Boycott of Protestants at Fethard-on-Sea, County Wexford, begins (13 May).

Gough Monument in Phoenix Park wrecked by explosion (23 July).

1958 Act providing for establishment of An Foras Talúntais (Agricultural Research Institute) (19 Feb.).

General election in Northern Ireland (20 Mar.): Unionists 37, Nationalists 7, Independent Nationalists 1, NILP 4, Independent Labour 1, Republican Labour 1, Independent 1 (See 1962).

Aer Lingus service to North America inaugurated (28 Apr.).

Economic Development, by T. K. Whitaker and others, completed (May; published Dec.).

Act for establishing Ulster Folk Museum (10 June; see 1964).

Fifty Irish officers appointed as observers with United Nations peacekeeping forces in Lebanon (July; see 1978).

First *Programme for Economic Expansion* laid by the government before each House of the Oireachtas (Nov.; see 1963).

First programme of economic expansion published (11 Nov.).

1959   Congress of Irish Trade Unions and Irish Trade Union Congress decide to combine in Irish Congress of Trade Unions, with separate committee for Northern Ireland (10 Feb.).

De Valera elected president of Republic (17 June) in succession to Seán T. O'Kelly (see 1952; continues till 1966).

Seán Lemass (FF), minister for industry and commerce, elected taoiseach in succession to de Valera (23 June; continues till Nov. 1966).

Rev Donald Soper prevented from delivering address at open-air meeting at Ballymena by heckling of Paisley and others (1 Aug.; Paisley fined £5 for causing breach of the peace).

General election in UK (8 Oct.): in GB – Con. 333, Lab. 258, Nat. Lib and Con. 20, Lib. 6, others 1; in Northern Ireland – Unionists 12 (see 1964)

Agreement between UK and Republic on Sir Hugh Lane pictures announced by Lemass (12 Nov.).

1960   Act of Oireachtas establishing broadcasting authority (Radio Éireann) of nine members to conduct national radio and television services (12 Apr.; see 1953; name altered to 'Radio Telefís Éireann' by act of 8 Mar. 1966).

Ireland sends troops to serve with UN forces in Congo (27 July).

Appointment of commission on higher education (Sept.; report, Feb. 1967).

1961   Ireland applies for membership of European Economic Community (1 Aug.).

Ireland enters UNESCO (3 Oct.).

General election in Republic (4 Oct.): FF 70, FG 47, Lab. 16, Clann na Talmhan 2, National Progressive Democratic Party 2, Clann na Poblachta 1, independents and others 6 (see 1957, 1965)

Television service of Radio Éireann inaugurated (31 Dec.).

1962   General election in Northern Ireland (31 May): Unionists 34, Nationalists 9, NILP 4, Independent Labour 1, Republican Labour 1, Irish Labour 1, independent 1 (see 1957, 1965).

First transmission of RTÉ television series *The Late, Late Show*: compère Gay Byrne (6 July).

Motorway (M1) from Belfast to Lisburn opened (10 July); first in Ireland.

1963   Capt. Terence O'Neill succeeds Viscount Brookeborough as PM of Northern Ireland (25 Mar.; continues till 28 Apr. 1969).

Pope John XXIII dies (3 June; Paisley leads protest against action of Belfast City Council in paying tribute to him, 4 June).

John F. Kennedy, President of USA, in Ireland (26–9 June).

Second Programme for Economic Expansion laid by the government before each House of the Oireachtas (Aug.); part II follows in July 1964; see 1969.

Second Programme of Economic Expansion in Republic published (22 Aug.).

Committee under Sir John Lockwood appointed to review facilities for higher education in Northern Ireland (20 Nov.; report, 10 Feb. 1965) .

Survey team under Patrick Lynch appointed, in association with OECD, to estimate technological needs of Republic (Nov.; see 23 Dec. 1965).

President John F. Kennedy assassinated in Dallas, Texas (22 Nov.).

1964   Republic decides to send troops to serve with UN forces in Cyprus (24 Mar.).

An Forus Forbartha (National Institute for Physical Planning and Construction Research) incorporated (26 Mar.).

Ulster Folk Museum opened, at Cultra, County Down (2 July).

Northern Ireland Committee of Irish Congress of Trade Unions recognised by Northern Ireland government (24 Aug.).

Rioting in Belfast (28 Sept.–3 Oct.).

General election in UK(15 Oct.): in GB – Lab. 317, Con . 292, Lib. 9; in Northern Ireland – Unionists 12; Harold Wilson (Lab.) succeeds Alec Douglas-Home (Con.) as PM (16 Oct.; continues till June 1970) (See 1959,1966).

1965   Lemass, taoiseach, visits O'Neill, PM of Northern Ireland, in Belfast (14 Jan.).
Nationalist Party decides to accept role of official opposition in Northern Ireland parliament, Edward McAteer leader in House of Commons (2 Feb.).
O'Neill visits Lemass in Dublin (9 Feb.).
Report of Lockwood Committee (10 Feb.) recommends second university for Northern Ireland, at Coleraine (see 1 Oct. 1968) and an Ulster polytechnic (see 1 Apr. 1971).
General election in Republic (7 Apr.): FF 72, FG 47, Lab. 22, Clann na Poblachta 1, others 2 (see 1961, 1969).
New Towns Act, Northern Ireland (24 June; leads to establishment of new town, Craigavon, near Portadown).
W. T. Cosgrave dies (16 Nov.).
General election in Northern Ireland (25 Nov.): Unionists 36, Nationalists 9, NILP 2, Republican Labour 2, National Democratic Party 1, Liberal 1, independent 1.
Anglo-Irish Free Trade Agreement (14 Dec.).
Act altering law relating to succession in Republic (22 Dec.).
Investment in Education: Report of the Survey Team Appointed. . . in October 1962, vol. i, published (23 Dec.; vol. ii, 8 August 1966).

1966   RTÉ television series, *The Course of Irish History*, edited by T. W. Moody and F. X. Martin (24 Jan.–13 June; published in book form, 26 Jan. 1967).
Nelson Pillar, Dublin, wrecked by explosion (8 Mar.).
General election in UK (31 Mar.): in GB – Lab. 364, Con. 239, National Lib. and Con. 3, Lib. 12; in Northern Ireland – Unionists 11, Republican Labour 1. (See 1964, 1970)
Commemoration of fiftieth anniversary of Easter rising begins (10 Apr.).
Ulster Volunteer Force, first of Protestant paramilitary organisations, founded (Apr./May).
Banks throughout Ireland closed by strike of junior officials (6 May; reopened to public, in Northern Ireland on 21 June, in Republic on 5 Aug.; see 1954, 1970).
De Valera re-elected president of Republic (1 June; continues till May 1973).
Paisley demonstrates outside Church House, Belfast, against 'Romeward trend in presbyterian church' (6 June).
Catholic bishops, as trustees of Maynooth College, announce proposal to develop it as 'an open centre of higher studies, admitting students of both sexes, clerical and lay'.
Peter Ward, Catholic barman (aged 18) shot dead in Malvern Street, Belfast (26 June; Gusty Spence and other UVF men convicted of the murder, 14 Oct.).
UVF declared illegal organisation by Northern Ireland government (28 June).
First public performance in new Abbey Theatre, Dublin (18 July).
Paisley and others each fined £30 for unlawful assembly on 6 June (19 July; refusing to pay fine and enter into recognisances to keep the peace, they are imprisoned, 26 July–19 Oct.).
First section of Belfast–Ballymena motorway (M2) opened (24 Oct.).
Ulster Council of Christian Churches and Religious Communions in Ireland (see 1923) renamed Irish Council of Churches (4 Nov.).
Lemass (see 1959) announces intention to resign as taoiseach (8 Nov.); Jack Lynch elected leader of Fianna Fáil party by 52 votes to 19 for George Colley, Charles J. Haughey having withdrawn his candidature (9 Nov.).
Lemass resigns; Jack Lynch elected to succeed him (10 Nov.; continues till Mar. 1973).
Seán T. O'Kelly, president of Republic, 1945–59, dies (25 Nov.).
Meeting in London between Lynch, taoiseach, and Wilson, PM, for discussion of common interests of Ireland and Great Britain in relation to European Economic Community (19 Dec.).

1967   Northern Ireland Civil Rights Association (NICRA) formed (29 Jan.).
Act to establish An Chomhairle Óiliuna (AnCo), industrial training authority (7 Mar.).
Commission on Higher Education, 1960–67, presentation and summary of report published (22 Mar.).; recommendations include: National University to be defederated and its constituent colleges to become independent universities; Trinity College Dublin to remain a separate university; university governing bodies to be reformed; Council of

Irish Universities and Commission for Higher Education to be set up.

Donogh O'Malley, Republic minister for education, announces government's intention to combine Trinity College Dublin and University College Dublin in one university of Dublin (18 Apr.; strong opposition to plan in both colleges eventually results in its abandonment).

Republic and UK reapply for membership of EEC (11 May; see 1972).

Agreement between Republic of Ireland and Northern Ireland for linking electricity system by line from Maynooth to Tandragee (5 Oct.).

Lynch visits O'Neill at Stormont, Belfast (11 Dec.).

O'Neill visits Lynch in Dublin (8 Jan.).

Sir Alfred Chester Beatty, first honorary citizen of Ireland (1956), dies aged 92 (20 Jan.); in his will his library (see 1953) becomes the property of the Irish nation (9 Sept.).

Donogh O'Malley dies (10 Mar.) aged 47.

Austin Currie, nationalist MP, 'squats' in house at Caledon, County Tyrone (20 June), after protesting against its allocation by Dungannon Rural District Council to a single girl, aged 19.

'Lenihan plan' for higher education announced by Republic minister for education (6 July): NUI to be dissolved; UCC and UCG to become separate universities; TCD and UCD to be combined but each to retain its identity; Higher Education Authority and Conference of Irish Universities to be established.

Paul VI encyclical, *Humanae Vitae*, condemning artificial forms of contraception (29 July).

Civil-rights march (first of a series) from Coalisland to Dungannon, County Tyrone (24 Aug.).

First meeting of Higher Education Authority (12 Sept.); Dr Tarlach Ó Raifeartaigh chairman.

Maynooth College admits first lay students for degree courses (14 Sept.).

New University of Ulster opened at Coleraine (1 Oct.).

William Craig, minister of home affairs, Northern Ireland, bans intended civil-rights march and Apprentice Boys' parade in Derry announced for 5 Oct. (3 Oct.).

Clash between civil rights marchers and police in Derry (5 Oct.), followed by rioting (5–6 Oct.).

Derry Citizens' Action Committee formed (9 Oct.).

Student demonstration in Belfast; People's Democracy formed (9 Oct.).

Referendum to amend Republic constitution so as to abolish proportional representation heavily defeated (16 Oct.).

O'Neill announces five-point reform programme for Northern Ireland (22 Nov.) conceding NICRA demands except 'one man one vote' in local-government elections. William Craig dismissed as Northern Ireland minister of home affairs (11 Dec.).

1969   People's Democracy march from Belfast to Derry (1–4 Jan.); marchers ambushed by militant Protestants at Burntollet Bridge, County Derry (4 Jan.).

Brian Faulkner, minister of commerce, resigns (23 Jan.), succeeded by Roy Bradford (24 Jan.).

New Ulster Movement launched (6 Feb.).

General election in Northern Ireland (24 Feb.): Unionists 36 (24 pro-O'Neill, 12 anti-O'Neill), Independent Unionists 3, Nationalists 6, NILP 2, Republican Labour 2, Independents 3 (see 1965, 1973).

Cameron commission appointed to investigate violence in Northern Ireland since 5 Oct. 1968 (3 Mar.); its report (12 Sept.) very critical of conduct of RUC.

Third programme: Economic and Social Development 1969–72, laid by the government before each House of the Oireachtas (Mar.).

Explosions at electricity substation at Castlereagh, near Belfast (30 Mar.), and at Belfast city reservoir (20 Apr.), caused by Protestant extremists.

Rioting in Derry (19 Apr., 12–16 July, 12–14 Aug.); at request of Northern Ireland government British troops move in.

O'Neill wins small majority of Unionist Party for 'one man one vote' principle in local government elections (23 Apr.).

O'Neill resigns as PM of Northern Ireland (28 Apr.); succeeded by James Chichester-Clark (1 May; continues till Mar. 1971).

General election in Republic (18 June): FF 75, FG 50, Lab. 18, independent 1 (see 1965, 1973).

UVF bomb explodes at RTÉ headquarters, Dublin, first of a series (5 Aug.).

Rioting in Belfast (2–5, 15 Aug.); British troops move in (15 Aug.).

'Downing Street Declaration' (19 Aug.), joint communiqué by UK and Northern Ireland ministers on responsibilities of UK government for Northern Ireland and on cooperation between the two governments to restore normality there.

Joint communiqué by PMs of UK and Northern Ireland: GOC will have overall responsibility for security in Northern Ireland (19 Aug.).

British government issues seven-point statement, 'The Downing Street Declaration' (19 Aug.), stating its ultimate responsibility for the protection of the people of Northern Ireland, welcoming reforms already made by the Northern Ireland government, and reaffirming that every citizen of Northern Ireland is 'entitled to the same equality of treatment and freedom from discrimination as obtains in the rest of the United Kingdom.'

Joint communiqué issued by governments of UK and Northern Ireland on measures being taken by Northern Ireland government to implement reforms indicated in Downing Street Declaration and marking out areas in which it is agreed that effective reforms are fundamental to the creation of confidence (29 Aug.).

Report of Hunt Committee (10 Oct.) on reform of police.

Northern Ireland Electoral Law Act (25 Nov.): qualifying age lowered to 18; 'one man one vote' in local government elections.

Act to establish Ulster Defence Regiment, part-time security force under army control (18 Dec.).

Press report (28 Dec.) of split in IRA between 'Officials' and 'Provisionals'.

1970   Split between 'Officials' and 'Provisionals' at Sinn Féin convention in Dublin (11 Jan.)

Banks in Republic restrict service owing to labour dispute (2 Mar.); banks closed (30 Apr.); reopened 17 Nov.; (see 1966, 1976).

Act establishing police authority etc. in Northern Ireland (26 Mar.). Easter rising commemorations lead to rioting in Derry, Armagh and Belfast (28 Mar.–2 Apr.); beginning of fighting between republicans and British army.

Agreement between TCD and NUI on distribution of certain faculties between them (7 Apr.).

Alliance Party, combining liberal Protestants and Catholics in Northern Ireland, founded 21 Apr.).

'B Specials' disbanded and their duties transferred to Ulster Defence Regiment (30 Apr.).

Macrory Report on new structure of local government in Northern Ireland (29 May); general acceptance by NI government announced (17 Dec.).

Bernadette Devlin, MP, arrested (26 June), leading to renewed demonstrations in Derry and Belfast (26–9 June); Provisional IRA in action for first time, in Belfast.

Charles J. Haughey, Republic minister for finance, and Neil Blaney, minister for agriculture, dismissed by Lynch (6 May); arrested on charges of illegal importation of arms for IRA (28 May); Blaney discharged (2 July); Haughey acquitted (23 Oct.).

General election in UK (18 June): in GB – Con. 322, Lab. 288, Lib. 6, others 2; in Northern Ireland – Unionists 8, Protestant Unionist 1, Republican Labour 1, Unity 2 (see Feb. 1974); Wilson (see 1964) succeeded as PM by Edward Heath (Con.) (19 June; continues till Mar. 1974).

Catholic bishops announce removal of restrictions on Catholics attending Trinity College, Dublin (25 June).

Social Democratic and Labour Party, Northern Ireland, formed by combination of opposition MPs (21 Aug.); leader Gerry Fitt.

Irish School of Ecumenics (director Rev Michael Hurley, SJ) inaugurated at Milltown Park by Rev Eugene Carson Blake, general secretary of World Council of Churches (9 Nov.).

1971   First British soldier killed in Belfast (6 Feb.).

Fighting between Provisional IRA and Officials in Belfast (10 Mar.).

Chichester-Clark (see 1969) resigns as PM (20 Mar.); succeeded by Brian Faulkner (23 Mar.; continues till 24 Mar. 1972).

Seán Lemass (taoiseach 1959–66) dies (11 May).

Reintroduction of internment without trial (9 Aug.): 342 arrested.

Ulster Defence Association (UDA), paramilitary organisation of working-class Protestants, emerges in Belfast (Aug.).

Tripartite talks at Chequers between Heath, Lynch and Faulkner (27–8 Sept.).

Discovery-well in gas field off Old Head of Kinsale completed (7 Nov.).

Senator John Barnhill shot dead at his home near Strabane by Officials (12 Dec.).

1972   Treaty of accession to EEC signed in Brussels by Republic, UK and Denmark (22 Jan.)

'Bloody Sunday': thirteen civilians shot dead by paratroopers in Derry, following banned civil rights march (30 Jan.); Lynch declares 2 Feb. day of national mourning (31 Jan.); British embassy in Dublin burned (2 Feb.).

Bomb explosion, work of Officials, at officers' mess in Aldershot, killing six civilians (22 Feb.).

Attempt to assassinate John Taylor, Northern Ireland minister of state, at Armagh (25 Feb.).

Explosion at Abercorn Restaurant, Belfast (4 Mar.).

Marcus McCausland shot dead near Derry by Officials (6 Mar.).

Faulkner's government resigns, having refused to accept transfer of responsibility for security from Stormont to Westminster; Northern Ireland parliament and government suspended; direct rule introduced under William Whitelaw as secretary of state for Northern Ireland (24 Mar.; Northern Ireland parliament abolished, 18 July 1973).

Republic sets up Special Criminal Court, to consist of three judges without a jury, under Offences against the State Act, 1939 (26 May).

Officials suspend operations in Northern Ireland (29 May).

Truce between Provisional IRA and British army (26 June; continues till 9 July).

'Bloody Friday' in Belfast (21 July): twenty-two explosions by Provisional IRA, killing 19 and injuring 130.

Whitelaw's green paper, *The Future of Northern Ireland*, published (30 Oct.).

Seán MacStíofáin, Provisional IRA chief of staff, arrested by Republic police (19 Nov.), after giving an interview to RTÉ reporter Kevin O'Kelly; interview broadcast later that day. RTÉ Authority dismissed by government (24 Nov.) over broadcast of MacStíofáin interview.

Referendum in Republic reduces minimum age for voting to 18 and approves omission from constitution of special position of Roman Catholic Church (7 Dec.).

1972 is peak year for violence in Northern Ireland: 467 killed, out of total killings of 678 since 1969.

1973   Republic becomes member of EEC along with UK and Denmark (1 Jan.).

Car bomb explosion in Dublin, killing one and injuring seventeen (20 Jan.).

General election in Republic (28 Feb.): FF 69, FG 54, Lab. 19, independents 2; majority for Fine Gael–Labour coalition; Lynch (see 1966) succeeded as taoiseach by Liam Cosgrave (FG) heading inter-party government (14 Mar.; continues till June 1977).

Two car-bomb explosions in London, killing one and injuring 180 (8 Mar.).

Act providing for assembly of seventy-eight in Northern Ireland, to be elected by proportional representation (3 May).

Erskine Hamilton Childers elected president of Republic (30 May; continues till 17 Nov. 1974).

Elections in Northern Ireland to new district councils, first to be held since 1967 (30 May); final results: Official Unionists 210, Loyalist coalition 81, SDLP 82, Alliance 63, others 83 (total 519).

General election for Northern Ireland assembly (28 June); final results: Official Unionists 23, Alliance 8, NILP 1, (total pro-assembly unionists 32); Unpledged Unionists 10, Loyalist Coalition 15, other loyalists 2 (total dissident unionists 27); SDLP 19 (total membership 78) (See 1969, 1975).

Northern Ireland Constitution Act (UK) (18 July).

First meeting of Northern Ireland Assembly ends in disorder (31 July).

Heath and Cosgrave meet at Baldonnell Aerodrome, County Dublin (17 Sept.).

First inter-church meeting at Ballymascanlon, County Louth, attended by representatives of all main churches in Ireland (26 Sept.); the first of an annual series of ecumenical conferences.

Six oil-producing countries in Persian Gulf increase price of crude oil from $3 to $8 per barrel (16 Oct.); to $11.50 on 23 Dec.; world economic recession follows.

Official Unionists, Alliance and SDLP agree to form 'power-sharing' executive under Faulkner (22 Nov.).

United Ulster Unionist Council, combination of loyalist parties, formed to oppose power-sharing (6 Dec.).

Whitelaw (see 1972) succeeded by Francis Pym as secretary of state for Northern Ireland (2 Dec.; continues till Mar. 1974).

Conference at Sunningdale, Berkshire, between representatives of Irish and British governments and of Northern Ireland executive designate (6–9 Dec.), resulting in agreement on status of Northern Ireland, setting up of a Council of Ireland and cooperation between the two Irish governments, including measures to bring to justice persons committing crimes of violence, however motivated, in any part of Ireland (9 Dec.).

1974	Northern Ireland executive takes office under Faulkner (1 Jan.).

Bomb kills eleven in bus carrying army personnel to Catterick, Yorkshire (4 Feb.).

General election in UK (28 Feb.): in GB – Lab. 301, Con. 297, Lib. 14, others 11; in Northern Ireland – Unionists 7, DUP 1, Vanguard Unionist Progressive Party 3, SDLP 1 (United Ulster Unionist Council (see 6 Dec. 1973) gain eleven out of twelve seats) (see 1970, Oct. 1974); Wilson succeeds Heath (see 1970) as PM (4 Mar.; continues till Apr. 1976); Merlyn Rees (Lab.) succeeds Pym (see 1973) as secretary of state for Northern Ireland (continues till Sept. 1976).

Ulster Workers' Council declares general strike (14 May). Three car-bomb explosions in Dublin kill twenty-five, and one in Monaghan kills six (17 May).

Faulkner and unionist members of executive resign (28 May).

Northern Ireland assembly prorogued and direct rule from Westminster reimposed (29 May); strike called off.

UK act providing for constitutional convention on Northern Ireland (17 July).

General election in UK (10 Oct.): in GB – Lab. 319, Con. 277, Lib. 13, others 14; in Northern Ireland – Unionists 6, DUP 1, Vanguard Unionist Progressive Party 3, SDLP 1, independent 1 (see Feb. 1974, 1979).

Erskine Childers (president of Republic 1973–4) dies (17 Nov.); Cearbhall Ó Dálaigh elected unopposed to succeed him (3 Dec.; continues till Oct. 1976).

Richard Burke, minister for education, announces new plan for higher education (16 Dec.): UCD to become independent university, TCD to retain independence with loss of certain faculties.

1975	General election for Northern Ireland convention (1 May): Unionist Party of Northern Ireland 5; Official Unionist Party 19; DUP 12; Vanguard Unionist Party 14; NILP 1; SDLP 17; Alliance 8; independents 2 (total membership 78); convention meets 8 May (see 1973, 1982).

Éamon de Valera dies, aged 92 (29 Aug.).

Dr Tiede Herrema kidnapped in Limerick (3 Oct.); released after eighteen days' siege of house in Monasterevin (7 Nov.).

Convention votes by 42 to 31 to present report of United Ulster Unionist Council (rejecting power-sharing) as report of convention, while appending minority report (7 Nov.).

Detention without trial in Northern Ireland ends (5 Dec.).

1976	John A. Costello, taoiseach 1948–51 and 1954–7, dies, aged 84 (5 Jan.).

Northern Ireland convention dissolved and report rejected by UK government (5 Mar.; see 23 Oct. 1982).

James Callaghan (Lab.), succeeds Wilson (see 1974) as PM of UK (5 Apr.; continues till May 1979).

National Trust Archive, for historical records of Irish architecture, established (12 April; title changed to Irish Architectural Archive, 9 June 1981).

Strike of bank officials closes banks in Republic (28 June); banks reopen 6 Sept. (See 1966, 1970).

Bomb explosions in Special Criminal Court, Dublin: 4 prisoners escape (15 July).

Christopher Ewart-Biggs, UK ambassador to Republic, and Judith Cooke, civil servant, killed by landmine at Sandyford, County Dublin (21 July).

Galway and Maynooth College to become independent universities (30 July).

Deaths of three children struck by car driven by Provo pursued by soldiers in Belfast (10 Aug.) leads to movement called 'Peace People' headed by Mairead Corrigan and Betty Williams.

Faulkner announces intention to retire from politics (18 Aug.; succeeded as leader of Unionist Party of Northern Ireland by Anne Letitia Dickson, 15 Sept.).

Roy Mason succeeds Rees (see 1974) as secretary of state for Northern Ireland (10 Sept.; continues till May 1979).

President Ó Dálaigh, after being described by Patrick Donegan, minister for defence, as 'a thundering disgrace' (18 Oct.), resigns to protect the dignity of his office (22 Oct.); Patrick Hillery returned unopposed to succeed him (9 Nov.).

Heritage Trust, to reconcile economic development and conservation of the physical heritage of Ireland, established (27 Oct.).

Rally of Peace People from North and South at new bridge over Boyne at Drogheda (5 Dec.).

1977   Treasures of Ireland, covering from 1500 BC to 1500 AD, loaned by National Museum, Trinity College Dublin and Royal Irish Academy, go on public exhibition to different centres in USA, 1979–82, to Paris, Cologne, Berlin, Amsterdam and Copenhagen, 1982–4.

Brian Faulkner (created Lord Faulkner, Jan.) dies in riding accident, aged 56 (3 Mar.).

General election in Republic (June): FF 84, FG 43, Lab. 17, others 4; Cosgrave (see 1973) succeeded as taoiseach by Lynch (FF) (5 July; continues till Dec. 1979); Cosgrave succeeded in leadership of Fine Gael by Garret FitzGerald (see 1973, 1981).

1978   Cearbhall Ó Dálaigh (president 1974–6) dies aged 67 (21 Mar.).

Lynch, taoiseach, addresses special session on disarmament at United Nations General Assembly (25 May).

Irish battalion sent to Lebanon to serve with United Nations peacekeeping forces there (June).

High Court declares portion of Wood Quay site, Dublin, to be a national monument, the first such declaration by an Irish court (30 June; see 1 June 1979).

1979   Whiddy Island disaster (8 Jan.): the 150,000-ton French oil-tanker Betelgeuse explodes at Gulf Oil terminal on Whiddy Island, Bantry Bay, killing fifty people; inquiry (May–Dec.), conducted by Judge Declan Costello in Dublin, finds owners of tanker and Gulf Oil responsible (report of inquiry published July 1980).

European Monetary System instituted (13 Mar.); Republic a member, UK not; Republic announces ending of one-for-one parity with sterling (30 Mar.).

General election in UK (3 May): in GB – Con. 339, Lab. 269, Lib. 11, others 4; in Northern Ireland – Official Unionists 5, DUP 3, SDLP 1, others 3; Callaghan (Lab.; see 1976) succeeded as PM by Margaret Thatcher (Con.; 4 May); Mason (see 1976) succeeded by Humphrey Atkins as secretary of state for Northern Ireland (continues till Sept. 1981) (See Oct. 1974).

To halt destruction of national monument at Wood Quay, Dublin, for building of civic offices, site occupied peacefully by group of distinguished citizens (1–20 June; see 30 June 1978).

Citizens of the nine member states of EEC vote for 410 representatives (MEPs) in first direct elections to European parliament (7 June): Republic returns 15 members (5 FF, 4 FG, 4 Lab., 2 independents); Northern Ireland returns 3 members (1 Official Unionist Party, 1 DUP, 1 SDLP).

Earl Mountbatten assassinated on his boat off Mullaghmore, County Sligo (27 Aug.).

Pope John Paul II in Ireland (29 Sept.–1 Oct.).

Lynch (see 1977) announces his intention to resign as taoiseach (5 Dec.); Charles J.

Haughey, minister for health and social welfare, elected to succeed him (11 Dec.; continues till June 1981).

1980 Chalice and accompanying objects unearthed at Derrynaflan, barony of Slieveardagh, County Tipperary (17 Feb.); Derrynaflan chalice is superb example of ninth-century Irish art.

Meeting in London of Haughey with Thatcher (21 May): friendly exchange of views on Northern Ireland situation.

Connemara National Park, Letterfrack, opened (Oct.).

Seven republican prisoners in Maze Prison, County Antrim, begin hunger strike as protest against prison regulations (27 Oct.); three women in Armagh prison join hunger strike 1 Dec.); twenty-three additional prisoners in Maze join (15 Dec.); strike ends at Maze (18 Dec.), at Armagh (19 Dec.; see Mar. 1981).

Meeting in Dublin of Haughey and Thatcher (8 Dec.): they agree to begin consideration of the totality of relationships within these islands.

1981 Stardust Ballroom, Artane, County Dublin, destroyed by fire (14 Feb.): 48 killed, over 160 injured.

'Bobby' Sands, OC Provisional IRA in Maze Prison, begins hunger strike (1 Mar.; see 27 Oct. 1980); later joined by other republican prisoners; elected Sinn Féin MP in by-election for Fermanagh–South Tyrone (20 Apr.); dies (5 May); nine other hunger-strikers die (12 May–10 Aug.); strike called off (3 Oct.); 64 killed in disturbances in Northern Ireland (1 Mar.–3 Oct.).

Atkins (see May 1979) succeeded by James Prior as secretary of state for Northern Ireland (Sept.).

General election in Republic of Ireland (11 June): FF 78, FG 65, Lab. 15, others 8; Haughey (see 1979) succeeded as taoiseach by Garret FitzGerald (FG), heading FG–Lab. coalition government (30 June; continues till Mar. 1982). (See 1977, Feb. 1982).

Official opening of new National Concert Hall in Earlsfort Terrace, Dublin, by President Hillery (9 Sept.).

Meeting between taoiseach and Mrs Thatcher (6 Nov.): Anglo-Irish Inter-governmental Council to be set up (first meeting of council 19 Jan. 1982).

1982 General election in Republic (18 Feb.): FF 81, FG 63, Lab. 15, others 7; FitzGerald (see 1981) succeeded as taoiseach by Haughey (FF) (9 Mar.). (See Nov. 1982).

Argentinian forces occupy Falkland Islands (2 Apr.); first ships of British task force sent to reoccupy them leave Portsmouth (5 Apr.); Republic government affirms Irish neutrality (2 May); announces that, in view of open hostilities in Falklands, it regards use of economic sanctions against Argentina by EEC as inappropriate (4 May); sanctions renewed by EEC (17 May), Republic and Italy refusing to concur; Argentinian forces in Falklands surrender to British (15 June).

Prior's white paper, *Northern Ireland: A Framework for Devolution*, published (6 Apr.): calls for 'rolling devolution' (see 20 Oct.).

Haughey, taoiseach, addresses second special session on disarmament at United Nations General Assembly (11 June).

Provisional IRA explode bombs in Hyde Park and Regent's Park, London, killing 10 British servicemen, members of mounted detachments of Household Cavalry and members of band of Royal Green Jackets (20 July).

FF parliamentary party reject by 58 to 22 a vote of no confidence in Haughey as taoiseach moved by Charles McCreevy (6 Oct.); minority includes Desmond O'Malley and Martin O'Donoghue, who resign as ministers of trade, commerce and tourism, and of education, in order to vote against Haughey.

General election for Northern Ireland Assembly (20 Oct.); final results: Official Unionist Party 26, DUP 21, other unionists 2, Alliance 10, SDLP 14, Sinn Féin 5 (total membership 78) (see 1975).

Bomb at Droppin Well Inn, Ballykelly, County Derry, kills sixteen (eleven British soldiers of Cheshire Regiment and five civilians) and injures many others (6 Dec.); Irish National Liberation Army claims responsibility.

General election in Republic (24 Nov.): FF 75, FG 70, Lab. 16, others 5; Haughey (see above, 9 Mar.) succeeded as taoiseach by FitzGerald, heading FG–Lab. coalition government (14 Dec.). (See Feb. 1982).

1983   Peter Barry, Republic minister for foreign affairs, pays a fact-finding visit to Belfast and Derry to acquaint himself with the Northern Ireland situation on the ground (18–20 Jan).

Garret FitzGerald, taoiseach, Charles Haughey, leader FF party, Dick Spring, tánaiste and John Hume, leader, SDLP, meet for the first session of New Ireland Forum, which invited the views of all people who wish for lasting peace and stability in a new Ireland (30 May). Chairman Colm Ó hEocha, president UCG. The Forum consisted of FG 8, FF 9, Lab. 5, SDLP 5.

Referendum to amend the constitution to prevent possibility of laws permitting abortion. In a poll of 54.59 per cent, 66.45 per cent voted for the amendment, and 32.87 per cent against.

Death of George Colley, TD, who served as minister in several FF governments, and twice contended for the leadership. He was tánaiste from 1977 to 1981 (17 Sept.).

Garret FitzGerald, taoiseach, and Margaret Thatcher, PM, meet at Chequers for the first session of the Anglo-Irish Intergovernmental Council (AIIC), which will discuss issues in Anglo-Irish relations (7 Nov.).

Michael Mills, political correspondent of the *Irish Press*, appointed to the new post of ombudsman, to examine complaints concerning the actions of public officials (8 Nov.).

Niels J. Haagerup, a Danish representative, presents a draft resolution on Northern Ireland to the European Parliament's Political Affairs Committee (12 Dec.). (This report is adopted in March 1984, and welcomed by the government of the Republic as a recognition of the problem as one of the gravest in the European community.)

Dr Patrick Hillery inaugurated as the seventh president for his second consecutive term (31 Dec.). He is an agreed candidate and no election is held.

1984   Death of Seán MacEntee (9 Jan.).

Death of Professor T. W. Moody. Co-editor of the first two editions of *The Course of Irish History*, 1967, 1984; he also planned the ambitious multi-volume, *A New History of Ireland* published jointly by the Royal Irish Academy and Oxford University Press, 1976 –.

Publication of the Report of the New Ireland Forum, which put forward three possibilities for discussion: a unitary state, a federal/confederal state and joint sovereignty (2 May).

John Stalker, deputy chief constable of Manchester, appointed to lead inquiry into the killing of six unarmed men in Northern Ireland (May).

US President Reagan visits Balyporeen, Ireland (1–4 June).

European election in Republic: FF 8, FG 6, ind. 1; in Northern Ireland: Ian Paisley, John Taylor and John Hume elected (18 June).

John Treacy wins a silver medal in the marathon at the Olympic Games (12 Aug.).

Death of writer Liam O'Flaherty (7 Sept.).

Douglas Hurd succeeds James Prior as secretary of state for Northern Ireland (10 Sept.).

Grand Hotel Brighton bombed during Conservative Party Conference; four people killed and one died later (12 Oct.).

1985   First commercial flight from Knock Airport (25 Oct).

Anglo-Irish Agreement signed by Garret FitzGerald and Margaret Thatcher at Hillsborough (15 Nov.)

Dáil passes Anglo-Irish Agreement (21 Nov.)

House of Commons passes Anglo-Irish Agreement (27 Nov.)

Progressive Democrat Party formed by Desmond O'Malley and Mary Harney (21 Dec.).

1986   John Stalker removed from inquiry (June; see 1984).

Divorce referendum in Republic – ban on divorce confirmed (June).

Republican Sinn Féin founded by R. Ó Brádaigh and D. Ó Conaill (Nov.).

1987   General election in Republic (19 Feb.): FF 81, FG 51, Lab 12, PD 14, others 5. Haughey is taoiseach.

Alan Dukes succeeds Garret FitzGerald as leader of FG (Mar.).

	SAS kill eight PIRA at Loughall, County Armagh (8 May).
	Referendum on Single European Act (24 May).
	Stephen Roche wins Tour de France cycle race (26 July).
	PIRA bomb kills eleven and injures sixty-three at Remembrance Day Service in Enniskillen (8 Nov.).
1988	Death of Seán MacBride, winner of Nobel and Lenin Peace Prizes (15 Jan.).
	SAS kill three unarmed members of PIRA in Gibraltar: Máiréad Farrell, Seán Savage and Daniel McCann (6 Mar.).
	European Court rules against seven-day detention; British government had sought 'temporary' derogation (Dec.).
1988–9	Bicentenary of foundation of Australia as a British convict settlement. Amongst the convicts, the Irish were prominent. Altogether, some 23,000 Irish were transported between 1788 and 1876.
1989	European elections in Republic: FF 6, FG 4, Lab. 1, ind. 2, WP 1, PD 1.
	General election in Republic: FF 77, FG 55, Lab. 15, PD 6, WP 7, DSP 1. Haughey is taoiseach of FF–PD coalition.
	Peter Brooke succeeds Tom King as secretary of state for Northern Ireland (24 July).
	University of Limerick opened (14 Sept).
	Guildford Four released (19 Oct.).
	Author Samuel Beckett, winner of Nobel Prize for Literature, dies (27 Dec.).
1990	Northern Ireland Fair Employment Act (1 Jan.).
	Cardinal T. Ó Fiaich dies on visit to Lourdes (8 May).
	Death of Terence O'Neill, prime minister of Northern Ireland 1963–9 (14 June).
	Brian Keenan released (24 Aug.).
	Painting by Michelangelo Merisi da Caravaggio (1571–1610) *The Taking of Christ* discovered in Dublin. Originally given to Jesuits by Dr Marie Lee-Wilson. Experts first called to examine it in August 1990. Information revealed to public in April 1993 by Noel Barber, SJ, and painting given on indefinite loan to the National Gallery. First exhibited in November 1993.
	Mary Robinson elected president of Republic (7 Nov.; installed 3 December).
	John Bruton succeeds Alan Dukes as leader of FG (Nov.).
	John Major succeeds Margaret Thatcher as leader of Conservative Party and prime minister (Nov.).
1991	Mortar bombs fired by PIRA at 10 Downing Street (7 Feb.).
	Release of Birmingham Six (14 Mar.).
	Maguire Seven convictions quashed (26 June).
1992	Haughey resigns as taoiseach; succeeded by Albert Reynolds (Feb.).
	Democratic Left Party formed after split in Workers' Party (Feb.).
	In Northern Ireland election, Gerry Adams of Sinn Féin loses his Westminster seat to Dr Joe Hendron of the SDLP; Conservatives elected in UK with twenty-one-seat majority (April).
	Patrick Mayhew succeeds Peter Brooke as secretary of state for Northern Ireland (April).
	Referendum on Maastricht Treaty (18 June).
	Nelson Mandela of ANC visits Ireland and addresses Dáil (July).
	Michael Carruth, boxer, wins a gold medal as a welterweight at the Olympic Games (Aug.).
	UDA banned (Aug.)
	General election in Republic: FF 88, FG 45, Lab. 33, PD 10, DL 4, others 5 (Nov.).
	Referendum on right to life (25 Nov.).
	Referendum on right to travel (25 Nov.).
	Referendum on right to information (25 Nov.).
1993	Albert Reynolds elected taoiseach of FF–Lab. coalition (12 Jan.).
	European Commission accepts case brought by relatives of the people killed in Gibraltar (Sept. see 1988).
	Mary Harney succeeds Desmond O'Malley as leader of the PDs (Oct.).
	Downing Street Declaration signed by Albert Reynolds and John Major (15 Dec.).
1994	Amnesty International Report on political killings in Northern Ireland published (Feb.).

European elections in Republic: FF 7, FG 4, Lab. 1, GP 2, ind. 1.

Sonia O'Sullivan's athletics victory at the Helsinki European Championships on 10 August wins her a gold medal (10 Aug.).

The IRA begins a ceasefire (30 August) 1994.

1995 New government – a 'Rainbow coalition' of FG, Lab and DL – takes office in the Republic; FG leader John Bruton elected Taoiseach (Jan).

Violence and conflict surround Orange Order marches in Drumcree, Portadown and Ormeau Road, Belfast (July–Aug.).

Gerry Adams tells Belfast rally the IRA 'haven't gone away, you know' (13 Aug.).

David Trimble replaces James Molyneaux as Ulster Unionist Party leader; the *Irish Press* closes down after 64 years in existence (8 Sept.).

Seamus Heaney awarded Nobel Prize for Literature (5 Oct.).

Divorce referendum passed by a narrow majority (24 Nov.).

US President Bill Clinton visits Belfast, Derry and Dublin (30 Nov. –1 Dec.).

1996 Publication of the Mitchell Report, which outlines six principles committing participants in all-party talks on the future of NI to non-violence (24 Jan.).

IRA ends its ceasefire with a huge bomb at Canary Wharf, London (9 Feb.).

Crime journalist Veronica Guerin shot dead by Dublin criminals (26 June).

Irish swimmer Michelle Smith wins three gold medals at the Olympic Games in Atlanta (July); her career ends in disgrace in 1998 amid doping allegations.

Brigid McCole dies of hepatitis C contracted from contaminated blood supplied by the Blood Transfusion Service (2 Oct.).

Revelations regarding the payment by businessman Ben Dunne for an extension to the home of Fine Gael TD Michael Lowry cause a scandal (Nov.).

1997 Former Taoiseach Charles Haughey embroiled in payments-to-politicians allegations.

A general election results in the formation of a FF–PD coalition with Bertie Ahern as taoiseach (6 June).

The IRA reinstates its ceasefire (20 July).

Sinn Féin subscribes to the Mitchell principles; all-party talks commence (Sept.– Oct.).

Ray Burke resigns as minister for foreign affairs over bribery allegations (7 Oct.); the Flood Tribunal is established to investigate planning irregularities in north County Dublin.

Mary McAleese wins the presidential election (31 Oct.); her predecessor, Mary Robinson, is appointed UN Commissioner for Human Rights.

1998 The Good Friday Agreement is signed by all NI parties participating in talks and the Irish and British governments (10 April).

The Good Friday Agreement is endorsed in referendums north and south of the border; the Amsterdam Treaty is endorsed by referendum in the Republic (22 May).

The 'Real IRA' kill twenty-nine people in a bomb attack in Omagh, County Tyrone (16 Aug.).

John Hume and David Trimble are awarded the Nobel Peace Prize (16 Oct.).

President McAleese and Queen Elizabeth II commemorate Irish war dead in Flanders (11 Nov.).

DL makes decision to merge with the Labour Party (13 Dec.).

1999 Launch of the euro (2 Jan.).

Record Exchequer surplus of over £1 billion in the Republic (April).

Gay Byrne presents *The Late Late Show*, the world's longest running chatshow, for the last time (May).

Privatisation of Telecom Éireann (July).

Devolved government takes office in NI, with David Trimble (UUP) as first minister and Seamus Mallon (SDLP) as deputy first minister; Sinn Féin has two ministerial positions; Irish government replaces Articles 2 and 3 of the Constitution and the British Government repeals the Government of Ireland Act, 1920; the IRA appoints an intermediary to enter discussions with arms decommissioning body (2 Dec.).

2000 Announcement by NI Secretary Peter Mandelson introducing legislation to create the new Police Service of Northern Ireland, replacing the RUC (19 Jan.).

Direct rule over Northern Ireland re-imposed by London (11 Feb.).

Four Irish soldiers killed in road accident in Lebanon while on peacekeeping duties (14 Feb.).

Saville Inquiry on Bloody Sunday opens in Derry (27 Mar.).

Shooting of John Carthy by armed gardaí at Abbeylara, County Longford (20 Apr.).

IRA states its commitment to put its arms beyond use 'completely and verifiably' in the context of the full implementation of the Good Friday Agreement (6 May).

Devolved government restored in Northern Ireland (29 May).

Train disruption following ILDA strike (June–August).

IRA announce opening of arms dumps to inspectors (26 June).

End of release programme under Good Friday Agreement for Maze prisoners; in total, 428 are released (28 July.)

Loyalist feuding in NI returns British soldiers to Belfast streets (21 Aug.).

Real IRA mount rocket attack on MI6 headquarters in London (21 Sept.).

Secondary schools forced to close by striking teachers demanding pay rises (Nov.–Apr.).

US President Bill Clinton visits Ireland at end of term of office (12–13 Dec.).

Ireland's national debt hits record low (30 Dec.).

2001   TD Liam Lawlor jailed for seven days for obstructing the Flood Tribunal (15 Jan.).

John Reid replaces Peter Mandelson as NI Secretary (15 Jan.).

Michael Noonan replaces John Bruton as leader of Fine Gael (9 Feb.).

EU Commission formally reprimands Irish government for permitting tax cuts and encouraging expansion (12 Feb.).

Archbishop of Dublin Desmond Connell is made a Cardinal (21 Feb.).

Outbreak of foot and mouth disease in UK (23 Feb.); border is patrolled; social and sporting events are cancelled in Ireland, including St Patrick's Day Festival (17 Mar.).

Outbreak of foot and mouth disease in NI (28 Feb.).

Outbreak of foot and mouth disease on Cooley peninsula, County Louth (22 Mar.); immediate action prevents spread of disease.

TD Beverley Cooper-Flynn expelled from Fianna Fáil after losing libel case (11 Apr.).

Electorate rejects Nice Treaty in referendum: 35 per cent turnout – 46 per cent for, 54 per cent against (7 June).

David Trimble announces resignation as First Minister in NI Assembly because of IRA failure to decommission (30 June).

Job losses hit multinational hi-tech firms in Ireland (July–Aug.).

Protestant eighteen-year-old Gavin Brett mistakenly killed by renegade loyalists in sectarian gun attack (29 July).

IRA release statement on plans to put weapons beyond use and cooperation with decommissioning body (6 Aug.).

IRA decommissioning plans rejected by David Trimble (7 Aug.).

NI Assembly suspended for twenty-four hours by British government to allow six-week pause for debate on election of new leader to replace David Trimble (10 Aug.).

Three suspected IRA men arrested in Colombia; trio are thought to have been working with FARC guerrillas (13 Aug.).

IRA withdraw decommissioning offer, blaming David Trimble's response (14 Aug.).

Population in Republic hits 120-year high at 3.84 million; immigration and birth-rate contribute to rise (29 Aug.).

Children and parents going to Catholic Holy Cross Primary School in Belfast are subjected to abuse as local loyalists blockade the school (3 Sept.).

Professor John H. Andrews is a Fellow Emeritus of Trinity College, Dublin, and formerly Associate Professor of Geography. He is the author of *A Paper Landscape: Ordnance Survey in Nineteenth Century Ireland* (1975), *Plantation Acres: A Historical Study of the Irish Land Surveyor and his Maps* (1985) and *Shapes of Ireland: Maps and their Makers 1564–1839* (1997). He is currently continuing his research on the history of Irish cartography.

F. J. Byrne held the position of Professor of Early Irish History, University College, Dublin. His published works include *The Rise of the Uí Néill and the High-kingship of Ireland* (1969) and *The Scholar Revolutionary: Eoin MacNeill, 1867–1945, and the Making of the New Ireland* (1973). He contributed to *A New History of Ireland*, writing *Vol. 3: Early Modern Ireland 1534–1691* (1976).

Professor Aidan Clarke is Erasmus Smith's Professor of Modern History at Trinity College, Dublin, and a past President of the Royal Irish Academy. He is the author of numerous articles on early modern Irish topics. His most recent book is *Prelude to Restoration in Ireland: The End of the Commonwealth, 1659–1660* (1999). His first book, *The Old English in Ireland, 1625–1642*, was reprinted in 2000.

Art Cosgrove took his doctorate at the Queen's University, Belfast and joined the staff of University College, Dublin, in 1963. He became an associate professor of the Medieval History department there in 1990 and was chairman of the combined departments of history from 1991 to 1993. In 1994, he became the President of UCD. His publications include *Late Medieval Ireland 1370–1541* (1981). He is a co-editor and contributor to *A New History of Ireland* (1987–).

Liam de Paor (1926–1998) worked for the Office of Public Works and became a lecturer in archaeology at University College, Dublin. His interest in historical conservation led him to spend a year as a UNESCO adviser in Nepal, after which he returned to UCD as a college lecturer in history. His publications include *Early Christian Ireland* (1958), *Archaeology: An Illustrated Introduction* (1967) and *Divided Ulster* (1970).

Richard English is Professor of Politics at Queen's University, Belfast. Educated at the universities of Oxford and Keele, his books include *Ernie O'Malley: IRA Intellectual* (Oxford University Press, 1998).

E. R. R. Green was Director of the Institute of Irish Studies at Queen's University, Belfast. He is the author of *The Lagan Valley 1800–50: A Local History of the Industrial Revolution* (1949) and *The Industrial Archaeology of County Down* (1963) and edited *Essays in Scotch-Irish History* (1969).

Dr G. A. Hayes-McCoy (1911–75) was on the staff of the National Museum of Ireland from 1939 to 1958, when he became Professor of History at University College, Galway, a position he held until his death. He co-founded the Military History Society and was the first editor of its journal, *The Irish* Sword. His books include *Scots Mercenary Forces in Ireland 1565–1603* (1937), *Irish Battles* (1969), *History of Irish Flags from Earliest Times* (1979) and *The Irish at War* (1964).

Kathleen Hughes held the position of Lecturer in the Early History and Culture of the British Isles at the University of Cambridge. She authored *Church and Society in Ireland, AD 400–1200* (1987), *Early Christian Ireland: An Introduction to the Sources* (1972) and *Celtic Britain in the Early Middle Ages: Studies in Scottish and Welsh Sources* (1980).

Dr Dermot Keogh is Professor of History at University College, Cork. He is the author of *Twentieth Century Ireland, Ireland and Europe* and *Jews and Twentieth Century Ireland*. He is currently working on biographies of Jack Lynch and John Charles McQuaid.

Professor J. F. Lydon was head of the Department of Medieval History at Trinity College, Dublin from 1980 to 1987. His publications include *England and Ireland in the Later Middle Ages* (1981), *Law and Disorder in Thirteenth-Century Ireland: The Dublin Parliament of 1297* (1997) and *The Making of Ireland: From Ancient Times to the Present* (1998).

Patrick Lynch is Professor Emeritus of Political Economy at University College, Dublin. His books include *Planning for Economic Development* (1959), *The Fenian Chief: A Biography of James Stephens* (1967) and Economic *Development and Planning* (1969).

Donal McCartney is Professor Emeritus of Modern Irish History at University College, Dublin. His major works include *Parnell: The Politics of Power* (1991), *W. E. H. Lecky, Historian and Politician, 1828–1903* (1994) and *UCD: A National Idea – The History of the University College, Dublin* (1999).

J. L. McCracken is Emeritus Professor of History in Coleraine at the University of Ulster. His publications include *Representative Government in Ireland: A Study of Dáil Éireann 1919–48* (1958), *The Irish Parliament in the Eighteenth Century* (1971) and *New Light at the Cape of Good Hope: William Porter, the Father of Cape Liberty* (1993).

R. B. McDowell is a Fellow Emeritus of Trinity College, Dublin and formerly Associate Professor of Modern History. His major works include *The Irish Administration, 1801–1914* (1964), *Ireland in the Age of Imperialism and Revolution, 1760–1801* (1979) and *Crisis and Decline: The Fate of the Southern Unionists* (1997).

F. X. Martin (1922–2000) became a member of the Augustinian order in 1941. He joined the staff of University College, Dublin in 1959 and was appointed professor of medieval history in 1962. As chairman of Friends of Medieval Dublin he was instrumental in preserving the city's archaeological heritage. His publications include *No Hero in the House: Diarmait Mac Murchada and the Coming of the Normans to Ireland* (1977). His most important work was the multi-volume *New History of Ireland* (1987–) of which he was joint-editor and a major contributor.

G. F. Mitchell was a Fellow of Trinity College, Dublin, and formerly Professor of Quaternary Studies. He was a founder member of An Taisce, president of the Royal Society of Antiquaries of Ireland, President of the Royal Irish Academy (1976–9) and was elected President of the International Quaternary Association. His publications include *The Irish Landscape* (1986); *The Great Bog of Ardee* (1985) and *Reading the Irish Landscape* (1997).

Professor T. W. Moody, Fellow Emeritus of Trinity College, Dublin, formerly Associate Professor of Modern History, was a founder of *The New History of Ireland*, published by Oxford University Press. He was one of the founders of *Irish Historical Studies*. Professor Moody's principal published works concerned Ireland from the seventeenth to the nineteenth centuries and included *Davitt and Irish Revolution, 1846–82* (1981).

Brian Ó Cuív (1916–99) was a noted Irish scholar who spent most of his career at the School of Celtic Studies in the Dublin Institute of Advanced Studies, where he was a Senior Professor. His contributions to scholarship include studies of the Irish of Muskerry, County Cork, and editions of Irish texts from all stages of the language. He had a particularly profound knowledge of bardic poetry. His catalogue of the Irish manuscripts in the Bodleian Library at Oxford was published posthumously in 2001.

Tomás Ó Fiaich (1923–90), was ordained to the priesthood in 1948 and studied in University College, Dublin and Belgium. A distinguished academic, he taught history at Maynooth before becoming President of the university in 1974. He was elevated to the primatial see of Armagh in 1977 and made a cardinal two years later. He was an authority on the missionaries of early Christian Ireland who rekindled the faith in a pagan Europe, as his two most significant publications, *Gaelscrínte i gCéin* (1960) and *Irish Cultural Influences in Europe* (1966) attest.

Maureen Wall was a College Lecturer in Modern Irish History at University College, Dublin. Her publications include *The Penal Law, 1691–1760: Church and State from the Treaty of Limerick to the Accession of George III* (1961) and *Catholic Ireland in the Eighteenth Century* (1989).

J. H. Whyte was educated at Ampleforth and Oxford. He was a lecturer in politics at University College, Dublin from 1961 to 1966, when he went to Queen's University, Belfast as a lecturer in political science. He later became the professor of Irish politics there. Published works include *The Independent Irish Party 1850–9* (1958), *Church and State in Modern Ireland 1923–70* (1971) and *Catholics in Western Democracies: A Study in Political Behaviour* (1981).